20th Nordic Conference of Computational Linguistics

(NODALIDA 2015)

NEALT Proceedings Series Volume 23

Vilnius, Lithuania
11 – 13 May 2015

Editor:

B. Megyesi

ISBN: 978-1-5108-0299-5

Printed from e-media with permission by:

Curran Associates, Inc.
57 Morehouse Lane
Red Hook, NY 12571

proceedings.com

Some format issues inherent in the e-media version may also appear in this print version.

Printed by Curran Associates, Inc. (2015)

Association for Computational Linguistics
209 N. Eighth Street
Stroudsburg, Pennsylvania 18360

Phone: 1-570-476-8006
Fax: 1-570-476-0860

acl@aclweb.org

Additional copies of this publication are available from:

Curran Associates, Inc.
57 Morehouse Lane
Red Hook, NY 12571 USA
Phone: 845-758-0400
Fax: 845-758-2634
Email: curran@proceedings.com
Web: www.proceedings.com

Proceedings of the 20th Nordic Conference of Computational Linguistics NODALIDA 2015

Editor
Beáta Megyesi

May 11-13, 2015
Institute of the Lithuanian Language
Vilnius, Lithuania

Published by

ACL Anthology
https://www.aclweb.org/anthology/

Linköping University Electronic Press, Sweden
Linköping Electronic Conference Proceedings #109
ISSN: 1650-3638

Sponsors

UNIVERSITY OF
COPENHAGEN

CLT
Centre for Language Technology
Gothenburg, Sweden

UNIVERSITY OF
GOTHENBURG

LIETUVIŲ KALBOS INSTITUTAS

Lingsoft®
LANGUAGE
MANAGEMENT

NEALT

UPPSALA
UNIVERSITET

Preface: Program Chair

We are very pleased to introduce the proceedings of the 20th Nordic Conference on Computational Linguistics (NODALIDA 2015), held at the Institute of the Lithuanian Language in Vilnius, Lithuania, between May 11 and May 13, 2015. The proceedings is published as part of the NEALT Proceedings Series by Linköping University Electronic Press, and is also publicly available in the ACL Anthology for the first time.

NODALIDA have been held bi-annually since 1977, first organized as a friendly gathering in Gothenburg, Sweden to discuss on-going research in computational linguistics in the Nordic countries. Nearly 30 years later, in 2006, the Northern European Association for Language Technology (NEALT) was founded to organize NODALIDA and other events in the Nordic countries, the Baltic states, and Northwest Russia to promote research, cooperation and information exchange in the field of language technology in a wide sense. Today, NODALIDA addresses all aspects of computational linguistics, natural language processing, and speech technology, including work in closely related neighboring disciplines. The conference has been internationally recognized outside the Nordic regions and submissions are received from all over the world. It is a great honor to serve as the Program Chair for NODALIDA 2015, to be held in Lithuania for the first time.

Following the pattern of previous years, the Program Committee invited paper submissions in four distinct tracks: *regular papers* on substantial, original, and unpublished research, including empirical evaluation results, where appropriate; *student papers* on completed or ongoing work, where at least the first author is a student; *short papers* on smaller, focused contributions, work in progress, negative results, surveys, or opinion pieces; and *demonstration papers* summarizing a software system or language resource, to be accompanied by a live demonstration at the conference.

The conference received 68 submissions from all over Europe as well as from Canada, India, Japan, and the US. We followed the standards of recent NODALIDAs–emerged since 2007–with high quality technical track with peer-review of all papers, and an acceptance rate of 61%. All submitted papers went through a rigorous review process. The regular, student and short papers were reviewed by three experts in the field while the demonstration papers were reviewed by two experts. The final selection was made by the Program Committee, which was not an easy task due to many submissions with high scores and overall positive reviews, and the time and space constraints of the two day long main conference. We aimed at achieving balance between regular and short papers, and was more lenient in the student and demo categories. Our goal was to include papers dealing with a wide variety of topics from various regions while maintaining NODALIDA's regional character as the major conference for Nordic research. 42 submissions were accepted for presentation either as long talks, poster presentations, lightning talks with poster presentations, or demos. In the final program, there are 22 regular, 5 student, 8 short, and 7 demonstration papers, all collected in this volume.

In addition to the accepted papers, we are proud to present three invited keynote speakers, distinguished researchers from France, Great Britain, and the US, to cover different areas of the conference.

Kevin Knight (University of Southern California) presents work on the use of redundancy information occurring in natural language by humans to improve automatic language processing applications, such as summarization or machine translation. Catherine Pelachaud (CNRS-LTCI, TELECOM-ParisTech) talks about how to model virtual agents with socio-emotional capabilities, in particular how we can animate laughter and virtual agents who can laugh when interacting with humans. Sebastian Riedel (University College London) presents his work on teaching machines to read and to reason about what was read. In addition, we followed the quite recent tradition of organizing a local language tutorial on Lithuanian.

The conference program also includes four worshops: i) NLP for Computer Assisted Language Learning, ii) Semantic resources and semantic annotation for Natural Language Processing and the Digital Humanities, iii) Constraint Grammar - Methods, Tools and Applications and iv) Innovative Corpus Query and Visualization Tools. Each workshop has been organized by their own committees, and produced their own proceedings published in the same series.

Organizing a conference with a good program is complex and relies on the goodwill of many researchers involved in the field. I would like to express my gratitude and appreciation to my fellows on the Program Committee for their hard and invaluable work for sharing the effort of creating the program. A special thanks goes to Stephan Oepen, the program chair of NODALIDA 2013, and NEALT's president, Bolette Sandford Pedersen, for generous advice. Wholehearted thanks go to the 62 reviewers for their time and effort to contribute to the reviewing and selection of papers. I am also grateful to the three keynote speakers, the presenter of the local language tutorial, and the workshop organizers! And of course, all the authors who submitted papers deserve special thanks. Without you, this conference would not take place! In addition, I would also like to acknowledge and thank Nils Blomqvist for professionally serving as the proceedings co-manager. I am also indebted to Lars Ahrenberg, the editor-in-chief of NEALT, for helping the publication of the proceedings in ACL anthology, in parallel with Linköping University Electronic Press, come true. My greatest debt goes to the Institute of the Lithuanian Language, Jolanta Zabarskaitė, and in particular Violeta Meiliūnaitė for carrying the heavy burden of the local organization, and for being a great host in the picturesque city of Vilnius. Lastly, I am grateful to my colleagues at Department of Linguistics and Philology at Uppsala University for their patience with me during the last year and generously letting me hide from time to time while organizing this conference, and to my nearest and dearest—my twins and friends—for generously giving me the space to disappear into our world of language technology.

I wish you all a fruitful conference and hope you will enjoy NODALIDA 2015!

Beáta Megyesi (Program Chair)

Preface: Local Organizer Chair

I would like to extend a warm welcome to the participants and guests at NODALIDA 2015.

The fact that this conference, with its highly acclaimed status and prominence in the academia, is taking place in Lithuania in 2015 is significant in several ways.

We find it very important that such a high-level event, which attracts a great many scientists and graduate students from all over the world, is taking place in a country that has its language classed as one of the less-used. It shows that NEALT understands and supports the involvement of the minor European languages that do not have big technological markets in the processes of supporting multilingualism and multiculturalism both in Europe and on a world-wide scale, which processes are in fact aimed at developing and upgrading language technologies. Needless to say, this kind of involvement is critical to the Lithuanian language.

What is more, in the digital age language acquires many new functions, evolving from a tool of communication and a persuader into something that creates added value in the society of knowledge and creative process. Figuratively speaking, the impalpability of the digital world brings forth perfectly tangible things. As John Searle, one of the most prominent contemporary linguistic philosophers, once said – words make things. And it is the rapidly developing language technologies that make it happen in the first place. Language technologies facilitate the retrieval of information, management of different things, communication, and exchange of creative ideas that are rooted in the unique nature of each and every language. Ideas are the backbone of innovation as the key precondition for global development. As a researcher of the Lithuanian language, I believe that eventually there will be no more minor and major languages in the world, as they all have equal opportunities. And all that thanks to language technologies alone.

Another important thing is that NODALIDA 2015 is taking place in a country whose language is considered one of the languages that have preserved the structure of the Indo-European parent language the best, and for a good reason. The structure of the Lithuanian language is indeed very complicated, and its digitalisation poses a significant challenge to scientists. I truly hope that as a result of this conference more researchers will discover a passion for tackling difficult problems, such as the Lithuanian language and its next-of-kin, the Latvian language.

The future of languages is in the hands of language technologists. Sharing scientific expertise, discovering new contacts, meeting old friends, setting up and updating scientific networks, developing and presenting new ideas is what we all expect from NODALIDA 2015.

Many thanks to all who have gathered here in Vilnius.

Jolanta Zabarskaitė (Local Organizer Chair)

Program Committee

- Filip Ginter, University of Turku, Finland
- Kristiina Jokinen, University of Helsinki, Finland
- Arne Jönsson, Linköping University, Sweden
- Violeta Meiliūnaitė, Institute of the Lithuanian Language, Lithuania
- Beáta Megyesi (Program Chair), Uppsala University, Sweden
- Costanza Navarretta, University of Copenhagen, Denmark
- Stephan Oepen, University of Oslo, Norway
- Oscar Täckström, Google Inc.

Organizing Committee

- Jolanta Zabarskaitė
- Violeta Meiliūnaitė

Reviewers

- Yvonne Adesam, University of Gothenburg, Sweden
- Lars Ahrenberg, Linköping University, Sweden
- Krasimir Angelov, University of Gothenburg, Sweden
- Bernd Bohnet, University of Stuttgart, Germany
- Janne Bondi Johannessen, University of Oslo, Norway
- Johan Boye, Royal Technical Institute (KTH), Sweden
- Diego Ceccarelli, National Research Council, Italy
- Lin Chen, University of Illinois, USA
- Koenraad De Smedt, University of Bergen, Norway
- Rodolfo Delmonte, Ca'Foscari University Venice, Italy
- Jens Edlund, Royal Technical Institute (KTH), Sweden
- Anna Esposito, Second University of Naples, Italy
- Björn Gambäck, Norwegian University of Science and Technology, Norway

- Gintare Grigonyte, University of Stockholm, Sweden
- Christian Hardmeier, Uppsala universitet, Sweden
- Petter Haugereid, NTNU, Trondheim, Norway
- Katarina Heimann Mühlenbock, University of Gothenburg, Sweden
- Anna Hjalmarsson, Royal Technical Institute (KTH), Sweden
- Angelina Ivanova, University of Oslo, Norway
- Richard Johansson, University of Gothenburg, Sweden
- Sofie Johansson Kokkinakis, University of Gothenburg, Sweden
- Jussi Karlgren, Gavagai and KTH, Sweden
- Mare Koit, University of Tartu, Estonia
- Marco Kuhlmann, Linköping University, Sweden
- Alessandro Lenci, University of Pisa, Italy
- Krister Lindén, University of Helsinki, Finland
- Christian Lindgren, Lund University, Sweden
- Diego Marcheggiani, Italian National Research Council, Italy
- Antonia Martí, University of Barcelona, Spain
- Mattias Nilsson, Karolinska Institutet, Sweden
- Joakim Nivre, Uppsala University, Sweden
- Pierre Nugues, Lund University, Sweden
- Gustav Öqvist Seimyr, Karolinska Institutet, Sweden
- Constantin Orasan, University of Wolverhampton, UK
- Robert Östling, Stockholm University, Sweden
- Lilja Øvrelid, University of Oslo, Norway
- Patrizia Paggio, University of Copenhagen, Denmark
- Eva Pettersson, Uppsala University, Sweden
- Tommi A Pirinen, Dublin City University, Ireland
- Barbara Plank, University of Copenhagen, Denmark
- Sampo Pyysalo, University of Turku, Finland

- Siva Reddy, University of Edinburgh, UK
- Fabio Rinaldi, University of Zurich, Switzerland
- Eirikur Rognvaldsson, School of Humanities, Iceland
- Rune Sætre, NTNU, Trondheim, Norway
- Giampiero Salvi, Royal Technical Institute (KTH), Sweden
- Marina Santini, Nordstedts, Sweden
- Arne Skjærholt, University of Oslo, Norway
- Anders Søgaard, University of Copenhagen, Denmark
- Sara Stymne, Uppsala University, Sweden
- Torbjørn Svendsen, Norwegian University of Science and Technology, Norway
- Nina Tahmasebi, University of Gothenburg, Sweden
- Joel Tetreault, Yahoo Labs, USA
- Jörg Tiedemann, Uppsala University, Sweden
- Olga Uryupina, University of Trento, Italy
- Erik Velldal, University of Oslo, Norway
- Sumithra Velupillai, Stockholm University, Sweden
- Martin Volk, University of Zurich, Switzerland
- Jürgen Wedekind, University of Copenhagen, Denmark
- Mats Wirén, Stockholm University, Sweden
- Roman Yangarber, University of Helsinki, Finland
- Heike Zinsmeister, University of Hamburg, Germany

INVITED TALK: How Much Information Does a Human Translator Add to the Original?

Kevin Knight

ISI, University of Southern California, USA

knight@isi.edu

Abstract

It is well-known that natural language has built-in redundancy. By using context, we can often guess the next word or character in a text. Two practical communities have independently exploited this fact. First, automatic speech and translation researchers build language models to distinguish fluent from non-fluent outputs. Second, text compression researchers convert predictions into short encodings, to save disk space and bandwidth. I will explore what these two communities can learn from each others' (interestingly different) solutions. Then I will look at the less-studied question of redundancy in bilingual text, addressing questions like "How well can we predict human translator behavior?" and "How much information does a human translator add to the original?" (This is joint work with Barret Zoph and Marjan Ghazvininejad.)

Bio

Kevin Knight is Director of Natural Language Technologies at the Information Sciences Institute (ISI) of the University of Southern California (USC), and a Professor in the USC Computer Science Department. He received a PhD in computer science from Carnegie Mellon University and a bachelor's degree from Harvard University. Prof. Knight's research interests include machine translation, automata theory, and decipherment of historical manuscripts. Prof. Knight co-wrote the textbook "Artificial Intelligence", served as President of the Association for Computational Linguistics, and was a co-founder of the machine translation company Language Weaver, Inc. He is a Fellow of the Association for the Advancement of Artificial Intelligence (AAAI), the Association for Computational Linguistics (ACL), and the Information Sciences Institute (ISI).

INVITED TALK:
Modeling Socio-Emotional Humanoid Agent

Catherine Pelachaud

CNRS-LTCI, TELECOM-ParisTech, France

catherine.pelachaud@telecom-paristech.fr

Abstract

In this talk, I will present our current work toward endowing virtual agents with socio-emotional capabilities. I will start describing an interactive system of an agent dialoging with human users in an emotionally colored manner. Through its behaviors, the agent can sustain a conversation as well as show various attitudes and levels of engagement. I will present our latest work on laughter. I will address several issues such as: how to animate laughter in a virtual agent looking particularly at rhythmic movements; how to laugh with human participant and how laughing agent is perceived.

Bio

Catherine Pelachaud is a Director of Research at CNRS in the laboratory LTCI, TELECOM ParisTech. Her research interest includes embodied conversational agent, nonverbal communication (face, gaze, and gesture), expressive behaviors and socio-emotional agents. She is associate editor of several journals among which IEEE Transactions on Affective Computing, ACM Transactions on Interactive Intelligent Systems and Journal on Multimodal User Interfaces. She has co-edited several books on virtual agents and emotion-oriented systems.

INVITED TALK:
Embedding Probabilistic Logic for Machine Reading

Sebastian Riedel

University College London, UK

sebastian.riedel@gmail.com

Abstract

We want to build machines that read, and make inferences based on what was read. A long line of the work in the field has focussed on approaches where language is converted (possibly using machine learning) into a symbolic and relational representation. A reasoning algorithm (such as a theorem prover) then derives new knowledge from this representation. This allows for rich knowledge to captured, but generally suffers from two problems: acquiring sufficient symbolic background knowledge and coping with noise and uncertainty in data. Probabilistic logics (such as Markov Logic) offer a solution, but are known to often scale poorly.

In recent years a third alternative emerged: latent variable models in which entities and relations are embedded in vector spaces (and represented "distributional"). Such approaches scale well and are robust to noise, but they raise their own set of questions: What type of inferences do they support? What is a proof in embeddings? How can explicit background knowledge be injected into embeddings? In this talk I first present our work on latent variable models for machine reading, using ideas from matrix factorisation as well as both closed and open information extraction. Then I will present recent work we conducted to address the questions of injecting and extracting symbolic knowledge into/from models based on embeddings. In particular, I will show how one can rapidly build accurate relation extractors through combining logic and embeddings.

Bio

Dr. Riedel is a Senior Lecturer in the Department of Computer Science at University College London, leading the Machine Reading lab. He received his MSc and PhD (in 2009) in Computer Science from the University of Edinburgh. He was a researcher at the University of Tokyo, and a postdoc with Andrew McCallum at the University of Massachusetts Amherst. He is an Allen Distinguished Investigator, a Marie Curie CIG fellow, was a finalist for the Microsoft Research Faculty Award in 2013 and recently received a Google Focused Research award. Sebastian is generally interested in the intersection of NLP and machine learning, and particularly interested in teaching machines to read, and to reason with what was read.

Table of Contents

Invited Keynotes

Regular Papers

Student Papers

Short Papers

Demonstration Papers

CONFERENCE PROGRAM

Monday, May 11, 2015 NODALIDA WORKSHOPS

09:00-13:00 **Constraint Grammar - Methods, Tools and Applications**

09:00-18:00 **4th Workshop on NLP for Computer Assisted Language Learning**

13:00-18:00 **Innovative Corpus Query and Visualization Tools**

13:00-17:30 **Semantic resources and semantic annotation for Natural Language Processing and the Digital Humanities**

19:30 **Welcome reception**

Tuesday, May 12, 2015 MAIN CONFERENCE

09:10 – 09:30 **Opening**

09:30 – 10:30 **Keynote**
Kevin Knight
How Much Information Does a Human Translator Add to the Original?

10:30-11:00 Coffee Break

11:00-12:30 **Regular papers**

Parallel session 1 *Syntax*

11:00-11:30 *Eckhard Bick and Tino Didriksen.*
CG-3 — Beyond Classical Constraint Grammar

11:30-12:00 *Jostein Lien, Erik Velldal and Lilja Øvrelid.*
Improving Cross-Domain Dependency Parsing with Dependency-Derived Clusters

12:00-12:30 *Jörg Tiedemann.*
Improving the Cross-Lingual Projection of Syntactic Dependencies

Parallel Session 2 *Annotation, Lithuanian NLP*

11:00-11:30 *Yvonne Adesam, Gerlof Bouma and Richard Johansson.*
Defining the Eukalyptus forest – the Koala treebank of Swedish

11:30-12:00 *Loïc Boizou, Jolanta Kovalevskaitė and Erika Rimkutė.*
Automatic Lemmatisation of Lithuanian MWEs

12:00-12:30	*Jurgita Kapočiūtė-Dzikienė, Ligita Šarkutė and Andrius Utka.* **The Effect of Author Set Size in Authorship Attribution for Lithuanian**

Parallel session 3 *Speech*

11:00-11:30	*Robert Reynolds and Francis Tyers.* **Automatic Word Stress Annotation of Russian Unrestricted Text**
11:30-12:00	*Dominik Sacha, Yuki Asano, Christian Rohrdantz, Felix Hamborg, Daniel Keim, Bettina Braun and Miriam Butt.* **Self Organizing Maps for the Visual Analysis of Pitch Contours**
12:00-12:30	*Julián Zapata and Andreas Søeborg Kirkedal.* **Assessing the Performance of Automatic Speech Recognition Systems When Used by Native and Non-Native Speakers of Three Major Languages in Dictation Workflows**
12:30-13:30	Lunch
13:30-14:30	**Lightning talks**

Parallel Session 1 *Syntax and Semantics*

13:30-13:50	*Johan Bos and Malvina Nissim.* **Uncovering Noun-Noun Compound Relations by Gamification**
13:50-14:10	*Héctor Martínez Alonso, Anders Johannsen, Barbara Plank and Anders Søgaard.* **Active Learning for Sense Annotation**
14:10-14:30	*Ildikó Pilán.* **Helping Swedish words Come to their Senses: Word-Sense Disambiguation Based on Sense Associations from the SALDO Lexicon**

Parallel Session 2 *Sign language and Speech*

13:30-13:50	*Robert Östling, Carl Börstell and Lars Wallin.* **Enriching the Swedish Sign Language Corpus with Part of Speech Tags Using Joint Bayesian Word Alignment and Annotation Transfer**
13:50-14:10	*Peter Juel Henrichsen.* **Talebob - an Interactive Speech Trainer for Danish**
14:10-14:30	*Askars Salimbajevs and Jevgenijs Strigins.* **Using Sub-Word N-Gram Models for Dealing with OOV in Large Vocabulary Speech Recognition for Latvian**

14:30-15:00 Coffee break

14:30-16:00 **Posters and demos**

Posters:
Johan Bos and Malvina Nissim.
Uncovering Noun-Noun Compound Relations by Gamification

Peter Juel Henrichsen.
Talebob - an Interactive Speech Trainer for Danish

Héctor Martínez Alonso, Anders Johannsen, Barbara Plank and Anders Søgaard.
Active Learning for Sense Annotation

Ildikó Pilán.
Helping Swedish words Come to their Senses: Word-Sense Disambiguation Based on Sense Associations from the SALDO Lexicon

Askars Salimbajevs and Jevgenijs Strigins.
Using Sub-Word N-Gram Models for Dealing with OOV in Large Vocabulary Speech Recognition for Latvian

Robert Östling, Carl Börstell and Lars Wallin.
Enriching the Swedish Sign Language Corpus with Part of Speech Tags Using Joint Bayesian Word Alignment and Annotation Transfer

Demos:
Magnus Birkenes, Lars Johnsen, Arne Lindstad and Johanne Ostad.
From Digital Library to N-Grams: NB N-gram

Janne Bondi Johannessen.
The Corpus of American Norwegian Speech (CANS)

Johan Bos.
Open-Domain Semantic Parsing with Boxer

Sam Hardwick, Miikka Silfverberg and Krister Lindén.
Extracting Semantic Frames using hfst-pmatch

Arne Neumann.
discoursegraphs: A Graph-Based Merging Tool and Converter for Multilayer Annotated Corpora

Tommi A Pirinen.
Omorfi–Free and Open Source Morphological Lexical Database of Finnish

Evelina Rennes and Arne Jönsson.
A Tool for Automatic Simplification of Swedish Texts

16:00-17:00 **Keynote**
Catherine Pelachaud
Modeling socio-emotional humanoid agent

19:00 Conference Dinner

Wednesday, May 13, 2015 MAIN CONFERENCE

09:00 -10:00 **Keynote**
Sebastian Riedel
Embedding Probabilistic Logic for Machine Reading

10:00 -10:30 Coffee break

10:30-12:00 **Regular and student papers**

Parallel Session 1 *Semantics*

10:30-11:00 *Juhani Luotolahti and Filip Ginter.*
Sentence Compression For Automatic Subtitling

11:00-11:30 *Sigrid Klerke,* Héctor Martínez Alonso *and Anders Søgaard.*
Looking hard: Eye Tracking for Detecting Grammaticality of Automatically Compressed Sentences

11:30-12:00 *Richard Johansson and Luis Nieto Piña.*
Combining Relational and Distributional Knowledge for Word Sense Disambiguation

Parallel Session 2 *Syntax and Semantics*

10:30-11:00 *Malin Ahlberg, Peter Andersson, Markus Forsberg and Nina Tahmasebi.*
A case study on supervised classification of Swedish pseudo-coordination

11:00-11:30 *Eva Pettersson and Joakim Nivre.*
Improving Verb Phrase Extraction from Historical Text by use of Verb Valency Frames

11:30-12:00 *Sampo Pyysalo, Jenna Kanerva, Anna Missilä, Veronika Laippala and Filip Ginter.*
Universal Dependencies for Finnish

Parallel Session 3 *Student Session*

10:30-11:00 *Max Berggren, Jussi Karlgren, Robert Östling and Mikael Parkvall.*
Inferring the Location of Authors from Words in their Texts

11:00-11:30	*Inari Listenmaa and Francis M. Tyers.* **Automatic Conversion of Colloquial Finnish to Standard Finnish**
11:30-12:00	*Scharolta Sienčnik.* **Adapting word2vec to Named Entity Recognition**
12:00-13:00	Lunch
13:00–14:00	**Business meeting**
14:00-14.30	Coffee break
14:00-15:30	**Poster session**

Long papers:

Héctor Martínez Alonso, Anders Johannsen, Sussi Olsen, Sanni Nimb, Nicolai Hartvig Sørensen, Anna Braasch, Anders Søgaard and Bolette Sandford Pedersen.
Supersense tagging for Danish

Alexandr Chernov, Volha Petukhova and Dietrich Klakow.
Linguistically Motivated Question Classification

Jana Götze and Johan Boye.
Resolving Spatial References using Crowdsourced Geographical Data

Veronika Laippala, Jenna Kanerva, Anna Missilä, Sampo Pyysalo, Tapio Salakoski and Filip Ginter.
Towards the Classification of the Finnish Internet Parsebank: Detecting Translations and Informality

Mihai Lintean and Vasile Rus.
An Optimal Quadratic Approach to Monolingual Paraphrase Alignment

Michael Nokel and Natalia Loukachevitch.
Topic Models: Accounting Component Structure of Bigrams

Short papers:

Katarina Heimann Mühlenbock, Sofie Johansson Kokkinakis, Caroline Liberg, Åsa af Geijerstam, Jenny Folkeryd, Arne Jönsson, Erik Kanebrant and Johan Falkenjack.
A Multivariate Model for Classifying Texts' Readability

Gustavo Henrique Paetzold.
Using Positional Suffix Trees to Perform Agile Tree Kernel Calculation

Steinþór Steingrímsson, Sigrún Helgadóttir and Eiríkur Rögnvaldsson.
Analysing Inconsistencies and Errors in PoS Tagging in two Icelandic Gold Standards

Student papers:

Vytautas Mickevičius, Tomas Krilavičius Vaidas Morkevičius and Aušra Mackutė-Varoneckienė.
Automatic Thematic Classification of the Titles of the Seimas Votes

Birgitta Ojamaa, Päivi Kristiina Jokinen and Kadri Muischenk.
Sentiment Analysis on Conversational Texts

15:30-16:30 **Tutorial on Lithuanian**
Algirdas Saugdargas.
Lithuanian Language in the Architecture of Knowledge

16:30-16:40 **Closing**

Defining the Eukalyptus forest – the Koala treebank of Swedish

Yvonne Adesam Gerlof Bouma Richard Johansson
Språkbanken
Department of Swedish
University of Gothenburg
{yvonne.adesam, gerlof.bouma, richard.johansson}@gu.se

Abstract

This paper details the design of the lexical and syntactic layers of a new annotated corpus of Swedish contemporary texts. In order to make the corpus adaptable into a variety of representations, the annotation is of a hybrid type with head-marked constituents and function-labeled edges, and with a rich annotation of non-local dependencies. The source material has been taken from public sources, to allow the resulting corpus to be made freely available.

1 Introduction

Corpora annotated with part-of-speech tags and syntactic structure are crucial for the development and evaluation of automatic tools for syntactic analysis, as well as for empirical research in syntax. For Swedish, annotated corpora have been available for quite a number of years. The venerable MAMBA treebank (Teleman, 1974) was created in the 1970s. It has formed the basis for a number of Swedish constituency and dependency treebanks such as Talbanken05 (Nivre et al., 2006), the more recent Swedish Treebank, and the Swedish part of the multilingual Universal Dependency Treebank (de Marneffe et al., 2014). The Stockholm–Umeå Corpus (SUC) (Ejerhed et al., 1992) with manually checked part-of-speech tags and base forms for roughly a million tokens, has been a de facto standard for Swedish part-of-speech tagging. The Swedish Treebank uses the SUC part-of-speech tags together with the automatically converted syntactic structures from MAMBA (Nivre et al., 2008).

In our project Koala, we develop new annotation tools to be used for the multi-billion token corpora of Korp, the corpus query infrastructure at Språkbanken. Part of our effort lies in evaluation of these annotation tools. For a number of reasons, the corpora mentioned and their annotation schemata are not suitable as our gold standard.

First, the texts in the corpora are quite dated, and do not reflect the text types available in Korp. Secondly, the MAMBA annotation would require several complex conversion heuristics to be used as a conventional constituency or dependency treebank. Due to technical limitations in the 1970s, attachment in MAMBA is underspecified in some cases, most notably in clause coordination, and its annotation does not have explicit phrase categories. On the other hand, its set of grammatical function categories is very fine-grained, and we consider some more semantic/pragmatic distinctions hard to apply. For the Swedish Treebank we further note that the part-of-speech tags and the syntactic categories were designed in separate projects, and there are several cases of redundancy, where grammatical function distinctions are also reflected in the set of part-of-speech tags.

In this paper, we describe the design of the syntactic layer, and to some extent the part-of-speech layer, of the new *Koala* multi-genre annotated Swedish corpus. In designing the annotation guidelines, we have aimed to address the above-mentioned shortcomings: First, the part-of-speech, phrase, and function categories have received clearly separated roles. Secondly, we use a syntactic annotation format that is less restrictive than MAMBA's. Thirdly, the annotation model has been designed with deterministic conversion into other formalisms in mind. Finally, the corpus consists of material from several genres. The texts have been collected from public-domain sources, so that the corpus can be made freely available. With the data release, we will also supply scripts for conversion to other standards.

2 The Koala corpus

The Koala corpus will consist of at least 100k tokens of modern Swedish text of various types, with about 20k tokens of each different text type.

- Novels: the first chapters from four novels
- Wikipedia: full articles from Swedish Wikipedia, 3k to 100 tokens per article
- Blogs: blog entries from the SIC corpus (Östling, 2013)
- Europarl: proceedings from the European parliament (Koehn, 2002)
- News/community information: we would have liked to add news text, but due to IPR restrictions, this is mainly community information (government information, health service information etc.)

Sentence segmentation and tokenization is based on orthographic words and sentences. This does not rule out the possibility of having syntactic tokens that span several graphic words, as the syntactic annotation readily allows multiword expressions (see Section 4.3: 'multiword expressions'). Graphic words containing several tokens, each with their own syntactic contribution – such as *serunte* for *ser (d)u (i)nte* 'don't you see', lit. 'see you not' – do however receive special treatment. The texts are manually annotated using an adapted version of the Synpathy tool.[1]

3 Lexical annotation

The part-of-speech tag set is a reduced version of the SUC tag set, with alterations to make it more consistent with the Swedish reference grammar SAG (Teleman et al., 1999). The labels are listed in Table 1. Nouns are marked for gender, number, and definiteness. Adjectives are marked for degree (POS/KOM/SUV), gender, number, and definiteness. Adverbs are marked for degree and whether they are relative or wh-pronouns (+FR). Verbs are marked for mood/finiteness, voice (where we, following SUC, distinguish between active and s-form, rather than active, passive, deponent, etc.), and in the case of indicative and subjunctive we also mark tense. Pronouns are marked for gender, number, definiteness, form (subject, object or possessive), and wh/relative. Proper nouns, numerals, interjections, subordinators, coordinators, prepositions, and foreign words are not further specified. Symbols are divided into punctuation and other.

Traditionally, the nominative-genitive case distinction is made for nominal parts-of-speech. However, in Swedish *-s* can either be the genitive suffix or it can be a phrase marking clitic, appearing on any NP-final word. In Koala we handle both these uses at the lexical level, using a single GEN feature that can appear on any part-of-speech. The example in (1) shows a GEN-marked preposition.

[1]http://www.mpi.nl/tools/synpathy.html

Part-of-speech	Features	
AB Adverb	degree	POS KOM SUV
	wh/rel	+FR
AJ Adjective	degree	POS KOM SUV
	gender	UTR NEU MAS
	number	SIN PLU
	species	IND DEF
EN Proper noun		
IJ Interjection		
KO Coordinator		
NN Noun	gender	UTR NEU
	number	SIN PLU
	species	IND DEF
NU Numeral		
PE Preposition		
PO Pronoun	gender	UTR NEU MAS
	number	SIN PLU
	species	IND DEF
	form	SUB OBJ PSS
	wh/rel	+FR
SU Subordinator		
SY Symbol	type	DEL SYM
UO Foreign word		
VB Verb	mod/fin	IND KON IMP SUP INF
	voice	AKT SFO
	tense	PRS PRT

Table 1: The Koala Part-of-speech tag set, with morphological features.

(1) gå till den man ska svara pås gästbok
PE.GEN
go to them one shall reply to's guest book
'go to the guest book of the person you want to reply to'

In addition, parts-of-speech are marked with specific morphological labels when they are abbreviations, or when they are the incomplete part in an elliptical coordination (such as the first part in *lång- och kortfristiga lån* 'long and short term loans', or *1930- och 1940-talet* 'the 1930s and 1940s').

Compared to SUC, several categories are removed. Wh-adverbs are added to adverbs, participles and ordinal numbers to adjectives, and the infinitival marker to subordinators. Determiners, wh-determiners, possessive pronouns, wh-pronouns, and possessive wh-pronouns are added to pronouns. Particles are no longer a separate category, the majority being adverbs or prepositions. Punctuation is subsumed into the category of symbols.

In addition to the part-of-speech and morphological tags, we link words to the large-scale semantic lexicon SALDO (Borin et al., 2013), which provides us with a lemma, the inflectional pattern and a sense distinction. We also follow SALDO in assuming that there is a multiword counterpart to each of the parts-of-speech. In the Koala syntax annotation schema, these multiword expressions reside between the lexical and the phrasal levels.

4 Syntactic annotation

4.1 Formalism

The syntactic structures in the Koala annotation schema follow the format introduced in Skut et al. (1997). It uses rooted trees, the 'primary graph', with additional, 'secondary', edges. All tokens part of the syntactic structure must occur as leaf nodes in the primary graph. Internal nodes in the primary graph represent phrases or (in our schema) multiword expressions. Unlike traditional phrase structure trees, linear order is not part of the encoding and phrases may be discontinuous. Word order variants therefore need not lead to different trees.

Edges, primary as well as secondary, carry grammatical function labels. Secondary edges are used for various kinds of sharing of syntactic material. With secondary edges included, syntactic structures can in principle be unrestricted directed graphs, however, in Koala we avoid cyclic structures.

Tokens are non-empty string segments, and the formalism does not allow for empty categories such as traces or null-pronouns. Discontinuous phrases and secondary edges together take care of most of the need for empty material.

The format has proven its suitability in several treebanks, including the German NEGRA (Brants et al., 1999), TIGER (Brants et al., 2004), and Tuba-D/Z (in restricted form) (Telljohann et al., 2012) treebanks, the Dutch CGN (spoken) (Hoekstra et al., 2001) and Lassy (written) (van Noord et al., 2013) corpora, the Swedish-German parts of the SMULTRON parallel treebank (Volk et al., 2010), and the Swedish Treebank (Nivre et al., 2006). It allows us to combine descriptive adequacy with ease of human annotation. It also allows us to convert the structures into dependency grammar or phrase structure grammar with as few heuristics as possible. The format ideally encodes the combined information found in analyses from either of these traditions.

4.2 Descriptive content

Our analysis of Swedish syntax is for important parts based on MAMBA and SAG. MAMBA contains a mix of elements from dependency grammar, topological field analysis and phrase structure grammar (see also Nivre (2002) for a brief description). The bulk of the dependency types Koala recognizes is taken from MAMBA, although Koala uses a much smaller set, especially in the adverbial and attributive modifier domain. Much of the grammatical argumentation is taken from SAG, as well as the set of phrase types. Of course, a reference grammar and an annotation model have very different goals: Whereas SAG can give a piecemeal description of different grammatical levels and domains and merely point out difficulties, ambiguities or non-discrete categorizations, the Koala schema needs to allow the annotator to assign a single complete tree to an annotation unit. On the other hand, Koala leaves much underspecified. Especially the rich semantic and pragmatic distinctions present in a comprehensive language description such as SAG's have been left out of Koala's system of functions and categories.

Phrasal categories, heads, and pseudoheads

Any of the part-of-speech categories of Section 3 may be used to construct a phrase with arguments and modifiers. The relation between a phrase and its head daughter (HD) is constrained by the following three properties:

Uniqueness There is at most one head in a phrase.
Lexicality The head daughter is a (multi)word.
Projection The phrase's category is determined by the head daughter's part-of-speech

In some cases, we wish to construct a phrase around a head-like element that violates one or more of these constraints. We then use the label pseudohead (PH). All allowed uses of PH are specified in the schema. Phrases are in principle allowed to be (pseudo-)headless, either just in terms of the primary graph or completely. The situations in which this may occur are specified (as much as possible) in the schema. An important motivation for the head constraints is ease of conversion to a dependency format[2] and increased possibilities for automatic error mining of the annotations.

[2]Of course, having a headed tree per se does not help in conversion to a format that uses different criteria for which part of a phrase functions as head.

	Category	Head	Pseudohead
S	Sentence	VB.IND|KON|IMP	
VP	Verb phrase	VB.SUP|INF	
NP	Noun phrase	NN, PO, EN	AJ, AjP, NU, NuP
NuP	Numeral phrase	NU	
KoP	Coordinator phrase		KO
SuP	Subordinator phrase	SU	PO.+FR, AB.+FR, or AbP, NP, AjP, PP dominating such
PP	Preposition phrase	PE	
AjP	Adjective phrase	AJ	
AbP	Adverb phrase	AB	
IjP	Interjection phrase	IJ	
— any of the above —		— UO, SY.SYM —	

Table 2: Phrase categories and head projection rules. Note that wherever a part-of-speech is listed, its multiword counterpart is also accepted.

The inventory of phrase labels, and the part-of-speech tags they are projected from, are given in Table 2. The set of phrases largely follows SAG, although notably, unlike SAG, we do not recognize a finite VP, but instead combine the finite verb with its subject and other dependants directly in S.

We allow both function words (functional parts-of-speech) and content words (lexical parts-of-speech) as heads, unlike for instance the Universal Dependency Treebank (de Marneffe et al., 2014), which for reasons of cross-linguistic parallelism prefers content word heads. To illustrate, we distinguish a PP from an NP, instead of attaching the preposition as a case-like marker in the NP; and we recognize the level of SuP (subordinator phrase) rather than considering the subordinator to be a marker on one of the verbal projections. Although the majority of cases can straightforwardly be converted to a content word head-oriented annotation, we do note that in the case of a PP which embeds another PP or a SuP another SuP, we do not lose the hierarchical structure if we consider the PE or SU to be the head. Examples of the two annotation styles are in (2). The Koala annotation (2a) explicitly encodes the hierarchical information. The alternative – on the assumption of head lexicality – is the flat (2b), where the hierarchical information is only encoded in the linear order of the markers.

(2) a. [$_{PP}$ sedan $_{HD}$ [$_{PP}$ innan $_{HD}$ jul]]
PE PE NN
since before christmas
'since before christmas'

b. [$_{NP}$ sedan $_{MARKER}$ innan $_{MARKER}$ jul $_{HD}$]]

In the same vein, we annotate modal and auxiliary verbs as heads rather than the main verbs, and copulas rather than the predicative complement (see also Section 4.3: 'the verbal domains').

The parts-of-speech SY and UO appear to violate the projection constraint: they may head any type of phrase and therefore do not determine the containing phrase's category. However, because of SY and UO's special status as marking lexical material outside Swedish morpho-syntactic conventions, they function as part-of-speech wild cards, and we do not consider phrases headed by SY or UO to violate projection. For instance, in (3), we have a symbol SY functioning as a verb heading an S, and a foreign multiword UOM functioning as a noun heading an NP.

(3) a. [$_{S}$:'($_{HD}$ inte för mig!]
SY AB PE PO
— not for me
'Don't cry for me!'

b. Det där är [$_{NP}$ ett [*sine qua non.*]$_{HD}$]
PO UOM
that is a —
'That is a *conditio sine qua non.*'

We use pseudoheads PH for head-like daughters in three types of phrases: coordinators in coordinations (Section 4.3: 'coordination'), non-subordinator material introducing relative clauses or subordinate questions (Section 4.3: 'subordinate clauses') and adjectives or numerals in headless NPs (Section 4.3: 'the noun phrase').

Finally, unary branching nodes are avoided. So, bare nouns, adjective phrases, pronouns or numerals can serve directly as, say, direct object, without intermediate NP node. Likewise, we do not posit a unary SuP for bare subordinate clauses – they are simply marked S. In (4), an AjP (arguably with nominal flavour to it) directly serves as object (OO).

(4) Det gäller enbart [$_{AjP}$ nyligen anställda.$_{HD}$]$_{OO}$
AB AJ
this applies only newly employed
'This only applies to new employees.'

By exception, the primary graph will contain unary branching nodes when they are needed to accommodate secondary edges. See (12) in Section 4.3 for an example.

Edge labels

Koala uses a set of 2 head labels, 18 grammatical functions, and 2 extra-syntactic functions. All of them can appear in the primary or secondary graph. Some grammatical functions appear in different phrase types, possibly with subtly different meanings. For instance, we use a rather general MD label for modifiers in any domain. This contrasts with the tradition where such modifiers are called *attributive* in the nominal domain but *adverbial* in other domains. Similarly, the label OO is used for (direct) objects of verbs and adjectives (e.g., *likt dig* 'resembling you', lit. 'alike.NEU you'), as well as the complement (Swe: *rektion*) of subordinators or prepositions. Not all grammatical functions appear in every phrase type. Table 3 lists all functions and their domains. In the table, the designation '*' means any phrasal node can have an outgoing edge with the label in question, '*M' refers to the special multiword nodes, which are lexical pre-terminal nodes (see Section 4.3: 'multiword expressions').

Basic usage of some of the grammatical functions is illustrated in the sections below. The two extra-syntactic functions ME and DF fullfill rather different roles. They are used to include material in the primary graph that would otherwise not enter it for lack of syntactic interactions between the material and the rest of the graph. The multiword element label ME (see Section 4.3: 'multiword expressions') combines leaf nodes into a node to be used as one lexical unit. The discourse function DF is used for material that is coupled to the utterance, but does not relate syntactically to it: vocatives, left/right-dislocations, parentheticals, decorations, tags, etc. Example (5) shows the use of DF for the interjection *eller*, a homonym with coordinator 'or', which has an established use as a question tag.

(5) [$_S$ E$_{HD}$ du go, eller?$_{DF}$]
VB PO AJ IJ
are you good or
'Are you out of your mind!?'

Label	Meaning and domain
HD	head: *
PH	pseudohead: NP, SuP, KoP
SB	subject: S raised subject: VP, only secondary
ES	extraposed subject, pivot: S, VP
OO	direct object: S, VP, AjP complement: PP, SuP
EO	extraposed direct object: S, VP, AjP extraposed complement: PP
IO	indirect object: S, VP, AjP
AG	demoted subject in passive: S, VP, AjP
AN	bound apposition: NP free apposition: * not IjP
KL	conjunct: KoP
DT	determiner: NP
IV	non-finite verbal complement with raised subject: S, VP
JF	comparison: S, VP, AjP, AvP
MD	modifier: *
PL	verb particle: S, VP
OA	adverbial complement: S, VP, AjP, AvP
OP	object-oriented predicative: S, VP, PP
SP	subject-orentied predicative: S, VP
RA	locative/directional adjunct or complement: S, VP
EF	subordinate part of cleft: S, VP
ME	element of a multiword: *M
DF	discourse function: *

Table 3: List of edge labels, and their meaning per applicable domain

The discourse function can admittedly be (ab)used to make the graph span a unit defined in other terms – for instance the graphic sentence – by choosing a main part and adding the rest to it as DF-daughters. In any case, the parts that are connected by DFs are themselves syntactically coherent units, à la Loman and Jörgensen's (1971) *macrosyntagm*.

4.3 Selected applications

Below we give examples of how the system of phrases and functions is employed in some prominent domains of the grammatical system.

The verbal domains S and VP

The phrases S and VP project from respectively finite and non-finite verbs. Phrases of the category S typically contain at least a subject and a verb, further complements and adverbial modifiers of the verb can all be attached in the S node. We use a flat S annotation, irrespective of word order: V2 main clauses, (unmarked) SVO subordinate clauses, and V1 questions, imperatives or conditionals are all S.

VPs are built around a non-finite verb, and never contain their own (formal) subject. For subject control, we use a secondary SB edge, in which case the whole VP receives the special IV function. Arbitrary implicit subjects are not marked at all.

Example (6), a V1-imperative with an *accusativus cum infinitivo*, shows both an S node and a VP-node, and illustrates the use of a secondary edge for the VP's subject.[3]

(6) [$_S$ Snälla$_{DF}$ hjälp$_{HD}$ mig$^{\boxed{1}}_{OO}$ [$_{VP}$ $\boxed{1}_{SB}$ fatta.$_{HD}$]$_{IV}$]
IJ VB PO VB
please help me understand
'Please, help me understand.'

Because of the gradual nature of the auxiliary-main verb distinction in Swedish, we treat auxiliaries as embedding, just like any other verbal complement taking verbs. For instance, composite tense is treated as control using the IV function and a secondary subject in the embedded VP. Non-finite verbal material marked with *att* 'to' is annotated as a SuP containing a VP, with the infinitive marker heading the SuP.

The noun phrase NP

Noun phrases are projected from nouns, pronouns or proper names. The determiner role DT is specific to NPs, and is used for attributes of definiteness (including possessives) and quantity. Otherwise, the MD function is used as a general label for attributive material. In (7) we see a full NP, with both a definiteness and a quantity attribute, and with a prenominal adjectival modifier and a postnominal relative clause.

(7) [$_{NP}$ de$_{DT}$ två$_{DT}$ bästa$_{MD}$ låtar$_{HD}$ [$_S$ han gjort]$_{MD}$]
PO PO AJ NN PO VB
the two best songs he made
'his two best songs'

When an NP lacks a head in a coordination or more generally in ellipsis, we leave it without a head daughter in the primary graph completely, in coordinations the head is indicated using a secondary edge. Some NPs can be argued to construct around a non-nominal core, and annotating these as headless would be undesirable: realization of such NPs without a nominal head is the typical or even only way. Consider the AjP in example (4) above. The adjective *anställd* 'employed', without any nominal head, is the standard way of referring to an employee in Swedish. When combined with a determiner, as in (8a), we know we are dealing with an NP. We thus build an NP on basis of the AjP, and use the PH label to indicate that projection and lexicality are violated.

(8) a. [$_{NP}$ de$_{DT}$ [$_{AjP}$ nyligen$_{MD}$ anställda$_{HD}$]$_{PH}$]
PO AB AJ
the newly employed

b. [$_{NP}$ de$_{DT}$ nya$_{MD}$ anställda$_{PH}$]
PO AJ AJ
the new employed
'the new employees'

In (8b), we see a variant in which the NP with an adjective pseudohead contains an attributive premodifier.

Subordinate clauses S and SuP

Subordinate clauses fall in one of two categories, depending on whether they have pre-adjoined material marking them as subordinate clauses or whether they are bare. First, bare subordinate clauses are labeled S, as in (9).

(9) Jag tror [$_S$ jag$_{SB}$ är$_{HD}$ kär.$_{SP}$]
PO VB AJ
I think I am in love
'I think I'm in love.'

Embedded sentences may have a different word order than main ones, but, as mentioned, this does not change the categorization.

Secondly, embedded clauses are labeled SuP when they are introduced by a subordinator (10a) or by a wh- or relative-marked constituent (10b). Note that the latter is never an SU and may be phrasal. The two types of SuP-introducers are also distinguished by whether they have a syntactic function in the S embedded in the SuP. Note the secondary edge in (10b).

(10) a. Jag tror [$_{SuP}$ att$_{HD}$ [$_S$ du$_{SB}$ förstår.$_{HD}$]$_{OO}$]
SU PO VB
I think that you understand
'I think you understand.'

b. Jag vet
I know
[$_{SuP}$ varför$^{\boxed{1}}_{HD}$ [$_S$ hon$_{SB}$ kom$_{HD}$ hit.$_{RA}$ $\boxed{1}_{MD}$]$_{OO}$]
AB PO VB AB
why she came here
'I know what she came for.'

It is common for SuPs with a pseudo-head to be optionally or obligatorily doubly marked using the

[3] To overcome the limitations of the single line textual representation of structure, we use indexing for secondary edges: *node*$^{\boxed{i}}$ means that *node* will be referred to with index *i*, $\boxed{i}_{FN}$ means node *i* secondarily has function FN. The indices should not be understood as traces or null pronouns.

subordinator *som*, for instance when the pseudo-head is also subject in the complement S: *Ingen anar* $[_{SuP}$ *vad som* $[_{S}$ *sker.*]] 'No-one knows what goes on.'

Coordination KoP

Coordinations get their own phrase category, to deal with coordination of unlike categories.[4] The phrase category KoP can be understood as projected from the coordinator's part-of-speech KO. Coordinators are pseudoheads because of the existence of polysyndeton, in which head uniqueness is violated, (11).

(11) $[_{KoP}$ pappa och_{PH} morfar och_{PH} farfar]
NN KO NN KO NN
dad and grandpa and grandpa
'dad and grandpa (on mother's side) and grandpa (on father's side)'

Next to subject sharing in the verbal domain, coordination is the other main application area for secondary annotations. They are used to distribute material over the conjuncts, as in (12).

(12) $[_{NP}$ $en^{\boxed{1}}_{DT}$ stuga] eller $[_{NP}$ $\boxed{1}_{DT}$ $lada_{HD}$]
PO NN NN
a cottage or barn
'a cottage or barn'

Multiword expressions *M

Multiword expressions are an important part of the Koala annotations, for two different reasons. First, in word sense annotation, multiword expressions as a whole will receive a single sense identifier from the SALDO lexicon. For singleword expressions, sense ids are attached to the token node, for multiword expressions, they are attached to a multiword node which connects to all elements of the expression using ME-labelled edges. Secondly, a part of the vocabulary of multiword expressions cannot be comfortably analyzed in syntactic terms using the general Koala schema – either because they show idiosyncratic properties or because they are part of expressions that can be said to have an expression specific grammar, for instance *Firstname Lastname* person names, street addresses, compound numerals, and so on.[5] We join all elements of such expressions directly under a (unstructured) multiword node, so that the whole may participate in the primary graph as if we were dealing with one token. On the one hand, this allows us to defer the question of whether such expressions should be one token or several (in terms of segmentation), on the other, it allows us to deal with a broader class of idiosyncratic expressions than a word-with-spaces approach, because material under a node need not be continuous. For instance, a discontinuous coordinator like *såväl ... som* 'both ... and' or a circumposition like *för ... sedan* 'ago' (lit. 'for ... since') is also gathered under one multiword node before participating in syntax as pseudo-head in a coordination or head in a PP.

Multiword expressions thus come in two flavours as far as Koala's annotation schema is concerned: analyzable and unanalyzable. Both types are annotated with the help of a multiword node to which we can attach a sense id. Unanalyzable multiword nodes have all their children in the primary graph. An example with a discontinuous coordinator is in (13).

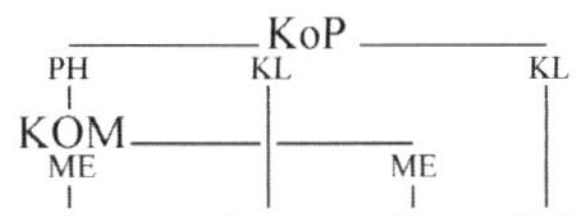

(13) varken kött eller fisk
— NN KO NN
neither meat or fish
varken_eller..1
'neither meat nor fish'

Analyzable multiword expressions first receive a regular syntactic analysis, after which a multiword node is placed in the primary graph directly above one of the elements and the other elements are connected using secondary edges. The multiword annotation here solely fulfils the purpose of having a node to attach the SALDO annotation to. An example of a multiword preposition is given in (14).

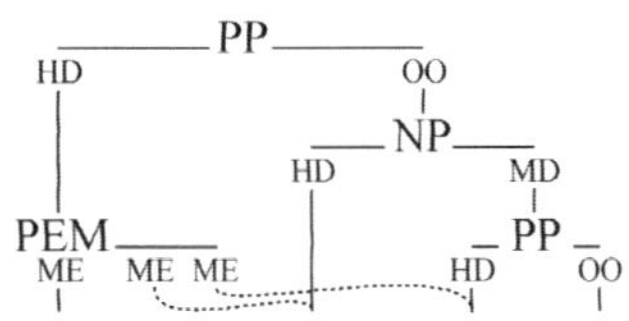

(14) på grund av det
PE NN PE PO
on ground of that
på_grund_av..1
'because of that'

The analyzable multiwords can participate in syn-

[4] Note that, if needed, a more informative phrase type for the coordination can easily be derived automatically from the conjuncts in a coordination of like categories.

[5] This is not to say that the internal structure of such expressions is uninteresting.

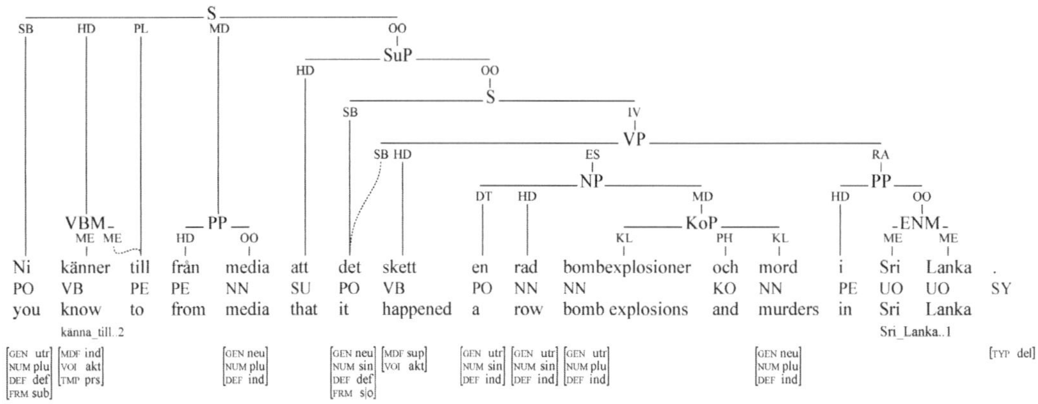

Figure 1: A full Koala sentence analysis.

tax to greater or lesser extent. Some, like the example in (14), are rather fixed, but others, like verb-object and -particle idioms, support-verb-constructions, etc., allow for more freedom, including modification of parts and flexible positioning of parts. Application of the distinction analyzable-unanalyzable has proven to be unproblematic for our annotators in practice, even though corner cases can be found.

4.4 A worked out example

We end this overview of Koala's morpho-syntactic annotation schema with a worked out complete example. Figure 1 shows the analysis of a sentence containing different types of subordinate clauses (S, SuP), two uses of secondary edges (in the multiword *känna till* 'know', lit. 'know to' vs subject control), two types of multiwords (the just mentioned vs *Sri Lanka*), so called *ha*-deletion (the missing temporal auxiliary governing the supine form *skett* 'happened'), a simple coordination, and a complex NP.

5 Conclusions

We have described the linguistic annotations of the 100k token mixed-genre Koala treebank, manually annotated with parts-of-speech and syntactic structures. The corpus will be freely available.

Both the inventory of parts-of-speech and the set of syntactic categories are more concise than in the de facto standards for annotating Swedish, SUC and MAMBA. This is because the simultaneous development of the two annotation levels has allowed us to carefully choose where to put which information. In particular, some part-of-speech distinctions that are purely based on function could be deferred to the syntactic level, with its hybrid structure of head-marked phrases and function labelled edges.

In addition, the structures should be easy to annotate, which means that the distinctions should be easy for the annotators to comprehend and apply. It also mean's that the structures are preferably compact: trees are relatively flat and do not contain empty nodes or unary nodes.

In contrast, we also want the syntactic structure to be easy to convert into other formalisms, which suggests a rich annotation. While the annotation is designed with an eye towards conversion into a bare constituency or dependency structure, we believe that the explicit annotation structure sharing and non-local relationships provided in the corpus can also make it usable as the basis for a conversion into linguistically richer formalisms (Cahill et al., 2004; Miyao et al., 2004).

Although the development of the annotation guidelines and the annotation itself is well underway, we have yet to do a thorough evaluation of the consistency of the annotation, the comprehensiveness of the annotation guidelines and the ease of annotating the described syntactic structures. However, at the time of writing we have annotations of parts-of-speech and syntactic structures for around 60k tokens. Our impression is that annotation is fast and the annotators enjoy the annotation work.

Acknowledgements

The Koala project is funded 2014–2016 by Riksbankens Jubilemsfond, grant number In13-0320:1.

References

Lars Borin, Markus Forsberg, and Lennart Lönngren. 2013. SALDO: a touch of yin to WordNet's yang. *Language Resources and Evaluation*, 47(4):1191–1211.

Thorsten Brants, Wojciech Skut, and Hans Uszkoreit. 1999. Syntactic annotation of a German newspaper corpus. In *Proceedings of the ATALA Treebank Workshop*, pages 69–76.

Sabine Brants, Stefanie Dipper, Peter Eisenberg, Silvia Hansen-Schirra, Esther König, Wolfgang Lezius, Christian Rohrer, George Smith, and Hans Uszkoreit. 2004. Tiger: Linguistic interpretation of a German corpus. *Research on Language and Computation*, 2(4):597–620.

Aoife Cahill, Michael Burke, Ruth O'Donovan Josef Van Genabith, and Andy Way. 2004. Long-distance dependency resolution in automatically acquired wide-coverage PCFG-based LFG approximations. In *Proceedings of the 42nd Meeting of the Association for Computational Linguistics (ACL'04), Main Volume*, pages 319–326.

Marie-Catherine de Marneffe, Timothy Dozat, Natalia Silveira, Katri Haverinen, Filip Ginter, Joakim Nivre, and Christopher Manning. 2014. Universal stanford dependencies: A cross-linguistic typology. In *Proceedings of LREC*.

Eva Ejerhed, Gunnel Källgren, Ola Wennstedt, and Magnus Åström. 1992. The linguistic annotation system of the Stockholm-Umeå corpus project - description and guidelines. Technical report, Department of Linguistics, Umeå University.

Helen Hoekstra, Michael Moortgat, Ineke Schuurman, and Ton van der Wouden. 2001. Syntactic annotation for the spoken Dutch corpus project (CGN). In Walter Daelemans, Khalil Sima'an, Jorn Veenstra, and Jakub Zavrel, editors, *Computational Linguistics in the Netherlands 2000. Selected Papers from the Eleventh CLIN Meeting*, pages 73–87. Rodopi.

Philipp Koehn. 2002. Europarl: A multilingual corpus for evaluation of machine translation.

Bengt Loman and Nils Jörgensen. 1971. *Manual för analys och beskrivning av makrosyntagmer*. Studentlitteratur, Lund.

Yusuke Miyao, Takashi Ninomiya, , and Jun'ichi Tsujii. 2004. Corpus-oriented grammar development for acquiring a head-driven phrase structure grammar from the Penn Treebank. In *Proceedings of the 1st International Joint Conference on Natural Language Processing (IJCNLP 2004)*, pages 684–693.

Joakim Nivre, Jens Nilsson, and Johan Hall. 2006. Talbanken05: A Swedish treebank with phrase structure and dependency annotation. In *Proceedings of the 5th International Conference on Language Resources and Evaluation (LREC)*, pages 1392–1395.

Joakim Nivre, Beáta Megyesi, Sofia Gustafson-Capková, Filip Salomonsson, and Bengt Dahlqvist. 2008. Cultivating a Swedish treebank. In *Resourceful Language Technology: Festschrift in Honor of Anna Sågvall Hein*. Uppsala University, Department of Linguistics and Philology.

Joakim Nivre. 2002. What kinds of trees grow in Swedish soil? a comparison of four annotation schemes for Swedish. In *Proceedings of the Workshop on Treebanks and Linguistic Theories, September 20-21 (TLT02)*.

Robert Östling. 2013. Stagger: an open-source part of speech tagger for swedish. *Northern European Journal of Language Technology*, 3:1–18.

Wojciech Skut, Brigitte Krenn, Thorsten Brants, and Hans Uszkoreit. 1997. An annotation scheme for free word order languages. In *Proceedings of the 5th Conference on Applied Natural Language Processing*, pages 88–95.

Ulf Teleman, Staffan Hellberg, and Erik Andersson. 1999. *Svenska Akademiens Grammatik*. Svenska Akademien, Stockholm.

Ulf Teleman. 1974. *Manual för grammatisk beskrivning av talad och skriven svenska*. Studentlitteratur, Lund.

Heike Telljohann, Erhard Hinrichs, Sandra Kübler, Heike Zinsmeister, and Kathrin Beck. 2012. Stylebook for the Tübingen treebank of written German (TüBa-D/Z). Technical report, Seminar für Sprachwissenschaft, Tübingen.

Gertjan van Noord, Gosse Bouma, Frank Van Eynde, Daniël de Kok, Jelmer van der Linde, Ineke Schuurman, Erik Tjong Kim San Sang, and Vincent Vandeghinste. 2013. Large scale syntactic annotation of written dutch: Lassy. In Peter Spyns and Jan Odijk, editors, *Essential Speech and Language Technology for Dutch*, Theory and Applications of Natural Language Processing, pages 147–164. Springer Berlin Heidelberg.

Martin Volk, Anne Göhring, Torsten Marek, and Yvonne Samuelsson. 2010. SMULTRON (version 3.0) — the Stockholm MULtilingual parallel TReebank. `http://www.cl.uzh.ch/research/parallelcorpora/paralleltreebanks_en.html`.

A case study on supervised classification of Swedish pseudo-coordination

Malin Ahlberg, Peter Andersson, Markus Forsberg, and Nina Tahmasebi
Språkbanken, Department of Swedish, University of Gothenburg
{firstname.lastname}@svenska.gu.se

Abstract

We present a case study on supervised classification of Swedish pseudo-coordination (SPC). The classification is attempted on the type-level with data collected from two data sets: a blog corpus and a fiction corpus. Two small experiments were designed to evaluate the feasability of this task. The first experiment explored a classifier's ability to discriminate pseudo-coordinations from ordinary verb coordinations, given a small labeled data set created during the experiment. The second experiment evaluated how well the classifier performed at detecting and ranking SPCs in a set of unlabeled verb coordinations, to investigate if it could be used as a semi-automatic discovery procedure to find new SPCs.

1 Introduction

This paper describes a case study on supervised classification of Swedish complex predicate constructions, namely pseudo-coordinations (SPCs). SPCs are light verb constructions of the form V_1 *och* V_2 'V_1 and V_2', with a semantically light V_1. An example of an SPC is *Han står och stirrar bort över havet* which could be literally translated into 'He stands and stares away over the sea', but a more correct translation would be 'He is staring away over the sea', i.e., the first verb mainly adds a progressive/durative aspect to the second verb. This example illustrates one of the reasons why SPCs, as well as constructions in general, may be worth studying from a practical language technology perspective – to improve machine translation.

We use the term 'construction' as it is used within the theoretical paradigm of construction grammar. The main tenet of construction grammar is that our grammatical knowledge is made up of a taxonomic network of constructions, i.e., pairings of form and meaning (Croft, 2001; Goldberg, 2006). Moreover, no level of grammar is considered autonomous (Fried and Östman, 2004). Constructions include all dimensions of language, form includes syntax as well as phonological aspects, and meaning includes semantics and pragmatics. Early works on construction grammar restrict the notion of constructions to form-meaning pairings with some non-predictable aspect (Goldberg, 1995), but today the concept of construction has been expanded to also include pairings with compositional meaning, which "are stored as constructions even if they are fully predictable, as long as they occur with sufficient frequency" (Goldberg, 2006). SPCs are complex constructions with a partially non-compositional meaning.

Previous work on automatic identification of Swedish constructions, e.g., Forsberg et al. (2014), focus on unsupervised classification of all constructions in a language. Forsberg et al. (2014) do this by using information-theoretic measures to rank automatically generated hybrid n-grams, where the constituents of an n-gram are either lemmas or a syntactic phrases. In this paper we are interested in a particular class of constructions, namely SPCs, where we explore the use of supervised methods that rely on available linguistic knowledge about SPCs in the classification process.

1.1 Swedish pseudo-coordination (SPC)

Pseudo-coordination is not unique to Swedish, it appears in all Scandinavian languages, as well as in other languages, such as English. If we turn our attention to pseudo-coordination in Swedish, the standard grammar reference for Swedish, Teleman et al. (1999), list five classes of SPC, based on the properties of the first verb (V_1).

1. V_1 is a position verb, e.g., *sitta* 'sit', *stå* 'stand', *ligga* 'lay'...

Kristian ***står och stirrar*** *bort över havet.*
'Kristian is staring (lit. 'stands and stares') out over the sea.'

2. V_1 is a verb of movement, e.g., *kom hit* 'come here', *åka* 'go', *går ut* 'go out', *kryper in* 'crawl inside' ...
Jag tror jag ***kryper in och sträcker ut mig*** *ett slag.*
'I think I will crawl inside and stretch myself out for a while.'

3. V_1 is a verb denoting different phases of an action, e.g., börja 'begin', fortsätta 'continue', hålla på 'keep on', sluta 'stop' ...
Folk ***håller på och tar ner*** *sina parasoller.*
'People keep on (lit. 'and') taking down their umbrellas.'

4. V_1 is a verb preceding a politeness expression, e.g., *vara (hygglig)* 'be (so kind)'.
Kan du inte ***vara hygglig och köpa*** *hem mat?*
'Could you be so kind and buy home some food?'

5. V_1 is a verb denoting the channel of communication, e.g., *skriva* 'write', *ringa* 'call', *telegrafera* 'telegraph' ...
Skriv och berätta *om dina glada upplevelser.*
'Write and tell me about your happy experiences.'

1.2 Linguistic properties of SPC

Central work related to SPCs are Teleman et al. (1999), Wiklund (2007), Kvist Darnell (2008), Blensenius (2014), and Hilpert and Koops (2008). SPCs are not as well understood as similar constructions, e.g., auxiliary constructions, which have been more extensively studied. Below you find the most prominent properties that distinguish SPCs from ordinary verb coordinations, as described in the litterature.

1. It is possible to front an object or bound adverbial of V_2 that is not compatible with V_1:
Hon satt och skrev en bok.
'She sat and wrote a book.'
$\Rightarrow$
Det var en bok som hon satt och skrev.
'It was a book that she sat and wrote.'

2. The order of V_1 and V_2 is fixed:
Mona satt och skrev
'Mona sat and wrote.'
$\Rightarrow$
?*Mona skrev och satt.*
'Mona wrote and sat'

3. Some paraphrasings are blocked:
Mona satt och sydde
'Mona sat and sewed.'
$\Rightarrow$
?*Mona satt och hon sydde.*
'Mona sat and she sewed'

4. *både* V_1 och V_2 'both V_1 and V_2' is blocked:
?*Mona både satt och sydde*
'Mona both sat and sewed.'

5. There are usually no or few arguments between V_1 and *och*.

6. Both verb forms have identical tense, with a few exceptions where V_1 is a modal auxiliary: *måste och handla* 'lit. must (present) and shop (infinitive)' and *vill och bada* 'lit. want (present) and bath (infinitive)'.

Other criteria are based on our own observations, or a result of discussions with colleagues. An example of what came out of these discussions is the negation test: If an SPC has a negation inserted after V_1, it also negates V_2. *Hon satt inte och skrev en bok* 'She did not (sit and) write a book'. This stands in contrast to ordinary verb coordination where the negation does not affect V_2. *Hon skrattade inte och sade ingenting* 'She did not laugh and said nothing'. Another example of what came out of these discussions was that frequency counts are very important, especially the count of the V_2 verb types; when the V_1 verb is light, it is more likely to occur with a large number of V_2 types.

Most, if not all criteria, need to be fulfilled in order for a verb coordination to qualify as a SPC. But as always when dealing with real language, between the clear cases, you find a lot of variation. One problem with using some of the above criteria is that they are all negative tests, which are known to be problematic in language classification tasks. E.g., not finding *både* V_1 *och* V_2 'both V_1 and V_2' in our data collection does not at all entail that it cannot occur, only that it has not been found in the data set.

Moreover, different SPCs seem to behave somewhat differently and the dividing line between SPCs and other complex predicates are not distinct. Both lexicalized verb constructions, such as *tycka och tänka*, 'think and reflect', and auxiliary constructions, such as *sluta och (att) spela*, 'lit. stop and (to) play', behave similarly with respect to syntactic and semantic features (Teleman et al., 1999). In fact, since 'och' and 'att' are typically pronounced in the same way, verb chains with a V_1 denoting the phase of an action are often pronounced in the same way both as SPCs and auxiliaries. Wiklund (2007) calls this group of verb chains an informal and dialectal class of SPCs.

2 Methodology

The experiments are designed for supervised classification on the type level, i.e., we do not try to decide whether a particular verb coordination in a given context is an SPC, but rather whether the verb coordination, given all its contexts, tends to function as a pseudo-coordination. For this we need a labeled data set and a suitable set of features. These features were derived from previous work and adapted to our settings. The values for each feature are based on all evidence for a verb coordination in the current data set.

Once we have trained and tested our classifier on the labeled data set, we then apply the classifier on unknown instances and evaluate the top SPC candidates according to the classifier, i.e., try to use the classifier as an SPC discovery procedure.

2.1 A random forest classifier

Using the Weka tool (Hall et al., 2009), we experimented with different types of machine learning algorithms, all with similar results. A requirement was that the classifier should be able to produce a real-valued classification to enable ranking. For no other strong reason, we ended up using a random forest classifier (Breiman, 2001). A random forest classifier consists of a combination of decision trees where features are randomly extracted to build a set of decision trees. A decision tree is a tree-structured graph where each node corresponds to a test on a feature. A path from the root to a leaf represents a classification rule.

The features are decided upon beforehand and the values for each node are learned based on training data, with the aim to best separate the positive instances from the negative instances. In our case, the instances to be classified are the verb coordinations, (V_i, V_j), that are considered positive if they are in the class SPC, and negative if they do not.

The classifier is trained and tested on labeled data from both the positive and negative class. Training and testing are performed on mutually exclusive parts of the labeled data in a stratified ten-fold cross validation. The classification results are then averaged over all ten folds.

The result according to the test data is presented in a confusion matrix with four classes: true positive (TP), true negative (TN), false positive (FP), and false negative (FN). The true positive and true negative classes contain those instances that have been correctly classified. The false positive class contains all non-SPC instances that have been misclassified as SPC, and conversly, the false negative class contains all SPC instances misclassified as non-SPC.

2.2 The feature set

For each verb coordination (V_i, V_j), we derived a set of features based on the evidence in our data set. Our features were derived from Hilpert and Koops (2008), Teleman et al. (1999), Tsvetkov and Wintner (2011) (a work on classifying multiword expressions, a task similar to this one), as well as our own observations.

The features generally measured closeness and order, as well as represented negative tests, and the features were real-valued features rather than binary, i.e., a test like "is the word *både* 'both' used before the verb coordination?" was translated into "how often is the word *både* used before the verb coordination?". In particular when working with unedited text such as blogs, real-valued features can help reduce the effects of noise.

The features used by our classifier are described below.

1. **frequency** Frequency of (V_1, V_2), normalized by
   - the maximum frequency of any verb coordination
   - the average frequency of all verb coordinations
2. **closeness** How often are V_1 and V_2 separated by words other than *och* 'and'?
3. **inverse order** How often does (V_2, V_1) occur in relation to the frequency of (V_1, V_2)?

4. **inverse frequency** Frequency of (V_2, V_1), normalized using the maximum frequency of any verb coordination.

5. **inverse closeness** Similar to test 2, but for (V_2, V_1).

6. **both** How often is *både* 'both' used in conjunction to the verb coordination?

7. **between** How many words appear on average between V_1 and V_2?

8. **spread** How many different V can be found with V_1? Normalized by the maximum spread of all V_1.

9. **PMI** Pointwise mutual information as $log(p(V_1, V_2)/(p(V_1) * p(V_2)))$ where $p(V_i)$ is the relative frequency of verb V_i and $p(V_1, V_2)$ is the relative frequency of the verb coordination.

10. **not** How often does the word *inte* 'not' follow V_1: V_1 *inte och* V_2?

11. **tense** How often do V_1 and V_2 share the same tense?

12. **pos tags before** Distribution of the three most common pos-tags before the verb coordination.

13. **pos tags after** Distribution of the three most common pos-tags after the verb coordination.

Since the classification is done on the type level, it is unavoidable that we sometimes misclassify individual instances. Moreover, since the extraction of verb coordinations is currently done without any sophistication, some chains of verb coordinations can be misinterpreted, e.g., *Jag var ute och gick och hittade min bok* 'I was out walking and found my book' will probably be misclassified as SPC, since *gick och hittade* is erroneously extracted, a verb coordination that tends to be an SPC.

3 Two SPC experiments

The aim of our experiments is twofold. First, we want to know how well the known properties of SPCs can be utilized for classification, i.e., can we build a classifier that can separate known SPCs from other verb coordinations? Secondly, we want to explore if a classifier trained on labeled data can be used to detect SPCs from a set of unknown verb coordinations. We do this by labeling all unknown verb coordinations as non-SPCs and feeding them to the classifier. If the classifier judges them as SPCs, they end up in the class of false positives, with confidence scores that we can use for ranking. We then evaluate if the method can be used as a semi-automatic SPC discovery procedure by investigating the top candidates of the ranking.

The experiments are performed on two different kinds of modern Swedish data sets: a blog corpus and a fiction corpus.

3.1 The data

The blog corpus, *Bloggmix*,[1] is a collection of Swedish blog texts consisting of around 505 million tokens spanning 16 years, starting in 1998. The data has been annotated automatically using the LT tools in the Korp pipeline (Borin et al., 2012).

Since blog texts are typically informal and unedited, they contain a high degree of noise, i.e., misspellings and ungrammatical language. However, since the language of blogs typically is closer to spoken language than edited texts, and SPCs tend to be more frequent in spoken language, they contain many SPCs as well as new SPC-like constructions.

The fiction corpus, *Bonniers Romaner I&II*,[2] is some decades older and contains a more standardized language use. It consists of around 11 million tokens of Swedish fiction published between 1976 and 1981.

From each of these data sets we have extracted a training set of verb coordinations occuring at least twice in the data, manually labeled as SPC or non-SPC. The SPC instances all have V_1 listed as typical SPC-verbs by Teleman et al. (1999, §17–22), such as *sitta* 'sit' and *ringa* 'call'. In the negative training set, we collected instances of the same V_1, but used with V_2 that will force a non-SPC reading, such as *ringa och skriva* 'call and write' and *sitta och ligga* 'sit and lie down'. The negative examples also consist of verb coordinations with first verbs randomly selected from the data set. To

[1]Browsable at `http://spraakbanken.gu.se/korp/`, and downloadable (in a sentence-scrambled format) at `http://spraakbanken.gu.se/eng/resources/corpus`.

[2]Browsable at `http://spraakbanken.gu.se/korp/#?corpus=romi,romii`, and downloadable (in a sentence-scrambled format) at `http://spraakbanken.gu.se/eng/resources/corpus`.

	SPC	Non-SPC
SPC	492 (TP)	55 (FN)
Non-SPC	71 (FP)	598 (TN)

Table 1: Confusion matrix for the blog data set

Precision	Recall	Class
0.874	0.899	SPC
0.916	0.894	Non-SPC
0.897	0.897	Weighted avg

Table 2: Classification results for the blog data set.

capture slight variations, we allow a maximum of three words separating V_1 and V_2, e.g., ***sitter** i soffan **och läser*** 'sits in the sofa and reads'.

The created data sets were small, but for our explorative purposes, sufficiently large to get an idea of the feasibility of the task. For the blog texts we had 669 verb coordinations marked as non-SPC with 298 unique V_1, and 547 verb coordinations marked as SPC with 16 unique V_1 that were collected from Teleman et al. (1999). For the fiction data set we had 193 verb coordinations marked as non-SPC with 121 unique V_1, and 121 verb coordinations marked as SPC with 11 unique V_1.

3.2 SPC classification: the blog data set

In order to investigate how well the classifier performs on the blog data set, we evaluated using a stratified 10-fold cross validation on the labelled data. Tables 1 and 2 show the results. The classifier was able to correctly identify 89.9% of all SPCs and 89.4% of all non-SPCs, giving us an F1-measure of 0.897.

3.3 SPC ranking of unknowns: the blog data set

In our second experiment we tested the classifier, trained on the labeled data set, on previously unknown verb coordinations that we added as non-SPC. Table 3 shows the top ranking of verb coordinations that ended up in the false positive, i.e., the verb coordinations in the unknown set that the classifier deemed SPC. We found a few SPCs in this manner, for example, V_1 such as *åka* 'go', *stanna* 'stay, stop', *dra* '(slang) go' and *fara* '(formal) go' are all examples of V_1-verbs that occur in SPCs.

After having analyzed the ranking, we found many of the verb coordinations interesting, even though not necessarily typical SPCs. To investigate this further, we conducted a manual analysis of the results and classified each verb coordination into one of five classes, defined as follows:

1. **Class 0** No SPCs, or incorrectly extracted verb coordination, e.g., V_2 is the first word in phrasal verb.

2. **Class 1** Additive lexicalized verb coordination, e.g., *äta och dricka* 'eat and drink'.

3. **Class 2** Lexicalized SPC-like verb coordination, where V_2 is semantically more prominent than V_1, e.g., *fnysa och säga* 'snort and say'.

4. **Class 3** Verb coordination with a strong tendency to be SPC.

5. **Class 4** Support verb constructions, where V_1 is a support verb. The most common use of V_1 *och* V_2 in informal texts is actually incorrectly written, and should have been V_1 *att* V_2. E.g., *försöka och träna* 'try and (meant: to) exercise'.

Since this task is hard in the general case, we decided to only evaluate a few verb coordinations, and to do it through a consensus discussion among at least three evaluators. When in doubt, sentences that contained the verb coordination were used to support a decision. For the blog data, we evaluated in total 78 of the top-ranked verb coordinations. The majority of the verb coordinations, 53 of 78 was marked as class 0, and for the remaining classes, class 1: 5, class 2: 2, class 3: 12, and class 4: 6. With the exception of class 0, the SPC class was the largest with its 12 verb coordinations. In total, 25 of the 78 verb coordinations were of interest for further analysis.

3.4 SPC classification: the fiction data set

For the fiction data set, the cross validation results in Table 5 differ only slightly from the results on the blog data set. The classifier correctly identifies 90.6% of all SPCs and 89.1% of all non-SPCs. The F1-measure of 0.898 shows that the results are comparable to those of the blog data set. The absolute number of instances that fall into different categories differ from blogs, Table 4, but are similar in relation.

Verb pair	First verb	Conf.	#pairs	Pairs
talk and decide*	prata	1.0	169	[bestämma, ljuga, trycka,...]
go and camp	åka	1.0	195	[campa, beställa, bidra,...]
work and enjoy	jobba	1.0	146	[roa, använda, stressa, ...]
see and squeeze	se	1.0	56	[klämma, uppleva, värdera, ...]
find and try	hitta	1.0	71	[prova, leka, se, ...]
go and shower	dra	1.0	73	[duscha, kolla, fortsätta, ...]
play and crack	spela	1.0	51	[spräcka, njuta, uppträda, ...]
use and put	använda	1.0	66	[ställa, upptäcka, fungera, ...]
look and laugh	kolla	1.0	72	[skratta, klappa, fylla, ...]
eat and scoff*	äta	1.0	91	[glufsade, lyssna, babbla,...]
stay and promise	stanna	1.0	57	[lova, slappa, käka, ...]

Table 3: An extract of highly ranked verb coordinations in the blog data set. **Verb coordinations** in **bold** have a strong tendency to be SPCs, and * marks interesting verb coordinations from class 1, 2 or 4.

	SPC	Non-SPC
SPC	163 (TP)	17 (FN)
Non-SPC	21 (FP)	172 (TN)

Table 4: Confusion matrix for the fiction data set

Precision	Recall	Class
0.886	0.906	SPC
0.91	0.891	Non-SPC
0.898	0.898	Weighted avg

Table 5: Classification results for the fiction data set.

3.5 SPC ranking of unknowns: the fiction data set

Table 6 shows all verb coordinations that are classified by the algorithm as a false positive with a confidence higher than or equal to 0.6.

There is one movement SPC V_1, *åka* 'go', and one phasal SPC, V_1: *stanna* 'stay, stop'. Furthermore, we find verb coordinations that show a tendency of acting in an SPC-like way, e.g., *vända och gå* 'turn around and go'. The top candidates, *kunna* 'be able to' and *ha* 'have', are errors occuring because of faulty coordination extraction – clausal coordinations have been misinterpreted as verb coordinations. For further discussion, see section 4.

We evaluated this data set in the same manner as for the blog data, through consensus voting of at least three evaluators. Again, we only evaluated a small data set, 61 verb coordinations. We found 31 of 61 in class 0; 7 in class 1; 7 in class 2; 14 in class 3; and 1 in class 4. In total, 30 of the 61 verb coordinations were of interest for further analysis. In comparison with the same experiment on blog texts, we get 20% more, however, since we are dealing we such small sets of data, it is not possible to conclude that the difference is statistically significant.

4 Discussion

Teleman et al. (1999) list a few more SPC tests. One such important test is whether the pronounciation of the first verb is stressed, but such features are unavailable in our data sets. Neither do we take into account features that require a correct parse tree, such as object extraction (see 1.2). This test was used by Hilpert and Koops (2008) in their manual classification, but the correctness of the syntactic parses available to us was not deemed high enough to measure this correctly, especially for the unstandardized language found in blog texts. Hilpert and Koops (2008) also consider adverb placement, which is a feature approximated by feature 7, see section 2.2.

The feature **spread**, which is related to the grammaticalization of V_1, counts the number of unique V_2. Frequent SPC V_1 verbs such as *sitta* 'sit' have a high V_2 count. Interestingly, empirical evidence shows that while removing this feature gives lower results in the classification, see table 7 and 8, the corresponding classifier seemed to find more interesting SPC candidates when applied to the unknown verb coordinations. Table 9 shows the ranking of the unknown verb coordinations for the blog data set, with a corresponding F1-score of 0.847 for the classifier. That is, a five point drop in F1-score gave us the possibility to better locate up-and-coming SPCs semi-automatically. Examples of first verbs found with a confidence score of 1.0 are *googla* 'to google, googling', *ramla* 'to

verb coordination	First verb	Conf.	#coordinations	Verb coordinations
can and take	kunna	1.0	12	[ta, böra, se...]
have and put	ha	0.9	4	[lägga, ge, ha...]
go and pick up	åka	0.8	5	[hämta, hälsa, spela,...]
stay and buy	stanna	0.7	8	[köpa, lyssna, ta, vänta...]
smile and say*	le	0.7	2	[säga, verka]
say and feel	säga	0.7	8	[känna, dra, visa,...]
see and feel	se	0.7	4	[känna, lära, erfara,...]
laugh and say*	skratta	0.6	1	[säga]
live and must	leva	0.6	1	[måste]
turn around and go*	vända	0.6	1	[gå]

Table 6: Ranking of unknown verb coordinations in the fiction data set with a confidence higher than or equal to 0.6. **Verb coordinations** in **bold** have a strong tendency to be SPCs. * marks interesting verb coordinations from class 1, 2 or 4.

fall', *fara* 'to go', *resa* 'to travel', *mejla* 'email', *maila* 'email (different spelling)', *trilla* 'to fall', *varda (vart)* 'to be', *vända* 'turn', and *testa* 'test'.

The verb coordination *mejla och fråga* 'email and ask' falls into the same category as *ringa och fråga* 'call and ask' or *telegrafera och skicka* 'to telegraph and send a message'. Further down the list we find the Swedish words for *emailing*, *googling*, *commenting*, and *blogging*, i.e., new forms of communication. We also find more lexicalized verb coordinations such as: *ramla och slå (sig)* 'to fall and hurt oneself', *vända och gå* 'to turn around and go'.

Similar analysis on the fiction data set did not change the ranking substantially, probably due to it being a smaller data set, possibly because the language use is more formal and less spoken-like than in blogs. This hypothesis remains to be further investigated.

Since the data sets are small, it is important to note that our results are indicative rather than conclusive. When building the labeled data set we aimed at including well-known SPCs, as described in the reference literature, into our data. To reduce the bias of the frequency of V_1 in the data set, we added verb coordinations where V_1 both occurs in SPCs and non-SPCs. E.g., both SPCs such as *sitta och titta* 'sit and look' and non-SPCs such as *sitta och ligga* 'sit and lie down' are included in our training data to reduce this bias. We also randomly sampled verb coordinations while excluding the V_1 occuring in known SPCs. A more fair sample could be created, and will be created in future work, by sampling the negative examples according to the frequency distributions of V_1 and V_2 for the SPCs.

Precision	Recall	Class
0.853	0.797	SPC
0.843	0.888	Non-SPC
0.847	0.847	Weighted avg

Table 7: Cross validation results for the blog data set without the spread feature.

Precision	Recall	Class
0.729	0.822	SPC
0.821	0.715	Non-SPC
0.772	0.767	Weighted avg

Table 8: Cross validation results for the fiction data set without the spread feature.

5 Conclusion and future work

We presented a case study on supervised classification of Swedish pseudo-coordination. The classification results with F1 measures of 0.9 based on two separate data set indicate that it is possible to automatically separate known SPCs from other verb coordinations. When applying the classifiers on unknown verb coordinations, we found that quite a few interesting verb coordinations could be captured semi-automatically using a simple discovery procedure. However, when evaluating the result manually, it became clear that many verb coordinations had as many positive as negative SPC instances, which suggests that individual instances often cannot be estimated using general tendencies. Therefore, our next step is to explore how to do the classification on the instance-level instead of the type-level, like we do here.

Instance-level judgments will be important for the future research that we have planned, which

Verb pair	First verb	Conf.	#pairs	Pairs
go and camp	åka	1.0	120	[campa, beställa, bidra,...]
wake and see*	vakna	1.0	63	[se, leva, ligga, ...]
stay and eat	stanna	1.0	65	[käka, städa, säga,...]
pack and prepare	packa	1.0	19	[förbereda, vänta, åka, ...]
eat and listen	äta	1.0	35	[lyssna, fixa, titta, ...]
fall and break*	ramla	1.0	9	[bryta, slå, skrapa, skada, skylla, ...]
go and check	dra	1.0	47	[kolla, storhandla, gymma, ...]
nod and say*	nicka	1.0	4	[säga, se, komma, ...]
go and eat	fara	1.0	30	[käka, fixa, fika, ...]
google and find	googla	1.0	9	[titta, hitta, upptäcka, ...]
mail and ask	maila	1.0	13	[vilja, tipsa, fråga, ...]
stand and wait	stog	1.0	7	[vänta, titta, kolla ...]
comment and share*	kommentera	0	14	[dela, motivera, fråga, ...]
mail and tell	mejla	1.0	7	[berätta, säga, kolla, ...]
text message and ask	messa	0.9	6	[vilja, undra, säga, ...]
talk and decide*	prata	0.9	25	[bestämma, räkna, låtsas, ...]

Table 9: An extract of highly ranked verb coordinations in the blog data set, without the spread feature. **Verb coordinations** in **bold** have a strong tendency to be SPCs. * marks interesting verb coordinations from class 1, 2 or 4.

is to investigate how to capture constructional change of SPCs by introducing a temporal dimension to the classification. If successful in this task, we will continue by investigating if we can construct a classifier that captures constructional change in general, e.g., by trying to target constructions that in some ways are similar to SPCs. An interesting question in this context becomes: given that we do not know anything at all about the existence and/or emergence of a class of SPC, is there a way to discover them?

When adding a temporal dimension, the most interesting cases are the ambiguous ones, together with the SPC-likeness of other complex predicate constructions, which may represent an ongoing change, e.g., a grammaticalization in a continuum starting from ordinary verb coordination to auxiliary-like SPCs.

Acknowledgments

The research presented here was supported by the Swedish Research Council (through the projects *Swedish FrameNet++*, contract no 2010-6013, *Towards a knowledge-based culturomics*, dnr 2012-5738), and by the Bank of Sweden Tercentenary Foundation (grant agreement P12-0076:1) (through *A Swedish Constructicon*, dnr 2010-6013), the University of Gothenburg through its support of the Centre for Language Technology and its support of Språkbanken.

References

Kristian Blensenius. 2014. Maintaining contact with pseudoprogressive pseudocoordinations: Swedish verbal coordinations with 'sit', 'stand', and 'lie' from a spatial perspective. Ms. Dept. of Swedish, University of Gothenburg.

Lars Borin, Markus Forsberg, and Johan Roxendal. 2012. Korp – the corpus infrastructure of Språkbanken. In *Proceedings of LREC 2012*, pages 474–478, Istanbul. ELRA.

Leo Breiman. 2001. Random forests. In *Machine Learning*, pages 5–32.

William Croft. 2001. *Radical construction grammar : syntactic theory in typological perspective*. Oxford University Press, New York.

Markus Forsberg, Richard Johansson, Linnéa Bäckström, Lars Borin, Benjamin Lyngfelt, Joel Olofsson, and Julia Prentice. 2014. From construction candidates to constructicon entries: An experiment using semi-automatic methods for identifying constructions in corpora. *Constructions and Frames*, 6(1):114–135.

Mirjam Fried and Jan-Ola Östman. 2004. *Construction grammar in a cross-language perspective*. John Benjamins Pub., Amsterdam.

Adele E. Goldberg. 1995. *Constructions : a construction grammar approach to argument structure*. Univ. of Chicago Press, Chicago.

Adele E. Goldberg. 2006. *Constructions at work : the nature of generalization in language*. Oxford Univ. Press, New York.

Mark Hall, Eibe Frank, Geoffrey Holmes, Bernhard Pfahringer, Peter Reutemann, and Ian H. Witten.

2009. The weka data mining software: An update. *SIGKDD Explor. Newsl.*, 11(1):10–18, November.

Martin Hilpert and Christian Koops. 2008. A quantitative approach to the development of complex predicates. The case of Swedish Pseudo-Coordination with sitta "sit". *Diachronica*, 25(2):242–261.

Ulrika Kvist Darnell. 2008. *Pseudosamordningar i svenska : särskilt sådana med verben sitta, ligga och stå*. Institutionen för lingvistik. Stockholms universitet, Stockholm.

Ulf Teleman, Staffan Hellberg, and Erik Andersson. 1999. *Svenska Akademiens grammatik*. Stockholm: Norstedts.

Yulia Tsvetkov and Shuly Wintner. 2011. Identification of multi-word expressions by combining multiple linguistic information sources. In *Proceedings of the Conference on Empirical Methods in Natural Language Processing*, EMNLP '11, pages 836–845, Stroudsburg, PA, USA. Association for Computational Linguistics.

Anna-Lena Wiklund. 2007. *The syntax of tenselessness : tense/mood/aspect-agreeing infinitivals*. Mouton de Gruyter, Berlin.

Supersense tagging for Danish

Héctor Martínez Alonso‡ Anders Johannsen Sussi Olsen Sanni Nimb†
Nicolai Hartvig Sørensen† Anna Braasch Anders Søgaard Bolette Sandford Pedersen‡
Njalsgade 140, Copenhagen (Denmark), University of Copenhagen
†Christians Brygge 1,Copenhagen (Denmark), Danish Society of Language and Literature
‡alonso@hum.ku.dk, bspedersen@hum.ku.dk

Abstract

We describe the creation of a new Danish resource for automated coarse-grained word sense disambiguation of running text (supersense tagging, SST). Based on corpus evidence we expand the sense inventory to incorporate new lexical classes. We add tags for verbal satellites like collocates, particles and reflexive pronouns, to give account for the satellite-framing properties of Danish. Finally, we evaluate the quality of our expanded sense inventory in terms of variation in F_1 on a state-of-the-art SST system. The SST systems uses type constraints and achieves performance just under the upper bound of inter-annotator agreement. The initial release is a 1,500-sentence corpus covering six genres, made available under an open-source license.[1]

1 Introduction

Supersense tagging is a coarse-grained word sense disambiguation task, which bases its sense inventory on the top level of Princeton Wordnet (Fellbaum, 1998), taken from *lexicographer files*. A supersense is more general than a synset, grouping many related sense distinctions together, while keeping important semantic distinctions. The smaller number of supersenses (comparable to the size of a typical POS tag set) makes it possible for state-of-the-art taggers to be trained on datasets of moderate size.
Supersense tagging is similar to Named Entity Recognition (NER) in that the labels are comprised within spans of one or more tokens. NER, however, only recognizes a handful of entity types and does not extend beyond nouns, while supersenses may be defined for all part of speech and permit more granular semantic distinctions.

While coarse-grained semantic types find use in a range of applications, such as information retrieval, question answering (QA), and relation extraction, one of the main intended uses of the annotated corpus is building a semantic concordancer in the style of SemCor (Miller et al., 1994).

We base our annotation effort on the set of supersenses derived from Princeton Wordnet, which makes our annotations interoperable across many languages through the already existing linkings to Princeton Wordnet. However, we found several cases where the Princeton supersenses made overly broad distinctions that caused large groups of lexemes to be grouped together (e.g. buildings and vehicles falling under the ARTIFACT class).

The original sense inventory comprises a total of 41 senses, spread over 26 noun senses, and 15 verb senses, plus a single "catch-all" sense for adjectives, which is grammatically rather than semantically motivated. Based on lexical data from the corpus-based Danish wordnet (Pedersen et al., 2009), we introduce seven new noun senses, two verb senses, and four adjective senses. A complete listing is shown in Table 3. Importantly, these additions do not break compatibility with supersenses, because the extended senses add more granularity to existing senses. An additional sense can thus always be unambiguously mapped to an original sense. For instance, a DISEASE is a STATE. Details about the newly introduced senses are given in Section 2.

After an annotation task, we experiment with SST in order to gauge the quality of automatic supersenses annotations for the aforementioned semantic concordancer.

[1]The data is available at `clarin.dk` under *Danish Supersense Corpus*

2 Extended sense inventory

The current standard supersense inventory is the list of WordNet lexicographer files.[2] However, the Danish wordnet (DanNet) is not organized in the WordNet lexicographer files. Instead, each synset in DanNet is described by an an *ontological type*, namely an array of ontological properties that we have mapped to the standard and new supersenses. Table 2 provides three examples of such mapping.

Ontological type	Supersense
Property+Physical+Colour	ADJ.PHYSICAL
Liquid+Natural	NOUN.SUBSTANCE
Dynamic+Agentive+Mental	VERB.COGNITION

Table 1: Ontological type to supersense projection.

The standard set of noun supersenses expresses very general lexical semantic properties such as *state*, *event*, *animal*, *person*, and *cognition*. We extend the standard set with a few more fine-grained types, translating DanNet ontological types to supersenses. The new noun supersenses are BUILDING, CONTAINER, VEHICLE, DISEASE, ABSTRACT, and DOMAIN (for fields of expertise like *philosophy*). The noun senses COGNITION and COMMUNICATION cover processes as well as contents, and might result in low-agreement annotations. We have added the ABSTRACT and DOMAIN specified senses for COGNITION, and disregarded extending COMMUNICATION—although it could potentially be extended into a supersense for linguistic units like *word* or *speech*, and another one for semiotic artifacts like *book* or titles like *Crime and Punishment*

For verbs, we choose to extend the set with the supersense PHENOMENON in order to cover general verb event senses like *happen*, in line with the corresponding ones for noun senses in the standard set (covering noun events and noun natural phenomena). Verbs of natural events are, in our annotation experience, only covered partly by the standard supersense WEATHER.

For adjectives, we introduce four supersenses: one PHYSICAL (*green*, *tall*, *hard*), one MENTAL (*jealous*, *sensible*, *clever*), one SOCIAL (*democratic*, *Arabic*, *economical*), and finally one for TIME (*early*, *contemporary*), which includes intensional adjectives like *former*.

[2] http://wordnet.princeton.edu/man/lexnames.5WN.html

New category	Subsumed by
Noun	
VEHICLE BUILDING CONTAINER	} ARTIFACT
DOMAIN ABSTRACT	} COGNITION
INSTITUTION	} GROUP
DISEASE	} STATE
Verb	
ASPECTUAL	} STATIVE
PHENOMENON	} CHANGE
Adj	
MENTAL PHYSICAL SOCIAL TIME	} ALL
Sat	
COLL PARTICLE REFLPRON	} -none-

Table 2: Extensions to the sense inventory.

Danish is a typical satellite-framing language in Talmy's (1985) terms, because the verb in combination with a satellite (such as a particle) typically expresses a composite and often non-transparent meaning. To give account for verb-headed collocations, phrasal verbs, and reflexive verbs, which often occur as discontinuous constituents in running text, we have introduced three verb-satellite tags: COLL, PARTICLE, and REFLPRON. These are rather to be understood as morphosyntactic tags indicating that the given satellite contribute to the composite meaning of the verb in question.

In other words, these three tags are interpreted in combination with the verb introducing them, as in *han slog ordet op i ordbogen* (lit. 'he hit the word up in the dictionary') meaning 'he looked up the word in the dictionary', and as in *han satte ham på plads* (lit: 'he put him in place') meaning 'he corrected him harshly'.

Tagging of satellites allows for a composite semantic intrepretation of the verb-headed multiword expressions, interpreting thus the collocation *sætte på plads* as communication and not as motion, which the verb *sætte* ('put') would indicate in isolation. This interpreta-

Domain	$\overline{SL}$	$\frac{\text{tokens}}{\text{types}}$	Sentences
Blog	16.44	2.95	100
Chat	14.61	3.70	200
Forum	20.51	3.85	200
Magazine	19.45	2.95	200
Newswire	17.43	3.28	600
Parliament	31.21	5.00	200

Table 4: Supersense tagging data sets.

tion is annotated in the corpus in the following way: *han satte*(VERB.COMMUNICATION) *ham på*(COLL) *plads*(COLL).

3 Annotation process

This section the describes the annotation task for supersenses, including detailes on corpus, guidelines and resulting agreement scores. For further information, cf. Olsen et al. (2015).

3.1 Corpus

We have chosen to annotate from the Danish CLARIN Reference Corpus (Asmussen and Halskov, 2012), which consists of newspapers, magazines, oral debates, blogs, and social media.[3]

Table 4 lists the amount of training data (1,500 sentences in total) currently annotated for each domain. We describe each domain in terms of its average sentence length ($\overline{SL}$) and proportion of tokens per type, namely the average amount of repetitions for a certain type.

The final release will be made up of 600 sentences from all of the domains in Table 4, plus the test section of the Danish Dependency Treebank (Buch-Kromann et al., 2003).

All the data has been POS-tagged using the Stanford POS-tagger (Toutanova et al., 2003) trained on the Danish PAROLE corpus.[4] Note that we strictly use predicted POS instead of gold-standard to provide a more realistic setup for the evaluation of our system in Section 5.

3.2 Annotation guidelines

Sense inventory The guidelines for the supersense annotation comprise the list of supersenses provided with an explanation and examples for each supersense.

[3]http://cst.ku.dk/Workshop311012/sprogtekno2012.pdf

[4]http://korpus.dsl.dk/e-resurser/paroledoc_en.pdf

Application rules The second part of the guidelines consists of a set of more specific rules for each part of speech. The rules for nouns concern the delimitation of units to be annotated, how to treat multiword units (e.g. names of people, places,or book titles), compounds, figurative senses and metaphors, but also clarifications of how to interpret some of the supersenses that are closely related.

The rules for adjectives treat the language-specific issues of determining when a word is a participle, an adverb or an adjective, and how to annotate it in the later case. The rules for verbs concern the identification of grammatical phenomena like auxiliary verbs, and modal verbs—which are not annotated, because we only assign a supersense to the main lexical verb, e.g. in constructions like *"would have found"* only *found* would be annotated—, and the identification of words that participate in verb-satellite constructions.

Decision trees The sense inventory and the application rules are vertebrated into three (one per main part of speech) decision trees, that illustrate the ontological structure of the supersenses to use in case of sense subsumption like ARTIFACT vs. VEHICLE or CHANGE vs. PHENOMENON.

3.3 Sense distribution

Figure 1 shows the distribution of tags across all the parts of speech in absolute frequency. The plot is divided in high and low-frequency bands. All the new adjective supersenses appear in the high-frequency band. The senses NOUN.BUILDING and NOUN.VEHICLE fall respectively in the high and low band. As regards the verbal satellites, SAT.COLL is ranked 12.

Sense distributions vary across domains. Figure 2 shows the variation of frequency for four supersenses in all domains. While NOUN.PERSON is the overall most frequent sense for nouns, it is not in Forum (where the most frequent noun sense is NOUN.COMMUNICATION), while Magazine—being made up of tabloid text, where the life of celebrities is discussed—is made of 10% of person-type nouns.

3.4 Agreement

Each sentence in our dataset has been annotated by two of the four native annotators with a background in linguistics, and reviewed by one of the

ADJ.ALL	NOUN.FOOD	**SAT.PARTICLE**
ADJ.MENTAL	NOUN.GROUP	**SAT.RELFPRON**
ADJ.PHYS	**NOUN.INSTITUTION**	VERB.ACT
ADJ.SOCIAL	NOUN.LOCATION	**VERB.ASPECTUAL**
ADJ.TIME	NOUN.MOTIVE	VERB.BODY
NOUN.TOPS	NOUN.OBJECT	VERB.CHANGE
NOUN.ABSTRACT	NOUN.PERSON	VERB.COGNITION
NOUN.ACT	NOUN.PHENOMENON	VERB.COMMUNICATION
NOUN.ANIMAL	NOUN.PLANT	VERB.COMPETITION
NOUN.ARTIFACT	NOUN.POSSESSION	VERB.CONSUMPTION
NOUN.ATTRIBUTE	NOUN.PROCESS	VERB.CONTACT
NOUN.BODY	NOUN.QUANTITY	VERB.CREATION
NOUN.BUILDING	NOUN.RELATION	VERB.EMOTION
NOUN.COGNITION	NOUN.SHAPE	VERB.MOTION
NOUN.COMMUNICATION	NOUN.STATE	VERB.PERCEPTION
NOUN.CONTAINER	NOUN.SUBSTANCE	**VERB.PHENOMENON**
NOUN.DISEASE	NOUN.TIME	VERB.POSSESSION
NOUN.DOMAIN	**NOUN.VEHICLE**	VERB.SOCIAL
NOUN.FEELING	**SAT.COLL**	VERB.STATIVE

Table 3: Sense inventory with new senses introduced in this article marked in bold.

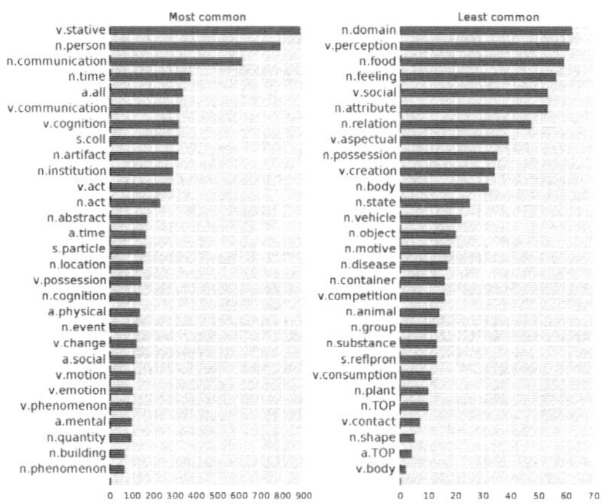

Figure 1: Distribution of senses in the high and low-frequency bands.

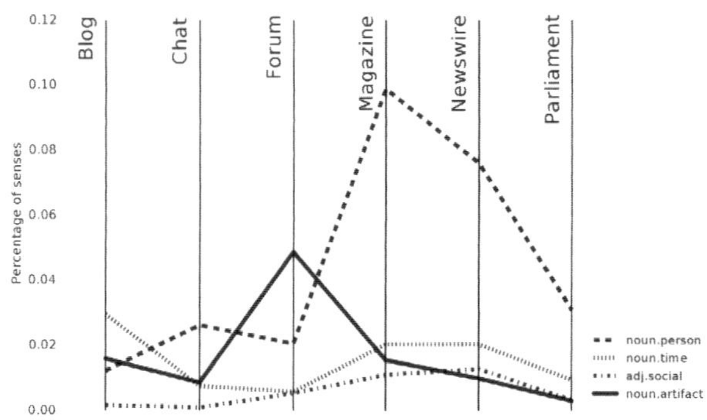

Figure 2: Variation of sense frequency across domains.

two adjudicators. We use WebAnno (Yimam et al., 2013) as annotation environment.

We calculate inter-annotator agreement using Cohen's κ. A first batch of documents were annotated by two of the annotators and later reviewed by one of the adjudicators. The agreement in the first documents was between 0.52 and 0.57. The causes of disagreement were principally verbal collocates, particle verbs and multiword units.

After discussion and refinement of the annotation guidelines, the agreement increased to 0.63. We also tested the agreement between adjudicators using the revised guidelines. The two adjudicators reached a κ of 0.7 on a 200-sentence sample. The remaining disagreement is mostly due to varying interpretations of the sentences (taken out of context) and to the delimitation of some of the abstract supersenses that overlap in some ways.

Figure 3 provides plots that illustrate the disagreement patterns between the annotators. Each row stands for the overall probability of any annotator assigning the sense listed. The size of the boxes indicate the probability that another annotator might have chosen another sense for the same word. We have calculated these probabilities on a 200-sentence sample from the Newswire domain.

Rows are sorted after the size of the diagonal value, and values in the diagonal indicate the proportion of agreement between two annotators for any given sense. Rows with many large, spread boxes indicate low-agreement senses. The sense NOUN.GROUP, for instance, has a smaller value in the diagonal than in the column for NOUN.QUANTITY. This difference indicates that these two senses are very often disagreeed upon, and that there is little agreement on when to assign the sense NOUN.GROUP. Other senses, like NOUN.FOOD have perfect or near-perfect agreement.

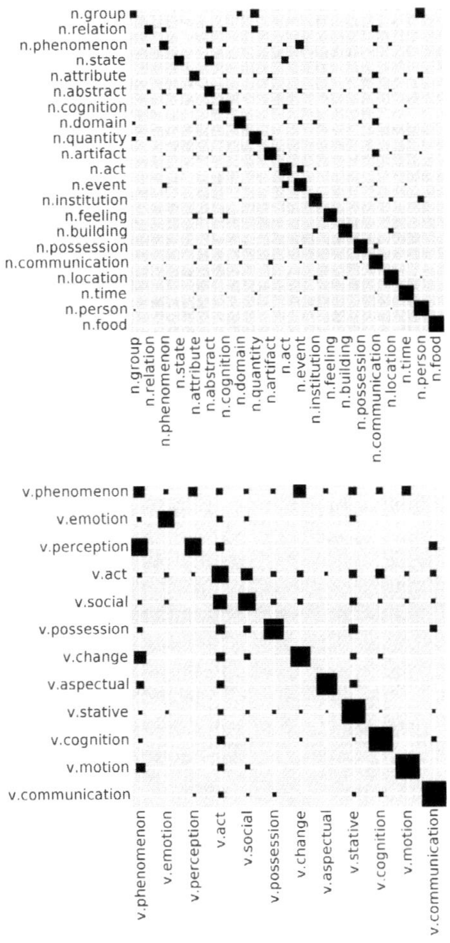

Figure 3: Disagreement plots for nouns and verbs.

We observe that there are some nouns with very good agreement, while there is much less general agreement on verb senses. The sense VERB.ACT has indeed a chance for being annotated with any other verb sense by the another annotator.

To compensate for the disagreement during the annotation step, there is an adjudication step. The following examples show cases of disagreement when annotating with our sense inventory. The word where annotators incur in disagreement is in italics, the two conflicting senses appear in brackets, with the adjudicated sense underlined.

(1) Findes der ikke et eneste stykke *papir* [<u>ARTIFACT</u>/COMMUNICATION] i Vatikanets kældre om alt det?
"Isn't there a single piece of *paper* in the Vatican's basements about all of this?"

(2) Så giver I bare fremmede frø mulighed for at *spire* [CHANGE/<u>PHENOMENON</u>].
"Then you are giving foreign seeds a chance to *sprout*."

(3) Togtrafikken mellem Vejle og Århus var i går *lammet* [<u>PHYS</u>/SOCIAL] i flere timer efter en personpåkørsel ved Horsens.
"The train traffic between Vejle and Århus was *paralyzed* yesterday for several hours after a human collision arounds Horsens."

(4) Thi først brød han *igennem* [COLL/<u>PARTICLE</u>] til det store publikum med den på mange måder uhyre vellykkede fimatisering af Umberto Ecos "Rosens Navn".
"Because of this, he broke *through* to the major audience with the, in many ways monstrously accomplished, filmatization of Umberto Eco's "Name of the Rose"."

4 SST model

The labels in supersense tagging are spans (defined using BIO notation) like *Hans/B-noun.person Hansen/noun.person*. Supersense tagging is typically cast as a sequential problem like POS tagging. However, the class distribution is more skewed than for POS tagging, given that in SST all the words that do not receive a supersense receive the outside-of-entity tag O. We use the feature model of Johannsen et al. (2014). For each word *w*, we calculate the following:

1. **The 2-token window** of forms, lemmas and POS tags around *w*, including *w*.
2. **2-token window** of forms, lemmas and POS tags around *w*, including *w*.
3. **The 2-token window** of forms, lemmas and POS tags around *w*, including *w*.
4. **Bag of words** of forms and lemmas at the *left* and *right* of *w*, marked for directionality so words at the left are different from words at the right.
5. **Morphology** of *w*, whether it is all alphanumeric, capitalized, contains hyphens, and its 3-letter prefix and suffix.
6. **Brown cluster** that *w* belongs to. We generate the 2-,4,6,8,10 and 12-bits long prefix

of the cluster bitstring from clusters from the ClarinDK corpus.[5]

7. **Embeddings** of w and its 2-word window context [6], using 100-dimension vectors, 5-word window sampling and 10-word negative sampling from the ClarinDK corpus. We calculate the weighted average of w and its four surrounding words, where w is weighted twice. For the five different embedding vectors, we also calculate the dimension-wise maximum and minimum. These three operations yield a total of 300 real-valued features. Moreover, we calculate the cosine similarity between w and its four context words.

The sequence-prediction algorithm for the system is on SEARN, search-based classification, with two passes over the data (Daumé et al., 2009).[7]

4.1 Type constraints

We implement distant supervision by only allowing a system to predict a certain supersense s for a given lemmatized word w with part of speech p with the following criteria:

1. If (w,s) has been observed in the training data, s is an allowed sense.

2. If (w) is not in the training data, but (w,p) appears in DanNet, we allow the most frequent sense for (w,p).

3. If w does neither appear in the training data or in DanNet, we make no assumptions and allow any sense to be assigned by the classifier.

We refer to this distant-supervision strategy as *type constraints*. Since SEARN decomposes sequential labelling into a series of binary classifications, we constrain the labels by simply picking the top-scoring sense for each token from the allowed set of senses.

5 Evaluation

In this section we evaluate the performance of the supersense tagging system (SST) against the MFS (most-frequent sense baseline). All our systems have been evaluated on 5-fold cross-validation on randomly shuffled sentences. All results are expressed in terms of micro-averaged F_1-score.[8]

We have trained and test the data using two variants of the training data: one where the verbal satellites where removed from the annotation replacing them with the O tag, and another where the annotations were kept intact. We evaluate only on the set of lexical supersenses (adjectives, nouns and verbs). The goal of this comparison is to establish whether adding the verb-satellite tags penalizes the performance of the system.

5.1 MFS baseline

For most word sense disambiguation studies, predicting the most frequent sense (MFS) of a word has been proven to be a strong baseline. Following this, our MFS baseline simply predicts the supersense for (w,p) in a manner similar to the one used to implement type constraints (Section 4.1), namely by calculating MFS from the training data and backing off to the value in DanNet if the word is not present in the training data. If a word is not present in either, it receives the most frequent sense for its part of speech.

5.2 System performace

Table 5 provides the micro-averaged F_1 for the SST system. The SEARN column reflects the classifier output before type contraints are applied, and +Constraints is the resulting F_1 after applying the type contraints described in 4.1.

	MFS	SEARN	+Constraints
SST	32.96	52.01	60.51

Table 5: F_1 scores for SST system.

The F_1 score between the two variants of the training data does not change, regardless of the presence of the verb-satellite tags. Thus, we consider that is viable to mantain the annotation of the verb satellites. Table 5 shows the micro-averaged F_1 score for the SST system with and without type contraints, and compared against the MFS baseline, using all the sense inventory (all the lexical senses and the verb satellites).

We have experimented with feature ablation, but the best final system contains the full feature set. In particular, embedding features provide an improvement of around 4.0 in F_1.

[5]We use Liang's implementation https://github.com/percyliang/brown-cluster

[6]We use Word2Vec https://code.google.com/p/word2vec

[7]SEARN in Vowpal Wabbit https://github.com/JohnLangford/vowpal_wabbit

[8]We have used the conlleval.pl script from the NER shared tasks

5.3 Constraint contribution

Applying type constraints contributes greatly to the performance of the system. Indeed, the +Constraints system has an F_1 score just below the expected maximum performance, namely the κ agreement coefficient of the data (0.63).

	SEARN	+Constraints
$\rho(\frac{\text{tokens}}{\text{types}}, F_1)$	0.74	0.27
$\rho(\text{tokens}, F_1)$	0.81	0.40

Table 6: Correlation scores for SST before and after applying type constraints.

Table 6 shows the Spearman's ρ between the F_1 of each individual supersense and its token-type ratio and number of tokens respectively, for both the SEARN and the +Constraints system. We observe that, before any constraint is applied, performance is highly correlated with token-type ratio, but even more so with the number of tokens.

Train	DanNet	Train+DanNet
0.49	0.34	0.16

Table 7: OOV rates for training data and DanNet.

Applying type contraints effective decorrelates the performance of the individual supersenses from the bias of the SST classifier. However, the correlation with the number of tokens remains higher, as it is also correlated with the coverage in DanNet for a certain supersense. That is, a high-frequency sense like NOUN.PERSON will contain more high-frequency words that will be covered in a wordnet (e.g. *person, child, sailor*).

5.4 POS-wise evaluation

This section provides tagwise evaluation in terms of precision (P), recall (R), and F_1. In addition, we provide the number of tokens (absolute frequency), the number of types, the token-type ratio for each supersense tag in tables 8, 10, 9 and 11.

Supersense	P	R	F_1	types	tokens	$\frac{\text{tokens}}{\text{types}}$
ADJ.ALL	59.8	62.1	60.9	246	341	1.39
ADJ.MENTAL	58.3	44.1	50.2	79	100	1.27
ADJ.PHYSICAL	56.5	46.3	50.9	98	138	1.41
ADJ.SOCIAL	68.8	69.4	69.1	92	114	1.24
ADJ.TIME	80.2	83.5	81.8	56	166	2.96

Table 8: Performance for adjectives.

Overall, the prediction of adjective supersenses fares fairly well, however ADJ.ALL makes up a 30% of the annotated adjectives senses, which is too large for a back-off sense. Also, ADJ.ALL is a low-agreement supersense tag. A further refinement of the annotation guidelines or an inclusion on an additional supersense—provided that we identify some internal semantic consistency—can reduce the amount of words labeled as ADJ.ALL.

Supersense	P	R	F_1	types	tokens	$\frac{\text{tokens}}{\text{types}}$
VERB.ACT	42.6	52.7	47.1	197	283	1.44
VERB.CHANGE	46.4	34.2	39.4	84	123	1.46
VERB.COGNITION	67.7	59.0	63.1	156	317	2.03
VERB.COMMUNICATION	75.5	72.7	74.1	158	323	2.04
VERB.CONSUMPTION	100.0	7.1	13.3	7	11	1.57
VERB.EMOTION	51.8	40.0	45.1	55	104	1.89
VERB.MOTION	39.8	48.5	43.7	76	114	1.5
VERB.PERCEPTION	47.4	51.4	49.3	25	61	2.44
VERB.PHENOMENON	39.3	34.2	36.5	75	103	1.37
VERB.POSSESSION	54.8	42.3	47.7	62	143	2.31
VERB.STATIVE	79.2	84.3	81.7	122	884	7.25

Table 9: Performance for the 10 most frequent verbs senses.

Overall performance for verbs is worse than for nouns. Even though there are fewer verbal senses, verbs are more difficult to annotate, as shown by the verb disagreement plot in Figure 3.

Supersense	P	R	F_1	types	tokens	$\frac{\text{tokens}}{\text{types}}$
NOUN.ABSTRACT	37.23	34.31	35.71	141	170	1.21
NOUN.ACT	56.9	61.34	59.03	189	233	1.23
NOUN.ARTIFACT	45.56	39.81	42.49	259	316	1.22
NOUN.COGNITION	49.44	53.61	51.45	112	141	1.26
NOUN.COMMUNICATION	41.24	52.49	46.19	399	618	1.55
NOUN.EVENT	43.21	29.41	35.0	107	128	1.2
NOUN.INSTITUTION	51.69	46.15	48.76	235	292	1.24
NOUN.LOCATION	67.37	70.09	68.7	130	155	1.19
NOUN.PERSON	66.72	75.04	70.64	579	795	1.37
NOUN.TIME	83.92	84.73	84.32	163	373	2.29

Table 10: Performance for the 10 most frequent noun senses.

The sense COMMUNICATION is the second most frequent noun sense, yet it fares much worse than that first sense, namely PERSON. Even though COMMUNICATION has lower support, its token-type ratio is higher than the one for PERSON, which should increase F_1. However, PERSON has a subset of well-defined proper names that are easy to identify automatically given features like capitalization.

For NOUN.COMMUNICATION, out of its 323 examples, 10% of them are hapaxes. The VERB.STATIVE class, however, with a 884 examples, is constituted by forms of the verb *være* (to be) in 76%. The low variety of lexical elements makes it an easy-to-predict sense, and yields an F_1 of 78.39, which is very high for word-sense disambiguation tasks. The three verbal satellites fare very differently from each other. The most common tag, COLL, has a very low F_1 (14.35). Besides the already commented factors of number of tokens and token-type ratio, the predictability of these senses is also determined by how many different POS tags they can be applied to: REFLPRON is only for pronouns, PARTICLE encompasses prepositions and adverbs, whereas COLL can also contain nouns, verbs, and adjectives.

Supersense	P	R	F_1	types	tokens	$\frac{tokens}{types}$
NOUN.ABSTRACT	37.2	34.3	35.7	141	170	1.21
NOUN.ARTIFACT	45.6	39.8	42.5	259	316	1.20
NOUN.BUILDING	47.9	37.0	41.7	58	67	1.15
NOUN.CONTAINER	91.7	64.7	75.9	12	16	1.33
NOUN.DISEASE	73.3	55.0	62.9	14	17	1.22
NOUN.DOMAIN	63.3	28.8	39.6	49	62	1.27
NOUN.INSTITUTION	51.7	46.2	48.8	235	292	1.25
NOUN.VEHICLE	53.9	33.3	41.2	20	22	1.10
VERB.ASPECTUAL	77.8	32.6	45.9	27	39	1.45
VERB.PHENOMENON	39.3	34.2	36.5	75	103	1.37
SAT.COLL	37.9	7.7	12.8	120	316	2.63
SAT.PARTICLE	59.4	47.9	53.0	34	165	4.76
SAT.REFLPRON	69.6	76.4	72.9	4	13	3.22

Table 11: Performance for extended noun and verb supersenses, and satellites.

6 Related work

There has been relatively little previous work on supersense tagging, and it has mostly been limited to English newswire and literature (namely running on SemCor and SensEval data).[9] Nevertheless, the interest in applying word-sense disambiguation techniques to reduced, coarser sense inventories has been a topic since the development of the first wordnets (Peters et al., 1998). Kohomban and Lee (2005) and Kohomban and Lee (2007) also propose to use lexicographer file identifers from Princeton WordNet senses (supersenses) and, in addition, discuss how to retrieve fine-grained senses from those predictions.

The task of supersense tagging was first introduced by Ciaramita and Altun (2006), who used a structured perceptron trained and evaluated on SEMCOR via 5-fold cross validation. Johannsen et al. (2014) extend the SST approach to the Twitter domain, and include the usage of word embeddings in their feature representation.

Supersenses have been used as features in various tasks, such as preposition sense disambiguation, noun compound interpretation, metaphor detection and relation extraction (Ye and Baldwin, 2007; Tratz and Hovy, 2010; Tsvetkov et al., 2013; Søgaard et al., 2015). Schneider et al. (2012) annotated supersenses on Arabic Wikipedia articles . Princeton WordNet only provides a fully developed taxonomy of supersenses for verbs and nouns. Tsvetkov et al. (2014) propose an extension for adjectives, along the lines of the adjective sense of the German wordnet(Hamp and Feldweg, 1997).

To the best of our knowledge, the current work is the first SST approach to Danish, which also extends to less canonical, characteristically web-based text types like chats or fora.

7 Conclusions

We have presented a resource for SST that includes an extension of the English supersense inventory that can be used for any language, plus three additional tags that give account for characteristics of the syntax-semantics interface of a satellite-framing language like Danish.

We have conducted an annotation task on 1,500 sentences, reaching 0.63 κ score after refining the annotation guidelines. After annotation, the supersenses in our data has been adjudicated to resolve systematic disagreements. Later, we have trained an SST model that we have evaluated before and after applying type constraints. Our best system reaches a micro-averaged F_1 of 60.51, which is very close to the theoretical maximum of prediction performance set by the agreement score. This leads us to conclude that the system is mature enough to be used productively when the annotation process has finished.

Nevertheless, the performance is not even across all supersenses. Some of the high-frequency, low-variation supersenses show very high scores (above 81%), while other infrequent senses with a lot of variation or low agreement show lower scores. Some frequent senses like NOUN.COMMUNICATION might benefit from extension.

To the best of our knowledge , this article represents the first attempt to incorporate verb-satellite annotation in sense annotation to give account for verb-headed multiword expressions, which present more practical and theoretical difficulties than the span annotation for nominal multiwords typical of NER.

[9] http://web.eecs.umich.edu/ mihalcea/senseval/senseval3/

References

Jørg Asmussen and Jakob Halskov. 2012. The CLARIN DK Reference Corpus. In *Sprogteknologisk Workshop*.

Matthias Buch-Kromann, Line Mikkelsen, and Stine Kern Lynge. 2003. Danish dependency treebank. In *TLT*.

Massimiliano Ciaramita and Yasemin Altun. 2006. Broad-coverage sense disambiguation and information extraction with a supersense sequence tagger. In *Proc. of EMNLP*, pages 594–602, Sydney, Australia, July.

Hal Daumé, John Langford, and Daniel Marcu. 2009. Search-based structured prediction. *Machine learning*, 75(3):297–325.

Christiane Fellbaum. 1998. *WordNet: an electronic lexical database*. MIT Press USA.

Birgit Hamp and Helmut Feldweg. 1997. Germanet-a lexical-semantic net for german. In *Proceedings of ACL workshop Automatic Information Extraction and Building of Lexical Semantic Resources for NLP Applications*, pages 9–15. Citeseer.

Anders Johannsen, Dirk Hovy, Héctor Martínez, Barbara Plank, and Anders Søgaard. 2014. More or less supervised supersense tagging of Twitter. In *Lexical and Computational Semantics (*SEM 2014)*.

Upali Kohomban and Wee Lee. 2005. Learning semantic classes for word sense disambiguation. In *ACL*.

Upali Kohomban and Wee Lee. 2007. Optimizing classifier performance in word sense disambiguation by redefining word sense classes. In *IJCAI*.

George A. Miller, Martin Chodorow, Shari Landes, Claudia Leacock, and Robert G. Thomas. 1994. Using a semantic concordance for sense identification. In *Proceedings of the workshop on Human Language Technology*, pages 240–243. Association for Computational Linguistics.

Sussi Olsen, Bolette Sandford Pedersen, Héctor Martínez Alonso, and Anders Johannsen. 2015. Coarse-grained sense annotation of danish across textual domains. In *COLING*.

Bolette Sandford Pedersen, Sanni Nimb, Jørg Asmussen, Nicolai Hartvig Sørensen, Lars Trap-Jensen, and Henrik Lorentzen. 2009. Dannet: the challenge of compiling a wordnet for danish by reusing a monolingual dictionary. *Language resources and evaluation*, 43(3):269–299.

Wim Peters, Ivonne Peters, and Piek Vossen. 1998. Automatic sense clustering in eurowordnet. In *LREC*. Paris: ELRA.

Nathan Schneider, Behrang Mohit, Kemal Oflazer, and Noah A Smith. 2012. Coarse lexical semantic annotation with supersenses: an arabic case study. In *Proceedings of the 50th Annual Meeting of the Association for Computational Linguistics*, pages 253–258. Association for Computational Linguistics.

Anders Søgaard, Barbara Plank, and Hector Martinez Alonso. 2015. Using frame semantics for knowledge extraction from twitter. In *AAAI*.

Leonard Talmy. 1985. Lexicalization patterns: Semantic structure in lexical forms. *Language typology and syntactic description*, 3:57–149.

Kristina Toutanova, Dan Klein, Chris Manning, and Yoram Singer. 2003. Feature-rich part-of-speech tagging with a cyclic dependency network. In *NAACL*.

Stephen Tratz and Eduard Hovy. 2010. Isi: automatic classification of relations between nominals using a maximum entropy classifier. In *Proceedings of the 5th International Workshop on Semantic Evaluation*, pages 222–225. Association for Computational Linguistics.

Yulia Tsvetkov, Elena Mukomel, and Anatole Gershman. 2013. Cross-lingual metaphor detection using common semantic features. *Meta4NLP 2013*, page 45.

Yulia Tsvetkov, Nathan Schneider, Dirk Hovy, Archna Bhatia, Manaal Faruqui, and Chris Dyer. 2014. Augmenting english adjective senses with supersenses. In *Proc. of LREC*.

Patrick Ye and Timothy Baldwin. 2007. Melb-yb: Preposition sense disambiguation using rich semantic features. In *Proceedings of the 4th International Workshop on Semantic Evaluations*, pages 241–244. Association for Computational Linguistics.

Seid Muhie Yimam, Iryna Gurevych, Richard Eckart de Castilho, and Chris Biemann. 2013. Webanno: A flexible, web-based and visually supported system for distributed annotations. In *ACL (Conference System Demonstrations)*, pages 1–6.

CG-3 - Beyond Classical Constraint Grammar

Eckhard Bick
University of Southern Denmark
eckhard.bick@mail.dk

Tino Didriksen
GrammarSoft ApS
tino@didriksen.cc

Abstract

This paper discusses methodological strengths and shortcomings of the Constraint Grammar paradigm (CG), showing how the classical CG formalism can be extended to achieve greater expressive power and how it can be enhanced and hybridized with techniques from other parsing paradigms. We present a new, largely theory-independent CG framework and rule compiler (CG-3), that allows the linguist to write CG rules incorporating different types of linguistic information and methodology from a wide range of parsing approaches, covering not only CG's native topological technique, but also dependency grammar, phrase structure grammar and unification grammar. In addition, we allow the integration of statistical-numerical constraints and non-discrete tag and string sets.

1 Introduction

Within Computational Linguistics, Constraint Grammar (CG) is more a methodological than a descriptive paradigm, designed for the robust parsing of running text (Karlsson et al., 1995). The formalism provides a framework for expressing contextual linguistic constraints allowing the grammarian to assign or disambiguate token-based, morphosyntactic readings. However, CG's primary concern is not the tag inventory itself, or the underlying linguistic theory of the categories and structures used, but rather the efficiency and accuracy of the method used to achieve a given linguistic annotation. Conceptually, a Constraint Grammar can be seen as a declarative whole of contextual possibilities and impossibilities for a language or genre, but in programming terms, it is implemented procedurally as a set of consecutively iterated rules that add, remove or select tag-encoded information. In its classical form (Karlsson, 1990; Karlsson et al., 1995), Constraint Grammar relies on a morphological analyzer providing so-called cohorts of possible readings for a given word, and uses constraints that are largely topological[1] in nature, for both part-of-speech disambiguation and the assignment of syntactic function tags. (a-c) provide examples for close context (a) and wide context (b) POS rules, and syntactic mapping (c).

(a) REMOVE VFIN IF (0 N) (-1 ART OR <poss> OR GEN); *remove a finite verb reading if self (0) can also be a noun (N), and if there is an article (ART), possessive (<poss>) or genitive (GEN) 1 position left (-1).*

(b) SELECT VFIN IF (NOT *1 VFIN) (*-1C CLB-WORD BARRIER VFIN); *select a finite verb reading, if there is no other finite verb candidate (VFIN) to the right (*1), and if there is an unambiguous (C) clause boundary word (CLB-WORD) somewhere to the left (*-1), with no (BARRIER) finite verb in between.*

(c) MAP (@SUBJ) TARGET N (*-1 >>> BARRIER NON-PRE-N) (1C VFIN) ; *map a subject reading (@SUBJ) on noun (N) targets if there is a sentence-boundary (>>>) left without non-prenominals (NON-PRE-N) in between, and an unambiguous (C) finite verb (VFIN) immediately to the right (1C).*

As can be seen from the examples, the original formalism refers only to the linear order of tokens, with absolute (>>>) or relative fields

[1] With "topological" we mean that grammar rules refer to relative, left/right-pointing token positions (or word fields), e.g. -2 = 2 tokens to the left, *1 = anywhere to the right.

counting tokens left (-) or right (+) from a zero/target position in the sentence. Though in principle a methodological limitation, this topological approach also has descriptive "side effects": For instance, it supports local syntactic function tags (such as the @SUBJ tag on the head noun of an NP), but it does not easily lend itself to structural-relational annotation. Thus, dependency relations or constituent brackets can neither be created or referred to by purely topological CG rules[2]. Even chunking constraints, though topologically more manageable than tree structures, have to be expressed in an indirect way (cp. the NON-PRE-N barrier condition in example rule (c), and syntactic phrases cannot be addressed as wholes, let alone subjected to rewriting rules.

A second design limitation in classical CG concerns the expression of vague, probabilistic truths about language. Thus, the formalism does not allow numerical tags or numerical feature-value pairs, and while many current main stream NLP tools are based on probabilistic methods and machine learning, classical CG is entirely rule-based, and the only way to integrate likelihoods is through lexical "Rare" tags or by ordering rules in batches with more heuristic rules applying last.

Third, classical CG tags and tokens are discrete units and are handled as string constants. While this design option facilitated efficient processing and even FST methods, it also limited the linguist, who was not allowed to use regular expressions, feature variables or unification. Another aspect of discreteness concerns tokenization: Classical CG regarded token form, number and order as fixed, so the formalism had difficulty in accommodating, for instance, the rule-based creation of a (fused) named-entitity token, the insertion or removal of tokens in spell and grammar checking, or the reordering of tokens needed for machine translation.

Finally, when classical CG was designed, it had isolated sentences in mind. Though rule scope can be arbitrarily defined by a "window" delimiter set, and though "global" window rules clearly surpass the scope of HMM n-grams, it was not possible to span several windows at a time or to link referents across sentence, nor was it possible to contextually trigger genre variables or in other ways to make a grammar interact with a given text type. Descriptively, this limitation meant that CG as such could not be used for higher-level annotation such as anaphora or discourse relations, and that grammars were agnostic of genre and task types.

Following Karlsson's original proposal, two standards for CG rule compilers emerged in the late 90'ies. The first, CG-1, was used by Karlsson's team at Helsinki University and commercially by the spin-off company LingSoft for English (ENGCG), Swedish and German (GERCG) taggers, as well as for applied products such as Scandinavian grammar checkers (Arppe, 2000; Birn, 2000 for Swedish, Hagen et al., 2001 for Norwegian). The second compiler, CG-2, was programmed and distributed by Pasi Tapainen (1996), who made several notational improvements[3] to the rule formalisms (in particular, regarding BARRIER conditions, SET definitions and REPLACE operations), but left the basic topological interpretation of constraints unchanged. Five years later, a third company, GrammarSoft ApS, in cooperation with the University of Southern Denmark, launched an open source CG compiler, vislcg, which was backward compatible with CG-2, but also introduced a few new features[4], in particular the SUBSTITUTE and APPEND operators designed to allow system hybridization where input from a probabilistic tagger could be corrected with CG rules in preparation of a syntactic or semantic CG stage, as implemented e.g. in the earliest version of the French FrAG parser (Bick, 2004). Vislcg, too, was used in spell and grammar checkers (Bick, 2006a), but because of its open-source environment it also marked the transition to a wider spectrum of CG users and research languages.

[2] As a work-around, attachment direction markers (arrows) were introduced in the syntactic function tags, such as @>N or @N> for pre-nominal and @N< or @<N for post-nominal NP-material.

[3] Tapanainen also created a very efficient compiling and run-time interpretation algorithm for cg2, involving fintite state transducers, as well as a finite state dependency grammar, FDG (Tapanainen, 1997), for his company Conexor and its Machinese parsers.

[4] The vislcg compiler was programmed over several years by Martin Carlsen for VISL and GrammarSoft. For a technical comparison of CG-2 and vislcg, cf. http://beta.visl.sdu.dk/visl/vislcg-doc.html .

But though constraint grammars using the CG-2/VISLCG compiler standard did achieve a tag granularity and accuracy that allowed them to support external modules for both constituent and dependency tree generation, they remained topological in nature and did not permit explicit reference to linguistic relations and structure in the formalism itself. The same is true for virtually all related work outside the CG community itself, where the basic idea of CG constraints has sometimes been exploited to enhance or hybridize HMM-style probabilistic methods (e.g. Graña et al., 2003) or combined with machine learning (Lindberg & Eineborg, 1998; Lager, 1999), but always in the form of (mostly close-context) topological rather than structural-relational rules and always with discrete tag and string constants. It is only with the CG-3 compiler presented here, that these and most of the other above-mentioned design issues have been addressed in a principled way and inside the CG formalism itself. CG-3[5] (or VISL CG-3 because of its backward compatibility with VISLCG) was developed over a period of 6 years, where new features were designed and implemented continually, while existing features were tested in real-life parsing applications. In the following sections we will discuss the most important of these features and compare the finished framework with other approaches.

2 Expressive power: Relational tags

In CG all information is expressed as token-based tags, and this is true of CG-3 relational tags, too. Though each token can be part of any number of relations, the individual relation is binary, linking a from- and a to-token. Dependency annotation can be seen as a special type of such a relation, where each dependent (daughter, child) is assigned exactly one head (mother, parent), but where each head can have any number of dependents. In CG-3, we mark dependency relations on the daughter token with a #n->m tag, where 'n' is the token id of the dependent, and 'm' the token id of the head. Thus, dependency is a tag field, just like the ".."-marked lemma field, the upper-case POS and inflection fields or the @-marke syntactic function field[6]:

Both "both" <quant> DET P @>N #1->2
companies "company" <HH> N P @SUBJ> #2->3
said "say" <speak> <mv> V IMPF @FS-STA #3->0
they "they" <clb> PERS 3P NOM @SUBJ> #4->5
would "will" <aux> V IMPF @FS-<ACC #5->3
lauch "launch" <mv> V INF @ICL-AUX< #6->5
an "a" <indef> ART S @>N #7->9
electric "electric" <jpert> ADJ POS @>N #8->9
car "car" <Vground> N S NOM @<ACC #9->6
. "." PU @PU #10->0

Instead of the "topological" left/right-pointing position markers, CG rules with dependency contexts can refer to three types of relations: p (parent/head), c (child/dependent) and s (sibling).

ADD (§AG) TARGET @SUBJ (p V-HUM LINK c @ACC LINK 0 N-NON-HUM) ;

*(Add an AGENT tag to a **subject** reading if its parent verb is a human verb that in turn has a child accusative **object** that is a non-human noun. E.g. "**BMW** launched an electric **car**.")*

In order to add dependency annotation to "virgin" input, the operators SETPARENT and SETCHILD are used together with a TO target. Thus, for the sentence *"We **know** for a fact **that** the flat **had** not been used in months."*

SETPARENT @FS-<ACC (*-1 ("that" KS) BARRIER CLB TO (**-1 <mv> LINK 0 V-COGNITIVE) (NOT 1 @<ACC);

will link a finite object clause (underlined, marked @FS-<ACC on *'had'*) with a that-conjunction to a main verb (<mv>) anywhere to the left (**-1) if the latter is a cognitive verb (V-COG) and is not followed by an ordinary direct object (@<ACC). Both the SET-target and the TO-target can have their own independent context conditions, and that these can either be traditional positional contexts, or exploit already established dependency relations. CG-3 has a built-in check against circularity, preventing attachments that would create a dependency loop[7]. Dependency operators can be combined with a number of options:

5 For detailed technical documentation on CG-3, cf. http://beta.visl.sdu.dk/cg3.html, for tutorials, associated tools, parser demos and resources, see http://visl.sdu.dk/constraint_grammar.html. Cagetories and tag abbreviations are explained at http://visl.sdu.dk/tagset_cg_general.html .

6 All of these fields can easily be converted into xml-encoded feature-value pairs for compatibility. The authors provide scripts for conversion into e.g. MALT xml and TIGER xml.

1.) * *(Deep scan)* allows a child- or parent-test to continue searching along a straight line of descendants and ancestors, respectively, until the test condition is matched or until the end of a relation chain is reached.

2.) *C (All scan)* requires a child- or sibling-relation to match *all children* or *all* siblings, respectively. Note that this is different from the ordinary C (= safe) option which applies to readings. Thus 'cC ADJ' means 'only adjectives as children' – e.g. no articles or PP's, while 'c (*) LINK 0C ADJ' means 'any one daughter with an unambiguous adjective reading'.

3.) *S (Self)* can be combined with c, p or s to look at the current target as well. For example, 'c @SUBJ LINK cS HUM' looks for a human subject NP – where either the head noun (@SUBJ) itself is human, or where it has a modifier that is tagged as human.

Apart from dependency relations, we also allow general *named* relations in CG-3, that can be used for arbitrary relation types, such as secondary dependencies between object and object complement, anaphora (Bick, 2010), discourse relations etc. Thus, the following establishes an identity relation between a relative pronoun and its noun antecedent:

```
SETRELATION (identity) TARGET (<rel>)
   TO (*-1 N)
```

Where matched, this will add a relational tag on the pronoun token: *ID:n R:identity:m*, where R: specifies the relation, and n and m are token id's for the pronoun and noun, respectively.

It is even possible to set bidirectional relations with separate labels, to be tag-marked at both ends of the relation arc. Thus, the example rule sets a relation between a human noun subject and a sense-verb object, labelling the former as "experiencer" and the latter as "stimulus":

```
SETRELATIONS (experiencer) (stimulus)
   TARGET N-HUM + @SUBJ TO (p V-SENSE
   LINK c @ACC) ;
```

[7] Though descriptively undesirable, loops can be explicitly allowed with the ALLOWLOOP and NEAREST options (cf. visl.sdu.dk/cg3.html)

3 Constituent structure: Inspiration from the generative paradigm

Because dependency syntax bases its structural description on tokens (words), it is inherently closer to the native CG approach than the competing generative family of syntactic formalisms, which operate with non-terminal nodes and constituent brackets.

3.1 Tree transformation

Classical CG does not support constituent brackets in any form, be it flat chunks or nested constituents, so external modules had to be used to create constituent trees. The oldest example are PSGs with CG functions as terminals (Bick, 2003), used for CALL applications within the VISL project, followed by dependency-to-constituent tree transformation employing an external dependency grammar (Bick, 2005; Bick, 2006b). Of course the same transformation could be used with our new, native CG dependency (cp. previous section), but CG-3 does offer more direct ways to express linguistic structure in generative terms, allowing linguists used to *think* along PSG lines to directly translate generative descriptions and constraints into the CG formalism.

3.2 Chunking

There are at least two distinct methods in CG-3 to perform chunking, using either (a) cohort insertion or (b) relation-adding. For traditional, shallow chunking, without overlaps and nesting, only about 20 rules are needed (Bick, 2013), inserting opening (a) and closing (b) edge marker tokens.

```
(a) ADDCOHORT ("<$np>" "CHUNK" NP)
BEFORE @>N OR N/PROP/PRON OR
DET/NUM/PERS - @ATTR (NOT -1 @>A OR
@>N) (NEGATE -1 IT LINK -1 @>N) ;

(b) ADDCOHORT ("<$/np>" "ENDCHUNK"
NP) AFTER N/PROP/PRON OR DET/NUM/PERS
- @ATTR (NOT 0 @>N) (*-1 CHUNK-NP
BARRIER CHUNK) ;
```

NP opening markers (a) are inserted before prenominal noun dependents (@>N) or NP heads (N/PROP/PRON), accepting even determiners and numerals if they have no attributive function (@ATTR). Likewise, NP closing markers (b) are inserted *after* the above NP head candidates, in the presence of the left-hand (*-1) NP-chunk opener. The NOT contexts in (a) make sure that the triggering prenominal is in fact the *first* element in the NP, and not preceded by an adverbial dependent of its own, or part of a coordination. The inserted chunk-opening and -closing tokens can then be interpreted as labelled brackets: **(np** *We_PRON* **/np)** *had* **(np** *very_@>A delicious_@>N icecream_N* **/np)** *with* **(np** *strawberries_N* **/np)**.

The second method is better suited for layered, deep chunking, because it uses relational tags to individually link chunk edges to each other or to the chunk head. With full layering, this approach can create complete xml-formated constituent trees from CG dependency-tagged input without the need of an external converter, if chunk brackets are expressed as xml opening/closing markers. However, using relations to delimit topological units such as chunks, introduces certain complexities in the face of crossing branches and needs to specify the "handedness" (left/right) and "outermostness" of dependency arcs, features that are normally left underspecified in dependency annotation. In CG3, we support these features as l/r- (left/right) and ll/rr- (leftmost/rightmost) additions:

(a) ADDRELATIONS (np-head-l) (np-start) TARGET (*) (c @>N OR @N<&) TO (llScc (*)) ;

(b) ADDRELATIONS (np-head-r) (np-stop) TARGET (*) (c @>N OR @N<&) (r:np-head-l (*)) TO (rrScc (*)) ;

Both rules are bidirectional and mark both chunk head and chunk edges. The head target is any word (*) with an adnominal dependent (c @>N OR @N<), and the TO-edge is the leftmost (ll) resp. rightmost (rr) descendant (cc) or self (S). This second method will yield complete, nested structures, including adjective phrases (adjp) and prepositional phrases (pp) in the NPs: ***(np-start (adjp-start*** *very_@>A delicious_@>N* ***adjp-stop)*** *icecream_N* ***(pp-start*** *with_PRP_@N< strawberries_@P<* ***pp-stop) np-stop)***[8].

3.3 Phrase templates

Both of the above chunking methods are intended to be used late in the annotation pipe, and exploit existing morphosyntactic markup or even dependencies, so the chunking cannot itself be seen as methodological part of parsing *per se*. However, CG-3 also offers another way of expressing chunks, the *template*, which can be integrated into CG rules also at early tagging stages. A template is basically a pre-defined sequence of tokens, POS or functions that can be referred to as a whole in rule contexts, or even in other templates. The basic idea goes back to Karlsson et al. (1995), but was not implemented in either CG-1 or CG-2.

For instance, an NP could be defined as

(a) TEMPLATE np = ([ART, N]) OR ([ART,ADJ,N])

(b) TEMPLATE np = (? ART LINK 1 N) OR (? ART LINK 1 ADJ LINK 1 N)

(c) TEMPLATE np = ? ART LINK *1 N BARRIER NON-PRE-N

and then used in ordinary rules with a T:-prefix

(*1 VFIN LINK *1 T:np).

(a) is closest to the original idea, and reminiscent of generative rewriting rules, while (b) and (c) are shorthand for ordinary CG contexts and harness the full power of the latter. Independently of the format, however, the linguistic motivation behind templates is to allow direct reference to constituent units, to *think* in terms of phrase structure and to subsume aspects of generative grammar into CG. Thus, constituent templates allow a direct conceptual transfer from generative rules, and a simple generative NP grammar for the NP *"a very delicious icecream with strawberries"*:

np = adjp? n pp? ;
adjp = adv? adj ;
pp = prp np ;

could be expressed in CG3 as:

TEMPLATE np = (N)
OR (T:adjp LINK 1 N)
OR (T:adjp LINK 1 N LINK 1 T:pp)
OR (N LINK 1 T:pp) ;
TEMPLATE adjp = (ADJ) OR (ADV LINK 1 ADJ) ;
TEMPLATE pp = PRP LINK 1 T:np ;

In the example, *"very_ADV delicious_ADJ"* matches T:adjp, and *"with_PRP icecream_N"* matches T:pp, and the whole expression could then be referred to as a T:np context by CG rules. CG-internally, templates could also simply be interpreted as shorthand (variables) for context parentheses, so-called *context templates*. As such, they logically need to allow *internal*, predefined

[8] For clarity, only phrases with 2 or more constituents were bracketed in the 2nd method.

positions, as in the following example for a human verb-template, where the motivation is not a constituent definition, but simply to integrate two context alternatives into one[9], and to label the result with one simple variable.

TEMPLATE v-hum = ((c @SUBJ + HUM) OR (*1 ("that" KS) BARRIER V)) ; *"human verb" defined as either having a subject (@SUBJ) child (c) that is human (HUM), or having a subordinating conjunction (KS) anywhere to the right (*1) without another verb (V) in between.*

Compiler-internally, both template types are processed in a similar way, which is why constituent templates have question marks or 0-positions as place holders for an external position marker, which will be inserted into the template by the compiler at run-time.

When using templates together with (external) BARRIER's or LINKed conditions, the template can be thought of as one token – meaning that right-looking contexts with a template (*1 T:x BARRIER) will be interpreted against the left edge of the template, while left-looking contexts (*-1 T:x) will be interpreted against the right edge of the template so as to avoid internal, unpredictable parts of the template itself to trigger the BARRIER condition.

4 Beyond discrete tags and string constants: Regular expressions, variables and unification

A formal grammar has to strike a balance between computational efficiency on the one hand, and linguistic ease and rule writing efficiency on the other. Thus, the "classical" CG compilers treated tags and strings (lemma & word form) as constants and CG-2, in particular, achieved very high processing speeds exploiting this fact in its finite state implementation. Some flexibility was introduced through set definitions, and vislcg went on to allow sets as targets, too, as well as multiple conditions for the same position, but many rules had still be to be written in multiple versions because of expressive limitations in the formalism:

(a) OR'ing only for tags/sets, not contexts
(b) no nesting of NOT conditions
(c) no C-restriction for BARRIERs

CG-3 adds all of the above[10], but while increasing rule-writing efficiency, these changes to not affect the discreteness of tags and strings. Methodologically more important, therefore, is our introduction of regular expressions and variables. The former can be used instead of sets for open-class items, primarily lemma and word class, e.g. ".*i[zs]e"r V in a transitivity set or ".*ist" N as a heuristic candidate for the <Hprof> or <Hideo> classes ("professional" or "ideological" humans). But the feature is useful even with a closed-class semantic set such as +HUM, and <H.*>r will work across grammars and languages leaving grammarians the option to introduce ad hoc sub-distinctions (e.g. <Hsick> for words like 'diabetic'). Finally, regular expressions can be used to substitute for, or enhance, morphological analysis, for instance in stemming or affix recognition, supporting the creation of so-called "barebones" Constraint Grammars without lexical resources (Bick, 2011).

Variables can be used in connection with regular expressions, when appending readings (a) or for instantiating valency conditions (b):

APPEND ("$1"v ADJ) TARGET ("<(.*(ic|oid|ous))>"r) ; # recognizing adjective endings

REMOVE (N) (0 (<(.+)^vp>r INF)) (-1 INFM) (1 ("$1"v PRP)) ; # e.g. *to minister to the tribe*

With the example given, the second rule can remove the noun reading for 'minister' because the 'to' in the valency marker <to^vp> of the verb 'minister' matches the lemma "to" of the following preposition, even if the infinitive marker is still unsafe and potentially a preposition itself (-1 rather than -1C).

The methodologically most important use of variables, however, resides in feature unification. Thus, CG3 allows the use of sets as to-be-unified variables by prefixing $$ before the set name. Set unification integrates yet another methodological feature, used in other parsing paradigms, such as HPSG, but so far accessible in CG only at the cost of considerable "rule explosion". Apart from the obvious gender/number/case-disambiguation of noun phrases, unification is also useful in for

[9] In traditional CG, this OR'ed expression could not even be expressed in one rule, let alone be referenced as one label.

[10] The nesting of NOT conditions is achieved by making a distinction between ordinary NOT, that only negates its immediate position, and NEGATE, which a scope over the whole context bracket - including other NOTs or NEGATEs.

instance coordination, as with the following LIST set of semantic roles (agent, patient, theme and location):

LIST ROLE = §AG §PAT §TH §LOC ;

SELECT $$ROLE (-1 KC) (-2C $$ROLE) ;

Sometimes unification has to be vague in order to work. This is the case when underspecified "Portmanteau" tags are used (e.g. nC - nocase unified with NOM or ACC cases), or in the face of very finegrained semantic distinctions. We therefore make a distinction between list unification ($$-prefix) and set unification (&&-prefix), where the former unifies "terminal" set members, while the latter unifies subsets belonging to a superset. Two contexts will set-unify if they have tags sharing the same subset. In the example below, N-SEMS is defined as a superset, with N-SEM as one of the subsets.

LIST N-SEM = <sem> <sem-l> <sem-r> <sem-w> <sem-c> <sem-s> <sem-e> <coll-sem> <sem-nons> <system> <system-h> ;

SET N-SEMS = N-HUM OR N-LOC ... OR N-SEM ... OR N-SUBSTANCE ;

REMOVE @SUBJ>
(0 $$@<ARG LINK 0 &&N-SEMS)
(*-1 KC BARRIER NON-PRE-N/ADV LINK *-1C $$@<ARG BARRIER CLB-ORD OR &MV OR @ARG/ADVL> LINK 0 &&N-SEMS) ; # *... offered the reader detailed* ***notes*** *and* ***instructions*** *on most of the prayers ...*

The example sentence has an ambiguous coordination, where it is not clear if 'and' starts a new clause, and the task of the REMOVE rule is to exclude a subject reading for 'instructions' (tagged <sem-s>) by semantically aligning it with 'notes' (tagged <sem-r>) because both <sem-r> and <sem-s> are part of the N-SEM subset of the &&N-SEMS superset, - and by checking if both nouns also have matching left-pointing argument readings ($$@<ARG), in this case @<ACC (direct objects).

5 Integrating statistical data: Numerical tags

CG-3 moves beyond traditional <Rare> sets and heuristic rule batching by allowing rules to make reference to statistical information. This is achieved by introducing numerical secondary tags of the type <LABEL:number>, which can be used to encode and use corpus-harvested frequencies. The simplified example rule (a) exploits relative lexical POS frequencies for bigram disambiguation in a way reminiscent of hidden Markov models (HMMs), while (b) is a spell checker fall-back rule selecting the word with the highest phonetical similarity value

REMOVE (<fr<10> N) (0 (<fr>60> V)) (1 N)

SELECT (<PHONSIM=MAX>)

A more complex example is the use of CG-annotated data to boot-strap statistical "wordnets" or "framenets", containing the likelihood of semantic types or roles given an established syntactic function. Thus, the Portuguese PALAVRAS parser (Bick, 2014) assigns and exploits tags like <fSUBJ/H:41>, <fSUBJ/org:27> and <fACC/deverbal:53> for the verb *"propor"* (suggest), meaning that *"propor"* has a 53% probability of having a deverbal direct object (action/activity/process/ event), and subject likelihoods of 41% and 27% for person and organization, respectively[11].

Obviously, numerical tags could be used for other ends than statistics, for instance to assign confidence values to mapped syntactic tags or semantic roles, or for similarity degrees in spell-checking. Finally, using only the equal-operator, numerical tags can be seen as a special case of (numerical) global variables, e.g. for numbered genre types or Wordnet synset id's.

6 Grammar-text interaction

The fourth and last design limitation of classical CG to be treated here concerns ways to let a constraint grammar mold itself on the fly and to adapt to the text (or speech transcript) it is used to annotate. In CG-3 we introduce 3 types of such self-organizing behaviour:

(a) scope control
(b) rule or section triggering
(c) parameter variables

Scope control is achieved by allowing the grammarian not only to define window (read: sentence) delimiters, but also a spanning width of n windows left or right of the rule focus. Unbounded context conditions can breach

[11] Simplifying, we here only list high-percentage semantic types for subjects and objects.

window boundaries by adding a 'W', e.g. *-1W for scanning left across the window boundary. This feature is especially useful for higher-order relations such as anaphora (Bick, 2010) or discourse relations. Another scope-related innovation are (definable) paired brackets that allow rules to scan across brackets in a first pass, and make reference to them in a second pass. Like templates, bracket eclipsing is meant to help reduce CG's topological complexity problem, i.e. allow syntactic function carriers to "see" each other more easily across intervening tokens.

CG-3, unlike earlier CG compilers, applies rules strictly sequentially, and each rule is run on *all* cohorts in a window before the next rule is tried. This makes rule tracing more predictable, but also facilitates grammar self-organisation. Thus, we allow context-triggered JUMPs to rule ANCHORs, to INCLUDE additional rules from a file or to call EXTERNAL programs. For instance, an early rule can scan the window for verbo-nominal ambiguities, and if there are none, bypass the rule section in question.

Because CG does not depend on training data, it is generally assumed to be more genre-robust than machine-learning systems[12], and a few manual rule changes will often have a great effect on genre tuning (e.g. allowing/forbidding imperative readings for recipes or science articles, respectively). In CG-3, we further enhance this methodological advantage by introducing parameter variables, that can be set or unset either in the data stream (e.g. corpus section headers) or dynamically-contextually by the grammar itself. The example rule below assigns the value "recipe" to a "genre" variable, when encountering imperatives followed by quantified food nouns.

SETVARIABLE (genre) (recipe) TARGET (IMP) (*1 N-FOOD LINK *-1 NUM OR N-UNIT BARRIER (*) - ("of"))

Finally, grammar-text interaction may take the form of rule-governed changes to the text itself. Thus, the ADDCOHORT feature used for chunking in section 3.2., and its REMCOHORT counterpart can be used for adding or removing commas in grammar checking, and the MOVE BEFORE, MOVE AFTER and SWITCH WITH operators can be used to express syntactic movement rules in machine translation. The example rule will change Danish VS into English SV in the presence of a fronted adverb: MOVE WITHCHILD[13] (*) @<SUBJ BEFORE (*-1 VFIN) (-1 ADV LINK -1 >>>).

Applied to the Danish sentence "I går *så jeg* et rensdyr", this will turn the literal translation "Yesterday *saw I* a reindeer" into the correctly ordered "Yesterday *I saw* a reindeer".

7 Efficiency and hybridization options

This paper is primarily concerned with design aspects and a linguistic discussion of the CG-3 formalism, and advances in expressive power have been the main focus of innovation during development. That said, the CG-3 rule parser compiles mature grammars with thousands of rules in fractions of a second and maintains the processing speed of VISLCG inspite of the added complexity caused by regular expressions, variables, templates and numerical tags. For a mature morphosyntactic core grammar with 6000 rules, on a single machine, this amounts to ~1000 words (cohorts) per second for each of the morphological and syntactic levels. However, Yli-Jyrä (2011) has shown that much higher speeds (by about 1 order of magnitude[14] on a comparable machine) are possible, at least for VISLCG-compatible rules without the above complexities, when using a double finite-state representation, where rule conditions are matched against a string of feature vectors that summarize compact representations of local ambiguity. Future work should therefore explore the possibility of sectioned grammars, where a distinction is made between FST-compatible rule sections on the one hand, and smaller specialized rule sections on the other hand, which for their part would allow the complete range of CG-3 features. This way, simpel "traditional" rules would run at the higher FST speed, and the current procedural compiler architecture would only be used where necessary, greatly reducing overall processing time.

[12] The rationale for this is that an ML system basically is a snapshot of the linguistic knowledge contained in its training data, and therefore will need new training data for each new genre in order to perform optimally.

[13] The WITHCHILD option means that heads are moved together with their dependents, in this case "reindeer" together with "a".

[14] The reported speed is 110,000 cohorts for FINCG, an open morphological CG with ~ 950 low-complexity CG-1 rules, originally developed by Fred Karlsson for Finnish.

References

Arppe, Antti. 2000. Developing a grammar checker for Swedish. In: Torbjørn Nordgård (ed.). *Proceedings of NODALIDA '99*. pp. 28-40. Trondheim: Department of Linguistics, University of Trondheim.

Bick, Eckhard. 2003. A CG & PSG Hybrid Approach to Automatic Corpus Annotation. In: Kiril Simow & Petya Osenova (eds.). *Proceedings of SProLaC2003* (at Corpus Linguistics 2003, Lancaster), pp. 1-12

Bick, Eckhard. 2004. Parsing and evaluating the French Europarl corpus, In: Patrick Paroubek, Isabelle Robba & Anne Vilnat (red.): *Méthodes et outils pour l'évaluation des analyseurs syntaxiques* (Journée ATALA, May 15, 2004). pp. 4-9. Paris: ATALA.

Bick, Eckhard. 2005. Turning Constraint Grammar Data into Running Dependency Treebanks. In: Civit, Montserrat & Kübler, Sandra & Martí, Ma. Antònia (red.). *Proceedings of TLT 2005* (4th Workshop on Treebanks and Linguistic Theory, Barcelona), pp.19-27

Bick, Eckhard. 2006a. A Constraint Grammar Based Spellchecker for Danish with a Special Focus on Dyslexics". In: Suominen, Mickael et.al. (ed.) *A Man of Measure: Festschrift in Honour of Fred Karlsson on his 60th Birthday*. Special Supplement to SKY Jounal of Linguistics, Vol. 19. pp. 387-396. Turku: The Linguistic Association of Finland

Bick, Eckhard. 2006b. Turning a Dependency Treebank into a PSG-style Constituent Treebank. In: Calzolari, Nicoletta et al. (eds.). *Proceedings of LREC 2000*. pp. 1961-1964

Bick, Eckhard. 2010. A Dependency-based Approach to Anaphora Annotation. In: (eds.) *Extended Activities Proceedings, 9th International Conference on Computational Processing of the Portuguese Language* (Porto Alegre, Brazil). ISSN 2177-3580

Bick, Eckhard. 2011. A Barebones Constraint Grammar. In: Helena Hong Gao & Minghui Dong (eds), *Proceedings of the 25th Pacific Asia Conference on Language, Information and Computation* (Singapore). pp. 226-235

Bick, Eckhard. 2013. Using Constraint Grammar for Chunking. In: S. Oepen, K. Hagen & J. B. Joannessen (Eds). *Proceedings of the 19th Nordic Conference of Computational Linguistics (NODALIDA 2013)*. Linköping Electronic Conference Proceedings Vol. 85, pp. 13-26. Linköping: Linköping University Electronic Press.

Bick, Eckhard. 2014. PALAVRAS, a Constraint Grammar-based Parsing System for Portuguese. In: Tony Berber Sardinha & Thelma de Lurdes São Bento Ferreira (eds.), *Working with Portuguese Corpora*, pp 279-302. London/New York: Bloomsburry Academic.

Birn, Jussi. 2000. Detecting grammar errors with Lingsoft's Swedish grammar checker. In: Torbjørn Nordgård (ed.). *Proceedings of NODALIDA '99*. p. 28-40. Trondheim: Deparment of Linguistics, University of Trondheim.

Graña, Jorge & Gloria Andrade & Jesús Vilares. 2003. Compilation of constraint-based contextual rules for part-of-speech tagging into finite state transducers. In: *Proceedings of the 7th Conference on Implementation and Application of Automata (CIAA 2002)*. pp. 128–137. Springer-Verlag, Berlin.

Hagen, Kristin & Pia Lane & Trond Trosterud. 2001. En grammatikkontrol for bokmål. In: Kjell Ivar VAnnebo & Helge Sandøy (eds). *Språkknyt 3-2001, pp.* 6-9. Oslo: Norsk Språkråd

Karlsson, Fred. 1990. Constraint Grammar as a Framwork for Parsing Running Text. In: Hans Karlgren (ed.). Proceedings of COLING-90, Vol. 3, pp. 168-173

Karlsson, Fred & Atro Voutilainen & Juha Heikkilä & Arto Anttila. 1995. *Constraint Grammar: A language-independent system for parsing unrestricted text.* Natural Language Processing 4. Berlin & New York: Mouton de Gruyter.

Lager, Torbjörn. 1999. The μ-TBL System: Logic Programming Tools for Transformation-Based Learning. In: *Proceedings of CoNLL'99 (Bergen).*

Lindberg, Nikolaj & Martin Eineborg. 1998. Learning Constraint Grammar-style Disambiguation Rules Using Inductive Logic Programming. In: *Proceedings of the 36th ACL / 17th COLING (Montreal, Canada)*. volume 2, pages 775–779

Tapanainen, Pasi. 1996. The Constraint Grammar Parser CG-2. No 27, Publications of the Department of Linguistics, University of Helsinki.

Tapanainen, Pasi. 1997. A Dependency Parser for English. Technical Reports No TR1. Department of Linguistics, University of Helsinki.

Yli-Jyrä, Anssi Mikael. 2011. An Efficient Constraint Grammar Parser based on Inward Deterministic Automata. In: *Proceedings of the NODALIDA 2011 Workshop ConstraintGrammar Applications*, pp. 50-60 NEALT ProceedingsSeries , vol. 14

Automatic Lemmatisation of Lithuanian MWEs

Loïc Boizou **Jolanta Kovalevskaitė** **Erika Rimkutė**
Centre of Computational Linguistics
Vytautas Magnus University
Kaunas, Lithuania
{l.boizou, j.kovalevskaite, e.rimkute}@hmf.vdu.lt

Abstract

This article presents a study of lemmatisation of flexible multiword expressions in Lithuanian. An approach based on syntactic analysis designed for multiword term lemmatisation was adapted for a broader range of MWEs taken from the Dictionary of Lithuanian Nominal Phrases. In the present analysis, the main lemmatisation errors are identified and some improvements are proposed. It shows that automatic lemmatisation can be improved by taking into account the whole set of grammatical forms for each MWE. It would allow selecting the optimal grammatical form for lemmatisation and identifying some grammatical restrictions.

1 Introduction

In Lithuanian, in addition to fully fixed multiword expressions (MWEs), there are many MWEs with one or more constituents (possibly all) which can be inflected. Therefore, these "flexible" MWEs appear in texts in several forms[1]: as shown by the corpus data, the Lithuanian verbal phraseme *pakišti koją*, meaning 'to put a spoke in somebody's wheel', has a form with the verb in definite past *pakišo koją*, a form with the verb in past frequentative (*pakišdavo koją*), and future (*pakiš koją*) (for more examples, see Kovalevskaitė (2014)). If we extract MWEs of a strongly-inflected language like Lithuanian from a raw text corpus using statistical association measures, we often get MWEs with their different grammatical forms (GF). However, in lexical databases and terminology banks, a single lemma is usually used in order to represent the MWE independently from its concrete forms which appear in the corpus.

In traditional Lithuanian dictionaries of idioms, there is no problem of MWE lemmatisation, because data are collected manually and represented following the rule that a verb of an idiom is provided in infinitive form (Paulauskas (ed), 2001), e.g.: *Savo vietą žinoti* 'to know one's place', *Vietos neturėti* 'to have nowhere to go'. The recent Dictionary of Lithuanian Nominal Phrases[2], which was compiled semi-automatically from a corpus, contains the unlemmatised list of MWEs. Therefore, automatic phrase lemmatisation could help in organizing the dictionary data and in improving the user interface.

This article describes the main problems occurring during the lemmatisation of Lithuanian MWEs. The concept of lemmatisation is quite clear for single words, but for MWEs, it can be understood differently as it will be discussed in part 3. Although the accuracy of lemmatisation of individual words is high (99% for lemmatisation and 94% for grammatical form identification (Rimkutė and Daudaravičius, 2007)), the lemmatisation of single words included in MWEs cannot produce well-formed MWE lemmas. Indeed, base forms of Lithuanian multiword terms which should occur in dictionaries and terminology databases are not the same as the sequences of lemmas of their constitutive words (Boizou et al., 2012, p. 28). For example, if we lemmatise each constitutive word in MWEs *taupomųjų bankų*, *taupomuoju banku* ('savings bank' in genitive plural and instrumental singular), the result is *taupyti bankas* (infinitive 'to save' and nominative singular 'bank'), because the morphological annotator of the Lithuanian language (Zinkevičius, 2000; Zinkevičius et al., 2005) assignes infinitive as the proper lemma for participles and other verb forms. The structure of such improperly lemmatised MWE fails to reflect the syntactic relations (agreement and gov-

[1]Grammatical forms of the same MWE (or phraseme) can be labelled as phraseme-types (Kovalevskaitė, 2014).

[2]http://donelaitis.vdu.lt/lkk/pdf/dikt_fr.pdf

ernment) which ensure the grammatical cohesion between the constitutive words of an MWE.

This work is focused on syntagmatic lemma, which is the form of the MWE where the MWE syntactic head is lemmatised and the necessary adaptations are made in order to ensure the morphosyntactic unity of the MWE. With a similar approach, a tool for automatic Lithuanian sintagmatic lemmatisation called JungLe was first developed and trained with multiword terms during the project ŠIMTAI 2 (semi-automatic extraction of education and science terms). The first experiments with the Lithuanian multiword terms showed accuracy close to 95% (Boizou et al., 2012), but it can be related to a relatively low variety of term structures. For this study, JungLe was adapted for a broader set of types of Lithuanian compositional and non-compositional MWEs, e.g. idioms, collocations, nominal compounds, MW terms, MW named entities, MW function words, proverbs, etc.

2 Data

This study is based on the data from the Dictionary of Lithuanian Nominal Phrases (further on, dictionary). The database of the dictionary[3] consists of 68,602 nominal phrases. It has to be mentioned, that the term nominal phrase refers to all MWEs which contain at least one noun: it can be phrases with a noun as a syntactic head, as well as phrases with a verb or an adjective as a syntactic head. In this article, the terms MWE and phrase are used interchangeably.

In the dictionary, the phrases are of different length: from two-word phrases (31,853 phrases) to phrases comprising 46 words (1 phrase). The major part of the dictionary phrases is made up of two-word phrases (46.4%), whereas three-word phrases and four-word phrases form accordingly 28.7% and 10.1% of the dictionary (Rimkutė et al., 2012, p. 19). The phrases are not lemmatised, but given in the form as they appear in the corpus, e.g.:

- *mobilaus ryšio telefonas, mobilaus ryšio telefono, mobilaus ryšio telefoną, mobilaus ryšio telefonus* ('mobile phone' in various grammatical forms: nominative singular, genitive singular, accusative singular and accusative plural);
- *nenuleisti rankų, nenuleido rankų, nenuleidžia rankų* ('not to give up', lit. 'not to lower hands', in various grammatical forms: infinitive, definite past, present tense).

[3]http://tekstynas.vdu.lt/page.xhtml?id=dictionary-db

As Lithuanian is a strongly inflected language, it is an advantage that users can see phrases in the form they are used in the corpus. Phrases were extracted by the method of Gravity Counts (Daudaravičius and Marcinkevičienė, 2004, p. 330) from the Corpus of Contemporary Lithuanian Language (100 m running words; made up of periodicals, fiction, non-fiction, and legal texts published in 1991-2002). Gravity Counts helps to evaluate the combinability of two words according to individual word frequencies, pair frequencies or the number of different words in a selected 3 word-span. As a result, it detects collocational chains as text fragments, not as a list of collocates for the previously selected node-words.

After automatic extraction of collocational chains from the corpus, manual procedures were performed: transformation of collocational chains into phrases (the procedure is described in detail in Marcinkevičienė (2010) and Rimkutė et al. (2012)). According to the lexicographical approach, linguistically well-formed collocational chains have to be grammatical, meaningful, and arbitrary. Therefore, some chains were shortened, complemented, joined or deleted manually. At present, the dictionary database contains phrases without additions (1) and with additions: additions can be explicitly specified (2) or not (3), e.g.:

1. *ne tuo adresu* 'under a wrong address';
2. (*gauti; suteikti*) *daugiau informacijos* '(get; give) more information';
3. *atkreipiant dėmesį į* (...) 'paying attention to (...)'.

Phrase type	Number of lemmas	Number of lemmas with 2 or more GF
2-word	18,581	6,585 (35,4%)
3-word	10,970	2,245 (20,5%)
4-word	3,333	477 (14,3%)
In total	32,884	9,307 (28,3%)

Table 1: Statistical information about MWEs from the type (1).

Only two-, three-, and four-word phrases from the type (1) were filtered out for this study (see Table 1). As already mentioned, these phrases make up 85% of the whole dictionary database, and thus can be considered as the most typical multiword units in Lithuanian (Marcinkevičienė, 2010; Rimkutė et al., 2012). Most of them are idioms, phraseologisms and collocations, although there are many multiword terms as well.

It was calculated that two-word expressions have on average 1.71 different grammatical forms, three-word expressions – around 1.35 different grammatical forms, and four-word expressions – 1.22 different grammatical forms. The maximum number of grammatical forms for one lemma are respectively 21 (*aukšta mokykla* 'high school'), 15 (*mobilaus ryšio telefonas* 'mobile phone') and 8 (*kandidatas į seimo narius* 'candidate as MP'). For this study, only the 9,307 MWEs with two or more grammatical forms were selected. The remaining MWEs, those for which only one form was identified automatically, are excluded, as they do not always need to be lemmatised and require a further study.

The next section describes the main approaches applied to the process of automatic lemmatisation of MWEs.

3 Approaches to Lemmatisation of MWEs

In Lithuanian, a great number of MWEs can appear in different grammatical forms. As such, they do not differ from variable simple words. Accordingly, a lot of Lithuanian MWEs consist of nouns, verbs and/or adjectives that are used in a particular grammatical form. Some of these word classes can have from a few to dozens of different grammatical forms. Traditionally, for the set of grammatical forms of each variable word, one basic form is assigned. The latter, a lemma, is a convenient representation of the whole set of grammatical word forms. Although in principle a lemma could be an artificial form (a stem, for example), the tradition is to select as a lemma one form from the whole set of grammatical forms, e.g. in Lithuanian:

- nominative singular form for nouns (except for plural nouns);
- nominative singular masculine positive indefinite form for adjectives;
- positive form for adverbs (if they vary in degree);
- infinitive for verbs (including participles).

In the field of computational linguistics, it is common to use artificial lemmas for MWEs, because they can be easily generated by automatic means. There are two main kinds of artificial lemmas:

a) It is possible to use a lemmatic sequence which is the sequence of lemmas of each constitutive word of the MWE[4]. Using the morphological annotation tool for Lithuanian (the tool is described in Zinkevičius (2000) and Zinkevičius et al. (2005)), each grammatical form of the multiword term, *bendrosioms mokslo programoms* 'framework programme', is annotated morphologically as follows:

- <word="bendrosioms" lemma="bendras" type="bdv., teig, nelygin. l., įvardž., mot. g., dgs., N."/>[5]
- <word="mokslo" lemma="mokslas" type= "dkt., vyr. g., vns., K."/>[6]
- <word="programoms" lemma="programa" type="dkt., mot. g., dgs., N."/>[7]

The lemmatic sequence, e.g. for the previous example *bendras mokslas programa*, is often used in the field of automatic term recognition (e.g., Loginova et al. (2012, p. 9)) to represent a term or another type of MWE. Nonetheless, such a substitute, which lacks grammatical cohesion between the parts of the MWE, appears as a heap of words, which is unnatural for human users[8].

[4]The difference between syntagmatic lemma (with morphosyntactic relations between constitutive words) and lemmatic sequence (the sequence of lemmas of constitutive words) is relevant only for MWEs, not for single words.

[5]The field *type* contains the following grammatical features: adjective, positive, undefined, positive degree, feminine, plural, dative.

[6]Grammatical features: noun, masculine, singular, genitive.

[7]Grammatical features: noun, feminine, plural, dative.

[8]In about 5% of the studied phrases, the sequences of isolated lemmas incidentally correspond to their natural lemma, e.g. *vyras ir moteris* 'man and woman', *valstybinis simfoninis orkestras* 'national symphony orchestra'. Such cases require the following conditions: the nominal syntactic head is masculine singular, the only syntactic relation inside the term is agreement or implies invariable words, degree and definiteness must not be retained in the lemma, no participle is implied.

b) The second frequent method is stemming, that is, dropping of endings. For example, the forms of the previously mentioned MWE *bendroji mokslo programa*, *bendrosios mokslo programos* and *bendrosioms mokslo programoms* can be represented as: *bendr moksl program*. This option is even more artificial for Lithuanian, since, in addition to the loss of syntactic cohesion, this approach generates shortened words without endings, which do not exist in Lithuanian.

Other approaches attempt to provide a natural lemma, i.e., by either choosing the most frequent form as a lemma, or generating a correct syntagmatic lemma from grammatical forms. Taking the most frequent form of the lemma avoids mistakes in generation, but the result is that the set of basic forms is heterogeneous: some MWEs will be in nominative, some will be in accusative, genitive or in some other case, some will be in the plural form, others - in the singular.

Automatic lemmatisation according to the syntactic structure of each MWE ensures the constitency of basic forms, but it is the most complicated process. The tool JungLe, which is described in Boizou et al. (2012), was specifically designed for this task. This software analyses an MWE and attempts to distinguish three types of syntactic components (as a concrete example the multiword term *individualus studijų grafikas* 'individual study plan/schedule' is provided):

- syntactic head (e.g., the noun *grafikas* 'plan/schedule');
- words congruent with the head (e.g., the adjective *individualus* 'individual');
- other words, that is, words governed by the head and their own dependents (e.g., the noun in genitive case *studijų* 'study').

The generation of the syntagmatic lemma requires the syntactic head to be lemmatised (for terms, the syntactic head is a noun, but there is more diversity with other types of MWEs). Words (usually in the genitive case) governed by the head and their own dependents remain in their grammatical form, e.g., *švietimo {lygmuo}* 'education level', *socialinių mokslų {sritis}* 'field of social sciences'.[9]

[9] Here and below the syntactic head is indicated in curly brackets.

The most difficult case concerns words congruent with the head, since they often have to be corrected to remain congruent with the head once it is lemmatised. If the head is masculine singular, the adaptation usually requires only taking lemmas for each congruent word, e.g., in the multiword term *individualus studijų grafikas* 'individual study plan/schedule' (the adjective *individualus* 'individual' agrees with the noun *grafikas* 'schedule', not with the noun *studijų* 'study'). When the syntactic head is feminine, congruent words must also be put in their feminine form, e.g., *nuotolinės studijos* 'distance studies' (instead of **nuotolinis studijos*, where the masculine singular indefinite positive form of the adjective *nuotolinis* is incongruent with the feminine plural head *studijos*).

Besides, some lexico-grammatical features, e.g., definiteness, comparative/superlative degrees, are usually semantically relevant, so that they have to be kept in the syntagmatic lemma, which requires to generate the proper form, even when the head is masculine and singular, e.g. *Senasis ir Naujasis testamentas* 'The Old and New Testament' (where the adjectives *Senasis* and *Naujasis* are in the definite form, instead of **Senas ir Naujas testamentas*), *aukštesnioji žemės ūkio mokykla* 'high school of agriculture' (where the adjective *aukštesnioji* is in the definite comparative form, instead of **aukštas žemės ūkio mokykla*).

Syntagmatic lemmatisation also requires to lemmatise participles in a different manner than single words. Indeed, participles are traditionally lemmatised as verbs in infinitive form. For example, the single word lemmatisation of the term *perkeliamieji gebėjimai* 'transferable skills' gives a result *perkelti gebėjimai*, that is a sequence of an infinitive (*perkelti* 'to transfer') and a noun in nominative (*gebėjimai* 'skills'). The correct syntagmatic lemmatisation requires participles to be corrected in gender, number and case only, in order to remain congruent with their lemmatised head, e.g. *perkeliamasis gebėjimas*.

All required generations are made by a lightweighted generative module. This module uses to the largest possible extent the information provided by the morphological analyser, which works on a single word basis. Its generative capacities are restricted to the nominative forms, since noun, adjective and participle lemmas are in the nominative form. Aiming at facilitation of the process, the generation proceeds either from a single lemma or a grammatical form. For example, lemmas for participles are generated from the grammatical form, because it helps to avoid the problem of numerous verbal paradigms in Lithuanian, while adjectives are generated from the lemma. Indeed, some endings of nouns and adjectives (e.g., *-(i)ų* genitive plural) hide the declension paradigm (which is necessary for the selection of the correct feminine ending), so that it is better to decide from the lemma, which expresses the adjectival declension paradigm by its ending[10], e.g., *nuotolinis* 'distant' (third adjectival declension paradigm) → *nuotolinė*. The whole process is very similar to Thurmair (2012, p. 257).

4 Syntagmatic Lemmatisation of Lithuanian MWEs: Evaluation and Results

In this part of the article, we present our results: what problems are solved by syntactic analysis, and what problems still remain and pose challenges for automatic MWE lemmatisation.

Two-, three- and four-word phrases were automatically lemmatised with the help of JungLe tool and the results were evaluated manually (see Table 2). JungLe generates a lemma for each MWE grammatical form separately, so that more than one lemma can be provided for the same MWE, especially when it is difficult to identify automatically to which word an attribute in genitive belongs, e.g., two lemmas, both inaccurate, were provided for the MWE *bendroji dalinės nuosavybės teisė* 'general partial ownership', where the first adjective *bendroji* 'general' is congruent with the MWE head *teisė* 'law' and the second adjective *dalinės* 'partial' with the noun *nuosavybės* 'property' (which depends on the MWE head). In the first provided lemma **bendroji dalinė nuosavybės teisė*, *dalinė* incorrectly agrees with *teisė*, and in the second one, **bendrosios dalinės nuosavybės teisė*, *bendrosios* incorrectly agrees with *nuosavybės*.

As each grammatical form is lemmatised separately, in some cases there is more than one lemma for the same MWE. Thus, lemmatisation accuracy was assessed for individual grammatical forms of MWEs. Table 2 shows that the highest accuracy is with two-word phrases; however, the number of incorrectly lemmatised MWEs increases for three- and four-word phrases. It shows that the syntactic complexity increases with the length of the MWEs.

Phrase type	Number of lemmas	Number of GF	Correctly lemmatised GF
2-word	6,585	19,822	91.56%
3-word	2,245	6,110	80.57%
4-word	477	1,206	76.43%
In total	9,307	27,138	

Table 2: Statistical information about the analysed MWEs (2 or more forms only).

The analysis of the automatic lemmatisation revealed three groups of errors[11]: a) agreement errors (number, gender); b) government errors; c) lexico-grammatical errors (degree, definiteness, lexical plural).

4.1 Agreement Errors

Many errors occur with numerals, e.g., **beveik du trečdalis* '*nearly two third' (it should be *beveik du trečdaliai*, 'nearly two thirds', with *trečdalis* 'third' in the plural form), also **aštuoni mėnuo* '*eight month' (while it should be *aštuoni mėnesiai*, 'eight months', with *mėnuo* 'month' in the plural form). Many of these errors can be eliminated by applying proper rules in the syntactic analysis.

During the syntactic analysis gender errors occur when the composition of an MWE is more complex, e.g., **vienas ar kita grupė* 'one or the other group'(instead of *viena ar kita grupė*, with *viena* 'one' and *kita* 'other' in the feminine form). We can see that the coordinating link could be the factor determining the agreement errors[12].

[10]Ending *-as* for the first adjectival declension, *-ias* for the second, *-is* and *-ys* for the third and fourth, and *-us* for the fifth.

[11]Some errors of lemmatisation occur due to errors of the previous morphological analysis, e.g., the lemma for the MWE *arbatinio šaukštelio* ('tea spoon', sing. Gen.) is provided incorrectly as **arbatinio šaukštelis* (genitive singular + nominative singular, instead of *arbatinis šaukštelis*, nominative singular for both the adjective and the noun), because of an improper morphological analysis: *arbatinis* was annotated as a noun, not an adjective.

[12]Some similar errors, which must be corrected, appear with the genitive case, e.g. *Afrikos ir Azija* (genitive and nominative, it should be *Afrika ir Azija* 'Africa and Asia', nominative and nominative), **daina ir šokių ansamblis* (nominative noun, conjunction, genitive noun, nominative noun), instead of *dainų ir šokių {ansamblis}* (genitive noun, conjunction, genitive noun, nominative noun) 'song and dance ensemble'.

It was observed that a large number of agreement errors take place when one of the attributes is an apposition, i.e., a noun which has to agree in a case (sometimes gender and number) with the adjacent noun, e.g., **šalies gavėja* (it should be *šalis gavėja*, 'the recipient party'), **mergelės Marija* (it should be *mergelė Marija*, 'the Virgin Mary', with both parts in nominative). One the other hand, such attributes are not numerous, and such errors could be solved by looking at other cases than genitive.

4.2 Government Errors

Problems mainly arise when the tool fails to correctly identify the syntactic head of a phrase. Such a problem usually occurs when the head is not at the end of an MWE, e.g. **paskolos {studijos}* (instead of *{paskola} studijoms* 'study loan'), **atliko savo {darbas}* 'carried out their work' (instead of *{atlikti} savo darbą*, where the verb is the head). Problems also occur in phrases, where the head is a half-participle or a gerund: **įsigaliojus naujasis civilinis {kodeksas}* 'when the new civil code came into effect' (it should be *{įsigaliojus} naujajam civiliniam kodeksui*, i.e. where dative is required).

It must be noticed that in some cases the representation of the lemma does not correspond to a natural linguistic form. It occurs in collocations which contain a conjugated verb (*pakilo*) with a (nominative) subject, e.g. *pakilo temperatūra* 'temperature rised'. In the assigned lemmas, conjugated verbs are substituted for infinitive forms (*pakilti*). Infinitives cannot have a subject in Lithuanian, and therefore the MWE subject could be presented in brackets in the nominative form (e.g. *pakilti (temperatūra)* 'to rise (temperature)'). A further exception comes from the MWEs with a gerund, since the logical subject of a gerund is not expressed as a nominative, but as a dative complement, e.g., *atsitikus nelaimei* 'a disaster occurs'. In such cases, we propose to assign two different lemmas: one lemma, which retains the grammatical form without change, *atsitikus nelaimei* (gerund + dative complement), as used in gerund grammatical form; and the second lemma, where the gerund is substituted for the infinitive and the dative complement is substituted for a nominative form in bracket, e.g. *atsitikti (nelaimė)* (infinitive + nominative), as in the previous example.

We should also mention, among other complicated lemmatisation instances, the loss of grammatical forms which carry the meaning of an MWE, e.g., *atstovų teigimas* ('representatives' assertion') could be considered as a correctly generated lemma; however, after a closer investigation of the grammatical forms, we can see that in this MWE the syntactic head is always used in the instrumental case (*teigimu*), i.e., *atstovų teigimu* ('according to the representatives'), thus the lemma should keep this form. Similarly, the lemma of an MWE *balsavimo paštas* ('voting post') is not accurate, as the syntactic head (*paštas*) should be in the instrumental case, i.e., *balsavimas paštu* ('voting by mail'), while the lemma of a phrase *visa išgalė* ('all possible measures') should be *visomis išgalėmis* ('by all possible measures'), because this phrase as an MWE is used only in the form of instrumental plural.

4.3 Lexico-grammatical Errors

There are many errors made by JungLe where a lemma has to be assigned to nouns which are used in plural in the phrase, e.g., **žmogaus teisė ir laisvė* 'human right and freedom', instead of *žmogaus teisės ir laisvės*, 'human rights and freedoms'; **jungtinė tauta* 'united nation', instead of *Jungtinės Tautos*, 'United Nations'; **visa Baltijos šalis* 'the whole Baltic country', instead of *visos Baltijos šalys* 'all Baltic countries', **Vilniaus ir Šalčininkų rajonas* 'Vilnius and Šalčininkai district', instead of *Vilniaus ir Šalčininkų rajonai* 'Vilnius and Šalčininkai districts'. As number errors were considered the examples when a lemma looked correct at first sight, i.e., a lemma is provided in the same number as in the dictionary. However, from the usage data (all forms of a phrase) one can see that certain MWEs are used only in plural, e.g., *meteorologinės sąlygos* 'meteorological conditions', *mineralinės trąšos* 'mineral fertilizers', *mirties aplinkybės* 'death circumstances'. All these phrases, which are made of an adjective or a genitive noun followed by a noun, are incorrectly lemmatised in the singular form, e.g. **meteorologinė sąlyga*, **mineralinė trąša*, **mirties aplinkybė*. Many of the above-mentioned nouns can be used in plural and singular, when they are used independently, but they can be restricted to one of these numbers inside MWEs. Traditional grammars and dictionaries do not provide necessary information to solve this problem, which could often be resolved if we take into account actual usage from the corpus.

There are two types of degree errors: a) in some phrases a particular degree form is used, thus, the same form should be in the lemma (*Aukščiausiasis Teismas* 'supreme court'; *daugiau kaip dveji metai* 'more than two years'); b) there are phrases, where an adverb or an adjective is used in several degrees: then different phrases can contain adjectives or adverbs of different degrees (cf. *įvairūs / įvairiausi būdai* ('various/ the most various ways') and *skirti daug/daugiau/daugiausia dėmesio* (to pay a lot of/more/ most attention)). Analysis of all forms of an MWE can help to distinguish a) and b) phrases.

Errors of definiteness often occur in phrases joined by coordination, when one adjective is provided in the definite form while the other one is indefinite, e.g., **Senas ir Naujasis testamentas* ('Old and New Testament').

After the examination of errors and problematic cases created by JungLe, we can draw a conclusion that automatic lemmatisation is aggravated by:

1. syntactic heads in the genitive form: when there are several nouns in the genitive in the MWE, it leads to attachment ambiguities;
2. the length of an MWE: the longer the phrase, the more complicated syntactic structure; the accuracy of lemmatisation decreases (see Table 2);
3. problems of lexico-grammatical nature, when a grammatical form depends on a lexical meaning (here, errors of number must be emphasized).

It must be emphasized that the numbers in Table 2 show the situation after the first extension of JungLe. The results can still be improved significantly. Some errors can be corrected by improving the grammar used by JungLe for syntactic analysis, some of them require adding new capacities to JungLe, other errors will be difficult to correct without human intervention.

5 Discussion and Recommendations

The traditional morphological analyser, which analyses every word individually, cannot produce natural lemmas for MWEs. It is necessary to carry out the syntactic analysis for automatic assignation of natural lemmas for different grammatical forms of MWEs. But beside syntactic analysis of MWEs, we often need to take into account the usage data of a particular MWE and to apply additional criteria. The automatic syntagmatic lemmatisation tool was tested on the data from the Dictionary of Lithuanian Nominal Phrases, which are characterized by a high variety. For this reason, it can be stated that the essential features, as well as problems, of automatic lemmatisation of Lithuanian MWEs were identified.

One of the most important lemmatisation issues that is difficult to solve is the problem of an attribute which is incongruent with a noun and usually expressed in genitive. Most commonly, such problems (in automatic lemmatisation) are inevitable, because ambivalent syntactic relations can exist in MWEs composed of the same words, e.g., the lemma for MWE grammatical forms *administracinės teisės pažeidimų*, *administracinės teisės pažeidimą*, *administracinės teisės pažeidimus* 'breach of administrative law' (where *administracinis* 'administrative' is congruent with *teisė* 'law') should be *administracinės teisės pažeidimas*, while the lemma for MWE grammatical forms *administracinį teisės pažeidimą*, *administracinių teisės pažeidimų*, *administracinius teisės pažeidimus* 'administrative breach of law' (where *administracinis* 'administrative' is congruent with *pažeidimas* 'breach') should be *administracinis teisės pažeidimas*. In order to set the right lemma, the noun with which the adjective agrees must be correctly assigned.

The head of a phrase in genitive can influence adjective agreement errors, too. For instance, the genitive grammatical form *periodinio mokslo leidinio*, where it is unclear if *periodinio* 'periodic' is congruent with *mokslo* 'science' or *leidinio* 'publication', could formally be lemmatised as **periodinio mokslo leidinys* 'a publication of periodic science' or *periodinis mokslo leidinys* 'a periodic scientific publication' by looking at the internal syntactic structure of the term. In order to disambiguate syntax correctly, we need to compare other (unambiguous, i.e., cases other than the genitive) forms of the term, e.g., *periodiniams mokslo leidiniams* (in dative plural), which shows that the adjective *periodinis* 'periodic' is congruent with the noun *leidinys* 'publication', therefore, this MWE should properly be lemmatised as *periodinis mokslo leidinys*.

The problems concerning the genitive case

would decrease, if the usage criterion was applied, i.e., if lemma was identified considering all forms of the MWE. For example, it is especially complicated to lemmatise an MWE with all genitive cases, e.g., it is impossible to identify an accurate lemma for MWEs *valstybinio socialinio draudimo biudžeto* ('the budget of state social insurance'), *fizinių asmenų pajamų mokesčių* ('income taxes of natural persons'). In such cases, a rule should be applied: if the same phrase is used in genitive and in other cases, the lemma should be identified on the basis of phrases with other cases than genitive.

The usage criterion would help to avoid the number errors. Quite often this criterion proved the rule that if different grammatical forms of an MWE are in plural, then the lemma should keep the plural form too. For example, a dictionary of nominal phrases provides two grammatical forms: *laužas ir atliekos*, *laužo ir atliekų* 'debris and waste', in both phrases the noun *laužas* is in the singular form, while *atliekos* is used in plural. Thus, when merging the two MWEs to one lemma, *atliekos* has to remain in the plural form. During the lemmatisation of the forms *žvėris ir paukščius*, *žvėrių ir paukščių*, *žvėrys ir paukščiai* ('beasts and birds', repectively accusative plural, genitive plural, nominative plural), we have to assign plural lemmas for both nouns – *žvėrys ir paukščiai*, because all forms of these nominal phrases are in the plural form. This is especially important for names, cf. **Lietuvos geležinkelis* (it should be *Lietuvos geležinkeliai*, 'Lithuanian Railways'), **Vilniaus šilumos tinklas* (it should be *Vilniaus šilumos tinklai*, 'Vilnius Heating Network').

Based on the usage data, it would be possible to distinguish between the MWEs where a certain word is used only in one form of the degree (*Aukščiausiasis Teismas*, superlative, 'Supreme Court'), and those where several forms of a degree are used (*įvairūs būdai* and *įvairiausi būdai*, positive and superlative, 'various ways').

When applying the usage criterion, it is important to remember that in this case the accuracy of the tool will be linked to the corpus data: the rarer the phrase, the higher the risk for the tool to make a mistake. For example, if we recognize only two forms of a particular phrase, and they are both in the plural form, the tool can come to a false conclusion that the lemma of that phrase is also in plural, although that phrase could also be used in singular. But such a risk is significant for rare MWEs only.

It is possible that next to the usage criterion, other criteria will have to be introduced. For example, in order to avoid lemmatisation errors related to definiteness, it would be worthwhile to invoke not only the usage, but, also, frequency criterion. Indeed, according to the data, *nekilnojamas turtas* (with the indefinite form of the adjective *nekilnojamas*) and *nekilnojamasis turtas* (with the definite form of the adjective *nekilnojamasis*), which both mean 'real property', are concurrently used. However, one can expect the standard form, the definite one, to be more frequent, as it is a term.

The evaluation of the research results has revealed that the accuracy of the MWE lemmatisation is not only influenced by the accuracy of the syntactic analyser, but, also, by the variability of MWEs. If we come across a phrase which has two variants, then a separate lemma will be assigned to each variant during the automatic lemmatisation, e.g., *užrašų knygutė* and *užrašų knygelė* ('a notebook', the difference lies in the diminutive suffix of the nouns). However, several forms of degree, different forms of definiteness could be used in the same MWE; for this reason, we have to discuss how to reflect all this in a lemma. The substituting component could be presented in angle brackets: *skirti* [*daug/daugiau*] *dėmesio* 'to pay [much/more] attention'; [*nekilnojamas/nekilnojamasis*] *turtas* 'real property' (with a definite or indefinite adjective). Thus, this would indicate that some syntagmatic lemmas contain substituting components.

References

Loïc Boizou, Gintarė Grigonytė, Erika Rimkutė, and Andrius Utka. 2012. Automatic Inference of Base Forms for Multiword Terms in Lithuanian. In *Proceedings of the Fifth International Conference Human Language Technologies – The Baltic Perspective*, pages 27–35.

Vidas Daudaravičius and Rūta Marcinkevičienė. 2004. Gravity Counts for the Boundaries of Collocations. *International Journal of Corpus Linguistics*, 9(2):321–348.

Jolanta Kovalevskaitė. 2014. Phraseme-type and Phraseme-token: a Corpus-driven Evidence for Morphological Flexibility of Phrasemes. *Res Humanitariae*, XVI, pages 126–143.

Elizaveta Loginova, Anita Gojun, Helena Blancafort, Marie Guégan, Tatiana Gornostay, and Ulrich Heid. 2012. Reference Lists for the Evaluation of Term

Extraction Tools. In *Proceedings of the 10th International Congress on Terminology and Knowledge Engineering (TKE)*, pages 177–192, Madrid, Spain.

Rūta Marcinkevičienė. 2010. *Lietuvių kalbos kolokacijos*. Vytauto Didžiojo universitetas, Kaunas, Lithuania.

Jonas Paulauskas (ed). 2001. *Frazeologijos žodynas*. Lietuvių kalbos institutas, Vilnius, Lithuania.

Erika Rimkutė and Vidas Daudaravičius. 2007. Morfologinis dabartinės lietuvių kalbos tekstyno anotavimas. *Kalbų studijos*, 11:30–35.

Erika Rimkutė, Agnė Bielinskienė, and Jolanta Kovalevskaitė (eds). 2012. *Lietuvių kalbos daiktavardinių frazių žodynas*. Vytauto Didžiojo universitetas, Kaunas, Lithuania.

Gregor Thurmair and Vera Aleksić. 2012. Creating Term and Lexicon Entries from Phrase Tables. In *Proceedings of the 16th EAMT Conference*, pages 253–260.

Vytautas Zinkevičius, Vidas Daudaravičius, and Erika Rimkutė. 2005. The Morphologically Annotated Lithuanian Corpus. In *Proceedings of The Second Baltic Conference on Human Language Technologies*, pages 365–370.

Vytautas Zinkevičius. 2000. Lemuoklis – morfologinei analizei. *Darbai ir Dienos*, 24:245–273.

Linguistically Motivated Question Classification

Alexandr Chernov **Volha Petukhova** **Dietrich Klakow**
Saarland University, Spoken Language Systems
Saarbrücken, Germany
{alexandr.chernov, v.petukhova, dietrich.klakow}@lsv.uni-saarland.de

Abstract

In this paper we describe a question interpretation module designed as a part of a Question Answering Dialogue System (QADS) which is used for an interactive quiz application. Question interpretation is achieved in applying a sequence of classification, information extraction, query formalization and query expansion tasks. The process of a question classification is performed based on a domain-specific taxonomy of semantic roles and relations. Our taxonomy was designed in accordance with the real spoken dialogue data. The SVM-based classifier is trained to predict the Expected Answer Type (EAT) with the precision of 82%. In order to retrieve a correct answer, focus word(-s) are extracted to augment the EAT identified by the system. Our hybrid algorithm for the extraction of focus words demonstrates the accuracy of 94.6%. EAT together with focus words are formalized in a query, which is further expanded with the synonyms from WordNet. The expanded query facilitates the search and retrieval of the information that is necessary to generate the system's responses.

1 Introduction

Any question answering (QA) system has to be able to give as precise as possible answers to natural language questions. In order to perform this task with a reasonably high accuracy, an adequate question interpretation is required. In the NLP field, this problem is often defined as the question classification. Due to the ambiguity of natural language utterances the task may become very complicated. For this reason the question classification phase has proven to be one of the most important parts of many QA system. If a question type is not correctly identified, the system will not be able to find the correct and/or complete answer. According to Razmara et al. (2007), correctly classified questions are answered correctly twice as often as misclassified ones.

The study conducted by Moldovan et al. (2000) set a new modern foundation in the QA task. An end-to-end open-domain QA system has been developed. In TREC-8[1], it achieved the highest result by demonstrating the accuracy of 77.7%. The designed system performs question processing, including question classification, focus and key words extraction, as well as the specification of an expected answer type.

In 2011, IBM Watson QA system (Ferrucci et al., 2010) won Jeopardy! quiz game, where it was able to beat two highest ranked players. The system includes a component responsible for the question analysis: the system needs to know what was asked in a question. Having this knowledge, the system generates candidate answers. In 2013 IBM made an attempt to adapt Watson QA to the healthcare domain (Ferrucci et al., 2013).

The scenario targeted in our application is comparable to the Jeopardy! quiz game. Our system, however, provides an interactive quiz game meaning that the returned answers are not just extracted information chunks or slot fillers, or database entries, but rather full-fledged dialogue utterances. The domain, on the other hand, is restricted to bibliographical facts about a famous person, and the player's task is to guess his/her identity by asking ten questions of various types. For such a close-domain, for the system to understand a question it is possible to narrow down the knowledge available to it. For example, structured knowledge bases can be used, e.g. Freebase[2]. They are however not complete to achieve sufficient cover-

[1] http://trec.nist.gov/pubs/trec8
[2] http://www.freebase.com/

age of factual information required for our game. Therefore, the content that the system operates on is a bigger collection of unstructured free texts, namely, Wikipedia articles[3]. This impacts search and retrieval tasks. As a consequence, the output of a question interpretation module should be a rather comprehensive query capturing various semantic information concerning events in question, entities involved in this event and their properties, and type of relations between entities and possibly between events. Thus, question interpretation is defined as a sequence of classification, information extraction, query formalization and query expansion tasks. Given the closeness of the domain, the system can operate on the basis of pre-defined domain-specific taxonomy of various semantic relations between different types of entities in order to compute an Expected Answer Type (EAT). The EAT is classified using statistical classifiers like Support Vector Machines (SVM) operating on multiple features, such as n-grams, part-of-speech and other syntactic information. The EAT is further augmented with question focus word(-s) information to determine the main event in question. Both, the EAT and focus word(-s), are formalized in a query which, on its turn, is expanded to cover as many as possible natural language variations.

The paper is structured as follows. Section 2 presents related work that has been reported in the area of general question answering and in question classification in particular. In Section 3 we outline performed experiments describing the data, tagset, features, algorithms and evaluation metrics that have been used. Section 4 reports on the experimental results, applying SVM on various feature combinations, to assess the automatic EAT classification. We also assess the semantic relations learnability by partitioning the training set and increasing a number of training instances in each next run. In Section 5 we describe an algorithm for automatic extraction of focus words. Section 6 explains how the query is generated and expanded. Section 7 summarizes our findings and outlines plans for the future work.

2 Related Work

Depending on the domain and task, QA systems may require different kinds of question type taxonomies. The main difference lies in the principle on which the question categorisation is performed.

[3]http://www.wikipedia.org

Lehnert (1986) developed a conceptual taxonomy with 13 conceptual classes (e.g. *causal antecedent, goal orientation, enablement, etc.*). This kind of categorization allows considering processes which occur within human memory during interpretation. Lehnert (1977) also pointed out that for the correct categorisation of ambiguous questions the context is very helpful.

Singhal et al. (1999) designed a very simple taxonomy based on the correspondence between question words and expected answer types. For instance, according to this taxonomy, questions containing *Who* or *Whom* belonged to the type *Person*. For more ambiguous words like *What* or *Which* the type of a question was identified by the head noun.

Li and Roth (2002) implemented a more advanced system. They created a hierarchical classifier relying on the answer type semantics, the taxonomy had 2 layers: 6 coarse classes (*abbreviation, entity, description, human, location, numeric value*) and 50 fine classes (subclasses of different coarse classes do not overlap). Using a hierarchical classifier they tried to get an increase in performance, but experimental results showed that the gained difference with a flat classifier turned out to be insignificant.

The system called Quarc performed a question categorisation relying exclusively on the presence of certain question words (e.g. *who, what, when, where, why*). For each question word the system had a set of heuristic rules which were applied to find out what kind of information an answer should contain. For example, *What*-questions may refer to objects (*What is on the picture?*), humans (*What was the name of the main character?*), or to time (*What year was America discovered in?*) (Riloff and Thelen, 2000).

Nowadays statistical machine learning is actively used for NLP tasks, also for the question classification. Many studies on machine learning indicate that there are no significant differences in performance of existing classification algorithms (Sebastiani, 2002). For example, Huang et al. (2008) applied classifiers based on linear SVM and Maximum Entropy models to the question classification problem. Almost identical accuracy has been achieved: 89.2% and 89.0% respectively. Panicker et al. (2012) used Naive Bayes and SVM classifiers for a comparable problem. Under different conditions the classifiers demonstrated similar results. However, the authors decided in favour of SVM because it was proved to be more effective for complex data.

Further, the question focus may be used to find an answer. Moldovan et al. (2000) defines the question focus as a word or a sequence of words which helps to identify what is asked in a question. Mikhailian et al. (2009) introduced two different types of the question focus:

1. Asking Point (AP) - the explicit question focus, e.g. in the question *Which books have you read?* the word *books* denotes AP;
2. Expected Answer Type (EAT) was used when the answer type was implicit but could be inferred from the information provided by the question, e.g. *person* is the EAT for the question *Who wrote "Pride and Prejudice"?*.

Focus words were applied as features to predict question types. Mikhailian et al. (2009) reported about accuracy of above 82%.

Ferret et al. (2001) defined the question focus as "a noun phrase that is likely to be present in the answer". The focus of a question consists of a head noun and a list of its modifiers. Their QALC system was able to correctly identify the focus for 85% of the questions from TREC10 dataset.

eatEntities	**29.21**		
creatorOf	9.74	partIn	2.46
activityOf	6.95	episodeOf	0.79
famousFor	3.16	interestOf	0.29
fieldOf	2.95	otherEntities	0.21
award	2.66		
eatHumanDescription	**28.76**		
title	11.9	nationality	1.46
name	7.49	religion	1.21
ageOf	2.08	gender	1.21
educationOf	1.66	otherHumanDescription	0.12
body	1.62		
eatHumanGroups	**10.61**		
memberOf	2.25	supporterOf	0.58
chargedFor	2.21	victimOf	0.25
employeeOf	1.79	causeOf	0.17
ownerOf	1.37	subordinateOf	0.12
founderOf	1.17	otherHumanGroups	0.04
superiorOf	0.62	chargeeOf	0.04
eatTime	**9.45**		
time	4.24	period	0.75
timeDeath	2.16	duration	0.67
timeBirth	1.62		
eatLocation	**9.4**		
loc	2.41	locActivityOf	0.92
locBirth	1.96	locDeath	0.83
locResidence	1.66	locFamousFor	0.29
locOrigin	1.33		
eatHumanRelations	**7.41**		
spouseOf	1.87	siblingOf	0.67
parentOf	0.96	friendOf	0.58
familyOf	0.92	enemyOf	0.54
childOf	0.83	otherHumanRelations	0.25
colleagueOf	0.79		
eatDescription	**4.12**		
typeOf	2.16	otherDescription	0.29
manner	0.75	definitionOf	0.21
reason	0.67	purpose	0.04
Multilabel	**1.04**		
fieldOf+spouseOf	0.12	activityOf+childOf	0.04
spouseOf+famousFor	0.12	spouseOf+gender	0.04
siblingOf+activityOf	0.12	spouseOf+founderOf	0.04
title+famousFor	0.08	spouseOf+award	0.04
title+childOf	0.08	otherHumanRelations+famousFor	0.04
title+spouseOf	0.08	title+loc	0.04
nationality+spouseOf	0.08	famousFor+otherHumanRelations	0.04
founderOf+activityOf	0.04		

Table 1: Distribution of semantic relation classes (in terms of relative frequencies in the corpus).

3 Experimental Set Up

3.1 Data and Tagset

It is generally known that spoken language differs from its written form in terms of grammaticality, syntax, vocabulary, etc. Our system is primarily focused on the spoken natural language processing. Unfortunately, publicly available corpora did not meet the requirements of our application.

In order to better understand the nature of spoken dialogue data and to obtain training data, the series of Wizard-of-Oz experiments were conducted. 338 dialogues were recorded, their total duration constitutes about 16 hours (Petukhova et al., 2014). 1342 unique questions were extracted and annotated with semantic relations. Two separate annotators were working on the labelling. To measure the agreement between them, we calculated Cohen's kappa score (Cohen, 1960) for all obtained labels. The kappa score equal to 0.85 was acquired, which indicated a very high degree of agreement between the annotators. Disputable questions were re-annotated together after a thorough discussion.

A preceding study on the question classification problem (see Faiz (2014) for more details) focused on automatically generated data. 1067 questions were obtained from the corresponding Wikipedia article using tool developed by Heilman (2011) and used for the training of an SVM-based classifier. The best precision of 80.18% was achieved on the combination of unigrams and bigrams of lemmas. We combined these two corpora, the resulting dataset contained 2403 (some questions were excluded due to the differences between the taxonomies).

We developed a hierarchical taxonomy of question types, which consists of two layers: coarse classes and fine classes. The full set of the defined relations is presented in Table 1 (see also Petukhova et al. (2014) for more details) with their relative frequency in the data (coarse classes are in bold).

3.2 Classifier

We used scikit-learn[4] (see Pedregosa et al. (2011) for more details), a machine learning library for

[4] http://scikit-learn.org

python, to build a question classifier based on the SVM algorithm and linear kernel function (linearSVC). Since we work in a quite specific domain, we could not obtain a separate dataset for testing. For this reason it was decided to apply a stratified 5-fold cross-validation. The number of folds was chosen based on the analysis of the data. According to Table 1, some classes in our dataset are under-represented. Dividing questions into 5 folds, we were able to equally distribute questions of each class (except for the ones represented by less than five instances).

Our classifier performs multi-class and multi-label classification. Thus, the classifier can handle questions containing several semantic relations which is often the case in real life situations.

We can use the hierarchical structure of our taxonomy to better discriminate between different question types. There are at least two possible ways of how it can be implemented:

1. Sequence of classifiers, where classifier#1 predicts coarse class labels and classifier#2 applies these labels as additional features.
2. Hierarchy of classifiers, where classifier#1 decides to which coarse class a question belongs and transfers it to the corresponding classifier trained specifically for these types of questions.

In our experiments we followed the first approach. According to (Li and Roth, 2002) who worked on a very similar problem there is no significant difference in performance between flat and hierarchical classifiers.

3.3 Features

No matter what learning algorithm or approach is applied, text-based features remain important for the classification task. The bag-of-words (BoW) approach, for example, is by far most widely used in text classification. This approach does not take into account the order of words and their co-occurrences. Therefore, apart from bow-models we constructed models based on bigrams, trigrams, and their combinations to assess their impact on the overall classifier performance. It is also of great interest to understand whether additional linguistic information helps to better discriminate between different classes.

The corpus of annotated questions was processed using the Stanford CoreNLP tools[5] to obtain part-of-speech and lemma information. In our experiments surface word forms, POS-tags, lemmas, as well as surface forms + POS-tags, lemmas + POS-tags, focus words and lemmas of focus words were used as features. Apart from that, we applied combinations of all the above mentioned features with coarse class labels to predict fine classes.

In order to extract focus words, we implemented an algorithm that preserves the main nominal phrase with the predicate, corresponding prepositions and conjunctions while removing everything else. The algorithm excludes stop words and stop phrases (from predefined lists), as well as some parts of speech (based on the Penn Tree Bank tagset[6] we remove existential *there*, interjections, interrogative pronouns and possessive endings), auxiliary verbs, and interrogative pronouns. Questions from the real dialogue data were manually annotated with focus words, which allowed to test this algorithm. It was able to extract focus words with the accuracy of 94.6%.

3.4 Evaluation Metrics

It is desirable, that in a quiz game the system provides the player with a correct answer, and rather acknowledge the fact if no answer is not found by generating utterances like "*Sorry, I do not have this information*".[7] In other words, to return the correct answer or acknowledge the fact that no answer is found is more important for the overall system performance than to return a wrong answer. That is why the precision for both question classification and answer detection tasks was more important than the recall. The precision metrics indicates how relevant the returned answers is to the question asked. Recall, by contrast, indicates how many relevant answers are returned by the classifier, which is not important information for the system to know, therefore disregarded in further evaluations. We calculated a weighted precision score taking into account the proportion of instances in each class. The weighted precision is computed by the following formula:

$$P_w = \frac{\sum_c P_c W_c}{\sum_c W_c}$$

[5]http://nlp.stanford.edu/downloads/corenlp.shtml

[6]http://www.cis.upenn.edu/~treebank/

[7]To make the game more entertaining, the system can always play with strategies to turn a negative situation in a system's favour. For example, if no answer is found, the system may ask the player to put another question claiming that the previous one was not eligible for whatever reasons or the answer to it would lead to quick game end, or alike.

where P_c - precision for a certain class of questions, W_c - weight associated with that class (number of instances in a individual class).

3.5 Experimental Design

As a baseline it is common practice to use the majority class tag, but for our data sets such a baseline is not very useful because of the relatively low frequencies of the tags for many classes (see Table 1). Instead, we computed a baseline that is based on a single feature, namely, bag-of-words when training the Naive Bayes classifier. The baseline classifier achieved the precision of 56%. It was implemented using Multinomial Naive Bayes algorithm from scikit-learn (Pedregosa et al., 2011). Naive Bayes has been chosen for several reasons. Firstly, it is considered to be one of the basic classification algorithms. Secondly, it can be easily implemented. Thirdly, Naive Bayes is relatively simple and works quite fast.

In the first experiment we intended to establish how the classifier performs on the following features: surface word forms, POS-tags, lemmas, surface forms + POS-tags, lemmas + POS-tags, focus words and lemmas of focus words.

Second experiment is based on the assumption that the classifier should be able to predict coarse classes with a higher precision, since coarse classes are better represented in our data. We added coarse class labels as complementary features to the existing ones to predict fine classes. Labels were taken from the annotated data. Unfortunately, this is not a realistic setting, since the classifier can hardly predict coarse class labels with the precision of 100%.

In the third experiment, the classifier was trained on the actual predicted coarse-class labels instead of the annotated ones.

4 Experimental results

We have conducted three experiments, each time using different feature sets. Our classifier outperformed the baseline (X^2 (1, n = 2403) = 293.181, p<.05). The highest precision of 82% was achieved by the model which had been trained on unigrams+bigrams of lemmas. In most cases models based on unigrams+bigrams demonstrated significantly better results than unigram, bigram, or trigram models. It means that the word order is important for the classifier, but not very crucial. In Table 2 we summarize results from all of the experiments.

Features	**n-grams range**				
	1,1	**1,2**	**2,2**	**2,3**	**3,3**
Experiment 1					
Words	0.81	0.81	0.72	0.72	0.68
POS-tags	0.27	0.4	0.4	0.46	0.44
Lemmas	0.8	**0.82**	0.74	0.73	0.71
Words+POS-tags	0.8	0.81	0.71	0.71	0.68
Lemmas+POS-tags	0.8	0.82	0.73	0.73	0.71
Focus	0.75	0.74	0.63	0.59	0.31
FocusLem	0.76	0.76	0.65	0.61	0.39
Experiment 2					
Words+CA	0.86	0.86	0.8	0.79	0.71
POS-tags+CA	0.55	0.66	0.65	0.64	0.61
Lemmas+CA	0.86	0.87	0.81	0.81	0.76
Words+POS-tags+CA	0.85	0.85	0.8	0.79	0.7
Lemmas+POS-tags+CA	**0.87**	0.86	0.81	0.81	0.76
Focus+CA	0.82	0.82	0.72	0.68	0.5
FocusLem+CA	0.83	0.83	0.75	0.71	0.52
Experiment 3					
Words+CP	0.82	0.81	0.77	0.76	0.7
POS-tags+CP	0.41	0.6	0.59	0.6	0.56
Lemmas+CP	0.81	**0.82**	0.78	0.78	0.75
Words+POS-tags+CP	0.81	0.81	0.77	0.76	0.7
Lemmas+POS-tags+CP	0.81	0.82	0.78	0.78	0.75
Focus+CP	0.79	0.77	0.68	0.65	0.44
FocusLem+CP	0.79	0.79	0.71	0.68	0.48

Table 2: Precision of the classifier for fine classes (CA - coarse class labels from the annotated data, CP - coarse class labels predicted by the classifier).

In Experiment 1 models based on unigrams and unigrams+bigrams of surface word forms achieved the precision 81%, while models based on unigrams+bigrams of lemmas - 82%. These are the two best results in the Experiment 1. However, it is necessary to say that there is no significant difference in performance between these models (X^2 (1, n = 2403) = 0.5745, p>.05).

Deviations in performance between the unigrams and unigrams+bigrams of lemmas turned out to be statistically insignificant (X^2 (1, n = 2403) = 2.2640, p>.05). However, the model based on unigrams+bigrams is more precise than the one based on bigrams (X^2 (1, n = 2403) = 33.3749, p<.05).

Unfortunately, by adding POS-tags we did not get any improvements. Words+POS-tags and Lemmas+POS-tags feature sets accounted for the same maximal values: 81% and 82% respectively.

Using exclusively POS-tags as features, the classifier was able to achieve the precision of 46%. It is a very poor result in comparison to the unigrams+bigrams of lemmas (X^2 (1, n = 2403) = 522.6607, p<.05).

Surface word forms and lemmas of focus words demonstrate similar results (X^2 (1, n = 2403) = 0.4674, p>.05), achieving maximal precision of 75% and 76% respectively. These values are significantly lower than the results achieved by question surface word forms (X^2 (1, n = 2403) = 12.4608, p<.05) or by question lemmas (X^2 (1, n = 2403) = 18.1542, p<.05).

We can see that in Experiment 2 unigrams, unigrams+bigrams of Words+CA and unigrams+bigrams of Lemmas+CA perform almost equally well (X^2 (1, n = 2403) = 0.7440, p>.05), demonstrating the highest precision of 86% and 87% respectively. There is no significant difference between unigrams and unigrams+bigrams of lemmas (X^2 (1, n = 2403) = 0.7440, p>.05). The difference is significant for unigrams+bigrams and bigrams of lemmas (X^2 (1, n = 2403) = 24.1152, p>.05), and for unigrams+bigrams and bigrams of surface words forms.

Combinations with POS-tags again were not beneficial for the classification process. They did not show any improvements.

Comparing the results of Experiment 2 with the results of Experiment 1, we may conclude that by adding coarse class labels as additional features a significantly higher precision was achieved.

In Experiment 3 we used coarse class labels predicted by the classifier (on unigrams+bigrams of lemmas) and did not observe any significant difference in comparison to the results from Experiment 1. Unigrams+bigrams of lemmas, unigrams+bigrams of Words+POS-tags and Lemmas+POS-tags demonstrated absolutely identical results.

As for separate classes, questions of the most prevailing classes were identified with a very high precision: *title* - 85%, *creatorOf* - 81%, *name* - 89%.

The most frequent questions in our corpus are related to the professional activity of a person. Most of the time this kind of questions belong to the class *acitivityOf* or to the class *title*. They turned out to be very similar: for example, by asking *What do you do for a living?*, the player expects to get as a potential answer either the description of a particular professional activity or the name of a title (position) the person holds. Moreover, very often the player does not care which of them will be chosen, both answers will be correct. As consequence, the classifier can confuse the classes *acitivityOf* and *title* with each other.

As we expected, the classifier achieved the best results by using lexical clues, i.e. the presence of absence of certain words is a strong feature to determine to which class or classes a question will be assigned. Unfortunately when a question contains words shared by questions belonging to different classes, it may cause prediction errors. For example, the classifier may assign several labels instead of one and vice versa. Based on the analysis of misclassified instances, we can tell that a question will receive more than one label, if wording representative for two (or more) classes is observed and extracted as features.

The analysis of false predictions indicates that most of them were caused by the imbalanced training set. There are also no strict borders between some classes. Questions with multiple labels are under-represented. According to Table 1 they comprise only 1.04%.

By applying coarse class labels as additional features we tried to get a higher precision. Unfortunately, it worked only when these labels were taken from the annotated corpus. The classifier was able to predict coarse class labels with the average precision of 90% (see Table 3). However, it was not enough to make the actual predicted labels useful for the next classifier.

Classes	Precision
eatEntities	0.86
eatTime	0.97
eatHumanRelations	0.92
eatHumanDescription	0.9
eatLocation	0.91
eatDescription	0.86
eatHumanGroups	0.88
avg/total	0.9

Table 3: Precision of the classifier for coarse classes (unigrams+bigrams of lemmas).

The precision for all coarse classes is already relatively high. Questions of the class *eatTime*, for example, were correctly identified in 97% of cases. It may be very problematic to make further improvements.

To explore learnability of the best performing classification model and to evaluate how the size of the training set affects the classifier's results, we divided the corpus of annotated questions into 20 parts. All partitions, except for the first one, contained the equal number of questions. Different question types were equally distributed among the partitions. We started with the training set consisting of 636 questions and gradually increased its size. Based the obtained results, the learning curve has been plotted presented in Figure 1.

As we can observe, the precision rose almost steadily until the size of the training set became

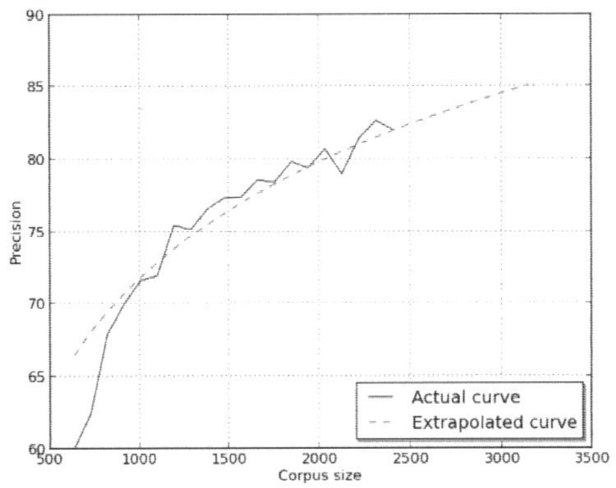

Figure 1: Learning curve.

bigger than 2000 questions. The growth stopped at the precision of around 81%. It was followed by a decrease of 2%. After that the precision grew by 3%, and then again dropped about 1%. These fluctuations, as we believe, were caused by the quality of the data.

The growth slows down gradually, i.e. in the range from about 700 till 1200 questions the precision increased from 65% till 75%, while to get another 5%, the classifier required 800 additional questions. Taking these calculations into account, we were able to obtain the formula, which allowed to extrapolate the learning curve:

$$y = 1.164396665 * 10^{-1} * ln(x) - 8.691998379 * 10^{-2}$$

We came to the conclusion that the classifier will need the training set including approximately 3100-3200 questions to achieve the precision of 85%. Thus, getting more data may potentially improve the performance of the classifier. However, given the obtained learnability results and since data collection and its annotation is a very time consuming task, the efforts may be better spent to explore other approaches additional to machine learning, e.g. pattern matching and bootstrapping from collected examples.

5 Question Focus Extraction

In line with Moldovan et al. (2000), the question focus describing the main event is typically expressed by a verb or eventive noun. Despite the fact that the focus is semantically defined, we use the knowledge of syntactic structures, since syntactic parsers are mature enough comparing to semantic ones to be used reliably. The following procedures have been applied to automatically extract focus words:

1. **Auxiliary verbs elimination**. OpenNLP chunker[8] detects VP-chunks. There is a predefined set of rules helping to identify which of them contains an auxiliary:
   - *Combinations of adjacent chunks like VP+NP+VP are glued together. The first verb in such combinations is usually an auxiliary, checked in the list of auxiliaries.*
   - *If there is only one verb in a sentence than it is not an auxiliary verb.*
   - *If a long chunk contains several verbs, at least one of them should be an auxiliary, checked in the list of auxiliaries.*
2. **Removal of opening and closing phrases using regular expressions**. For example, *"Could you tell me what are you doing for living?"*, *"You are an American, aren't you?"*.
3. **Stop words and stop phrases removal.**
4. **Postprocessing**. Removal of extra spaces, conjunctions left at the beginning or at the end of the focus.

This algorithm demonstrated the accuracy of 94.6% when evaluating on the manually annotated reference data.

6 Query Generation and Expansion

Question	What do you do as a job?
Focus words	do as job
Expanded focus	do [make, perform, cause, practice, act], as, job [activity, occupation, career, employment, position]
EAT	Title_do(do as job)
Query	(Z, E, ?X) :: Title_do(Z, doAs, ?job) :: QUALITY(String) :: QUANTITY(List) :: FOCUS(do as job)
Expanded query	(Z, E, ?X) :: Title_do(Z, doAs, ?job) :: QUALITY(String) :: QUANTITY(List) :: FOCUS(do [make, perform, practice, act], as, job [activity, occupation, career, employment, position])

Table 4: Example of an expanded query.

Query generation is the last data processing operation that is performed in the question interpretation module. The query is generated according to the pre-defined set of rules. It captures the results of the question classification (labels) process as well as the extracted focus words and transfers this information to the next module.

[8]https://opennlp.apache.org

The query generation processes, the semantic representation of its components in particularly, partially based on the Discourse Representation Theory (DRT) (Kamp and Reyle, 1993). It incorporates semantic information that is necessary to find the correct answer. Table 4 demonstrates an example of such a query.

In natural languages the same message has a number of realizations. So far, our QA system misses many answers when the answer is expressed by different lexical units. To solve this problem, we used WordNet[9] synonyms to elaborate the extracted question focus words.

7 Conclusions and Future Work

To implement a question classifier for our system, we used SVM algorithm. This algorithm performs quite accurate classification, has a mechanism to avoid overfitting, can be customized by changing its kernel function, and is able to handle high dimensional spaces.

We have annotated a corpus of questions, which will become publicly available in the nearest future. Although our corpus has been designed for a quite specific gaming application, it may be of interest for researchers working on various topics. Regardless of the domain, annotated spoken dialogue data may help in studying of different linguistic phenomena such as, for example, ellipsis or co-reference resolution.

The corpus has been used as a training set for a question classifier. The classifier was able to predict EAT with the precision of 82%. This result was achieved by the model based on the unigrams and bigrams of lemmas.

Having analysed misclassified questions, we drew several conclusions. First, the classifier confuses semantically similar classes. Second, it has difficulty to identify EATs for under-represented classes. Third, questions simultaneously belonging to several classes were often misclassified.

Additional to the EAT, focus words are important to find correct answers. Moldovan et al. (2000) defines the question focus as a word or a sequence of words which helps to identify what is asked in a question. In order to automatically extract focus words, we have implemented an algorithm that performs with the accuracy of 94.6%.

Once EAT and focus words are specified, this information needs to be formalized in a form of a query, in order to be processed by next modules, in particular for answer retrieval and generation, and for dialogue manager to update the latest information state and decide on further dialogue actions. To address this problem, the question classification module generates a query which incorporates various linguistic information such as one or multiple semantic relations, events, named entities mentioned in a question, the entity or event for which information (slot filler) has to be found.

Our findings confirmed that by increasing the training set we can slightly improve the precision of the classifier. However, due to the specificity of our data, this task becomes quite difficult. Wizard-of-Oz experiments involve human participants and are conducted in a controlled setting. All participants have to be instructed in advance. After experiments dialogue data should be analysed, transcribed, and manually annotated by at least several trained annotators. The listed actions require considerable amount of efforts and time.

The easiest way to achieve a higher precision is probably to increase the number of instances for the under-represented classes. Of course, it is impossible to force the users to ask only certain types of questions. However, new instances can be generated based on the existing ones using bootstrapping. The training set, which has been used to learn the classifier, is unbalanced. Ideally, all question types should be equally represented.

It is also possible to apply bootstrapping to generate synonymous questions for the whole corpus. In this case we will not discover any new phenomena, but we will get a better lexical coverage.

By querying search engines we can extract questions that match regular expressions. However, it should be noted that not all questions types can be encoded using regular expression. Data obtained in such a way may require some manual post-processing.

While testing/evaluating with the system, players produce a lot of questions. Saving each gaming session could help to enrich the training set.

The analysis of false predictions suggests that the taxonomy requires some refinements. Many classes were never used during the annotation. Certain classes appeared to be very similar to other classes or simply too general. They should be either merged together of divided into several more specific subclasses respectively.

[9] http://wordnet.princeton.edu

References

J. Cohen. 1960. A coefficient of agreement for nominal scales. *Educational and Psychological Measurement*, 20(1):37–46.

H. Faiz. 2014. Question classification module for question answering gaming application. Master's thesis, Saarland University, Germany.

O. Ferret, B. Grau, M. Hurault-Plantet, G. Illouz, L. Monceaux, R. Robba, and A. Vilnat. 2001. Finding an answer based on the recognition of the question focus. In *TREC*.

D. Ferrucci, E. Brown, J. Chu-Carroll, J. Fan, D. Gondek, A. A. Kalyanpur, A. Lally, J. W. Murdock, E. Nyberg, J. Prager, et al. 2010. Building watson: An overview of the deepqa project. *AI magazine*, 31(3):59–79.

D. Ferrucci, A. Levas, S. Bagchi, D. Gondek, and E. T. Mueller. 2013. Watson: Beyond jeopardy! *Artif. Intell.*, 199:93–105.

M. Heilman. 2011. *Automatic Factual Question Generation from Text. PhD thesis*. Carnegie Mellon University, USA.

Z. Huang, M. Thint, and Z. Qin. 2008. Question classification using head words and their hypernyms. In *Proceedings of the Conference on Empirical Methods in Natural Language Processing*, EMNLP '08, pages 927–936, Stroudsburg, PA, USA. Association for Computational Linguistics.

H. Kamp and U. Reyle. 1993. From discourse to logic. Introduction to modeltheoretic semantics of natural language, formal logic and Discourse Representation Theory. *Studies in Linguistics and Philosophy*, 42.

W. Lehnert. 1977. *The Process of Question Answering. Research Report No. 88 [microform] / Wendy Lehnert*. Distributed by ERIC Clearinghouse [Washington, D.C.].

W. Lehnert. 1986. A conceptual theory of question answering. In Barbara J. Grosz, Karen Sparck-Jones, and Bonnie Lynn Webber, editors, *Readings in Natural Language Processing*, pages 651–657. Morgan Kaufmann Publishers Inc., San Francisco, CA, USA.

X. Li and D. Roth. 2002. Learning question classifiers. In *Proceedings of the 19th International Conference on Computational Linguistics - Volume 1*, COLING '02, pages 1–7, Stroudsburg, PA, USA. Association for Computational Linguistics.

A. Mikhailian, T. Dalmas, and R. Pinchuk. 2009. Learning foci for question answering over topic maps. In *Proceedings of the ACL-IJCNLP 2009 Conference Short Papers*, ACLShort '09, pages 325–328, Stroudsburg, PA, USA. Association for Computational Linguistics.

D. Moldovan, S. Harabagiu, A. Harabagiu, M. Pasca, R. Mihalcea, R. Girju, R. Goodrum, V. Rus, and I. Background. 2000. The structure and performance of an open-domain question answering system. In *Proceedings of the Conference of the Association for Computational Linguistics (ACL-2000)*, pages 563–570.

A. D. Panicker, A. U, and S. Venkitakrishnan. 2012. Article: Question classification using machine learning approaches. *International Journal of Computer Applications*, 48(13):1–4, June. Published by Foundation of Computer Science, New York, USA.

F. Pedregosa, G. Varoquaux, A. Gramfort, V. Michel, B. Thirion, O. Grisel, M. Blondel, P. Prettenhofer, R. Weiss, V. Dubourg, J. Vanderplas, A. Passos, D. Cournapeau, M. Brucher, M. Perrot, and E. Duchesnay. 2011. Scikit-learn: Machine learning in Python. *Journal of Machine Learning Research*, 12:2825–2830.

V. Petukhova, M. Gropp, D. Klakow, G. Eigner, M. Topf, S. Srb, P. Moticek, B. Potard, J. Dines, O. Deroo, R. Egeler, U. Meinz, and S. Liersch. 2014. The DBOX corpus collection of spoken human-human and human-machine dialogues. In *Proceedings of the 9th Language Resources and Evaluation Conference (LREC)*. ELDA, Reykjavik, Iceland.

M. Razmara, A. Fee, and L. Kosseim. 2007. Concordia university at the TREC 2007 QA Track. In *TREC*.

E. Riloff and M. Thelen. 2000. A rule-based question answering system for reading comprehension tests. In *Proceedings of the 2000 ANLP/NAACL Workshop on Reading Comprehension Tests As Evaluation for Computer-based Language Understanding Sytems - Volume 6*, ANLP/NAACL-ReadingComp 00, pages 13–19, Stroudsburg, PA, USA. Association for Computational Linguistics.

F. Sebastiani. 2002. Machine learning in automated text categorization. *ACM Comput. Surv.*, 34(1):1–47, March.

A. Singhal, S. P. Abney, M. Bacchiani, M. Collins, D. Hindle, and F. C. N. Pereira. 1999. AT&T at TREC-8. In *TREC*.

Resolving Spatial References using Crowdsourced Geographical Data

Jana Götze and Johan Boye
KTH, School of Computer Science and Communication
100 44 Stockholm, Sweden
jagoetze,jboye@csc.kth.se

Abstract

We present a study in which we seek to interpret spatial references that are part of in-situ route descriptions. Our aim is to resolve these references to actual entities and places in the city using a crowdsourced geographic database (OpenStreetMap). We discuss the problems related to this task, and present a possible automatic reference resolution method that can find the correct referent in 68% of the cases using features that are easily computable from the map.

1 Introduction

When humans give route instructions to each other, such instructions typically involve a wide range of references, such as references to landmarks ("Turn at the church."), to the spatial configuration ("The road is bending to the left."), to the current path of movement ("Keep walking along this road."), or to the direction of movement ("You should turn to the right."). Determining which places and objects are referred to is a significant part of designing geographical information systems that aim at interacting with the user in natural language. A long-term goal for our automatic navigation system (Boye et al., 2014) is to be able to ground that a route instruction was understood or to enable the user to ask questions about a particular landmark. This requires resolving the user's geographic references.

Resolving referring expressions (REs) to entities in the world is an ongoing area of research.[1] In written text, including web pages and search queries, references are often to geographic entities such as cities or countries (Amitay et al., 2004; Martins et al., 2006; Pouliquen et al., 2006). In spoken language, the domain is typically restricted to a task that one or more speakers are solving by referring to the objects that are involved, e.g. the pieces of a puzzle (Funakoshi et al., 2012; Matuszek et al., 2014).

This paper addresses the problem of mapping from linguistic REs that refer to aspects of space to objects in a map representation of that space. We collected a number of path descriptions from pedestrians, similar to the corpus of (Blaylock, 2011). The REs we are interested in refer to entities in a real urban environment and the map representation is general rather than tailored to this particular problem. We give an overview of the kinds of knowledge needed to resolve different kinds of references that speakers use to describe their environment while navigating in it. We discuss the challenges that occur when real language data meets real spatial data and suggest ways to address them.

2 Representing Space: OpenStreetMap

OpenStreetMap (OSM) is a crowdsourcing project that creates a geographical knowledge base (Haklay and Weber, 2008). Similar to Wikipedia, the data is open[2] and has been used for research projects in different areas, as well as for education and to create maps for special needs, such as bicycle or hiking maps.[3]

The geographic data can be downloaded in an xml format, Figure 1 shows a short extract. There are two basic data types that are used to represent objects in the OSM database: *nodes* and *ways*. *Ways* are sequences of *nodes*, used for representing a wide variety of objects, such as roads,

[1] Note that this is different from coreference resolution, where the objective is to identify those expressions in a text that refer to the same entity, but not to identify what that entity is (Mitkov, 2010).

[2] `http://www.openstreetmap.org/copyright`

[3] For an overview of OSM-based applications for research, education, and other purposes, cf. `http://wiki.openstreetmap.org`

```
<node id="485981500" lat="59.3360310" lon="18.0510617">
  <tag k="amenity" v="bench"/>
</node>
<node id="674212016" lat="59.3380430" lon="18.0529256">
  <tag k="addr:housenumber" v="15"/> <tag k="addr:street" v="Upplandsgatan"/>
</node>
<way id="39228957">
  <nd ref="469951578"/> <nd ref="469955649"/> <nd ref="469952066"/>
  <tag k="highway" v="footway"/> <tag k="surface" v="paved"/>
</way>
```

Figure 1: An extract of OpenStreetMap data. Each entity has an ID and can be annotated with several tags. This extract shows two *nodes* (a bench and a street address), and a *way*, consisting of several nodes.

squares, areas and buildings (in the three latter cases, the first node in the sequence is the same as the last node, and hence the way forms the perimeter of a polygon). An intersection between two streets is represented by the node where the ways corresponding to the streets meet. Both nodes and ways can be annotated with a set of tags to specify names and types, and additional information such as opening times or links to homepages.

The OSM wiki explains the available set of tags[4] and how they should be used. However, the geographical situation is often not as clear as the given examples and the same kind of object can be represented in different ways, as we will describe further in Section 5. Furthermore, the data is also incomplete: Not all things that speakers mention are mapped, not all details about entities are mapped, and there are errors, e.g. spelling mistakes or wrong tags.

On the other hand, OSM often provides a fine level of detail in urban areas for objects that can be useful for pedestrian navigation. This includes information about many kinds of landmarks and smaller objects such as artworks or benches. The crowdsourced nature of the data also makes it possible for the crowd to correct mistakes in spellings or positions, as well as to keep the map updated.

3 Spatial Descriptions

In order to obtain REs that are used while the speaker is moving in the environment on foot, we carried out the following study.

[4] http://wiki.openstreetmap.org/wiki/Map_Features

3.1 Data Collection

For this study, we used data from a previous data collection (Götze and Boye, 2013) in which subjects were asked to walk a specific route and describe their path in a way that would make it possible for someone to follow them. We thereby put participants into the same environment in which we would later like to guide them. Instead of reading from a 2-dimensional map, our participants can now see the environment in the same way as users of a route-giving system experience it.

The experiment was set up as a Wizard-of-Oz situation in which the participants were asked to describe to a spoken dialog system with the task of making it understand. They were told that the system, like them, had a 3-dimensional and 1st-person view of the environment. The participants were not instructed to interact with the system in any special language but were advised to try out what they thought was suitable and that the system would ask them if it needed clarification, in which case they should stop until the situation was clarified. In this way, the experimenter was able to interfere in situations where an instruction was evidently ambiguous. Otherwise, the experimenter took as little initiative as possible in order to avoid influencing them in their choice of REs.

The data was collected in English,[5] in which all participants reported to be fluent. All were slightly familiar or familiar with the area and all were able to complete the task.

The route that the participants were asked to walk was a round tour that started and ended outside the doors of our laboratory. The route was approximately two kilometers long and was given

[5] The data collection was carried out as part of the European Spacebook project: www.spacebook-project.eu

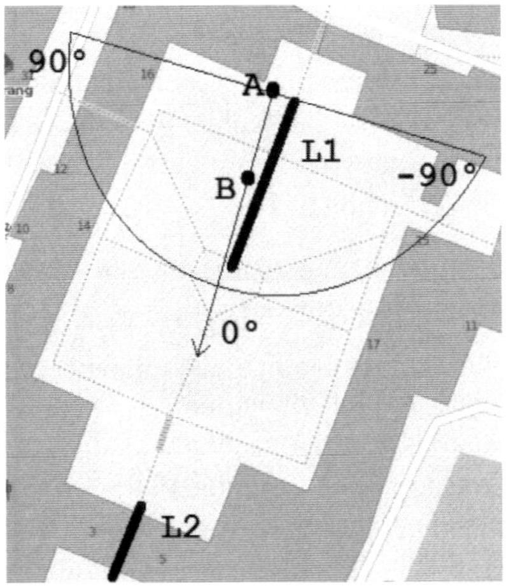

Figure 2: An example segment for the utterance: "I continue in a this direction down *the steps* [L1] towards *the arch* [L2]" A and B indicate the start and the goal position respectively. The lines indicate the speaker's direction and field of view.

to the participants on an unlabelled map. The map had street and other names removed, as well as common symbols, e.g. for churches or bus stops.

The recorded speech was transcribed and segmented into utterances, and aligned with the GPS signal. Figure 2 shows an example utterance, the GPS coordinates (the points A and B) indicate where the instruction was given and where the next instruction followed. In this example, the participant referred to two objects, "the steps" and "the arch". Both of these objects are OSM ways and indicated by the lines L1 and L2 in the figure.

Here, we consider the route descriptions of three of the study participants. Note that none of the descriptions contain any names of streets because we asked participants to avoid them. The original purpose of collecting this data was to investigate what landmarks are used for guiding someone and street names are known to be hard to recognize in a route finding scenario (Tom and Denis, 2004). We are extracting all REs they used, but restrict ourselves here to noun phrases that refer to entities that could in principle be represented on a map (explicitly or implicitly), such as "a junction" or "the church". Noun phrases that refer to directions ("to *the left*") or that are referring to the task ("I made *a mistake*") are excluded. This results in a total of 398 REs, 150 by participant *A*, 122 by participant *B*, and 126 by participant *C*.

3.2 Common Referring Expressions

Many REs (ca. 97%) contain the **type** of the entity as interpreted by the describer, e.g. "a small tunnel", "the parking lot", "the street ahead".

Names, e.g. "Baldersgatan", "Engelbrektsskolan", "the Algerian embassy", can occur in REs, usually for streets or for objects whose names are clearly visible. In our data, the describers use names in 2–15% of the REs.

In around 3–9% of the REs in our data the description is more detailed and specifies a certain **part of an entity**, e.g. "the middle of the park", "an entrance to the station", "the end of the road".

A RE includes the object's **location relative** to the speaker in around 27% of the cases, e.g. "a fountain to my left", "ahead of me is the bus station", "on the right hand side of the building", "a building to my right".

Plurals and sets, e.g. "some steps", "a collection of trees", can occur in the REs. Several objects can be referred to as one or one object can be perceived as many.

Some references (ca. 3%) describe **topographical features** of the terrain, e.g. "the hill", "a slight incline", "the arch at the bottom".

4 What we Need to Resolve Spatial References

We can now look at the different kinds of information that we need to resolve the example references and check whether this information is in principle inferrable from the OSM geographical representation.

4.1 Types of Knowledge Needed

Position, distance, and angles

We need to know the placement of objects on the map as well as the speaker's current and previous position to determine distances and relative directions. For example, in expressions like "I'm walking toward the street." where we want to exclude entities that are behind the speaker.

Visibility

In our dataset, speakers are describing the way they are walking and we can therefore assume that they are referring to objects they can see. This assumes knowledge about the height and extension of objects as well as topographical knowledge to know whether the speaker or an object is located on e.g. a hill.

Type information

Most often, objects are referred to by their type. Describers can use different expressions to refer to the same type: "I am crossing the *street/road*", and describers can use the same expression to refer to different types: A *street* could also be a bike lane or a footway. Information about how types are related to one another as well as which expressions can designate which types in the map is needed to resolve such ambiguities.

Names

Although not many of the REs in our corpus contain names, they can be useful to reduce the number of possible referents. A method is needed to map colloquial or shortened names to those in the database, as well as to resolve ambiguities where several entities have the same name, e.g. a bus stop may be named after the hospital where it is located.

Topography

In order to resolve REs that refer to topographical features, knowledge about elevation is needed.

Discourse history

We are dealing with continuous descriptions and speakers who are moving through the environment as they are speaking. Speakers are referring to some objects several times, e.g. to describe them in more detail. This results in the use of pronouns and short descriptions that we can only resolve by taking into account previous utterances (as well as already found referents):

Position	Utterance
P_t	"So I'm right in front of *the arcs*."
P_{t+1}	"and I'm walking through *them*."

4.2 When to Reject a Solution

No map of a real urban environment can be assumed to be complete. We therefore need a mechanism to decide that we cannot resolve the reference to anything in the map representation. This can be decided on the basis of e.g. distance, visibility, and type. If the describer is talking about a pedestrian crossing, and there is none within a small radius, we can reject the expression as unresolvable. If the describer is talking about a building, it might be visible from further away and we can extend the radius to look for possible referents.

4.3 Using OpenStreetMap

Let us now consider how we can obtain this kind of knowledge from OpenStreetMap (OSM). Recall that we are assuming knowledge about the speaker's position.

Knowledge that can be obtained directly

Recall from Section 2, that OSM entities (*nodes* and *ways*) are tagged with their **position** in terms of latitude and longitude, as well as information about their **type** and their **name** (cf. Figure 1).

Information about **topography** is in principle possible to obtain from OSM. The tag `incline` can be used to specify the steepness of a way. The tags `natural` and `ele` can be used to specify a peak and a point's elevation above sealevel. To specify the height of buildings, OSM provides the tag `height`. However, these topographical tags are rarely used in the urban environment that corresponds to the REs from our data.

Knowledge that can be inferred

Both **distance** and **angles** can easily be inferred using the speaker's and the entities' positions. As mentioned above, the concept of an *intersection* can be inferred by checking how many streets (or OSM ways) are meeting in a node. If more than two streets meet, we can assume that the node is a junction. This knowledge is needed for descriptions that specify a certain part of a street, such as "the end of the street" or "the corner of street X and street Y".

Information about **visibility** can be computed from knowledge about topography and distance if it is available. In order to approximate knowledge on visibility where it is not available, we can check whether there is a free line of sight from the speaker to an entity, i.e. whether there is a building in between the speaker and the entity.

Some **types** do not have to be explicitly represented in the form of tags, but can be inferred. For example, in order to determine which buildings make up a university campus or a hospital complex, it may be possible to group them on the basis of their name.

4.4 Other Sources of Knowledge

When speakers describe something by its type ("I can see *a fountain*."), then this type does not necessarily correspond to the type as used in OSM. For example, what describers call a "street" corresponds to many different types in OSM, as tags

a) A building that is named directly

```
<way id="21572801">
  <tag k="building" v="church"/>
  <tag k="name"
    v="Engelbrektskyrkan"/> </way>
```

b) A building with an additional node placed inside that has its name associated to it

```
<way id="163966736">
  <tag k="building" v="yes"/> </way>
<node id="1340902455"
  lat="59.345" lon="18.067">
  <tag k="name" v="Tyskaskolan"/>
</node>
```

Figure 3: Ambiguity in representation: How entities are name-tagged.

specify the size and function of the street, e.g. residential or cycleway. Likewise, describers can use a variety of expressions to refer to the same type, e.g. they could also refer to a street as "a road". Therefore, we need an appropriate mapping to infer the possible matches.

Besides geographic knowledge, more general knowledge about certain objects can be useful to infer their properties even when they are not explicitly mapped. Consider a user that interacts with a navigation system saying "I am following the footpath" but the matching OSM entity is tagged as a bicycle path. In this kind of application, it is useful to assume that bicycle paths can usually be accessed by pedestrians and the RE can be resolved to it.

5 Mismatches Between Map Representation and Speakers' Conceptualization

As mentioned before, OpenStreetMap contains a number of inconsistencies in how entities are tagged. This implies that several strategies can be needed to resolve the same kind of reference. Figure 3 shows the case of names for buildings. A building of any kind (an OSM way), can be tagged with a name directly (3a), or there can be an additional node placed inside the building, that is tagged with the name (3b). In the map representation, there is no direct link between the way and the named node. This connection has to be inferred by computing whether the node's position is inside the building.

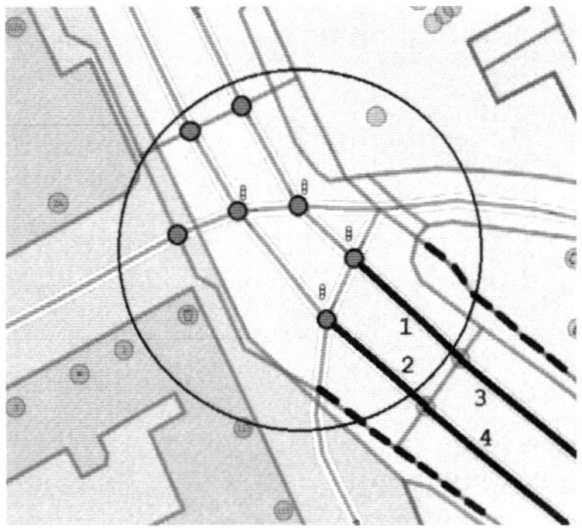

Figure 4: Granularity in OpenStreetMap: an intersection consisting of many street segments and nodes where they meet. The highlighted nodes inside the circle are all part of "an intersection". The highlighted street segments (1-4) belong to the same named street, that is also mapped with a footway and a cycleway running next to it (indicated by the discontinuous lines)

Another problematic case is the granularity with which objects are mapped. Figure 4 shows a major intersection, containing many street segments and nodes where they meet. In the description "I am approaching a junction" it is not at once clear which entities an algorithm should pick.

Grouping larger objects together, such as street segments or buildings that form a unit such as a university campus, is challenging as well. At first sight, this problem could be solved on the basis of the entities' names. Consider however the mapping of large roads, where sometimes the pedestrian walkway is mapped separately, parallely to the road. These pedestrian ways frequently do not contain a name tag and can thus not be associated to the road easily. Additionally, ways can (and often do) consist of several segments, each an own entity in OSM. In Figure 4, each thick black line corresponds to the segment of a street that stretches further in both directions, and has a pedestrian way mapped next to it. Speakers will often refer to the whole structure as "the street" and we need to decide which entities this should correspond to.

6 Resolving References

Keeping the above difficulties in mind, the task is now to map from a referring expression to the user's intended referent, which may be one or more OSM entities.

Referring Expression	OSM tag/value
"road", "street"	highway={tertiary, secondary, primary, residential, pedestrian}
"path", "footpath"	highway={footway, cycleway}
"cycle path", "bike lane"	highway=cycleway
"trees"	natural=tree_row, leisure=park
"traffic lights"	highway=traffic_signals, crossing=traffic_signals
"bus station"	highway=bus_stop
"stairs", "staircase"	highway=steps
"parking lot", "parking space"	amenity=parking
"arches", "archway"	tunnel=yes

Table 1: A set of mappings from referring expressions to features of the OSM entities that the expressions refer to

We can distinguish the following cases:

1. There are zero referents in the database (i.e. the intended referent is not in the database).

2. The intended referent is a unique OSM entity with a single OSM identifier.

3. The intended referent is a unique set of referents in the database ("the two bus stops").

4. A referent can be chosen from a set of interchangeable (equally good) entities in the database.

In the latter case, we either need to devise a mechanism to group the entities together, or we can pick one of them, as the following two examples show:

- "the intersection" can refer to a group of several nodes where street segments meet to form what the speaker perceives as a unit. In this case, we do not want to pick out one of the nodes, but treat them as a unit so that they reflect the extension of the intersection as in expressions like "Cross the intersection".

- "an entrance to the tunnelbana station" can be the building that is the actual entrance, or the node inside it, that is tagged as subway_entrance.

6.1 OSM Features for Resolving References

We have matched all 398 REs in our data with the OSM entity or entities that we judge correspond to the user's intended referent. In 354 cases (89%) the intended referent is present in the database. For all of these 354 REs and correponding referents, we computed the following binary features:

osmName True if the name used in the RE matches the OSM name. We count only exact matches, i.e. the OSM tag name has to exactly match the string in the RE. This serves to give a first overview of how many expressions can be resolved purely by checking the name.

osmName+ True if the name used in the RE matches the OSM name, with some simple normalization using a robust parser. Here, we are applying simple rewriting rules (the RE "the Serbian embassy" is mapped to name="Embassy of the Republic of Serbia") as well as translations of type specifications, such as mapping "Engelbrekt's church" to name="Engelbrektskyrkan"). Note that we are only considering a small part of OSM and additional rules may be needed for cases that we did not come across in this dataset.

osmType True if the type used in the RE (e.g. "restaurant") exactly matches the OSM type. In OSM, types are represented as tags, either as the tag name (building=yes), or as its value (tourism=artwork).

osmType+ True if the type used in the RE matches the OSM type modulo the taxonomy in Table 1 (i.e. the RE "street" matches all the OSM types tertiary, secondary, etc., and "car park" matches entities that are tagged as amenity=parking etc.)

closest True if the entity is the closest of its type to the speaker.

direction True if the entity is located in the speaker's walking direction. For this feature, we are using the previous location of the speaker to define her current bearing. An entity is in her walking direction if it is located within an angle from -90 to 90 degrees (cf. Figure 2).

	Describer		
	A	B	C
# ref. expr.	150	122	126
# in OSM*	134	109	111
name references	14	3	17
osmName	3	2	8
osmName+	13	3	16
type references	128	106	111
osmType	29	45	49
osmType+	117	100	102
closest	101	75	84
direction	130	106	109
visibility	125	106	105

Table 2: Counts of referring expressions that can be linked to OSM features as described in Section 6.1 *the OSM data was downloaded in June 2013

visibility True if the entity is visible from where the speaker is. This feature reflects actual visibility, i.e. as judged by the annotators from their knowledge of the environment. An entity can also be visible if it is behind the speaker.

6.2 Results

Table 2 shows the result of the annotation. We can see that the majority of REs contain a type, but that they exactly match the type names and tags in OSM in less than half of the cases. For describer C, all REs contain a type identifier (111), but only 49 of them can be related to their referent without further processing. Applying the mappings shown in Table 1 can improve the matching to more than twice the amount. This is the case for the describers A and B as well.

Very few names were used. However, recall that the describers were asked not to use street names. Consequently, the amount of names might have been higher if they had been allowed to do so.

Furthermore, the table shows that most of the objects are in front of and visible for the speaker (e.g. 97% and 93% for describer A, respectively). In fewer cases (ca. 69–75%), the object was the closest of its type. Note that these three features depend on the position of the speaker and that the GPS signal on which we base these features, varies in accuracy.

The counts in Table 2 show that we can map the type and name of an entity as they are used in the RE with the annotation used in OSM, for a large number of cases. This will limit the number of possible referents, but not suffice to find the actual referent.

Feature combination	Referents found
osmType, osmName, closest	.27
osmType, closest	.30
osmType+, osmName+, closest	.67
osmType+, closest	.68
osmType+, closest, visibility	.65
osmType+, closest, visibility, osmName+	.65
osmType+, closest, visibility, osmName+, direction	.63

Table 3: Applying different combinations of features to resolve references.

In Table 3, we are considering different subsets of the features. We are considering the 354 REs of all three speakers, for which we know that the referent is in the database. The combination of features that covers most mappings uses only the type feature along with the taxonomy in Table 1 (osmType+), combined with the distance information (closest).

Based on these counts, a baseline method can proceed in the following way to find a referent:

1. Compute the set of geographic entities in the vicinity of the speaker's position.
2. From this set, compute the set of possible referents by determining how the entitites are related to one another. At this step, potential referents can be added for entities that make up a unit, e.g. nodes of an intersection as depicted in Figure 4.
3. Filter away entities that do not match the RE in name or type.
4. Pick the closest of the remaining entities.

Note that visibility can be handled in different ways: When computing the initial set of available referents, or at a later point. The counts in Table 3 reflect a lower number of matches when including information about visibility. This may be because of inaccuracies in the GPS signal, or simply an artefact of the small dataset.

7 Discussion and Future Work

The ultimate aim of this work is to develop a robust reference resolution method that can be incorporated into our pedestrian navigation system (Boye et al., 2014). Therefore, it is important to point out that the above results were all obtained using data where users described the way as they were walking, and consequently it was natural to resolve a spatial reference to a matching entity closest to the user's position. However, there are situations where users would refer to entities and places that are possibly far away (e.g. "How do I get to X street?"). Therefore any realistic spatial reference algorithm must take the user's dialogue act into account: For instance, if the user is making a request ("Give me directions to X"), proximity to X should not be given much weight.

Furthermore, in this paper we have only considered how many of the intended referents we can find, but it is also important to identify the references that have no referent in the database, as to avoid false positives. Such a procedure needs to make an assumption about the coverage of OSM in a particular area as well.[6]

As discussed before, it is often far from obvious what the intended referent is. In particular this is true in situations where the user conceptualizes her surroundings differently from how the database is organized (as in Figure 4). A possibility would be to add an extra layer on top of OpenStreetMap, in which nodes are grouped into super-concepts like "intersection", "roundabout", etc. Such super-concepts could be formed on the basis of actual data, like the verbal route descriptions we are using in this study. This would have the advantage of resolving references to entities that more closely correspond to the user's mental map, but the disadvantage of requiring extra computation.

Additional processing is also required when the reference resolution is to be carried out in other languages than English. In our features, we exploited the fact that OSM tags and values are in English and therefore match natural language expressions in some cases. Further linguistic processing and algorithms that map OSM concepts to language resources such as WordNet, like *Voc2WordNet* (Ballatore et al., 2014), may be a useful resource to bridge the gap between commonly used terms and map concepts.

[6]A visualization of the OSM coverage can be found at `https://www.mapbox.com/osm-data-report/`

Acknowledgment

The authors were supported by Swedish national grant VR 2013-4854 "Personalized spatially-aware dialogue systems".

References

E. Amitay, N. Har'El, R. Sivan, and A. Soffer. 2004. Web-a-where: Geotagging Web Content. In *Proc. of SIGIR*, pages 273–280.

A. Ballatore, M. Bertolotto, and D. C. Wilson. 2014. Linking geographic vocabularies through WordNet. *Annals of GIS*, 20(2):73–84.

N. Blaylock. 2011. Semantic Annotation of Street-level Geospatial Entities. In *Proc. of the IEEE ICSC Workshop on Semantic Annotation for Computational Linguistic Resources*.

J. Boye, M. Fredriksson, J. Götze, J. Gustafson, and J. Königsmann. 2014. Walk This Way: Spatial Grounding for City Exploration. In *Natural Interaction with Robots, Knowbots and Smartphones*, pages 59–67. Springer New York.

K. Funakoshi, M. Nakano, T. Tokunaga, and R. Iida. 2012. A unified probabilistic approach to referring expressions. In *Proc. of SIGdial*, pages 237–246.

J. Götze and J. Boye. 2013. Deriving Salience Models from Human Route Directions. In *Workshop on Computational Models of Spatial Language Interpretation and Generation 2013 (CoSLI-3)*, pages 36–41.

M. Haklay and P. Weber. 2008. OpenStreetMap: User-Generated Street Maps. *Pervasive Computing, IEEE*, 7(4):12–18, Oct.

B. Martins, M. J. Silva, S. Freitas, and A. P. Afonso. 2006. Handling Locations in Search Engine Queries. In *Workshop on Geographical Information Retrieval, SIGIR*.

C. Matuszek, L. Bo, L. Zettlemoyer, and D. Fox. 2014. Learning from Unscripted Deictic Gesture and Language for Human-Robot Interactions. In *Proc. of the 28th National Conference on Artificial Intelligence*.

R. Mitkov, 2010. *Computational Linguistics and Natural Language Handbook*, chapter Discourse processing, pages 599–629. Blackwell Publishers.

B. Pouliquen, M. Kimler, R. Steinberger, C. Ignat, T. Oellinger, K. Blackler, F. Fuart, W. Zaghouani, A. Widiger, A.-C. Forslund, and C. Best. 2006. Geocoding multilingual texts: Recognition, disambiguation and visualisation. *Proc. of LREC-2006*.

A. Tom and M. Denis. 2004. Language and spatial cognition: comparing the roles of landmarks and street names in route instructions. *Applied Cognitive Psychology*, 18(9):1213–1230.

Combining Relational and Distributional Knowledge for Word Sense Disambiguation

Richard Johansson **Luis Nieto Piña**
Språkbanken, Department of Swedish, University of Gothenburg
Box 200, SE-40530 Gothenburg, Sweden
{richard.johansson, luis.nieto.pina}@svenska.gu.se

Abstract

We present a new approach to word sense disambiguation derived from recent ideas in distributional semantics. The input to the algorithm is a large unlabeled corpus and a graph describing how senses are related; no sense-annotated corpus is needed. The fundamental idea is to embed meaning representations of *senses* in the same continuous-valued vector space as the representations of *words*. In this way, the knowledge encoded in the lexical resource is combined with the information derived by the distributional methods. Once this step has been carried out, the sense representations can be plugged back into e.g. the skip-gram model, which allows us to compute scores for the different possible senses of a word in a given context.

We evaluated the new word sense disambiguation system on two Swedish test sets annotated with senses defined by the SALDO lexical resource. In both evaluations, our system soundly outperformed random and first-sense baselines. Its accuracy was slightly above that of a well-known graph-based system, while being computationally much more efficient.

1 Introduction

For NLP applications such as word sense disambiguation (WSD), it is crucial to use some sort of representation of the meaning of a word. There are two broad approaches commonly used in NLP to represent word meaning: representations based on the structure of a formal knowledge representation, and those derived from co-occurrence statistics in corpora (*distributional* representations). In a knowledge-based word meaning representation, the meaning of a word string is defined by mapping it to a symbolic concept defined in a knowledge base or ontology, and the meaning of the concept itself is defined in terms of its relations to other concepts, which can be used to deduce facts that were not stated explicitly: a *mouse* is a type of *rodent*, so it has prominent *teeth*. On the other hand, in a data-driven meaning representation, the meaning of a word in defined as a point in a geometric space, which is derived from the word's cooccurrence patterns so that words with a similar meaning end up near each other in the vector space (Turney and Pantel, 2010). The most important relation between the meaning representations of two words is typically *similarity*: a *mouse* is something quite similar to a *rat*. Similarity of meaning is often operationalized in terms of the geometry of the vector space, e.g. by defining a distance metric.

These two broad frameworks obviously have very different advantages: while the symbolic representations contain explicit and very detailed relational information, the data-driven representations handle the notion of graded similarity in a very natural way, and the fact that they typically have a wide vocabulary coverage makes it attractive to integrate them in NLP systems for additional robustness (Turian et al., 2010). However, there are many reasons to study how these two very dissimilar approaches can complement each other. Mikolov et al. (2013c) showed that vector spaces represent more structure than previously thought: they implicitly encode a wide range of syntactic and semantic relations, which can be recovered using simple linear algebra operations. For instance, the geometric relation between *Rome* and *Italy* is similar to that between *Cairo* and *Egypt*. Levy and Goldberg (2014) further analyzed how this property can be explained.

One aspect where symbolic representations seem to have an advantage is in describing *word sense ambiguity*: the fact that one surface form may correspond to more than one underlying concept. For instance, the word *mouse* can refer to a *rodent* or an *electronic device*. Except for scenarios where a small number of senses are used, lexical-semantic resources such as WordNet (Fellbaum, 1998) for English and SALDO (Borin et al., 2013) for Swedish are crucial in applications that rely on sense meaning, WSD above all.

Corpus-derived representations on the other hand typically have only one representation per surface form, which makes it hard to search e.g. for a group of words similar to the rodent sense of *mouse*[1] or to reliably use the vector in machine learning methods that generalize from the semantics of the word (Erk and Padó, 2010). One straightforward solution could be to build a vector-space semantic representation from a sense-annotated corpus, but this is infeasible since fairly large corpora are needed to induce data-driven representations of a high quality, while sense-annotated corpora are small and scarce. Instead, there have been several attempts to create vectors representing the senses of ambiguous words, most of them based on some variant of the idea first proposed by Schütze (1998): that senses can be seen as clusters of similar contexts. Further examples where this idea has reappeared include the work by Purandare and Pedersen (2004), as well as a number of recent papers (Huang et al., 2012; Moen et al., 2013; Neelakantan et al., 2014; Kågebäck et al., 2015). However, sense distributions are often highly imbalanced, it is not clear that context clusters can be reliably created for senses that occur rarely.

In this work, we build a word sense disambiguation system by combining the two approaches to representing meaning. The crucial stepping stone is the recently developed algorithm by Johansson and Nieto Piña (2015), which derives vector-space representations of word senses by embedding the graph structure of a semantic network in the word vector space. A scoring function for selecting a sense can then be derived from a word-based distributional model in a very intuitive way simply by reusing the scoring function used to construct the original word-based vector space. This approach to WSD is attractive because it can leverage corpus statistics similar to a supervised method trained on an annotated corpus, but also use the lexical-semantic resource for generalization. Moreover, the sense representation algorithm also estimates how common the different senses are; finding the predominant sense of a word also gives a strong baseline for WSD (McCarthy et al., 2007), and is of course also interesting from a lexicographical perspective.

We applied the algorithm to derive vector representations for the senses in SALDO, a Swedish semantic network (Borin et al., 2013), and we used these vectors to build a disambiguation system that can assign a SALDO sense to ambiguous words occurring in free text. To evaluate the system, we created two new benchmark sets by processing publicly available datasets. On these benchmarks, our system outperforms a random baseline by a wide margin, but also a first-sense baseline significantly. It achieves a slightly higher score than UKB, a highly accurate graph-based WSD system (Agirre and Soroa, 2009), but is several orders of magnitude faster. The highest disambiguation accuracy was achieved by combining the probabilities output by the two systems. Furthermore, in a qualitative inspection of the most ambiguous words in SALDO for each word class, we see that the sense distribution estimates provided by the sense embedding algorithm are good for nouns, adjectives, and adverbs, although less so for verbs.

2 Representing the meaning of words and senses

In NLP, the idea of representing word meaning geometrically is most closely associated with the *distributional* approach: the meaning of a word is reflected in the set of contexts in which it appears. This idea has a long tradition in linguistics and early NLP (Harris, 1954).

The easiest way to create a geometric word representation is to implement the distributional idea directly: for each word, we create a vector where each dimension corresponds to a feature describing the frequency of contexts where the target word has appeared. Typically, such a feature corresponds to the document identity or another word with which the target word has cooccurred (Sahlgren, 2006), but in principle we can define arbitrary contextual features, for instance the syntactic context (Padó and Lapata, 2007). In addition, a dimensionality reduction step may be used to map the high-dimensional sparse vector space onto a smaller-dimensional space (Landauer and

[1] According to Gyllensten and Sahlgren (2015), this problem can be remedied by making better use of the topology of the neighborhood around the search term.

Dumais, 1997; Kanerva et al., 2000).

As an alternative to context-counting vectors, geometric word representations can be derived indirectly, as a by-product when training classifiers that predict the context of a focus word. While these representations have often been built using fairly complex machine learning methods (Collobert and Weston, 2008; Turian et al., 2010), such representations can also be created using much simpler and computationally more efficient log-linear methods that seem to perform equally well (Mnih and Kavukcuoglu, 2013; Mikolov et al., 2013a). In this work, we use the *skip-gram* model by Mikolov et al. (2013a): given a focus word, the contextual classifier predicts the words around it.

2.1 From word meaning to sense meaning

The crucial stepping stone to WSD used in this work is to *embed* the semantic network in a vector space: that is, to associate each sense s_{ij} with a *sense embedding*, a vector $E(s_{ij})$ of real numbers, in a way that makes sense given the topology of the semantic network but also reflects that the vectors representing the lemmas are related to those corresponding to the underlying senses (Johansson and Nieto Piña, 2015).

Figure 1 shows an example involving an ambiguous word. The figure shows a two-dimensional projection[2] of the vector-space representation of the Swedish word *rock* (meaning either 'coat' or 'rock music') and some words related to it: *morgonrock* 'dressing gown', *jacka* 'jacket', *kappa* 'coat', *oljerock* 'oilskin coat', *långrock* 'long coat', *musik* 'music', *jazz* 'jazz', *hårdrock* 'hard rock', *punkrock* 'punk rock', *funk* 'funk'. The words for styles of popular music and the words for pieces of clothing are clearly separated, and the polysemous word *rock* seems to be dominated by its music sense.

The sense embedding algorithm will then produce vector-space representations of the two senses of *rock*. Our lexicon tells us that there are two senses, one related to clothing and the other to music. The embedding of the first sense ('coat') ends up near the other items of clothing, and the second sense ('rock music') near other styles of music. Furthermore, the embedding of the lemma consists of a mix of the embeddings of the two senses: mainly of the music sense, which reflects the fact that this sense is most frequent in corpora.

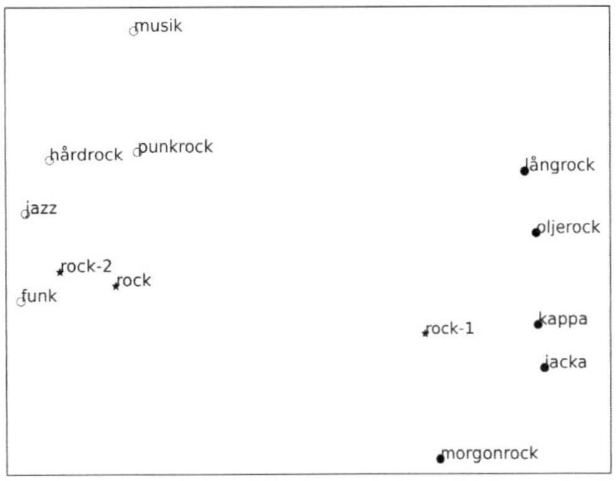

Figure 1: Vector-space representation of the Swedish word *rock* and its two senses, and some related words.

2.2 Embedding the semantic network

We now summarize the method by Johansson and Nieto Piña (2015) that implements what we described intuitively above,[3] and we start by introducing some notation. For each lemma l_i, there is a set of possible underlying concepts (senses) $s_{i1}, \ldots, s_{im_i}$ for which l_i is a surface realization. Furthermore, for each sense s_{ij}, there is a *neighborhood* set consisting of concepts semantically related to s_{ij}. Each neighbor n_{ijk} of s_{ij} is associated with a weight w_{ijk} representing the degree of semantic relatedness between s_{ij} and n_{ijk}. How we define the neighborhood, i.e. what we mean by the notion of "semantically related," will obviously have an impact on the result of the embedding process. In this work, we simply assume that it can be computed from any semantic network, e.g. by picking a number of hypernyms and hyponyms in a lexicon such as WordNet for English, or primary and secondary descriptors if we are using SALDO for Swedish.

We assume that for each lemma l_i, there exists a D-dimensional vector $F(l_i)$ of real numbers; these vectors can be computed using any method described in Section 2. Finally, we assume that there exists a *distance function* $\Delta(x,y)$ that returns a non-negative real number for each pair of vectors in $\mathbb{R}^D$; in this work, this is assumed to be the squared Euclidean distance.

[2]The figures were computed in `scikit-learn` (Pedregosa et al., 2011) using multidimensional scaling of the distances in a 512-dimensional vector space.

[3]`http://demo.spraakdata.gu.se/richard/scouse`

The goal of the algorithm is to associate each sense s_{ij} with a sense embedding, a real-valued vector $E(s_{ij})$ in the same vector space as the lemma embeddings. The lemma embeddings and the sense embeddings will be related through a *mix constraint*: the lemma embedding $F(l_i)$ is decomposed as a convex combination $\sum_j p_{ij}E(s_{ij})$, where the $\{p_{ij}\}$ are picked from the probability simplex. Intuitively, the mix variables correspond to the occurrence probabilities of the senses, but strictly speaking this is only the case when the vectors are built using context counting.

We now have the machinery to state the optimization problem that formalizes the intuition described above: the weighted sum of distances between each sense and its neighbors is minimized, and the solution to the optimization problem so that the mix constraint is satisfied for the senses for each lemma. To summarize, we have the following constrained optimization program:

$$\begin{aligned} \underset{E,p}{\text{minimize}} \quad & \sum_{i,j,k} w_{ijk}\Delta(E(s_{ij}),E(n_{ijk})) \\ \text{subject to} \quad & \sum_j p_{ij}E(s_{ij}) = F(l_i) \quad \forall i \\ & \sum_j p_{ij} = 1 \quad \forall i \\ & p_{ij} \geq 0 \quad \forall i,j \end{aligned} \tag{1}$$

This optimization problem is hard to solve with off-the-shelf methods, but Johansson and Nieto Piña (2015) presented an approximate algorithm that works in an iterative fashion by considering one lemma at a time, while keeping the embeddings of the senses of all other lemmas fixed.

It can be noted that the vast majority of words are monosemous, so that the procedure will leave the embeddings of these words unchanged. These will then serve as as anchors when creating the embeddings for the polysemous words; the requirement that lemma embeddings are a mix of the sense embeddings will also constrain the solution.

3 Using the skip-gram model to derive a scoring function for word senses

When sense representations have been created using the method described in Section 2, they can be used in applications including WSD. Exactly how this is done in practice will depend on the properties of the original word-based vector space; in this paper, we focus on the *skip-gram* model by Mikolov et al. (2013a).

In its original formulation, the skip-gram model is based on modeling the conditional probability that a context feature c occurs given the lemma l:

$$P(c|l) = \frac{e^{F'(c)\cdot F(l)}}{Z(l)}$$

The probability is expressed in terms of lemma embeddings $F(l)$ and context $F'(c)$: note that the word and context vocabularies can be distinct, and that the corresponding embedding spaces F and F' are separate. $Z(l)$ is a normalizer so that the probabilities sum to 1.

The skip-gram training algorithm then maximizes the following objective:

$$\sum_{i,j} \log P(c_{ij}|l_i)$$

Here, the l_i are the lemmas occurring in a corpus, and c_{ij} the contextual features occurring around l_i. In practice, a number of approximations are typically applied to speed up the optimization; in this work, we applied the *negative sampling* approach (Mikolov et al., 2013b), which uses a few random samples instead of computing the normalizer $Z(l)$.

By embedding the senses in the same space as the words using the algorithm in Section 2, our implicit assumption is that contexts can be predicted by senses in the same way they can be predicted by words: that is, we can use the sense embeddings $E(s)$ in place of $F(l)$ to model the probability $P(c|s)$. Assuming the context features occurring around a token are conditionally independent, we can compute the joint probability of a sense and the context, conditioned on the lemma:

$$\begin{aligned} P(s,c_1,\ldots,c_n|l) &= P(s|l)P(c_1,\ldots,c_n|s) \\ &= P(s|l)P(c_1|s)\cdots P(c_n|s). \end{aligned}$$

Now we have what we need to compute the posterior sense probabilities[4]:

$$\begin{aligned} P(s|c_1,\ldots,c_n,l) &= \frac{P(s|l)P(c_1,\ldots,c_n|s)}{\sum_{s_i} P(s_i|l)P(c_1,\ldots,c_n|s_i)} \\ &= \frac{P(s|l)e^{(F'(c_1)+\ldots+F'(c_n))\cdot E(s)}}{\sum_{s_i} P(s_i|l)e^{(F'(c_1)+\ldots+F'(c_n))\cdot E(s_i)}} \end{aligned}$$

[4]We are using unnormalized probabilities here. Including $Z(s)$ makes the computation much more complex, but changes the result very little.

Finally, we note that we can use a simpler formula if we are only interested in ranking the senses, not of their exact probabilities:

$$\text{score}(s) = \log P(s|l) + \sum_{c_i} F'(c_i) \cdot E(s) \quad (2)$$

We weighted the context vector $F'(c_i)$ by the distance of the context word from the target word, corresponding to the random window sizes commonly used in the skip-gram model. We leave the investigation of more informed weighting schemes (Kågebäck et al., 2015) to future work. Furthermore, we did not make a thorough investigation of the effect of the choice of the probability distribution $P(s|l)$ of the senses, but just used a uniform distribution throughout; it would be interesting to investigate whether the accuracy could be improved by using the mix variables estimated in Section 2, or a distribution that favors the first sense.

4 Application to Swedish data

The algorithm described in Section 2 was applied to Swedish data: we started with lemma embeddings computed from a corpus, and then created sense embeddings by using the SALDO semantic network (Borin et al., 2013).

4.1 Creating lemma embeddings

We created a corpus of 1 billion words downloaded from Språkbanken, the Swedish language bank.[5] The corpora are distributed in a format where the text has been tokenized, part-of-speech-tagged and lemmatized. Compounds have been segmented automatically and when a lemma was not listed in SALDO, we used the parts of the compounds instead. The input to the software computing the lemma embedding consisted of lemma forms with concatenated part-of-speech tags, e.g. *dricka..vb* for the verb 'to drink' and *dricka..nn* for the noun 'drink'. We used the `word2vec` tool[6] to build the lemma embeddings. All the default settings were used, except the vector space dimensionality which was set to 512. We made a small modification to `word2vec` so that it outputs the context vectors as well, which we need to compute the scoring function defined in Section 3.

[5] `http://spraakbanken.gu.se`
[6] `https://code.google.com/p/word2vec`

4.2 SALDO, a Swedish semantic network

SALDO (Borin et al., 2013) is the most comprehensive open lexical resource for Swedish. As of May 2014, it contains 125,781 entries organized into a single semantic network. Compared to WordNet (Fellbaum, 1998), there are similarities as well as considerable differences. Both resources are large, manually constructed semantic networks intended to describe the language in general rather than any specific domain. However, while both resources are hierarchical, the main lexical-semantic relation of SALDO is the *association* relation based on centrality, while in WordNet the hierarchy is taxonomic. In SALDO, when we go up in the hierarchy we move from specialized vocabulary to the most central vocabulary of the language (e.g. 'move', 'want', 'who'); in WordNet we move from specific to abstract (e.g. 'entity'). Every entry in SALDO corresponds to a specific sense of a word, and the lexicon consists of word senses only. There is no correspondence to the notion of synonym set as in WordNet. The sense distinctions in SALDO are more coarse-grained than in WordNet, which reflects a difference between the Swedish and the Anglo-Saxon traditions of lexicographical methodologies.

Each entry except a special root is connected to other entries, its *semantic descriptors*. One of the semantic descriptors is called the *primary* descriptor, and this is the entry which better than any other entry fulfills two requirements: (1) it is a semantic neighbor of the entry to be described and (2) it is more central than it. That two words are semantic neighbors means that there is a direct semantic relationship between them, for instance synonymy, hyponymy, antonymy, meronymy, or argument–predicate relationship; in practice most primary descriptors are either synonyms or hypernyms. Centrality is determined by means of several criteria. The most important criterion is frequency: a frequent word is more central than an infrequent word. Other criteria include stylistic value (a stylistically unmarked word is more central) and derivation (a derived form is less central than its base form), semantic criteria (a hypernym being more central than a hyponym).

To exemplify, here are a few instances of entries in SALDO and their descriptors.

Entry	Primary	Secondary
bröd 'bread'	*mat* 'food'	*mjöl* 'flour'
äta 'eat'	*leva* 'to live'	
kollision 'collision'	*kollidera* 'to collide'	
cykel 'bicycle'	*åka* 'to go'	*hjul* 'wheel'

When using SALDO in the algorithm described in Section 2, we need to define a set of neighbors n_{ijk} for every sense s_{ij}, as well as weights w_{ijk} corresponding to the neighbors. We defined the neighbors to be the primary descriptor and inverse primaries (the senses for which s_{ij} is the primary descriptor); we excluded neighbors that did not have the same part-of-speech tag as s_{ij}. The secondary descriptors were not used. For instance, *bröd* has the primary descriptor *mat*, and a large set of inverse primaries mostly describing kinds (e.g. *rågbröd* 'rye bread') or shapes (e.g. *limpa* 'loaf') of bread. The neighborhood weights were set so that the primary descriptor and the set of inverse primaries were balanced: e.g. 1 for *mat* and $1/N$ if there were N inverse primaries. After computing all the weights, we normalized them so that their sum was 1. We additionally considered a number of further heuristics to build the neighborhood sets, but they did not seem to have an effect on the end result.

5 Inspection of predominant senses of highly ambiguous words

Before evaluating the full WSD system in Section 6, we carry out a qualitative study of the mix variables computed by the algorithm described in Section 2. Determining which sense of a word is the most common one gives us a strong baseline for word sense disambiguation which is often very hard to beat in practice (Navigli, 2009). McCarthy et al. (2007) presented a number of methods to find the predominant word sense in a given corpus.

In Section 2, we showed how the embedding of a lemma is decomposed into a mix of sense embeddings. Intuitively, if we assume that the mix variables to some extent correspond to the occurrence probabilities of the senses, they should give us a hint about which sense is the most frequent one. For instance, in Figure 1 the embedding of the lemma *rock* is closer to that of the second sense ('rock music') than to that of the first sense ('coat'), because the music sense is more frequent.

For each lemma, we estimated the predominant sense by selecting the sense for which the corresponding mix variable was highest. To create a dataset for evaluation, an annotator selected the most polysemous verbs, nouns, adjectives, and adverbs in SALDO (25 of each class) and determined the most frequent sense by considering a random sample of the occurrences of the lemma. Table 1 shows the accuracies of the predominant sense selection for all four word classes, as well as the average polysemy for each of the classes.

Part of speech	Accuracy	Avg. polysemy
Verb	0.48	6.28
Noun	0.76	6.12
Adjective	0.76	4.24
Adverb	0.84	2.20
Overall	0.71	4.71

Table 1: Predominant sense selection accuracy.

For nouns, adjectives, and adverbs, this heuristic works quite well. However, similar to what was seen by McCarthy et al. (2007), verbs are the most difficult to handle correctly. In our case, this has a number of reasons, not primarily that this is the most polysemous class. First of all, the most frequent verbs, which we evaluate here, often participate in multi-word units such as particle verbs and in light verb constructions. While SALDO contains information about many multi-word units, we have not considered them in this study since our preprocessing step could not deterministically extract them (as described in Section 4). Secondly, we have noticed that the sense embedding process has a problem with verbs where the sense distinction is a distinction between transitive and intransitive use, e.g. *koka* 'to boil'. This is because the transitive and intransitive senses typically are neighbors in the SALDO network, so their context sets will be almost identical and the algorithm will try to minimize the distance between them.

6 WSD evaluation

To evaluate our new WSD system, we applied it to two test sets and first compared it to a number of baselines, and finally to UKB, a well-known graph-based WSD system.

Our two test sets were the *SALDO examples* (SALDO-ex)[7] and the *Swedish FrameNet examples* (SweFN-ex)[8]. Both resources consist of sentences selected by lexicographers for illustration of word senses. At the time of our experiments, SALDO-ex contained 4,489 sentences. In each

[7] http://spraakbanken.gu.se/resurs/saldoe
[8] http://spraakbanken.gu.se/resurs/swefn

sentence, one of the tokens (the target word) has been marked up by a lexicographer and assigned a SALDO sense. SweFN-ex contained 7,991 sentences, and as in SALDO-ex the annotation consists of disambiguated target words: the difference is that instead of a SALDO sense, the target word is assigned a FrameNet frame (Fillmore and Baker, 2009). However, using the Swedish FrameNet lexicon (Friberg Heppin and Toporowska Gronostaj, 2012), frames can in most cases be deterministically mapped to SALDO senses: for instance, the first SALDO sense of the noun *stam* ('trunk' or 'stem') belongs to the frame PLANT_SUBPART, while the second sense ('tribe') is in the frame AGGREGATE.

We preprocessed these two test sets using Språkbanken's annotation services[9] to tokenize, compound-split, and lemmatize the texts and to determine the set of possible senses in a given context. All unambiguous instances were removed from the sets, and we also excluded sentences where the target consisted of more than one word. We then ended up with 1,177 and 1,429 instances in SALDO-ex and SweFN-ex, respectively. Figure 2 shows the distribution of the number of senses for target word in the combination of the two sets.

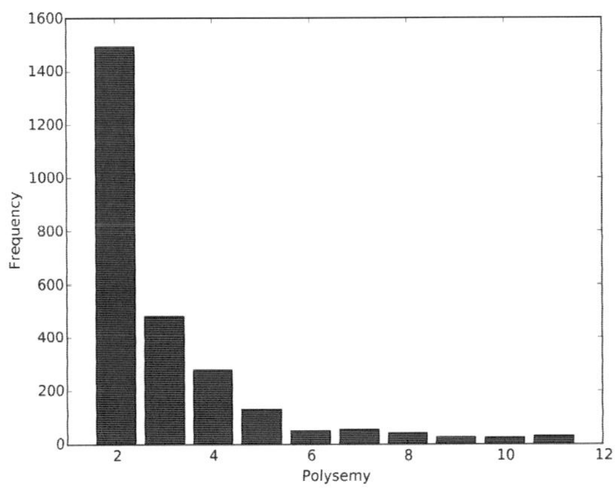

Figure 2: Histogram of the number of senses for target words in the test sets.

6.1 Comparison to baselines

We applied the contextual WSD method defined by Eq. 2 to the two test sets. As the simplest baseline, we used a random selection. A much more difficult baseline is to select the first sense[10] in the inventory; this baseline is often very hard to beat for WSD systems (Navigli, 2009). Furthermore, we evaluated a simple approach that selects the sense whose value of the mix variable in Section 2 is highest. Table 2 shows the result.

System	SALDO-ex	SweFN-ex
Random	39.3	40.3
Sense 1	52.5	53.5
By mix variables	47.6	53.9
Contextual WSD	62.7	63.3

Table 2: Comparison to baselines.

We see that our WSD system clearly outperforms not only the trivial but also the first-sense baseline. Selecting the sense by the value of the mix variable (which can be regarded as a prior probability) gives a result very similar to the first-sense baseline: this can be useful in sense inventories where senses are not ranked by frequency or importance. (This result is lower in SALDO-ex, which is heavily dominated by verbs; as we saw in Section 5, the mix variables seem less reliable for verbs.)

6.2 Analysis by part of speech

The combined set of examples from SALDO-ex and SweFN-ex contains 1,723 verbs, 575 nouns, 287 adjectives, and 15 adverbs. We made a breakdown of the result by the part of speech of the target word, and we show the result in Table 3.

PoS tag	Accuracy	Avg. polysemy
Adjective	62.3	2.7
Adverb	80.0	2.4
Noun	71.1	2.6
Verb	60.5	3.3

Table 3: Results for different parts of speech.

Again, we see that verbs pose the greatest difficult for our methods, while disambiguation accuracy is higher for nouns. Adjectives are also difficult to handle, with an accuracy just slightly higher than what we had for the verbs. (There are too few adverbs to allow any reliable conclusion to be drawn about them.) To some extent, the differences in accuracy might be expected to be correlated with the degree of polysemy, but there are

[9]`http://spraakbanken.gu.se/korp/annoteringslabb/`

[10]Unlike in WordNet, SALDO's senses are not explicitly sorted by frequency. The first sense is the one that the lexicographers regarded as the most important, which will often but not always be the same as the most frequent one.

also other factors involved, such as the structure of the SALDO network. We leave an investigation of the causes of these differences to future work.

6.3 Comparison to graph-based WSD

To find a more challenging comparison than the baselines, we applied the UKB system, a WSD system based on personalized PageRank in the sense graph, which has achieved a very competitive result for a system without any annotated training data (Agirre and Soroa, 2009). Because of limitations in the UKB software, the test sets are slightly smaller (1,055 and 1,309 instances, respectively), since we only included test instances where the lemmas could be determined unambiguously. The result is presented in Table 4. This table also includes the result of a combined system where we simply added Eq. 2 to the log of the probability output by UKB.

System	SALDO-ex	SweFN-ex
Contextual WSD	64.0	64.2
UKB	61.2	61.2
Combined	66.4	66.0

Table 4: Comparison to the UKB system.

Our system outperforms the UKB system by a slight margin; while the difference is not statistically significant, the consistent figures in the two evaluations suggest that the results reflect a true difference. However, in both evaluations, the combination comes out on top, suggesting that the two systems have complementary strengths.

Finally, we note that our system is much faster: UKB processes the SweFN-ex set in 190 seconds, while our system processes the same set in 450 milliseconds, excluding startup time.

7 Conclusion

We have presented a new method for word sense disambiguation derived from the skip-gram model. The crucial step is to embed a semantic network consisting of linked word senses into a continuous-vector word space. Unlike previous approaches for creating vector-space representations of senses, and due to the fact that we rely on the network structure, we can create representations for senses that occur very rarely in corpora. Once the senses have been embedded in the vector space, deriving a WSD model is straightforward. The word sense embedding algorithm (Johansson and Nieto Piña, 2015) takes a set of embeddings of lemmas, and uses them and the structure of the semantic network to induce the sense representations. It hinges on two ideas: 1) that sense embeddings should preserve the structure of the semantic network as much as possible, i.e. that two senses should be close geometrically if they are neighbors in the graph, and 2) that lemma embeddings can be decomposed into separate sense embeddings.

We applied the sense embedding algorithm to the senses of SALDO, a Swedish semantic network, and a vector space trained on a large Swedish corpus. These vectors were then used to implement a WSD system, which we evaluated on two new test sets annotated with SALDO senses. The results showed that our new WSD system not only outperforms the baselines, but also UKB, a high-quality graph-based WSD implementation. While the accuracies were comparable, our system is several hundred times faster than UKB.

Furthermore, we carried out a qualitative inspection of the mix variables estimated by the embedding algorithms and found that they are relatively good for predicting the predominant word senses: more so for nouns, adjectives and adverbs, less so for verbs. This result is consistent with what we saw in the quantitative evaluations, where selecting a sense based on the mix variable gave an accuracy similar to the first-sense baseline.

In future work, we will carry out a more systematic evaluation of the word sense disambiguation system in several languages. For Swedish, a more large-scale evaluation requires an annotated corpus, which will give more reliable quality estimates than the lexicographical examples we have used in this work. Fortunately, a 100,000-word multi-domain corpus of contemporary Swedish is currently being annotated on several linguistic levels in the KOALA project (Adesam et al., 2015), including word senses as defined by SALDO.

Acknowledgments

This research was funded by the Swedish Research Council under grant 2013–4944, *Distributional methods to represent the meaning of frames and constructions*, and grant 2012–5738, *Towards a knowledge-based culturomics*. We also acknowledge the University of Gothenburg for its support of the Centre for Language Technology and Språkbanken.

References

Yvonne Adesam, Gerlof Bouma, and Richard Johansson. 2015. Defining the Eukalyptus forest – the Koala treebank of Swedish. In *Proceedings of the 20th Nordic Conference of Computational Linguistics*, Vilnius, Lithuania.

Eneko Agirre and Aitor Soroa. 2009. Personalizing PageRank for word sense disambiguation. In *Proceedings of the 12th Conference of the European Chapter of the ACL (EACL 2009)*, pages 33–41, Athens, Greece.

Lars Borin, Markus Forsberg, and Lennart Lönngren. 2013. SALDO: a touch of yin to WordNet's yang. *Language Resources and Evaluation*, 47(4):1191–1211.

Ronan Collobert and Jason Weston. 2008. A unified architecture for natural language processing: Deep neural networks with multitask learning. In *Proceedings of the 25th International Conference on Machine Learning*, pages 160–167.

Katrin Erk and Sebastian Padó. 2010. Exemplar-based models for word meaning in context. In *Proceedings of the ACL 2010 Conference Short Papers*, pages 92–97, Uppsala, Sweden.

Christiane Fellbaum, editor. 1998. *WordNet: An electronic lexical database*. MIT Press.

Charles J. Fillmore and Collin Baker. 2009. A frames approach to semantic analysis. In B. Heine and H. Narrog, editors, *The Oxford Handbook of Linguistic Analysis*, pages 313–340. Oxford: OUP.

Karin Friberg Heppin and Maria Toporowska Gronostaj. 2012. The rocky road towards a Swedish FrameNet – creating SweFN. In *Proceedings of the Eighth conference on International Language Resources and Evaluation (LREC-2012)*, pages 256–261, Istanbul, Turkey.

Amaru Cuba Gyllensten and Magnus Sahlgren. 2015. Navigating the semantic horizon using relative neighborhood graphs. *CoRR*, abs/1501.02670.

Zellig Harris. 1954. Distributional structure. *Word*, 10(23).

Eric H. Huang, Richard Socher, Christopher D. Manning, and Andrew Y. Ng. 2012. Improving word representations via global context and multiple word prototypes. In *Association for Computational Linguistics 2012 Conference (ACL 2012)*, Jeju Island, Korea.

Richard Johansson and Luis Nieto Piña. 2015. Embedding a semantic network in a word space. In *Proceedings of the 2015 Conference of the North American Chapter of the Association for Computational Linguistics – Human Language Technologies*, Denver, United States.

Mikael Kågebäck, Fredrik Johansson, Richard Johansson, and Devdatt Dubhashi. 2015. Neural context embeddings for automatic discovery of word senses. In *Proceedings of the Workshop on Vector Space Modeling for NLP*, Denver, United States. To appear.

Pentti Kanerva, Jan Kristoffersson, and Anders Holst. 2000. Random indexing of text samples for latent semantic analysis. In *Proceedings of the 22nd Annual Conference of the Cognitive Science Society*.

Thomas K. Landauer and Susan T. Dumais. 1997. A solution to Plato's problem: The latent semantic analysis theory of acquisition, induction and representation of knowledge. *Psychological Review*, 104:211–240.

Omer Levy and Yoav Goldberg. 2014. Linguistic regularities in sparse and explicit word representations. In *Proceedings of the Eighteenth Conference on Computational Natural Language Learning*, pages 171–180, Ann Arbor, United States.

Diana McCarthy, Rob Koeling, Julie Weeds, and John Carroll. 2007. Unsupervised acquisition of predominant word senses. *Computational Linguistics*, 33(4):553–590.

Tomáš Mikolov, Kai Chen, Greg Corrado, and Jeffrey Dean. 2013a. Efficient estimation of word representations in vector space. In *International Conference on Learning Representations, Workshop Track*, Scottsdale, USA.

Tomáš Mikolov, Ilya Sutskever, Kai Chen, Greg Corrado, and Jeff Dean. 2013b. Distributed representations of words and phrases and their compositionality. In *Advances in Neural Information Processing Systems 26*.

Tomáš Mikolov, Wen-tau Yih, and Geoffrey Zweig. 2013c. Linguistic regularities in continuous space word representations. In *Proceedings of the 2013 Conference of the North American Chapter of the Association for Computational Linguistics: Human Language Technologies*, pages 746–751, Atlanta, USA.

Andriy Mnih and Koray Kavukcuoglu. 2013. Learning word embeddings efficiently with noise-contrastive estimation. In *Advances in Neural Information Processing Systems 26*, pages 2265–2273.

Hans Moen, Erwin Marsi, and Björn Gambäck. 2013. Towards dynamic word sense discrimination with random indexing. In *Proceedings of the Workshop on Continuous Vector Space Models and their Compositionality*, pages 83–90, Sofia, Bulgaria.

Roberto Navigli. 2009. Word sense disambiguation: a survey. *ACM Computing Surveys*, 41(2):1–69.

Arvind Neelakantan, Jeevan Shankar, Alexandre Passos, and Andrew McCallum. 2014. Efficient non-parametric estimation of multiple embeddings per word in vector space. In *Proceedings of the 2014 Conference on Empirical Methods in Natural Language Processing (EMNLP)*, pages 1059–1069, Doha, Qatar.

Sebastian Padó and Mirella Lapata. 2007. Dependency-based construction of semantic space models. *Computational Linguistics*, 33(1).

Fabian Pedregosa, Gaël Varoquaux, Alexandre Gramfort, Vincent Michel, Bertrand Thirion, Olivier Grisel, Mathieu Blondel, Peter Prettenhofer, Ron Weiss, Vincent Dubourg, Jake VanderPlas, Alexandre Passos, David Cournapeau, Matthieu Brucher, Matthieu Perrot, and Edouard Duchesnay. 2011. Scikit-learn: Machine learning in Python. *Journal of Machine Learning Research*, 12:2825–2830.

Amruta Purandare and Ted Pedersen. 2004. Word sense discrimination by clustering contexts in vector and similarity spaces. In *HLT-NAACL 2004 Workshop: Eighth Conference on Computational Natural Language Learning (CoNLL-2004)*, pages 41–48, Boston, United States.

Magnus Sahlgren. 2006. *The Word-Space Model*. Ph.D. thesis, Stockholm University.

Hinrich Schütze. 1998. Automatic word sense discrimination. *Computational Linguistics*, 24(1):97–123.

Joseph Turian, Lev-Arie Ratinov, and Yoshua Bengio. 2010. Word representations: A simple and general method for semi-supervised learning. In *Proceedings of the 48th Annual Meeting of the Association for Computational Linguistics*, pages 384–394, Uppsala, Sweden.

Peter D. Turney and Patrick Pantel. 2010. From frequency to meaning: Vector space models of semantics. *Journal of Artificial Intelligence Research*, 37:141–188.

Talebob - an interactive speech trainer for Danish

Peter Juel Henrichsen
DanCAST - Danish Center for Applied Speech Technology
Copenhagen Business School
pjh.ibc@cbs.dk

Abstract

Talebob ("*Speech Bob*") is an interactive language learning tool for pupils (10+ years) helping them practice their pronunciation of simple, highly frequent phrases in Danish. Talebob's feedback is based on acoustic measurements (for pitch and intensity), presented to the user as helpful instructions for improvement. Talebob is currently being tested in schools in Nuuk, Hafnarfjörður and Tórshavn where Danish is taught as a second language (L2); we present some preliminary results. We conclude with a discussion of the didactic relevance of Talebob and computer-assisted language learning in general, exploiting the IT-curiosity of modern pupils.

1 Introduction

Talebob - presented to the public for the first time in this paper - is an internet-based language learning tool assisting Nordic pupils train their spoken Danish. Talebob helps students (from 10 years) practice the pronunciation of short phrases frequently occurring in everyday conversation. Such informal phrases are often rich in function words (such as pronouns, connectives, adverbs and prepositions). Their pronunciation may be highly conventionalized and are often in conflict with the general and productive rules of Danish pronunciation. For this reason they are often difficult to master for the L2 learner, who will nevertheless be confronted with them in any informal conversation. Many Greenlandic, Faroese, and Icelanding children report the Danes to be unexpectedly difficult to understand at their first encounter, even after several years of Danish studies, especially because the informal phrases occur so frequently. Unfortunately, West-Nordic teachers of Danish report that no teaching materials are available training this particular aspect of spoken Danish.

Talebob is meant as a remedy. It is conceived and designed by Danish computational linguists in cooperation with Icelandic researchers in didactics and West-Nordic school teachers. Talebob (ver. 1) is currently being tested in public schools in Nuuk, Hafnarfjörður and Tórshavn. Early experiments are also being carried out in Denmark with adult L2-learners.

Sections 2-5 below cover the technological and linguistic aspects of Talebob's design (front-end, back-end, and system architecture). In section 6 we report from the practical test sessions (mainly in Iceland) and discuss the linguistic properties and cross-language portability of Talebob. We conclude in section 7 with some remarks on Talebob (and interactive language learning tools in general) as an approach to screening large populations of pupils.

A note for the reader: Pronouns he/she are used randomly for the generic pupil and teacher. Example phrases are quoted in Danish and (being highly idiomatic) translated only when strictly necessary.

2 Talebob as a CALL tool

Talebob is a tool for computer-assisted language learning (CALL), and it can be seen as a technically updated continuation of the classic language lab. Many readers will probably remember from their school days the setup with study booths equipped with a cassette deck for recording and playback, enabling oral communication with the language teacher on a one-to-one basis. The language lab (e.g. Thorborg (2003, 2006)) stimulated the pupil's spoken language production and in this respect was a huge improvement over L2 exercises based on rehearsed dialogues. Of course the attention from the teacher was a scarce resource, and each pupil could not expect more than a few minutes of personal instruction during a lesson.

One of our main goals with Talebob is to take the language lab a step further towards interactivity such that each language production will yield an informed comment, either an appreciation or a constructive correction. In other words, Talebob should give the pupil a feeling of being heard.

3 Talebob's front-end (hello, pupil!)

School children are used to computer games with a visual side approaching virtual reality. Rather than competing on graphics we wanted to attract our users through a carefully designed interactivity offering meaningful replies on all contacts. Talebob should thus behave as an attentive listener and competent evaluator.

The Talebob challenge consists of 30 tasks, each focused on a specific Danish phrase such as greeting formulae (*godmorgen*), common requests (*gi'r du en kop kaffe?*), and emotional expressions (*er du rigtig klog?!*). Common to such phrases is that their communicative effects may change radically with the smallest twists of the pronunciation. An inconspicuously looking phrase like "tak skal du have" (*thank you*) may be perceived as being ironic, impressed, tired, cordial, hateful, or just plainly informative depending on subtle prosodic modifications (e.g. changing the relative weight of the main stresses slightly). Being able to control such details is an intrinsic part of one's L1 competence, but is often difficult for L2 learners to acquire. Talebob allows the pupil to repeat each phrase as many times as needed, informed by Talebob's feedback. The phrase prompts are produced by a native speaker aiming for an 'ecological' pronunciation that no Dane would object to.

For each Talebob-task the pupil

1. selects a phrase,
2. listens to the phrase prompt (using the Lyt-Til-Frasen button),
3. reproduces the prompt orally (using Optag/Stop buttons for recording), mimicking it closely wrt. articulation, prosody, and tempo,
4. compares prompt and own production auditorily (pressing Lyt-Til-Optagelsen),
5. repeats steps 2-4 until entirely satisfied, then presses Send for evaluation,
6. consults the returned Talebob comment (either a success message sending the pupil to the next task, or a try-again advising the pupil how to improve)

Pressing Send invokes the Talebob acoustic analyzer, returning a smiley, either happy, neutral, or sad. With a happy smiley **:-)** the pupil has completed the task and may continue with the next phrase. Level-1 is done when the first five tasks are completed, level-2 has ten tasks, and level-3 fifteen. The phrases are ordered progressively, from single words and simple phrases in level-1 (*godmorgen, værsgo!*), frequent idioms in level-2 (*hvordan går det?, tak i lige måde*), to more expressive phrases in level-3 (*det siger du ikke?, hellere end gerne!*). When all tasks in level-3 are done, the Talebob challenge is passed.

Talebob's front-end is illustrated in fig. 1-3.

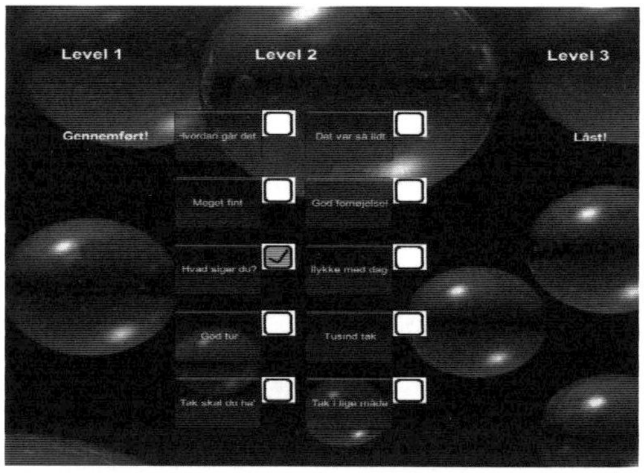

Figure 1. Screenshot (excerpt) from Talebob task-page, level 2, with one phrase passed.

Figure 2. Screenshot (excerpt) from Talebob return-page, level 2, not-passed.

Figure 3. Screenshot (excerpt) from Talebob return-page, level 2, passed.

4 Talebob's back-end (acoustic analysis)

The two sound files submitted (with the Send button) are evaluated in the Talebob back-end application. The acoustic analysis compares the prompt version (P) and the user's own production (U) sampling both files for F0 (pitch in Hz) and INT (intensity in dB), being uanimously considered as the most relevant parameters for acoustic-phonetic evaluation.[1] The linguistic evaluation is focused on the concordance of P and U wrt. speech tempo, global prosody, and articulation.

The speech tempo factor (*STF*) is determined as the ratio of durations for P and U,

$$STF = \text{duration}(P) : \text{duration}(U)$$

[1] F0 and INT are measured using the Praat toolkit (www.fon.hum.uva.nl/praat), window size 5 ms, filter settings = *Pitch (ac)... 0.005 75 15 yes 0.03 0.45 0.01 0.4 0.14 600; Intensity... 75 0.005 yes.* We also experimented with HNR (harmonicity-to-noise ratio) and various spectral filterings, but found them to be too noise sensitive. Classrooms are not quiet places!

STF is calculated from INT data. First the zero level for INT in U is estimated, corresponding to 'no speech' in the given signal (this calibration can be tricky, especially for noise-prone samples, and is always a matter of heuristics). Then the zero level (0 dB after calibration) is used to delimit the speech production in U. By definition the optimum value for *STF* is 1.0, and productions approaching this value will trigger the comment "Meget fint taletempo" (*excellent speech tempo*). Lesser or greater values return instructions to speak faster or slower, respectively.

Prosody and articulation analyses are based on F0 measurements. Only the 'sonorant' parts of P and U are sampled - that is, the segments of the speech signals where a pitch value can be meaningfully estimated, thus excluding obstruent sounds and moments of silence (e.g. between words). All frequency data are stored as logarithmic values (more convenient for statistical use). Many of Talebob's users are children, and their speech productions will often be higher-pitched than the phrase prompt on average. This global difference in pitch is of course irrelevant to the Talebob evaluation, so the F0 dataset for U is normalized (each sample multiplied with a derived constant) equalizing the average pitch of U and P.

After these preparatory steps, the prosodic evaluation is done. The calculation is based on 10 qualified datapoints for each (normalized) dataset U and P, in a procedure best explained by an example. Say 130 valid pitch samples were derived from P; the first datapoint for P (call it $f_{1,P}$) is then derived as the mean value for the first 13 samples; the 2nd datapoint ($f_{2,P}$) for samples 14..26, et cetera, up to ($f_{10,P}$) and ($f_{10,U}$). Finally the prosodic deviation (*ProsDev*) of U wrt. P is calculated by summation of 'errors',

$$ProsDev = |f_{1,P}-f_{1,U}| + |f_{2,P}-f_{2,U}| + .. + |f_{10,P}-f_{10,U}|$$

This particular *ProsDev* formula was designed to meet two special requirements. Firstly it abstracts away any temporal incongruities between U and P (already addressed by the *STF* score); secondly it copes well with the unpredictable number of valid F0 samples for U (sometimes as few as 15-20 for short speech productions in noisy surroundings, while P may produce 3-4 times more), preserving commensurability. For low *ProsDev* values, Talebob returns a praising comment "Dit tonefald er fint", and otherwise an instruction how to improve, e.g. "Prøv at tale mere livligt" (*try speaking more lively*).

The articulation is evaluated (*ArtEval*) along the same lines, but focusing on local incongruities rather than the phrase as a whole. First 30 qualified datapoints are derived following the procedure above, using numerical interpolation if necessitated by data sparseness. Error analyses (calculated as for *ProsDev*, mutatis mutandis) are done for datapoints 1..10, 11..20, and 21..30,

$$ArtEval(a,b)=\sum_{n=a}^{b}(F_{n,P}-F_{n,U})\quad,$$

F being is the 30-point dataset (otherwise as f above). The results for *ArtEval*(1,10), *ArtEval*(11,20), and *ArtEval*(21,30) represents the first, middle, and last part of the utterance as reflected in the returned comments: "Prøv at tale tydeligere i de første/midterste/sidste ord" (*try to speak more clearly in the first/middle/final/all words*). Such a message is, admittedly, a very blunt linguistic description, but faced with the impatience and limited academic vocabulary of pupils, we had to prioritize didactive effect over descriptive accuracy.

Summing up, feedback from Talebob consists in three comments, one for each of the evaluation criteria (tempo, prosody, and pronunciation), and in addition a smiley representing the overall performance. The *happy* smiley ('task completed') is given when each of the three evaluation results has met a (pre-set) acceptable limit, the *sad* smiley is given if none of the limits are met, and the *medium* smiley otherwise.

See the discussion below on the linguistic relevance and scientific testability of the Talebob acoustic-phonetic design.

4.1 An example - phrase "hej med dig"

The graphs in fig. 4 and 5 both cover the phrase *hej med dig* in three speech productions, (*i*) the prompt, (*ii*) an Islandic pupil (boy, 7th grade) on 2nd attempt, and (*iii*) same pupil on 5th attempt. Notice that INT graphs are continuous, intensity being defined everywhere, while F0 graphs are interruped at non-sonorant passages (e.g. the stopped [d] in *dig*).

The huge difference in speech tempo between 2nd and 5th attempt is easily appreciated in fig. 4. The very slow tempo in #2 (2nd attempt) triggered the Talebob comment "Du taler alt for langsomt" (*you speak much too slowly*); the pupil sped up and - as seen - eventually matched the prompt's tempo in #5. His pronunciation had also become more fluent, without the unwarranted separation of *hej* and *med* (cf. the INT dip around t=0.45" in the #2 graph, absent from both #5 and the prompt). Concerning the prosodic contour, notice that the F0 envelope for #2 and #5 (cf. fig. 5) both match the prompt quite closely when abstracting away from the different tempi: two stable pitch inclinations with an intervening resetting, corresponding to the two stress groups in the (most common) Danish pronunciation. Consequently, *ProsDev* is relatively low in both cases, having Talebob praise the pronunciation in both cases: "Meget fint tonefald" (*very good tone-of-voice*). At the same time, though, the *ArtEval*-based analysis shows a 'lack' of pitch modulation in #2 (preceived as mumbling, and producing a relatively poor *ArtEval* value), in this case triggering the comment for #2: "Prøv at tale tydeligere" (*try to pronounce the words more clearly*). Through his next attempts, the pupil improved his pronunciation gradually, and by #5, the *ArtEval* value passed the accept limit, allowing Talebob to issue a happy smiley (notice though in fig. 5 that the pitch range is still somewhat limited for #5).

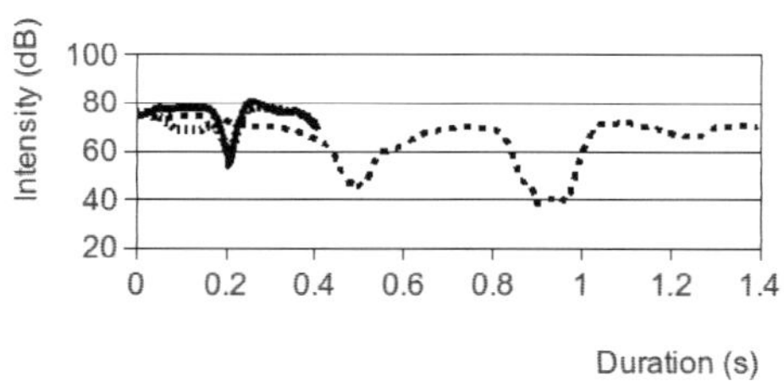

Figure 4. Phrase "hej med dig", intensity data; prompt (solid line), Icelandic pupil's 2nd/5th attempt (close/dispersed dots)

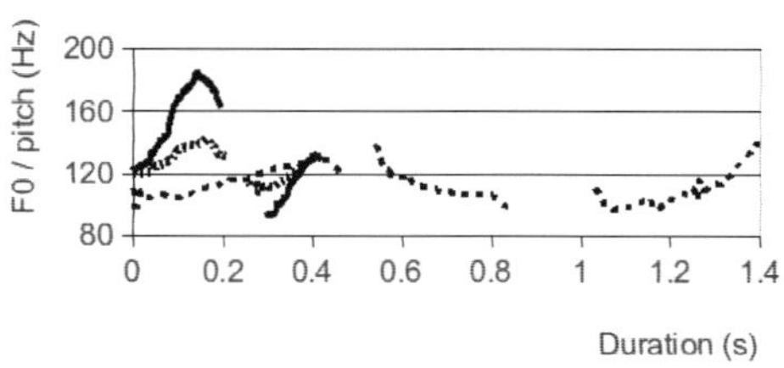

Figure 5. Phrase "hej med dig", pitch data; prompt (solid line), Icelandic pupil's 2nd/5th *attempt (close/dispersed dots)*

5 System architecture

The Talebob development had three phases. First an appropriate set of phrases was selected and recorded, largely recycling materials and selection criteria from earlier CALL projects including Allwood et al. (2005), Selsøe et al. (2004), Henrichsen (2004, 2004b). Then the back-end was programmed and tested (Perl-code and standard open-source modules). The front-end, however, presented us with an unexpected challenge. Nobody could update us on the IT situation in West-Nordic schools, neither for hardware, software, operating system, local IT-assistance, or even internet connectivity. Yet we did not want any potential user to go down on equipment. Also we did not want to preclude any working places. Some pupils prefer to train in the privacy of their home while others like to share. We did not want to force any limitations on the user on purely technical grounds. This led us to consider three front-end/back-end architectures.

A1. Stand-alone (program installed on user's own hardware: pc, tablet, or smartphone)

PRO:

- Independent of internet connectivity
- Quick query-response cycle

CON:

- Programming/maintenance of back-end for a range of unknown hardware is demanding
- Technical support (from developer to pupil, teacher and/or local IT helpdesk) is hard due to physical and time-zone distance
- Monitoring of users' performance and progress is difficult
- System updates are hard to communicate

A2. Browser-based

PRO:

- Contacts between users and server can be logged (easier maintenance & development)
- Developers can make performance data available to teachers and others online
- Browser-based front-end using HTML5 and CSS is hardware independent (well, almost!)

CON:

- Stands or falls with user's connectivity
- 100% server uptime is mandatory
- HTML5 audio, especially for recording, is currently not fully supported in all browsers

A3. Internet-based, but dedicated front-end

The advantages are the same as for *A2*, and in addition the HTML5 problem can be avoided. Also we do not need to instruct users to download this or that internet-browser. The main hurdle is that users have to install a dedicated program prior to their first positive Talebob experience.

Even if *A2* seemed to us to be the best alternative overall, we settled on *A3* for practical reasons. Many potential users are Explorer fans and did not care to install a new browser with better HTML5 support, such as Chrome, Firefox, or even IE 9+.

As the developer team had some experience with Unity4 (www.unity4.com), in particular its strong audio support and graphics drivers, we settled for this programming workbench. Unity4 is freely available (in the open-source version) and so does not compromize Talebob as a shareable application. Unity4 programs compile to all common operating systems (even older versions) including Linux, Mac, Win, Android, etc. The flip side of the coin is that potential Talebob users have to download an executable (via Dropbox, as explained in the Taleboblen homepage, www.taleboblen.hi.is), unzip it, and invoke it using their own operating system. Simple as these procedures may be for skilled IT-users, they showed to be problematic for many language teachers and even local IT-helpdesks. We intend to launch a purely browser-based Talebob-version in the near future, as a supplement to the current version.

For an interesting discussion on CALL design principles for tools training spoken language, see Appel (2012). González (2012) and Mbah (2013) have experimented with minimalistic CALL applications for English teaching.

6 Talebob meets the world

Before launching our test programme in Iceland, Greenland, and the Faroese Islands we wanted to assess Talebob's competence as a Danish language teacher, so we evaluated Talebob with a panel of native Danish speakers (18 pupils aged 9-18), in surroundings chosen to match the typical Talebob user's (school, car, living room). 16 out of 18 panel members completed the 30 phrases in less than 50 attempts, meaning that most tasks were completed on the first attempt. This seemed to be a satisfactory result.

For comparison, our current log of L2 users at the time of writing shows an average of 84 attempts for the Talebob challenge as a whole (2.80 attempts per phrase), with a global best-score of 55 attempts. Danes and non-Danes thus seem to be clearly distinguished, suggesting that Talebob's automatic feedback is linguistically non-arbitrary as well as didactically useful.

6.1 The case of Iceland

Table 1 summarizes all contacts made to the Talebob back-end during our (still ongoing) test period. For technical and practical reasons, Greenland and the Faroes have only been able to access Talebob systematically for a considerably shorter time than Iceland. We therefore have to postpone cross-country comparisons to a later paper.[2]

The pupils taking part in the experiment were not urged to finish the Talebob challenge. They were simply invited by their teacher to try it out. It's therefore interesting to notice that approximately half of the users who have taken up the Talebob challenge (i.e. passed at least one phrase task), do finish the course as well. In other words, we don't see signs of 'early fatigue'.

When consulting the performance data, we see that level-1 phrases took 2.64 attemps to pass on average, level-2 took 2.54, and level-3 took 3.48. As level-3 puts the user under much heavier demand (15 several-word phrases, compared to level-1's 5 very short phrases), we conclude that pupils, in general, are not scared off by the harder struggle. Out of 19 pupils entering level-3, almost 70% completed the level as well. This is an encouraging result, convincing us that Talebob - even in it's earliest version, with crude graphics, canned messages, an adult prompt voice, and no personalization at all - can be appreciated as a fun and meaningful challenge by young children used to the far more advanced interaction of computer games.

Log-data (TB=Talebob)	**All**	**Iceland**
TB contacts	2508	1888
TB phrase evaluations	2203	1773
Level-1 commenced	39	27
Level-1 passed	30	23
Level-2 passed	24	19
Level-3 passed	16	13
Smiley-1 (*happy*)	738	571
Smiley-2 (*medium*)	1355	1123
Smiley-3 (*sad*)	110	79
TB-eval. per Smiley-1	2.99	3.11

Table 1. Log-data for Icelandic users as per 18/12 2013. Column 'All' includes Faeroese and Greenlandic contacts.

6.2 What's *Danish* about Talebob?

There is nothing intrinsically 'Danish' about Talebob. The acoustic analysis and scoring procedures do not contain any language-specific

[2]The cross-country study could be an interesting one given the extremely different attitudes towards Danish as an L2 encountered in the West-Nordic area. Running a risk of premature generalization, we observe that Greenlandic pupils are highly motivated learners (being heavy users of Danish media) as opposed to the Icelandic children who may have an easier time pronouncing the Danish sounds, but are generally much less motivated anyway (Iceland being in some respects more culturally self-sufficient). Faroese children don't seem to question the necessity of learning Danish at all (many of them preparing for studies in mainland Denmark).

parts. Hence no re-programming will be needed when porting Talebob to new L2 scenaria, only an editorial process of selecting 30 (or more) suitable phrases followed by a recording session with one or more native speakers with a flair for 'ecological pronunciation'. The technical integration of these materials are fairly trivial (though some languages may require slight changes in the acoustic setup). In this respect, Talebob's simplistic speech evaluation differs from the technologically far more sophisticated CALL tools for L2 conversational training available in the market, such as Guiliana (2004), Wang (2011), de Vries (2014), and Mirzaei et al. (2014), and commercial CALL-programs like Cooori (www.cooori.com), all including a fully-fledged ASR component (automatic speech recognition).

6.3 Talebob as a scientific enterprise

Our current evaluation regime (based on *STF*, *ProsDev*, and *ArtEval*) has worked well, providing a useful compromise between linguistic precision and communicable (age-appropriate) advise. However, we are aware that this particular setup has not proved itself in a strict scientific sense. Maybe different formulae or new scoring procedures would allow even more useful feedback from Talebob. For example, we suspect that *ProsDev* and *ArtEval* definitions based on standard deviation rather than numerical distance may allow more specific corrections. New batteries of formulae is constantly being tested - still without this being driven by ideal linguistic criteria, but rather as a pragmatic and feedback-informed activity.

Actually, it's not clear to us that an 'ideal' configuration could be obtained at all. The most effective evaluation procedures, from a didactic point of view, would not rely solely on ideal linguistic criteria, but include the personal profiles of the pupils (degree of motivation, prior knowledge of Danish, own first language, general IT-experience, and more).

7 Concluding remarks

Our perhaps most significant conclusion is that pupil users *like* Talebob and spend far more time (at home and in school) training Danish pronunciation than ever before (Hauksdottir and Henrichsen, in prep.). We have not performed any objective evaluations of the didactic effects yet, and so we do not know whether Talebob can actually teach pupils a better Danish. Nevertheless, teachers in our test group (especially Icelanders) report that most of their pupils never practiced spoken Danish before unless forced. A majority of pupils report that they feel more confident now when using Danish speech productively (Hauksdottir 2015). This seems to be an important result in itself.

Finally we wish to point to Talebob as an example of CALL-based screening of large groups of pupils. Access to statistical information about the progress of individual pupils, classes, or even populations of classes may of course be useful for teachers, but perhaps even more so for researchers and political decision-makers.

Such considerations are highly relevant in Denmark right now, the 2014 school reform being currently implemented. For the first time ever English is now taught from first grade. Spokesmen for the teachers are constantly expressing concerns about the lack of training programmes for teachers new to the challenge of teaching English to minors. Objective means for assessing the learning patterns are frequently called for in the press and in the parliament. We believe that cleverly designed CALL-tools could play a decisive role in this debate.

We are currently working preparing a Talebob version adapted for English phrases, planning experiments with first graders in late 2015, hopefully laying the ground for a longitudinal study. We do hope that Nordic researchers and Danish politicians will pick up on this unique historical opportunity.

Acknowledgments

The presented work is a part of the ongoing Nordic project "Talehjælp til Dansk som Nabosprog" 2013-2015, supported by NorFA and Nordisk Ministerråd/Nordplus. We gratefully acknowledge their contributions. The project combines didactic and computational-linguistic research in Iceland, Denmark, and Sweden with practical implementation work by language teachers in Nuuk, Hafnarfjörður and

Tórshavn (visit http://www.taleboblen.hi.is). Many have thus contributed, from a geographical area spanning five time zones. One, however, outshines all others: project leader and initiator Auður Hauksdóttir. Thanks to Auður for her many years as a powerstation in Nordic L2 didactics.

References

Allwood, J., Henrichsen, P. J. (eds). 2005. *SweDanes for CALL - A corpus and computer-based student's aid for comparison of Swedish and Danish spoken language.* NorFA CALL NET (cd med manual)

Appel, C., Robbins, J., Moré, J., Mullen, T. 2012. *Task and Tool Interface Design for L2 Speaking Interaction Online.* EUROCALL 2012

Giuliani, D., Mich, O., Gerosa, M. 2004. *Parling, a CALL System for Children.* InSTIL/ICALL2004 – NLP and Speech Technologies in Advanced Language Learning Systems

González, J.F. 2012. *Can Apple's iPhone Help to Improve English Pronunciation Autonomously? State of the App.* EUROCALL 2012

Hauksdottir, A., Henrichsen, P.J. (in prep.) *Dansk som Fremmedsprog i Vestnorden*

Henrichsen, P. J. 2004b. *"CALL for the Nordic Languages - tools and methods for Computer Assisted Language Learning;* Cph. Studies in Language 30/2004

Mbah, E.E., Mhab, B.M., Iloene, M.I., Iloene, G.O. 2013. *Podcasts for Learning English Pronunciation in Igboland: Students' Experiences and Expectations.* EUROCALL 2013

Mirzaei (2014) *Partial and synchronized captioning: A new tool for second language listening development;* EUROCALL 2014.
Henrichsen, P. J. 2004. *The Twisted Tongue; Tools for Teaching Danish Pronunciation Using a Synthetic Voice*; in Henrichsen 2004b

Selsøe Sørensen, H., Henrichsen, P. J., Hansen, C. 2004. *NorFA CALL net: Nordisk Netværk om Computerstøttet Unvervisning i Nordiske Sprog*; Nordisk Sprogteknologisk Forskningsprogram 2000-2004, Samfundslitteratur Press, 224pp

Thorborg, L. 2003. *Dansk Udtale - Øvebog.* Synope, ISBN 87-988509-4-6 (cd and book)

Thorborg, L. 2006. *Dansk Udtale i 49 Tekster.* Synope, ISBN 87-91909-01-5 (cd and book)

de Vries, B. P., Cucchiarini, C., Bodnar, S.. 2014. *Automatic Feedback on Spoken Dutch of Low-Educated Learners: An ASR-based CALL study.* Proceed. of EUROCALL 2014 (to appear)

Wang, H., T. Kawahara and Y. Wang. 2011. *Improving Non-native Speech Recognition Performance by Discriminative Training for Language Model in a CALL System;* INTERSPEECH 2011, 27-31

The Effect of Author Set Size in Authorship Attribution for Lithuanian

Jurgita Kapočiūtė-Dzikienė
Vytautas Magnus University
K. Donelaičio 58, LT-44248,
Kaunas, Lithuania
jurgita.k.dz@gmail.com

Ligita Šarkutė
Kaunas University of Technology
K. Donelaičio 73, LT-44029,
Kaunas, Lithuania
ligita.sarkute@ktu.lt

Andrius Utka
Vytautas Magnus University
K. Donelaičio 58, LT-44248,
Kaunas, Lithuania
utka@hmf.vdu.lt

Abstract

This paper reports the first authorship attribution results based on the effect of the author set size using automatic computational methods for the Lithuanian language. The aim is to determine how fast authorship attribution results are deteriorating while the number of candidate authors is gradually increasing: i.e. starting from 3, going up to 5, 10, 20, 50, and 100. Using supervised machine learning techniques we also investigated the influence of different features (lexical, character, morphological, etc.) and language types (normative parliamentary speeches and non-normative forum posts).

The experiments revealed that the effectiveness of the method and feature types depends more on the language type rather than on the number of candidate authors. The content features based on word lemmas are the most useful type for the normative texts, due to the fact that Lithuanian is a highly inflective, morphologically and vocabulary rich language. The character features are the most accurate type for forum posts, where texts are too complicated to be effectively processed with external morphological tools.

1 Introduction

Authorship Attribution (AA) is the task of identifying who, from a set of candidate authors, is an actual author of a given anonymous text document. This prediction is based on a human "stylometric fingerprint" notion: i.e. a specific, individual, persistent, and uncontrolled habit to express thoughts with a unique set of linguistic means. Van Halteren (2005) has gone so far as to name this phenomenon a "human stylome" in the deliberate analogy to the DNA "genome". However, Juola (2007) argues that such strict implications may not be absolutely correct, because the "genome" is stable, but the human style tends to evolve over time. Nevertheless a "stylome" can still be added to human biometrics, next to voice, gait, keystroke dynamics, handwriting, etc.

Starting from Mendenhall (1887) AA is one of the oldest computational linguistics problems, which is especially highly topical nowadays. For a long time in the past the main AA applications were restricted to the literary texts only. But the constant influx of anonymous electronic text documents, especially on the Internet, and the popularity of automatic methods opened the gate to a number of new applications in forensic analysis and electronic commerce. In addition to literary research the practical problems from the plagiarism detection (Stamatatos, 2011), the identification of harassment and threatening (Tan et al., 2013) to tracking authors of malicious source code (Alrabaee et al., 2014) gained even greater prominence. This led to experiments with different datasets, such as e-mails (de Vel et al., 2001; Abbasi and Chen, 2008), web forum messages (Solorio et al., 2011), online chats (Cristani et al., 2012; Inches et al., 2013), Internet blogs (Koppel et al., 2011) or tweets (Sousa-Silva et al., 2011; Schwartz et al., 2013), which, in turn, contributed to a progress of the development of computational linguistic methods that are able to cope with the emerged problems.

Despite that many computational linguistic tasks can be solved accurately only relying on efforts of domain-experts, it is very time consuming, expensive, and perhaps the most limiting way for AA, moreover, which provides no explicit measure how attributions are made. The alternative way is a manually composed set of rules capable to take attribution decisions automatically. Unfortunately, rule-based systems usually are very complex, unwieldy, and thus not robust to any changes in the domain, language or author characteristics, therefore it is rather difficult to make any updates. Moreover, when dealing with hundreds (e.g. in Luyckx and Daelemans (2008), Luyckx (2010)) or thousands of candidate authors (e.g. in Koppel et al. (2011) 10,000 authors; in Narayanan et al. (2012) – 100,000) the possibility to create an effective rule set goes far beyond human potential limits. Ultimately, AA task can be solved using the machine learning (Sebastiani, 2002): i.e. by training the classifiers and later using them to predict the authorship of unseen texts. Moreover, it can be easily adjusted to new applications or domains and even generalized well to drifts in the author characteristics. Due to all these advantages, the machine learning paradigm became dominant and remained the most popular till nowadays. Therefore our focus in this paper is also on the machine learning methods.

2 Related Work

Despite rare attempts to deal with unlabeled data, e.g. Nasir et al. (2014), Qian et al. (2014), a typical AA problem fits the standard paradigm of the supervised machine learning. It means that the training dataset containing texts of known authors is available and can be used to create the model able to predict the authorship of unknown texts from the same closed-set of the candidate authors in the future. Algorithmically, it involves a variety of different methods (for the detailed review see Stamatatos (2009)) ranging from probabilistic approaches (Seroussi et al., 2011), compression models (Oliveira et al., 2013) to Vector Space Models (Stamatatos, 2008). In general all methods can be distinguished according to whether they treat each training text individually (instance-based) or cumulatively by concatenating texts written by the same author into one (profile-based). Intuitively, profile-based approaches should have advantages over instance-based when text documents are very concise, thus concatenation helps to create sufficiently long document for capturing its style; but on the other hand instance-based approaches are better suited for the sparse data scenario. Some comparative experiments on the AA after testing Decision Trees (DTs), Back Propagation Neural Networks (BPNNs) and Support Vector Machines (SVMs) revealed that SVMs and BPNNs achieved significantly better performance compared to DTs (Zheng et al., 2006). Zhao and Zobel (2005) proved that k-Nearest Neighbor (kNN) approach produces better results compared to both Naïve Bayes (NB) and DTs. Jockers and Witten (2010) report that Delta method outperforms popular SVMs. Savoy (2012) proposes new classification scheme based on the specific vocabulary and experimentally proves that it performs better than Principal Component Analysis (PCA) and slightly better than Delta approach; Savoy (2013) also shows that LDA (Latent Dirichlet Allocation) classification scheme can surpass two classical AA approaches – i.e. Delta rule and chi-squared distance. Nevertheless, the precise comparison of methods is still difficult due to the lack of suitable benchmark data. Besides, the results are affected not only by the selected classification method itself, but by preprocessing techniques, author set sizes, language characteristics, etc. However the most crucial factor is probably the selected type of features.

The first modern work in AA (different from traditional human-expert techniques) was described by Mosteller and Wallace (1963). They demonstrated promising AA results on *The Federalist papers* using Bayesian methods applied on frequencies of a small set of function words (including articles, prepositions and conjunctions) as stylistic features in the text. Since this pioneering study and until 1990s AA was based on quantitative features (so-called style markers) such as a sentence or word length, syllables per word, type-token ratio, vocabulary richness functions, lexical repetition, etc. In fact all these stylometric features are considered to be suitable only for homogeneous long texts (>1,000 words) and for datasets where the number of candidate authors is limited. Lately other feature types– in particular, lexical, syntactic, semantic, or character –treating texts as the sequence of tokens or characters became more popular. A huge number of these features have been presented so far, but we will focus only on the most popular and the most accurate ones. The most common example of the lexical feature type is a simple bag-of-words representation which is considered to be topic-dependent therefore should be avoided when the distribution over authors coincides the distribution over different topics (not to solve topic-classification problem instead of AA). Besides token n-grams are also considered to capture content-specific instead of stylistic information. The most popular topic-neutral lexical solution, carrying no semantic information, is the function words (articles, conjunctions, prepositions, pronouns, etc.). Various authors use different lists of function words, varying from 150 (Abbasi and Chen, 2005) to 675 (Argamon et al., 2007) words, but providing very little information about how these lists were composed. The effectiveness of syntactic and semantic features usually rely on the accuracy of external linguistic tools (e.g. part-of-speech taggers, parsers) or exhaustiveness of additional data resources (e.g. thesauruses or databases). Although used alone they hardly can outperform lexical features, but often improve the results used in the combination (Gamon, 2004). However, character features (character n-grams, in particular) are considered the most important document representation type in authors' style detection: they are topic-neutral, language-independent, able to capture style through lexical and contextual information, and are tolerant to grammatical errors. Application-specific features are highly dependent on the solvable problem, e.g. positions of hashtags, smileys, punctuation are important style detectors in tweets (Sousa-Silva et al., 2011).

The majority of surveyed research works deal with Germanic languages, providing no guidance what could work the best with morphologically rich, highly inflective, derivationally complex, and relatively free word order languages such as Lithuanian. Starting from 1971 (Pikčilingis, 1971) lots of descriptive linguistic works are done on the AA for the Lithuanian language (the review in Žalkauskaitė (2012)). Besides, the pioneering and as far as we know the only work using automatic methods on the Lithuanian texts is described in (Kapočiūtė-Dzikienė et al., 2014). However, their experiments have been made only with the normative Lithuanian language, few authors, and small training data; therefore findings are not robust to make the generalizations about which method is the best and which feature type is the most reliable for solving AA problem in general. Consequently in this research we will try to overcome all mentioned shortcomings by experimenting with different language types (normative and Internet forum data) and increasing number of candidate authors (up to one hundred).

3 Methodology

In essence, AA problem is a task which can be formally described as follows.

The dataset D contains text documents d_i attributed to a closed-set of candidate authors (defined as classes) $C = \{c_j\}$.

The training dataset D^T (where $D^T \subset D$) is composed of training instances: i.e. documents d_i with a known authorship c_j: $\{\langle d_i, c_j \rangle\}$.

The function φ determines the mapping (about characteristics in styles of the authors) how each d_i is attributed to c_j in D^T.

Our goal is using D^T to train a classifier and to create the model φ', which could be as close approximation of φ as possible.

3.1 The Datasets

All our experiments were carried out on 2 datasets to make sure that findings generalize over different domains and language types:

- *ParlTranscr*[1] (see Table 1) contains unedited transcripts of parliamentary speeches and debates, thus representing formal spoken but normative Lithuanian language. All transcripts are from regular parliamentary sessions and cover the period of 7 parliamentary terms starting on March 10, 1990 and ending on December 23, 2013. Very long (>1,000 words) and very short (<100 words) texts were removed from the dataset to avoid speeches written by non-parliamentarians, but by someone else and to avoid less informative text samples, respectively. Afterwards we selected 100 authors with the largest number of texts, but making sure that the selected candidates are distributed over different parliamentary terms (to avoid topic classification) and party groups (to avoid ideology-based classification).

- *LRytas*[2] (see Table 2) contains forum data full of informal words, foreign language insertions, word shortenings, emoticons, and diacritic eliminations, thus represents the informal non-normative Lithuanian language. The forum has 11 general topics (such as "Business", "Politics", "Sports", etc.). Very short texts (<10 words) were not included into

[1] Downloaded from http://www3.lrs.lt/pls/inter/w5_sale.

[2] Crawled on March 19, 2014 from http://forum.lrytas.lt/forum_show.pl.

the dataset. Afterwards we selected 100 authors having the largest number of texts, but making sure that selected candidates would be distributed over different topics (to avoid topic classification).

3.2 Classification

In this paper we focus on the supervised machine learning techniques (Kotsiantis, 2007) applied to the text categorization (Sebastiani, 2002) and used for the AA (Stamatatos, 2009).

The aim of our task is to find a method, which could distinguish the distinct authors from each other by creating a model for the best approximation of the authors' style. For this reason we explored two supervised machine learning approaches:

- *Support Vector Machine* (SVM) (introduced by Cortes and Vapnik (1995)) is a discriminative instance-based approach, which is currently the most popular text classification technique, efficiently handling a high dimensional feature spaces (e.g. maximum ~295 thousand features in the imbalanced 100 authors *ParlTrascr* dataset, ~84,4 thousand in *LRytas*); sparseness of the feature vectors (only ~215 non-zero feature values among ~295 thousand in *ParlTranscr* and ~42 among ~84,4 thousand in *LRytas*); and does not perform aggressive feature selection, which may result in a loss of information and degrade the accuracy (Joachims, 1998).

- *Naïve Bayes Multinomial* (NBM) (introduced by Lewis and Gale (1994)) is a generative profile-based approach, which is often selected due to its simplicity: Naïve Bayes assumption about the feature independence allows parameters of each feature to be learned separately; the method performs especially well when the number of features having equal significance is large; it is very fast and does not require huge data storage resources; besides, this Bayesian method is often selected as the baseline approach.

However, it is important to notice that the choice of classification algorithm is not more important than the choice of feature types by which texts have to be represented.

3.3 Feature Extraction

In our research we explored the impact of the most popular or/and accurate individual and compound feature types, covering stylistic, character, lexical, and morpho-syntactic levels:

- *usm* – ultimate style markers: average sentence and word length in a text document; standardized type/token ratio (STTR). Although we assume that this archaic stylometric feature type will definitely give very poor classification results, it still has to be tested for comparison reasons.

- *chrN* – document-level character n-grams: context-free character feature type (where *N* = [2;7] in our experiments). It considers successions of *N* characters including spaces and punctuation marks, e.g., *chr7* of phrase "authorship attribution" produces the following character n-grams: "authors", "uthorsh", "thorshi", "horship", "orship_", "rship_a", etc.[3] By many researchers this feature type was proved to be one of the best (or even the best) to tackle AA problems.

- *fwd* – function words: the content-free lexical feature type which includes prepositions, pronouns, conjunctions, particles, interjections, and onomatopoeias. Instead of relying on the pre-established and stable list of the function words, we identified them by applying the Lithuanian morphological analyzer-lemmatizer "Lemuoklis" (Zinkevičius, 2000; Daudaravičius et al., 2007). This feature type by consensus is considered as the topic-neutral and was proved to be a relatively good identifier of the writing style by many researchers.

- *lexN* – token n-grams: the most popular content-specific lexical feature type which involves a bag-of-words (*N* = 1) or interpolation of token n-grams (*N* = [2;3] in our experiments), e.g., *lex1* of the phrase "authorship attribution problem" produces 3 bag-of-words: "authorship", "attribution", and "problem"; *lex2*: 3 bag-of-words plus token bigrams "authorship attribution", and "attribution problem"; *lex3*: 3 bag-of-words, 2 to-

[3] This and the following examples will be given in English instead of Lithuanian for the clarity reasons.

Numb. of classes	Numb. of text documents	Numb. of tokens	Numb. of distinct tokens (types)	Numb. of distinct lemmas	Avg. numb of tokens in a doc.
3	600 16,804	156,107 3,457,093	21,439 107,950	8,608 35,525	260.18 205.73
5	1,000 22,476	239,288 4,585,493	27,983 132,623	10,864 42,620	239.29 204.02
10	2,000 34,307	451,638 6,821,083	38,952 157,409	14,076 49,470	225.82 198.82
20	4,000 50,532	927,411 10,254,271	63,456 204,043	21,310 61,443	231.85 202.93
50	10,000 77,005	2,475,615 16,478,475	107,029 254,966	33,308 75,563	247.56 213.99
100	20,000 98,999	4,728,411 21,295,515	151,836 295,046	45,441 86,770	236.42 215.11

Table 1: Composition of *ParlTranscr*: the upper value in each cell represents a balanced dataset (200 instances in each class), the lower – imbalanced (full). The set of authors is identical in the both datasets.

Numb. of classes	Numb. of text documents	Numb. of tokens	Numb. of distinct tokens (types)	Numb. of distinct lemmas	Avg. numb of tokens in a doc.
3	30 3,567	1,252 137,768	792 30,830	615 16,726	41.73 38.62
5	50 4,579	1,722 166,512	1,049 36,267	781 19,271	34.44 36.36
10	100 6,209	3,913 244,947	2,191 49,648	1,572 26,603	39.13 39.45
20	200 8,470	8,876 351,285	4,287 63,363	2,910 33,377	44.38 41.47
50	500 11,155	21,942 468,466	8,980 76,861	5,725 40,057	43.88 42.00
100	1,000 12,888	44,375 545,405	15,290 84,482	9,443 44,211	44.38 42.32

Table 2: Composition of *LRytas*: the upper value in each cell represents a balanced dataset (10 instances in each class), the lower – imbalanced (full). The set of authors is identical in the both datasets.

ken n-grams plus one trigram "authorship attribution problem".

- *lemN* – n-grams of token lemmas: the content-specific lexical feature type which involves lemmas based on the word tokens (N = 1) or their interpolation (N = [2;3] in our experiments). "Lemuoklis" replaces words with their lemmas, transforms recognized generic words into the lower-case and replaces all numbers with a special tag. We assume that this feature type should reduce the number of types significantly (especially for *ParlTranscr*) which should result in creation of more robust models and higher classification accuracy.

- *posN* – n-grams of part-of-speech tags: the content-free morpho-syntactic feature type which involves coarse-grained part-of-speech tags based on word tokens (N = 1) or their interpolation (N = [2;3] in our experiments). Coarse-grained part-of-speech tags (such as noun, verb, adjective, etc.) are also determined by "Lemuoklis".

- *lexposN*, *lemposN*, *lexmorfN*, *lemmorfN* – the aggregated features which involve unigrams (N = 1) of concatenated features or their interpolation (N = [2;3] in our experiments): *lex&pos*, *lem&pos*, *lex&morf*,

lex&morf, respectively, where *morf* indicates the string of the concatenated fine-grained morphological values for case, gender, tense, mood, etc., determined by "Lemuoklis", e.g., *lexpos2* of phrase "interesting problem" produces two unigrams "interesting_ADJ", "problem_NOUN" plus one bigram "interesting_ADJ problem_NOUN".

4 Experimental Set-Up and Results

Our aim is to explore different classification methods (see Section 3.2), feature types (see Section 3.3) and to answer the main questions:

- How the author set size affects results, when having 3, 5, 10, 20, 50, and 100 candidate authors? The candidate author selection is done depending on the number of their texts: the authors with the most texts are selected first.
- How the language type influences results, when *ParlTranscr* contains texts of normative, but *LRytas* of non-normative language?

All experiments were carried out with the stratified 10-fold cross-validation and evaluated using accuracy and micro/macro average F-score metrics. Since F-scores showed the same accuracy trend in all our experiments, we do not present them in the following figures and tables. For each dataset random ($\sum P^2(c_j)$) and majority ($\max P(c_j)$) baselines (where $P(c_j)$ is the probability of class c_j) were calculated, but only the higher values were presented in the following figures. In order to determine whether the differences between obtained values are statistically significant we performed McNemar's (McNemar, 1947) test with one degree of freedom.

In our experiments we used chi-squared feature extraction method, SMO polynomial kernel (because it gave the highest accuracy in our preliminary control experiments) with SVM and NBM implementations in the WEKA machine learning toolkit (Hall et al., 2009), version 3.6. All remaining parameters were set to their default values.

For the effect of used method see Figure 1 and feature type see Table 3 and Table 4.

5 Discussion

Zooming into the results presented in Figure 1, allows us to report the following statements:

All obtained results are reasonable and appropriate for our solving task, because they exceed random and majority baselines. However, SVM is a much better selection, as it always outperformed NBM, except for a couple of cases when the both methods achieved the same accuracy.

If compared the same number of candidate authors, the accuracy of *LRytas* is always much lower compared to *ParlTranscr*. This could be due to the language type, text length, and training dataset size. The comprehensive expert analysis revealed that parliamentarians use official language with the larger but more steady dictionary. Moreover, their speeches or debates are carefully transcribed, thus there are no grammatical errors and diacritic eliminations. Whereas in *LRytas* different forum texts posted by even the same author are written in different manners, thus the quality of texts varies (sometimes more typing errors or abbreviations). Since the non-normative language is always much harder to deal with, the accuracy is lower. The second reason is the length of classified texts: it is always easier to predict the author from longer text samples. As we can see from the Table 1 and Table 2 the texts in *ParlTranscr* are more than 5 times longer compared to *LRytas* texts. Besides, in our experiments we were using 10-fold cross-validation, thus having 9/10 of all text samples for training, e.g., when dealing with the imbalanced datasets and 100 candidate authors, *ParlTransc* has 7 times more text documents and 3 times more different tokens (types) compared to *LRytas* (see Table 1 and Table 2). Consequently, the bigger variety in the training data helps to create more comprehensive models which in turn are more robust in the classification stage.

When increasing the number of candidate authors, we are also making the task more difficult, thus the accuracy is gradually dropping. However the decline is much steeper for *LRytas* compared to *ParlTranscr*, e.g. the increase from 3 to 100 candidate authors using SVM for balanced and imbalanced *ParlTranscr* produces the decrease of 26.9% and 22.9%, respectively; while for *LRytas* it is 46.6% and 40.1%. Having more candidate authors the task becomes more difficult, therefore all previously mentioned problems (language type, text length, training dataset size), become even more detriment.

The balancing decreases training data, thus negatively affects AA results for *LRytas* and SVM's results with 100 authors for *ParlTranscr* (this confirms a statement in Manning and Schütze (1999)),

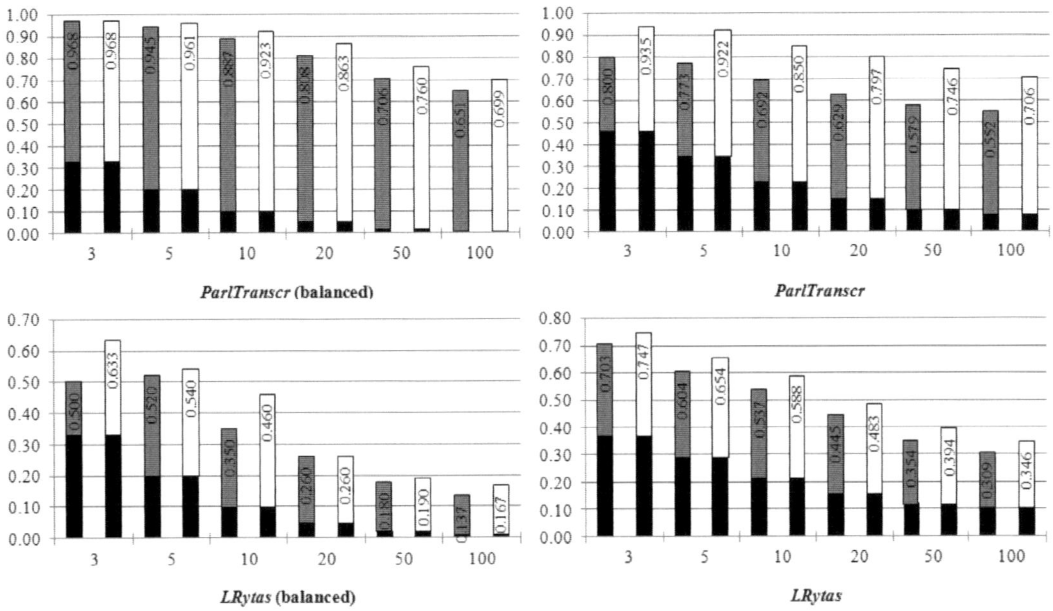

Figure 1: The accuracy (y axis) dependence on the number of the candidate authors (x axis). Grey columns represent NBM, white – SVM, black lower parts represent higher of the random/majority baselines. Each column shows the maximum achieved accuracy over all explored feature types.

but has opposite effect on *ParlTranscr*. This might happened due to a successful random selection of instances for the balanced dataset. In the imbalanced experiment the major 3 authors already has the texts which are not appropriate to express their style as good as in the balanced dataset, thus a negative influence not only persists, but may increase when adding more authors to the dataset.

In our experiments we tested all the most popular currently known feature types (29 in total) used for AA. Zooming into the results reported in Table 3 and Table 4 allows us to make the following statements.

When analyzing the normative Lithuanian language (as it is in *ParlTranscr*) the content information is very important for achieving high classification accuracy. Moreover, the feature type based on word lemmas is marginally the best in 8 of 12 times (with 5, 10, 20, 50 and 100 candidate authors with balanced and 10, 50 and 100 authors with imbalanced dataset). When having 5 or 20 authors with imbalanced dataset a bit longer patterns $N = 2$ and $N = 3$, respectively, of word lemmas give the best results. Despite that the part-of-speech information when used alone is definitely not the best selection, but in concatenation with lemmas (when $N = 2$) it can boost the performance and become the best feature type with 3 authors. Considering information about statistical significance between different results, and ignoring small variations depending on the number of authors, we can state that in general the best feature type for *ParlTranscr* dataset is based on the lemma and part-of-speech information. It is not surprising due to the fact that we were dealing with the Lithuanian language which is highly inflective, morphologically and vocabulary rich; moreover we were dealing with the normative language; therefore morphological tools were maximally helpful for this dataset.

When dealing with forum posts in *LRytas*, the picture is absolutely different. Marginally the best feature type in most of the cases is not based on the content information, thus, it is not based on the lemma information. Document-level character bigrams give the best results in 9 of 12 cases with the small exceptions (100 candidate authors with balanced and 3 and 5 authors with imbalanced datasets), where the credit is given to the content lemma information again. It is not surprising, since we were dealing with the non-normative Lithuanian language texts full of errors, diacritic eliminations, and words out of the standard Lithuanian language dictionary; moreover,

Feature type	ParlTranscr (balanced)						ParlTranscr					
	3	5	10	20	50	100	3	5	10	20	50	100
usm	0.488	0.430	0.272	0.155	0.069	0.037	0.581	0.435	0.299	0.202	0.133	0.103
fwd	0.792	0.763	0.662	0.518	0.392	0.324	0.801	0.753	0.642	0.555	0.461	0.398
chr3	0.938	0.945	0.901	0.819	0.699	0.627	0.904	0.890	0.804	0.747	0.680	0.633
chr4	0.938	0.945	0.893	0.813	0.685	0.601	0.906	0.887	0.802	0.743	0.674	0.625
lex1	0.953	0.936	0.900	0.816	0.708	0.635	0.927	0.911	0.832	0.774	0.706	0.659
lem1	0.960	**0.961**	**0.922**	**0.862**	**0.760**	**0.699**	0.931	0.920	**0.850**	0.796	**0.746**	**0.706**
lem2	0.962	0.958	0.910	0.852	0.753	0.691	0.932	**0.922**	0.847	0.797	0.740	0.702
lem3	0.957	0.954	0.914	0.849	0.753	0.690	0.933	0.921	0.847	**0.797**	0.737	0.701
pos3	0.742	0.715	0.643	0.509	0.359	0.261	0.807	0.755	0.655	0.558	0.439	0.364
lexpos1	0.962	0.943	0.906	0.815	0.705	0.637	0.926	0.912	0.835	0.774	0.708	0.659
lempos1	0.960	0.956	0.918	0.851	0.750	0.690	0.934	0.921	0.847	0.795	0.742	0.701
lempos2	**0.968**	0.954	0.913	0.841	0.741	0.682	**0.935**	0.919	0.846	0.795	0.738	0.698
lexmorf1	0.953	0.941	0.900	0.812	0.703	0.632	0.922	0.911	0.831	0.771	0.705	0.657
lemmorf1	0.958	0.936	0.907	0.822	0.708	0.646	0.925	0.913	0.835	0.778	0.715	0.671

Table 3: Accuracy values with SVM and various feature types for *ParlTrascr* dataset. Only the best results in terms of *N* of each feature type are reported. The best results for different author set sizes (in columns) are in bold; results that do not statistically significant differ from the best result are underlined.

Feature type	LRytas (balanced)						LRytas					
	3	5	10	20	50	100	3	5	10	20	50	100
usm	0.267	0.360	0.250	0.085	0.038	0.027	0.443	0.343	0.251	0.183	0.139	0.121
fwd	0.300	0.280	0.170	0.105	0.078	0.045	0.587	0.459	0.375	0.293	0.225	0.197
chr2	**0.500**	**0.520**	**0.350**	**0.260**	**0.180**	0.135	0.698	0.584	**0.537**	**0.445**	**0.354**	**0.309**
lex1	0.467	0.400	0.320	0.175	0.136	0.103	0.695	0.578	0.512	0.397	0.323	0.281
lem1	0.433	0.380	0.310	0.165	0.172	0.128	0.696	**0.604**	0.525	0.418	0.336	0.230
lem2	0.400	0.280	0.210	0.205	0.152	0.127	0.687	0.583	0.506	0.409	0.328	0.287
pos1	0.400	0.340	0.220	0.180	0.106	0.060	0.609	0.486	0.407	0.304	0.233	0.202
pos2	0.367	0.280	0.260	0.150	0.082	0.063	0.649	0.536	0.469	0.353	0.275	0.238
lexpos1	0.467	0.440	0.290	0.225	0.128	0.097	0.689	0.570	0.500	0.394	0.316	0.281
lempos1	0.467	0.380	0.280	0.140	0.144	**0.137**	0.692	0.592	0.526	0.413	0.337	0.298
lempos2	0.367	0.260	0.200	0.190	0.146	0.118	0.697	0.586	0.508	0.407	0.327	0.289
lexmorf1	0.400	0.400	0.240	0.220	0.124	0.087	0.695	0.571	0.501	0.396	0.315	0.276
lemmorf1	0.367	0.340	0.240	0.140	0.130	0.105	**0.703**	0.570	0.506	0.395	0.318	0.278

Table 4: Accuracy values with SVM and various feature types for *LRytas* dataset. For other notations see the caption of Table 3.

even in forums for the registered users the identity of the author is not 100% certain. Despite all these findings about character n-grams, we cannot strongly state that it is the very best feature type for our non-normative texts, because the differences between other content-based feature types are not always statistically significant.

6 Conclusions and Future Work

In this paper we report the first authorship attribution results based on the exploration of the effect of the author set size when dealing with normative and non-normative Lithuanian language texts and using supervised machine learning techniques.

We experimentally have determined that the effect of feature types depend more on the language type used in the dataset than on the number of candidate authors. Using parliamentary data (thus normative Lithuanian language) the best feature types are based on the morpho-syntactic information generated by the external grammatical tools. The results exceed baseline by 62.7% and reach even 70.6% of accuracy with 100 of candidate authors. Using forum posts (thus non-normative texts) the best feature types are however based on the character n-grams. The results exceed baseline by 20.7% and reach 30.9% of accuracy.

In the future research we are planning to further expand the number of candidate authors up to several thousands or even tens of thousands; to experiment more with non-normative Lithuanian language (blog data, tweets, etc.) and to reveal if the same statements about feature types and methods are still valid.

Acknowledgments

Research was funded by a grant (No. LIT-8-69) from the Research Council of Lithuania.

References

Ahmed Abbasi and Hsinchun Chen. 2005. Applying Authorship Analysis to Extremist-Group Web Forum Messages. *IEEE Intelligent Systems*, 20(5):67–75.

Ahmed Abbasi and Hsinchun Chen. 2008. Writer-prints: A Stylometric Approach to Identity-Level Identification and Similarity Detection in Cyberspace. *ACM Transactions on Information Systems*, 26(2):1–29.

Saed Alrabaee, Noman Saleem, Stere Preda, Lingyu Wang, and Mourad Debbabi. 2014. OBA2: An Onion approach to Binary code Authorship Attribution. *Digital Investigation*, 11(1):S94–S103.

Shlomo Argamon, Casey Whitelaw, Paul Chase, Sobhan Raj Hota, Navendu Garg, and Shlomo Levitan. 2007. Stylistic Text Classification Using Functional Lexical Features: Research Articles. *Journal of the American Society for Information Science and Technology*, 58(6):802–822.

Corina Cortes and Vladimir Vapnik. 1995. Support-Vector Networks. *Machine Learning*, 20(3):273–297.

Marco Cristani, Giorgio Roffo, Cristina Segalin, Loris Bazzani, Alessandro Vinciarelli, and Vittorio Murino. 2012. Conversationally-inspired Stylometric Features for Authorship Attribution in Instant Messaging. In *Proceedings of the 20th ACM International Conference on Multimedia*, pages 1121–1124.

Vidas Daudaravičius, Erika Rimkutė, and Andrius Utka. 2007. Morphological annotation of the Lithuanian corpus. In *Proceedings of the Workshop on Balto-Slavonic Natural Language Processing: Information Extraction and Enabling Technologies*, pages 94–99.

Olivier de Vel, Alison M. Anderson, Malcolm W. Corney, and George M. Mohay. 2001. Mining e-Mail Content for Author Identification Forensics. *SIGMOD Record*, 30(4):55–64.

Michael Gamon. 2004. Linguistic Correlates of Style: Authorship Classification with Deep Linguistic Analysis Features. In *Proceedings of the 20th International Conference on Computational Linguistics*, pages 611–617.

Mark Hall, Eibe Frank, Holmes Geoffrey, Bernhard Pfahringer, Peter Reutemann, and Ian H. Witten. 2009. The WEKA Data Mining Software: An Update. *SIGKDD Explorations*, 11(1):10–18.

Giacomo Inches, Morgan Harvey, and Fabio Crestani. 2013. Finding Participants in a Chat: Authorship Attribution for Conversational Documents. In *International Conference on Social Computing*, pages 272–279.

Thorsten Joachims. 1998. Text Categorization with Support Vector Machines: Learning with many Relevant Features. In *10th European Conference on Machine Learning*, volume 1398, pages 137–142.

Matthew L. Jockers and Daniela M. Witten. 2010. A Comparative Study of Machine Learning Methods for Authorship Attribution. *Literary and Linguistic Computing*, 25(2):215–223.

Patrick Juola. 2007. Future Trends in Authorship Attribution. In *Advances in Digital Forensics III IFIP – The International Federation for Information Processing*, volume 242, pages 119–132.

Jurgita Kapočiūtė-Dzikienė, Andrius Utka, and Ligita Šarkutė. 2014. Feature Exploration for Authorship Attribution of Lithuanian Parliamentary Speeches. In *17th International Conference on Text, Speech, and Dialogue*, pages 93–100.

Moshe Koppel, Jonathan Schler, and Shlomo Argamon. 2011. Authorship attribution in the wild. *Language Resources and Evaluation*, 45(1):83–94.

Sotiris B. Kotsiantis. 2007. Supervised Machine Learning: A Review of Classification Techniques. In *Proceedings of the 2007 Conference on Emerging Artificial Intelligence Applications in Computer Engineering: Real Word AI Systems with Applications in eHealth, HCI, Information Retrieval and Pervasive Technologies*, pages 3–24.

David D. Lewis and William A. Gale. 1994. A Sequential Algorithm for Training Text Classifiers. In *17th Annual International ACM-SIGIR Conference on Research and Development in Information Retrieval*, pages 3–12.

Kim Luyckx and Walter Daelemans. 2008. Authorship Attribution and Verification with Many Authors and Limited Data. In *Proceedings of the 22Nd International Conference on Computational Linguistics*, volume 1, pages 513–520.

Kim Luyckx. 2010. *Scalability Issues in Authorship Attribution*. Ph.D. thesis, University of Antwerp, Belgium.

Christopher D. Manning and Hinrich Schütze. 1999. *Foundations of Statistical Natural Language Processing*. MIT Press, Cambridge, MA, USA.

Quinn Michael McNemar. 1947. Note on the Sampling Error of the Difference Between Correlated Proportions or Percentages. *Psychometrika*, 12(2):153–157.

Thomas Corwin Mendenhall. 1887. The Characteristic Curves of Composition. *Science*, 9:237–246.

Frederik Mosteller and David L. Wallace. 1963. Inference in an authorship problem. *Journal Of The American Statistical Association*, 58(302):275–309.

Arvind Narayanan, Hristo Paskov, Neil Zhenqiang Gong, John Bethencourt, Emil Stefanov, Eui Chul Richard Shin, and Dawn Song. 2012. On the Feasibility of Internet-Scale Author Identification. In *Proceedings of the 2012 IEEE Symposium on Security and Privacy*, pages 300–314.

Jamal Abdul Nasir, Nico Görnitz, and Ulf Brefeld. 2014. An Off-the-shelf Approach to Authorship Attribution. *The 25th International Conference on Computational Linguistics*, pages 895–904.

Walter Ribeiro Oliveira, Edson Justino, and Luiz S. Oliveira. 2013. Comparing compression models for authorship attribution. *Forensic Science International*, 228(1-3):100–104.

Juozas Pikčilingis. 1971. *Kas yra stilius?[What is the style?]*. Vaga, Vilnius, Lithuania. (in Lithuanian).

Tieyun Qian, Bing Liu, Li Chen, and Zhiyong Peng. 2014. Tri-Training for Authorship Attribution with Limited Training Data. In *Proceedings of the 52nd Annual Meeting of the Association for Computational Linguistics*, volume 2, pages 345–351.

Jacques Savoy. 2012. Authorship Attribution: A Comparative Study of Three Text Corpora and Three Languages. *Journal of Quantitative Linguistics*, 19(2):132–161.

Jacques Savoy. 2013. Authorship Attribution Based on a Probabilistic Topic Model. *Information Processing and Management*, 49(1):341–354.

Roy Schwartz, Oren Tsur, Ari Rappoport, and Moshe Koppel. 2013. Authorship Attribution of Micro-Messages. In *Empirical Methods in Natural Language Processing*, pages 1880–1891.

Fabrizio Sebastiani. 2002. Machine Learning in Automated Text Categorization. *ACM Computing Surveys*, 34(1):1–47.

Yanir Seroussi, Ingrid Zukerman, and Fabian Bohnert. 2011. Authorship Attribution with Latent Dirichlet Allocation. In *Proceedings of the Fifteenth Conference on Computational Natural Language Learning*, pages 181–189.

Thamar Solorio, Sangita Pillay, Sindhu Raghavan, and Manuel Montes-y Gómez. 2011. Modality Specific Meta Features for Authorship Attribution in Web Forum Posts. In *The 5th International Joint Conference on Natural Language Processing*, pages 156–164.

Rui Sousa-Silva, Gustavo Laboreiro, Luís Sarmento, Tim Grant, Eugénio C. Oliveira, and Belinda Maia. 2011. 'twazn me!!! ;(' automatic authorship analysis of micro-blogging messages. In *Proceedings of the 16th International Conference on Natural Language Processing and Information Systems*, pages 161–168.

Efstathios Stamatatos. 2008. Author Identification: Using Text Sampling to Handle the Class Imbalance Problem. *Information Processing and Management*, 44(2):790–799.

Efstathios Stamatatos. 2009. A Survey of Modern Authorship Attribution Methods. *Journal of the Association for Information Science and Technology*, 60(3):538–556.

Efstathios Stamatatos. 2011. Plagiarism Detection Using Stopword N-Grams. *Journal of the American Society for Information Science and Technology*, 62(12):2512–2527.

Enhua Tan, Lei Guo, Songqing Chen, Xiaodong Zhang, and Yihong Zhao. 2013. UNIK: Unsupervised Social Network Spam Detection. In *Proceedings of the 22Nd ACM International Conference on Conference on Information & Knowledge Management*, pages 479–488.

Hans Van Halteren, R. Harald Baayen, Fiona Tweedie, Marco Haverkort, and Anneke Neijt. 2005. New Machine Learning Methods Demonstrate the Existence of a Human Stylome. *Journal of Quantitative Linguistics*, 12(1):65–77.

Gintarė Žalkauskaitė. 2012. *Idiolekto požymiai elektroniniuose laiškuose. [Idiolect signs in e-mails]*. Ph.D. thesis, Vilnius University, Lithuania. (in Lithuanian).

Ying Zhao and Justin Zobel. 2005. Effective and Scalable Authorship Attribution Using Function Words. In *Proceedings of the Second AIRS Asian Information Retrieval Symposium*, pages 174–189.

Rong Zheng, Jiexun Li, Hsinchun Chen, and Zan Huang. 2006. A framework for authorship identification of online messages: Writing-style features and classification techniques. *Journal of the American Society for Information Science and Technology*, 57(3):378–393.

Vytautas Zinkevičius. 2000. Lemuoklis – morfologinei analizei [Morphological analysis with Lemuoklis]. In *Darbai ir Dienos*, volume 24, pages 246–273. (In Lithuanian).

Looking hard: Eye tracking for detecting grammaticality of automatically compressed sentences

Sigrid Klerke
University of Copenhagen
Copenhagen, Denmark
skl@hum.ku.dk

Héctor Martínez Alonso
University of Copenhagen
Copenhagen, Denmark
alonso@hum.ku.dk

Anders Søgaard
University of Copenhagen
Copenhagen, Denmark
soegaard@hum.ku.dk

Abstract

Natural language processing (NLP) tools are often developed with the intention of easing human processing, a goal which is hard to measure. Eye movements in reading are known to reflect aspects of the cognitive processing of text (Rayner et al., 2013). We explore how eye movements reflect aspects of reading that are of relevance to NLP system evaluation and development. This becomes increasingly relevant as eye tracking is becoming available in consumer products. In this paper we present an analysis of the differences between reading automatic sentence compressions and manually simplified newswire using eye-tracking experiments and readers' evaluations. We show that both manual simplification and automatic sentence compression provide texts that are easier to process than standard newswire, and that the main source of difficulty in processing machine-compressed text is ungrammaticality. Especially the proportion of regressions to previously read text is found to be sensitive to the differences in human- and computer-induced complexity. This finding is relevant for evaluation of automatic summarization, simplification and translation systems designed with the intention of facilitating human reading.

1 Introduction

Intuitively, the readability of a text should reflect the effort that a reader must put into recognizing the meaning encoded in the text. As a concept, readability thus integrates both content and form.

Sentence-level readability assessment is desirable from a computational point of view because smaller operational units allow systems to take rich information into account with each decision. This computer-centric approach is in contrast to traditional human-centric readability metrics which are explicitly constructed for use at text level (cf. Bjornsson (1983) and Flesch (1948)) and are by their own definitions unsuitable for automatic application (cf. Benjamin (2012) for an evaluation of readability-formula usability).

The standard approach to assessing text readability in natural language processing (NLP) is to ask readers to judge the quality of the output in terms of comprehensibility, grammaticality and meaning preservation (cf. Siddharthan and Katsos (2012)). An alternative is to use existing text collections categorized by readability level for learning models of distinct categories of readability e.g. age or grade levels (Schwarm and Ostendorf, 2005; Vajjala and Meurers, 2014).

In this paper we seek to establish whether readers share an intuitive conceptualization of the readability of single sentences, and to what extent this conceptualization is reflected in their reading behavior. We research this by comparing subjective sentence-level readability judgments to recordings of readers' eye movements and by testing to what extent these measures co-vary across sentences of varying length and complexity. These analyses enable us to evaluate whether sentence-level simplification operations can be meaningfully and directly assessed using eye tracking, which would be of relevance to both manual and automated simplification efforts.

1.1 Automatic Simplification by Compression

Amancio et al. (2014) found that more than one fourth of the transformations observed in sentence pairs from Wikipedia and Single English Wikipedia were compressions. To obtain automatically simplified sentences we therefore train a sentence-compression model.

With inspiration from McDonald (2006), we train a sentence compression system on a corpus of parallel sentences of manually expert-simplified and original newswire text where all simplifications are compressions. The system is described in detail in section 2.

Sentence compression works by simply dropping parts of a sentence and outputting the shorter sentence with less information content and simpler syntax. This approach allows us to control a number of variables, and in particular, it guarantees that each expert simplification and each system output are true subsets of the original input, providing three highly comparable versions of each sentence. Further the system serves as a proof of concept that a relatively small amount of task-specific data can be sufficient for this task.

Sentence compression is, in addition, an important step in several downstream NLP tasks, including summarization (Knight and Marcu, 2000) and machine translation (Stymne et al., 2013).

Below, we present the automatic simplification setup, including the parallel data, features and model selection and details on how we select the data for the eye-tracking experiment. The following section details the eye movement recording and subjective evaluation setup. Section 4 presents our results followed by a discussion and our conclusions.

2 Automatic Simplification Setup

2.1 Training and Evaluation Corpus

For the sentence compression training and evaluation data we extracted a subset of ordinary and simplified newswire texts from the Danish DSim corpus (Klerke and Søgaard, 2012). In Figure 1 we give a schematic overview of how the data for our experiments was obtained.

For model development and selection we extracted all pairs of original and simplified sentences under the following criteria:

1. No sentence pair differs by more than 150 characters excluding punctuation.
2. The simplified sentence must be a strict subset of the original and contain a minimum of four tokens.
3. The original sentence must have at least one additional token compared to the simplified sentence and this difference must be non-punctuation and of minimum three characters' length.

This results in a corpus of 2,332 sentence pairs, close to 4% of the DSim corpus. Descriptive statistics of this corpus are shown in Table 1.

We followed the train-dev-test split of the DSim corpus forming a training set of 1,973 sentence pairs, a development set of 239 pairs, and a test set of 118 pairs.[1]

For our experiment with eye tracking and subjective evaluation we created a similar dataset, denoted "augmented compressions" in Figure 1, from sentence pairs displaying similar compressions and in addition exactly one lexical substitution. We augmented these pairs by simply changing the synonym back to the original word choice, resulting in a valid compression. We obtained an automatically compressed version of these sentences from the trained model[2]. This results in a corpus of sentence triples consisting of an **original**, an **expert** simplification and a **system** generated version. In some cases the system output was identical to either the original input or to the expert simplification. We therefore selected the evaluation data to include only sentence triples where all three versions were in fact different from one another resulting in 140 sentence triples, i.e. 420 individual stimuli. On average the system deleted 15 tokens per sentence while the experts average around 12 token deletions per sentence.

2.2 Compression Model and Features

The compression model is a conditional random field (CRF) model trained to make a sequence of categorical decisions, in each determining whether the current word should be left out of the compression output while taking into account the previous decision. We used CRF++ (Lafferty et al., 2001) trained with default parameter settings.

Below, we describe the features we implemented. The features focus on surface form, PoS-tags, dependencies and word frequency information. Our initial choice of features is based on the comparisons in Feng et al. (2010) and Falkenjack and Jönsson (2014), who both find that parsing

[1] The corpus was PoS-tagged and parsed using the Bohnet parser (Bohnet, 2010) trained on the Danish Dependency Treebank (Kromann, 2003) with Universal PoS-tags (Petrov et al., 2011).

[2] Note that this dataset did not contribute to training, tuning or choosing the model.

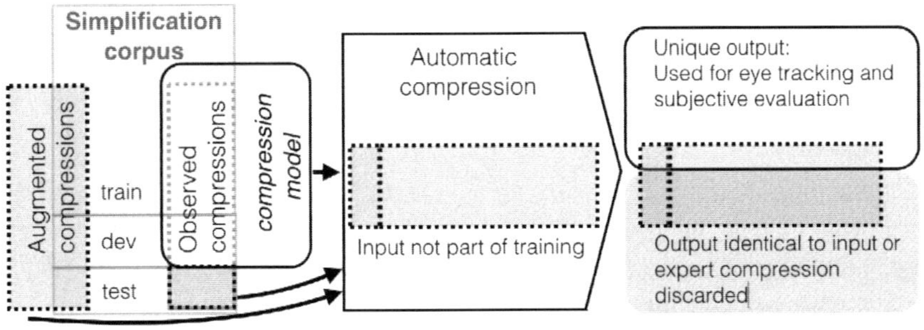

Figure 1: We extract observed compressions from the simplification corpus and train an automatic compression model. For the eye tracking and subjective evaluation we run the model on data that was not used for training. We only keep automatic compressions that are different from both the input and the expert compression. Augmented compressions are similar to compressions, but in addition they display one lexical substitution. We augment these by substituting the original synonym back in the expert simplification, thereby making it a compression.

	Original newswire		Expert compressions		Difference
	Characters	Tokens	Characters	Tokens	% deleted tokens
Total	288,226	46,088	133,715	21,303	53.8%
Mean	123.6	19.8	57.3	9.1	51.0%
Std	43.2	7.1	24.5	4.0	18.2%
Range	24 – 291	5 – 45	15 – 178	4 – 33	4.4% – 86.2%

Table 1: Statistics on the full specialized corpus, 2.332 sentence pairs in total. Except for the row "Total", statistics are per sentence. "Difference Tokens" report the average, standard deviation and range of the proportional change in number of tokens per sentence.

features are useful while the gain from adding features beyond shallow features and dependencies is limited. In the CRF++ feature template we specified each feature to include a window of up to +/- 2 tokens. In addition we included all pairwise combinations of features and the bigram feature option which adds the model's previous decision as a feature for the current token.

Shallow FORM, POS, CASE: This group consists of the lowercase word form, universal PoS-tag and the original case of the word.

Length W_LENGTH, S_LENGTH: This group registers the word length (characters) and sentence length (tokens).

Position PLACE, NEG_PLACE, REL_TENTH, THIRDS: This group records the token indices from both the beginning and end of the sentence, as well as each token's relative position measured in tenths and in thirds of the sentence length.

Morphology BIGRAM, TRIGRAM, FOURGRAM: The group records the final two, three and four characters of each token for all tokens of at least four, five and six characters' length, respectively.

Dependencies DEP_HEAD, DEP_LABEL: These two features capture the index of the head of the token and the dependency label of this dependency relation.

Vocabulary OOV, FREQ_3, FREQ_5, FREQ_10PS, FREQ_10EXP: This feature group records a range of frequency-counts[3]. The first feature records out-of-vocabulary words, the remaining features assign the token to one of 3, 5 or 10 bins according to it's frequency.[4] In the 10-bin cases "Pseudo tenths" (PS) assigns the token to one of 10 bins each representing an equal number of word forms[5], while "Exponential"

[3]We used the Danish reference corpus KorpusDK (Asmussen, 2001) concatenated with the training part of the DSim corpus

[4]3 bins: in 1K most frequent tokens (mft), 5K mft or outside 5K mft. 5 bins: in 100 mft, 500 mft, 1K mft, 5K mft or outside 5K mft.

[5]Three large bins were assigned word forms occurring 1, 2 and 3 times respectively while the remaining word forms were sorted in seven bins of equal number of word forms

splits the vocabulary into 10 bins containing a decreasing number of word forms as the contained word form frequencies rise exponentially.

2.3 Feature Selection

We tested five types of feature selection on the development set of the corpus, namely single best feature, single best feature group, add-one, and feature-wise and group-wise feature ablation. On the development set the single best feature was POS alone, the single best feature group was the Shallow group alone, while the add-one-approach returned the combination of the three features FORM, PLACE and FREQ_10PS, and single feature ablation returned all individual features minus FREQ_10EXP, OOV, REL_TENTHS, and group-wise ablation favored all groups minus the Vocabulary and Shallow groups. Of these, the last model, chosen with group-wise feature ablation, obtained the best F1-score on the test set. We use this model, which include the feature groups Length, Position, Morphology and Dependencies, to generate system output for the subsequent experiments.

3 Human Evaluation

The experiment described in the following section consisted of an eye tracking part and a subjective evaluation part. The eye tracking part of the experiment was carried out first and was followed by the subjective evaluation part, which was carried out by email invitation to an online survey.

We recruited 24 students aged 20 to 36 with Danish as first language, 6 male and 18 female. All had normal or corrected-to-normal vision. None of the participants had been diagnosed with dyslexia. A total of 20 participants completed the evaluation task. The experiment was a balanced and randomized Latin-square design. This design ensured that each participant saw only one version from each sentence-triple from one half of the dataset while being eye-tracked. Afterwards participants were asked to assign relative ranks between all three versions in each sentence-triple in the half of the dataset which they had not previously seen. In total, each version of each sentence was read by four participants in the eye-tracking experiment and ranked by 9-11 other participants.

In the subjective evaluation task participants had to produce a strict ordering by readability of all three versions of each sentence, with the rank '1' designating the most readable sentence. Presentation order was fully randomized.

3.1 Eye Tracking Design

The stimuli were presented on a screen with 1080 x 1920 resolution, and eye movements were recorded with a Tobii X120 binocular eye tracker at 60hz. We used the IV-T fixation filter with standard parameter settings (Olsen, 2012). The eye tracker was calibrated to each participant.

Each stimulus was presented on one screen with left, top and right margins of 300 px and 1-6 lines per slide[6]. The font vas Verdana, size 60px and line spacing was 0.8em[7].

Participants were given written instructions and three demo trials before they were left alone to complete the experiment. All participants completed 72 trials in three blocks, with the option to take a short break between blocks. Each trial consisted of a fixation screen visible for 1.5 seconds, followed by stimulus onset. The participants were instructed to try to notice if each sentence was comprehensible and to press a key to proceed to the following trial as soon as they had finished reading.

This setup only encourages but does not require participants to read for comprehension. Through data inspection and informal questions after the experiment, we ascertained that all participants were in fact reading and trying to decide which sentences were comprehensible.

3.2 Eye-movement Measures

Eye movements in reading can be divided into fixations and saccades. Saccades are rapid eye movements between fixations, and fixations are brief periods of relatively stationary eye positions where information can be obtained from an area covering the central 1-2 degrees of the visual field. Because reading is largely sequential, we can observe regressions, which denote episodes of re-reading, that is, fixations directed at text which is located earlier in the text than the furthest fixated word (Holmqvist et al., 2011).

In our analyses we include the measures of eye movements described below. All measures are calculated per single sentence reading and averaged

[6] After recording, sentences with seven lines were discarded due to data quality loss at the lower edge of the screen

[7] Following Blache (2012) who show that the viewing patterns with large text sizes are comparable to smaller text sizes and can be detected with this type of eye tracker.

over all four individual readings of each version of each sentence.

Fixation count (Fix), the average total number of fixations per sentence. This measure is expected to vary with sentence length, with more text requiring more fixations.

Total duration (ms), the average time spent reading the entire sentence. This measure is expected to increase with sentence length and with sentence complexity.

Fixations per word (Fix/w), the average number of fixations per word. This measure is sensitive to the number of saccades relative to the sentence length and is expected to reflect the reader's confusion as more fixations are needed to collect additional information. It should also be expected to be sensitive to high amounts of long words.

Reading time per word (ms/w), the average time spent per word. This measure increases with slower paced reading, regardless of the number of fixations. Reading time is considered a measure of processing cost and is influenced by both lexical and syntactic complexity.

Proportion regressions (%-regr), the proportion of fixations spent on parts of the text that were already passed once. This measure is typically 10-15% in full paragraphs, and is expected to increase with sentence complexity. (Rayner et al., 2006)

We include the sentence length as number of words (n-words) in our analyses for comparison because sentence length can influence the reading strategy (Holmqvist et al., 2011).

Longer sentences will typically have a more complex syntax than short sentences due to the number of entities that need to be integrated into both the syntactic and mental representation of the sentence. However, unfamiliar or even erroneous words and syntax can add processing difficulties as well, leaving the reader to guess parts of the intended message. We consider all these cases under the term *complexity* as they are all likely to appear in automatically processed text. This is a natural consequence of the fact that statistical language processing tools are typically not able to distinguish between extremely rare, but admissible text use and text that would be judged as invalid by a reader.

4 Results

We first analyze the correlation of the subjective evaluations followed by analyses that compare eye movement measures, subjective rankings and sentence version.

4.1 Ranking

First we test whether the subjective rankings are similar between subjects. We estimate agreement with Kendall's τ_B association statistic, which is a pairwise correlation coefficient appropriate for comparing rank orderings. The range of τ_B is $[-1, 1]$ where -1 indicates perfect disagreement, i.e. one ranking is the precise opposite order of the other, 1 indicates perfect agreement and 0 indicates no association, that is, the order of two elements in one ranking is equally likely to be the same and the opposite in the other ranking. The odds-ratio of a pair of elements being ranked concordantly is $(1+\tau_B)/(1-\tau_B)$. The metric τ_B compares pairs of rankings, and we therefore calculate the average over all pairs of participants' agreement on each ranking task. We use the one-tailed one-sample student's t-test to test whether the average agreement between all 91 unique pairs of annotators is significantly different from 0. If the rankings are awarded based on a shared understanding and perception of readability, we expect the average agreement to be positive.

We find that the average τ_B is $0.311 (p < 0.0001)$. This corresponds to a concordance odds-ratio of 1.90 which means that it is almost twice as likely that two annotators will agree than disagree on how to rank two versions of a sentence. Although this result is strongly significant, we note that it is a surprisingly low agreement given that the chance agreement is high for two people ranking three items.

The relatively low systematic agreement could arise either from annotators ranking only a few traits systematically (e.g. syntax errors rank low when present and otherwise ranking is random) or it could result from annotators following fully systematic but only slightly overlapping strategies for ranking (e.g. one ranks by number of long words while another ranks by sentence length which would tend to overlap).

4.2 Eye Tracking

Our second analysis tests how well the subjective ranking of sentences correspond to eye movements. We expect that more complex text will slow down readers, and we want to know whether the perceived readability reflects the variation we observe in eye-movement measures. Again using

	Difference in medians									
	System – Expert		System – Original		Original – Expert		Expert – Broken		Broken – Original	
avg. rank	**0.25**	*	**-0.47**	***	**-0.73**	***	**-1.51**	***	**0.78**	***
ms	-7.5 ms	–	**-190.0 ms**	***	**182.5 ms**	***	-2 ms	–	**-168 ms**	***
Fix	-0.8 fix	–	**-14.0 fix**	***	**13.3 fix**	***	-1.3 fix	–	**-11 fix**	***
ms/w	3.0 ms	–	-3.0 ms	–	**6 ms**	**	**-13 ms**	**	-3 ms	–
fix/w	0.1 fix	–	**0.4 fix**	***	**-0.27 fix**	**	-0.19 fix	–	**0.36 fix**	**
%-regr	**4 pp**	**	1 pp	–	**5 pp**	***	**11 pp**	***	2 pp	–
n-words	**-1 word**	*	**-2 words**	*	1 word	–	0 words	–	-5 words	–

Table 2: Influence of sentence variant and brokenness on perceived readability and eye movements. When comparing Expert, Original and System 109 sentences are included while for Broken only 27 sentences are compared. Stars denote significance levels: *: $p < .05$, **: $p < .01$, ***: $p < .001$

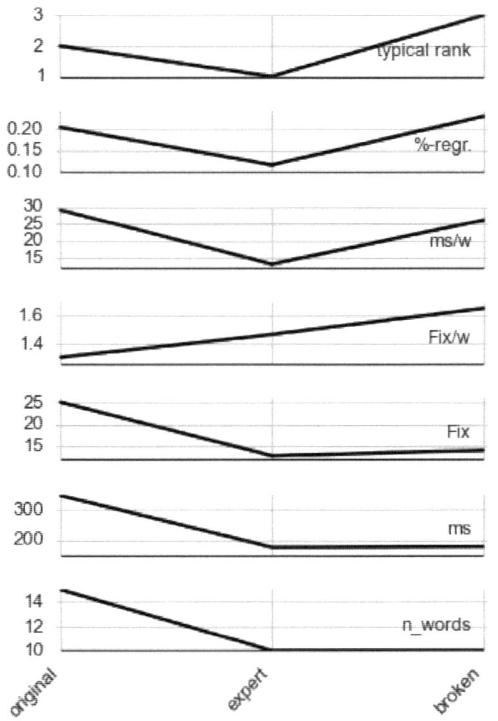

Figure 2: Interaction of sentence type and brokenness on perceived readability and eye movements. (N=27)

the τ_B association, we now assign ranks within each sentence-triple based on each eye-tracking measure and compare these pseudo-rankings to the *typical rank* assigned by the annotators.[8] We find that neither sentence length or any of the eye tracking measures are significantly associated with the *typical rank*. This means that we do not observe any correlation between sentences' perceived readability and the sentence length, the time it takes to read it or the speed or number of fixations or proportion of regressions recorded.

One potential reason why we do not observe the expected association between rank and eye movements can be that several of our eye tracking measures are expected to vary differently with sentence length and complexity, whereas readers' readability rankings are not necessarily varying consistently with any of these dimensions as participants are forced to conflate their experience into a one-dimensional evaluation.

In order to investigate whether the eye movements do in fact distinguish between length and complexity in sentences, we compare how readers read and rank long original sentences, short expert simplifications and short, syntactically broken system output.

The system output was post hoc categorized by syntactic acceptability by the main author and a colleague, resulting in a sample of 27 sentence triples with syntactically unacceptable system and a sample of 109 fully syntactically acceptable sentence triples. This allows us to compare the following four groups, Original, Expert, Unbroken System and Broken System.

We compare all eye-movement measures and ranking for each pair of groups[9] and test whether the measures differ significantly between groups using the Wilcoxon signed-rank test. We report the comparisons as the difference between the medians in Table 2. This is similar to an unnormalized Cohen's d effect size, but using the median as estimate of the central tendency rather than the mean. We observe that all group-wise comparisons receive significantly different average ranks, ranging from the Unbroken System scoring a quarter of a

[8]This approach introduces ties which are handled by the τ_B statistic but influences the result notably since each ranking task only includes 3 items.

[9]We use the larger sample whenever the group Broken System is not part of the comparison.

rank-position better than the Expert compressions to the Broken System output fairing 1.51 rank positions worse than the Expert group.

Note that Broken System is also ranked significantly below the Original newswire sentences, signaling that bad syntax has a stronger impact on perceived readability than length. Even though the sample of Broken System sentences is small, overall reading time and number of fixations distinguish the long Original sentences from both the short Expert simplifications and Broken System outputs, that are comparably short. We also observe that the number of fixations per word is consistently lower for the long Original sentences compared to the other, shorter groups. Importantly, we observe that two measures significantly distinguish Expert simplifications from syntactically Broken System output, namely reading time per word, which is slower for Broken System syntax and proportion of regressions which is much higher in Broken System sentences. In addition and as the only eye-tracking measure, proportion of regressions also distinguishes between Unbroken System output and Expert simplifications, indicating a 4 percentage point increase in proportion of regressions when reading Unbroken System output.

In Figure 2 we show how the medians of all the measures vary in the small subset that contain Broken System output, Expert compressions and Original newswire. The figure illustrates how the different aspects of reading behavior reflect length and syntax differently, with regressions most closely following the subjective ranking (top).

5 Discussion

In the following section we discuss weaknesses and implications of our results.

5.1 Learning and Scoring the Compression Model

It is important to note that the compression model inherently relies on the expert compressed data, which means it penalizes any deviation from the single gold compression. This behavior is suboptimal given that various good simplifications usually can be produced by deletion and that alternative good compressions are not necessarily overlapping with the gold compression. One example would be to pick either part of a split sentence which can be equally good but will have zero overlap and count as an error. Our results suggest that the framework is still viable to learn a useful model, which would need a post-processing syntax check to overcome the syntax errors arising in the deletion process.

We note that the model produces more aggressive deletions than the experts, sometimes producing sentences that sound more like headlines than the body of a text. It is surprising that this is the case, as it is typically considered easier to improve the readability slightly, but we speculate that the behavior could reflect that the parts of the training data with headline-like characteristics may provide a strong, learnable pattern. However, from an application perspective, it would be simple to exploit this in a stacked model setup, where models trained to exhibit different characteristics present a range of alternative simplifications to a higher-level model.

From inspections of the output we observe that the first clause tends to be kept. This may be domain-dependent or it may reflect that PoS-tags and parsing features are more reliable in the beginning of the sentence. This could be tested in the future by applying the model to text from a domain with different information structure.

5.2 Implications for System Development

We found that the very simple compression model presented in this paper was performing extensive simplifications, which is important in light of the fact that humans consider it harder to produce more aggressive simplifications. We trained our model on a relatively small, specialized compression corpus. The Simple English Wikipedia simplification corpus (SEW) (Coster and Kauchak, 2011), which has been used in a range of statistical text simplification systems (Coster and Kauchak, 2011; Zhu et al., 2010; Woodsend and Lapata, 2011), is far bigger, but also noisier. We found fewer than 50 sentence pairs fitting our compression criteria when exploring the possibility of generating a similar training set for English from the SEW. However, in future work, other, smaller simplification corpora could be adapted to the task, providing insight into the robustness of using compression for simplification.

5.3 Implications for Evaluation Methodology

In many natural language generation and manipulation setups, it is important that the system is able to recognize acceptable output, and it is typical of this type of setup that neither system-intrinsic scoring functions or as standard automatic evaluation procedures are reliably meeting this requirement. In such cases it is common to obtain expensive specialized human evaluations of the output. Our results are encouraging as they suggest that behavioral metrics like regressions and reading time that can be obtained from nave subjects simply reading system output may provide an affordable alternative.

5.4 Brokenness in NLP output

The experiments we have presented are targeting a problem specific to the field of computer manipulation of texts. In contrast to human-written text, language generation systems typically cannot fully guarantee that the text will be fluent and coherent in both syntax and semantics. Earlier research in readability has focused on how less-skilled readers, like children, dyslectic readers and second-language readers, interact with natural text, often in paragraphs or longer passages. It is important to determine to what extent the existing knowledge in these fields can be transferred to computational linguistics.

6 Conclusion

We have compared subjective evaluations and eye-movement data and shown that human simplifications and automatic sentence compressions of newswire produce variations in eye movements.

We found that the main source of difficulty in processing machine-compressed text is ungrammaticality. Our results further show that both the human simplifications and the grammatical automatic sentence compressions in our data are easier to process than the original newswire text.

Regressions and reading speed were found to be good candidates for robust, transferrable measures that, with increasing access to eye-tracking technology, are strong candidates for being directly incorporated into language technologies.

We have shown that these measures can capture significant differences in skilled readers' reading of single sentences across subjects and with ecologically valid stimuli. In future research we wish to explore the possibility of predicting relevant reading behavior for providing feedback to NLP systems like automatic text simplification and sentence compression.

References

Marcelo Adriano Amancio, UK Sheffield, and Lucia Specia. 2014. An analysis of crowdsourced text simplifications. In *Proceedings of the 3rd Workshop on Predicting and Improving Text Readability for Target Reader Populations (PITR)@ EACL*, pages 123–130.

Jørg Asmussen. 2001. Korpus 2000. *Korpuslingvistik (NyS30)*.

Rebekah George Benjamin. 2012. Reconstructing readability: Recent developments and recommendations in the analysis of text difficulty. *Educational Psychology Review*, 24(1):63–88.

Carl-Hugo Bjornsson. 1983. Readability of Newspapers in 11 Languages. *Reading Research Quarterly*, 18(4):480–497.

Philippe Blache, Stephane Rauzy. 2012. Robustness and processing difficulty models. a pilot study for eye-tracking data on the french treebank. In *24th International Conference on Computational Linguistics*, page 21.

Bernd Bohnet. 2010. Very high accuracy and fast dependency parsing is not a contradiction. In *Proceedings of the 23rd International Conference on Computational Linguistics*, pages 89–97. Association for Computational Linguistics.

William Coster and David Kauchak. 2011. Simple English Wikipedia: a new text simplification task. In *Proceedings of the 49th Annual Meeting of the Association for Computational Linguistics: Human Language Technologies: short papers-Volume 2*, volume 2, pages 665–669. Association for Computational Linguistics.

Johan Falkenjack and Arne Jönsson. 2014. Classifying easy-to-read texts without parsing. In *Proceedings of the 3rd Workshop on Predicting and Improving Text Readability for Target Reader Populations (PITR)@ EACL*, pages 114–122.

Lijun Feng, Martin Jansche, Matt Huenerfauth, and Noémie Elhadad. 2010. A comparison of features for automatic readability assessment. In *Proceedings of the 23rd International Conference on Computational Linguistics: Posters*, pages 276–284. Association for Computational Linguistics.

Rudolph Flesch. 1948. A new readability yardstick. *Journal of applied psychology*, 32(3):221.

Kenneth Holmqvist, Marcus Nyström, Richard Andersson, Richard Dewhurst, Halszka Jarodzka, and Joost Van de Weijer. 2011. Eye tracking: A comprehensive guide to methods and measures.

Sigrid Klerke and Anders Søgaard. 2012. DSim , a Danish Parallel Corpus for Text Simplification. In *Proceedings of Language Resources and Evaluation (LREC 2012)*, pages 4015–4018.

Kevin Knight and Daniel Marcu. 2000. Statistics-based summarization-step one: Sentence compression. In *AAAI/IAAI*, pages 703–710.

Matthias T Kromann. 2003. The Danish Dependency Treebank and the DTAG treebank tool. In *Proceedings of the Second Workshop on Treebanks and Linguistic Theories (TLT)*, page 217.

John Lafferty, Andrew McCallum, and Fernando CN Pereira. 2001. Conditional random fields: Probabilistic models for segmenting and labeling sequence data.

Ryan McDonald. 2006. Discriminative sentence compression with soft syntactic evidence. In *EACL*.

Anneli Olsen. 2012. The tobii i-vt fixation filter. *Tobii Technology*.

Slav Petrov, Dipanjan Das, and Ryan McDonald. 2011. A universal part-of-speech tagset. *Arxiv preprint ArXiv:1104.2086*.

Keith Rayner, Kathryn H Chace, Timothy J Slattery, and Jane Ashby. 2006. Eye movements as reflections of comprehension processes in reading. *Scientific Studies of Reading*, 10(3):241–255.

Keith Rayner, Alexander Pollatsek, and D Reisberg. 2013. Basic processes in reading. *The Oxford Handbook of Cognitive Psychology*, pages 442–461.

Sarah E Schwarm and Mari Ostendorf. 2005. Reading Level Assessment Using Support Vector Machines and Statistical Language Models. In *Proceedings of the 43rd Annual Meeting of the ACL*, pages 523–530.

Advaith Siddharthan and Napoleon Katsos. 2012. Offline sentence processing measures for testing readability with users. In *Proceedings of the First Workshop on Predicting and Improving Text Readability for target reader populations*, pages 17–24. Association for Computational Linguistics.

Sara Stymne, Jörg Tiedemann, Christian Hardmeier, and Joakim Nivre. 2013. Statistical machine translation with readability constraints. In *Proceedings of the 19th Nordic Conference on Computational Linguistics (NODALIDA'13)*, pages 375–386.

Sowmya Vajjala and Detmar Meurers. 2014. Exploring measures of readability for spoken language: Analyzing linguistic features of subtitles to identify age-specific tv programs. In *Proceedings of the 3rd Workshop on Predicting and Improving Text Readability for Target Reader Populations (PITR)@ EACL*, pages 21–29.

Kristian Woodsend and Mirella Lapata. 2011. WikiSimple: Automatic Simplification of Wikipedia Articles. In *Twenty-Fifth AAAI Conference on Artificial Intelligence*.

Zhemin Zhu, Delphine Bernhard, and I. Gurevych. 2010. A monolingual tree-based translation model for sentence simplification. In *Proceedings of The 23rd International Conference on Computational Linguistics*, pages 1353–1361. Association for Computational Linguistics.

Towards the Classification of the Finnish Internet Parsebank: Detecting Translations and Informality

Veronika Laippala[1 2] **Jenna Kanerva**[3] **Anna Missilä**[2]
Sampo Pyysalo[3] **Tapio Salakoski**[3] **Filip Ginter**[3]
[1] Turku Institute for Advanced Studies, University of Turku, Finland
[2] School of Languages and Translation Studies, University of Turku, Finland
[3] Department of Information Technology, University of Turku, Finland
first.last@utu.fi

Abstract

This paper presents the first results on detecting informality, machine and human translations in the Finnish Internet Parsebank, a project developing a large-scale, web-based corpus with full morphological and syntactic analyses. The paper aims at classifying the Parsebank according to these criteria, as well as studying the linguistic characteristics of the classes. The features used include both lexical and morpho-syntactic properties, such as syntactic n-grams. The results are practically applicable, with an AUC range of 85–85% for the human, $\sim 98\%$ for the machine translated texts and 73% for the informal texts. While word-based classification performs well for the in-domain experiments, delexicalized methods with morpho-syntactic features prove to be more tolerant to variation caused by genre or source language. In addition, the results show that the features used in the classification provide interesting pointers for further, more detailed studies on the linguistic characteristics of these texts.

1 Introduction

With its growing size and coverage, the Internet has become an attractive source of material for linguistic resources, used both for linguistics and natural language processing (NLP) applications (Baroni et al., 2009; Kilgarriff and Grefenstette, 2003). However, automatically collected, very large corpora covering all the text that can be found are very heterogeneous, which may complicate their usage. In linguistics, the origin of the corpus texts is of primary importance (Biber et al., 1998; Sinclair, 1996), and also in many NLP applications, such as automatic syntactic analysis, linguistic variation across different domains affects the results significantly (Laippala et al., 2014).

This paper presents the first results on the linguistic variation in the Finnish-language Internet by analyzing informality, machine translations and human translations in the Finnish Internet Parsebank[1], an on-going project aiming at a large-scale, web-based corpus of Finnish with full morphological and syntactic analyses. The current version consists of 3.2 billion tokens and 241 million sentences.

This article has two main objectives. The first aim is to develop classification methods in order to detect informality, machine translations and human translations from the Parsebank. This would facilitate the use of the Parsebank, as searches or applications could be targeted only at certain parts of the corpus. In the classification, the features used include syntactic n-grams, little subtrees of dependency syntax analyses developed for Finnish by Kanerva et al. (2014), originally produced for English by Goldberg and Orwant (2013).

Secondly, the study points research directions for the analysis of the linguistic characteristics of the text classes. The automatic classification based on the data-driven combination of lexical, syntactic and morphological features offers a new approach to the linguistic study of these texts and their characteristics, as traditional linguistic studies often concentrate on the analysis of a limited number of preselected features.

The study consists of three sets of classification experiments and their analyses. In the first, texts are classified according to the level of formality to standard and informal. In the second, the classification is done to human translated texts and texts originally written in Finnish, and in the last, to machine translated texts and texts originally written in Finnish.

[1] http://bionlp.utu.fi/finnish-internet-parsebank.html

Proceedings of the 20th Nordic Conference of Computational Linguistics (NODALIDA 2015)

2 Related Work

Regarding human translation detection, *translationese* is a term originally coined by linguists to refer to features typical of translated texts. Baker (1993) was the first to define potential *translation universals*: features that all translated texts hypothetically share.

The existence of translationese has also been tested by studies applying machine learning. Baroni and Bernardini (2006) use monolingual corpora to experiment with for instance lemmas and POS tags, providing evidence that an algorithm can perform better than humans in recognizing human translated texts. Other similar studies include Ilisei et al. (2010) presenting a language-independent system based on average sentence length or lexical richness, Popescu (2011) using solely character 5-grams (ignoring sentence boundaries) to detect English translations, and Avner, Ordan and Wintner (2014) concentrating on morphological properties in Hebrew.

Previous studies on classifying machine translated texts mostly rely on different combinations of lexical and grammatical features as well. Aharoni, Koppel, and Goldberg (2014) use a set of function words, POS tags and a mix of the two to classify texts, whereas Arase and Zhou (2013) concentrate on indicators based on sentence-internal coherence, also called the *phrase salad* phenomenon (Lopez, 2008).

Despite their relative infrequency, some previous work also concentrate on classifying informality. Unlike those concerning translation classification, these concentrate on lexical rather than morphological features. Lahiri, Mitra, and Lu (2011) explore the *Formality Score*, a frequency list based on the differences of word classes in a corpus. Mosquera and Moreda (2011) define the most relevant features of informality to be the frequencies of spelling mistakes, interjections, and emoticons. These same individual features have also been studied as signs of informality in many linguistic studies (Lehti and Laippala, 2014).

3 Data

3.1 Finnish Internet Parsebank and Syntactic N-grams

The current version of the Finnish Internet Parsebank consists of 3.2 billion tokens and 241 million sentences. It is produced by crawling the Finnish web with the Spiderling web crawler[2]. Being designed for collecting text corpora, it can be targeted to crawl only pages in a specific language. In addition, it can automatically remove boilerplate text, such as lists and menus from the output. The output is deduplicated at the web page level and fully morphologically and syntactically analyzed using the parsing pipeline by Haverinen et al˙ (2013).

Syntactic n-grams are little subtrees of dependency syntax analyses, originally produced for English by Goldberg and Orwant (2013) and recently for Finnish by Kanerva et al. (2014). Instead of the linear context used with flat n-grams, the context for syntactic n-grams is defined by the syntactic representation. Possible configurations include combinations from one to four arcs. In addition to the syntactic and lexical information, complete syntactic n-grams include the part-of-speech (POS) categories of the words together with their morphological features (see Figure 1). Some of these analyses and/or the words can be also be deleted in order to obtain the desired level of description granularity.

3.2 Translations

The source data for machine translation comes for most part from WaCky (Baroni et al., 2009). The corpora used were ukWaC for English, frWaC for French, and deWaC for German. These languages were chosen based on both their common usage and availability. A random sample was taken from each of the corpora and machine translated using Google Translate (2015). The resulting translation was then parsed using the parsing pipeline by Haverinen et al. (2013). The part of data marked "randomPB" in Table 1 is a random selection from the Parsebank, manually identified as machine translated.

The Finnish human translations are taken from the *Corpus of Translated Finnish* (CTF) (Mauranen, 2000). The 10-million-word CTF is categorised into different genres based on the classifications by publishers and reviewers. It can be divided into three different sub-corpora: firstly, a corpus of translated Finnish where English is the source language, secondly, a corpus of original Finnish, and thirdly, a substantially smaller corpus of translated Finnish with multiple source languages (for example Russian, French, and Ger-

[2] http://nlp.fi.muni.cz/trac/spiderling

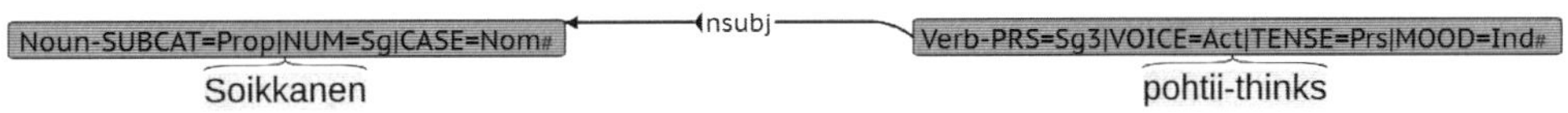

Figure 1: Syntactic 2-gram with word-level, POS-level and morphological analyses.

man). The question of data availability governed the text selection, and therefore only translations with English as the source language were chosen as training set.

In order to expand the available test data and ensure the performance of the algorithm, the biography section with English as the source language was kept as as an out-of-domain test corpus not used in the training.

3.3 Standard and Informal Data

While standard language is relatively simple to define as a variant following the recommendations and guidelines of a language, informality is less so.

In Finnish, the language variant defined as more free and less premeditated (Institute of Languages of Finland, 2014) is generally referred to as "everyday language / arkikieli". Despite its somewhat misleading name, the term is used for language variants that could also be called informal, regardless of the topic of the discussion or text (Grönros, 2006). Typical instances of informality are for instance playful and subjective expressions (Mäkinen, 1989).

In this paper, we adopt the term informality to refer to language that does not follow the general language guidelines and/or includes other structural or lexical instances untypical for standard language. As noted by Grönros (2006), informality is subjective with frequent borderline cases. In order to operationalize the concept, we rely both on human annotation and on data representing informal texts and apply two sources of data: the weak data set, a collection of large unannotated corpora that are expected to be biased towards standard or informal sentences based on their venue of publication, and second, the gold data set, a smaller corpus of sentences drawn at random from the Parsebank and manually annotated to identify sentence formality.

The annotation process is described in Section 3.4 and the unannotated data used in Table 2. The different parts of the standard language section of the unannotated data are derived from two sources: the news and the Europarl sections from

Standard language corpora	Words
News text	27 121
Europarl	18 946
Academic research papers	1 400 281
Biographies	337 642
Popular science	632 102
Total	2 416 092
Informal language corpora	Words
Popular blogs	21 791
Online discussion forums:	
- the Finnish yellow press	54 091
- the main Finnish newspaper	93 425
- a big Finnish online community	65 966
Total	236 083

Table 2: Informal and standard language corpora.

Turku Dependency Treebank (TDT) (Haverinen et al., 2013), and the academic research articles, biographies and popular science books from CTF (Mauranen, 2000). On the informal side, the blogs are from TDT, and the forum discussions from the main Finnish newspaper website from a private corpus collected by a research group from the School of Languages and Translation Studies from the University of Turku. The rest of the forum discussions are collected for the purposes of this study.

3.4 Formality Annotation

For the formality classification task, we annotated a random sample of sentences from the Finnish Parsebank. The manual annotation involved assigning each sentence into one of three categories: standard Finnish, informal Finnish, or not Finnish. Only the former two categories were considered in the experiments, with sentences identified as not being Finnish discarded after initial annotation.

The manual annotation effort started with simple initial guidelines (approximately one page) that were applied by two annotators working independently on the same sample of sentences. The two sets of annotations were then compared, differences resolved to generate merged consensus annotation, and the guidelines refined to identify the desired annotation in cases where disagree-

	Genre+Lang	Train	Devel	Test	Total
MT	DE	12 166	12 165	7228	31 559
	EN	17 664	17 663	14 511	49 838
	FR	23 662	23 662	19 117	66 441
	RandomPB			4468	4468
	TotalMT	53 492	53 490	40 856	147 842
MT OOD	DE	12 166	12 165		24 331
	EN	17 664	17 663		35 327
	FR			66 441	66 441
MT OOD2	DE			31 559	31 559
	EN	17 664	17 663		35 327
	FR	23 662	23 662		47 324
HT	AcadDE			66 774	66 774
	AcadEN	428 365	428 364	158 215	1 014 944
	AcadFR			57 373	57 373
	BioEN			151 517	151 517
	ChildEN	306 856	306 856	43 437	657 149
	DetEN	72 243	72 243	200 746	345 232
	EntEN			270 332	270 332
	FicEN	537 904	537 903	188 935	1 264 742
	PopEN	133 355	133 355	188 587	455 297
	TotalHT	1 478 723	1 478 721	1 407 628	4 365 072
HT OOD	BioEN			151 517	151 517
Orig	AcadFI	525 326	525 326	267 418	1 318 070
	BioFI			309 941	309 941
	ChildFI	256 768	256 767	94 590	608 125
	DetFI	31 374	31 374	176 251	238 999
	EntFI			235 885	235 885
	FicFI	551 318	551 318	105 244	1 207 880
	PopFI	193 554	193 554	203 143	590 251
	TotalFI	1 558 340	1 558 339	1 392 472	4 509 151
Orig OOD	BioFI			309 941	309 941
Orig-PB	WebFI	53 493	53 492	40 640	147 625
Total		**3 144 048**	**3 144 042**	**2 804 352**	**9 092 442**

Table 1: Translation detection statistics: number of words. (MT - machine translation, HT - human translation, Orig - original, Orig-PB - original from Parsebank, OOD - out of domain; DE - German, EN - English, FI - Finnish, FR - French; Acad - academic, Bio - biography, Child - children, Det - detective, Ent - fictional entertainment, Fic - fiction, Pop - popular non-fiction.)

ment was found. This double annotation protocol was repeated until an 89% intern-annotator agreement was reached on a batch of 100 sentences. After this initial development and refinement of annotation guidelines and annotator training, annotation proceeded independently to categorize a total of 3300 sentences.

After the primary annotation, the final training, development and test sets were prepared as follows. First, 218 sentences identified as *not Finnish* and 27 sentences that were duplicates of other sentences in the data were discarded. The remaining sentences were then down-sampled to 3000, which were split into a training set of 1500, a development set of 500, and a test set of 1000 sentences. The random split was stratified to roughly preserve the distribution of standard and informal sentences in each subset. Table 3 shows the final statistics of the annotated corpus.

	Train	Devel	Test	Total
Standard	957	321	639	1917
Informal	543	179	361	1083
Total	1500	500	1000	3000

Table 3: Formality annotation statistics: number of sentences

4 Experiments & Results

4.1 Experimental setup

We evaluate performance using two standard sets of metrics. First, we report classification precision, recall and their balanced harmonic mean, the F_1-score (*F-score* for short). As these metrics are sensitive to the distribution of positive and negative instances in the test data, we also report the area under the receiver operating characteristic curve (AUC), which corresponds to the probability that a randomly chosen negative and a randomly chosen positive example will be correctly ranked by the classifier. As AUC is invariant with respect to the positive-negative distribution, it is more readily applicable for comparing performance across datasets that have a different balance of examples of these classes.

In the sentence formality classification task, we consider the informal class positive and the standard class negative for the purposes of calculating precision, recall and F-score.[3] In the translation recognition task, we similarly consider the translation classes positive and the original Finnish class negative. In the informality detection, the classification is done at the sentence-level, where as the translations are classified in segments of five sentences.

In all three classification tasks, a bag-of-words (BOW) approach is used as a simple baseline method. Leaning purely on lexical items can however lead to a topic-wise classification which would decrease the performance when classifying texts with wide range of topics, such as Internet texts from the Finnish Parsebank. Therefore, we also run two delexicalized approaches giving linguistically interesting results on the morpho-syntactic characteristics of the corpora as well. First, we derive features from the morphology of the tokens, using combined POS and morphological feature uni-, bi- and trigrams. During the preliminary experiences, we noticed that the fine-grained morphology carries some features that signal very reliably the text class but do not carry any linguistically interesting information, such as morphological features indicating proper nouns, capitalization and whether the Finnish morphological analyzer recognized the token. As our aim is not only to classify the texts but also to analyze the linguistic characteristics of the resulting classes, these analyses are discarded from the morphology. In the second delexicalized approach, the feature set is expanded to include syntactic information giving the opportunity to recognize more complex sentence structures (see Figure 1).

The machine learning is carried out using a linear classifier trained with the stochastic gradient descent method.[4] We optimized the learning rate in preliminary experiments and set it constant throughout the rest of the study, since a per-experiment grid search is unlikely to result in any substantial gains. This allows us a very fast turnaround in the various runs, and the classifier is performance-wise roughly equal to linear SVMs on our data — which we verified in preliminary experiments as well.

4.2 Standard / Informality Classification

Table 4 presents the results of the informality classification task trained with different feature combinations on different data sets. All the methods are tested on the manually annotated gold standard.

For the system trained on the manually annotated gold data set, the best AUC, 73%, is produced by the simple BOW method, indicating that the vocabulary is the most distinguishing characteristic of informality, as already proposed by previous studies discussed in Sections 2 and 3.3. For the system trained on the more heterogeneous weak data set, the delexicalized methods are slightly better. This could suggest that the delexicalized methods are more robust and better adapted to variation in the test setting, and also proves that informal text does have morpho-syntactic characteristics as well. In addition, even if the performance of the systems trained on the weak data set is not excellent, its performance on the gold data set proves that the training of such a system without manual annotation is possible.

Although outperformed by the BOW method, the results of the classification based on morpho-

[3]The assignment of positive and negative label does not affect AUC.

[4]Implemented in the well-known *Vowpal Wabbit* package (Agarwal et al., 2011).

	Train	AUC	Pre	Rec	F-score
Bag-of-words	Weak	64.23	47.50	47.37	47.43
POS+feat	Weak	63.25	48.01	46.81	47.41
POS+feat+syntax	Weak	66.22	49.86	49.31	49.58
Bag-of-words	Gold	73.34	66.67	39.89	49.91
POS+feat	Gold	69.71	59.84	41.27	48.85
POS+feat+syntax	Gold	70.03	60.00	40.72	48.51

Table 4: Results for the detection of informal sentences. *POS+feat* refers to unigram, bigram and trigram sequences including the POS and other morphological tags of the tokens. *Syntax* refers to sequences of syntactic relations generated from the delexicalized syntactic n-grams.

logical and syntactic features are also reasonable and provide interesting information on the structural characteristics of the classes. Table 5 shows some of the most significant morphological + syntactic features of the informal text class with similar features grouped together. The tendency is clear with interjections and pronouns forming the majority of the ten most important features. In fact, this supports the findings by Mosquera et Moreda (2011).

Rank	Feature
1	Interj / Punct
2	Interj
5	Interj / ROOT
3	Pron+NUM_Sg_CASE_Nom
6	Pron+NUM_Pl+CASE_Nom
10	Pron+NUM_Sg+CASE_Nom / N+NUM_Sg+CASE_Gen

Table 5: Most significant features for the informal class grouped together. The rank means the significance rank of the feature in the classification.

4.3 Human Translated / Original Text Classification

The results of the human translation detection, shown in Table 6, support the existence of translationese: especially in the general training setting where the test set includes both domain and out-of-domain data, the best detection AUC is 87.19%. For the general test setting, the best results are obtained with the simple BOW method. However, when tested against an out-of-domain data set consisting of biographies, a genre not included in the training data set, the other methods perform clearly better, showing that a delexicalized method is more easily generalizable than the ones based on lexicon, and that the classification is also possible based on morphological and syntactic structures. Furthermore, these structural features are more interesting for the linguistic study of the characteristics of the classes than simple words.

Table 7 and Table 8 show some of the most significant features of human translated texts and texts originally written in Finnish, with similar features grouped together. Some of them reflect translation universals found in previous studies. In particular, the noun+verb combinations (ranks 2 and 14) in the translations, and the pronoun+verb combinations (rank 1) in the original Finnish support the previous results (Nevalainen, 2003; Laviosa-Braithwaite, 1995) on the frequency of pronouns on original texts on one hand, as well as on the lexical repetition on the other.

However, some of the results also contest previous studies. In the original Finnish data, many n-grams (ranks 5,7,8) seem to describe simple verb+argument fragments, which could easily reflect simplification, a typical feature of translationese studied by Blum-Kulka and Levenston (1983) and Laviosa (2002). Also nonfinite structures appear in both classes, even though according to a previous study by Puurtinen (2003), these would be typical of translated texts.

4.4 Machine Translated / Original Text Classification

The results of the machine translation detection are shown in Table 9. They reflect the effortlessness of the task: the results attain an $\sim 98\%$ AUC and a $\sim 91\%$ F-score for all data sets. For the out-of-domain tasks where the test sets are composed of translations from a language not included in the training set, the results are equally good, indicating that the source language does not have a significant effect. This has practical advantages, as machine translations can be detected without collecting training data from all possible languages.

	Train	Test	AUC	Pre	Rec	F-score
Bag-of-words	HT + Orig	HT + Orig	87.19	75.71	79.90	77.75
POS+feat	HT + Orig	HT+ Orig	84.98	75.28	74.17	74.72
POS+feat+syntax	HT + Orig	HT + Orig	86.26	75.17	77.76	76.57
Bag-of-words	HT + Orig	HT OOD + Orig OOD	81.80	61.20	58.82	59.99
POS+feat	HT + Orig	HT OOD + Orig OOD	86.05	60.99	72.84	66.39
POS+feat+syntax	HT + Orig	HT OOD + Orig OOD	85.00	59.16	73.15	65.42

Table 6: Results for the detection of human translations. *POS+feat* refers to unigram, bigram and trigram sequences including the POS and other morphological tags of the tokens. *Syntax* refers to sequences of syntactic relations generated from the delexicalized syntactic n-grams. The data sets are presented in Table 1.

Rank	N-gram
1	**C+SUBCAT_CC / Pron+SUBCAT_Dem+NUM_Pl+CASE_Ill**
	and / to-those
15	V+NUM_Sg+CASE_Nom+VOICE_Act+PCP_PrfPrc+CMP_Pos /...
	V+PRS_Sg3+VOICE_Act+TENSE_Prt+MOOD_Ind / **C+SUBCAT_CC**
	broken / took / and
2	**N+ / V+PRS_Sg3+VOICE_Act+TENSE_Prt+MOOD_Ind**
	/A / took
14	Punct **N+ / V+PRS_Sg3+VOICE_Act+TENSE_Prt+MOOD_Ind**
	/. / A / took
4	**Pron+SUBCAT_Rel+NUM_Pl+CASE_Nom /...**
	Pron+SUBCAT_Pers+NUM_Pl+CASE_Gen / Adv+POSS_Px3
	who / ours / together-with
6	N+NUM_Pl+CASE_Ins / N+NUM_Sg+CASE_Ela / **Pron+SUBCAT_Rel+NUM_Sg+CASE_Nom**
	with-fingers / from-town / which
5	Punct / **V+NUM_Sg+CASE_Ine+POSS_Px3+VOICE_Act+INF_Inf2 /...**
	V+NUM_Sg+CASE_Ine+VOICE_Act+INF_Inf3
	. / while-he-was-going / taking
7	N+NUM_Sg+CASE_Ade / **V+NUM_Sg+CASE_Abe+VOICE_Act+INF_Inf3 / N+NUM_Pl+CASE_Par**
	at-the-table / without-understanding / dogs

Table 7: Most significant features in the human translation class, followed by example lexicalizations. The features are POS n-grams with morphological features. The first column refers to the feature ranks in the classification, 1 being the most significant feature.

The best results for the general test setting are obtained with the syntactic n-grams, while the weakest ones are obtained with the BOW method. Although the BOW's AUC is comparable to other methods, the recall for the general setting is 81.58%, and 66.34% and 58.54% for the out-of-domains. This implies that the most significant features of the machine translations are not lexical and that the structural information included in the POS, morphological and syntactic analyses is needed, most importantly when generalizing to domains not included in the training data.

5 Conclusion

This paper proves that a reliable detection of informality, human and machine translations is realistic. As shown already by Aharoni et al. (2014), machine translations can be detected at an extremely high level of accuracy. In addition, our results indicate that the source language does not affect the results significantly. For human translations, the detection task is obviously more difficult. However, our results achieve a very applicable AUC of $\sim 86\%$, both for the general setting and the out-of-domain one, showing that genre variation has some but not a dramatic effect on the results. For the informality detection, the results are applicable, although they can still be improved. For this class in particular, more studies on genre variation is needed in order to improve the classification features and thereby results.

For the machine translation experiment in the general setting, the features composed of POS, morphological and syntactic information performed the best, while for the human translation and informality detection, the BOW reached better results. However, in out-of-domain settings, the BOW is clearly outperformed by the other

Rank	N-gram
1	**Pron+NUM_Sg+CASE_Nom / V+PRS_Sg1+VOICE_Act+TENSE_Prt+MOOD_Ind** *I / ran*
4	**V+CASE_Ine+VOICE_Pass+INF_Inf2 / /...** **V+PRS_Pe4+VOICE_Pass+TENSE_Prs+MOOD_Ind / A+NUM_Pl+CASE_Par+CMP_Pos** *if-it-is-needed / we-put / more-funny*
9	N+NUM_Pl+CASE_Nom / N+NUM_Sg+CASE_All / **V+NUM_Sg+CASE_Ill+VOICE_Act+INF_Inf3** *children / to-the-school / to-read*
12	A+NUM_Pl+CASE_Tra+CMP_Pos / **V+PRS_Sg1+VOICE_Act+MOOD_Pot /...** **V+NUM_Sg+CASE_Ins+VOICE_Act+INF_Inf2** *to-wise / might / resulting-from*
5	N+NUM_Pl+CASE_Nom / **V+PRS_Sg2+VOICE_Act+TENSE_Prt+MOOD_Ind** *children / you-said*
7	Pron+NUM_Sg+CASE_All / **V+PRS_Sg3+VOICE_Act+TENSE_Prt+MOOD_Ind / Punct** *for-him / he-said / .*
8	N+NUM_Pl+CASE_Par / **V+PRS_Pl3+VOICE_Act+TENSE_Prt+MOOD_Ind / N+NUM_Sg+CASE_Ine** *dogs / they-said / in-house*

Table 8: Most significant features in the original Finnish class, followed by example lexicalizations. The features are POS n-grams with morphological features.

	Train	Test	AUC	Pre	Rec	F-score
Bag-of-words	MT + Orig-PB	MT + Orig-PB	98.03	99.10	80.58	88.88
POS+feat			98.06	96.22	86.41	91.05
POS+feat+syntax			98.35	98.89	86.17	92.09
Bag-of-words	MT OOD + Orig-PB	MT OOD + Orig-PB	95.37	99.51	66.34	79.61
POS+feat			97.56	98.64	82.84	90.05
POS+feat+syntax			98.17	97.56	85.37	91.06
Bag-of-words	MT OOD2 + Orig-PB	MT OOD2 + Orig-PB	97.31	97.96	58.54	73.28
POS+feat			97.56	98.64	82.84	90.05
POS+feat+syntax			98.03	99.40	82.51	91.57

Table 9: Results for classifying machine translated text and text originally written in Finnish. *POS+feat* refers to unigram, bigram and trigram sequences including the POS and other morphological tags of the tokens. *Syntax* refers to sequences of syntactic relations generated from the delexicalized syntactic n-grams. The data sets used are described in Table 1.

approaches. This demonstrates that while word-based methods can be useful for well defined contexts, different levels of delexicalizations are more tolerant for linguistic variation caused by for instance differences in genre or the source language, making them further applicable for the Parsebank classification.

In addition, it is important to notice that even if they were not ranked first for all the tasks, the delexicalized methods reached good results. indicating that morpho-syntactic differences between the texts classes can be captured by automatic classification. From a linguistic perspective studying the characteristics of the text classes, this is very promising. Also our findings on the distinguishing features of the studied classes reflect this: by supporting some previous findings and contesting others, the delexicalized classification method provides material for linguistic studies. Even if a detailed analysis of all of the features is not possible in the scope of this article, the utility of the approach is demonstrated.

The article offers multiple possibilities for future studies. In particular, the most significant text class features pointed out by the classification offer several research directions. In addition, the method can be extended to the study of other lexical and morpho-syntactic characteristics of other genres. Naturally, an obvious next step would also be the classification of the entire Internet Parsebank.

Acknowledgments

This work has been supported by the Kone foundation and Emil Aaltonen foundation. We also thank CSC - IT Center for Science.

References

Alekh Agarwal, Olivier Chapelle, Miroslav Dudík, and John Langford. 2011. A reliable effective terascale linear learning system. *CoRR*, abs/1110.4198.

Roee Aharoni, Moshe. Koppel, and Yoav Goldberg. 2014. Automatic detection of machine translated text and translation quality estimation. In *Proceedings of the 52nd Annual Meeting of the Association for Computational Linguistics: Short Papers*, pages 289–295.

Yuki Arase and Ming Zhou. 2013. Machine translation detection from monolingual web-text. In *Proceedings of the 51st Annual Meeting of the Association for Computational Linguistics: Long Papers*, pages 1597–1607.

Alexander Ehud Avner, Noam Ordan, and Shuly Wintner. 2014. Identifying translationese at the word and sub-word level. In *Proceedings of the 49th Annual Meeting of the Association for Computational Linguistics: Human Language Technologies*.

Mona Baker. 1993. Corpus linguistics and translation studies: implications and applications. In Gill Francis and Elena Tognini-Bonelli, editors, *Text and Technology: In Honour of John Sinclair*, pages 233–252. John Benjamins.

Marco Baroni and Silvia Bernardini. 2006. A new approach to the study of translationese: Machine-learning the difference between original and translated text. *Literary and Linguistic Computing*, 21(3):259–274.

Marco Baroni, Silvia Bernardini, Adriano Ferraresi, and Eros Zanchetta. 2009. The WaCky wide web: a collection of very large linguistically processed web-crawled corpora. *Language Resources and Evaluation*, 43(3):209–226.

Douglas Biber, Susan Conrad, and Randi Reppen. 1998. *Corpus Linguistics: Investigating Language Structure and Use*. Cambridge University Press, Cambridge.

Soshana. Blum-Kulka and Edwards Levenston. 1983. Universals of lexical simplification. *Language Learning*, 28:399–415.

Yoav Goldberg and John Orwant. 2013. A dataset of syntactic-ngrams over time froma a very large corpus of english books. In *Second Joint Conference on Lexical and Computational Semantics (*SEM), Volume 1: Proceedings of the Main Conference and the Shared Task: Semantic Textual Similarity*, pages 241–247. Association for Computational Linguistics.

Google. 2015. Google Translate.

Eija-Riitta Grönros. 2006. Arkikielesta yleiskieleen (From everyday language to standard language). *Kielikello*, 4.

Katri Haverinen, Jenna Nyblom, Timo Viljanen, Veronika Laippala, Samuel Kohonen, Anna Missilä, Stina Ojala, Tapio Salakoski, and Filip Ginter. 2013. Building the essential resources for Finnish: the Turku Dependency Treebank. *Language Resources and Evaluation*, pages 1–39.

Iustina Ilisei, Diana Inkpen, Gloria Corpas Pastor, and Ruslan Mitkov. 2010. Identification of translationese: A machine learning approach. In Alexander F. Gelbukh, editor, *Computational Linguistics and Intelligent Text Processing*, volume 6008 of *Lecture Notes in Computer Science*, pages 503–511. Springer.

Institute of Languages of Finland. 2014. *Kielitoimiston sanakirja / Dictionary of the Institute for Languages of Finland*. Number 35 in Kotimaisten kielten keskuksen verkkojulkaisuja. Kotimaisten kielten keskus / Institute for Languages of Finland.

Jenna Kanerva, Juhani Luotolahti, Veronika Laippala, and Filip Ginter. 2014. Syntactic n-gram collection from a large-scale corpus of internet finnish. In *Proceedings of the Sixth International Conference Baltic HLT*.

Adam Kilgarriff and G. Grefenstette. 2003. Introduction to the special issue on web as corpus. *Computational Linguistics*, 29:333–347.

Shibamouli Lahiri, Prasenjit Mitra, and Xiaofei Lu. 2011. Informality judgment at sentence level and experiments with formality score. In Alexander Gelbukh, editor, *Computational Linguistics and Intelligent Text Processing*, volume 6609 of *Lecture Notes in Computer Science*, pages 446–457. Springer Berlin Heidelberg.

Veronika Laippala, Timo Viljanen, Antti Airola, Jenna Kanerva, Sanna Salanterä, Tapio Salakoski, and Filip Ginter. 2014. Statistical parsing of varieties of clinical Finnish. *Artificial Intelligence in Medicine*, 61(3):131–136.

Sara Laviosa-Braithwaite. 1995. Comparable corpora: towards a corpus linguistic methodology for the empirical study of translation. In M. Thelen and B. Lewandowska-Tomaszczyzk, editors, *Translation and Meaning Part 3. Proceedings of the Maastricht Session of the 2nd International Maastricht-Lodz Duo Colloquium on "Translation and Meaning"*., pages 153–163. Hoogeschool Maastricht, Maastricht.

Sara Laviosa. 2002. *Corpus-based Translation Studies: Theory, Findings, Applications*. Rodopi, Amsterdam, New York.

Lotta Lehti and Veronika Laippala. 2014. Style in french politicians' blogs: Degree of formality. *Language at Internet*, 11.

Adam Lopez. 2008. Statistical machine translation. *ACM Computing Surveys*, 40(3):1–49.

Kirsti Mäkinen. 1989. Sanojen tyyliväri. In *Nykysuomen sanavarat*, pages 200–212. WSOY.

Anna Mauranen. 2000. Strange strings in translated language: A study on corpora. In *Intercultural Faultlines. Research Models in Translation Studies 1*, pages 119–141. St. Jerome Publishing, Manchester.

Alejandro Mosquera and Paloma Moreda. 2011. The use of metrics for measuring informality levels in web 2.0 texts. In *Proceedings of the 8th Brazilian Symposium in Information and Human Language Technology*.

Sampo Nevalainen. 2003. Käännöskirjallisuuden puhekielisyyksistä - kaksinkertaista illuusiota? (on the informality of translated literature - a double illusion?). *Virittäjä*, (1):2–26.

Marius Popescu. 2011. Studying translationese on the character level. In *Proceedings of Recent Advances in Natural Language Processing*, pages 634–639.

Tiina Puurtinen. 2003. Genre-specific features of translationese? Linguistic differences between translated and non-translated Finnish children's literature. *Literary and Linguistic Computing*, 18(4):389–406.

John M. Sinclair. 1996. *Preliminary recommendations on Corpus Typology*. http://www.ilc.cnr.it/EAGLES/corpustyp/corpustyp.html.

Improving cross-domain dependency parsing with dependency-derived clusters

Jostein Lien **Erik Velldal** **Lilja Øvrelid**
Department of Informatics
University of Oslo, Norway
{josteili, erikve, liljao}@ifi.uio.no

Abstract

This paper describes a semi-supervised approach to improving statistical dependency parsing using dependency-based word clusters. After applying a baseline parser to unlabeled text, clusters are induced using K-means with word features based on the dependency structures. The parser is then re-trained using information about the clusters, yielding improved parsing accuracy on a range of different data sets, including WSJ and the English Web Treebank. We report improved results using both in-domain and out-of-domain data, and also include a comparison with using n-gram–based Brown clustering.

1 Introduction

Several recent studies have attempted to improve dependency parsers by including information about word clusters into their statistical parsing models. This is typically motivated by at least two concerns, both of which relate to the shortage of labeled training data. As argued by Koo et al. (2008), the lexicalized statistics important to disambiguation in parsing are often sparse, and modeling relationships on a more general level than the words themselves may therefore be helpful. The other motivation is domain adaptation, attempting to leverage a parsing model for use on data from a new domain. By including information about word clusters estimated from unlabeled in-domain data, one can hope to reduce the loss in performance expected from using a parser trained on an out-of-domain treebank.

While previous approaches have typically relied on the n-gram–based Brown clustering (Brown et al., 1992), this paper instead describes experiments using dependency-based word clusters formed using the generic clustering algorithm K-means. After applying a baseline dependency parser to unlabeled text, K-means is applied to form word clusters with features based on the dependency structures produced by the parser. The parser is then re-trained using features that record information about the dependency-derived clusters, thereby introducing an element of self-training. The re-trained parser obtains improved parsing accuracy on a range of different data sets, including the five web domains of the English Web Treebank (EWT) (Bies et al., 2012) and the Wall Street Journal (WSJ) portion of the Penn Treebank (PTB) (Marcus et al., 1993). We document improvements using both in-domain and out-of-domain data, and also when compared to using Brown clusters. All our parsing experiments use MaltParser (Nivre et al., 2007), a data-driven transition-based dependency parser.

The rest of the paper is structured as follows. Section 2 provides an overview of previous work. Section 3 details the data sets we use, including comments on the pre-processing. Section 4 then describes the experimental set-up, while the actual experiments and results are described in Section 5. A summary with thoughts about future directions is provided in Section 6.

2 Related work

The task of assigning word-to-word relations is at the core of dependency parsing, and statistics regarding relations between different words in the training data therefore provide vital information. These lexical statistics are, however, often sparse, and there exists a growing body of work which examines various strategies for generalizing over the distributions of words and using different kinds of lexical categories. This section reviews relevant previous work in this direction based on the use of word clusters.

Several prior studies on using word clusters for improving statistical parsers have relied on the Brown algorithm (Brown et al., 1992) to produce the clusters. The Brown algorithm produces a hierarchical clustering, with each node in the tree corresponding to a pairwise merge operation. The criterion for merging clusters in the Brown algorithm is to minimize the decrease in the likelihood of a given corpus according to a class-based bigram language model. As with any hierarchical clustering method, the result is actually a set of nested partitions, and in order to produce a final set of flat clusters, a cut must somehow be defined on the tree (i.e., selecting all nodes at a certain depth from the root and collapsing all nodes below them).

One of the reports on using Brown clusters is the study presented by Koo et al. (2008). In experiments with dependency parsing of PTB and the Prague Dependency Treebank (PDT) (Hajič, 1998), Koo et al. (2008) showed substantial performance gains for both English and Czech when incorporating cluster-based features in their discriminative learner (averaged perceptron). The English word clusters were derived from the BLLIP corpus (Charniak et al., 2000), which contains roughly 30 million words of Wall Street Journal text (and overlaps with the Penn Treebank). Czech word clusters were derived from the raw text section of the PDT 1.0, reported to contain about 39 million words of newswire text. In both cases the clustering is performed on data overlapping with what is used for parsing.

Koo et al. (2008) experiment with different feature configurations, extending the baseline feature sets of McDonald et al. (2005; Carreras (2007), but only generate cluster-based features for the top N=800 most frequent words in the corpus, and set the Brown algorithm to only recover at most 1,000 distinct clusters. Koo et al. (2008) reports relative error reductions of up to 14% for unlabeled parsing of PTB when adding cluster features to their baseline parser. Looking at learning curves, Koo et al. (2008) show that the use of word clusters can also be used to compensate for reduced training data for the parser.

Candito and Seddah (2010) apply Brown clusters in the context of statistical constituent parsing for French, experimenting with creating clusters of lemmas and PoS-tagged lemmas. The clusters themselves are created from the L'Est Républicain corpus (using up to 1,000 clusters), comprising 125 million words of news text, and cluster-based features are then added to the Berkeley PCFG parser with latent annotations (Petrov et al., 2006), before parsing the French Treebank (Abeillé et al., 2003). Candito and Seddah (2010) analyze the results with respect to word frequency and find improvements in performance for all strata; unseen or rare words, as well as medium- to high-frequency words. Adding PoS-information to the lemmas also appeared beneficial, though depending on the quality of the tagger.

Øvrelid and Skjærholt (2012) apply Brown clusters to improve dependency parsing of English web data using MaltParser. Augmenting a WSJ-trained parser with Brown clusters – using the cluster labels of Turian et al. (2010) computed for the Reuters corpus – is shown to improve parsing accuracy on a range of web texts, including the Twitter and user forum data from the web 2.0 data sets described by Foster et al. (2011) and web data from various sources in the OntoNotes corpus, release 4 (Weischedel et al., 2011). In the experiments of Øvrelid and Skjærholt (2012), cluster information was found to be more beneficial for parsing with automatically assigned PoS tags (using SVMTool), while less so when using gold PoS tags. Improvements were also more pronounced for the web data than on WSJ. Experimenting with different tree cut-offs, producing different numbers of clusters, Øvrelid and Skjærholt (2012) found that using a smaller number of large and general clusters (100–320) worked better than using a higher number of smaller and more fine-grained clusters (experimenting with up to 3200 clusters).

As an alternative to the above approaches using n-gram-based Brown clusters, the current paper documents experiments with using syntactically informed clusters instead, generated with a generic clustering algorithm. One previous study following a related line of investigation is that of Sagae and Gordon (2009) who also used parsed data for creating syntactically informed clusters. The clustering is there performed by applying the general method of (average-link) hierarchical agglomerative clustering to the 5,000 most frequent words of the BLLIP WSJ corpus, containing approximately 30 million words of WSJ news articles, parsed with the Charniak (2000) parser. The features used for the clustering encode phrase-structure tree paths that include direction information and non-terminal node labels, but does not include lexical information or part-of-speech tags. The clusters are then added as features in a data-driven transition-based dependency parser which is again used to identify predicate-argument dependencies extracted from the HPSG Treebank developed by Miyao et al. (2004) comprising the standard PTB WSJ sections. The pipeline described by Sagae and Tsujii (2008) thus include several layers of cross-framework interactions. Cutting the cluster hierarchy to include 600 clusters was shown to given the highest F-score, significantly improving the accuracy of the predicate-argument dependency parser.

The goal of Sagae and Gordon (2009) is to improve the accuracy of a fast dependency parser by using a corpus which has previously been automatically annotated using a more accurate but slower phrase-structure parser. In our experiments we seek to improve a baseline dependency parser by using clusters formed directly on the basis of the annotations of the baseline parser itself, without the complexity of involving a second parser. Using the method of K-means we will define a flat partition directly, without the need to cut the tree formed by a hierarchical method. While Sagae and Gordon (2009) focus on cross-framework leveraging, all testing is for in-domain models only, like for Koo et al. (2008), whereas the current paper will also investigate the benefit of dependency-based word clusters for porting a parser to new domains and text-types. The following section presents the various data sets we use, before moving on to describe the experimental set-up and the results.

3 Data sets

We experiment with using several different data sets, both for forming the word clusters and for evaluating the re-trained cluster-informed parser. We describe the data sets as well as the relevant pre-processing steps below.

The shared task[1] on parsing English web data hosted by the First Workshop on Syntactic Analysis of Non-Canonical Language (SANCL 2012) provided both unlabeled and labeled data for the five different domains from the English Web Treebank (EWT): weblogs, emails, question-answers, newsgroups, and reviews (Petrov and McDonald, 2012). In addition to the web texts, the SANCL data also contains the WSJ portion of the OntoNotes corpus, release 4.0 (Weischedel et al., 2011). (The OntoNotes version of WSJ differs slightly from the original PTB in terms of tokenization and noun-phrases analysis in certain places.) For the shared task, the data for weblogs and emails were used for development testing, while answers, newsgroups, and reviews were reserved for held-out testing. We will be following that same structure here.

The SANCL data comprises both labeled and unlabeled data. The labeled web data, corresponding to the EWT,[2] is what we will be using for our parser evaluations in addition to WSJ sections 22 (dev.) and 23 (held-out). The unlabeled SANCL data will be used for clustering, in addition to the newswire collection of the Reuters Corpus Volume I (RCV1) (Lewis et al., 2004). All the unlabeled data sets are summarized in Table 1. Note that the SANCL data is provided pre-segmented, tokenized and converted to Stanford dependencies in the CoNLL06/07 data format. For Reuters we segmented and tokenized the data using NLTK (Bird et al., 2009).

Various other pre-processing steps are applied to the unlabeled data prior to clustering. First, PoS-tagging is performed using SVMTool (Giménez and Màrquez, 2004) (using version 1.3.1 with the pre-trained WSJ model and the following options: '`-S LRL -T 0`'). Note that we are clustering lemmas rather than word forms, and lemmatization is performed using the NLTK WordNet lemmatizer (Bird et al., 2009). Finally, a baseline configuration of MaltParser is applied using the parse model of Foster et al. (2011) and Øvrelid and Skjærholt (2012) – more information about the parser and the feature set is provided in Section 4.2.

In Section 5.4 we also compare results to Øvrelid and Skjærholt (2012) for using Brown clusters rather than K-means with dependency features. For this comparison we use some additional data

[1] https://sites.google.com/site/sancl2012/home/shared-task

[2] Despite the separation into development and test domain, the SANCL data still defines development and test splits for the labeled data in all five domains, but we will simply merge all the labeled data for each domain.

	Reuters	Weblogs	Emails	Answers	Newsgroups	Reviews
Sentences	12,515,901	524,834	1,194,172	27,274	1,000,000	1,965,350
Tokens	217,635,636	10,356,138	17,046,119	424,292	18,424,049	29,288,947

Table 1: The number of sentences and tokens in the unlabeled corpora used for clustering.

	WSJ 02-21	WSJ 22	WSJ 23	Weblogs	Emails	Answers	Newsgr.	Reviews
Sentences	30,060	1,336	1,640	4,060	4,900	6,976	4,782	7,627
Tokens	731,678	32,092	39,590	88,762	57,807	108,006	86098	111,182

Table 2: The number of sentences and tokens in the labeled corpora used for parsing.

from the OntoNotes corpus: general English web data (Eng.: 71,500 tokens) and a larger set of sentences originally selected to improve sense coverage in the corpus (Sel.: 279,000 tokens).

4 Experimental set-up

In this section we present the set-up of the experimental process. We start by describing the set-up for the clustering before turning to how the parser is trained and applied. The actual experiments and results are the provided in Section 5.

4.1 K-means word clustering with dependency features

We experiment with forming word clusters of lemmas in several different data sets: Reuters and the unlabeled SANCL data for five different web domains. The web data is clustered per-domain as well as all together. To run clustering on a given corpus, we first extract the 50,000 most frequent lemmas, only considering verbs, nouns and adjectives.[3] The next step – after the initial pre-processing with the SVMTool PoS tagger and MaltParser – is to record features for the various lemma occurrences across the corpus.

The features we use for the K-means clustering record information about the target lemma, its head, its leftmost / rightmost siblings, and its leftmost / rightmost dependents. The *siblings* of a target are defined as the tokens having the same head as the target. The *dependents* of a target are all the tokens having the target as the head. For both these notions, the leftmost or rightmost token corresponds to the one furthest to the left or right in the sentence, respectively. The clustering features record the following information for each lemma token:

- PoS
- Dependency label
- PoS of head
- Dependency label of head
- Lemma of head
- PoS leftmost/rightmost sibling
- Dependency label of leftmost/rightmost sibling
- Lemma of leftmost/rightmost sibling
- PoS leftmost/rightmost dependent
- Dependency label of leftmost/rightmost dependent
- Lemma of leftmost/rightmost dependent

The actual clustering is performed using the K-means implementation of the Python-based toolkit *scikit-learn* (Pedregosa et al., 2011), using its *mini-batch* version of the algorithm – an alternative online implementation optimized for large samples (Sculley, 2010). We perform clustering for K (i.e., the pre-defined number of clusters) set to 10, 50 and 100 (using higher values for K failed due to memory constraints).

4.2 Parser set-up

As said, our experiments our based on MaltParser (Nivre et al., 2007) (v. 1.7.2), a system for data-driven dependency parsing which is based on a deterministic parsing strategy in combination with treebank-induced classifiers for predicting parse transitions. It supports a rich feature representation of the parse history and can easily be extended to take additional features into account. We choose to use MaltParser primarily due to its easily extendable feature model which facilitates experimentation with additional features during parsing. As our baseline parser, we use the parse model described by Foster et al. (2011) and Øvrelid and

[3] More specifically, we only consider lemmas with a PoS tag from one of the sets {NN, NNS, NNP, NNPS}, {VB, VBD, VBG, VBN, VBP, VBZ} or {JJ, JJR, JJZ}.

Feature set	Feature templates
Baseline	S_0p, S_1p, S_2p, S_3p, L_0p, L_1p, L_2p, I_0p, $S_{0l}p$, $S_{0r}p$, $S_{1r}p$, $S_{0l}d$, $S_{1r}d$, S_0w, S_1w, S_2w, L_0w, L_1w, $S_{0l}w$, $S_{1r}w$, S_0pS_1p, S_0wL_0w, S_0pS_0w, S_1pS_1w, L_0pL_0w, $S_{1r}dS_{0l}d$, $S_{1r}pS_{1l}p$, $S_0pS_1pL_0p$, $S_0pS_1pS_2p$, $S_0pL_0pL_1p$, $L_0pL_1pL_2p$, $L_1pL_2pL_3p$, $S_0pL_0pI_0p$, $S_1pS_{1l}dS_{1r}d$
PoS simple	+ S_0l, S_1l, S_2l, S_3l, L_0l, L_1l, L_2l, I_0l, $S_{0l}l$, $S_{0r}l$, $S_{1r}l$
Form simple	+ S_0l, S_1l, S_2l, L_0l, L_1l, $S_{0l}l$, $S_{1r}l$
Form all	+ S_0l, S_1l, S_2l, L_0l, L_1l, $S_{0l}l$, $S_{1r}l$, S_0lL_0l, S_0pS_0l, S_1pS_1l, L_0pL_0l,

Table 3: Feature models for the baseline and the re-trained parser, where p = PoS-tag, w = word form, d = dependency label in the graph constructed so far (if any), and l = cluster label. MaltParser's stacklazy algorithm operates over three data structures: a stack (S) of partially processed tokens, a list (I) of nodes that have been on the stack, and a "lookahead" list (L) of nodes that have not been on the stack. We refer to the top of the stack using S_0 and subsequent nodes using S_1, S_2, etc., and the leftmost/rightmost dependent of S_0 with S_{0l}/S_{0r}.

Skjærholt (2012). It employs the stacklazy algorithm (Nivre, 2009), along with the LIBLINEAR package (Fan et al., 2008) for inducing parse transition SVM classifiers.

4.2.1 Parser features

Table 3 describes the baseline feature set, along with three additional feature sets based on the models described in Øvrelid and Skjærholt (2012) and that in various ways include information about cluster labels: *PoS simple*, *Form simple* and *Form all*. These augmented feature sets are constructed by copying the full baseline feature set (*all*) or only the features that pertain to a single token (*simple*) and involve either the PoS-tag or the word form respectively. (Note that a *PoS all* feature set was also tried but proved to be too large for practical experimentation.) Preliminary experimentation on the development sets showed that the *Form all* feature model consistently outperformed the other two cluster-based feature set, so we will only be reporting results for this feature set in the paper, in addition to the baseline.

We evaluate the parser outputs in terms of Labeled Attachment Score (LAS) – computed using the evaluation script[4] of the CoNLL-X shared task on multi-lingual dependency parsing – and compare them using Dan Bikel's Randomized Parsing Evaluation Comparator with $p \leq \alpha = 0.05$ considered statistically significant.

	PoS in training	
	Gold	Predicted
WSJ 22	81.54	**84.88**
WSJ 23	81.88	**84.79**

Table 4: The effect on LAS for training on gold vs. predicted PoS tags, when testing on predicted PoS tags.

4.2.2 Gold vs. predicted PoS tags

In preliminary experiments we assessed the effect of using gold standard versus automatically assigned part-of-speech-tags tags when training the parser, in both cases testing on automatically tagged text. (These experiments used the baseline MaltParser without cluster information and using only default parameter settings, including $C = 0.1$ for the SVM.) We trained two versions of the parser on WSJ sections 02–21 (from OntoNotes/SANCL) using (1) the gold PoS tags provided in the treebank and (2) replacing these with tags automatically predicted by SVMTool. We then applied the parsers to WSJ 22 and 23, for both parsers using SVMTool tags during testing. The results are shown in Table 4.2.2 and reveal that there is a clear advantage to training on predicted tags (all differences are statistically significant at $\alpha = 0.05$). For all parsing results reported elsewhere in this paper automatically predicted PoS tags are used in both training and testing.

5 Experiments and results

The development results reported below are obtained by; parsing unlabeled data using the baseline feature set trained on WSJ 02-21; computing lemma clusters from dependency features; retraining the parser on WSJ 02-21 with the augmented *Form all* feature set; and finally tuning the number of clusters (K) and the C parameter[5] of

[4] http://ilk.uvt.nl/conll/software.html

[5] The penalty factor C governs the trade-off between training error and margin. It can have a large impact on the resulting model and, in our case, parser performance. In our empirical tuning on the dev. set we first tested values in the interval $[2^{-7}, 2^{-6} \ldots 2^6, 2^7]$ and after identifying the appropriate neighborhood further fine-tuned the value using in-

	WSJ 22	Weblogs	Emails
Baseline	86.72	80.00	72.85
Reuters clusters	**86.79**	**80.34**	73.11
SANCL clusters, per-domain	n/a	80.20	**73.35**
SANCL clusters, all	n/a	80.26	73.27

Table 5: LAS results for the development data – WSJ 22 and the two SANCL test domains – comparing the baseline parser to parsers re-trained using word clusters from various sources of unlabeled data: the Reuters corpus, the unlabeled SANCL data for the respective domains, or clustering all the unlabeled SANCL data from all five domains together. (All data sets are PoS-tagged automatically using SVMTool.)

	Answers	Newsgroups	Reviews
Baseline	73.10	76.13	75.01
Reuters	**73.58**	**76.97**	75.43
SANCL per-domain	73.39	76.87	75.51
SANCL all	73.52	76.94	**75.53**

Table 6: Held-out LAS evaluation on the three SANCL test domains using the baseline parser compared to parsers re-trained with information about word clusters generated from various sources: the Reuters corpus, the unlabeled SANCL data for the respective test domains, or clustering all the unlabeled SANCL data from all five domains together. (All data sets are PoS-tagged automatically using SVMTool.)

the parser's SVM classifier to find the configuration with the highest LAS. The best configuration found for the development data is then applied to the held-out data.

5.1 Reuters clusters

Instantiating the clustering features described in Section 4.1 for the top 50k lemmas of Reuters resulted in a total of 1,673,744 feature types. Specifying a feature frequency cut-off of $>= 10$ brought this down to a more manageable set of 339,473 features. After running K-means for 10, 50 and 100 clusters and tuning the SVM penalty parameter of the parser, the best configuration for all the development data sets was found to be $K = 50$ and $C = 0.0625$. The results can be seen in Table 5, including the scores of the initial baseline parser.[6] Looking at the baseline scores, the results clearly demonstrates the difficulty in applying parsers to text outside the domain of the training data, combined with the added noise we can expect to find in web data text types compared to newswire text: There is a clear drop in performance for the web data compared to WSJ 22. While we see that the cluster-informed parser improves over the baseline across all data sets, we also see that the improvements are larger for the web data than for WSJ 22: For Weblogs and Emails the relative reductions of error rate (RER) are 1.7% and 0.96% respectively, compared to RER = 0.53% for WSJ. When applying these models to the held-out data, the gains of the cluster-informed models are even larger, as shown in Table 6, with error reductions of up to 3.52%. When testing on WSJ 23 (not included in the table), the baseline obtained LAS = 86.88, compared to 87.16 for the cluster model, amounting to RER = 2.13%. The differences in held-out performance where detected as statistically significant across all the data sets.

Note that one complication with respect to assessing the effect of K-means clustering is the fact that the algorithm is sensitive to the initial random seeding of the cluster centers. Using the mini-batch implementation in scikit-learn alleviates this problem to some degree in that it will compute a handful of different seedings and choose the one with the lowest inertia (i.e., within-cluster sum-of-squares) before starting the clustering. Still, repeated runs with the same parameters and the same input can generate different outputs. In order to quantify the extent of this effect we run K-means for $K = 100$ clusters 10 times on the Reuters data and parsed WSJ 22 with the re-trained parser (fixing the SVM parameter C to 0.0625). This resulted in mean and median LAS scores of 86.78 and 86.81 respectively, with a variance of 0.009 and a standard deviation of 0.095.

5.2 Per-domain SANCL clusters

While we already see improvements in parsing accuracy for the web data, one could expect to see even greater gains when using clusters generated from texts in the same domain that is to be parsed.

crements of 0.015: The best performance was typically found for $C = 0.0625$.

[6]For the baseline model, the best C value varied slightly across the different development sets, with $C = 0.0625$ for WSJ 22, 0.0775 for Weblogs, and 0.0925 for Emails. In subsequent held-out testing for the baseline we use the model trained with $C = 0.0625$ for the WSJ data and 0.0775 for the web data.

We therefore tried running K-means on the unlabeled SANCL data from respective test domains[7] (while still training the parser on WSJ like above). This means that, for example, the 4,060 sentences in the labeled Weblogs data is parsed using clusters generated for the 50K most frequent lemmas of the 524,834 sentences in the unlabeled Weblogs data. After empirically tuning the parameters, the highest LAS scores on the development sets were observed for the configuration of $K = 100$ and $C = 0.0625$. (As for all clustering results reported here we use the *Form all* feature set of Table 3.)

Development results are provided in Table 5 and held-out results in Table 6, see the row *SANCL per-domain*. Although the re-trained parser with per-domain clusters again significantly outperforms the baseline across all data sets, there is no clear advantage to using per-domain clusters compared to the Reuters cluster of the news domain. The parser using per-domain web clusters improves on the parser using Reuters clusters for two out of five domains: Emails (development) and Reviews (held-out). Interestingly, these are also the two domains with the largest unlabeled data sets, as shown in Table 1. At the same time, we see that the Reuters corpus is vastly larger than any of the unlabeled SANCL corpora. For our next round of experiments we therefore wanted to see whether we could compensate for this difference in size by clustering all the unlabeled SANCL data combined, while still hoping to see positive effects of using data closer to the test domain.

5.3 All-in-one SANCL clusters

The motivation of the experiments in this section is to see whether using word clusters generated from all the five unlabeled SANCL sections together yields better parsing performance than using clusters from each domain individually. Using a feature cut-off of ≥ 3, a total of 375,793 feature types are extracted for clustering the 50K most frequent noun/verb/adjective lemmas in the concatenated SANCL data. Using 100 clusters generated by K-means and setting $C = 0.0625$ for the SVM classifier in MaltParser, the results are shown as *SANCL all* in Tables 5–6.

We see that for all but one data set, the use of all-in-one SANCL clusters yield better results than per-domain clusters. The exception is the Emails (development) data, where the per-domain clusters still yields the highest LAS overall. At the same time, we see that the initial Reuters clusters still provide the highest score for three of the data sets, while the all-in-one SANCL model has the highest overall score for the (held-out) Reviews section. It is also worth noting that at 75 million tokens, the concatenated unlabeled SANCL data is still a third of the size of Reuters. When testing for statistical significance on the held-out data, none of the differences between the Reuters and SANCL runs are detected as being significant.

In sum, it is not possible to conclude anything about which data set provides the optimal source for generating the dependency-based word clusters for the parser, although it is clear that whichever data set is used, the re-trained parser with cluster features improves significantly on the baseline parser. For the final round of experiments, we investigate the use of the dependency-based clusters compared to n-gram Brown clusters as used in most previous studies.

5.4 Comparison to using Brown clusters

In this section, we report the results of parsing the English web data of the OntoNotes corpus as described in Section 3, in addition to the OntoNotes version of WSJ section 23, mirroring the data sets used by Øvrelid and Skjærholt (2012). The purpose is to compare the results obtained using our dependency-based clusters and the Brown clusters used by Øvrelid and Skjærholt (2012) and several previous studies. As to isolate the effect of the clustering approach as best as possible, we here use the same version of MaltParser as used by Øvrelid and Skjærholt (2012) (i.e., v.1.4.1). We otherwise apply the model configuration that was found to give the best results for the development experiments in Table 5, i.e., $K = 100$ and $C = 0.0625$, and apply models based on both the Reuters clusters and the all-in-one SANCL clusters.

The LAS results for the different models are compared in Table 7. It is important to note that while the scores for the dependency-based clusters represent strict held-out results, the results for Øvrelid and Skjærholt (2012) are to be regarded as development results: The scores of Øvrelid and Skjærholt (2012) are maximums after tuning the model parameters directly on the given data. The

[7] The frequency cut-off on the dependency features for the clustering was set to ≥ 2 for these runs. Note also that the vocabulary extracted for the unlabeled Answers data only comprises 22,227 lemmas, due to the smaller size of this data set.

	WSJ 23	Eng	Sel
Baseline, Øvrelid (2012)	86.24	76.99	74.84
Baseline	86.67	78.45	76.02
Brown, Øvrelid (2012)	86.67	78.30	75.82
Reuters	**86.98**	78.71	76.23
SANCL all	86.90	**78.79**	**76.30**

Table 7: Comparing LAS with Øvrelid and Skjærholt (2012), using data sets with automatic part-of-speech tags generated by SVMTool.

parameters include the number of clusters and the choice of feature set for the parser, corresponding to the various options listed in Table 3. In spite of this, we find that all the models using dependency-based clusters yield quite a bit higher LAS than the Brown-based models of Øvrelid and Skjærholt (2012). At the same time, even our baseline models perform on par with or better than the Brown models, so it is likely that other factors not accounted for are also affecting the results reported in Øvrelid and Skjærholt (2012). Note that the table include baseline results for both our own set-up and the scores provided in Øvrelid and Skjærholt (2012). Despite our efforts to replicate the set-up described by Øvrelid and Skjærholt (2012) we were not able to reproduce the results. The scores shown for our own baseline in Table 7 were produced using our tuned C parameters fpr the SVMs (though using the same version of the parser and tagger), but even when using the default parameters like reported by Øvrelid and Skjærholt (2012) our scores diverged.

6 Summary and future work

This paper has described a semi-supervised approach for improving a data-driven dependency parser using dependency-based clusters. The parser is first applied to a large corpus of unlabeled text, providing the input to K-means clustering of lemmas using features extracted from the dependency structures. The parser is the re-trained with new features that include information about the word clusters, thereby introducing an element of self-training. The cluster-informed parser is shown to improve significantly over the baseline on both in- and out-of-domain tests, including a wide range of web texts. For held-out tests on the web data the use of clusters yields error reductions of up to 3.52% relative to the baseline. The results of using our dependency-based clusters also compare favorably to previous studies using the n-gram based Brown clusters.

There are several directions we wish to pursue in follow-up work. The experiments in this paper were based on the feature set described by Øvrelid and Skjærholt (2012). Further work will give priority to the design and experimentation with additional cluster-based features in the parser, preferably informed by an analysis of the parser errors. The clustering described above comprise a fairly large vocabulary of 50,000 lemmas. In future experiments we would like to gauge the trade-off between the vocabulary size N and the number of clusters K: Decreasing N would allow us to specify a higher K. Moreover, when inspecting the the word clusters many of them can be seen to be fairly specific to distinct parts-of-speech – unsurprisingly, given the feature templates described in Section 4.1. In further experiments we therefore plan on performing the clustering separately for lemmas of different parts-of-speech. This will also be beneficial in terms of scalability: Computational considerations otherwise enforce limitations on vocabulary size, the number of clusters, and the size of the feature space, but running multiple and separate K-means clusterings for different PoS classes means we can increase the number of total clusters used and the lexical coverage of the clusters.

References

Anne Abeillé, Lionel Clément, and François Toussenel, 2003. *Treebanks: Building and Using Parsed Corpora*, chapter Building a Treebank for French. Kluwer, Dordrecht.

Ann Bies, Justin Mott, Colin Warner, and Seth Kulick. 2012. English Web Treebank LDC2012T13.

Steven Bird, Edward Loper, and Ewan Klein. 2009. *Natural Language Processing with Python*. O'Reilly Media Inc.

Peter F. Brown, Peter V. deSouza, Robert L. Mercer, Vincent J. Della Pietra, and Jenifer C. Lai. 1992. Class-based n-gram models of natural language. *Computational Linguistics*, 18(4):467–479, December.

Marie Candito and Djame Seddah. 2010. Parsing word clusters. In *Proceedings of the NAACL HLT 2010 First Workshop on Statistical Parsing of Morphologically-Rich Languages*, pages 76–84, Los Angeles, CA.

Xavier Carreras. 2007. Experiments with a higher-order projective dependency parser. In *Proceedings of the 2007 Joint Conference on Empirical Methods in Natural Language Processing and Computational Natural Language Learning*, pages 957–961, Prague, Czech Republic.

Eugene Charniak, Don Blaheta, Niyu Ge, Keith Hall, John Hale, and Mark Johnson. 2000. Brown laboratory for linguistic information processing (BLLIP) 1987–89 WSJ corpus release 1 LDC2000T43.

Eugene Charniak. 2000. A maximum-entropy-inspired parser. In *Proceedings of the 1st Meeting of the North American Chapter of the Association for Computational Linguistics*, pages 132–139, Seattle, WA.

Rong-En Fan, Kai-Wei Chang, Cho-Jui Hsieh, Xiang-Rui Wang, and Chih-Jen Lin. 2008. LIBLINEAR: A library for large linear classification. *Journal of Machine Learning Research*, (9).

Jennifer Foster, Özlem Çetinoğlu, Joachim Wagner, Joseph Le Roux, Stephen Hogan, Joakim Nivre, Deirdre Hogan, and Josef van Genabith. 2011. #hardtoparse: POS tagging and parsing the twitterverse. In *Proceedings of the AAAI Workshop on Analysing Microtext*, pages 20–25, San Francisco, CA.

Jesús Giménez and Lluís Màrquez. 2004. SVMTool: A general POS tagger generator based on Support Vector Machines. In *Proceedings of the 4th International Conference on Language Resources and Evaluation*, Lisbon, Portugal.

Jan Hajič. 1998. Building a syntactically annotated corpus: The Prague Dependency Treebank. In Eva Hajičová, editor, *Issues of Valency and Meaning. Studies in Honor of Jarmila Panevová*, pages 12–19. Prague Karolinum, Charles University Press.

Terry Koo, Xavier Carreras, and Michael Collins. 2008. Simple semi-supervised dependency parsing. In *Proceedings of the 46th Annual Meeting of the Association for Computational Linguistics: Human Language Technologies*, pages 595–603, Columbus, OH.

David D. Lewis, Yiming Yang, Tony G. Rose, and Fan Li. 2004. RCV1: A new benchmark collection for text categorization research. *Journal of Machine Learning Research*, 5:361–397.

Mitchell P. Marcus, Beatrice Santorini, and Mary Ann Marcinkiewicz. 1993. Building a large annotated corpus of English. The Penn Treebank. *Computational Linguistics*, 19(2):313–330.

Ryan McDonald, Koby Crammer, and Fernando Pereira. 2005. Online large-margin training of dependency parsers. In *Proceedings of the 43rd Annual Meeting of the Association for Computational Linguistics*, pages 91–98, Ann Arbor, MI.

Yusuke Miyao, Takashi Ninomiya, and Jun'ichi Tsujii. 2004. Corpus-oriented grammar development for acquiring a Head-driven Phrase Structure Grammar from the Penn Treebank. In *Proceedings of the 1st International Joint Conference on Natural Language Processing*, pages 684–693, Hainan Island, China.

Joakim Nivre, Johan Hall, Jens Nilsson, Gülsen Eryigit, Sandra Kübler, Marinov Svetoslav, Erwin Marsi, and Atanas Chanev. 2007. MaltParser: A language-independent system for data-driven dependency parsing. *Natural Language Engineering*, 13(2):95–135.

Joakim Nivre. 2009. Non-projective dependency parsing in expected linear time. In *Proceedings of the 47th Meeting of the Association for Computational Linguistics*, pages 351–359, Suntec, Singapore.

Lilja Øvrelid and Arne Skjærholt. 2012. Lexical categories for improved parsing of web data. In *Proceedings of the 24th International Conference on Computational Linguistics (COLING)*, pages 903–912, Bombay, India.

Fabian Pedregosa, Gaël Varoquaux, Alexandre Gramfort, Vincent Michel, Bertrand Thirion, Olivier Grisel, Mathieu Blondel, Peter Prettenhofer, Ron Weiss, Vincent Dubourg, Jake Vanderplas, Alexandre Passos, David Cournapeau, Matthieu Brucher, Matthieu Perrot, and Édouard Duchesnay. 2011. Scikit-learn: Machine learning in Python. *Journal of Machine Learning Research*, 12:2825–2830.

Slav Petrov and Ryan McDonald. 2012. Overview of the 2012 shared task on parsing the web. In *Notes of the First Workshop on Syntactic Analysis of Non-Canonical Language (SANCL)*.

Slav Petrov, Leon Barrett, Romain Thibaux, and Dan Klein. 2006. Learning accurate, compact, and interpretable tree annotation. In *Proceedings of the 21st International Conference on Computational Linguistics and 44th Annual Meeting of the Association for Computational Linguistics*, pages 433–440, Sydney, Australia, July.

Kenji Sagae and Andrew S. Gordon. 2009. Clustering words by syntactic similarity improves dependency parsing of predicate-argument structures. In *Proceedings of the 11th International Conference on Parsing Technologies (IWPT)*, pages 192–201, Paris, France.

Kenji Sagae and Jun'ichi Tsujii. 2008. Shift-reduce dependency DAG parsing. In *Proceedings of the 22nd International Conference on Computational Linguistics*, pages 753–760, Manchester.

David Sculley. 2010. Web-scale K-means clustering. In *Proceedings of the 19th International Conference on World Wide Web*, pages 1177–1178, Raleigh, NC.

Joseph Turian, Lev Ratinov, and Yoshua Bengio. 2010. Word representations: a simple and general method for semi-supervised learning. In *Proceedings of the 48th Meeting of the Association for Computational Linguistics*, pages 384–394, Uppsala, Sweden.

Ralph Weischedel, Martha Palmer, Mitchell Marcus, Eduard Hovy, Sameer Pradhan, Lance Ramshaw, Nianwen Xue, Ann Taylor, Jeff Kaufman, Michelle Franchini, Mohammed El-Bachouti, Robert Belvin, and Ann Houston. 2011. OntoNotes release 4.0 LDC2011T03.

An Optimal Quadratic Approach to Monolingual Paraphrase Alignment

Mihai Lintean
Department of Computer Science
The University of Memphis
Memphis, TN 38138, USA
`linteanm@yahoo.com`

Vasile Rus
Department of Computer Science
The University of Memphis
Memphis, TN 38138, USA
`vrus@memphis.edu`

Abstract

We model the problem of monolingual textual alignment as a Quadratic Assignment Problem (QAP) which simultaneously maximizes the global lexico-semantic and syntactic similarities of two sentence-level texts. Because QAP is an NP-complete problem, we propose a branch-and-bound approach to efficiently find an optimal solution. When compared with other methods and studies, our results are competitive.

1 Introduction

Textual alignment between two sentences involves the identification of words and phrases considered to be semantically equivalent or very close in meaning (within the context of the respective sentences). Monolingual alignment is particularly useful for the task of text-to-text semantic similarity (Agirre et al., 2012; Rus et al., 2013). Figure 1 shows an example of human generated alignments between two sentences from the corpus used by Thadani et al. (2012), which is a modified corpus of human-aligned paraphrases initially described in Cohn et al. (2008).

While monolingual text alignment has been tackled as a task of its own only recently (MacCartney et al., 2008; Thadani and McKeown, 2011; Yao et al., 2013; Sultan et al., 2014), text alignment has been explored intensely in the area of machine translation (Och and Ney, 2003; Brunning, 2010). Brunning (2010) distinguishes among three levels of alignment in machine translation: document alignment, sentence alignment, and word/phrase level alignment. We focus here on word-level alignment. Furthermore, we focus on monolingual word alignment in the context of sentence-to-sentence similarity tasks such as textual entailment and paraphrase identification.

We focus on word-level (as opposed to phrase-level) alignment for a number of reasons. First, the vast majority of gold alignments in the two datasets we use (95-96%) are word-level alignments (the rest are phrase-level). Similarly, Yao et al. (2013) report that word-level alignments constitute more than 95% of the alignments in recent human-annotated corpora. A second reason is the fact that our formulation of the monolingual alignment task based on the Quadratic Assignment Problem (QAP) (Burkard et al., 1998; Lawler, 1963; Koopmans and Beckmann, 1957) fits well with word-level alignment. Third, the key ingredients in our solution (the word-to-word semantic similarity measures and dependency relations) apply directly to words.

The role of word-to-word semantic similarity measures and contextual information for monolingual alignment has been explored in the past. However, the jury is still out there with respect to how to best combine these types of information for monolingual alignment as one of the most recent work in this area has illustrated (Sultan et al., 2014). Sultan et al. (2014) showed that use of local contextul information in combination with hand-crafted dependency type equivalences yields better results than methods that exploit local context, e.g. Yao et al. (2013). Indeed, our approach combines in unique ways word-to-word semantic similarity measures with contextual information in the form of dependency-relations among words and with a combinatorial optimization formulation based on the QAP problem. As dependencies can capture longer-distance relationships between words in a sentence, we can say that our method uses more than just local context for aligning texts. Furthermore, because the QAP formulation provides a global optimal solution, our method is indeed accounting for the full sentential context.

Indeed, our QAP formulation simultaneously accounts for word-level similarities and similari-

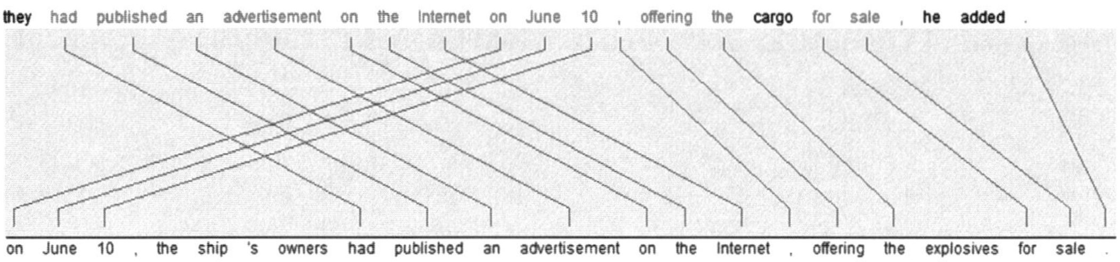

Figure 1: Example of Monolingual Text Alignment (instance #28 of the Edinburg corpus)

ties between corresponding syntactic/grammatical relations in a globally optimal manner. In contrast, Chambers et al. (2007) method for sentence level monolingual alignment finds a local maximum, which only in certain, lucky circumstances may also be a global maximum. Optimization methods have been proposed for phrase-level monolingual alignment (MacCartney et al., 2008; Thadani and McKeown, 2011; Thadani et al., 2012) in the context of a paraphrase task that rely on integer linear programming. Our optimization method is based on a different paradigm, the QAP formulation, and we rely on word-to-word semantic similarity measures, some of which are totally unsupervised such as Latent Semantic Analysis, and syntactic relation identity as opposed to edit distances. Thadani et al. (2011; 2012) used string similarity and WordNet for computing semantic relatedness.

We evaluated the proposed method on two datasets. The first one is the SEMILAR corpus (Rus et al., 2013), a subset of 701 randomly selected pairs from the Microsoft Research Paraphrase Corpus (MSRP) (Dolan et al., 2004). The pairs were manually annotated with tokens and phrase alignments. The second dataset is the evaluation corpus used by Thadani et al. (2012), called the Edinburg corpus, a modified corpus of human-aligned paraphrases, initially described in Cohn et al. (2008).

2 Related Work

The Quadratic Assignment Problem (QAP) is a classical combinatorial optimization problem (Burkard et al., 1998; Lawler, 1963; Koopmans and Beckmann, 1957). QAP has been originally formulated to minimize the overall cost of economic activities. QAP is an NP-hard problem (Sahni and Gonzalez, 1976).

We adapted the QAP formulation to our monolingual sentence-level alignment problem. In our case, we want to find a mapping between words in one sentence to words in another sentence that maximizes the similarity between two texts in terms of word-level similarity and simultaneously accounting for the relations between the matched words. That is, we prefer matchings between words in two texts T_1 and T_2 that not only lead to best word-level similarities but also the dependencies among words in T_1 and the corresponding matched words in T_2 must be optimally accounted for. We use word-to-word similarity measures for quantify the degree to which two words semantically match each other. We experimented with WordNet word-to-word similarity metrics (Pedersen et al., 2004) and the algebraically-derived Latent Semantic Analysis vectorial representation. To extract dependency relations we employed the Stanford CoreNLP Library.

Efforts to optimize the lexico-semantic, i.e. word-level, similarity between texts have been reported. Chan and Ng (2008) proposed a machine translation evaluation metric based on the optimal algorithm for bipartite graph matching also known as the assignment problem (Kuhn, 1955; Munkres, 1957). The assignment problem ignores interdependencies between words in a text although they could be accounted for indirectly, as Chan and Ng did. However, the indirect account of interdependencies among words in a text does not lead to an optimal solution that simultaneously maximizes overall word-level similariy while accounting for their contextual relations as encoded by, for instance, dependency information. QAP has been applied to the problem of word alignment by Lacoste-Julien and colleagues (2006), though their study is applied on pairs of bilingual sentences (i.e. French and English) and it does not consider syntactic dependencies between words in a sentence.

As already mentioned, QAP is an NP-hard problem. Efficient solutions work in general up to problem sizes of 25 using dynamic programming or branch-and-bound methods. In our case, we propose a branch-and-bound method which guarantees the finding of optimal solutions for short texts, i.e. typical sentences as those found in the SEMILAR and Edinburg corpora, our target datasets.

3 Alignment Approaches

We present in this section the details of the proposed optimal solution to the task of textual alignment in the context of semantic similarity of two sentences based on the QAP formulation. We start by describing two simpler solutions for monolingual text alignment: a greedy approach and an optimal solution based on the assignment problem for which a polynomial algorithm exists – the Kuhn-Munkres algorithm (Kuhn, 1955; Munkres, 1957). We evaluated and compared these simpler alignment methods to the proposed QAP solution. In our experiments, we followed a train-test methodology in which we first learnt the parameters of the various approaches on the training part of the data sets and then used the trained approaches to evaluate the QAP method on the test portion of the data.

3.1 Greedy Word-to-Word Alignment (GRD)

In the greedy approach to monolingual alignment, words from one sentence (usually the shorter sentence) are greedily matched, one by one, starting from the beginning of the sentence, with the most similar word from the other sentence. In case of duplicates, because we require that words must be part of at most one pair the order of the duplicate words in the two sentences becomes important such that the first occurrence in one sentence matches with the first occurrence in the other sentence and so on. Otherwise, the order in which the matching words appear in the two sentences does not matter. While simple and fast, the obvious drawback of the greedy method is that it can mistakenly match words if there are two or more ways to pair them, simply because of the order in which they were processed. The next method tries to solve this problem by searching for an alignment that leads to a global maximum similarity score across all pairs of aligned words.

3.2 Optimal Word-to-Word Alignment via Assignment Problem (w-OPT)

The job assignment problem or sailor assignment problem or just the assignment problem is one of the fundamental combinatorial optimization problems and consists of finding a maximum weight matching in a weighted bipartite graph. Given a complete bipartite graph, $G = (S, T, E)$, with n sailor vertices (S), n ships vertices (T), and each edge $e_{s \in S, t \in T} \in E$ has a non-negative weight $w(s,t)$ indicating how qualified a sailor is for a certain job, the task is to find a matching M from S to T with maximum weight. In case of different numbers of sailors or ships, dummy vertices could be used.

The assignment problem can be thus formulated as finding a permutation π for which $S_{w-OPT} = \sum_{i=1}^{n} w(s_i, t_\pi(i))$ is maximum. Such an assignment is called optimum assignment. An algorithm, the Kuhn-Munkres method (Kuhn, 1955), has been proposed that can find a solution to in polynomial time.

In our case, we model the semantic similarity problem as finding the optimum assignment between words in one text, T_1, and words in another text, T_2, where the fitness between words belonging in opposite texts can be measured by any word-to-word semantic similarity function. That is, we are after a permutation π for which $S_{w-OPT} = \sum_{i=1}^{n} \Theta_{sim}(v_i, w_{\pi(i)})$ is maximum where we note Θ_{sim} to be any word-to-word similarity measure, and v and w are words from the texts T_1 and T_2, respectively.

The assignment problem only focuses on optimally matching words in one sentence S to words in the other sentence T based only on how the words in S match the words in T. Interdependencies among words in S or among words in T are not taken into account. A solution that simultaneously accounts for such inter-dependencies, thus capturing the context of each word in their corresponding sentences, is presented next.

3.3 Optimal Sentence Alignment via Quadratic Assignment (QAP)

QAP has two well-known, historically important, formulations: the Koopmans-Beckmann (1957) formulation, and the more general Lawler (1963) formulation. We adapted the Koopmans-Beckmann (1957) formulation as it more clearly fits our task.

The goal is to find the optimum placement function π that maximizes the objective function $QAP(F, D, B)$ defined below where F and D describe syntactic dependencies between words in one sentence (S) and the other (T), respectively, while B captures the word-to-word similarity between words across the two sentences, all of them being symmetric, non-negative matrices. It should be noted that in the original formulation the objective function was about minimizing an economic cost while in our formulation we maximize the semantic similarity between two sentences. We further extend the objective function QAP by adding relative weighs to both terms in the above formulation resulting in the formulation below:

$$\max QAP_{(F,D,B)} = \alpha \sum_{i=1}^{n} \sum_{j=1}^{n} f_{i,j} d_{\pi(i)\pi(j)} + \\ +(1-\alpha) \sum_{i=1}^{n} b_{i,\pi(i)}$$

The $f_{i,j}$ term quantifies the syntactic relation between words i and j in text T_1 which are mapped to words $\pi(i)$ and $\pi(j)$ in text T_2, respectively. The distance $d_{\pi(i)\pi(j)}$ quantifies the syntactic relation between words π_i and π_j. For words i and j that have a direct dependency relation, $f_{i,j}$ is set to 1 and 0 in case there is no direct dependency between the two words. Similarly, the distance $d_{\pi(i)\pi(j)}$ between words $\pi(i)$ and $\pi(j)$ is set to 1 in case there is a direct dependency relation among them and 0 otherwise. We also experimented with a variant in which we enforced that the dependency between words i and j and the dependency between the corresponding words in the other text, $\pi(i)$ and $\pi(j)$, be of same type. That is, we prefer matchings between words in two texts T_1 and T_2 that not only lead to direct dependencies between words in T_1 and direct dependencies between corresponding matched words in T_2 but those dependencies must be of the same type. We obtained best results with this latter version which we used to generate all results in this paper.

The α parameter can be used to bias the search, to look for solutions that give more weight to matching dependencies (represented in the first term of the objective function) than to word similarities (represented in the second term), or vice-versa. When $\alpha = 0.5$, equal importance is given to both alignment criteria.

Solution Space

A brute force solution to the QAP problem, which would generate all possible mappings from words in a sentence to words in the other sentence, i.e. all permutations, is infeasible as the solution space is too big. When considering all possible pairings of words between sentence A, of size n, and sentence B of size m, where $n < m$, and we pose no limitations on the type of pairings that can be made, there are $m!/(m-n)!$ possible solutions. It should be noted that exact proposed solutions to the QAP problem can only handle instances up to $n = 25$ (Christofides and Benavent, 1989) or in special cases up to $n = 30$ (Anstreicher, 2003).

In the case of sentences of average size n=m=20 words, there are $2.4*10^{18}$ possible pairings, which is too large. We have taken a number of steps to reduce the solution space in our case. We know that words can only be paired with other words that are semantically similar. Given a word-to-word similarity metric, Θ_{sim}, which outputs a normalized similarity value between 0 and 1 (0 means not similar, 1 indicates equivalent meaning), we can impose to pair only words with Θ_{sim} greater than a similarity threshold value, which we will denote Ω. For instance, it does not make sense to consider matching a verb with a determiner even if the similarity is non-zero (but very close to zero, e.g. LSA similarity score between *provide* and *the* is 0.042). Moreover, in regard to the initial QAP search, we can further reduce the space by focusing on pairing only numbers and content words (i.e. nouns, verbs, adjectives and adverbs), as these, along with their associated dependencies, carry most of the relevant semantic content in a sentence. We also chose to pair words that have either identical lemma forms (i.e. *tell* vs. *told*, *gains* vs. *gain*) or the same part of speech. These constraints reduce considerably the QAP search space.

The average size of a sentence in the SEMILAR corpus is 21 tokens, with a maximum of 38, while the Edinburg corpus contains sentences with an average length of 22 tokens and a maximum of 50. Our branch and bound search allowed us to find an optimal solution in under a second for all instances on both corpora, when $\alpha \leq 0.5$.

Solving QAP via Branch & Bound

Branch-and-bound is one of the widely used paradigms for handling NP-hard optimization problems such as QAP. The gist of the branch-and-bound paradigm is to avoid explicitly exploring the entire solution space, which is too big for NP-hard optimization problems, while assuring that the unexplored parts of the space cannot contain the optimal solution. This is possible by defining a bounding function that always overestimates or underestimates solutions, depending on what type of optimal solution is sought, maximum or minimum cost, respectively.

The proposed branch-and-bound method starts with an initial solution, e.g. the optimal word-to-word matching approach obtained using the Kuhn-Munkres algorithm (w-OPT). We call this the current optimal QAP solution (C; optimal solution so far) and we denote C_{QAP} the value of the $QAP(F, D, B)$ objective function for this solution. Next, the method iteratively explores new solutions comparing at each step the current optimal solution with new ones. The exploration follows a search tree where each node represents a subspace of solutions. In our case, a subspace is defined by a partial pairing, P, with p word-to-word assignments ($p < n$). We define a bounding function $F(P)$ to compute an upper bound for the partial pairing and therefore for the entire subspace of solutions that contains this partial pairing. That is, any solution S containing the partial pairing P will have a QAP score that is guaranteed to be less than the value of the bounding function for the current node in the search tree, $S_{QAP} \leq F(P)$, for $\forall S, S \supseteq P$. If $F(P)$ is not greater than the best solution found so far, i.e. $F(P) \leq C_{QAP}$, it means there is no better solution than C_{QAP} within the subspace of complete solutions that contain the partial pairing P, as $F(P)$ always overestimates the QAP score of the solutions in this subspace. Thus, the entire subspace can be further ignored from the search. The details of the bounding function $F(P)$ are not presented here due to space reasons.

Comparing QAP Alignment with GRD and w-OPT

In this subsection, we exemplify how quadratic assignment (QAP) is more powerful when it comes to aligning words in two sentences than the other two methods described earlier: greedy (GRD) and optimal word matching (w-OPT). We take the example previously shown in Figure 1, an actual sample instance extracted from the Edinburg corpus. Its greedy alignment is shown in Figure 2. Because of the selective order in which the greedy method picks the matchings, notice that the two

Θ_{sim}	Ω	Method	Prec	Recall	F1
LCH	0.8	GRD	93.45	84.18	88.04
		w-OPT	93.94	84.62	88.51
		QAP	95.39	86.44	90.17
LSA	0.4	GRD	93.42	84.01	87.95
		w-OPT	94.07	84.56	88.55
		QAP	95.55	86.14	90.10
JCN	0.1	QAP	90.78	87.82	88.75
	0.2		94.70	87.15	**90.26**
	0.4		95.24	86.62	90.21
	0.6		95.39	86.45	90.18
	0.8		95.37	86.39	90.14
	0.9		95.45	86.38	90.17
		METEOR	94.22	84.77	**88.64**

Table 1: Alignment percent scores on SEMILAR corpus

'*the*' determiners, the '*on*' prepositions and both commas are mistakenly matched between the two texts. The word optimal (w-OPT) method does not perform any better in this case. The QAP method however, through the right use of the syntactic dependencies, is almost identical with the human annotations shown in Figure 1, except that it finds one extra unneeded pair between commas.

Though for our example, the w-OPT method does not perform any different than the greedy method, from our experiments we found that it does perform better overall, but not consistently better. This is due to the high-lexical overlap between sentences to be aligned in the datasets we used.

4 Experiments and Results

We evaluated and compared the three alignment methods presented in the previous section (GRD, w-OPT and QAP) on two datasets that were manually annotated with alignments between sentences: the SEMILAR corpus (Rus et al. 2013) and the Edinburg corpus (Thadani et al. 2012). The SEMILAR corpus consists of a set of 701 instances extracted from the MSRP corpus and which were tokenized, tagged and parsed with the Stanford Core NLP library and then manually annotated with tokens and phrase alignments. The Edinburg corpus contains 714 annotated instances used for training, and 306 instances used for evaluation, also pre-processed and parsed for syntactic dependencies using the Stanford NLP Parser.

As in Thadani et al. (2012), we used

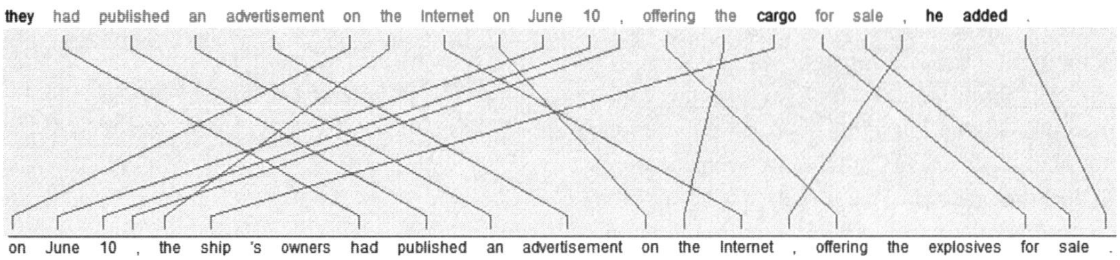

Figure 2: Greedy alignment on training instance #28 of the Edinburg corpus

METEOR's maximum accuracy alignment (Denkowski and Lavie, 2011) as a baseline to compare with our alignments. The evaluation scores for the alignments are also similarly computed as macro-average results: precision, recall, and F-score values are computed for each instance, then these scores are averaged across all instances. Because we do word-level alignments and the human-annotated data and METEOR output include phrase-level alignments we have to have a way to consistently assess the output of the method. We assessed the phrase-level alignments using word-level alignments as explained next. If the gold data contains a phrase-level alignment then if the output of a method contains an alignment between any two words in the gold-aligned phrases then we consider the system word-level alignment as a hit. Using this method, the METEOR alignments are evaluated at word-level and therefore can be directly compared to our methods' alignments. It should be noted that phrase-level alignments are very few. On the Edinburg corpus there are only 95 phrase alignments produced by METEOR out of 5,046 alignments (word- and phrase-level) and on the SEMILAR corpus METEOR produces only 30 phrase-level alignments out of 10,112 alignments. This method of evaluating neither penalizes nor rewards METEOR.

4.1 Results on the SEMILAR Corpus

Table 1 shows the alignment performance results on the SEMILAR corpus, for all three alignment methods and the METEOR baseline. For space reasons, we picked two representative word-to-word similarity metrics, JCN (Pedersen et al., 2004) and LSA, and report comparative results among the three alignment methods. Also, we illustrate the impact of the Ω parameters using the QAP method and a third word-to-word metric, JCN (Pedersen et al., 2004). Note that by changing the Ω value within some restrictive bounds, one could control for a better precision, at the expense of the recall, or viceversa, while keeping the overall F-score more or less the same. The other word-to-word metrics that we experimented with, show a similar trend in performance, with very small variations from the ones we reported. It is important to note that for the QAP method we used $\alpha = 0.5$ which was chosen following the same process explained in the next section. The QAP method significantly outperforms both GRD and w-OPT alignments for both JCN and LSA word-to-word similarity metrics ($p < 0.0018$). The difference in performance between GRD and w-OPT is significant only on the LSA metric ($p < 0.0058$). Note that the high performance scores for all methods are due to the high lexical overlap, a characteristic of the SEMILAR instances, which was inherited from the original MSRP corpus.

4.2 Results on the Edinburg Corpus

We present now results when evaluating the three alignment methods on the Edinburg corpus. As a first step, we used the optimal method (w-OPT) on the training subset to find the optimal word-to-word threshold (Ω) for seven word similarity (Θ_{sim}) metrics. Six of them are WordNet based: LIN, PATH, JCN, LCH, RES and WUP (Pedersen et al., 2004); and one is LSA. Word-to-word threshold values between 0 to 1 were evaluated in increments of 0.01 and the ones that gave the best F-Score on the training set, when using the w-OPT method, were selected: $\Omega(LIN) = 0.73$, $\Omega(PATH) = 0.3$, $\Omega(JCN) = 0.23$, $\Omega(LCH) = 0.69$, $\Omega(RES) = 0.47$, $\Omega(WUP) = 0.85$, $\Omega(LSA) = 0.1$.

Next, we searched for a good parameter α value to use in the QAP alignment. We evaluated QAP on the training set for several α values, from 0 to

Θ_{sim}	Ω	Method	Prec	Recall	F1
LIN	0.73	GRD	88.06	78.64	82.51
		w-OPT	89.18	79.14	83.30
		QAP	90.95	84.15	**86.87**
JCN	0.23	GRD	88.17	78.52	82.47
		w-OPT	89.33	79.02	83.27
		QAP	90.92	83.9	86.70
PATH	0.30	QAP	89.42	84.86	86.51
LCH	0.69		90.39	84.39	86.73
RES	0.47		92.82	80.57	85.61
WUP	0.85		90.75	84.19	**86.78**
LSA	0.10		88.94	84.63	86.24
		METEOR	88.10	83.37	**85.22**

Table 2: Alignments percent scores on Edinburg corpus

1 in increments of 0.1, and various word-to-word metrics. We found that $\alpha = 0.5$, which gives equal importance to both word and dependency relations, is the optimal value that maximizes F-measure on training and therefore we used this value for the test data.

Finally, we evaluated all three alignments methods on the testing part of the Edinburg corpus. We ran paired t-tests on the alignment performances (w-OPT against GRD, and QAP against w-OPT). We found QAP results to be statistically significantly better than w-OPT ($p < 0.0001$), and w-OPT to be significantly statistically better than GRD ($0.005 > p > 0.0004$) across all the seven word metrics that we used.

We also ran t-tests between the results given by our best word metric, LIN, and the other metrics. We found the differences were not statistically different, except on the LSA metric ($p = 0.0281$), and RES ($p < 0.0001$).

Table 2 shows comparative performance results for all three alignment methods on only two word metrics, LIN and JCN, for space reasons, and QAP comparative results for all the other word metrics, along with the METEOR alignment results.

It should be noted that the results reported by Thadani et al. (2012) consider phrase-level alignment and therefore their results are not directly comparable to ours. They report results slightly worse than METEOR on precision (-5%) and considerably better on recall ($+10\%$). For our case, we found that the QAP method is consistently better than METEOR, in terms of all measures, on all the word metrics except RES, which although gives best precision, it is highly penalized on recall.

5 Discussion and Conclusions

We proposed in this paper a novel approach to the task of aligning monolingual texts in the context of semantic similarity tasks based on an efficient branch and bound approach. We showed that our optimal solution provides state-of-the-art performance. Although the proposed method is computationally more expensive, it consistently outperforms other alignment methods and provides optimal solutions for sentences of average size (< 40 words). The proposed QAP solution can be useful for a number of tasks such as semantic similarity assessment and phrase level semantic equivalence extraction and in many applications such as intelligent tutoring systems, question answering, and automated essay scoring.

Acknowledgments

This research was supported in part by the Institute for Education Sciences under award R305A100875. Any opinions, findings, and conclusions or recommendations are solely the authors'.

References

Eneko Agirre, Daniel Cel, Mona Diab, and Aitor Gonzalez-Agirre. 2012. SemEval-2012 Task 6: A Pilot on Semantic Textual Similarity. *Proceedings of SemEval 2012, in conjunction with *SEM 2012.* Montreal, Canada, June 7-8, 2012.

Kurt M. Anstreicher. 2003. Recent advances in the solution of quadratic assignment problems. *Mathematical Programming*, volume 97(1-2):27–42. Springer.

James Brunning. 2010. *Alignment Models and Algorithms for Statistical Machine Translation.* Ph.D. Thesis, Cambridge University Engineering Department.

Rainer E. Burkard, Eranda Çela, Panos M. Pardalos, and Leonidas S. Pitsoulis. 1998. The Quadratic Assignment Problem. In P.M. Pardalos and D.Z. Zu, editors, *Handbook of Combinatorial Optimization*, volume 3:241–337. Kluwer Academic Publishers.

Nathanael Chambers, Daniel Cer, Trond Grenager, David Hall, Chloe Kiddon, Bill MacCartney, Marie-Catherine De Marneffe, Daniel Ramage, Eric Yeh, and Christopher D. Manning. 2007. Learning Alignments and Leveragning Natural Logic. In *Proceedings of the ACL-07 Workshop on Textual Entailment and Paraphrasing*.

Yee S. Chan and Hwee T. Ng. 2008. MAXSIM: A maximum similarity metric for machine translation evaluation. In *Proceedings of ACL-08: HLT*, pages 55–62.

Nicos Christofides and Enrique Benavent. 1989. An exact algorithm for the quadratic assignment problem. *Operations Research*, volume 37(5):760–768.

Trevor Cohn, Chris Callison-Burch, and Mirella Lapata. 2008. Constructing corpora for the development and evaluation of paraphrase systems. *Computational Linguistics*, volume 34(4):597–614.

Michael Denkowski and Alon Lavie. 2011. Meteor 1.3 Automatic Metric for Reliable Optimization and Evaluation of Machine Translation Systems. In *EMNLP 2011 - Workshop on Statistical Machine Translation*.

Bill Dolan, Chris Quirk, and Chris Brockett. 2004. Unsupervised construction of large paraphrase corpora: Exploiting massively parallel news sources. In *Proceedings of the 20th International Conference on Computational Linguistics*. Geneva, Switzerland.

Tjalling C. Koopmans and Martin Beckmann. 1957. Assignment Problems and the Location of Economic Activities. *Econometrica*, volume 25(1):53–76.

Harold W. Kuhn. 1955. The Hungarian Method for the assignment problem. *Naval Research Logistics Quarterly*, volume 2:83–97.

Simon Lacoste-Julien, Ben Taskbar, Dan Klein, and Michael I. Jordan. 2006. Word Alignment via Quadratic Assignment. In *Proceedings of HLT-NAACL '06*, pages 112–119. New York, June 2006.

Eugene L. Lawler. 1963. The quadratic assignment problem. *Management Science*, volume 9:586–599.

Bill MacCartney, Michel Galley, and Christopher D. Manning. 2008. A Phrase-Based Alignment Model for Natural Language Inference. In *Proceedings of the 2008 Conference on Empirical Methods in Natural Language Processing*. Honolulu. October, 2008.

Marie-Catherine de Marneffe, Bill MacCartney, and Christopher D. Manning. 2006. Generating Typed Dependency Parses from Phrase Structure Parses. In *LREC 2006*.

James Munkres. 1957. Algorithms for the assignment and transportation problems. *Journal of the Society for Industrial and Applied Mathematics*, 5(1):32–38. Society for Industrial and Applied Mathematics.

Franz J. Och and Hermann Ney. 2003. A systematic comparison of various statistical alignment models. *Computational Linguistics*, volume 29:19–51.

Ted Pedersen, Siddharth Patwardhan, and Jason Michelizzi. 2004. WordNet::Similarity - Measuring the Relatedness of Concepts. In *NAACL-2004*.

Vasile Rus, Mihai Lintean, Rajendra Banjade, Nobal Niraula, and Dan Stefanescu. 2013. SEMILAR: The Semantic Similarity Toolkit. In *Proceedings of ACL 2013*. Sofia, Bulgaria. August 4-9, 2013.

Sartaj Sahni and Teofilo Gonzalez. 1976. P-complete approximation problems. *Journal of the Association for Computing Machinery*, volume 23:555–565.

Arafat Md Sultan, Steven Bethard, and Tamara Summer 2014. Back to Basics for Monolingual Alignment: Exploiting Word Similarity and Contextual Evidence. *Transactions of the Association of Computational Linguistics*, volume 2(1):219–230.

Kapil Thadani, Scott Martin, and Michael White. 2012. A Join Phrasal and Dependency Model for Paraphrase Alignment. In *Proceedings of COLING-2012*

Kapil Thadani and Kathleen McKeown. 2011. Optimal and syntactically-informed decoding for monolingual phrase-based alignment. In *Proceedings of ACL-HLT, HLT '11*, pages 254–259.

Xuchen Yao, Benjamin Van Durme, Chris Callison-Burch and Peter Clark 2013. A Lightweight and High Performance Monolingual Word Aligner. In *ACL (2)*. The Association for Computer Linguistics, pages 702–707.

Sentence Compression For Automatic Subtitling

Juhani Luotolahti and Filip Ginter
Department of Information Technology
University of Turku, Finland
mjluot,figint@utu.fi

Abstract

This paper investigates sentence compression for automatic subtitle generation using supervised machine learning. We present a method for sentence compression as well as discuss generation of training data from compressed Finnish sentences, and different approaches to the problem. The method we present outperforms state-of-the-art baseline in both automatic and human evaluation. On real data, 44.9% of the sentences produced by the compression algorithm have been judged to be useable as-is or after minor edits.

1 Introduction

Automated broadcast programme subtitling is an important task, especially with the recent introduction of legislation which mandates all programmes of the Finnish national broadcasting corporation to be subtitled, even in cases where the programme is in Finnish, and not in a foreign language. Providing such a subtitling is a resource-intensive task, requiring human editors to manually transcribe the programme and produce the subtitles. There is an obvious motivation to automate this process to increase the subtitling throughput and drive the costs down. While ultimately aiming at a fully automated pipeline from speech recognition to screen-ready subtitles, in this paper we focus specifically on the task of text compression for subtitling.

The need for this task arises from the fact that the whole spoken content of the programme cannot be displayed in the area of the screen devoted to subtitles while respecting the standards setting the maximum number of characters per line and the minimum amount of time the subtitles must be shown. The subtitling naturally also needs to remain in time synchronisation with the spoken programme. In practice, the subtitling editors thus need to compress the text of the subtitles, removing or abridging parts which are less critical for the understandability of the programme.

2 Sentence Compression

The goal of automatic sentence compression is to create a shorter version of the input sentence, in a way preserving its meaning. Sentence compression is most often extractive, formed by dropping words from a sentence that are not needed for the sentence to be grammatical and do not importantly contribute to the meaning of the sentence. Many sentence compression methods are based on supervised learning using parallel corpora as training material (Knight and Marcu, 2002; Turner and Charniak, 2005; McDonald, 2006; Cohn and Lapata, 2009). Some methods don't require parallel corpora, but are either based on rules (Gagnon and Da Sylva, 2005) or use language models or statistics gathered from non-parallel sources (Chiori and Furui, 2004; Filippova and Strube, 2008, Clarke and Lapata, 2006). While some systems prune the sentence based on the linear order of the words, others prune the parse trees or modified parse trees. Language models are commonly used to ensure grammatical output.

3 Data and its pre-processing

We draw our data from subtitles of the Finnish national broadcasting corporation television programs provided to us by Lingsoft Inc. From Lingsoft, we have obtained the texts both before and after the compression step of the subtitling process, extracted from the internal processing pipeline. As illustrated in Figure 1, each programme consists of the subtitle texts and the associated time-stamps which define the time period in which the subtitle is shown on the screen. The full, unabridged

Subtitle	Original
13 10:01:31,12 --> 10:01:35,24 Jaro has returned to Finland after a victorious racing trip.	11 00:01:48,000 --> 00:01:51,600 Jaro has returned to Finland after a victorious racing trip to Estonia.
14 10:01:36,01 --> 10:01:41,01 Champion Toni Gardemaister awaits him with a surprise.	12 00:01:52,400 --> 00:01:56,000 Champion Toni Gardemaister awaits him with a surprise.
15 10:01:42,00 --> 10:01:44,15 Oh, hello. -Hi there	13 00:01:57,700 --> 00:02:00,000 Oh, hello hello. Hi there. What's up? Nothing much.
16 10:01:44,17 --> 10:01:49,21 Let's go to the kart racing track and let's see how good you are.	15 00:02:00,600 --> 00:02:05,100 Let's, you know, go cruising a little to the kart racing track. And let's see how good you are at kart racing.

Figure 1: Example document excerpt from the data, translated to English.

Pertti	hei	,	mä	käyn	näyttämäs	näitä	dioja	yhelle	asiantuntijalle	.
Pertti	hey	,	I	will_go	show	these	slides	one	to_expert	.
*	*	*	Mä	käyn	näyttämässä	näitä	dioja	*	asiantuntijalle	.
-	-	-	I	will_go	show	these	slides	-	to_expert	.
D	D	D	+	-	=	-	-	D	-	-

*	Mites	tää	puhelin	,	onks	tää	toiminu	?
-	How_about	this	phone	,	has	it	worked	?
Onko	*	tää	puhelin	*	*	*	toiminu	?
Has	-	this	phone	-	-	-	worked	?
I	D	-	+	D	D	D	-	-

Figure 2: Example alignments

version of the programme is used for internal purposes of the company and is the result of manual correction of speech recognition output. The compressed version of the programme consists of completed subtitles, exactly as delivered and subsequently aired. The subtitles often include spoken language, with incomplete words and slang terms, making them different in style from the strictly grammatical text which would be ideal.

The first step in pre-processing the data is to obtain a good alignment of the texts so that the individual edits can be identified. The data was received as raw subtitle files. A subtitle file consists of text units to be shown on a screen at a particular moment and the time to show it. Because the unabridged version was a result of speech recognition, its timing didn't correspond with the abridged version's timing. The subtitles and the amount of sentences they include are also different in size, because in many cases whole sentences were removed or introduced in the abridging process.

To identify the edits made to the subtitles, especially tokens being removed, it was necessary to obtain token to token level alignments between the two versions of the subtitles. String alignment was created using a distance matrix generated by calculating Levenshtein distance between the two subtitles on a token level. The edits were extracted from the distance matrix the method generates. Tokens with only minimal modifications (eg. 'ohjelma', 'program' and 'ohjelmamme', 'our program') were aligned instead of counting as a substitution. Minimal modification of tokens was defined as being sufficiently close to each other, when calculated with a string matching algorithm.

Because of the edits made in the abridging pro-

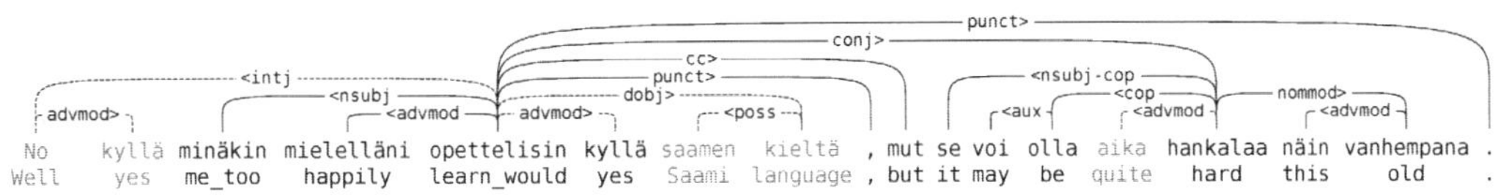

Figure 3: An example of the extended SD scheme.

cess, sometimes sentences were combined and sometimes cut in the abridged version. After we had the alignments the original subtitles with the abridged ones the subtitles were sentence split and the sentences were aligned with sentences of the abridged text.

Each sentence was parsed using the recently published Finnish statistical dependency parsing pipeline (Haverinen et al., 2014). The parser produces full dependency parse trees in a minor modification of the well-known Stanford Dependencies (SD) scheme (de Marneffe and Manning, 2008).

4 Methods

Since we have the appropriate training data at our disposal, we will approach the task as a supervised machine learning problem, whereby a classifier will predict which words will be removed from each sentence. We will test a few different approaches to the task, all based on supervised learning, but using different sentence reduction strategies. The feature set consists mainly of features based on the dependent token and features derived from the dependency tree, which we will describe later.

The first approach is to prune the dependency trees of the sentences. The goal of this approach is to produce more syntactically valid output than reducing the sentence based on its linear order. This, however, does not guarantee the syntactic validity of the sentence. Consider, for instance the subtree headed by *hankalaa (hard)* in Figure 3. Removing the word, together with its subtree will leave the conjunction *mut (but)* orphaned, resulting in an ungrammatical sentence. We will address the most common such cases with a set of straightforward post-processing rules. For dependency tree pruning we have the following strategies:

The first strategy is to let the classifier decide which dependencies (edges) to prune from the dependency tree and remove the complete subtree along with the removed dependency. For this we train an SVM classifier to recognize the dependencies to remove and clean the training data from dependencies which would be removed by a removal of a dependency higher up in the tree. The SVM implementation used is libSVM (Chang and Lin, 2011). In the results table, we refer to this approach as *mp svm*.

Another strategy is to remove a dependency only if all of the dependencies under it in the dependency tree have been removed as well. For this an SVM classifier is trained which for each dependency makes a prediction on whether to keep or remove it. Unlike previously, this time the training data contains all dependencies. The motivation behind this strategy is to conserve important subtrees of the tree. In the results table, we refer to this approach as *mk svm*.

The second approach for compressing the sentence is to let a classifier freely remove tokens from the sentence without limitations of the dependency tree structure. To gain advantage from the linear order of the sentence we cast the problem as a sequence classification problem and use Conditional Random Fields (CRF), as implemented in CRFSuite (Okazaki, 2007) with the same feature set as previously to predict which tokens to keep and which to drop. We refer to the CRF model as *crf*.

We also train another CRF model (referred to as *crf pos*) without the dependency tree features to see how well it fares against the full feature set and to judge the extent to which syntax contributes to the classification.

We will also implement a baseline system based on the work of Filippova and Strube (2008), which is based on finding an optimal abridged tree using Integer Linear Programming and unsupervised learning. This will be referred as *base ilp* in the evaluation tables.

The last system we build is a modification of the mentioned baseline system, described in detail in a later chapter. In this system we replace the statistical scores used by the baseline with those given by the *crf* model, such that basically the probability of token being removed is decided by the CRF classifier and is used by the ILP process to make the final decisions. The appeal of this strategy is the use of ILP, and a direct comparison with the baseline since it uses a qualitatively different removal scheme than our systems. This is referred as *crf ilp* in the evaluation.

All of these systems allow their rate of removal to be fixed by altering the classifier threshold and in the case of the Integer Linear Programming based method by setting a fixed rate of removal. The score used to adjust the rate of removal for SVM is simply the classifier score and for CRF, the marginal probabilities for token removal. It is to be noted that for the CRF based methods altering the threshold is very important, since without threshold manipulation the classifier produces too low compression rates (~5% of tokens removed in the dev-set with full feature set).

As with any similar supervised machine learning method, feature engineering is an important part of the development. The first class of features we use is derived from the morphological analysis of the target word. The second class of features is based on the surrounding structure of the parse tree. These features model the syntactic context of the target word to capture its immediate syntactic neighbourhood. We also add combination features where appropriate, since the underlying classifier is linear. The third class of features includes those that encode information about the target word's position in the sentence and within the tree. We also employ features from the Semantic Role Labeling system of Kanerva et al. (2014). We list the exact features used below, and in Section 5 we will present a feature ablation study to demonstrate their relative merits.

Features

The exhaustive list of features is described in the following:

Features based on the token

- Morphological tags
- The morphological tags of the next and the previous token in the sentence
- Word and lemma of the token
- Next and previous word and lemma of the token
- Next and previous pos-tags of the token

Tree structure based Features

- Dependency type
- The dependency types of the next and the previous token in the sentence
- The types of dependencies that have the dependent token as a governor and also this feature combined with the dependency type of the dependent token
- Dependency type combined with the dependent token's morphological tags
- The dependency types of the tokens which are siblings of this token in the dependency tree with information about whether the tokens are to the left or to the right of the dependent token in the sentence. This is also combined with the dependency type of the token.
- The morphological tags of the governing token
- The dependency type of the governing token with and without the dependent token's dependency type combined
- How many tokens depend on the current token
- How large a subtree would be removed if this dependency was pruned
- Whether this token is a leaf in the tree
- Whether this token has incoming semantic edges

Location and sentence based Features

- Whether sentence length is over 5, 10, or 15 tokens with and without the dependency type
- How long a path in the dependency tree is to the root node from this node
- Whether the number of dependencies above this dependency in the path to the root node is in the first, second, third or fourth quarter of the longest path to the root node in the tree
- Whether the dependent token is located in the first, second, third or fourth quarter of the sentence
- The two above features combined into one

5 Evaluation

Problem setting

The data is divided into training, development and test sets, with the division carried out by sampling sentences randomly. The development and test sets were both 3247 sentences long (roughly 18%

of all sentences). In the training data, only sentences with removals and no other edits such as substitutions are used, to ensure the classifier does not learn to remove tokens that are in fact substituted for another token, possibly at some later point in the sentence. The development and test sets are, however, preserved exactly as-is, containing all sentences from the original data. The compression experiments are done with compression rate of 85% (i.e. 15% token removal) to be in line with the test data and also 70% to see how the systems fare with a higher rate of removal.

Baseline

As the baseline, we have re-implemented the method of Filippova and Strube (2008). Like our method, the baseline is based on the removal of dependency sub-trees, however, it is an unsupervised method, requiring only a dependency treebank for its training. This will allow us to study to what extent the availability of supervised data affects the overall performance on the compression task, as compared to an unsupervised baseline previously shown to have a good performance and based on the same principle of dependency subtree removal.

The baseline method has three steps: transforming the source tree by adding additional edges, compression, and tree linearisation. The method assigns a score for each edge of a dependency tree and tries to find optimal edges to remove, maximizing the score of the remaining edges and at the same time maintaining a correct tree structure. The edge scores are calculated from statistics derived from a treebank. The method uses integer linear programming to find a globally optimal solution.

In our experiment, statistics of the dependencies and tokens are calculated from an approximately 500 million token corpus obtained by extracting Finnish text from the CommonCrawl[1] Internet crawl data and automatically parsed using the Finnish dependency parsing pipeline of Haverinen et al. (2014).

The trees are first pre-processed by creating a dummy root node and adding an edge from the dummy root to each finite verb in the sentence, making the trees graphs. Then, auxiliary verbs, negation markers and function words are merged with their governors to ensure they are not removed separately. And finally, coordination structures are decomposed by propagating the governor of the first coordinated element to every other element in the coordination, preserving the dependency type.

Tree compression is then cast as an optimization problem and solved using integer linear programming. Each dependency from a governor word g to a dependent d with type l is assigned a binary variable:

$$x^l_{g,d} = \begin{cases} 1 & \text{if edge preserved;} \\ 0 & \text{if edge not preserved.} \end{cases}$$

The method then optimizes the objective function

$$f(X) = \sum_x x^l_{g,d} \cdot P(l|g) \cdot I(d) \qquad (1)$$

where $P(l|h)$ is the conditional probability of the dependency type l, given that g is the governor. $I(d)$ is an importance score defined as:

$$I(d_i) = \frac{l}{N} f_i \cdot \log(\frac{F_a}{F_i}) \qquad (2)$$

where l is the number of clause nodes above the dependency, N is the maximum level of embedding, f_i is the frequency of the word in current document, F_a is the sum of frequencies of topic words in the corpus and F_i is the frequency of the word in corpus.

Constraints are added into the integer linear programming problem in order to ensure that a correct structure is produced, making sure that each word has a governor. The maximal number of tokens in the resulting tree is also encoded as a constraint to the problem, allowing the control of the compression ratio. The pruned tree is then linearized in the original order of words in the sentence.

Test Set Evaluation

First, we compare the performance of our proposed methods and the baseline in terms of F-score on the test set. Precision is defined as the proportion of predicted removed tokens which were also removed in gold standard, and recall is conversely defined as the proportion of removed tokens in the gold standard, whose removal is also predicted by the system. The main results in Table 1 show that with essentially equal compression ratios, the feature-rich CRF (referred to as *crf*) results in the highest F-score in both rates of

[1] http://www.commoncrawl.org

	F	CR(tkn)	CR(chr)
gold	1.0	0.863	0.884
crf ilp85	0.2346	0.847	0.844
base ilp85	0.1983	0.845	0.819
crf85	**0.3809**	0.850	0.879
crf pos85	0.3511	0.850	0.884
mk svm85	0.3613	0.849	0.883
mp svm85	0.3258	0.849	0.872
crf ilp70	0.2611	0.715	0.712
base ilp70	0.2504	0.714	0.683
crf70	**0.3758**	0.700	0.761
crf pos70	0.3527	0.700	0.777
mk svm70	0.3640	0.700	0.759
mp svm70	0.3408	0.699	0.741

Table 1: F1-Scores for the test set. CR(tkn) is token level rate of compression and CR(chr) is character level compression rate of the system output.

Feature Set	Dev-set@85% F-score
Token	34.10
Token+location	35.96
Token+tree structure	36.31
All	37.16

Table 2: CRF feature ablation table on development set with 85% compression rate.

Gold		Base		crf	
advmod	26.0%	advmod	18.9%	advmod	36.8%
punct	17.9%	nommod	13.0%	punct	10.8%
nommod	7.3%	punct	9.0%	det	8.4%
det	5.6%	amod	6.7%	intj	6.1%
nsubj	5.4%	dobj	5.8%	cc	5.4%
intj	4.4%	det	5.5%	nommod	4.6%
cc	3.9%	poss	5.3%	nsubj	3.7%
amod	3.1%	cc	4.0%	complm	3.3%
conj	2.7%	conj	3.5%	amod	2.8%
dobj	2.6%	cop	3.4%	conj	2.3%

Table 3: Dependency types pruned in the test set

removal, followed by the SVM classifier (which makes independent predictions, unlike the CRF sequence classifier). The baseline performs substantially worse. As a further insight into the methods, we present in Table 3 the ten most often removed dependency types for the best scoring *crf* model, the baseline, and in the test set. As expected, with few exceptions we see dependency types associated with modifiers and functional words rather than core semantic arguments. Most of these types will also tend to have a single, leaf dependent. We can also observe a rather wide overlap (7/10) of the commonly removed dependency types between the two methods, showing that the systems target similar points of compression.

Further, we perform a small-scale feature ablation study with a CRF classifier. The most important feature groups are those related to the token itself, such as its POS-tag and lemma. The features gathered from the syntactic trees, and related location group of features both contribute positively to the classification, even though the contribution is not major.

The F-score measure can be evaluated on as many runs as necessary, for instance in parameter selection, but it does not necessarily reflect the ability of the system to produce fluent and meaning-preserving compressions. The underlying problem is that any given sentence can have a number of valid compressions, but only one of them will be counted as a true positive, all others will be counted as false positives. To address these issues, we perform also a manual evaluation of the result, discussed in the following section.

Manual evaluation

In this evaluation, we focus on the ability of the systems to produce fluent output and preserve important, content-bearing parts of the sentence (i.e. its "main message"). These two qualities are to some degree independent (although clearly not entirely so) and we thus evaluate them separately.

We selected 399 random sentences which had been compressed by the systems from the test section of the corpus, and for each sentence we produced four compressed versions: one using the baseline method, one using the *crf* model which got the highest F-score on the test set. In addition we test *crf pos* and *crf ilp*. The *crf pos* set is selected because of its relatively high F-score on the test set, even though it does not employ the syntax of the sentence. The *crf ilp* is selected to test both the integer linear programming method and to provide the baseline with a comparison using the same approach to sentence reduction. For the test, compression rates were aligned. In the end all systems had a rate of token removal of 75% for the sentences being tested.

The compressed versions of the sentences were subsequently evaluated by a native speaker in

	Fluency
3	Readable as is
2	Minor revisions needed
1	Major revisions needed
0	Incomprehensible
	Meaning
3	Message preserved perfectly
2	Important message preserved
1	Minor revisions needed
0	Important message lost

Table 4: Manual evaluation scales.

	Fluency	Meaning
crf	799 (66.7%)	609 (50.8%)
crf pos	796 (66.5%)	579 (49.9%)
crf ilp	795 (66.4%)	487 (40.7%)
Baseline	720 (60.2%)	383 (32.0%)

Table 5: Sum of the scores over all test sentences given by the evaluator. The percentages are given in terms of maximum possible value, which for all quantities is 399 sentences × maximum score of 3, i.e. 1197.

terms of fluency and in terms of content preservation using the scales shown in Table 4. The order in which the compressed versions were presented for evaluation was randomly changed for every sentence separately, i.e. it was not possible to distinguish the methods by the evaluator. Further, the evaluator was not involved in the development of the methods in any manner and was thus not primed to recognize features typical of compressions produced by any of these methods.

To gain an initial insight into the evaluation results, we show in Table 5 the sum of scores given across all sentences. We can see that the *crf* gains on top of the baseline in terms of both measures: 6.5pp (percent points) in terms of fluency and 18.8pp in terms of meaning. These correspond to 16.3% and 27.6% of relative error decrease over the baseline. Both differences are statistically significant with $p < 0.02$ (two-tailed paired t-test).

For practical deployment, the proportion of sentences which need no, or only minor corrections is a crucial measure. For the best performing CRF method, 75.4% and 44.9% (fluency and meaning) were assigned score of 2 or 3, i.e. usable as-is or with only minor corrections. For the baseline method, the corresponding proportions are 68.2% and 15.3%, reflecting a notable gain of the proposed method over the baseline.

When both fluency and meaning had to be assigned score of 2 or 3, 44.9% of the sentences produced by the *crf* method required only minor modifications for fluency or were readily usable. For the baseline method only 15.0% of the sentences were rated as readily usable or requiring only minor modifications for fluency. The 29.9pp gain of the proposed method corresponds to a 35.1% relative decrease in error, and ultimately manual effort saved by the proposed method. 74.2% of the *crf* produced sentences are usable as-is or require minor fixing in terms of fluency and/or meaning, when using a more relaxed criteria and requiring fluency to be scored 2 or 3 and meaning to be 1 (Minor revisions needed for maintaining meaning) or greater, while baseline produces such sentences 63.9% of the time. This difference of 10.3pp corresponds to a relative decrease in error rate of 28.5%. The difference of performance between *crf* and *crf pos* when it comes to fluency or meaning is not statistically significant, although *crf* is rated higher on both measures. Human evaluation would suggest the *crf pos* performs slightly worse in maintaining the meaning of the sentence (0.9pp) than *crf*, while the difference in fluency is very small (0.2pp). This would suggest the syntax of the sentence might help the system deciding which tokens are important for the meaning of the sentence.

The difference in fluency between *crf* and *crf ilp* is not statistically significant, but difference between meaning is statistically significant ($p <$ 0.02 on two-tailed paired t-test). Because this system is identical in all respects but the scores used to prune the tree, to the baseline of which difference of fluency is statistically significant to the *crf*, this shows the CRF based scores do help with the fluency of the output. The comparison between *crf ilp* and the baseline is interesting, because they are essentially the same system except one is based on supervised learning and the other is based on statistics. The *crf ilp* outperforms the baseline on both metrics and the results are statistically significant. This speaks in favour of the supervised approach.

Human agreement

Earlier in the development process, we also performed another human evaluation to test both the process of human evaluation and the performance of the system. We were especially interested in the subjectivity of the task and the human agreement. While in this earlier experiment the test data, system and rate of removal are different from the above final test setting, it still offers insight into the evaluation process and especially the level of agreement of the human evaluators. For this human evaluation round, two evaluators were used, and rate of token compression for both classifiers was set to 85%. The participants of this evaluation are *mp svm* against the ILP-based baseline. 200 sentences were selected and all judged independently by both evaluators.

The Kappa score of the inter-annotator agreement over all 800 annotation data points (2 tasks $\times$ 2 methods $\times$ 200 sentences) is 0.32. When measured per method and task, Kappa varies from 0.25 (baseline method, meaning task) to 0.36 (proposed method, meaning task). For the specific binary decision of whether the score of an individual sentence is ≥ 2 or not, the overall Kappa score is 0.39. The overall scores of 0.32 and 0.39 would be interpreted as "fair" using the criteria of Viera et al. (2005).

6 Discussion and conclusions

Comparison of the F-score evaluation between the supervised method and the unsupervised baseline shows that the supervised training gives a rather substantial benefit over the unsupervised baseline. Numerically, the F-scores remained very low, which, however, can be largely attributed to the rather arbitrary nature of the sentence compression task where any sentence of a reasonable length may have a number of alternative compressions. Of these, one was selected when producing the sub-titles and the alternatives count as errors in the F-score based evaluation. This cannot be addressed without a major data curation effort which, in our practical setting, is not possible.

The manual evaluation not only shows considerably more promising results in the numeric sense, but also shows correlation with the F-score based evaluation. This suggests that it is possible to use the F-score evaluation to develop and optimize the method, while a manual evaluation is clearly necessary to gain insight into the practical usability of the output compressions.

Interestingly, we find a clearly better performance of the CRF-based method also in terms of fluency, even though the baseline method uses linear programming to find a globally optimal solution and the statistics it relies on were gathered on a parsed corpus of a substantial size.

From a practical point of view, the manual evaluation shows that about one half of the compressed sentences are acceptable as-is or nearly as-is. If deployed in a setting where the necessary minor edits are technically easily carried out, it would seem feasible that the sentence compression would lead to a streamlining of the subtitling process and subsequent cost reduction.

The lack of training data is an often cited problem for sentence compression. We have shown that subtitling data is a good source for sentence compression method development, even though non-trivial pre-processing is necessary to align the textual corpora and produce suitable training data. With the increasing pressure on the availability of subtitling and textual transcriptions, this task represents an important use case for text compression and increases the chance that such data can become available through industry collaboration.

There are many future work opportunities. The method currently does not take into account context beyond a single sentence. We thus lose the opportunity to model whether a particular sentence element has been discussed in the preceding sentence and may be pruned with a higher likelihood. There is also room for improvement in ensuring the grammaticality of the output. Others have used for instance language models to improve the grammaticality and fluency of the output. Modelling subcategorization frames could also be applied for this purpose.

Studying the data, we have noticed that often long words are replaced with their shorter synonyms to compress the sentence without any loss of information. Finding shorter synonyms and learning to substitute words and phrases would be very helpful for the sentence compression task, possibly applying the recent advancements in vector space representations and modelling phrase compositionality.

Acknowledgments

This work was supported by the Kone Foundation. Computational resources were provided by CSC – IT Center for Science. We thank Simo Vihjanen from Lingsoft Inc. for the data and the overall problem setting.

References

Chih-Chung Chang and Chih-Jen Lin. 2011. LIBSVM: A library for support vector machines. *ACM Transactions on Intelligent Systems and Technology*, 2:27:1–27:27. Software available at `http://www.csie.ntu.edu.tw/~cjlin/libsvm`.

HORI Chiori and Sadaoki Furui. 2004. Speech summarization: An approach through word extraction and a method for evaluation. *IEICE TRANSACTIONS on Information and Systems*, 87(1):15–25.

James Clarke and Mirella Lapata. 2006. Constraint-based sentence compression: An integer programming approach. In *Proceedings of the COLING/ACL 2006 Main Conference Poster Sessions*, pages 144–151.

Trevor Cohn and Mirella Lapata. 2009. Sentence compression as tree transduction. *Journal of Artificial Intelligence Research*, 34:637–674.

Marie-Catherine de Marneffe and Christopher D. Manning. 2008. The Stanford typed dependencies representation. In *Coling 2008: Proceedings of the workshop on Cross-Framework and Cross-Domain Parser Evaluation*, pages 1–8.

Katja Filippova and Michael Strube. 2008. Dependency tree based sentence compression. In *Proceedings of the Fifth International Natural Language Generation Conference*, pages 25–32.

Michel Gagnon and Lyne Da Sylva. 2005. Text summarization by sentence extraction and syntactic pruning. In *Proceedings of Computational Linguistics in the North East (CliNE05)*.

Katri Haverinen, Jenna Nyblom, Timo Viljanen, Veronika Laippala, Samuel Kohonen, Anna Missilä, Stina Ojala, Tapio Salakoski, and Filip Ginter. 2014. Building the essential resources for Finnish: The Turku Dependency Treebank. *Language Resources and Evaluation*, 48(3):493–531.

Jenna Kanerva, Juhani Luotolahti, and Filip Ginter. 2014. Turku: Broad-coverage semantic parsing with rich features. In *Proceedings of the 8th International Workshop on Semantic Evaluation (SemEval 2014)*, pages 678–682.

Kevin Knight and Daniel Marcu. 2002. Summarization beyond sentence extraction: A probabilistic approach to sentence compression. *Artificial Intelligence*, 139(1):91–107, July.

Ryan T McDonald. 2006. Discriminative sentence compression with soft syntactic evidence. In *Proceedings of the 11th conference of EACL*, pages 297–304.

Naoaki Okazaki. 2007. CRFsuite: A fast implementation of Conditional Random Fields (CRFs).

Jenine Turner and Eugene Charniak. 2005. Supervised and unsupervised learning for sentence compression. In *Proceedings of the 43rd Annual Meeting on Association for Computational Linguistics(ACL)*, pages 290–297.

Anthony Viera and Joanne Garrett. 2005. Understanding interobserver agreement: The Kappa statistic. *Family Medicine*, 37(5):360–363.

Topic Models: Accounting Component Structure of Bigrams

Michael Nokel
Lomonosov Moscow State University,
Russian Federation
mnokel@gmail.com

Natalia Loukachevitch
Lomonosov Moscow State University,
Russian Federation
louk_nat@mail.ru

Abstract

The paper describes the results of an empirical study of integrating bigram collocations and similarities between them and unigrams into topic models. First of all, we propose a novel algorithm PLSA-SIM that is a modification of the original algorithm PLSA. It incorporates bigrams and maintains relationships between unigrams and bigrams based on their component structure. Then we analyze a variety of word association measures in order to integrate top-ranked bigrams into topic models. All experiments were conducted on four text collections of different domains and languages. The experiments distinguish a subgroup of tested measures that produce top-ranked bigrams, which demonstrate significant improvement of topic models quality for all collections, when integrated into PLSA-SIM algorithm.

1 Introduction

Topic modeling is one of the latest applications of machine learning techniques to the natural language processing. Topic models identify which topics relate to each document and which words form each topic. Each topic is defined as a multinomial distribution over terms and each document is defined as multinomial distribution over topics (Blei et al., 2003). Topic models have achieved noticeable success in various areas such as information retrieval (Wei and Croft, 2006), including such applications as multi-document summarization (Wang et al., 2009), text clustering and categorization (Zhou et al., 2009), and other natural language processing tasks such as word sense disambiguation (Boyd-Graber et al., 2007), machine translation (Eidelman et al., 2012). Among most well-known models are Latent Dirichlet Allocation (LDA) (Blei et al., 2003), which is based on Dirichlet prior distribution, and Probabilistic Latent Semantic Analysis (PLSA) (Hofmann, 1999), which is not connected with any parametric prior distribution.

One of the main drawback of the topic models is that they utilize "bag-of-words" model that discards word order and is based on the word independence assumption. There are numerous studies, where the integration of collocations, n-grams, idioms and multi-word terms into topic models is investigated. However, it often leads to a decrease in the model quality due to increasing size of a vocabulary or to a serious complication of the model (Wallach, 2006; Griffiths et al., 2007; Wang et al., 2007).

The paper proposes a novel approach taking into account bigram collocations and relationship between them and unigrams in topic models (such as *citizen – citizen of country – citizen of union – European citizen – state citizen*; *categorization – document categorization – term categorization – text categorization*). This allows us to create a novel method of integrating bigram collocations into topic models that does not consider bigrams being as "black boxes", but maintains the relationship between unigrams and bigrams based on their component structure. The proposed algorithm leads to significant improvement of topic models quality measured in perplexity and topic coherence (Newman et al., 2010) without complications of the model.

All experiments were carried out using PLSA algorithm and its modifications on four corpora of different domains and languages: the English part of Europarl parallel corpus, the English part of JRC-Acquis parallel corpus, ACL Anthology Reference corpus, and Russian banking magazines.

The rest of the paper is organized as follows. In the section 2 we focus on related work. Section 3 proposes a novel algorithm PLSA-SIM that incorporates bigrams and similarities between them and unigrams into topic models. Section 4 describes the datasets used in experiments, all preprocessing steps and metrics used to evaluate the quality. In the section 5 we perform an extensive analysis of a variety of measures for integrating top-ranked bigrams into topic models. And in the last section we draw conclusions.

2 Related Work

The idea of using collocations in topic models is not a novel one. Nowadays there are two kinds of methods proposed to deal with this problem: creation of a unified probabilistic model and preliminary extraction of collocations and n-grams with further integration into topic models.

Most studies belong to the first kind of methods. So, the first movement beyond "bag-of-words" assumption has been made by Wallach (2006), where the Bigram Topic Model was presented. In this model word probabilities are conditioned on the immediately preceding word. The LDA Collocation Model (Griffiths et al., 2007) extends the Bigram Topic Model by introducing a new set of variables and thereby giving a flexibility to generate both unigrams and bigrams. Wang et al. (2007) proposed the Topical N-Gram Model that adds a layer of complexity to allow the formation of bigrams to be determined by the context. Hu et al. (2008) proposed the Topical Word-Character Model challenging the assumption that the topic of an n-gram is determined by the topics of composite words within the collocation. This model is mainly suitable for Chinese language. Johnson (2010) established connection between LDA and Probabilistic Context-Free Grammars and proposed two probabilistic models combining insights from LDA and Adaptor Grammars to integrate collocations and proper names into the topic model.

While all these models have a theoretically elegant background, they are very complex and hard to compute on real datasets. For example, Bigram Topic Model has W^2T parameters, compared to WT for LDA and $WT + DT$ for PLSA, where W is the size of vocabulary, D is the number of documents, and T is the number of topics. Therefore such models are mostly of theoretical interest.

The algorithm proposed in Lau et al. (2013) belongs to the second type of methods that use collocations in topic models. The authors extract bigram collocations via t-test and replace separate units by top-ranked bigrams at the preprocessing step. They use two metrics of topic quality: perplexity and topic coherence (Newman et al., 2010) and conclude that incorporating bigram collocations into topics results in worsening perplexity and improving topic coherence.

Our current work also belongs to the second type of methods and distinguishes from previous papers such as Lau et al. (2013) in that our approach does not consider bigrams as "black boxes", but maintains information about the inner structure of bigrams and relationships between bigrams and component unigrams, which leads to improvement in both metrics: perplexity and topic coherence.

The idea to utilize prior natural language knowledge in topic models is not a novel one. So, Andrzejewski et al. (2009) incorporated domain-specific knowledge by Must-Link and Cannot-Link primitives represented by a novel Dirichlet Forest prior. These primitives control that two words tend to be generated by the same or separate topics. However, this method can result in an exponential growth in the encoding of Cannot-Link primitives and thus has difficulty in processing a large number of constraints (Liu, 2012). Another method of incorporating such knowledge is presented in Zhai (2010) where a semi-supervised EM-algorithm was proposed to group expressions into some user-specified categories. To provide a better initialization for EM-algorithm the method employs prior knowledge that expressions sharing words and synonyms are likely to belong to the same group. Our current work distinguishes from these ones in that we incorporate similarity links between unigrams and bigrams into the topic model in a very natural way counting their co-occurrences in documents. The proposed approach does not increase the complexity of the original PLSA algorithm.

3 PLSA-SIM algorithm

As mentioned above, original topic models utilize the "bag-of-words" assumption that assumes word independence. And bigrams are usually added to topic models as "black boxes" without any ties with other words. So, bigrams are added to the vocabulary as single tokens and in each document containing any of added bigrams the frequencies of unigram components are decreased by the frequencies of bigrams (Lau et al., 2013). Thus "bag-of-words" assumption holds.

However, there are many similar unigrams and bigrams that share the same lemmas (i.e, *correction – correction of word – error correction – spelling correction*; *rail – rail infrastructure – rail transport – use of rail*) and others in documents. We should note such bigrams do not only have identical words, but many of them maintain semantic and thematic similarity. At the same time other bigrams with the same words (i.e., idioms) can have significant semantic differences. To take into account these different situations, we hypothesized that similar bigrams sharing the same unigram components should often belong to the same topics, if they often co-occur within the same texts.

To verify this hypothesis we precompute sets of similar unigrams and bigrams sharing the same lemmas and propose novel PLSA-SIM algorithm that is the modification of the original PLSA algorithm. We will rely on the description found in Vorontsov and Potapenko (2014) and use the following notations (further in the paper we will use notation "term" when speaking about both unigrams and bigrams):

- D – the collection of documents;
- T – the set of inferred topics;
- W – the vocabulary (the set of unique terms found in the collection D);
- $\Phi = \{\phi_{wt} = p(w|t)\}$ – the distribution of terms w over topics t;
- $\Theta = \{\theta_{td} = p(t|d)\}$ – the distribution of topics t over documents d;
- $S = \{S_w\}$ – the sets of similar terms (S_w is the set of terms similar to w, that is $S_w = \{w \bigcup_v wv \bigcup_v vw\}$, where w is the lemmatized unigram, while wv and vw are lemmatized bigrams);
- n_{dw}, n_{ds} – the number of occurrences of the terms w, s in the document d;
- $\hat{n}_{wt}$ – the estimate of frequency of the term w in the topic t;
- $\hat{n}_{td}$ – the estimate of frequency of the topic t in the document d;
- $\hat{n}_t$ – the estimate of frequency of the topic t in the text collection D;
- n_d – the number of words in the document d.

The pseudocode of PLSA-SIM algorithm is presented in the Algorithm 1. The only modifications of the original algorithm concern lines 6 and 9, where we introduce auxiliary variable f_{dw}, which takes into account pre-computed sets of similar terms. Thus, the weight of such terms is increased within each document.

Algorithm 1: PLSA-SIM algorithm: PLSA with similar terms

Input: collection of documents D, number of topics $|T|$, initial distributions Θ and Φ, sets of similar terms S

Output: distributions Θ and Φ

1 **while** *not meet the stop criterion* **do**
2   **for** $d \in D,\ w \in W,\ t \in T$ **do**
3         $\hat{n}_{wt} = 0,\ \hat{n}_{td} = 0,\ \hat{n}_t = 0,\ n_d = |d|$
4   **for** $d \in D,\ w \in W$ **do**
5         $Z = \sum_t \phi_{wt}\theta_{td}$,
6         $f_{dw} = n_{dw} + \sum_{s \in S_w} n_{ds}$
7   **for** $t \in T$ **do**
8   **if** $\phi_{wt}\theta_{td} > 0$ **then**
9                 $\delta = f_{dw}\phi_{wt}\theta_{td}/Z$
10                 $\hat{n}_{wt} = \hat{n}_{wt} + \delta,\ \hat{n}_{td} = \hat{n}_d + \delta,\ \hat{n}_t = \hat{n}_t + \delta$
11   **for** $w \in W,\ t \in T$ **do**
12         $\phi_{wt} = \hat{n}_{wt}/\hat{n}_t$
13   **for** $d \in D,\ t \in T$ **do**
14         $\theta_{td} = \hat{n}_{td}/n_d$

So, if similar unigrams and bigrams co-occur within the same document, we try to carry them to the same topics. We consider such terms having semantic and thematic similarities. However, if unigrams and bigrams from the same set S_w do not co-occur within the same document, we do no modifications to the original algorithm PLSA. We consider such terms having semantic differences.

4 Datasets and Evaluation

4.1 Datasets and Preprocessing

In our experiments we used English and Russian text collections obtained from different sources:

- For the English part of our study we took three different collections:
  - Europarl multilingual parallel corpus. It was extracted from the proceedings of the European Parliament (`http:`

//www.statmt.org/europarl). The English part includes almost 54 mln. words and 9672 documents.

 - JRC-Acquis multilingual parallel corpus. It represents selected texts of the EU legislation written between the 1950s and 2005 (http://ipsc.jrc.ec.europa.eu/index.php?id=198). The English part contains almost 45 mln. words and 23545 documents.
 - ACL Anthology Reference Corpus. It contains scholarly publications about Computational Linguistics (http://acl-arc.comp.nus.edu.sg/). The corpus includes almost 42 mln. words and 10921 documents.

- For the Russian part of our study we took 10422 Russian articles from several economics-oriented magazines such as Auditor, RBC, Banking Magazine, etc. These documents contain almost 18.5 mln. words.

At the preprocessing step documents were processed by morphological analyzers. For the English corpus we used Stanford CoreNLP tools (http://nlp.stanford.edu/software/corenlp.shtml), while for the Russian corpus we used our own morphological analyzer. All words were lemmatized. We consider only Adjectives, Nouns, Verbs and Adverbs since function words do not play significant role in forming topics. Besides, we excluded words occurring less than five times per the whole text collection.

In addition, we extracted all bigrams in forms of *Noun* + *Noun*, *Adjective* + *Noun* and *Noun* + *of* + *Noun* for all English collections, and *Noun* + *Noun in Genitive* and *Adjective* + *Noun* for the Russian collection. We consider only such bigrams since topics are mainly identified by nouns and noun groups (Wang et al., 2007).

4.2 Evaluation Framework

As for the inferred topics quality, we consider four different intrinsic measures. The first measure is **Perplexity** since it is the standard criterion of topic models quality (Daud et al., 2010):

$$Perplexity(D) = \exp\left(-\frac{1}{n}\sum_{d\in D}\sum_{w\in d} n_{dw} \ln p(w|d)\right), \quad (1)$$

where n is the number of all considered words in the collection, D is the set of documents in the collection, n_{dw} is the number of occurrences of the word w in the document d, $p(w|d)$ is the probability of appearing the word w in the document d.

The less the value of perplexity is the better the model predicts words w in documents D. Although there were numerous studies arguing that perplexity is not suited to topic model evaluation (Chang et al., 2009; Newman et al., 2010), it is still commonly used for comparing different topic models. Since it is well-known that perplexity computed on the same training collection is susceptible to over-fitting and can give optimistically low values (Blei et al., 2003) we use the standard method of computing hold-out perplexity described in Asuncion et al. (2009). In our experiments we split the collections randomly into the training sets D, on which models are trained, and the validation sets D', on which hold-out perplexity is computed.

Another method of evaluating topic model quality is using **expert opinions**. We provided annotators with inferred topics from the same text collections and instructed them to decide whether the topic was to some extent coherent, meaningful and interpretable. The indicator of topic usefulness is the ease by which one could think of a short label to describe a topic (Newman et al., 2010). In the Table 1 we present incoherent topic that can not be given any label and coherent one with label given by experts.

Top words from topic	Label
have, also, commission, state, more, however	–
vessel, fishing, fishery, community, catch, board	*fishing*

Table 1: Examples of incoherent and coherent topics

Since involving experts is time-consuming and expensive, there were several attempts to propose a method for automatic evaluation of topic models quality that would go beyond perplexity and would be correlated with expert opinions. The formulation of such a problem is very complicated since experts can quite strongly disagree with each other. However, it was recently shown that it is possible to evaluate topic coherence automatically using word semantics with precision, almost coinciding with experts (Newman et al., 2010; Mimno et al., 2011). The proposed metric measures interpretability of topics based on human judgement (Newman et al., 2010). As topics are usually presented to users via their top-N topic terms, the *topic coherence* evaluates whether these top terms correspond to the topic or not. Newman et al. (2010) proposed an automated variation of the coherence score based on pointwise mutual information (**TC-PMI**):

$$TC\text{-}PMI(t) = \sum_{j=2}^{10} \sum_{i=1}^{j-1} \log \frac{P(w_j, w_i)}{P(w_j)P(w_i)}, \quad (2)$$

where $(w_1, w_2, \ldots, w_{10})$ are the top-10 terms in a topic, $P(w_i)$ and $P(w_j)$ are probabilities of unigrams w_i and w_j respectively, while $P(w_j, w_i)$ is the probability of bigram (w_j, w_i). The final measure of topic coherence is calculated by averaging $TC\text{-}PMI(t)$ measure by all topics t.

This score is proven to demonstrate high correlation with human judgement (Newman et al., 2010). The proposed metric considers only top-10 words in each topic since they usually provide enough information to form the subject of the topic and distinguishing features from other topics. Topic coherence is becoming more widely used to evaluate topic model quality along with perplexity. For example, Stevens et al. (2012) showed that this metric is strongly correlated with expert estimates. Also Andrzejewski et al. (2011) simply used it for evaluating topic model quality.

Following the approach proposed by Mimno et al. (2011) we compute probabilities by dividing the number of documents where the unigram or bigram occurred by the number of documents in the collection. To avoid optimistically high values we use external corpus for this purpose – namely, Russian and English Wikipedia. We should note that we do not consider another variation of topic coherence based on log conditional probability (*TC-LCP*) proposed by Mimno et al. (2011) since it was shown in Lau et al. (2013) that it works significantly worse than *TC-PMI*.

We should note that while incorporating the knowledge of similar unigrams and bigrams into topic models in the proposed algorithm, we encourage such terms to be in the top-10 terms in inferred topics. Therefore, we increase TC-PMI metric unintentionally since such terms are likely to co-occur within the same documents. So we decided to use also modification of this metric to consider not top-10 terms in topics but top-10 non-similar terms in topics (this metric will be further called as **TC-PMI-nSIM**).

5 Integrating bigrams into topic models

To compare proposed algorithm with the original one we extracted all bigrams found in each document of collections. For ranking bigrams we utilized *Term Frequency (TF)* or one of the following 19 word association measures:

1. *Mutual Information (MI)* (Church and Hanks, 1990);
2. *Augmented MI* (Zhang, 2008);
3. *Normalized MI* (Bouma, 2009);
4. *True MI* (Deane, 2005);
5. *Cubic MI* (Daille, 1995);
6. *Symmetric Conditional Probability* (Lopes and Silva, 1999);
7. *Dice Coefficient (DC)* (Smadja et al., 1996);
8. *Modified DC* (Kitamura and Matsumoto, 1996);
9. *Lexical Cohesion* (Park et al., 2002);
10. *Gravity Count* (Daudarvičius and Marcinkevičienė, 2003);
11. *Simple Matching Coefficient* (Daille, 1995);
12. *Kulczinsky Coefficient* (Daille, 1995);
13. *Ochiai Coefficient* (Daille, 1995);
14. *Yule Coefficient* (Daille, 1995);
15. *Jaccard Coefficient* (Jaccard, 1901);
16. *T-Score*;
17. *Z-Score*;
18. *Chi Square*;
19. *Loglikelihood Ratio* (Dunning, 1993).

According to the results of Lau et al. (2013) we decided to integrate top-1000 bigrams into all topic models under consideration. We should note that in all experiments described in the paper we fixed the number of topics and the number of iterations of algorithms to 100.

We conducted experiments with all **20** aforementioned measures on all four text collections in order to compare the quality of the original algorithm PLSA, PLSA with top-1000 bigrams added as "black boxes", and PLSA-SIM algorithm with the same top-1000 bigrams.

According to the results of experiments we have revealed two groups of measures.

The first group contains *MI*, *Augmented MI*, *Normalized MI*, *DC*, *Chi-Square*, *Symmetrical Conditional Probability*, *Simple Matching Coefficient*, *Kulczinsky Coefficient*, *Yule Coefficient*, *Ochiai Coefficient*, *Jaccard Coefficient*, *Z-Score*, and *Loglikelihood Ratio*. We got nearly the same levels of perplexity and topic coherence when top bigrams ranked by these measures were integrated into all tested topic models. This is explained by the fact that these measures rank up very special, non-typical and low frequency bigrams. In the Table 2 we present results of integrating top-1000 bigrams ranked by *MI* for all text collections.

Corpus	Model	Perplexity	TC-PMI	TC-PMI-nSIM
Banking	*PLSA*	1724.2	86.1	86.1
	PLSA + bigrams	1714.1	84.2	84.2
	PLSA-SIM + bigrams	1715.4	84.1	84.1
Europarl	*PLSA*	1594.3	53.2	53.2
	PLSA + bigrams	1584.6	55	55
	PLSA-SIM + bigrams	1591.3	55.2	55.2
JRC	*PLSA*	812.1	67	67
	PLSA + bigrams	815.4	66.3	66.3
	PLSA-SIM + bigrams	815.6	66.4	66.4
ACL	*PLSA*	2134.7	74.8	74.8
	PLSA + bigrams	2138.1	75.5	75.5
	PLSA-SIM + bigrams	2144.8	75.8	75.8

Table 2: Results of integrating top-1000 bigrams ranked by MI into topic models

The second group includes *TF*, *Cubic MI*, *True MI*, *Modified DC*, *T-Score*, *Lexical Cohesion* and *Gravity Count*. We got worsened perplexity and improved topic coherence, when top bigrams ranked by these measures were integrated into PLSA algorithm as "black boxes". But when they were used in PLSA-SIM topic models, it led to significant improvement of all metrics under consideration. This is explained by the fact that these measures rank up high frequent, typical bigrams. In the Table 3 we present results of integrating top-1000 bigrams ranked by *TF* for all text collections.

So, we succeed to achieve better quality for both languages using the proposed algorithm and the second group of measures.

For the expert evaluation of topic model quality we invited two linguistic experts and gave them topics inferred by the original PLSA algorithm and by the proposed PLSA-SIM algorithm with top-1000 bigrams ranked by TF (term frequency). The task was to classify given topics into 2 classes: whether they can be given a subject name (we will further mark such topics as '+') or not (we will further mark such topics as '–'). In the Table 4 we present results for all text collections except ACL Anthology Reference Corpus because for the correct markup advance knowledge in computational linguistics is required.

Corpus	Model	Perplexity	TC-PMI	TC-PMI-nSIM
Banking	*PLSA*	1724.2	86.1	86.1
	PLSA + bigrams	2251.8	98.8	98.8
	PLSA-SIM + bigrams	**1450.6**	**156.5**	**102.6**
Europarl	*PLSA*	1594.3	53.2	53.2
	PLSA + bigrams	1993.5	57.3	57.3
	PLSA-SIM + bigrams	**1431.6**	**127.7**	**84.7**
JRC	*PLSA*	812.1	67	67
	PLSA + bigrams	1038.9	72	72
	PLSA-SIM + bigrams	**743.7**	**108.4**	**76.9**
ACL	*PLSA*	2134.7	74.8	74.8
	PLSA + bigrams	2619.3	73.7	73.7
	PLSA-SIM + bigrams	**1806.4**	**152.7**	**87.8**

Table 3: Results of integrating top-1000 bigrams ranked by TF into topic models

Corpus	Model	Expert 1		Expert 2	
		+	–	+	–
Banking	*PLSA*	93	7	92	8
	PLSA + bigrams	92	8	95	5
	PLSA-SIM + bigrams	**95**	**5**	**97**	**3**
JRC	*PLSA*	92	8	90	10
	PLSA + bigrams	94	6	97	3
	PLSA-SIM + bigrams	**97**	**3**	**100**	**0**
Europarl	*PLSA*	97	3	99	1
	PLSA + bigrams	95	5	99	1
	PLSA-SIM + bigrams	**98**	**2**	**100**	**0**

Table 4: Results of expert markup of topics

As we can see, in the case of PLSA-SIM algorithm with top-1000 bigrams ranked by TF the amount of inferred topics, for which labels can be given, is increased for all text collections. It is also worth noting that adding bigrams as "black boxes" does not increase the amount of such inferred topics. This result also confirms that the proposed algorithm improves the quality of topic models.

In the Table 5 we present top-5 words from one random topic for each corpus for original

PLSA and PLSA-SIM algorithms with top-1000 bigrams ranked by TF. Within each text collection we present topics discussing the same subject.

Banking		**Europarl**	
PLSA	PLSA-SIM	PLSA	PLSA-SIM
Banking	*Financial system*	*Financial*	*Economic crisis*
Bank	*Financial market*	*Crisis*	*Financial crisis*
Sector	*Financial sector*	*Have*	*European economy*
Financial	*Financial*	*European*	*Time of crisis*
System	*Financial institute*	*Market*	*Crisis*
JRC-Acquis		**ACL**	
PLSA	PLSA-SIM	PLSA	PLSA-SIM
Transport	*Transport*	*Tag*	*Tag*
Road	*Transport service*	*Word*	*Tag set*
Nuclear	*Road transport*	*Corpus*	*Tag sequence*
Vehicle	*Transport sector*	*Tagger*	*Unknown word*
Material	*Air transport*	*Tagging*	*Speech tag*

Table 5: Top-5 words from topics inferred by PLSA and PLSA-SIM algorithms

We should note that we used only intrinsic measures of topic model quality in the paper. In the future we would like to test improved topic models in such applications of information retrieval as text clustering and categorization.

6 Conclusion

The paper presents experiments on integrating bigrams and similarities between them and unigrams into topic models. At first, we propose the novel algorithm PLSA-SIM that incorporates similar unigrams and bigrams into topic models and maintains relationships between bigrams and unigram components. The experiments were conducted on the English parts of Europarl and JRC-Acquis parallel corpora, ACL Anthology Reference corpus and Russian banking articles distinguished two groups of measures ranking bigrams. The first group produces top bigrams, which, if added to topic models either as "black boxes" or not, results in nearly the same quality of inferred topics. However, the second group produces top bigrams, which, if added to the proposed PLSA-SIM algorithm, results in significant improvement in all metrics under consideration.

Acknowledgements

This work is partially supported by RFBR grant N14-07-00383.

References

David Andrzejewski, Xiaojin Zhu, and Mark Craven. 2009. *Incorporating Domain Knowledge into Topic Modeling via Dirichlet Forest Priors*. Proceedings of the 26th Annual International Conference on Machine Learning: 25–32.

David Andrzejewski and David Buttler. 2011. *Latent Topic Feedback for Information Retrieval*. Proceedings of the 17th ACM SIGKDD International Conference on Knowledge Discovery and Data Mining: 600–608.

Arthur Asuncion, Max Welling, Padhraic Smyth, Yee Whye Teh. 2009. *On Smoothing and Inference for Topic Models*. Proceedings of the 25th International Conference on Uncertainty in Artificial Intelligence: 27–34.

David M. Blei, Andrew Y. Ng, and Michael I. Jordan. 2003. *Latent Dirichlet Allocation*. Journal of Machine Learning Research, volume 3: 993–1022.

Gerlof Bouma. 2009. *Normalized (Pointwise) Mutual Information*. Proceedings of the Biennial GSCL Conference: 31–40.

Jordan Boyd-Graber, David M. Blei, and Xiaojin Zhu. 2007. *A Topic Model for Word Sense Disambiguation*. Proceedings of the 2007 Joint Conference on Empirical Methods in Natural Language Processing and Computational Natural Language Learning: 1024–1033.

Jonathan Chang, Jordan Boyd-Graber, Sean Gerrish, Chong Wang, David M. Blei. 2009. *Reading Tea Leaves: How Human Interpret Topic Models*. Proceedings of the 24th Annual Conference on Neural Information Processing Systems: 288–296.

Kenneth Ward Church, and Patrick Hanks. 1990. *Word Association Norms, Mutual Information, and Lexicography*. Computational Linguistics, volume 16: 22–29.

Beatrice Daille. 1995. *Combined Approach for Terminology Extraction: Lexical Statistics and Linguistic Filtering* PhD Dissertation. University of Paris, Paris.

Ali Daud, Juanzi Li, Lizhu Zhou, Faqir Muhammad. 2010. *Knowledge discovery through directed probabilistic topic models: a survey*. Frontiers of Computer Science in China, 4(2): 280–301.

Vidas Daudaravičius and Rūta Marcinkevičienė. 2003. *Gravity Counts for the Boundaries of Collocations*. International Journal of Corpus Linguistics, 9(2): 321–348.

Paul Deane. 2005. *A Nonparametric Method for Extraction of Candidate Phrasal Terms*. Proceedings of the 43rd Annual Meeting of the ACL: 605–613.

Ted Dunning. 1993. *Accurate Methods for the Statistics of Surprise and Coincidence*. International Journal of Computational Linguistics, 19(1): 61–74.

Vladimir Eidelman, Jordan Boyd-Graber, and Philip Resnik. 2012. *Topic Models for Dynamic Translation Model Adaptation*. Proceedings of the 50th Annual Meeting of the Association of Computational Linguistics, volume 2: 115–119.

Thomas L. Griffiths, Mark Steyvers, and Joshua B. Tenenbaum. 2007. *Topics in Semantic Representation*. Psychological Review, 114(2): 211–244.

Thomas Hofmann. 1999. *Probabilistic Latent Semantic Indexing*. Proceedings of the 22nd Annual International SIGIR Conference on Research and Development in Information Retrieval: 50–57.

Wei Hu, Nobuyuki Shimizu, Hiroshi Nakagawa, and Huanye Shenq. 2008. *Modeling Chinese Documents with Topical Word-Character Models*. Proceedings of the 22nd International Conference on Computational Linguistics: 345–352.

Paul Jaccard. 1901. *Distribution de la flore alpine dans le Bassin des Dranses et dans quelques regions voisines*. Bull. Soc. Vaudoise sci. Natur. V. 37. Bd. 140: 241–272.

Mark Johnson M. 2010. *PCFGs, Topic Models, Adaptor Grammars and Learning Topical Collocations and the Structure of Proper Names*. Proceedings of the 48th Annual Meeting of the ACL: 1148–1157.

Mihoko Kitamura, and Yuji Matsumoto. 1996. *Automatic Extraction of Word Sequence Correspondences in Parallel Corpora*. Proceedings of the 4th Annual Workshop on Very Large Corpora: 79–87.

Jey Han Lau, Timothy Baldwin, and David Newman. 2013. *On Collocations and Topic Models*. ACM Transactions on Speech and Language Processing, 10(3): 1–14.

Bing Liu. 2012. *Sentiment Analysis and Opinion Mining*. Synthesis Lectures on Human Language Technologies, Morgan & Claypool Publishers.

Jose Gabriel Pereira Lopes, and Joaquim Ferreira da Silva. 1999. *A Local Maxima Method and a Fair Dispersion Normalization for Extracting Multiword Units*. Proceedings of the 6th Meeting on the Mathematics of Language: 369–381.

David Mimno, Hanna M. Wallach, Edmund Talley, Miriam Leenders, Andrew McCallum. 2011. *Optimizing Semantic Coherence in Topic Models*. Proceedings of EMNLP'11: 262–272.

David Newman, Jey Han Lau, Karl Grieser, and Timothy Baldwin. 2010. *Automatic Evaluation of Topic Coherence*. Proceedings of Human Language Technologies: The 11th Annual Conference of the North American Chapter of the Association for Computational Linguistics: 100–108.

Youngja Park, Roy J. Byrd, and Branimir K. Boguraev. 2002. *Automatic Glossary Extraction: Beyond Terminology Identification*. Proceedings of the 19th International Conference on Computational Linguistics: 1–7.

Frank Smadja, Kathleen R. McKeown, and Vasileios Hatzivassiloglou. 1996. *Translating Collocations for Bilingual Lexicons: A Statistical Approach*. Computational Linguistics, 22(1): 1–38.

Keith Stevens, Philip Kegelmeyer, David Adnrzejewski, and David Buttler. 2012. *Exploring Topic Coherence over Many Models and Many Topics*. Proceedings of EMNLP-CoNLL'12: 952–961.

Konstantin V. Vorontsov, and Anna A. Potapenko. 2014. *Tutorial on Probabilistic Topic Modeling: Additive Regularization for Stochastic Matrix Factorization*. Proceedings of AIST'2014. LNCS, Springer Verlag-Germany, volume CCIS 439: 28–45.

Hanna M. Wallach. 2006. *Topic Modeling: Beyond Bag-of-Words*. Proceedings of the 23rd International Conference on Machine Learning: 977–984.

Xuerui Wang, Andrew McCallum, and Xing Wei. 2007. *Topical N-grams: Phrase and Topic Discovery, with an Application to Information Retrieval*. Proceedings of the 2007 Seventh IEEE International Conference on Data Mining: 697–702.

Dingding Wang, Shenghuo Zhu, Tao Li, and Yihong Gong. 2009. Multi-Document Summarization using Sentence-based Topic Models. Proceedings of the ACL-IJCNLP 2009 Conference Short Papers: 297–300.

Xing Wei and W. Bruce Croft. 2006. *LDA-Based Document Models for Ad-hoc Retrieval*. Proceedings of the 29th International Conference on Research and Development in Information Retrieval: 178–185.

Zhongwu Zhai, Bing Liu, Hua Xu, and Peifa Jia. 2010. *Grouping Product Features Using Semi-Supervised Learning with Soft-Constraints*. Proceedings of the 23rd International Conference on Computational Linguistics: 1272–1280.

Wen Zhang, Taketoshi Yoshida, Tu Bao Ho, and Xijin Tang. 2008. *Augmented Mutual Information for Multi-Word Term Extraction*. International Journal of Innovative Computing, Information and Control, 8(2): 543–554.

Shibin Zhou, Kan Li, and Yushu Liu. 2009. *Text Categorization Based on Topic Model*. International Journal of Computational Intelligence Systems, volume 2, No. 4: 398–409.

Improving Verb Phrase Extraction from Historical Text by use of Verb Valency Frames

Eva Pettersson and Joakim Nivre
Department of Linguistics and Philology
Uppsala University
firstname.lastname@lingfil.uu.se

Abstract

In this paper we explore the idea of using verb valency information to improve verb phrase extraction from historical text. As a case study, we perform experiments on Early Modern Swedish data, but the approach could easily be transferred to other languages and/or time periods as well. We show that by using verb valency information in a post-processing step to the verb phrase extraction system, it is possible to remove improbable complements extracted by the parser and insert probable complements not extracted by the parser, leading to an increase in both precision and recall for the extracted complements.

1 Introduction

Information extraction from historical text is a challenging field of research that is of interest not only to language technology researchers but also to historians and other researchers within the humanities, where information extraction is still to a large extent performed more or less manually due to a lack of NLP tools adapted to historical text and insufficient amounts of annotated data for training such tools.

In the *Gender and Work* project (GaW), historians are building a database with information on what men and women did for a living in the Early Modern Swedish society, i.e. approximately 1550–1800 (Ågren et al., 2011). This information is currently extracted by researchers manually going through large volumes of text from this time period, searching for relevant text passages describing working activities. In this process, it has been noticed that working activities often are described in the form of verb phrases, such as *hugga ved* ("chop wood"), *sälja fisk* ("sell fish") or *tjäna som piga* ("serve as a maid"). Based on this observation, Pettersson et al. (2012) developed a method for automatically extracting verb phrases from historical documents by use of spelling normalisation succeeded by tagging and parsing. Using this approach, it is possible to correctly identify a large proportion of the verbs in Early Modern Swedish text. Due to issues such as differences in word order and significantly longer sentences than in present-day Swedish texts (combined with sentence segmentation problems due to inconsistent use of punctuation), it is however still hard for the parser to extract the correct complements associated with each verb.

In this work we propose a method for improving verb phrase extraction results by providing verb valency information to the extraction process. We describe the effect of removing improbable complements from the extracted verb phrases, as well as adding probable complements based on verb valency frames combined with words and phrases occurring in close context to the head verb.

2 Related Work

Syntactic analysis of historical text is a tricky task, due to differences in vocabulary, spelling, word order, and grammar. Sánchez-Marco (2011) trained a tagger for Old Spanish, based on a 20 million token corpus of texts from the 12th to the 16th century, by expanding the dictionary and modifying tokenisation and affixation rules. An accuracy of 94.5% was reported for finding the right part-of-speech, and an accuracy of 89.9% for finding the complete morphological tag.

In many cases, there is a lack of large corpora for training such tools, and alternative methods are called for. Schneider (2012) presented a method for adapting the Pro3Gres dependency parser to analyse historical English text. In this approach, spelling normalisation is a key factor, transforming the historical spelling to a modern spelling by use of the VARD2 tool (Baron and Rayson, 2008) before parsing. In addition to spelling normalisation, a set of handwritten grammar rules were added to capture unseen interpretations of specific words, for relaxing word order constraints, and for ignoring commas in a sentence. Schneider concluded that spelling normalisation had a large impact on parsing accuracy, whereas the grammar adaptations where easy to implement but lead to small improvements only.

Pettersson et al. (2013) also presented an approach to automatic annotation of historical text based on spelling normalisation. In this approach, the historical spelling is translated to a modern spelling employing character-based statistical machine translation (SMT) techniques, before tagging and parsing is performed by use of standard natural language processing tools developed for present-day language. The method was evaluated on the basis of verb phrase extraction results from Early Modern Swedish text, where the amount of correctly identified verb complements (including partial matches) increased from 32.9% for the text in its original spelling to 46.2% for the text in its automatically modernised spelling. Earlier work by the same authors showed that using contemporary valency dictionaries to remove extracted complements not adhering to the valency frame of a specific verb had a positive effect on verb phrase extraction precision (Pettersson et al., 2012).

In the context of valency-based parsing of modern language, Jakubíček and Kovář (2013) introduced a verb valency-based method for improving Czech parsing. Their experiments were based on the Synt parser, which is a head-driven chart parser with a hand-crafted meta-grammar for Czech, producing a list of ranked phrase-structure trees as output. They used two different dictionaries with valency information to rerank the suggested parses in accordance with the valency frames suggested for the verb in the dictionaries. Evaluation was performed on the Brno Phrasal Treebank using the leaf-ancestor assessment metric, and an improvement from 86.4% to 87.7% was reported for the highest-ranked tree when comparing the Synt parser in its original setting to the inclusion of valency frames for reranking of the output parses.

For modern Swedish, Øvrelid and Nivre (2007) experimented on ways to improve parsing accuracy for core grammatical functions including for example object, subject predicative, and prepositional argument. They found that by providing the parser with linguistically motivated features such as animacy, definiteness, pronoun type and case, a 50% error reduction could be achieved for the syntactic functions targeted in the study.

3 Approach

In this work, we adopt the verb phrase extraction method presented in Pettersson et al. (2013), where verbs and complements are extracted from historical text based on output from NLP tools developed for present-day Swedish. In addition to their approach, we also include a post-processing step, removing and/or inserting verbal complements based on the valency frame of the head verb.

The full process is illustrated in Figure 1, where the first step is tokenisation of the source text by use of standard tools. The tokenised text is then to be linguistically annotated in the form of tagging and parsing. To the best of our knowledge, there is however no tagger nor parser available trained on Early Modern Swedish text. Since these tools are sensitive to spelling, the tokenised text is therefore normalised to a more modern spelling by use of character-based SMT methods, before tagging and parsing is performed using tools trained for modern Swedish. For tagging, we use HunPOS (Halácsy et al., 2007) with a Swedish model based on the Stockholm-Umeå corpus, SUC version 2.0 (Ejerhed and Källgren, 1997). For parsing, we use MaltParser version 1.7.2 (Nivre et al., 2006a) with a pre-trained model based on the Talbanken section of the Swedish Treebank (Nivre et al., 2006b).

After tagging and parsing, the annotations given by the tagger and the parser are projected back to the text in its original spelling, resulting in a tagged and parsed version of the historical text, from which the verbs and their complements are extracted. The complements included for extraction are the following: subject (for passive verbs only, where the subject normally corresponds to the direct object in an active verb construction), direct object, indirect object, prepositional complement, infinitive complement, subject predicative, verb particle, and reflexive pronoun. As mentioned, we also add a post-processing filter as a complementary step, using valency information to

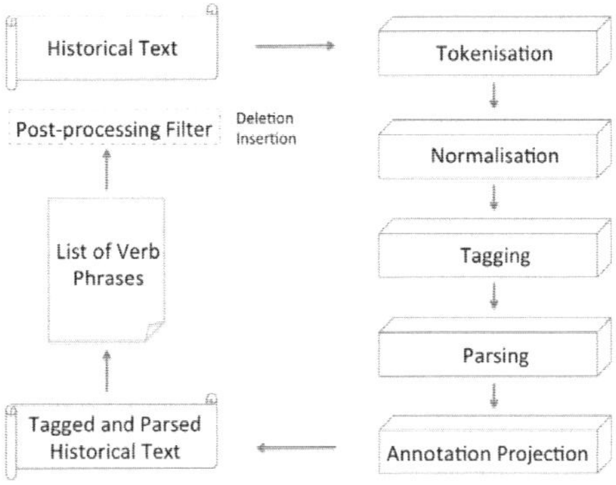

Figure 1: Method overview.

modify the complements suggested by the parser.

3.1 Deletion of Improbable Complements

As discussed in Section 1, certain characteristics of historical text make it difficult for the parser to correctly extract the complements of a verb. Therefore, we add valency information in a post-processing step, filtering away extracted complements that do not conform to the valency frame of the verb. A similar idea was presented in Pettersson et al. (2012), where filtering was based on valency frames given in two contemporary dictionaries, i.e. Lexin[1] and Parole[2]. However, some word forms in historical text are not frequent enough in contemporary language to occur in modern dictionaries. Examples from the GaW training corpus are *absentera* (old word for "be absent"), *umgälla* (old word for "suffer for"), and *ärna* (old word for "intend to"). Moreover, the meaning of verbs tend to change over time, and it is not obvious that verb valency frames for present-day Swedish also holds for historical Swedish. An example from the GaW corpus is the verb *slå* ("hit") which in both Lexin and Parole is listed as a monotransitive verb ("to hit someone"). In the GaW corpus however, it is repeatedly used as a ditransitive verb, as in *Sedhan hadhe Erich OluffSon slaghit Pelle Pederssonn tre blånader* ("Then Erich OluffSon had hit Pelle Pederssonn three bruises"). A comparison between the valency frames present in the GaW corpus and the frames present in the Lexin dictionary shows that only 16% of the verb forms that are present in both the old and the modern resource (108 out of 675 verb forms) have equal valency frames. In our approach to deletion of improbable complements, we therefore base the valency frames not only on the contemporary valency dictionaries, but also on the verbal complements occurring in the training part of the GaW corpus.

[1]http://spraakbanken.gu.se/lexin/valens_lexikon.html
[2]http://spraakbanken.gu.se/swe/resurs/parole

Deletion experiments are performed for all complement types extracted from the parser except for subjects, since a verb is typically expected to have a subject. We present deletion experiments for the following five settings:

1. **Lexin**
   For each extracted complement, if the head verb is present in the Lexin valency dictionary and the valency frame in Lexin does not allow for a complement of the type indicated by the parse label, the complement is removed from the extracted verb phrase.

2. **Parole**
   For each extracted complement, if the head verb is present in the Parole valency dictionary and the valency frame in Parole does not allow for a complement of the type indicated by the parse label, the complement is removed from the extracted verb phrase.

3. **GaW Corpus**
   For each extracted complement, if the head verb is present in the training part of the GaW corpus, and none of the occurrences in the corpus contain a complement of the type indicated by the parse label, the complement is removed from the extracted verb phrase.

4. **All combined**
   For each extracted complement, if the head verb is present in all three resources men-

tioned above, and none of these resources allow for a complement of the type indicated by the parse label, the complement is removed from the extracted verb phrase. Likewise, if the head verb is present in only two of these three resources, and none of these two resources allow for a complement of the type indicated by the parse label, the complement is removed from the extracted verb phrase. Finally, if the head verb is present in one resource exclusively, and this resource does not allow for a complement of the type indicated by the parse label, the complement is removed from the extracted verb phrase.

5. **All one-by-one**
   For each extracted complement, if the head verb is present in the best-performing resource, i.e. the resource yielding the highest complement extraction f-score in the first three experiments, and the valency frame in this resource does not allow for a complement of the type indicated by the parse label, the complement is removed from the extracted verb phrase. Otherwise, if the head verb is present in the second best-performing resource, and the valency frame in this resource does not allow for a complement of the type indicated by the parse label, the complement is removed from the extracted verb phrase. Only if the head verb is not present in any of the two best-performing resources, the third resource is consulted.

3.2 Insertion of Probable Complements

Apart from filtering away unlikely complements extracted by the parser, we also aim at inserting probable complements not found by the parser, by searching the parsed sentence for words and phrases that match the valency frame of the head verb, but which have not been extracted by the parser. Since the word order is more varying in Early Modern Swedish than in present-day Swedish, all complements are searched for both to the left and to the right of the head verb.

In the insertion experiments, we focus on phrasal verbs in the broader sense, including particles, reflexives, and prepositional complements. We believe that these complement types are relatively easy to recognise in a sentence. Furthermore, if for example a reflexive pronoun is found close to the head verb in the sentence, and the valency frame suggests a reflexive pronoun, then the probability that this reflexive belongs to the verb is rather high. The same argument holds for prepositional phrases containing the expected preposition to form a prepositional complement, and for prepositions or adverbials identical to a particle expected by the valency frame of the head verb. For direct and indirect objects on the other hand, even if we find a noun phrase close to the verb, it would still be hard to determine whether this noun phrase actually corresponds to a direct or indirect object, since noun phrases may occur with many different functions in a clause, and the word order is not fixed, particularly not for historical text. Therefore we would run a high risk of extracting for example the subject noun phrase instead of the direct or indirect object noun phrase, especially for languages like Swedish, where subject/object distinctions are not manifested morphologically other than for pronouns. Furthermore, direct objects are not always expressed in the form of noun phrases, but are quite often expressed as for instance clauses, as in the following example from the GaW corpus: *fordra at Barnet skal döpas hemma* ("demand that the Child should be christened at home"). Similarly, subject predicatives may also be expressed in varying ways and infinitive complements are often ambiguous to other functions. Thus, these categories are excluded from the insertion experiments.

In accordance with the arguments given above, the following three experiments are performed for insertion of probable complements:

1. **Insertion of prepositional complement**
   If the valency frame of the head verb (in any of the three valency resources) allows for a prepositional complement, and a prepositional phrase containing the expected preposition is found either to the left or to the right of the head verb, this prepositional phrase is added to the extracted verb phrase with a prepositional complement label.

2. **Insertion of particle**
   If the valency frame of the head verb allows for a particle, and a word that is identical to the expected particle and tagged as preposition or adverb is found either to the left or to the right of the head verb, this preposition or adverb is added to the extracted verb phrase with a particle label.

3. **Insertion of reflexive**
   If the valency frame of the head verb allows for a reflexive pronoun, and the word form *sig* ("oneself"), or the alternative historical spelling *sigh*, is found either to the left or to the right of the head verb, this word form is added to the extracted verb phrase with a reflexive label.

4 Data

Verb valency frames are extracted from three sources: the contemporary Lexin valency dictionary, the contemporary Parole valency dictionary, and the training and development parts of the GaW corpus of Early Modern Swedish court records and church documents. Evaluation is performed on the evaluation part of the GaW corpus. All the verbs in the GaW corpus have been manually annotated as such, and all complements adhering to the verbs have been annotated with labels denoting subject (for passive verbs only), direct object, indirect object, prepositional complement, infinitive complement, subject predicative, verb particle, and reflexive pronoun. Furthermore, the training and development parts of the corpus have been annotated with information on the manually modernised spelling for each original word form occurring in the text.

Both in the Lexin dictionary and in the Parole dictionary, verb valency frames are connected to the present tense form of the verb only, without information on other inflectional forms of the verb. In the verb phrase extraction process however, we need to connect whatever inflectional form of the verb that is used in the sentence to the correct valency frame. For broader coverage of the valency dictionaries, the present tense forms were therefore expanded to other inflectional forms based on the Saldo dictionary and the SUC corpus. The Saldo dictionary is a dictionary of present-day Swedish word forms, with morphological and inflectional information (Borin et al., 2008). By comparing the present tense verb form in Lexin or Parole to the Saldo dictionary, it is thus possible to extract a lemma corresponding to the verb form, and from that lemma all the inflectional forms adhering to that lemma. For verb forms not found in the Saldo dictionary, the SUC corpus was consulted. Since this corpus has been manually annotated with lemma information, all inflectional forms of the same lemma occurring in the corpus may thus be extracted. For Lexin and Parole verb forms not found in neither Saldo nor SUC, only the present tense form of the verb is stored with its corresponding valency frame.

For the GaW corpus, we have a similar problem in that only those verb forms that occur in the corpus will be assigned a valency frame, and if several forms of the same verb occur in the corpus, these will be assigned valency frames separate from each other. To deal with this, we use the same method of comparison to Saldo and SUC for retrieving the full set of word forms associated with a verb form, assigning the same valency frame to all verb forms belonging to the same lemma. In this process, we use the manually normalised form of each verb for comparison towards Saldo and SUC, to avoid mismatches due to spelling variation in the historical corpus.

It could be argued that instead of generating all fullforms for a verb, it would be more efficient to perform lemmatisation prior to comparison. This would however potentially impose more ambiguity to the valency frames, since word forms in the SUC corpus are associated with their base form rather than the actual lemma. This means that present tense forms such as *är* ("is") and *varar* ("lasts") are both associated with the same base form *vara* ("to be/to last"), even though their inflectional paradigms and valency frames differ significantly. For properly lemmatised sources, these word forms would instead have been associated with different lemmas, e.g. *vara1* and *vara2*.

Table 1 shows the number of verb forms found in Saldo and SUC respectively, during the process of expanding the valency frames to more inflectional forms. The GaW corpus has been divided into training (train), development (dev) and test sets, where the training part is the same data set as was used for training and tuning in Pettersson et al. (2013), and the development set is the same data set as was used for evaluation in the same paper. In total, the training and development parts contain 600 sentences each, whereas the test set contains 300 sentences. Since the test set will only be used for evaluation, no expansion to inflectional forms is needed for this particular data set.

Table 2 lists the total number of entries in the language resources, before and after word form expansion. We will use the training part of our corpus as a basis for valency frames during model selection, where the development part is used for

	Verbs	Saldo	SUC	Not found
Lexin	3,281	3,181	33	67
Parole	4,304	4,263	26	15
GaW Train	1,329	1,168	14	147
GaW Dev	1,410	1,245	15	150
GaW Test	987	n/a	n/a	n/a

Table 1: Verb forms found in Saldo and SUC during the process of expanding the valency frames to more inflectional forms.

repeated testing. In the final evaluation, the training and development sets are merged to a combined valency resource, and evaluation scores are given for the test part of the corpus.

	verb forms	expanded forms
Lexin	3,281	42,545
Parole	4,304	32,640
GaW Train	1,329	10,032
GaW Dev	1,410	10,394
GaW Test	987	n/a

Table 2: Number of verb forms in the language resources, before and after word form expansion.

5 Evaluation

Evaluation is performed in terms of precision, recall and f-score based on the extracted complements, where the baseline case is the original verb phrase extraction system without any of the above specified amendments. We define true positives as correctly extracted complements. Likewise, false positives are complements extracted by the system that are not present in the gold standard, whereas false negatives are complements that are present in the gold standard but not extracted by the system. Since we are specifically aiming at extracting the correct complements, intransitive verbs that were also identified as intransitive by the extraction system will not contribute to the set of true positives. Intransitive verbs for which the system has extracted complements will however contribute to the set of false positives, whereas verbs identified as intransitive by the system though complements are present in the gold standard will add to the set of false negatives.

We also make a distinction between labelled and unlabelled precision and recall, where labelled precision and recall requires that the correct label for the complement has been assigned, i.e. direct object, prepositional complement etc, whereas unlabelled precision and recall only concerns the extracted word sequences, regardless of what label the parser has assigned to the complement.

Since the overall aim of the verb phrase extraction process is to present to historians text passages that may be of interest, partial matches are also regarded as true positives, as these would still point the user to the right text passage. True positives thus include the following cases, with authentic examples from the GaW corpus:

- **Exact match**
  Gold complement: *2 klimpar smör*
  Extracted complement: *2 klimpar smör*
  "2 lumps of butter"
- **Substring type A**
  Gold complement: *de penningar och* ***medel***
  Extracted complement: ***medel***
  "(the money and) **resources**"
- **Substring type B**
  Gold complement: ***detta***
  Extracted complement: ***detta*** *efter honom*
  "**this** (after him)"
- **Overlap**
  Gold complement: ***förswagat*** *ock förtrygt*
  Extracted complement: *nogh* ***förswagat***
  "(probably) **weakened** (and oppressed)"

6 Model Selection

In the model selection phase, we try different strategies for deletion and insertion of complements, using the training part of the corpus as a basis for valency frames, and the development part of the corpus for testing.

6.1 Deletion of Improbable Complements

For deletion of improbable complements, we first need to decide which of the five settings listed in Section 3.1 that should be chosen. We therefore ran experiments where deletion is performed for all complement types (except subject), evaluating the results for each setting separately. The results for unlabelled complement extraction are summarized in Table 3.

	Precision	Recall	F-score
Baseline	53.30	51.22	52.24
Lexin	59.76	35.44	44.49
Parole	55.22	38.49	45.36
GaW corpus	57.51	46.77	51.59
All combined	56.62	47.76	51.81
All one-by-one	57.64	46.01	51.17

Table 3: Unlabelled results for deletion of improbable complements with different settings.

As seen from the results, all settings improve precision as compared to the original system. However, recall varies to a great extent. For the largest resource, i.e. the Lexin dictionary, precision is the highest, but recall is very low. This indicates that a great amount of verb forms are found in the Lexin dictionary, but with valency frames that do not correspond to the way the verbs are used in historical texts, meaning that complements are erroneously deleted. This confirms our initial hypothesis that due to language change, contemporary dictionaries are not sufficient for guiding a parser with valency information. Further arguments for this hypothesis is the fact that even though the GaW training corpus is by far the smallest valency resource, using only this resource for defining verb valency frames results in a substantially higher f-score value than using Lexin or Parole. In fact, the f-score results for using the GaW corpus only are almost as high as for using all resources combined.

Since all methods improve precision as compared to the baseline, we choose the combined method for further experiments, since this method has the highest recall and also the highest f-score.

In the next round of experiments, we want to find out which complement types should be candidates for deletion. The hypothesis is that some complement types may be more thoroughly covered in the valency resources than others. If so, deletion of complements may only be a successful method for some complement types, whereas others should be left unmodified in the deletion process. To test this hypothesis, we tried deletion for each complement type separately, keeping only those that improve f-score as compared to the baseline system. These experiments were run with the combined setting, in accordance with the arguments given above. The results are presented in Table 4, where it can be noticed that only deletion of direct objects and subject predicatives are successful in improving the f-score value as compared to the baseline. Keeping these two categories as candidates for deletion, a precision of 54.96% is achieved, with a recall of 50.25%, as compared to the baseline precision of 53.30 and recall of 51.22.

	Precision	**Recall**	**F-score**
Baseline	53.30	51.22	52.24
A) direct object	54.29	50.62	52.39
B) indirect object	53.37	50.92	52.12
C) prep compl	56.06	47.51	51.43
D) inf compl	53.34	51.02	52.15
E) subj predicative	53.93	50.84	52.34
F) particle	53.45	50.84	52.11
G) reflexive	53.19	50.50	51.81
A + E	54.96	50.25	52.50

Table 4: Unlabelled results for deletion of improbable complements for the setting "all combined", varying the complements included for deletion.

6.2 Insertion of Probable Complements

As described in Section 3.2, the insertion experiments are targeted at particles, reflexives, and prepositional objects. Whenever the valency frame of the head verb in the extracted phrase allows for a complement of the specified type, the parsed sentence is searched for words and phrases matching the complement at hand. In the insertion experiments, we tried the following enhancements of the original insertion strategy:

1. Inclusion of stopwords, for which no complements are to be added. The set of stopwords were empirically defined as word forms belonging to any of the lemmas *vara* ("be"), *bli* ("become"), *ha* ("have") and *finnas* ("exist").

2. Prohibiting punctuation to occur between the head verb and the candidate complement.

3. Inclusion of a distance threshold, defining how many tokens that may come in between the head verb and the candidate complement. We tried a number of different thresholds, out of which a threshold of 5 tokens turned out to yield the best results.

The insertion results are presented in Table 5, showing that without any restrictions in the insertion process, recall can be increased from 51.22% to 53.63%. This is however at the expense of a substantial drop in precision from 53.30% to 37.47% as compared to the baseline system. Restrictions in the form of A) stopwords for which no complements are inserted, B) prohibition of punctuation between the head verb and the candidate complement, and C) defining a threshold for how many tokens are allowed to occur between the head verb and the candidate complement, all had a positive effect on precision and f-score. Thus, in the best setting, i.e. where all three restrictions are implemented, a precision of 52.57% is achieved, with a recall of 52.45%.

To find out which complements should be included for insertion, we also tried insertion for each complement type separately. As seen from Table 6, the best results are achieved when all

	Precision	Recall	F-score
Baseline	53.30	51.22	52.24
Original	37.47	53.63	44.12
A) Stopwords	45.69	53.41	49.25
B) Punctuation	47.81	53.04	50.29
C) Threshold	51.42	52.54	51.97
A + B + C	52.57	52.45	52.51

Table 5: Unlabelled results for insertion of probable complements.

three complement types are included for insertion.

	Precision	Recall	F-score
Baseline	53.30	51.22	52.24
A) prep compl	52.70	51.86	52.28
B) particle	53.23	51.28	52.24
C) reflexive	53.20	51.75	52.46
A + C	52.60	52.39	52.49
A + B + C	52.57	52.45	52.51

Table 6: Unlabelled results for insertion of probable complements, varying the complements included for insertion.

7 Results

Table 7 presents the complement extraction results on the test corpus, with the training and development part of the GaW corpus merged into a single historical valency resource. Results are presented for the baseline system (without additional deletion or insertion), for the best deletion setting as argued in Section 6.1, for the best insertion setting as argued in Section 6.2, and for both deletion and insertion combined.

	Unlabelled		
	Precision	Recall	F-score
Baseline	61.82	48.68	54.47
Deletion	63.02	47.61	54.24
Insertion	61.88	50.80	55.80
Delete + Insert	63.04	49.74	55.61
	Labelled		
	Precision	Recall	F-score
Baseline	53.25	38.34	44.58
Deletion	54.75	37.97	44.84
Insertion	53.67	40.45	46.13
Delete + Insert	55.12	40.08	46.41

Table 7: Complement extraction results.

As expected, performing only deletion of complements leads to an increase in precision at the expense of a decrease in recall. Performing only insertion on the other hand leads to an increase in recall without decreasing precision, demonstrating that inserting complements introduces true positives to a higher extent than false positives, which is satisfactory. In fact, insertion of complements results in a slightly higher f-score value than the combination of deletion and insertion. However, the best precision is achieved when both deletion and insertion are performed, yielding a precision of 63.04%, as compared to 61.82% for the baseline system. This setting also improves both precision and recall as compared to the baseline.

8 Conclusion

We have presented a method for improving verb phrase extraction from historical text, by automatically deleting improbable verbal complements extracted by the parser, while at the same time inserting probable complements not extracted by the parser. Our approach is based on verb valency frames rendered from historical corpora and from contemporary valency dictionaries, where the historical corpus had the largest positive effect even though the contemporary dictionaries covered more verb forms. This supports our hypothesis that since language changes over time, valency frames for present-day language may not be enough to cover the syntax in historical text. By automatically deleting and inserting complements based on a combination of the historical corpus and the contemporary dictionaries, an increase in both precision and recall is achieved, as compared to the baseline system.

For historians working with old texts, there is a need for NLP tools to effectively search large volumes of text automatically for text passages of special interest. We believe our method for verb phrase extraction from historical text to be a useful tool for this purpose. Still, there is room for improvement, since the best precision achieved for complement extraction is 63.04%, with a recall of 49.74%. In the current approach, verb valencies are exploited in a post-processing phase, with the original extracted verb phrases as input. Future work includes to explore the possibility of providing valency information already in the parser training phase, enriching the part-of-speech tags with information on whether a certain verb is likely to occur with e.g. a particle or prepositional complement. The hypothesis is that a parser trained on this kind of data will be keen to search harder for the expected complements. It would also be interesting to explore the use of lexical semantics for identifying specific types of complements.

References

Maria Ågren, Rosemarie Fiebranz, Erik Lindberg, and Jonas Lindström. 2011. Making verbs count. The research project 'Gender and Work' and its methodology. *Scandinavian Economic History Review*, 59(3):271–291. Forthcoming.

Alistair Baron and Paul Rayson. 2008. Vard2: A tool for dealing with spelling variation in historical corpora. In *Postgraduate Conference in Corpus Linguistics*, Aston University, Birmingham.

Lars Borin, Markus Forsberg, and Lennart Lönngren. 2008. Saldo 1.0 (svenskt associationslexikon version 2). Språkbanken, University of Gothenburg.

Eva Ejerhed and Gunnel Källgren. 1997. Stockholm Umeå Corpus. Version 1.0. Produced by Department of Linguistics, Umeå University and Department of Linguistics, Stockholm University. ISBN 91-7191-348-3.

Péter Halácsy, András Kornai, and Csaba Oravecz. 2007. HunPos - an open source trigram tagger. In *Proceedings of the 45th Annual Meeting of the Association for Computational Linguistics*, pages 209–212, Prague, Czech Republic.

Miloš Jakubíček and Vojtěch Kovář. 2013. Enhancing czech parsing with verb valency frames. In *CICLing 2013*, pages 282–293, Greece. Springer Verlag.

Joakim Nivre, Johan Hall, and Jens Nilsson. 2006a. MaltParser: A data-driven parser-generator for dependency parsing. In *Proceedings of the 5th international conference on Language Resources and Evaluation (LREC)*, pages 2216–2219, Genoa, Italy, May.

Joakim Nivre, Jens Nilsson, and Johan Hall. 2006b. Talbanken05: A Swedish treebank with phrase structure and dependency annotation. In *Proceedings of the 5th international conference on Language Resources and Evaluation (LREC)*, pages 24–26, Genoa, Italy, May.

Lilja Øvrelid and Joakim Nivre. 2007. When word order and part-of-speech tags are not enough – Swedish dependency parsing with rich linguistic features. In *Proceedings of the International Conference on Recent Advances in Natural Language Processing (RANLP)*, pages 447–451.

Eva Pettersson, Beáta Megyesi, and Joakim Nivre. 2012. Parsing the Past - Identification of Verb Constructions in Historical Text. In *Proceedings of the 6th EACL Workshop on Language Technology for Cultural Heritage, Social Sciences, and Humanities*, pages 65–74, Avignon, France, April. Association for Computational Linguistics.

Eva Pettersson, Beáta Megyesi, and Joakim Nivre. 2013. An SMT approach to automatic annotation of historical text. In *Proceedings of the Workshop on Computational Historical Linguistics at NODALIDA. NEALT Proceedings Series 18; Linkping Electronic Conference Proceedings.*, volume 87, pages 54–69.

Cristina Sánchez-Marco, Gemma Boleda, and Lluís Padró. 2011. Extending the tool, or how to annotate historical language varieties. In *Proceedings of the 5th ACL-HLT Workshop on Language Technology for Cultural Heritage, Social Sciences, and Humanities*, pages 1–9, Portland, OR, USA, June. Association for Computational Linguistics.

Gerold Schneider. 2012. Adapting a parser to Historical English. In *Outpost of Historical Corpus Linguistics: From the Helsinki Corpus to a Proliferation of Resources.*

Universal Dependencies for Finnish

Sampo Pyysalo[1] **Jenna Kanerva**[1,2] **Anna Missilä**[4] **Veronika Laippala**[3,4] **Filip Ginter**[1]
[1]Department of Information Technology [2]University of Turku Graduate School (UTUGS)
[3]Turku Institute for Advanced Studies (TIAS) [4]School of Languages and Translation Studies,
University of Turku, Finland
`first.last@utu.fi`

Abstract

There has been substantial recent interest in annotation schemes that can be applied consistently to many languages. Building on several recent efforts to unify morphological and syntactic annotation, the Universal Dependencies (UD) project seeks to introduce a cross-linguistically applicable part-of-speech tagset, feature inventory, and set of dependency relations as well as a large number of uniformly annotated treebanks. We present Universal Dependencies for Finnish, one of the ten languages in the recent first release of UD project treebank data. We detail the mapping of previously introduced annotation to the UD standard, describing specific challenges and their resolution. We additionally present parsing experiments comparing the performance of a state-of-the-art parser trained on a language-specific annotation schema to performance on the corresponding UD annotation. The results show improvement compared to the source annotation, indicating that the conversion is accurate and supporting the feasibility of UD as a parsing target. The introduced tools and resources are available under open licenses from `http://bionlp.utu.fi/ud-finnish.html`.

1 Introduction

The Universal Dependencies (UD) initiative seeks to develop cross-linguistically consistent annotation guidelines and apply them to many languages to create treebank annotations that are uniform in e.g. their theoretical basis, label sets, and structural aspects. Such resources could substantially advance cross-lingual learning, improve comparability of evaluation results, and facilitate new approaches to automatic syntactic analysis.

UD builds on the Google Universal part-of-speech (POS) tagset (Petrov et al., 2012), the Interset interlingua of morphosyntactic features (Zeman, 2008), and Stanford Dependencies (de Marneffe et al., 2006; Tsarfaty, 2013; de Marneffe et al., 2014). In addition to the abstract annotation scheme, UD defines also a treebank storage format, CoNLL-U. A first version of UD treebank data, building on the Google Universal Dependency Treebanks (McDonald et al., 2013) and many other previously released resources (Bosco et al., 2013; Haverinen et al., 2013b), was recently released[1] (Nivre et al., 2015).

In this paper, we present the adaptation of the UD guidelines to Finnish and the creation of the UD Finnish treebank by conversion of the previously introduced Turku Dependency Treebank (TDT) (Haverinen et al., 2013b). We also provide a first set of experiments comparing the parsing scores of language-specific treebank annotation to that of a UD treebank, providing an evaluation of both the conversion quality and the feasibility of UD annotation as a parsing target. In a related but separate effort within the UD initiative, the FinnTreeBank 1[2] (ftb-1) (Voutilainen, 2011) is also being converted into the UD format. The *ftb-1* is a treebank based on all grammatical examples from the VISK[3] Finnish grammar reference (Hakulinen et al., 2004), and will thus complement the TDT-based UD Finnish treebank in the set of UD treebanks.

2 Treebank conversion

The conversion of TDT into the UD Finnish treebank was implemented following the UD specification (Nivre et al., 2014) (version 1, Oct 2014),

[1]Available from `http://universaldependencies.github.io/docs/`

[2]`http://www.ling.helsinki.fi/kieliteknologia/tutkimus/treebank/sources/`

[3]`http://scripta.kotus.fi/visk`

the Finnish grammar of Hakulinen et al. (2004) and the TDT annotation guidelines (Haverinen et al., 2013b) as the primary references. The initial stages of the work involved identifying similarities and differences between the TDT and UD annotation guidelines, adapting the general UD guidelines to Finnish, and planning the implementation of the conversion. Technically, the conversion was implemented as a pipeline of processing components, each of which consumed and produced CoNLL-U-formatted data. The following sections present the source data and primary stages of processing in detail.

2.1 Turku Dependency Treebank

As the source data for the conversion, we selected the most recent published distribution of TDT.[4] The source treebank contains 15,000 sentences (200,000 words) drawn from a variety of sources and annotated in a Finnish-specific version of the Stanford Dependencies (SD) scheme, and it has previously been demonstrated to be applicable e.g. for training broad-coverage dependency parsers for Finnish (Kanerva et al., 2014).

In addition to converting the annotation to UD standards, we also addressed a number of instances where tokenization differed from UD specifications, corrected a small number of sentence-splitting errors, and updated the lemmas to improve both treebank-internal consistency and conformance with the UD specification. We further introduced a fully manually annotated morphology layer, replacing the automatically generated morphological annotation of the initial data. This modified TDT not only serves as the basis for conversion but is also made available as a separate contribution.

2.2 Part-of-speech annotation

The UD specification defines 17 POS tags, and requires that all conforming treebanks use only these tags.[5] The TDT annotation uses a comparatively coarse-grained set of 12 POS tags, of which approximately half correspond straightforwardly to one of the 17 UD POS tags (Table 1). Several other TDT tags could be assigned the appropriate UD tag based on the value of the SUBCAT feature, which distinguishes e.g. coordinating conjunctions from subordinating conjunctions (CONJ and SCONJ in UD, respectively). Just four TDT tags, marking pronouns, punctuation, symbols and verbs, required further information to resolve correctly.

TDT	UD	TDT type
A	ADJ	adjective
Adp	ADP	adposition
Adv	ADV	adverb
C[SUBCAT=CC]	CONJ	coord. conj.
C[SUBCAT=CS]	SCONJ	subord. conj.
Foreign	X	foreign word
Interj	INTJ	interjection
N[SUBCAT=Prop]	PROPN	proper noun
N[!SUBCAT=Prop]	NOUN	common noun
Num[SUBCAT=Card]	NUM	cardinal number
Num[SUBCAT=Ord]	ADJ	ordinal number
Pron	PRON or ADJ	pronoun
Punct	PUNCT or SYM	punctuation
Symb	PUNCT or SYM	symbol
V	VERB or AUX	verb

Table 1: Part-of-speech tag mapping from TDT to UD. TAG[FEATURE=VALUE] specifies a mapping that applies only in cases where a word has both the given tag and the feature value, TAG[!FEATURE=VALUE] in cases where the feature is absent or has a different value.

Punctuation and symbols The guidelines covering the use of the Punct and Sym tags in the TDT annotation differed to such an extent from the UD specification of PUNCT and SYM that the Punct/Sym distinction in the original treebank was ignored in creating the mapping. Instead, words assigned either of these tags in TDT were assigned UD POS based on newly implemented surface form-based heuristics, with e.g. currency symbols, mathematical operators, URLs and emoticons assigned SYM and other non-alphabetical character sequences PUNCT.

Verbs All verbs that can serve as auxiliaries were assigned AUX or VERB based on the presence of an aux dependency. This is the only rule concerning the morphological annotation layer that refers to the syntactic annotation. It should be noted that this rule cannot be applied deterministically in a standard syntactic analysis pipeline where morphological analysis precedes dependency analysis, but will instead require these verbs to be assigned both a VERB and AUX reading.

Pronouns The TDT POS tag Pron maps to PRON for UD Finnish in most cases, but pro-

[4] Available from http://bionlp.utu.fi/

[5] While no language-specific POS tags can thus be defined in the primary POS annotation, the CoNLL-U format allows a secondary POS tag to be assigned to each word to preserve treebank-specific information.

adjectives such as *millainen* "like-what" are analyzed as Pron in TDT but assigned to ADJ in UD Finnish following the reference grammar and the UD specification. The annotation of related cases such as pro-adverbs was already consistent with the reference resources and could thus be processed using the general mapping rules.

Finally, we note that UD Finnish excludes by design two of the UD POS tags, DET (determiner) and PART (particle). As Finnish has no true articles (Sulkala and Karjalainen, 1992) and words (primarily pronouns) that play a determiner role syntactically can be identified using the dependency annotation layer (namely, the det relation), we opted not to apply DET in UD Finnish annotation. Similarly, although various words have been categorized as particles in different descriptions of Finnish, the reference grammar (Hakulinen et al., 2004) does not assign any Finnish words to the category covered by PART in the UD specification. This POS tag is correspondingly excluded from use in UD Finnish.

2.3 Morphological features

The UD specification defines a set of 17 widely attested morphological features such as Case, Person, Number, Voice and Mood. However, by contrast to the POS tag annotation, the specification allows conforming treebanks to introduce language-specific features that are not included in this universal inventory, suggesting that such features be drawn when possible from the extended Interset compilation of morphological feature names and labels (Zeman, 2008).

The morphological annotation of TDT draws directly on the rich features provided by the OMorFi morphological analyzer (Pirinen, 2008), and many of the generally applicable UD features can be generated by direct mapping from TDT POS tags and features (Table 2). For brevity, we refer to UD documentation for descriptions of UD standard features, focusing in the following on UD Finnish features not among the basic 17.

To minimize information loss from the conversion, we made liberal use of the possibility to introduce language-specific features to mark aspects of the TDT morphological annotation that were not captured by the basic 17 UD features. We aimed to primarily apply extended Interset features, drawing from this inventory the features Abbr (abbreviation or acronym), Style (colloquial or archaic style), Typo (typographic error), Foreign (foreign word or script) and AdpType (adposition type: pre- or postposition). Finally, we added features to capture aspects of TDT annotation that did not have representation in Interset: InfForm (differentiates between Finnish infinitives), PartForm (similar for participles), Connegative (verb in connegative form) and Clitic and Derivation, identifying steps in the morphological derivation and modification processes to create the wordform.

TDT	UD
CASE	Case
CLIT	Clitic
CMP	Degree
DRV	Derivation
INF	InfForm and VerbForm=Inf
MOOD	Mood
NEG=ConNeg	Connegative=Yes
OTHER=Coll	Style=Coll
OTHER=Arch	Style=Arch
OTHER=Err	Typo=Yes
PCP	PartForm and VerbForm=Part
POSS	Person[psor] and Number[psor]
V[SUBCAT=Neg]	Negative=Yes
SUBCAT=Pfx	-
Pron[SUBCAT]	PronType or Reflex
Adp[SUBCAT]	AdpType
SUBCAT=Card|Ord	NumType
NUM	Number
TENSE	Tense
VOICE	Voice
PRS	Person and Number
ABBR	Abbr
ACRO	Abbr
not INF and not PCP	VerbForm=Fin
FOREIGN[...]	Foreign

Table 2: Morphological feature mapping. FEATURE denotes a mapping that applies for all features with the given name, FEATURE=VALUE for a specific name-value pair, and TAG[FEATURE=VALUE] also for a specific POS tag. Person[psor] and Number[psor] are layered UD features for Person and Number of possessor, respectively.

While the great majority of UD Finnish features could be deterministically generated by reference only to the TDT POS tag and features, there were a few cases that required more complex heuristics to meet UD requirements. For example, the value of the Person feature is assigned to personal pronouns based on a lemma lookup table as OMorFi does not generate it, and the value of the Foreign value is assigned based on comparison of characters in the surface form against Unicode script tables.

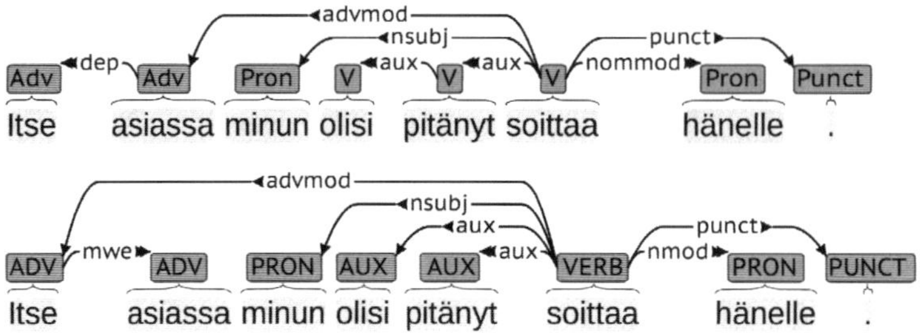

Figure 1: Top: TDT-style syntax and part-of-speech annotation for a Finnish sentence. Bottom: The same sentence converted to the UD Finnish scheme. Analyses visualized using BRAT (Stenetorp et al., 2012).

2.4 Dependency annotation

UD defines as set of 40 broadly applicable dependency relations, further allowing language-specific subtypes of these to be defined to meet the needs of specific resources. Unlike the fairly straightforward mappings for morphological annotations, the conversion from TDT dependency annotation to UD often required not only relabeling types, but also changes to the tree structure. This mapping is summarized in Table 3 and presented in detail below.

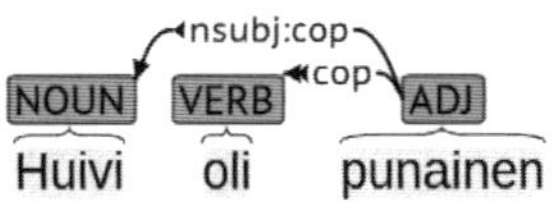

Figure 2: Annotation of *Huivi oli punainen* "The scarf was red".

The UD syntactic annotation is based on the universal Stanford Dependencies (SD) scheme (de Marneffe et al., 2014). One of the key properties of these schemes is that they emphasize direct relations between content words, treating function words as dependents of content words rather than as their heads. For example, this leads to a structure where a copula subject is attached directly to the predicative with the copular verb also becoming a dependent of the predicative (Figure 2). Furthermore, function words can only have a very limited set of dependents, with strong preference given to attachment of function words to content words rather than to other function words. This will tend to produce relatively flat tree structures.

The UD emphasis on content words is not universally shared with other dependency annotation schemes, many of which mediate connections between content words through function words. However, TDT is originally annotated using a language-specific variant of the SD scheme, and thus already applies an annotation scheme with predicatives as heads in copular expressions and content-word heads in prepositional phrases. The conversion of the syntactic annotation to UD thus involved fewer challenges than might be encountered for other treebanks.

During the conversion, relatively few structural reconfigurations were required. In the original TDT annotation, function words were allowed to have dependents of their own, permitting e.g. chains of auxiliary verbs (see Figure 1). These modifiers were reattached to the upper-level content words. Additionally, multi-word expressions and names were annotated with head-final structures in TDT, but UD specifies head-initial annotation for all expressions that do not have internal structure of their own. For UD Finnish, multi-word expressions were revised to follow the UD head-initial approach. However, the head-final structure was kept for names. This decision reflects the fact that in Finnish multi-word names, only the last word carries the morphological inflections, providing evidence that it is the head of the phrase. By contrast, fixed multi-word expressions (UD `mwe`) do not typically inflect, and thus do not provide sufficient cause to diverge from the UD guideline of head-initial annotation.

One problematic issue arose from the fact that UD makes a systematic distinction between core arguments and other modifiers, which are only partly distinguished in TDT annotation. For example, participial modifiers of predicates, which usually include also secondary predication, were annotated simply as participial modifiers in TDT, while in UD these are seen as clausal dependents and a distinction must thus be made between com-

Unchanged types
advcl, amod, appos, aux, auxpass, cc, conj, cop, csubj, det, dobj, mark, name, nsubj, neg, root, parataxis, xcomp
Simple mapping
acomp → xcomp, adpos → case, compar → advcl, comparator → mark, complm → mark, csubj-cop → csubj:cop, gobj → nmod:gobj, gsubj → nmod:gsubj, iccomp → xcomp:ds, infmod → acl, intj → discourse, nommod-own → nmod:own, nsubj-cop → nsubj:cop, num → nummod, number → compound, poss → nmod:poss, preconj → cc:preconj, prt → compound:prt, quantmod → advmod, rcmod → acl:relcl, voc → vocative, xsubj → nsubj, xsubj-cop → nsubj:cop
More complex mapping
advmod → advmod, cc, mark
ccomp → ccomp, xcomp:ds
dep → dep, mwe
nommod → nmod, xcomp, xcomp:ds
nn → compound:nn, goeswith
partmod → acl, advcl, ccomp, xcomp, xcomp:ds
punct → discourse, punct
∅ → remnant
Unmapped TDT types (removed)
ellipsis, rel
Unused UD types
csubjpass, dislocated, foreign, expl, iobj, list, nsubjpass, reparandum

Table 3: Dependency type mapping from TDT to UD Finnish.

plements and adjuncts. To implement the conversion for cases like these, we made reference to the manually annotated predicate-argument structures of the Finnish Propbank (Haverinen et al., 2013a). Since the Finnish Propbank and the Turku Dependency Treebank are built on top of the same texts, we had access to semantic information where each argument is marked to identify whether it serves as a core argument or a modifier.

In some cases the original TDT annotation is more fine-grained than the relation types defined in the UD guidelines. We use two approaches to resolve this issue in UD Finnish. First, most of the more specific dependency types not defined in UD are simply dropped from UD Finnish, replacing occurrences of the types with their more general UD types. This is done in particular for TDT types that are not specific to Finnish and encode distinctions not targeted in UD syntactic relations, such as the difference between finite and non-finite clauses (cf. SD partmod and infmod). However, some fine-grained dependencies were defined in the TDT variant of the SD scheme to capture properties that are unique or especially important to the Finnish language. We introduce some of these relations also in UD Finnish as subtypes of UD relations. This allows us to preserve the information while allowing a fully comparable UD analysis to be generated by simply replacing detailed types with those that they are subtypes of. For example, Finnish does not have a specific verb expressing ownership (such as *to have* in English), and typically the verb *olla* "to be" is used instead with the owner expressed with a nominal modifier. The surface forms of possessive clauses and existential clauses are similar (*Minulla on koira* "I have a dog", lit. *At_me is a dog* and *Pihalla on koira* "These is a dog in the yard"), and using the standard nominal modifier type nmod for both would fail to distinguish these constructions. Thus, UD Finnish carries over the original TDT distinction and defines a language-specific subtype nmod:own to address this issue. nmod:own can then trivially be mapped to nmod when the distinction is not required.

The total number of dependency relation types defined in UD Finnish is 43, consisting of 32 universal relations and 11 language-specific subtypes. In the original TDT annotation, 46 dependency types are used, with an additional 4 types to mark non-tree structures used in the second annotation layer of TDT. In UD Finnish, the second annotation layer does not expand the set of dependency types. Although not currently formalized in UD, the *extended* layer of annotation from TDT (Haverinen et al., 2013b) was converted as well and is included in the UD version of TDT. This extended TDT layer includes (1) conjunct propagation, where dependencies of the head of a coordination structure are propagated where applicable also to the other coordinated elements, (2) external subjects (xsubj) of open clausal complements,

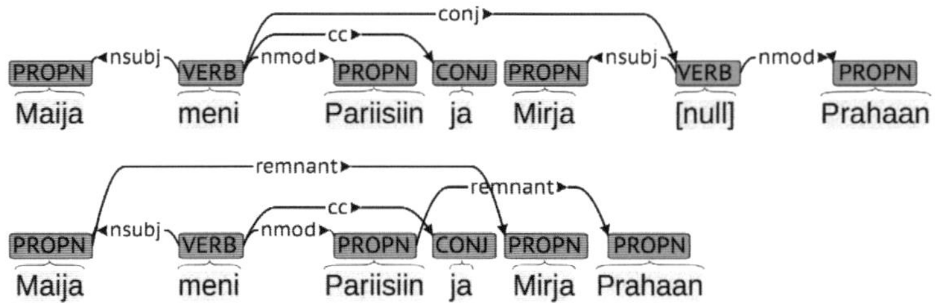

Figure 3: TDT-style (top) and UD-style (bottom) analysis for the sentence *Maija meni Pariisiin ja Mirja Prahaan* "Maija went to Paris and Mirja to Prague".

(3) `name` dependencies marking named entities spanning several words and having some internal syntactic structure, (4) dependencies marking the syntactic function of relativizers, and (5) the `ellipsis` dependency marking constructions involving ellipsis. Of these, conjunct propagation is converted using the same rules as the base syntax dependencies, external subjects are renamed to the standard subject relation `nsubj` or the language-specific `nsubj:cop` copula subject relation, the `name` dependencies are preserved, dependencies marking the syntactic function of relativizers are converted and placed into the base layer, replacing the `rel` dependency type (which is eliminated) and `ellipsis` dependencies are removed together with the `null` nodes they marked. (We refer to the UD Finnish documentation for further details.)

2.4.1 Implementation

While POS tags and morphological features could be mapped with rules affecting a single word and only referencing properties of that word, the dependency annotation mapping requires changes to the tree structure and the ability to refer to a wider syntactic context in mapping rules. The conversion is implemented using the *dep2dep* tool which allows rules that produce dependencies in the output tree based on an input tree context that can be specified in considerable detail: it can match subtree structures, specify negations (e.g. *does not have a property, dependent, or subtree*), refer to the morphological layer, the linear order of tokens, and to additional meta-data such as PropBank argument roles. The tool is implemented as a compiler that converts the source expressions into predicates in Prolog, which is then used to apply the rules.

As an illustration, consider the rule below, which specifies that an `advcl` UD dependency is to be produced between a verb and its participial modifier `partmod` in the transitive case, providing that the participle is not a core argument of the verb in the PropBank.

```
[v p ('advcl')] : [
  @[v-"POS_V" p-"CASE=Tra" ("partmod")]
  ![v p ("Arg_.*")]
]
```

In total, the conversion consists of 116 such rules, of which 22 are simple direct dependency renamings, and the remaining refer to a broader context. We note that these rules did not aim to be universal or exhaustive: a small number of dependencies, on the order of 250, were not covered by the rules and were edited manually upon conversion. This was more efficient than writing rules that only apply to generate very few or only single dependencies.

2.4.2 Null tokens

In many situations sentences can be incomplete and elements obvious from the context can be omitted. In *gapping*, an elliptic sentence element is omitted to avoid unnecessary repetition, whereas in *sentence fragments* the main predicate is absent. The analysis of fragments and sentences including gapping is difficult, and many different approaches have been proposed. In TDT the omitted token, most commonly a verb, is replaced with a *null* token, which is given a full morphological analysis and which acts as a normal token in the syntactic analysis.

UD takes a different approach to analyzing omitted sentence elements. UD aims in general to avoid representing things that are absent, and does not define a way to introduce null tokens. Instead, for example to address coordination with ellipsis, UD introduces a special dependency type `remnant`. Thus, e.g. *Maija meni Pariisiin ja Mirja Prahaan* "Maija went to Paris and Mirja to Prague" is analysed with an empty token representing *meni* "went" in the second constituent in

Language	Tokens	Source treebank
Czech	1,506,490	Prague Dependency Treebank 3.0 (PDT) (Bejček et al., 2012)
Spanish	432,651	Universal Dependency Treebank v2.0 (UDT) (McDonald et al., 2013)
French	400,620	Universal Dependency Treebank v2.0 (UDT) (McDonald et al., 2013)
German	298,614	Universal Dependency Treebank v2.0 (UDT) (McDonald et al., 2013)
English	254,830	English Web Treebank v1.0 (EWT) (Silveira et al., 2014)
Italian	214,748	Italian Stanford Dependency Treebank (ISDT) (Simi et al., 2014)
Finnish	**202,085**	Turku Dependency Treebank (TDT) (Haverinen et al., 2013b)
Swedish	96,819	Talbanken (Nivre, 2014)
Hungarian	26,538	Szeged Treebank (Farkas et al., 2012)
Irish	23,686	Irish Dependency Treebank (IDT) (Lynn et al., 2014)

Table 4: Statistics of the UD Finnish treebank in comparison to the other treebanks included in the first UD data release.

TDT, but with `remnant` relations between *Maija* and *Mirja* and between *Pariisiin* and *Prahaan* in UD Finnish (see Figure 3). We applied a combination of custom scripts and manual reannotation to resolve empty nodes in the conversion of TDT to UD Finnish.

2.5 Annotation statistics

Table 4 shows token statistics for the 10 languages for which treebanks were included in the initial UD data release. With over 200,000 tokens, the UD Finnish treebank is in a mid-size cluster among the UD version 1 languages together with German, English and Italian. This is a relatively prominent position for Finnish, which until recently had no publicly available treebanks. We hope that the availability of this corpus will encourage further interest in Finnish dependency parsing.

3 Experiments

As discussed by de Marneffe et al. (2014) in the context of the Universal Stanford Dependencies which formed the basis on which UD was built, parsing accuracy has not been a major consideration in the definition of the scheme. In fact, a number of the design choices taken, such as the attachment of auxiliaries and prepositions as dependents rather than governors of their semantic head is known to result in a numerically worse parsing accuracy. Additionally, as the conversion is an automatic process, the resulting noise may have a detrimental effect on parsing accuracy as well. To quantify these effects, we carry out several parsing experiments, comparing the Stanford Dependencies annotation in TDT with its conversion to the UD format. Further, since TDT now contains also fully manually annotated morphology, we will pay extra attention to morphological processing in the evaluation.

We base the experiments on the publicly available Finnish parsing pipeline.[6] The pipeline uses the CRF-based tagger Marmot (Müller et al., 2013), in conjunction with the two-level morphological analyzer OMorFi (Pirinen, 2008; Lindén et al., 2009). The morphological analyzer is used to provide the set of possible morphological readings (lemma, POS, and features) of every recognized word, which are subsequently given as features to the Marmot tagger. We initially apply a *hard* constraint approach, where the output of the tagger is used to select one of these readings (the reading with the highest overlap of tags and a priority for readings matching the main POS), effectively disambiguating OMorFi output. For words not recognized by OMorFi, the reading produced by Marmot is used as-is, and the wordform itself is used in place of the lemma. This has so far been the strategy taken when learning to parse Finnish (Bohnet et al., 2013). The tagged text is then parsed with the Mate tools graph-based dependency parser (Bohnet, 2010).[7]

As baseline, we consider the most recent Finnish dependency parser trained and evaluated on the original distribution of TDT. Note that the test sets differ: the baseline is evaluated on a test set matching the data it was trained on, which differs from the new test set in several aspects such as the treatment of named entities. The results are thus broadly comparable, but not directly so.

[6] `http://turkunlp.github.io/Finnish-dep-parser/`

[7] `https://code.google.com/p/mate-tools`

	POS	PM	FM	LAS	UAS
Baseline (Haverinen et al., 2013b)	94.3	90.5	89.0	81.4	85.2
Stanford Dependencies (SD)	96.3	93.4	90.3	80.1	84.1
Universal Dependencies (UD)	96.0	93.1	90.5	81.0	85.0
Pure Universal Dependencies (Pure UD)	96.0	93.1	90.5	81.5	84.7

Table 5: Results of the parsing experiments. *SD* refers to the morphological tagset and dependency relations as defined in TDT, *UD* to the universal tagset and relations, and *pure UD* to UD relations with no language-specific extensions. *POS* is the POS tagging accuracy, *PM* the accuracy of POS and all features, *FM* the accuracy of full morphology (including the lemma), and *LAS* and *UAS* are the standard labeled and unlabeled attachment score metrics.

	POS	PM	FM	LAS	UAS
Universal Dependencies (soft)	97.0	93.0	89.3	81.5	85.4
Universal Dependencies (hard-pos)	97.0	94.0	90.7	82.1	85.8
Pure Universal Dependencies (soft)	97.0	93.0	89.3	82.0	84.9
Pure Universal Dependencies (hard-pos)	97.0	94.0	90.7	82.7	85.4

Table 6: Results of the UD parsing experiments with the *soft* and *hard-pos* morphological tagging strategies.

The results are summarized in Table 5. Firstly, we see that all results are roughly comparable, meaning that the conversion to UD has had no major effect on the parsing accuracy. However, the attachment scores are somewhat lower compared to the baseline, likely due at least in part to the different treatment of named entities in the previously published baseline parser as opposed to both the newly introduced SD and UD versions of TDT. Unsurprisingly, the labeled attachment score is slightly higher for the pure UD scheme with no language-specific relations.

We additionally focused on morphological tagging. As TDT now contains manual morphological annotation, the analyses are no longer tightly bound to OMorFi as they were in the original release of TDT. We therefore consider also a *soft* constraint approach, where the tags given by Marmot are preserved, and OMorFi is only used to select the lemma (from the reading with the highest overlap of tags). This results in morphological analyses superior in POS accuracy but inferior in the prediction of full features. To address this issue, we implemented a new tagging strategy that applies the hard constraint only in cases where the predicted POS can be found among the analyses given by OMorFi (referred to as *hard-pos*). The results show an across-the-board improvement for this strategy as well as numerically the best scores for Finnish with the graph-based parser of Bohnet (2010) (Table 6).

4 Conclusions

We have presented Universal Dependencies (UD) for Finnish, detailing the application of general UD guidelines to the annotation of parts-of-speech, morphological features, and dependency relations in Finnish and introducing a conversion from the previously released Turku Dependency Treebank corpus into the UD Finnish treebank released in the first UD data release. We also performed experiments evaluating a state-of-the-art parser on both the source treebank, TDT, and the target UD Finnish treebank, finding that performance is slightly improved in the conversion, which supports both the accuracy of the conversion and the feasibility of UD as a parsing target.

All of the tools and resources described in this work are available under open licenses from `http://bionlp.utu.fi/ud-finnish.html`.

Acknowledgments

This work was supported by the Kone Foundation and the Emil Aaltonen Foundation. Computational resources were provided by CSC - IT Center for Science. This paper builds on joint work with Jinho Choi, Marie-Catherine de Marneffe, Tim Dozat, Yoav Goldberg, Jan Hajič, Christopher Manning, Ryan McDonald, Joakim Nivre, Slav Petrov, Natalia Silveira, Reut Tsarfaty, and Dan Zeman.

References

Bejček, E., Panevová, J., Popelka, J., Straňák, P., Ševčíková, M., Štěpánek, J., and Žabokrtský, Z. (2012). Prague dependency treebank 2.5 – a revisited version of pdt 2.0. In *Proceedings of the 24th International Conference on Computational Linguistics (Coling 2012)*, pages 231–246.

Bohnet, B. (2010). Top accuracy and fast dependency parsing is not a contradiction. In *Proceedings of COLING'10*, pages 89–97.

Bohnet, B., Nivre, J., Boguslavsky, I., Farkas, R., Ginter, F., and Hajič, J. (2013). Joint morphological and syntactic analysis for richly inflected languages. *Transactions of the Association for Computational Linguistics*, 1:415–428.

Bosco, C., Montemagni, S., and Simi, M. (2013). Converting italian treebanks: Towards an italian stanford dependency treebank. In *Proceedings of the 7th Linguistic Annotation Workshop and Interoperability with Discourse*, pages 61–69.

de Marneffe, M.-C., Dozat, T., Silveira, N., Haverinen, K., Ginter, F., Nivre, J., and Manning, C. D. (2014). Universal Stanford Dependencies: A cross-linguistic typology. In *Proceedings of the 9th International Conference on Language Resources and Evaluation (LREC)*, volume 14, pages 4585–4592.

de Marneffe, M.-C., MacCartney, B., and Manning, C. D. (2006). Generating typed dependency parses from phrase structure parses. In *Proceedings of the Fifth International Conference on Language Resources and Evaluation (LREC)*, volume 6, pages 449–454.

Farkas, R., Vincze, V., and Schmid, H. (2012). Dependency parsing of hungarian: Baseline results and challenges. In *Proceedings of the 13th Conference of the European Chapter of the Association for Computational Linguistics*, pages 55–65.

Hakulinen, A., Korhonen, R., Vilkuna, M., and Koivisto, V. (2004). *Iso suomen kielioppi*. Suomalaisen kirjallisuuden seura.

Haverinen, K., Laippala, V., Kohonen, S., Missil, A., Nyblom, J., Ojala, S., Viljanen, T., Salakoski, T., and Ginter, F. (2013a). Towards a dependency-based propbank of general finnish. In *Proceedings of the 19th Nordic Conference on Computational Linguistics (NoDaLiDa'13)*, pages 41–57.

Haverinen, K., Nyblom, J., Viljanen, T., Laippala, V., Kohonen, S., Missilä, A., Ojala, S., Salakoski, T., and Ginter, F. (2013b). Building the essential resources for finnish: the Turku Dependency Treebank. *Language Resources and Evaluation*, pages 1–39.

Kanerva, J., Luotolahti, J., Laippala, V., and Ginter, F. (2014). Syntactic n-gram collection from a large-scale corpus of internet finnish. In *Proceedings of the Sixth International Conference Baltic HLT*, pages 184–191.

Lindén, K., Silfverberg, M., and Pirinen, T. (2009). HFST tools for morphology — an efficient open-source package for construction of morphological analyzers. In *State of the Art in Computational Morphology*, volume 41 of *Communications in Computer and Information Science*, pages 28–47.

Lynn, T., Foster, J., Dras, M., and Tounsi, L. (2014). Cross-lingual transfer parsing for low-resourced languages: An Irish case study. In *Proceedings of the First Celtic Language Technology Workshop*, pages 41–49.

McDonald, R., Nivre, J., Quirmbach-Brundage, Y., Goldberg, Y., Das, D., Ganchev, K., Hall, K., Petrov, S., Zhang, H., Täckström, O., Bedini, C., Bertomeu Castelló, N., and Lee, J. (2013). Universal dependency annotation for multilingual parsing. In *Proceedings of the 51st Annual Meeting of the Association for Computational Linguistics (ACL)*, pages 92–97.

Müller, T., Schmid, H., and Schütze, H. (2013). Efficient higher-order CRFs for morphological tagging. In *Proceedings of the 2013 Conference on Empirical Methods in Natural Language Processing*.

Nivre, J. (2014). Universal Dependencies for Swedish. In *SLTC 2014*.

Nivre, J., Bosco, C., Choi, J., de Marneffe, M.-C., Dozat, T., Farkas, R., Foster, J., Ginter, F., Goldberg, Y., Hajič, J., Kanerva, J., Laippala, V., Lenci, A., Lynn, T., Manning, C., McDonald, R., Missilä, A., Montemagni, S., Petrov, S., Pyysalo, S., Silveira, N., Simi, M., Smith, A., Tsarfaty, R., Vincze, V., and Zeman, D. (2015). Universal dependencies 1.0.

Nivre, J., Choi, J., de Marneffe, M.-C., Dozat, T.,

Ginter, F., Goldberg, Y., Hajič, J., Manning, C., McDonald, R., Petrov, S., Pyysalo, S., Silveira, N., Tsarfaty, R., and Zeman, D. (2014). Universal dependencies documentation 1.0.

Petrov, S., Das, D., and McDonald, R. (2012). A universal part-of-speech tagset. In *Proceedings of the Eight International Conference on Language Resources and Evaluation (LREC)*, pages 2089–2096.

Pirinen, T. (2008). Suomen kielen äärellistilainen automaattinen morfologinen jäsennin avoimen lähdekoodin resurssein. Master's thesis, University of Helsinki.

Silveira, N., Dozat, T., de Marneffe, M.-C., Bowman, S., Connor, M., Bauer, J., and Manning, C. D. (2014). A gold standard dependency corpus for English. In *Proceedings of the Ninth International Conference on Language Resources and Evaluation (LREC-2014)*.

Simi, M., Bosco, C., and Montemagni, S. (2014). Less is more? towards a reduced inventory of categories for training a parser for the italian stanford dependencies. In *Proceedings of LREC 2014*.

Stenetorp, P., Pyysalo, S., Topić, G., Ohta, T., Ananiadou, S., and Tsujii, J. (2012). Brat: a web-based tool for nlp-assisted text annotation. In *Proceedings of the Demonstrations at the 13th Conference of the European Chapter of the Association for Computational Linguistics*, pages 102–107.

Sulkala, H. and Karjalainen, M. (1992). *Finnish*. Descriptive Grammar Series. Routledge, London.

Tsarfaty, R. (2013). A unified morpho-syntactic scheme of stanford dependencies. In *Proceedings of the 51st Annual Meeting of the Association for Computational Linguistics (ACL)*, pages 578–584.

Voutilainen, A. (2011). FinnTreeBank: Creating a research resource and service for language researchers with Constraint Grammar. In *Proceedings of the NODALIDA 2011 workshop Constraint Grammar Applications*.

Zeman, D. (2008). Reusable tagset conversion using tagset drivers. In *Proceedings of the Sixth International Conference on Language Resources and Evaluation (LREC)*, pages 213–218.

Automatic word stress annotation of Russian unrestricted text

Robert Reynolds
HSL Faculty
UiT The Arctic University of Norway
N-9018 Tromsø
robert.reynolds@uit.no

Francis Tyers
HSL Faculty
UiT The Arctic University of Norway
N-9018 Tromsø
francis.tyers@uit.no

Abstract

We evaluate the effectiveness of finite-state tools we developed for automatically annotating word stress in Russian unrestricted text. This task is relevant for computer-assisted language learning and text-to-speech. To our knowledge, this is the first study to empirically evaluate the results of this task. Given an adequate lexicon with specified stress, the primary obstacle for correct stress placement is disambiguating homographic wordforms. The baseline performance of this task is 90.07%, (known words only, no morphosyntactic disambiguation). Using a constraint grammar to disambiguate homographs, we achieve 93.21% accuracy with minimal errors. For applications with a higher threshold for errors, we achieved 96.15% accuracy by incorporating frequency- based guessing and a simple algorithm for guessing the stress position on unknown words. These results highlight the need for morphosyntactic disambiguation in the word stress placement task for Russian, and set a standard for future research on this task.

1 Introduction

Lexical stress and its attendant vowel reduction are a prominent feature of spoken Russian; the incorrect placement of stress can render speech almost incomprehensible. This is because Russian word stress is phonemic, i.e. many wordforms are distinguished from one another only by stress position. This is the cause of considerable difficulty for learners, since the inflecting word classes include complex patterns of shifting stress, and a lexeme's stress pattern cannot be predicted from surface forms. Furthermore, standard written Russian does not typically mark word stress.[1] Without information about lexical stress position, correctly converting written Russian text to speech is impossible. Half of the vowel letters in Russian change their pronunciation significantly, depending on their position relative to the stress. For example the word *dogovórom* 'contract.SG-INS' is pronounced /dəgʌvɔrəm/, with the letter *o* realized as three different vowel sounds. Determining these vowel qualities is impossible without specifying the stress position. This is a problem both for humans (e.g. foreign language students) and computers (e.g. text-to-speech).

We identify three different types relations between word stress ambiguity and morphosyntactic ambiguity. First, *intraparadigmatic* stress ambiguity refers to homographic wordforms belonging to the same lexeme, as shown in (1).[2]

(1) Intraparadigmatic homographs
 a. *téla* 'body.SG-GEN'
 b. *telá* 'body.PL-NOM'

The remaining two types of stress ambiguity occur between lexemes. *Morphosyntactically incongruent* stress ambiguity occurs between homographs that belong to separate lexemes, and whose morphosyntactic values are different, as shown in (2).

(2) Morphosyntactically incongruent homographs
 a. *nášej* 'our.F-SG-GEN/LOC/DAT/INS'
 našéj 'sew on.IMP-2SG'
 b. *dορóga* 'road.N-F-SG-NOM'
 dorogá 'dear.ADJ-F-SG-PRED'

[1] Texts intended for native speakers sometimes mark stress on words that cannot be disambiguated through context. Theoretically, a perfect word stress placement system could help an author identify tokens which should be stressed for natives: any token that cannot be disambiguated by syntactic or semantic means should be marked for stress.

[2] Throughout this article, cyrillic is transliterated using the scientific transliteration scheme.

Morphosyntactically congruent stress ambiguity occurs between homographs that belong to separate lexemes, and whose morphosyntactic values are identical, as shown in (3). This kind of stress ambiguity is relatively rare, and resolving this ambiguity would require the use of technologies such as word sense disambiguation.

(3) Morphosyntactically congruent homographs

a. *zámok* 'castle.$_{SG\text{-}NOM}$'
zamók 'lock.$_{SG\text{-}NOM}$'

b. *zámkov* 'castle.$_{PL\text{-}GEN}$'
zamkóv 'lock.$_{PL\text{-}GEN}$'

c. ...
...

It should be noted that most morphosyntactic ambiguity in unrestricted text does not result in stress ambiguity. For example, *novyj* 'new' (and every other adjective) has identical forms for F-SG-GEN, F-SG-LOC, F-SG-DAT and F-SG- INS: *nóvoj*. Likewise, the form *vypej* has multiple possible readings (including 'drink.$_{IMP}$', 'bittern.$_{PL\text{-}GEN}$'), but they all have the same stress position: *výpej*. We refer to this as *stress-irrelevant* morphosyntactic ambiguity, since all readings have the same stress placement.

In the case of unrestricted text in Russian, most stress placement ambiguity is rooted in intraparadigmatic and morphosyntactically incongruent ambiguity. Detailed part-of-speech tagging with morphosyntactic analysis can help determine the stress of these forms, since each alternative stress placement is tied to a different tag sequence. In this study we focus on the role of detailed part-of-speech tagging in improving automatic stress placement. We leave morphosyntactically congruent stress ambiguity to future work because it is by far the least common type of stress ambiguity (less than 1% of tokens in running text), and disambiguating morphosyntactically congruent stress requires fundamentally different technology from the other approaches of this study.

1.1 Background and task definition

Automatic stress placement in Russian is similar to diacritic restoration, a task which has received increasing interest over the last 20 years. Generally speaking, diacritics disambiguate otherwise homographic wordforms, so missing diacritics can complicate many NLP tasks, such as text-to-speech. For example, speakers of Czech may type emails and other communications without standard diacritics. In order to generate speech from these texts, they must first be normalized by restoring diacritics. A slightly different situation arises with languages whose standard orthography is underspecified, like vowel quality in Arabic or Hebrew. For such languages, the 'restoration' of vowel diacritics results in less ambiguity than in standard orthography. For languages with inherently ambiguous orthography, it may be more precise to refer to this as 'diacritic enhancement', since it produces text that is less ambiguous than the standard language. In this sense, Russian orthography is similar to Arabic and Hebrew, since its vowel qualities are underspecified in standard orthography.

Many studies of Russian text-to-speech and automatic speech recognition make note of the difficulties caused by the shortcomings of their stress-marking resources (e.g. Krivnova (1998)). Text-to-speech technology must deal with the inherent ambiguity of Russian stress placement, and many articles mention disambiguation of one kind or another, but to our knowledge no studies have empirically evaluated the success of their approach. Several studies have investigated methods for predicting stress position on unknown words. For example, Xomicevič et al. (2008) developed a set of heuristics for guessing stress placement on unknown words in Russian. More recently, Hall and Sproat (2013) trained a maximum entropy model on a dictionary of Russian words, and evaluated on wordlists containing 'known' and 'unknown' wordforms.[3] Their model achieved 98.7% accuracy on known words, and 83.9% accuracy on unknown words. The task of training and evaluating on wordlists is different from that of placing stress in running text. Since many of the most problematic stress ambiguities in Russian occur in high-frequency wordforms, evaluations of wordform lists encounter stress ambiguity seven times less frequently than in running text (see discussion in Section 4). Furthermore, working with running text includes the possibility of disambiguating homographs based on syntactic context.

[3]Hall and Sproat (2013) randomly selected their training and test data from a list of wordforms, and so a number of lexemes had wordforms in both the training and test data. Wordforms in the test data whose sibling wordforms from the same lexeme were in the training set were categorized as 'known' wordforms.

So far, the implicit target application of the few studies related to automatic stress placement in Russian has been text-to-speech and automatic speech recognition. However, the target application of our stress annotator is in a different domain: language learning. Since standard Russian does not mark word stress, learners are frequently unable to pronounce unknown words correctly without referencing a dictionary or similar resources. In the context of language learning, marking stress incorrectly is arguably worse than not marking it at all. Because of this, we want our stress annotator to be able to abstain from marking stress on words that it is unable to resolve with high confidence.

1.2 Stress corpus

Russian texts with marked word stress are relatively rare, except in materials for second language learners, which are predominantly proprietary. Our gold-standard corpus was collected from free texts on Russian language-learning websites. This small corpus (7689 tokens) is representative of texts that learners of Russian are likely to encounter in their studies. These texts include excerpts from well-known literary works, as well as dialogs, prose, and individual sentences that were written for learners.

Unfortunately, the general practice for marking stress in Russian is to *not* mark stress on monosyllabic tokens, effectively assuming that all monosyllabics are stressed. However, this approach is not well-motivated. Many words – both monosyllabic and multisyllabic – are unstressed, especially among prepositions, conjunctions, and particles. Furthermore, there are many high-frequency monosyllabic homographs that can be either stressed or unstressed, depending on their part of speech, or particular collocations. For example, the token *čto* is stressed when it means 'what' and unstressed in the conjunction *potomu čto* 'because'. For such words, one cannot simply assume that they are stressed on the basis of their syllable count.

Based on these considerations, we built our tools to mark stress on every word, both monosyllabic and multisyllabic. However, because our gold-standard corpus texts do not mark stress on monosyllabic words, we cannot evaluate our annotation of those words.

Similarly, some compound Russian words have secondary stress, but this is rarely marked, if at all, even in educational materials. Therefore, even though our tools are built to mark secondary stress, we cannot evaluate secondary stress marks, since they are absent in our gold-standard corpus.

In order to test our word stress placement system, we removed all stress marks from the gold-standard corpus, then marked stress on the unstressed version using our tools, and then compared with the original.

2 Automatic stress placement

State-of-the-art morphological analysis in Russian is based on finite-state technology (Nožov, 2003; Segalovich, 2003). To our knowledge, no existing open-source, broad-coverage resources are available for analyzing and generating stressed wordforms. Therefore, we developed free and open-source finite-state tools capable of analyzing and generating stressed wordforms, based on the well-known *Grammatical Dictionary of Russian* (Zaliznjak, 1977). Our Finite-State Transducer[4] (FST) generates all possible morphosyntactic readings of each wordform, and our Constraint Grammar[5] (Karlsson, 1990; Karlsson et al., 1995) then removes some readings based on syntactic context. The ultimate success of our stress placement system depends on the performance of the constraint grammar. Ideally, the constraint grammar would successfully remove all but the correct reading for each token, but in practice some tokens still have more than one reading remaining. Therefore, we also evaluate various approaches to deal with the remaining ambiguity, as described below. Table 1 shows two possible sets of readings for the token *kosti*, as well as the output of each approach described below. The first column exhibits stress ambiguity between the noun readings and the imperative verb reading. The second column shows a similar set of readings, after the constraint grammar has removed the imperative verb reading. This results in only stress-irrelevant ambiguity.

The `bare` approach is to not mark stress on words with more than one reading. Since both sets of readings in Table 1 have more than one reading, `bare` does not output a stressed form.

[4]Using two-level morphology (Koskenniemi, 1983; Koskenniemi, 1984), implemented in both xfst (Beesley and Karttunen, 2003) and hfst (Linden et al., 2011)

[5]Implemented using vislcg3 constraint grammar parser (http://beta.visl.sdu.dk/cg3.html).

Readings:	кость-N-F-SG-GEN *kósti* кость-N-F-SG-DAT *kósti* костить-V-IPFV-IMP *kostí*	кость-N-F-SG-GEN *kósti* кость-N-F-SG-DAT *kósti*
`bare`	*kosti*	*kosti*
`safe`	*kosti*	*kósti*
`randReading`	*kósti* (p=0.67) or *kostí* (p=0.33)	*kósti*
`freqReading`	*kósti*	*kósti*

Table 1: Example output of each stress placement approach, given a particular set of readings for the token *kosti*

The `safe` approach is to mark stress only on tokens whose morphosyntactic ambiguity is stress-irrelevant. In Table 1, the first column has readings that result in two different stress positions, so `safe` does not output a stressed form. However, in the second column, both readings have the same stress position, so `safe` outputs that stress position.

The `randReading` approach is to randomly select one of the available readings. In the first column of Table 1, a random selection means that *kósti* is twice as likely as *kostí*. The second column of Table 1 contains stress-irrelevant ambiguity, so a random selection of a reading has the same result as the `safe` approach.

The `freqReading` approach is to select the reading that is most frequent, with frequency data taken from a separate hand-disambiguated corpus. If none of the readings are found in the corpus, then `freqReading` selects the reading with the tag sequence (lemma removed) that is most frequent in our corpus. If the tag sequence is not found in our frequency list, then `freqReading` backs off to the `randReading` algorithm. In the first column of Table 1, `freqReading` selects *kósti* because the tag sequence N-F-SG-GEN is more frequent than the other alternatives. Note that for tokens with stress-irrelevant ambiguity (e.g. the second column of Table 1), `randReading` and `freqReading` produce the same result as the `safe` method.

So far, the approaches discussed are dependent on the availability of readings from the FST. The focus of our study is on disambiguation of known words, but we also wanted to guess the stress of unknown tokens in order to establish some kind of accuracy maximum for applications that are more tolerant of higher error rates. To this end, we selected a simple guessing method for unknown words. A recent study by Lavitskaya and Kabak (2014) concludes that Russian has default final stress in consonant-final words, and penultimate stress in vowel-final words.[6] Based on this conclusion, the `guessSyll` method places the stress on the last vowel that is followed by a consonant.[7] This method is applied two unknown wordforms in two approaches, `randReading+guessSyll` and `freqReading+guessSyll`, which are otherwise identical to `randReading` and `freqReading`, respectively.

For our baseline, we take the output of our morphological analyzer (without the constraint grammar) in combination with the `bare`, `safe`, `randReading`, `freqReading`, `randReading+guessSyll`, and `freqReading+guessSyll` approaches. We also compare our outcomes with the RussianGram[8] plugin for the Google Chrome web browser. RussianGram is not open-source, so we can only guess what technologies support the service. In any case, it provides a meaningful reference point for the success of each of the methods described above.

3 Results

We evaluated all multisyllabic words with marked stress in the gold-standard corpus (N = 4048). Since our approach is lexicon-based, some of our results should be interpreted with respect to how many of the stressed wordforms in the gold-standard corpus can be found in the output of the finite-state transducer. We refer to this measure as *recall*.[9] Out of 4048 tokens, 3949 were

[6]There is some disagreement over how to define default stress in Russian, cf. Crosswhite et al. (2003).

[7]Although this approach is simplistic, unknown words are not the central focus of this study. More sophisticated heuristics and machine-learning approaches to unknown words are discussed in Section 4.

[8]http://russiangram.com/

[9]Our method of computing recall assumes that if even one reading is output by the FST, then all possible readings are present. We have not attempted to formally estimate how frequently this assumption fails, but we expect such cases to be rare.

approach	accuracy%	error%	abstention%	totTry%	totFail%
`noCG+bare`	30.43	0.17	69.39	30.61	69.57
`noCG+safe`	90.07	0.49	9.44	90.56	9.93
`noCG+randReading`	94.34	3.36	2.30	97.70	5.66
`noCG+freqReading`	95.53	2.59	1.88	98.12	4.47
`noCG+randReading+guessSyll`	94.99	4.05	0.96	99.04	5.01
`noCG+freqReading+guessSyll`	95.83	3.46	0.72	99.28	4.17
`CG+bare`	45.78	0.44	53.78	46.22	54.22
`CG+safe`	93.21	0.74	6.05	93.95	6.79
`CG+randReading`	95.50	2.59	1.90	98.10	4.50
`CG+freqReading`	95.73	2.40	1.88	98.12	4.27
`CG+randReading+guessSyll`	95.92	3.33	0.74	99.26	4.08
`CG+freqReading+guessSyll`	96.15	3.14	0.72	99.28	3.85
`RussianGram`	90.09	0.79	9.12	90.88	9.91

Table 2: Results of stress placement task evaluation

found in the FST, which is equal to 97.55%. This number represents the ceiling for methods relying on the FST. Higher scores are only achievable by expanding the FST's lexicon or by using syllable-guessing algorithms. After running the constraint grammar, recall was 97.35%, a reduction of 0.20%.

Results were compiled for each of the 13 approaches discussed above: *without* the constraint grammar (`noCG`) x 6 approaches, *with* the constraint grammar (`CG`) x 6 approaches, and RussianGram (`RussianGram`). Results are given in Table 2. Each token was categorized as either an accurate output, or one of two categories of failures: errors and abstentions. If the stress tool outputs a stressed wordform, and it is incorrect, then it is counted as an 'error'. If the stress tool outputs an unstressed wordform, then it is counted as an 'abstention'. Abstentions can be result of either unknown wordforms, or known wordforms with no stress specified in our lexicon.

The two right-most columns in Table 2 combine values of the basic categories. The term 'totTry' refers to the sum of the accuracy and error rate. This number represents the proportion of tokens on which our system output a stressed wordform. In the case of `noCG+bare`, the accuracy% (30.43) and error% (0.17) sum to the totTry% value of 30.61. The term 'totFail' refers to the sum of error rate and abstention rate, which is the proportion of tokens for which the system failed to output the correct stressed form. In the case of `noCG+bare`, the error% (0.17) and abstention% (69.39) sum to the totFail% value of of 69.57 (rounded).

The `noCG+bare` approach achieves a baseline accuracy of 30.43%, so roughly two thirds of the tokens in our corpus are morphosyntactically ambiguous. The error rate of 0.17% primarily represents forms whose stress position varies from speaker to speaker (e.g. *zavílis'* vs. *zavilís'* 'they crinkled'), or errors in the gold-standard corpus (e.g. *verím* 'we believe').

The `noCG+safe` approach achieves a 60% improvement in accuracy (90.07%), which means that 89.39% of morphosyntactic ambiguity on our corpus is stress-irrelevant. Interestingly, the RussianGram web service achieves results that are very close to the `noCG+safe` approach.

Since the ceiling recall for the FST is 97.55%, and since the `noCG+safe` approach achieves 90.07%, the maximum improvement that a constraint grammar could theoretically achieve is 7.48%. A comparison of `noCG+safe` and `CG+safe` reveals an improvement of 3.14%, which is about 42% of the way to the ceiling recall.

The `CG+randReading` and `CG+freqReading` approaches are also limited by the 97.55% ceiling from the FST, and their accuracies achieve improvements of 2.29% and 2.52%, respectively, over `CG+safe`. However, these gains come at the cost of error rates as much as 3.5 times higher than `CG+safe`: +1.85% and +1.66%, respectively. It is not surprising that `CG+freqReading` has higher accuracy and a lower error rate than `CG+randReading`, since frequency-based guesses are by definition more likely to occur. The frequency data were taken from a very small corpus, and it is likely that frequency from a larger corpus would yield better results.

The `guessSyll` approach was designed to make a guess on every wordform that is not found in the FST, which would ideally result in an abstention rate of 0%. However, the abstention rates of approximately 0.7% are a manifestation of the fact that some words in the FST, especially proper nouns, have not been assigned stress. Because the FST outputs a form – albeit unstressed – the `guessSyll` algorithm is not called. This means that `guessSyll` is only guessing on about 2% of the tokens. The improvement on overall accuracy from `CG+freqReading` to `CG+freqReading+guessSyll` is 0.42%, which means that the `guessSyll` method guess was accurate 21% of the time.

4 Discussion

One of the main points of this paper is to highlight the importance of syntactic context in the Russian word stress placement task. If your intended application has a low tolerance for error, the `noCG+safe` approach represents the highest accuracy that is possible without leveraging syntactic information for disambiguation (90.07%). In other words, a system that is blind to morphosyntax and contextual disambiguation cannot significantly outperform `noCG+safe`. It would appear that this is the method used by `RussianGram`, since its results are so similar to `noCG+safe`. Indeed, this result can be achieved most efficiently without any part-of-speech tagging, but through simple dictionary lookup.

We noted in Section 1.1 that Hall and Sproat (2013) achieved 98.7% accuracy on stress placement for individual wordforms in a list (i.e. *without* syntax). This result is 8.63% higher than `noCG+safe`, but it is also a fundamentally different task. Based on the surface forms in our FST – which is based on the same dictionary used for Hall and Sproat (2013) – we calculate that only 29 518 (1.05%) of the 2 804 492 wordforms contained in our FST are stress-ambiguous. In our corpus of unrestricted text, at least 7.5% of the tokens are stress-ambiguous. Therefore, stress ambiguity is more than seven times more prevalent in our corpus of unrestricted text than it is in our wordform dictionary. Since the task of word stress placement is virtually always performed on running text, it seems prudent to make use of surrounding contextual information. The experiment described in this paper demonstrates that a constraint grammar can effectively improve the accuracy of a stress placement system without significantly raising the error rate. Our Russian constraint grammar is under continual development, so we expect higher accuracy in the future.

We are unaware of any other empirical evaluations of Russian word stress placement in unrestricted text. The results of our experiment are promising, but many questions remain unanswered. The experiment was limited by properties of the gold-standard corpus, including its size, genre distribution, and quality. Our gold-standard corpus represents a broad variety of text genres, which makes our results more generalizable, but a larger corpus would allow for evaluating each genre individually. For example, the vast majority of Russian words with shifting stress are of Slavic origins, so we expect a genre such as technical writing to have a lower proportion of words with stress ambiguity, since it contains a higher proportion of borrowed words, calques, and neologisms with simple stress patterns.

In addition to genre, it is also likely that text complexity affects the difficulty of the stress placement task. The distribution of different kinds of syntactic constructions vary with text complexity (Vajjala and Meurers, 2012), and so we expect that the effectiveness of the constraint grammar will be affected by those differences.

The resources needed for machine-learning – such as a large corpus of Russian unrestricted text with marked stress – are simply not available at this time. Even so, lexicon- and rule-based approaches have some advantages over machine-learning approaches. For example, we are able to abstain from marking stress on tokens whose morphosyntactic ambiguity cannot be adequately resolved. In language-learning applications, this reduces the likelihood of learners being exposed to incorrect wordforms, and accepting them as authoritative. Such circumstances can lead to considerable frustration and lack of trust in the learning tool. However, in error-tolerant applications, machine-learning does seem well-suited to placing stress on unknown words, since morphosyntactic analysis is problematic.

The syllable-guessing algorithm `guessSyll` used in this experiment was overly simplistic, and so it was not surprising that it was only moderately successful. More rigorous rule-based approaches have been suggested in other studies (Church, 1985; Williams, 1987; Xomicevič et al., 2008). For example, Xomicevič et al. (2008) attempt to parse the unknown token by matching known prefixes and suffixes.

Other studies have applied machine-learning to guessing stress of unknown words (Pearson et al., 2000; Webster, 2004; Dou et al., 2009; Hall and Sproat, 2013). For example, Hall and Sproat (2013) achieve an accuracy of 83.9% with unknown words. Their model was trained on a full list of Russian words, which is not representative of the words that would be unknown to a system like ours, so it would be possible modify their approach to fit our application. Most of the complicated word stress patterns are closed classes[10], so we could exclude closed classes of words from the training data, leaving only word classes that are likely to be similar to unknown tokens, such as those with productive derivational affixes.

5 Conclusions

We have demonstrated the effectiveness of using a constraint grammar to improve the results of a Russian word stress placement task in unrestricted text by resolving 42% of the stress ambiguity in our gold-standard corpus. We showed that stress ambiguity is seven times more prevalent in our corpus of running text than it is in our lexicon, suggesting the importance of context-based disambiguation for this task. As with any lexicon- and rule-based system, the lexicon and rules can be expanded and improved, but our initial results are promising, especially considering the short timespan over which they were developed.

As this is the first empirical study of its kind, we also discussed methodological limitations and possibilities for subsequent research, including collecting stressed corpora of varying text complexity and/or genre, as well as implementing and/or adapting established word stress-guessing methods for unknown words.

Acknowledgments

We are very grateful to Laura Janda, Tore Nesset and other members of the CLEAR research group at UiT The Arctic University of Norway for comments on an earlier draft of this paper. We are also grateful to three anonymous reviewers for thoughtful criticism. All remaining errors are our own.

[10]The growing number of masculine nouns with shifting stress (*dóktor*∼*doktorá* 'doctor'∼'doctors') is one exception to this generalization.

References

Kenneth R. Beesley and Lauri Karttunen. 2003. *Finite State Morphology: Xerox tools and techniques*. CSLI Publications, Stanford.

Kenneth Church. 1985. Stress assignment in letter to sound rules for speech synthesis. *Association for Computational Linguistics*, pages 246–253.

Katherine Crosswhite, John Alderete, Tim Beasley, and Vita Markman. 2003. Morphological effects on default stress in novel Russian words. In *WCCFL 22 Proceedings*, pages 151–164.

Qing Dou, Shane Bergsma, Sittichai Jiampojamarn, and Grzegorz Kondrak. 2009. A ranking approach to stress prediction for letter-to-phoneme conversion. In *Proceedings of the Joint Conference of the 47th annual meeting of the ACL and the 4th International Joint Conference on Natural Language Processing of the AFNLP*, pages 118–126, Suntec, Singapore. Association for Computational Linguistics.

Kieth Hall and Richard Sproat. 2013. Russian stress prediction using maximum entropy ranking. In *Proceedings of the 2013 Conference on Empirical Methods in Natural Language Processing*, pages 879–883, Seattle, Washington, USA. Association for Computational Linguistics.

Fred Karlsson, Atro Voutilainen, Juha Heikkilä, and Arto Anttila, editors. 1995. *Constraint Grammar: A Language-Independent System for Parsing Unrestricted Text*. Number 4 in Natural Language Processing. Mouton de Gruyter, Berlin and New York.

Fred Karlsson. 1990. Constraint grammar as a framework for parsing running text. In *Proceedings of the 13th Conference on Computational Linguistics (COLING), Volume 3*, pages 168–173, Helsinki, Finland. Association for Computational Linguistics.

Kimmo Koskenniemi. 1983. Two-level morphology: A general computational model for word-form recognition and production. Technical report, University of Helsinki, Department of General Linguistics.

Kimmo Koskenniemi. 1984. A general computational model for word-form recognition and production. In *Proceedings of the 10th International Conference on Computational Linguistics*, COLING '84, pages 178–181, Stroudsburg, PA, USA. Association for Computational Linguistics.

Olga F. Krivnova. 1998. Avtomatičeskij sintez russkoj reči po proizvol'nomu tekstu (vtoraja versija s ženskim golosom) [Automatic Russian speech synthesis with unrestricted text (version 2 with female voice)].

In *Trudy meždunarodnogo seminara Dialog [Proceedings of the international seminar Dialog]*, pages 498–511.

Yulia Lavitskaya and Barış Kabak. 2014. Phonological default in the lexical stress system of Russian: Evidence from noun declension. *Lingua*, 150:363–385, Oct.

Krister Linden, Miikka Silfverberg, Erik Axelson, Sam Hardwick, and Tommi Pirinen. 2011. Hfst—framework for compiling and applying morphologies. In Cerstin Mahlow and Michael Pietrowski, editors, *Systems and Frameworks for Computational Morphology*, volume Vol. 100 of *Communications in Computer and Information Science*, pages 67–85. Springer.

Igor Nožov. 2003. *Morfologičeskaja i sintaksičeskaja obrabotka teksta (modeli i programmy) [Morphological and Syntactic Text Processing (models and programs)] also published as Realizacija avtomatičeskoj sintaksičeskoj segmentacii russkogo predloženija [Realization of automatic syntactic segmentation of the Russian sentence]*. Ph.D. thesis, Russian State University for the Humanities, Moscow.

Steve Pearson, Roland Kuhn, Steven Fincke, and Nick Kibre. 2000. Automatic methods for lexical stress assignment and syllabification. In *International Conference on Spoken Language Processing*, pages 423–426.

Ilya Segalovich. 2003. A fast morphological algorithm with unknown word guessing induced by a dictionary for a web search engine. In *International Conference on Machine Learning; Models, Technologies and Applications*, pages 273–280.

Sowmya Vajjala and Detmar Meurers. 2012. On improving the accuracy of readability classification using insights from second language acquisition. In Joel Tetreault, Jill Burstein, and Claudial Leacock, editors, *In Proceedings of the 7th Workshop on Innovative Use of NLP for Building Educational Applications*, pages 163—-173, Montréal, Canada, June. Association for Computational Linguistics.

Gabriel Webster. 2004. Improving letter-to-pronunciation accuracy with automatic morphologically-based stress prediction. In *Eighth International Conference on Spoken Language Processing*, pages 2573–2576.

Briony Williams. 1987. Word stress assignment in a text-to-speech synthesis system for british english. *Computer Speech and Language*, 2:235–272.

Olga Xomicevič, Sergej Rybin, Andrej Talanov, and Ilya Oparin. 2008. Avtomatičeskoe opredelenie mesta udarenie v neznakomyx slovax v sisteme sinteza reči [Automatic determination of the place of stress in unknown words in a speech synthesis system]. In *Materialy XXXVI meždunarodnoj filologičeskoj konferencii [Proceedings of the XXXVI International Philological Conference]*, Saint Petersburg.

Andrej Anatoljevič Zaliznjak. 1977. *Grammatičeskij slovar' russkogo jazyka: slovoizmenenie: okolo 100 000 slov [Grammatical dictionary of the Russian language: Inflection: approx 100 000 words]*. Russkij jazyk.

Self Organizing Maps for the Visual Analysis of Pitch Contours

Dominik Sacha Yuki Asano Christian Rohrdantz Felix Hamborg
Daniel Keim Bettina Braun Miriam Butt
Data Analysis and Visualization Group & Department of Linguistics
University of Konstanz
forename.lastname@uni-konstanz.de

Abstract

We present a novel interactive approach for the visual analysis of intonation contours. Audio data are processed algorithmically and presented to researchers through interactive visualizations. To this end, we automatically analyze the data using machine learning in order to find groups or patterns. These results are visualized with respect to meta-data. We present a flexible, interactive system for the analysis of prosodic data. Using real-world application examples, one containing preprocessed, the other raw data, we demonstrate that our system enables researchers to interact dynamically with the data at several levels and by means of different types of visualizations, thus arriving at a better understanding of the data via a cycle of hypothesis generation and testing that takes full advantage of our visual processing abilities.

1 Introduction and Related Work

Traditionally, linguistic research on F_0 contours has been conducted by manually annotating the data using an agreed-upon set of pitch accents and boundary tones such as the ToBI system (Beckman et al., 2005). However, the manual categorization of F_0 contours is open to subjectiveness in decision making. To overcome this disadvantage, recent research has focused on functional data analysis of F_0 contour data (Gubian et al., 2013). The F_0 contours are smoothed and normalized resulting in comparable pitch vectors for different utterances of the same structure. However, with this method, the original underlying data is abstracted away from and cannot be easily accessed (or visualized) for individual analysis.

One of the typical tasks in prosodic research is to determine specific F_0 contours that signal certain functions. State of the art analysis is time intensive and not ideal, because statistics or projections are applied to the data leading to a possible loss of important aspects of original data. To overcome these problems, we offer a visual analytics system that allows for the use of preprocessed F_0 pitch vectors in data analysis as well as the ability to work with the original, individual data points. Moreover, the linguistic researcher is interactively involved in the visual analytics process by guiding the machine learning and by interacting with the visualization according to the visual analytics mantra "*Analyze first, Show the Important, Zoom, filter and analyze further, Details on demand*" (Keim et al., 2008).

Our system consists of three components. The *Data Input* where all input files are read and converted into the internal data model. The second part covers *Machine Learning* where we make use of Self Organizing Maps (SOM) in order to find clusters of similar pitch contours. The visualization based on the SOM result is realized within our last component, the *Interactive Visualization*. The researcher can interpret the data directly via this visualization, but may also interact with the system in order to steer the underlying model. The overall work flow is illustrated in Figure 1. This combination of human knowledge and reasoning with automated computational processing is the key idea of visual analytics (Thomas and Cook, 2006) and supports human knowledge generation processes (Sacha et al., 2014). Our contribution builds on existing previous work on SOM based visual analysis (Vesanto, 1999; Moehrmann et al., 2011), but also on previous attempts to visually investigate data from the domain of prosodic research (Ward and Mccartney, 2010; Ward, 2014). Furthermore, we profit from approaches to analyze speech using the SOM algorithm (Mayer et al., 2009; Silva et al., 2011; Tadeusiewicz et al.,

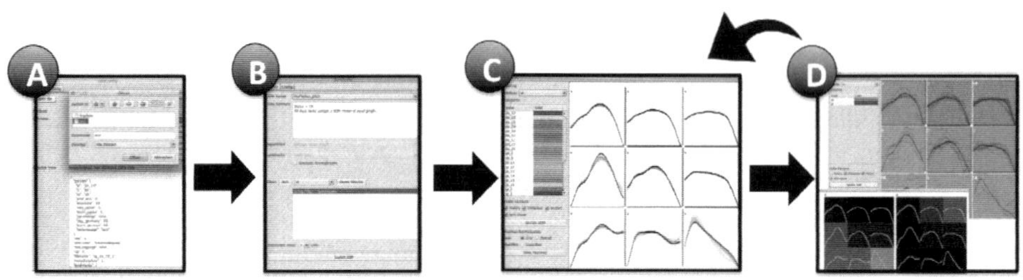

Figure 1: Work flow in four steps. A-Data Input, B-Configuration, C-Training, D-Visualization.

1999), but open up a new domain within this field as we allow for a visualization of pitch contours directly on a SOM-grid. We furthermore do not just produce one SOM, but also compute and visually present several dependent/derivative SOMs.

2 System

The system pipeline consists of three main components: 1) Data-Input; 2) Machine-Learning; 3) Interactive Visualizations.

2.1 Data Input

Our system is able to process and visualize any kind of data that satisfies the following restrictions. The data set needs to consist of a list of *data items*, where each item contains a set of key-value pairs, also called *data attributes*. The value of a data attribute must be a primitive, i.e., either a number, text string, or an array consisting of primitives. Except for primitive-arrays we do not allow nested data, thus we flatten the input data if necessary. Overall, data items should be comparable and contain attributes with equal keys (and different values).

The system also expects comparable feature vectors to which a distance measure can be applied. Furthermore, additional (meta) data can be part of the input. In the use cases presented here, each F_0 data is connected with speaker information such as the native language of the speaker, the level of second language (L2) proficiency and the context the data was produced in.

Vector Preprocessing After having loaded in the data, our system allows for the inspection of data prior to the actual analysis. Figure 1-A shows the inspection view that is typically used in the work flow at first. As part of the configuration work flow, the user selects an attribute as the *Input Vector* (Figure 1-B). This forms the basis of the machine learning component.

Before entering the machine learning of training phase, our system performs a validation of the *Input Vector* and allows for its adjustment if necessary. Whereas normalized and smoothed data, i.e., data items with vectors of equal length, can be processed directly, our system also offers the functionality to perform basic preprocessing of raw *Input Vectors*. If it is found that not all vectors have equal length, we offer several preprocessing techniques from which one can be chosen: Besides simple approaches of adding mean-values (mean-padding) or 0s (zero-padding), we also offer an approach that makes use of linear interpolation (pairwise). If time and landmark-information is available, it is also possible to divide the vectors into parts and adjust each of the parts separately. As a result, all the parts have equal length and are therefore better suited for comparison. The *Input Vectors* values can be normalized using *Semitone-Normalization*. The mean value can also be subtracted from each contour, in order to minimize gender effects.

In sum, we offer a very flexible preprocessing functionality for the *Input Vectors*. The available techniques can be combined flexibly and dynamically according to what is most suitable for the analysis task at hand. However, there are still methods that could be added. For example, one could additionally enhance the vector processing by a stronger leveraging of the time information in order to prepare the data for duration focused analysis tasks.

2.2 Machine Learning

We make use of Machine Learning (ML) for the detection of groups/clusters that are present in the data based on the *Input Vectors*. Additionally, the system detects correlations to the meta data. In our use cases this included information about the

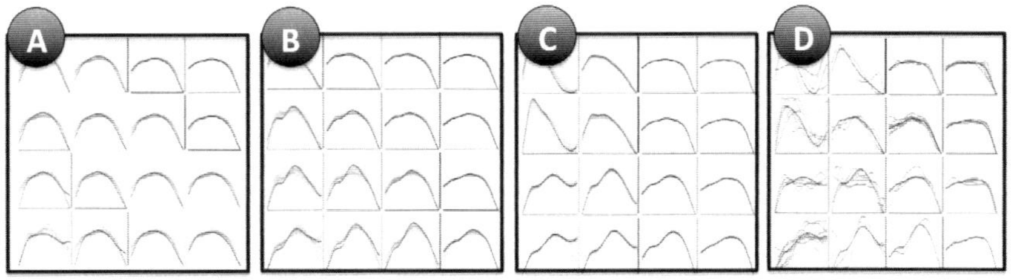

Figure 2: SOM-Training illustrated by 4 steps. For each cluster the prototype and the distances between adjacent cells are visualized by black lines in between. In step 4 the training has finished and the dedicated F_0 contours are also drawn in each cell.

native language of the speakers and the level of their language proficiency.

In principle, any distance function, projection or clustering method could be applied in our extensible framework. The central problem that needs to be resolved is that the high dimensional data from the *Input Vectors* needs to be reduced to a two-dimensional visualization that can be rendered on a computer screen or a piece of paper. We experimented with several different methods and found that SOMs, also known as Kohonen Maps (Kohonen, 2001), match the demands of this task best. SOMs are a well established ML technique that can be used for clustering or as a classifier based on feature vectors. SOMs are very suitable for our purpose for several reasons. First we can use SOMs as an unsupervised ML-technique to find a fixed number of clusters subsequent to a training phase. SOMs also provide a topology where similar clusters are adjacent. Finally, the algorithm adapts to the given input data depending on the amounts of desired clusters and data.

Furthermore, in our system, the clustering and dimensionality reduction are integrated in one step. This stands in contrast to other clustering and dimensionality reduction techniques like Multi Dimensional Scaling (MDS), Principal Component Analysis (PCA) or Non-negative Matrix Factorization (NMF). A disadvantage found with these other methods is that they tend to lead to clutter in the two-dimensionsal space (when there is high degree of overlap in the data). It is also unclear when to perform the clustering: in the high dimensional space before projection or in the two-dimensional space afterwards.

Our system proceeds as follows. First, the SOM-grid is initialized with random cluster centroids, which are feature vector prototypes for each cluster. Afterwards each feature vector is used to train the SOM in a random order. For each vector the SOM algorithm determines the best matching unit (BMU) and adjusts the BMU and adjacent clusters prototypes based on the input vector. This process is repeated n-times until the SOM is in a stable state (Figure 2, steps A-C). After the training phase the resulting grid can be used for clustering. Each vector is assigned to the cluster with the least distance to the cluster prototype (BMU). In Step D of Figure 2 each cell represents a cluster containing the cluster prototype (black vector) and the cluster members (colored vectors).

Note that we did not rely on existing software libraries like the SOM-toolbox, but instead implemented the algorithm from scratch. The reason for this is that we aim at being able to visualize and steer the algorithm at every step (see Section 2.4).

2.3 Visualizations

We build on Schreck et al.'s work on SOM-based visual analysis (Schreck, 2010). Within the basic SOM-grid, we provide several different ways of visualizing the information of interest to the researcher. As shown in Figure 3-A, we provide an overview visualization which shows the SOM-grid (Figure 3-A) filled by the clustered pitch contours. The individual cells also show the cluster centroid and the vectors (contours) that belong to that cell in relation to the centroid (Figure 3-F). We also visualize the training history of a cluster in the background in each cell (Figure 3-A) in order to keep track of the training phase.

Beyond the clustered contours, we furthermore provide possible visualizations (these can be selected or not), which add in simple highlighters or bar charts to the SOM result (Figure 3-C). We also experimented with heatmaps,[1] which turned out

[1] In our approach a color overlay for the SOM grid

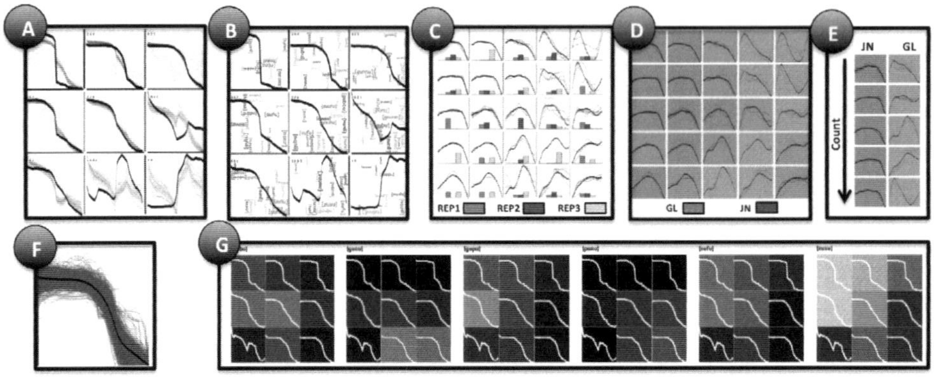

Figure 3: Different approaches to visualize SOM-results according to available meta data. (A) Grid visualization, (B) word cloud, (C) bar charts, (D) mixed color cells, (E) ranked group clusters, (F) one single cell that visualizes contained vectors and the cluster prototype, (G) separated heatmaps for all values of a categorical attribute.

to be good for visualizing the distribution of data attributes among the SOM-grid (3-G). The color-intensity of a node depends on the number of data items it contains; the more data items, the stronger the intensity.

We offer several normalization options. One approach takes the global maximum (of all groups/grids), whereas the other one takes a local maximum for each single group/grid. Different kinds of normalizations can also be chosen in order to handle outliers or small variabilities in the data. Depending on the underlying data, an adequate normalization technique is needed to obtain visible patterns in the data.

A drawback of the heatmaps is that it is not easy to detect if cells are homogeneous or heterogeneous. That means that it is hard to determine whether a cell contains only vectors of a specific group (i.e., in our use cases just native Japanese or native Germans) or if it is a mixed cell. For that reason we also offer another visualization. For each cell we derive the color depending on the number of group members. Therefore we assign a color (e.g. red vs. blue) to each group and mix them accordingly. As a result homogeneous (red vs. blue) and heterogeneous (purple) clusters are easy to detect (see Figure 3-D, where GL stands for "German learner" and "JN" for Japanese native). Finally, we also offer word cloud visualizations for each cell (Figure 3-B). These allow the user an overview of the values contained in a cell if the selected attribute has many categories/values.

Each of these visualizations offers different perspectives on the data and the user is able to interact dynamically with each of the different visualization possibilities.

2.4 Interaction

The system offers various possibilities for interaction: 1) Configuration/Encoding Interactions; 2) SOM Interactions; 3) Selection Interactions.

Configuration/Encoding Interactions: The algorithm and the visualization techniques offer many possibilities for individualized configuration, e.g., the grid dimensions of the SOM or the normalization techniques that are applied by the visualization techniques. Furthermore the cell layout can be toggled interactively from the SOM-grid to a grouped alignment. An advantage of the grouped alignment is that the typical feature clusters for each group can be determined by their position. In combination with our coloring approach, the analysts are thus able to locate the top group clusters and detect if they are homogeneous or heterogeneous (Figure 3-E). Users may also define and change visual mappings like the colors that are assigned to the attribute values.

SOM Interactions: We incorporate the idea that the analyst should be able to steer the training phase of the algorithm as well (Schreck et al., 2009). The analyst is able to enter into an iterative process that refines the analysis in each step. In each step the SOM result can be manipulated and serves as an input for the next iteration. For one, it is possible to delete cells directly on the grid. Another interactive possibility is to move cells to a desired position and to "pin" them to this position. That means that for the next SOM training this cell is fixed. We make use of these interactions to steer the SOM-algorithm to deliver visually similar outputs. For example, if we fix a cell near the upper right corner, in the next round of training this cell and the cells similar to it will be in the same corner (e.g., in Figure 4-E the two gray cells are fixed). Finally, it is possible to break off the current training process and to restart or to investigate the current state in more detail if the analyst already perceives a pattern or discovers problems.

Selection Interactions: These interactions help to filter and select the data during the analysis process. The data that are contained in the current SOM visualization serve as input for the next iteration of the analysis work flow. Besides removing data elements directly on the SOM grid, data can be selected to be removed directly in the attribute table (Figure 4-D). This feature allows the analyst to drill down into selected data subspaces. *Details on Demand* operations also enable the user to inspect subsets of clusters. Furthermore, single cells can be selected and investigated in a separate linked detail view.

By enabling these interactions we present the analyst with the flexible possibilities for an iterative analysis process. The system first provides an overview of the data, the analyst is able to interact with the data in iterations of hypothesis formation and testing. The hypothesis testing can be done with respect to the entire data set, or with respect to a selected subset. In order to keep track of the various visualizations and interactions conducted by the analyst, we offer a visualization history that displays the developed SOM grids next to one another (e.g., Figure 5). Clicking on one of these grids will automatically bring the selected SOM to the front of the screen.

3 Use Cases

We demonstrate the added value that our approach brings to prosodic research with respect to two linguistic experiments that were originally conducted independently of this work. We take a "paired analytics" approach for an evaluation of the potential of our system (Arias-Hernandez et al., 2011). In this approach, an expert for visual analytics collaborates with a domain expert. The domain expert places their focus on tasks, hypotheses and ideas while an analysis expert operates the system.

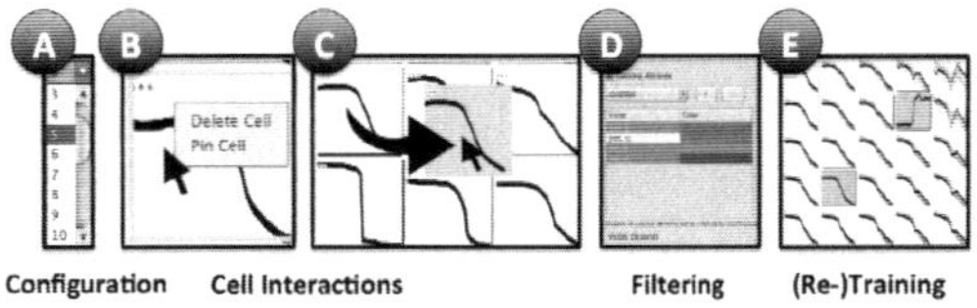

Figure 4: Interaction techniques that enable for an iterative data exploration. *Configuration Interactions* can be used to define parameters like the grid dimensions or visual mappings (e.g., selecting the attribute colors). *SOM Interactions* include the direct manipulation of the SOM-visualization (move, delete, or pin cells, begin or stop SOM training). *Selection Interactions* enable the analyst to dismiss data in each step in order to drill down into interesting data subspaces.

We are well aware that the standards for evaluation in natural language processing are quantitative in nature. There is an inherent conflict between quantitative evaluation and the rationale for using a visual analytics system in the first place. Visual analytics has the overall aim of allowing an interactive, exploratory access to an underlying complex data set. It is very difficult to quantify data exploration and cycles of hypothesis testing in the absence of a bench mark or gold standard. This is a known problem within visual analytics (Keim et al., 2010; Sacha et al., 2014), but one which cannot be addressed within the scope of this paper. The two use cases presented here should be seen as an initial test as to the added value of our system. An application to other scenarios and other use cases is planned as future work.

The use cases discussed below consist of experiments that were concerned with whether linguistic structures of a native language (henceforth L1) influence second language (henceforth L2) learning. The experiments involved Japanese native speakers vs. German learners of Japanese. The latter group had varying degrees of L2 competence. The data set consists of F_0 contours and meta data about the speakers.

3.1 Experiment 1

The first experiment investigated how native speakers of an intonation language (German) produce attitudinal differences in an L2 that has lexically specified pitch movement (Japanese).

Methods

15 Japanese native speakers and 15 German native speakers, who were proficient in the respective languages participated in the experiment. They produced the German word *Entschuldigung* and the Japanese word *sumimasen*, which both mean 'excuse me'. The Japanese word contains a lexically specified pitch fall associated with the penultimate mora in the word, /se/. Materials were presented with descriptions of short scenes. The task was to produce the target word three times in order to attract an imaginary waiter's attention in a crowded and noisy bar.

Our hypotheses were that Japanese native speakers would not change the F_0 contours across the three attempts, because the Japanese falling pitch accent is lexically fixed. German learners would change them, because German F_0 can be changed in order to convey attitude or emotion.

Segmental boundary annotation was carried out on the recorded raw data using Praat (Boersma and Weenink, 2011) as the first step. In Experiment 1, segmental boundaries were put between the Japanese smallest segmental unit, morae, which resulted in *—su—mi—ma—se—n—* (the straight lines signal the segmental boundaries). Then, F_0 contours were computed from the annotated data using the F_0 tracking algorithm in the Praat toolkit with the default range of 70-350 Hz for males and 100-500 Hz for females. Following the procedures of Functional Data Analysis (Ramsay and Silverman, 2009), we first smoothed the sampled F_0 contours into a continuous curve represented by a mathematical function of time $f(t)$ adopting B-splines (de Boor, 2001). Values of F_0 were expressed in semitones (=st) and the mean value was subtracted from each value, in order to minimize gender effects. After smoothing the curves we automatically carried out *landmark registration* in order to align corresponding segmental boundaries in time (Gubian et al., 2013; Ramsay et al., 2009). After these steps, the smoothed F_0 data all had the same duration.

Analysis

The analysis process of analyzing Experiment 1 is shown in Figure 5. The first SOM offers an overview for the whole dataset. The word cloud visualization additionally shows the utterances that occur in the cells (*sumimasen*, *Entschuldigung*). In a next step the data set was filtered to show only the data for *sumimasen* (Figure 5-A) and a second SOM with only this data was trained. In the 2nd SOM in Figure 5 the cells are coloured according to the number of speaker groups in each cell. Our analyst was able to discover different pitch contours per group (blue-German cells on the left-hand side and red-Japanese cells on the right-hand side).

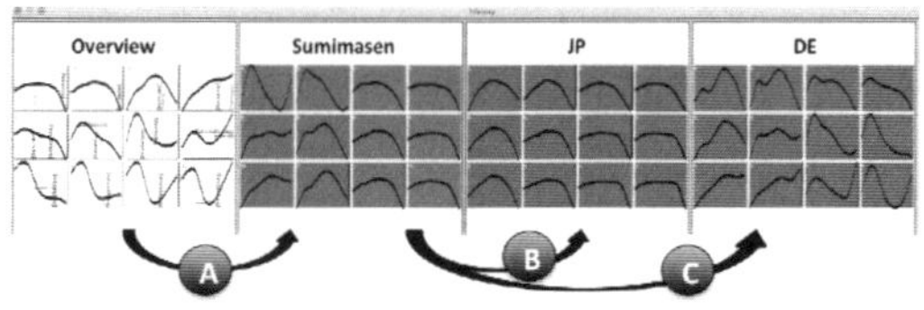

Figure 5: Experiment 1 work flow history: An overview is shown first. In the following steps data is filtered and the analysis refines stepwise into an interesting subspace. First, only the utterances *sumimasen* 'excuse me' are selected (A). These are then further subdivided according to speaker group (B/C): Japanese Native (JN) vs. German (DE).

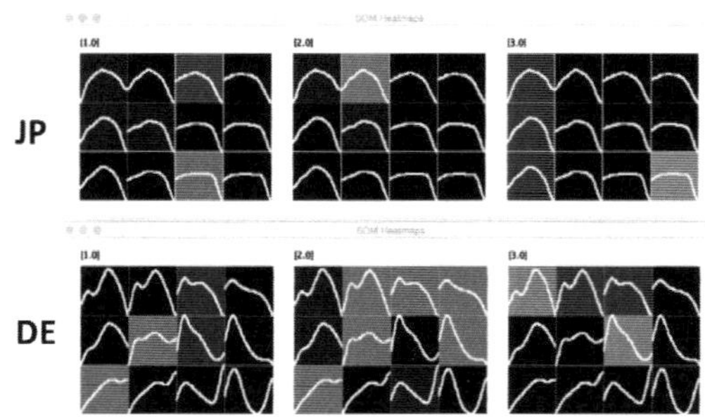

Figure 6: Experiment 1: Heatmaps for the repetition attribute for each speaker group. German learner contours clearly include more variations compared to native speaker contours.

In order to get more details we decided to train an additional SOM for each speaker group. We simply added the relevant filters and began a new SOM training for each group (Figure 5-B/C). As a result the two visualizations now clearly show that the F_0 produced by the groups look different. For further analysis, we also opened a heatmap visualization for another attribute for each group based on the SOM-grids B and C. In Figure 6 the repetitions (1st, 2nd, or 3rd) are shown for each group. One can clearly discover that the Japanese native speakers' (top) F_0 contours rarely vary in comparison with the German speakers (bottom).

3.2 Experiment 2

In Experiment 1 we were able to determine that German learners did not produce typical Japanese F_0 contours, namely flat F_0 followed by a drastic pitch fall, just on the basis of unannotated F_0 data. The second experiment examined whether German learners can produce this typical Japanese F_0 phonetic form in an imitation experiment. The experiment was originally conducted independently of Experiment 1.

Methods

24 Japanese native speakers and 48 German learners were asked to imitate Japanese disyllabic nonwords consisting of three-morae (/CV:CV/) with a long-vowel. All stimuli were recorded either with a flat pitch (high-high, HH) or with a falling pitch (high-low, HL) that occurs after the long-vowel. F_0 contours produced by Japanese native speakers are expected to imitate the stimuli correctly by realizing the typical phonetic form of a Japanese pitch accent, namely a drastic pitch fall preceded by a flat F_0. In contrast, as per the results of Experiment 1, German learners are expected not to produce this phonetic form.

In analogy to Experiment 1, segmental annotation was carried out. Segmental boundaries were put between consonants and vowels, which resulted in *—c—v—(c)c—(v)v—*. Then, F_0 contours were computed as in Experiment 1. The data contained the raw Hertz values of F_0 and additional information included data about segments, speaker information, time and landmark information for the produced pitch contour. In total 2393 data records were put into the SOM system.

Analysis

The analysis workflow for Experiment 2 is shown in Figure 7. The first SOM offers an overview for the whole dataset. This overview clearly shows two clusters for flat and falling F_0 contours ("HH"-blue and "HL"-red). On the lower most right corner, there is a red cell in the blue cluster. This type of pattern could be indicative of an error or noise in the data set.

Note that the SOM system did not know which experimental conditions the data contained. Without any information about the experimental variables, SOM detected differences across conditions. Furthermore, no other current analysis techniques enable an overview of F_0 data in this manner. Since we were interested in the phonetic realization of Japanese pitch accent, we further analyzed only the data of the falling F_0 condition.

As a consequence, a second SOM containing only the "HL" contours was trained (Figure 7-A). The next step was to remove the noise from the data (Figure 7-2nd SOM). In the second SOM we discovered one cell that contains non falling F_0 contours (lower left corner). We deleted this cell and fixed/pinned the other corner cells in order to steer the SOM algorithm to produce a similar SOM in the next training phase (Figure 7-B). In the next SOM the cells are colored according to the number of speaker groups in each cell (blue-German, red-Japanese). The three cells in the lower left corner were the most frequent F_0 contours produced only by German learners of Japanese. To analyze this further, we also changed the grid based layout to the ranked group layout to show the three most frequent F_0 contours in each language group (Figure 7-C). As a result, the last SOM visualization now clearly shows that the F_0 produced by the groups look different: Japanese native speakers produced typical Japanese F_0 contours consisting of a flat F_0 before a drastic F_0 fall (Gussenhoven, 2004). The third cells from above in both of the language groups show the same F_0 forms, suggesting that some German native speakers produced F_0 contours that were very similar to those of Japanese native speakers. Note however, that the most frequent contours produced by German learners clearly differed from the Japanese contours. Finally, one of the most important contributions of the SOM system was that it delivered us the findings without the necessity of having first manually annotated a large amount of data, saving personell costs.

4 Conclusion

We provide an interactive system for the analysis of prosodic feature vectors. To complement other state of the art techniques we make use of machine learning in combination with interactive visualizations. We implemented an iterative process using chains of SOM-trainings for a step-by-step refinement of the analysis. We show with real experiment data that the system supports linguistic research. Importantly, the analysis allows for a clustering of F_0 contours that works without time-intensive and possibly subjective manual intonational analysis. The clustered contours can be subjected to intensive phonological analy-

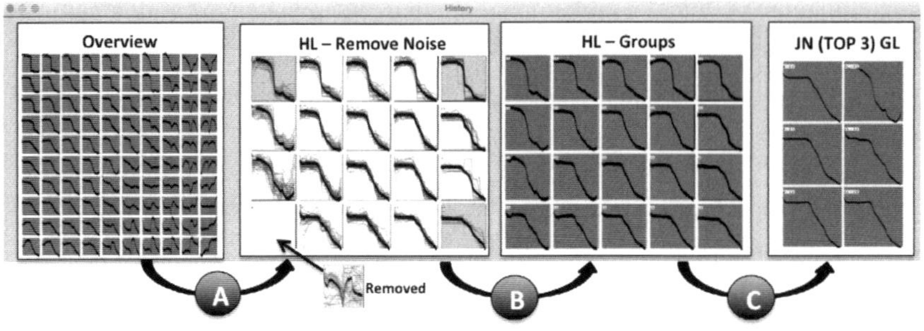

Figure 7: Experiment 2 work flow history: An overview is shown first. Then only "HL" F_0 contours (red colored cells) are selected (A). The researcher interacted directly with the second SOM: The noise cluster was removed (bottom left corner) and the other corner cells were fixed in order to steer the SOM algorithm to produce a visually similar SOM for the next training (B). The resulting SOM reveals blue clusters on the left hand side. Changing the layout to the top clusters per group (C) allows for a better comparison.

sis and furthermore allow the potential detection of more fine-grained phonetic differences across conditions. The analyses hence provide an important first step that the linguist can then focus on for subsequent analysis. For example, it is very easy to filter the data (e.g., examine only a subset of the data) or to adjust the grid size. More importantly, the approach is advantageous for an analysis of L2 data, since the learners' language has a dynamic character (Selinker, 1972) and it is difficult to determine intonational categories beforehand. Our SOM approach is generalizable to all kinds of data for which feature vectors can be derived, including other linguistic features as intensity, amplitude or duration.

We learned that the visualization of F_0 contours provides the most intuitive access for an understanding of the underlying data. One reason is that the F_0 contour can be visually inspected and directly related to meta data (e.g., through colors). Even without time-intensive manual annotation of F_0 contours, we could clearly see the differences between L1 and L2 performance despite the different characteristics of the two experimental data sets. We visualizaed and animated the SOM training phase and presented this to the researcher as well. This may seem unnecessary, but experience has shown that it helps users that are not experienced with ML to better understand the processes.

We applied our technique to two different datasets. A comparison of the achieved results shows that our approach works very well "out of the box" with preprocessed data and also with less effort on the preprocessing. To overcome the problem of handling less preprocessed data we added simple methods that turned out to be sufficient in order to reveal new insights. The system helped us to handle unexpected outliers or noise in the data. All the F_0 contours that do not match the major clusters of the SOM-algorithm are assigned to a few single cells. The data in these cells could easily be removed.

We plan to make the system available for other researchers in the future and are considering several expansions as well. For one, other machine learning and visualization techniques could be added for additional or further tasks. We also could try to support the user more in detecting interesting subspaces in the data. It is possible, for instance to visualize an overview of attribute-heatmaps that enables the human to detect patterns in each iteration.

In sum, this paper has presented an innovative and promising new approach for the automatic analysis of prosodic data. Key components are that prosodic data is translated into vectors that can be processed and analyzed further by SOM techniques and presented to the user as an interactive visual analytic system.

Acknowledgments

We gratefully acknowledge the funding for this work, which comes from the Research Initiative LingVisAnn and the research project "Visual Analytics of Text Data in Business Applications" of the University of Konstanz.

References

Richard Arias-Hernandez, Linda T Kaastra, Tera Marie Green, and Brian Fisher. 2011. Pair analytics: Capturing reasoning processes in collaborative visual analytics. In *System Sciences (HICSS), 2011 44th Hawaii International Conference on*, pages 1–10. IEEE.

Mary E. Beckman, Julia Hirschberg, and Stefanie Shattuck-Hufnagel. 2005. The original ToBI system and the evolution of the ToBI framework. In S.-A. Jun, editor, *Prosodic Typology – The Phonology of Intonation and Phrasing*. Oxford University Press.

Paul Boersma and David Weenink. 2011. Praat: Doing phonetics by computer [computer program] version 5.2.20.

Carl de Boor. 2001. *A Practical Guide to Splines*. Springer, New York.

Michele Gubian, Yuki Asano, Salomi Asaridou, and Francesco Cangemi. 2013. Rapid and smooth pitch contour manipulation. In *Proceedings of the 14th Annual Conference of the International Speech Communication Association, Lyon, France*, pages 31–35.

Carlos Gussenhoven. 2004. *The Phonology of Tone and Intonation*. Research surveys in linguistics. Cambridge University Press, Cambridge. 2003065202 Carlos Gussenhoven. ill. ; 24 cm. Includes bibliographical references (p. 321-344) and index.

Daniel Keim, Gennady Andrienko, Jean-Daniel Fekete, Carsten Görg, Jörn Kohlhammer, and Guy Melançon. 2008. *Visual analytics: Definition, process, and challenges*. Springer.

Daniel A. Keim, Jörn Kohlhammer, Geoffrey P. Ellis, and Florian Mansmann. 2010. *Mastering the Information Age - Solving Problems with Visual Analytics*. Eurographics Association.

Teuvo Kohonen. 2001. *Self-organizing Maps*, volume 30. Springer.

Rudolf Mayer, Jakob Frank, and Andreas Rauber. 2009. Analytic comparison of audio feature sets using self-organising maps. In *Proceedings of the Workshop on Exploring Musical Information Spaces, in Conjunction with ECDL*, pages 62–67.

Julia Moehrmann, Andre Burkovski, Evgeny Baranovskiy, Geoffrey-Alexeij Heinze, Andrej Rapoport, and Gunther Heidemann. 2011. A discussion on visual interactive data exploration using self-organizing maps. In *Advances in Self-Organizing Maps - 8th International Workshop, WSOM 2011, Espoo, Finland, June 13-15, 2011. Proceedings*, pages 178–187.

James Ramsay and Bernard. W. Silverman. 2009. *Functional Data Analysis*. Springer.

James Ramsay, Giles Hookers, and Spencer Graves. 2009. *Functional Data Analysis with R and MATLAB*. Springer.

Dominik Sacha, Andreas Stoffel, Florian Stoffel, Bum Chul Kwon, Geoffrey P. Ellis, and Daniel A. Keim. 2014. Knowledge generation model for visual analytics. *IEEE Transactions on Visualization and Computer Graphics*, 20(12):1604–1613.

Tobias Schreck, Jürgen Bernard, Tatiana Tekuov, and Jörn Kohlhammer. 2009. Visual cluster analysis of trajectory data with interactive Kohonen maps. *Palgrave Macmillan Information Visualization*, 8:14–29.

Tobias Schreck, 2010. *Visual-Interactive Analysis With Self- Organizing Maps — Advances and Research Challenges*, pages 83–96. Intech.

Larry Selinker. 1972. Interlanguage. *IRAL-International Review of Applied Linguistics in Language Teaching*, 10(1-4):209–232.

Ana Cristina C Silva, Ana Cristina P Macedo, and Guilherme A Barreto. 2011. A SOM-based analysis of early prosodic acquisition of English by Brazilian learners: preliminary results. In *Advances in Self-Organizing Maps*, pages 267–276. Springer.

Ryszard Tadeusiewicz, Wieslaw Wszolek, Antoni Izworski, and Tadeusz Wszolek. 1999. The methods of pathological speech visualization [using Kohonen neural networks]. In *Engineering in Medicine and Biology, 1999. 21st Annual Conference and the 1999 Annual Fall Meetring of the Biomedical Engineering Society, BMES/EMBS Conference, 1999. Proceedings of the First Joint*, volume 2, pages 980 vol.2–, Oct.

James J. Thomas and Kristin A. Cook. 2006. A visual analytics agenda. *IEEE Computer Graphics and Applications*, 26(1):10–13.

Juha Vesanto. 1999. SOM-based data visualization methods. *Intelligent Data Analysis*, 3(2):111–126.

Nigel G Ward and Joshua L Mccartney. 2010. Visualization to support the discovery of prosodic contours related to turn-taking.

Nigel G Ward. 2014. Automatic discovery of simply-composable prosodic elements. In *Speech Prosody*, volume 2014, pages 915–919.

Improving the Cross-Lingual Projection of Syntactic Dependencies

Jörg Tiedemann
Uppsala University
Department of Linguistics and Philology
firstname.lastname@lingfil.uu.se

Abstract

This paper presents several modifications of the standard annotation projection algorithm for syntactic structures in cross-lingual dependency parsing. Our approach reduces projection noise and includes efficient data sub-set selection techniques that have a substantial impact on parser performance in terms of labeled attachment scores. We test our techniques on data from the Universal Dependency Treebank and demonstrate the improvements on a number of language pairs. We also look at treebank translation including syntax-based models and data combination techniques that push the performance even further. We achieve absolute improvements of up to over seven points in labeled attachment scores pushing the state-of-the art in cross-lingual dependency parsing for all language pairs tested in our experiments.

1 Introduction

State-of-the art dependency parsing is mainly based on annotated data and supervised learning techniques. This, however, restricts the use of parsing technology to a few languages for which sufficient amounts of training data is available. Fully unsupervised techniques still fall far behind in their performance and cannot produce labels that are necessary for many downstream applications. Cross-lingual learning techniques have, therefore, been proposed as a quick solution to bootstrap tools for otherwise unsupported languages. There are basically two strategies that can be found in the literature: annotation projection and model transfer.

Model transfer has attracted a lot of interest recently due to the availability of cross-lingually harmonized annotation (Petrov et al., 2012) that makes it possible to use universal features across languages. The most straightforward technique is to train delexicalized parsers that heavily rely on universal POS tags. This simple technique has shown some success for closely related languages (McDonald et al., 2013). Several improvements can be achieved by using multiple source languages (McDonald et al., 2011; Naseem et al., 2012) and additional cross-lingual features that can be used to transfer models to a new language such as cross-lingual word clusters (Täckström et al., 2012) or word-typology information (Täckström et al., 2013).

Annotation projection has already a long tradition in NLP. Initially proposed for tasks like POS tagging (Yarowsky et al., 2001), the seminal work for annotation projection in dependency parsing is presented by Hwa et al. (2005). The general idea is to make use of parallel corpora and automatic word alignment to transfer information from the source language to a target language translation that can then be used for training parsers. In most cases, treebanks are not taken from parallel corpora and, therefore, one has to rely on automatic annotation of the source language part of another (usually unrelated) bitext. Together with the noise in automatic word alignment, these steps are bottlenecks in the projection strategy. Hwa et al. (2005) propose the basic projection heuristics (which they call the direct correspondence assumption algorithm or DCA for short) that can handle various types of word alignments. In this paper we revisit this algorithm and include a systematic comparison of projection heuristics together with various modifications and data-set selection techniques. We can show that these methods lead to significant improvements for all languages tested in our experiments.

Finally, we also look at the recently proposed treebank translation approach (Tiedemann et al., 2014), which can be used as an alternative to annotation projection on existing parallel data sets. Automatic translation has the advantage that we can use the manually verified annotation of the source language treebank instead of noisy machine-annotated parallel data and also the given word alignment, which is an integral part of the translation model. We present additional improvements when using our modifications of the projection algorithm and also show a positive effect when combining projected data from parallel corpora and machine translated treebanks.

2 Projection Using Parallel Corpora

Our first batch of experiments is based on the projection of syntactic information using existing parallel corpora. The basic setup is as follows:

1. Parse the source side of the parallel corpus with a parser trained on the source language treebank.
2. Project the syntactic information (including POS labels) to the target side of the parallel corpus using word alignment links and the direct correspondence assumption.
3. Train a parser on the projected data and evaluate its performance on the test sets of the universal treebank for the target language.

Word alignments are produced using IBM model 4 as implemented in GIZA++ (Och and Ney, 2003) trained in the typical pipeline as it is common in statistical machine translation using the Moses toolbox (Koehn et al., 2007). The asymmetric alignments are symmetrized with the intersection and the grow-diag-final-and heuristics (Koehn et al., 2003). We use the latter for the basic annotation projection presented in the next section.

For evaluation, we use the test sets provided by the Universal Dependency Treebank (UDT) version 1 (McDonald et al., 2013). The harmonized annotation makes it possible to perform a fair evaluation across languages including labeled attachment scores, which we use as our essential evaluation metric. Note that all scores include attachments of punctuation which makes our results directly comparable to the results presented in the related literature (Tiedemann, 2014).

2.1 Baseline

For our experiments, we use 40,000 sentences from Europarl (Koehn, 2005) for each language pair following the basic setup of Tiedemann (2014). The baseline model applies the projection heuristics as presented by Hwa et al. (2005):

one-to-one: For one-to-one alignments between the source words s_i and s_j and the target words t_x and t_y: Copy the relation $R(s_i, s_j)$ to $R(t_x, t_y)$.

unaligned source: Add dummy nodes in the target language that take all incoming and outgoing arcs of the unaligned source language word.

one-to-many: Add a dummy node in the target sentence and attach the aligned target words to this node (using a dummy label as well) and remove the original word alignments. Align the newly created dummy word with the corresponding source language word.

many-to-one: Retain only the link between the target language word and the source language word that is the highest up in the source language tree and delete all other links.

many-to-many: Perform the rule for one-to-many alignments first and then perform the rule for many-to-one alignments.

unaligned target: Remove all unaligned target words.

These heuristics ensure that the projected structures are proper trees and that we can train dependency parsers that are capable of handling non-projective structures without modification. Note that POS tags are also projected along the remaining word alignments and that some words obtain dummy tags if there is no relation to a source language token that could be used for projection.

In all our experiments, we apply MaltParser (Nivre et al., 2006) to train transition-based dependency parsers and we optimize feature models and learning parameters using MaltOptimizer (Ballesteros and Nivre, 2012). The parameters and feature models for the cross-lingual models are directly copied from the source language model in order to apply a realistic scenario for which no tuning data for the target language would be available. Table 1 lists the results in terms of labeled attachment scores of our baseline models for all language pairs in the test set. Rows correspond to each source language and columns represent the target language used for testing. Note that we restrict all our experiments to the languages for which the same kind of parallel data is available in Europarl.

The baseline scores are mainly in the range of 50-60% LAS with closely related languages (like French and Spanish) performing slightly better. This is on par with previously reported scores.

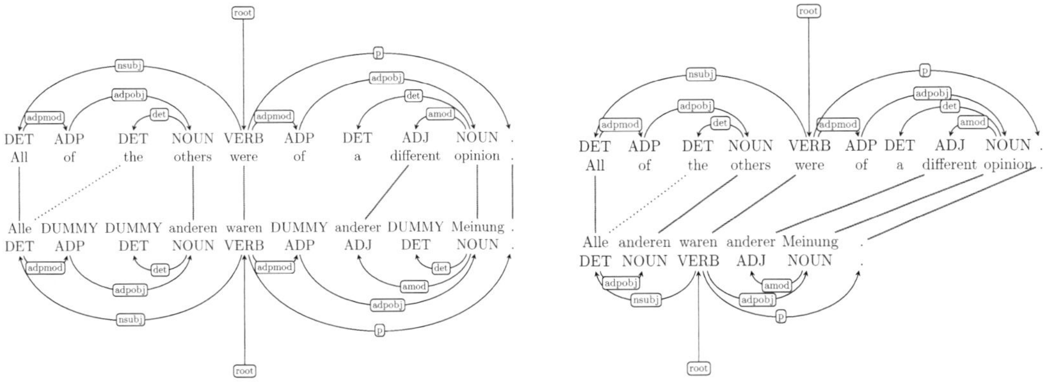

Figure 1: Removing unnecessary dummy nodes (right image) from standard DCA-based annotation projection (left image).

	DE	EN	ES	FR	SV
DE	(72.13)	48.81	56.76	58.52	60.33
EN	55.78	(87.50)	60.27	61.86	61.41
ES	52.94	47.74	(78.54)	65.12	60.97
FR	53.08	50.55	64.41	(77.51)	57.60
SV	55.12	48.76	60.76	61.60	(81.28)

Table 1: Baseline performance in LAS of a DCA-based annotation projection with 40,000 sentences (models trained on the original treebanks in grey).

2.2 Removing Unnecessary Dummy Nodes

A consequence of the projection heuristics is the appearance of dummy nodes and dummy labels. This may have a significantly negative impact on the performance of the model that is trained on this kind of data. Tiedemann et al. (2014) already discuss this problem and they propose an alternative projection algorithm, which, however, is not very successful in their experiments. In this work, we propose some different techniques that can be used to reduce or even remove all dummies from the data and we can show that these techniques are very effective.

The first method is similar to the approach presented by Tiedemann (2014). Arcs that run over dummy nodes that connect to a single daughter node only can simply be collapsed without any changes in the remaining structure. Figure 1 illustrates an example with two such unary dummy nodes that can be removed. The main difficulty with this method is to decide on the label for the arc that corresponds to the two collapsed ones. In some cases, one of the arcs is labeled as dummy as well and could, therefore, easily be ignored. This is not the case in our example and we decided to always use the label of the outgoing arc as illustrated in Figure 1.

In addition to collapsing unary dummy nodes, we can also ignore dummy nodes that are leaves of the dependency tree. Here, we assume that these nodes do not contribute much to the information projected from the source and rather confuse the learning algorithm. Figure 1 illustrates this procedure as well with two dummy determiners removed from the projected tree.

	DE	EN	ES	FR	SV
DE	–	**48.87**$^{(0.06)}$	**57.52**$^{(0.76)}$	**58.83**$^{(0.31)}$	**61.62**$^{(1.29)}$
EN	**56.64**$^{(0.86)}$	–	60.12$^{-0.15}$	**62.13**$^{(0.27)}$	**62.89**$^{(1.48)}$
ES	**53.77**$^{(0.83)}$	47.24$^{-0.50}$	–	**66.00**$^{(0.88)}$	60.65$^{-0.32}$
FR	**53.44**$^{(0.36)}$	49.69$^{-0.86}$	**64.69**$^{(0.28)}$	–	**59.16**$^{(1.56)}$
SV	**55.62**$^{(0.50)}$	**49.23**$^{(0.47)}$	60.47$^{-0.29}$	**61.86**$^{(0.26)}$	–

Table 2: Collapsing arcs over unary dummy nodes and removing dummy leaves (difference to baseline in superscript).

Table 2 summarizes the LAS scores after transforming our data sets in the way described above. We can see that this rather trivial change has positive effects on most models. In some cases there are substantial gains in LAS. However, we can also observe slight drops in performance for a few language pairs, which we should investigate in more details in future work.

2.3 Alternative Treatment of MWU's

Another consequence of the DCA algorithm is the insertion of dummy nodes which serve as heads of multi-word units that are aligned to single words in the source language. The left tree in Figure 2 illustrates this behavior with a dummy noun that

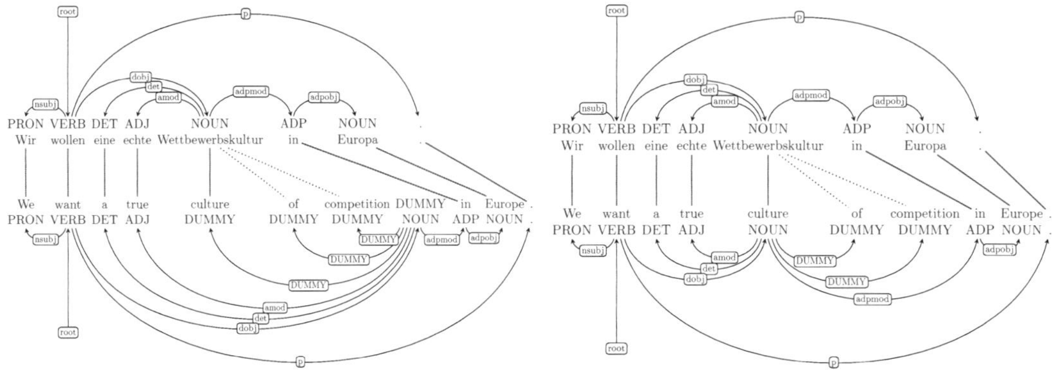

Figure 2: Projecting from German to English using the default DCA algorithm (left image) and using the new treatment for one-to-many word alignments (right image). Dotted lines are links from the grow-diag-final-and symmetrization heuristics and solid lines refer to links in the intersection of word alignments.

covers the noun phrase "culture of competition" which is aligned to "Wettbewerbskultur" in German. However, in contrast to the original setup of the DCA-based annotation projection, we have several word alignments at our disposal based on different symmetrization heuristics. The idea in our approach is now to make use of high-precision links to determine the head connection between source and target and to use other links to attach the remaining tokens. Figure 2 illustrates the procedure with the given example. In the figure, solid lines refer to high-precision links coming from the intersection of directional word alignments whereas dotted lines refer to additional links coming from the grow-diag-final-and heuristics that gives higher coverage. As we can see in the figure, "culture" is then chosen as the head of the multi-word unit and the other tokens in the NP are attached as dummy relations. This treatment is certainly not ideal but lacking more information we have at least eliminated yet another dummy node in our projected tree in a reasonable way.

The results of this procedure are summarized in Table 3. We can see that the new treatment of one-to-many links has again an overall positive effect on parsing performance with modest gains in most cases. It should be noted that the head selection heuristics is by far not perfect and that not all multi-word units can be resolved in this way. In many cases, none of the links is part of the intersection of links and, consequently, the projection algorithm has to fall back to the standard treatment with additional dummy nodes.

	DE	EN	ES	FR	SV
DE	–	**49.62**$^{(0.81)}$	**57.54**$^{(0.78)}$	**59.60**$^{(1.08)}$	**61.80**$^{(1.47)}$
EN	56.47$^{(0.69)}$	–	**60.57**$^{(0.30)}$	**62.71**$^{(0.85)}$	**62.94**$^{(1.53)}$
ES	**53.94**$^{(1.00)}$	**48.02**$^{(0.28)}$	–	65.74$^{(0.62)}$	**61.33**$^{(0.36)}$
FR	53.36$^{(0.28)}$	50.22$^{-0.33}$	64.54$^{(0.13)}$	–	**59.27**$^{(1.67)}$
SV	**56.34**$^{(1.22)}$	**49.30**$^{(0.54)}$	60.66$^{-0.10}$	**62.56**$^{(0.96)}$	–

Table 3: Using the intersection of word alignments to resolve one-to-many links without creating dummy head nodes. Bold numbers are also better than Table 2.

2.4 Data Sub-Set Selection

Yet another possibility for improvements is data selection or instance weighting. Here, we opt for subset selection techniques based on simple heuristic filters, which prove to be very effective for our task. The first idea is to simply discard any projected tree that includes dummy nodes. Our assumption is that such dummy nodes have a negative influence on the learning algorithm but also that sentence pairs, which require complex projection heuristics due to difficult word alignments are in general less suited to be used for annotation projection.

	DE	EN	ES	FR	SV
DE	–	**50.05**$^{(1.24)}$	**58.30**$^{(1.54)}$	**59.67**$^{(1.15)}$	**62.33**$^{(2.00)}$
EN	**58.33**$^{(2.55)}$	–	**61.01**$^{(0.74)}$	**63.34**$^{(1.48)}$	**63.70**$^{(2.29)}$
ES	**55.46**$^{(2.52)}$	**48.05**$^{(0.31)}$	–	65.90$^{(0.78)}$	**61.44**$^{(0.47)}$
FR	**54.39**$^{(1.31)}$	**50.69**$^{(0.14)}$	**65.08**$^{(0.67)}$	–	**60.23**$^{(2.63)}$
SV	**57.84**$^{(2.72)}$	**50.42**$^{(1.66)}$	**60.86**$^{(0.10)}$	62.47$^{(0.87)}$	–

Table 4: Discarding all projected trees that include dummy nodes (bold numbers are also better than Tables 2 and 3).

Table 4 shows the results when applying this simple filter on the data set of 40,000 projected sentences for each language pair. We can see that we obtain some significant improvements over the previous projection even though we reduce the training data substantially. To quantify this reduction, Table 5 lists the sizes of the remaining data sets we obtain. In several cases, the data is reduced to less than 10% of the original set but still performs as well or even better than the full data set of projected trees, which is quite remarkable. Note that all scores are also better than the baseline models.

	DE	EN	ES	FR	SV
DE	–	3778	3069	2557	7966
EN	6166	–	5010	3755	8169
ES	4114	5127	–	4332	4814
FR	5773	6917	7552	–	7104
SV	4661	3198	2484	1671	–

Table 5: Successfully projected trees out of 40,000 sentences when discarding trees with dummy nodes.

In order to perform a fair comparison, we ran another experiment with additional sentences coming from the same parallel corpus that fill up the projected training data to the same size of 40,000 trees as it is used in the other experiments. Table 6 lists the final results after training parser models on these extended data sets. We can see that we obtain yet another significant improvement and the best results for our task so far in almost all cases. Some scores are slightly below the performance of the reduced data set which is a bit surprising.

	DE	EN	ES	FR	SV
DE	–	**50.45**$^{(1.64)}$	**58.65**$^{(1.89)}$	**59.77**$^{(1.25)}$	**62.78**$^{(2.45)}$
EN	58.05$^{(2.27)}$	–	**60.77**$^{(0.50)}$	**64.71**$^{(2.85)}$	**64.34**$^{(2.93)}$
ES	**56.14**$^{(3.20)}$	**48.39**$^{(0.65)}$	–	65.91$^{(0.79)}$	**61.52**$^{(0.55)}$
FR	**55.47**$^{(2.39)}$	**51.15**$^{(0.60)}$	**65.27**$^{(0.86)}$	–	**59.99**$^{(2.39)}$
SV	**57.91**$^{(2.79)}$	**50.10**$^{(1.34)}$	**61.33**$^{(0.57)}$	**62.78**$^{(1.18)}$	–

Table 6: The same setting as in Table 4 but projecting the same number of sentences as in all other experiments (40,000) (bold numbers are higher than all previous settings).

Finally, we also define yet another simple filter that removes all trees that include any kind of dummy relation. Using this filter together with the one above dramatically reduces the size of the data and the scores obtained when training on the projected trees that remain from the original 40,000 sentences is not worthwhile to show here. However, filling up the data with additional sentences pushes the performance yet another step and the final scores are shown in Table 7. For some reason, French as a target language was not very successful with this strategy but in most other cases we can see considerable improvements over the previously noted top scores.

	DE	EN	ES	FR	SV
DE	–	**50.72**$^{(1.91)}$	**58.82**$^{(2.06)}$	59.37$^{(0.85)}$	62.78$^{(2.45)}$
EN	**59.34**$^{(3.56)}$	–	60.72$^{(0.45)}$	64.01$^{(2.15)}$	**64.52**$^{(3.11)}$
ES	**56.29**$^{(3.35)}$	**49.05**$^{(1.31)}$	–	64.62$^{-0.50}$	**62.28**$^{(1.31)}$
FR	**56.07**$^{(2.99)}$	**51.25**$^{(0.70)}$	**65.58**$^{(1.17)}$	–	**60.36**$^{(2.76)}$
SV	**58.04**$^{(2.92)}$	**50.55**$^{(1.79)}$	60.11$^{-0.65}$	61.35$^{-0.25}$	–

Table 7: Discarding all trees that include dummy nodes or dummy labels on any dependency relations but still projecting 40,000 sentences (bold numbers are higher than any previous setting).

3 Translated Treebanks

Treebank translation has been proposed by Tiedemann et al. (2014). In this paper, we would like to explore the impact of our modifications of the projection algorithm on that approach as well. For this, we use the training sets of the Universal Dependency Treebank and translate them with standard SMT models to the target languages we would like to test. Our setup is very generic and uses the Moses toolbox for training, tuning and decoding. The translation models are trained on the entire Europarl corpus version 7 without language-pair-specific optimization. For tuning we use MERT (Och, 2003) and the newstest 2011 data provided by the annual workshop on statistical machine translation.[1] The language model is a standard 5-gram model and is based on a combination of Europarl and News data provided from the same source. We apply modified Kneser-Ney smoothing without pruning, applying KenLM tools (Heafield et al., 2013) for estimating the LM parameters.

3.1 Phrase-based SMT

Our baseline system is a standard phrase-based model and we use the standard DCA projection algorithm as proposed by Hwa et al. (2005). The results are shown in Table 8.

With this, we can confirm the findings of Tiedemann (2014) that the translation approach has some

[1] http://www.statmt.org/wmt14. For Swedish we use a sample from the OpenSubtitles2012 corpus (Tiedemann, 2012).

	DE	EN	ES	FR	SV
DE	–	$\mathbf{53.36}^{(4.55)}$	$54.72^{-2.04}$	$58.07^{-0.45}$	$59.84^{-0.49}$
EN	$53.09^{-2.69}$	–	$\mathbf{60.81}^{(0.54)}$	$\mathbf{64.23}^{(2.37)}$	$\mathbf{63.43}^{(2.02)}$
ES	$50.54^{-2.40}$	$\mathbf{50.39}^{(2.65)}$	–	$\mathbf{66.10}^{(0.98)}$	$60.56^{-0.41}$
FR	$49.89^{-3.19}$	$\mathbf{53.65}^{(3.10)}$	$\mathbf{65.05}^{(0.64)}$	–	$\mathbf{58.38}^{(0.78)}$
SV	$53.83^{-1.29}$	$\mathbf{50.93}^{(2.17)}$	$60.61^{-0.15}$	$60.46^{-1.14}$	–

Table 8: Treebank translation with DCA-based projection (compared to the projection of parallel data from Table 1).

advantages over the projection of automatically annotated parallel corpora. For some language pairs, the labeled attachment scores are significantly above the projection results even though the parsers are trained on much smaller data sets (the treebanks are typically much smaller than 40,000 sentences for most language pairs). Very striking is also the outcome for German as a target language, which seems to be the hardest language to translate to in this data set.

In the next experiment we apply the same modifications of the projection algorithm as presented in Section 2.2. Once again, we can see that we obtain considerable improvements for most language pairs, which nicely re-assures the general utility of these techniques (see Table 8).

	DE	EN	ES	FR	SV
DE	–	$\mathbf{54.69}^{(1.33)}$	$\mathbf{56.72}^{(2.00)}$	$57.63^{-0.44}$	$\mathbf{60.07}^{(0.23)}$
EN	$\mathbf{53.50}^{(0.41)}$	–	$\mathbf{61.39}^{(0.58)}$	$\mathbf{64.63}^{(0.40)}$	$\mathbf{63.85}^{(0.42)}$
ES	$50.33^{-0.21}$	$49.90^{-0.49}$	–	$\mathbf{66.37}^{(0.27)}$	$59.96^{-0.60}$
FR	$\mathbf{51.81}^{(1.92)}$	$\mathbf{54.85}^{(1.20)}$	$\mathbf{66.32}^{(1.27)}$	–	$\mathbf{59.34}^{(0.96)}$
SV	$\mathbf{53.90}^{(0.07)}$	$\mathbf{51.18}^{(0.25)}$	$\mathbf{60.99}^{(0.38)}$	$\mathbf{61.01}^{(0.55)}$	–

Table 9: Collapsing relations over unary dummy nodes and removing dummy leave nodes (same approach as in Section 2.2; improvements over Table 8 in superscript)

Unfortunately, it is not possible to straightforwardly test the alternative treatment of multi-word-units presented in Section 2.3 as we do not have alternative word alignments readily available from the translation model. Certainly, additional alignments could be produces but for this, we would need to concatenate the translated treebanks with larger parallel corpora to obtain reasonable statistics for unsupervised word alignment, which still might not work very well. In our current experiments we, therefore, excluded this setup and may return to this idea in future work.

Furthermore, we do not include results with data selection techniques that we discussed in Section 2.4. This strategy is not very successful in the translation-based setup and the reason for this is that the data size drops substantially (having small treebanks to start with already) which causes significant drops in parsing performance.

3.2 Syntax-Based SMT

Previous research focused on phrase-based translation models and the projection through word alignments as described in the previous sections. In this paper, we also look at syntax-based SMT, which intuitively provides a better fit for syntactic annotation projection. The main motivation for this is the clear connection between syntax-based translation and syntactic annotation projection.

Syntax-based MT models supported by Moses are based on synchronous context-free grammars which are induced from aligned parallel data. Several modes are available. In our case, we are mostly interested in the tree-to-string models that require syntactic parse trees on the source language side (which we would like to project). Our assumption is that the structural relations that are induced from the parallel corpus with a fixed given source-side analysis improve the projection of syntactic relations when used in combination with syntax-based translation.

In order to make it possible to use dependency information in the framework of synchronous CFGs we convert projective dependency trees to the phrase structures required for training tree-to-string models with Moses. Figure 3 shows an example of an automatically parsed German sentence from Europarl and its conversion. We use the yield of each word to define a span over the sentence which forms a constituent with the label taken from the relation of that word to its head. Certainly, dependency trees using this conversion approach are not optimal for syntax-based SMT as they are usually very flat and do not provide the deep hierarchical structures that are common in phrase-structure trees. However, we still believe that valuable information can be pushed into the model in this way that may be beneficial for projecting dependency relations. Note that we use part-of-speech tags as additional pre-terminal nodes to enrich the information given to the system. The entire procedure in our approach is then as follows:

- We tag the source side of a parallel corpus with a POS tagger trained on the UDT training

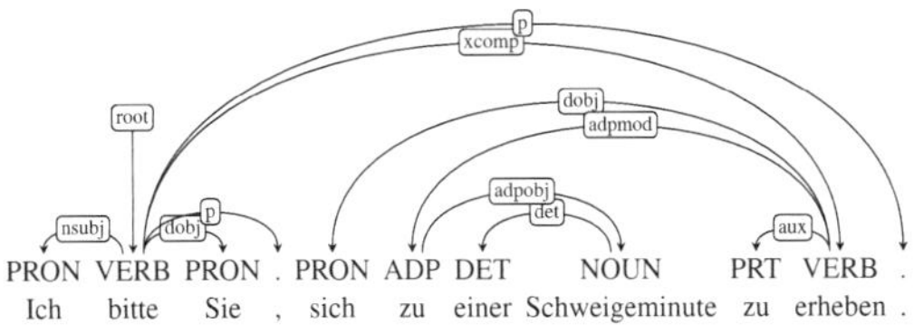


```
<tree label="ROOT">
 <tree label="nsubj"><tree label="PRON">Ich</tree></tree>
 <tree label="VERB">bitte</tree>
 <tree label="dobj"><tree label="PRON">Sie</tree></tree>
 <tree label="p"> <tree label=".">,</tree> </tree>
 <tree label="xcomp">
  <tree label="dobj"><tree label="PRON">sich</tree></tree>
  <tree label="adpmod">
   <tree label="ADP">zu</tree>
   <tree label="adpobj">
    <tree label="det"><tree label="DET">einer</tree></tree>
    <tree label="NOUN">Schweigeminute</tree>
   </tree>
  </tree>
  <tree label="aux"><tree label="PRT">zu</tree></tree>
  <tree label="VERB">erheben</tree>
 </tree>
 <tree label="p"><tree label=".">.</tree></tree>
</tree>
```

Figure 3: A dependency tree taken from the automatically annotated parallel data and its conversion to a nested phrase-structure tree in Moses format.

data using HunPos (Halácsy et al., 2007).

- We parse the tagged corpus using a MaltParser model trained on the UDT with a feature model optimized with MaltOptimizer (Ballesteros and Nivre, 2012).
- We projectivize all trees using MaltParser and convert to nested tree annotations.
- We extract synchronous rule tables from the word aligned bitext with source side syntax and score rules using Good Turing discounting. We do not use any size limit for replacing sub-phrases with non-terminals at the source side and restrict the number of non-terminals on the right-hand side of extracted rules to three. Furthermore, we allow consecutive non-terminals on the source side to increase coverage, which is not allowed in the default settings of the hierarchical rule extractor in Moses.
- We tune the model using MERT and the same data sets as before.
- Finally, we parse the training data of the UDT in the source language and translate it to the target language using the tree-to-string model created above.

Similar to the previous section, we then test the performance of our models on the target language test sets from the UDT. Table 10 lists the results in terms of labeled attachment scores.

	DE	EN	ES	FR	SV
DE	–	**54.72**$^{(5.91)}$	**59.87**$^{(3.11)}$	**59.77**$^{(1.25)}$	**63.15**$^{(2.82)}$
EN	**56.56**$^{(0.78)}$	–	**62.29**$^{(2.02)}$	**64.79**$^{(2.93)}$	**63.90**$^{(2.49)}$
ES	*52.40*$^{-0.54}$	**51.39**$^{(3.65)}$	–	65.48$^{(0.36)}$	**61.26**$^{(0.29)}$
FR	*52.56*$^{-0.52}$	**55.17**$^{(4.62)}$	**65.29**$^{(0.88)}$	–	**58.42**$^{(0.82)}$
SV	**55.48**$^{(0.36)}$	50.80$^{(2.04)}$	**61.34**$^{(0.58)}$	*60.52*$^{-1.08}$	–

Table 10: Annotation projection using tree-to-string models for translating treebanks (differences in LAS scores to the projection baseline are in superscript numbers). Results in bold are better than the phrase-based translation (Table 8). Scores in italics are worse than the annotation projection baseline (Table 1).

The results of the syntax-based translation projection are quite impressive. Almost all cases outperform the phrase-based MT approach which shows the potentials of these models for syntactic annotation projection. Furthermore, only three cases are below the annotation projection baseline and for the majority of language pairs we can observe a substantial improvement of up to 5.91 points in LAS compared to that baseline. It is difficult to say why the approach did not work as well for translating Spanish and French to German and Swedish to French but this may be related to specific properties of the treebanks involved and the domain mismatch with the data used for SMT training. Note that phrase-based models performed even worse for these language pairs and that only two other cases are slightly below the phrase-based translation projection whereas other language pairs obtain increased LAS's of several points (see, for example, German-Spanish and German-Swedish) compared to phrase-based SMT.

	DE	EN	ES	FR	SV
DE	–	**54.89**$^{(0.17)}$	**60.11**$^{(0.24)}$	**60.06**$^{(0.29)}$	**63.82**$^{(0.67)}$
EN	56.45$^{-0.11}$	–	**62.57**$^{(0.28)}$	**64.95**$^{(0.16)}$	63.72$^{-0.18}$
ES	**52.90**$^{(0.50)}$	**51.80**$^{(0.41)}$	–	**65.86**$^{(0.38)}$	60.24$^{-1.02}$
FR	**55.03**$^{(2.47)}$	**56.09**$^{(0.92)}$	**66.00**$^{(0.71)}$	–	**59.29**$^{(0.87)}$
SV	**55.70**$^{(0.22)}$	**51.18**$^{(0.38)}$	**61.64**$^{(0.30)}$	**60.91**$^{(0.39)}$	–

Table 11: Treating dummy nodes as described in Section 2.2.; improvements over Table 10)

Finally, we can use the same techniques for removing dummy nodes as described in Section 2.2. The results are shown in Table 11. Again, we can see consistent improvements in LAS with only a few exceptions.

4 Discussions

One of the questions that we have is whether there is a correlation between translation quality and the performance of the cross-lingual parsers based on translated treebanks. As an approximation for treebank translation quality we computed BLEU scores over well-established MT test sets from the WMT shared task, in our case newstest 2012.[2]

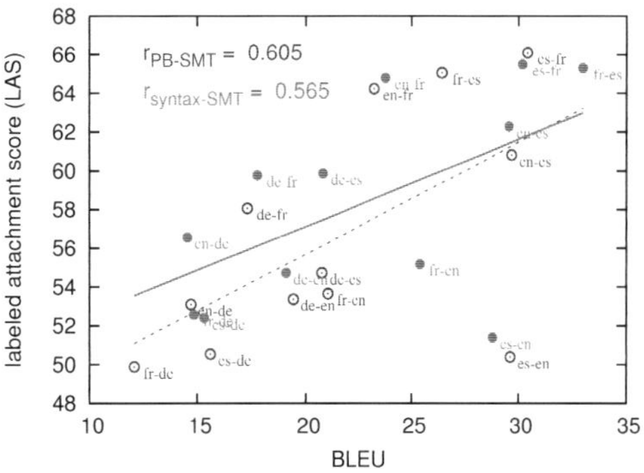

Figure 4: Correlation between BLEU scores and cross-lingual parsing accuracy.

Figure 4 illustrates the correlation between BLEU scores obtained on newstest data and LAS's of the corresponding cross-lingual parsers. First of all, we can see that the MT performance of phrase-based and syntax-based models is quite comparable with some noticeable exceptions in which syntax-based SMT is significantly better (French-English and French-Spanish, which is rather surprising). However, looking at most language pairs we can see that the increased parsing performance does not seem to be due to improvements in translation but rather due to the better fit of these models for syntactic annotation projection (see German, for example). Nevertheless, we can observe a correlation between BLEU scores and LAS within a class of models with one notable outlier, Spanish-English. This correlation may be explained by the fact that language relation is a crucial factor for both tasks, machine translation and annotation projection, with French and Spanish as the top-performing language pair in our experiments.

Another interesting question is whether the different data sets can successfully be combined. In order to test this possibility, we conducted a final experiment in which we concatenated all projected data sets coming from all source languages in our data set. The results are shown in Table 12. In all cases, we obtain the best score for cross-lingual dependency parsing so far which demonstrates the benefits of different projection algorithms. In our case, we only used a very simple concatenation approach and we expect that better combination techniques would work even better.

[2]Note that we have to leave out Swedish for this test as there is no test set available for this language.

	DE	EN	ES	FR	SV
LAS	**60.94**	**56.58**	**68.45**	**69.15**	**68.95**
UAS	67.89	63.89	75.33	74.75	76.48
LACC	79.02	73.26	81.99	83.18	80.85

Table 12: Combining projected data of all source languages to train target language parsing models. Additionally to LAS we also includes unlabeled attachment scores (UAS) and label accuracy (LACC).

5 Conclusions

In this paper, we propose several modifications and data sub-set selection techniques that can be used to improve the projection of syntactic annotation for cross-lingual dependency parsing. We show that it is beneficial to remove unnecessary dummy nodes from the projected trees and that it is useful to filter out sentences with uninformative annotation. These techniques lead to substantial improvements in labeled attachment scores when applied to automatically annotated bitexts and machine-translated text. We also introduce syntax-based SMT as yet another alternative to cross-lingual parsing and demonstrate its advantage over phrase-based models. Furthermore, a combination of projected resources leads to further gains and overall we present the highest scores for the cross-lingual parsing task so far.

There are several directions for future work. The most obvious question is related to data combination and multi-source transfer. A simple concatenation is certainly not optimal and more sophisticated data selection or instance weighting schemes are promising ideas for future research. Furthermore, the translation approach can be developed in various ways. First of all, we could look at improved translation that is optimized for the task of projection rather than translation quality. N-best lists could be explored as well and factored models may also help to improve the projection of POS tags.

References

Miguel Ballesteros and Joakim Nivre. 2012. MaltOptimizer: An Optimization Tool for MaltParser. In *Proceedings of EACL 2012*, pages 58–62.

Péter Halácsy, András Kornai, and Csaba Oravecz. 2007. Poster paper: Hunpos – an open source trigram tagger. In *Proceedings of the 45th Annual Meeting of the Association for Computational Linguistics Companion Volume Proceedings of the Demo and Poster Sessions*, pages 209–212, Prague, Czech Republic.

Kenneth Heafield, Ivan Pouzyrevsky, Jonathan H. Clark, and Philipp Koehn. 2013. Scalable Modified Kneser-Ney Language Model Estimation. In *Proceedings of ACL 2013*, pages 690–696.

Rebecca Hwa, Philip Resnik, Amy Weinberg, Clara Cabezas, and Okan Kolak. 2005. Bootstrapping Parsers via Syntactic Projection across Parallel Texts. *Natural Language Engineering*, 11(3):311–325.

Philipp Koehn, Franz Josef Och, and Daniel Marcu. 2003. Statistical Phrase Based Translation. In *Proceedings of NAACL-HLT 2003*, pages 48–54.

Philipp Koehn, Hieu Hoang, Alexandra Birch, Chris Callison-Burch, Marcello Federico, Nicola Bertoldi, Brooke Cowan, Wade Shen, Christine Moran, Richard Zens, Christopher J. Dyer, Ondřej Bojar, Alexandra Constantin, and Evan Herbst. 2007. Moses: Open Source Toolkit for Statistical Machine Translation. In *Proceedings of ACL 2007*, pages 177–180.

Philipp Koehn. 2005. Europarl: A Parallel Corpus for Statistical Machine Translation. In *Proceedings of MT Summit 2005*, pages 79–86.

Ryan McDonald, Slav Petrov, and Keith Hall. 2011. Multi-Source Transfer of Delexicalized Dependency Parsers. In *Proceedings of EMNLP 2011*, pages 62–72.

Ryan McDonald, Joakim Nivre, Yvonne Quirmbach-Brundage, Yoav Goldberg, Dipanjan Das, Kuzman Ganchev, Keith Hall, Slav Petrov, Hao Zhang, Oscar Täckström, Claudia Bedini, Núria Bertomeu Castelló, and Jungmee Lee. 2013. Universal Dependency Annotation for Multilingual Parsing. In *Proceedings of ACL 2013*, pages 92–97.

Tahira Naseem, Regina Barzilay, and Amir Globerson. 2012. Selective Sharing for Multilingual Dependency Parsing. In *Proceedings of ACL 2012*, pages 629–637.

Joakim Nivre, Johan Hall, and Jens Nilsson. 2006. MaltParser: A Data-Driven Parser-Generator for Dependency Parsing. In *Proceedings of LREC 2006*, pages 2216–2219.

Franz Josef Och and Hermann Ney. 2003. A Systematic Comparison of Various Statistical Alignment Models. *Computational Linguistics*, 29(1):19–52.

Franz Josef Och. 2003. Minimum Error Rate Training in Statistical Machine Translation. In *Proceedings of ACL 2003*, pages 160–167.

Slav Petrov, Dipanjan Das, and Ryan McDonald. 2012. A Universal Part-of-Speech Tagset. In *Proceedings of LREC 2012*, pages 2089–2096.

Oscar Täckström, Ryan McDonald, and Jakob Uszkoreit. 2012. Cross-lingual Word Clusters for Direct Transfer of Linguistic Structure. In *Proceedings of NAACL 2012*, pages 477–487.

Oscar Täckström, Ryan McDonald, and Joakim Nivre. 2013. Target Language Adaptation of Discriminative Transfer Parsers. In *Proceedings of NAACL 2013*, pages 1061–1071.

Jörg Tiedemann, Željko Agić, and Joakim Nivre. 2014. Treebank translation for cross-lingual parser induction. In *Proceedings of the 18th Conference Natural Language Processing and Computational Natural Language Learning (CoNLL)*, Baltimore, Maryland, USA.

Jörg Tiedemann. 2012. Parallel Data, Tools and Interfaces in OPUS. In *Proceedings of LREC 2012*, pages 2214–2218.

Jörg Tiedemann. 2014. Rediscovering annotation projection for cross-lingual parser induction. In *Proceedings of COLING 2014*, Dublin, Ireland, August.

David Yarowsky, Grace Ngai, and Richard Wicentowski. 2001. Inducing Multilingual Text Analysis Tools via Robust Projection Across Aligned Corpora. In *Proceedings of HLT 2011*, pages 1–8.

Assessing the Performance of Automatic Speech Recognition Systems When Used by Native and Non-Native Speakers of Three Major Languages in Dictation Workflows

Julián Zapata
School of Translation and Interpretation
University of Ottawa, Canada
jzapa026@uottawa.ca

Andreas Søeborg Kirkedal
Copenhagen Business School
& Mirsk Digital ApS
Denmark
andreas@mirsk.com

Abstract

In this paper, we report on a two-part experiment aiming to assess and compare the performance of two types of automatic speech recognition (ASR) systems on two different computational platforms when used to augment dictation workflows. The experiment was performed with a sample of speakers of three major languages and with different linguistic profiles: non-native English speakers; non-native French speakers; and native Spanish speakers. The main objective of this experiment is to examine ASR performance in translation dictation (TD) and medical dictation (MD) workflows without manual transcription vs. with transcription. We discuss the advantages and drawbacks of a particular ASR approach in different computational platforms when used by various speakers of a given language, who may have different accents and levels of proficiency in that language, and who may have different levels of competence and experience dictating large volumes of text, and with ASR technology. Lastly, we enumerate several areas for future research.

1 Introduction

Speech has been a popular input mode for several years in a number of domains and applications, from automated telephone customer services to legal and clinical documentation. Today, the general problem of automatic recognition of speech by any speaker in any environment is still far from being solved. Nevertheless, speech-enabled interfaces are proven to be more effective than keyboard-and-mouse interfaces for tasks for which full natural language communication is useful or for which keyboard and mouse are not appropriate (Jurafsky and Martin, 2009). Now, although it was implicit in the earliest efforts in natural language processing (NLP) that speech was expected to completely replace — rather than enhance — other input modes, it was soon proposed that, for many tasks, speech input achieved better performance in combination with other input modes (Pausch and Leatherby, 1991).

Clinical documentation and professional translation are two domains in which large volumes of texts are produced on a daily basis worldwide. We carried out an experiment to assess the performance of ASR-augmented dictation workflows using two different computational platforms: a speaker-adapted (SA) PC-based system on a Windows laptop, and a speaker-independent (SI) cloud-based system on an Android tablet. The experimental results of this study may also inform further developments in other areas such as respeaking and live subtitling, where interest in ASR technology has increased in recent years (Romero-Fresco, 2011). The experiment was performed with a small sample of speakers of three different languages and with different linguistic profiles: non-native English (Indian-accented and Spanish-accented) speakers; non-native French (Russian-accented and Spanish-accented) speakers; and native Spanish (Iberian-accented and Latin-American-accented) speakers. The main objective of this experiment was to examine the potential advantages and drawbacks of ASR-augmentation in different computational platforms and for various users, who may have different accents and levels of proficiency in their working languages, and who may have different levels of competence and experience dictating large volumes of text, and with ASR technology. The general conclusion is that, although some technical challenges still need to be overcome, speech-enabled interfaces have the potential to become one of the most efficient and ergonomic environments to perform translation and documentation tasks (including information retrieval) for an array of users, in addition to other emerging input modes such as gaze, touch and stylus, which may also be combined with speech in multimodal environments (Oviatt, 2012; Zapata, 2014). Lastly, this paper enumerates several areas for future research.

2 Dictation background

As mentioned above, clinical documentation and translation are two domains in which large volumes of texts are produced on a daily basis, and constitute the focus for the present paper. In this section, we provide some background on the use of medical dictation (MD) and translation dictation (TD).

2.1 Medical dictation

A clinical documentation workflow has the following steps: Patient consultation, diagnosis, dictation of diagnosis (using a recording device), transcription and documentation, as illustrated below:

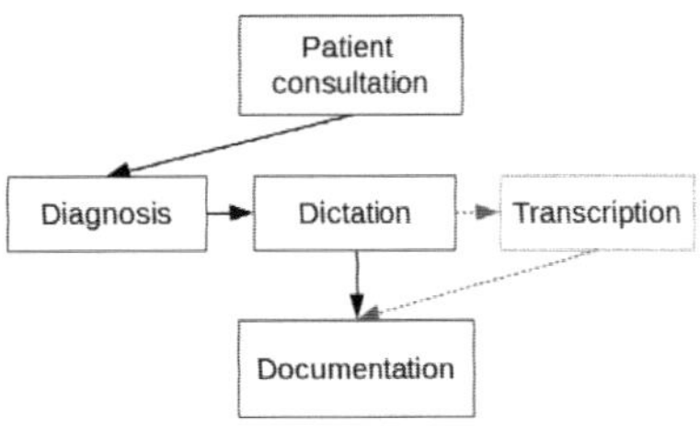

Figure 1. Clinical documentation workflow

The patient is involved during consultation; the physician is involved during all steps except transcription, which is handled by a specially-trained secretary or transcriptionist. The attending physician should approve the transcription before the documentation step, which the secretary also handles. However, this rarely happens in practice since the transcription is not immediate and the physician will have attended other patients in the meantime. In recent years, most hospitals have moved from paper-based clinical records to electronic medical records (EMR) systems where all documentation is stored. When stored in electronic format, information about patient history, medication, etc., and can be immediately shared with other hospitals in case of emergencies. The actual transcription of dictations is commonly handled on a computer using mouse and keyboard.

2.2 Translation dictation

In a professional translation setting, the scenario is similar. In TD, a translator or a team of translators work in collaboration with a transcriptionist or team of transcriptionists. The translator sight-translates a text and records it into a voice recorder. The recording is then sent (via email or a common server) to a transcriptionist, who transcribes the text as instructed by the translator (the latter also dictates punctuation marks and formatting instructions, etc.). It is the translator who makes the final revision to the text manually. Major modifications or additions to the text, if necessary, are dictated and sent again to the secretary for transcription. Figure 2 illustrates the TD workflow:

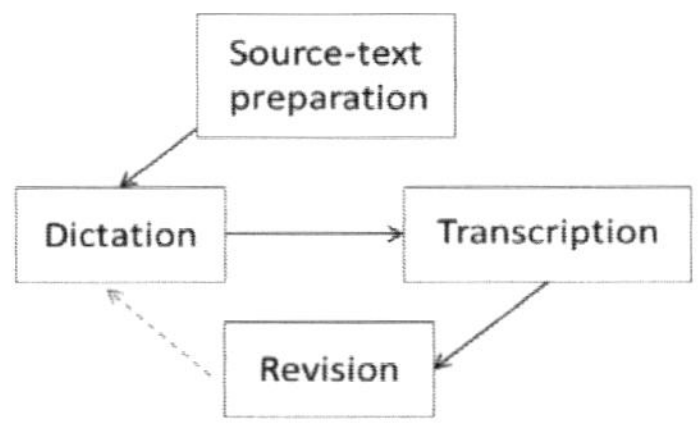

Figure 2. Translation dictation workflow

TD was a very popular – and effective – technique in the 1960s and 1970s (Gingold, 1978), but started to fade away as professional translators' workstations experienced the massive influx of typewriters and personal computers: it was no longer necessary to train and pay additional staff to transcribe translated texts; translators were now able to carry out the transcription by themselves. This being said, a few translation services still opt for this technique in an effort to provide translators with more ergonomic solutions and to increase productivity (Gouadec, 2007; Hétu, 2012). Today, the tremendous improvements in ASR technology provide a golden opportunity to bring back dictation to the profession; in the words of Gouadec (2007), TD "will become the norm once again".

In MD and TD, the transcription step is slow and expensive. For instance, in MD, the transcription can take between hours and months to complete. Training secretaries to transcribe dictations is expensive and transcription takes up to 60% of secretaries' working hours. Likewise, in TD, it has become difficult to find skilled personnel to type large volumes of texts in a way that the translator-transcriptionist collaboration is cost-effective. Because the transcription will be automatized and immediate with ASR-augmentation, physicians and translators will have the time and the possibility to proofread and approve the transcriptions. In the next section, we provide a brief historical overview of the interest in ASR for TD, and an overview of the different types of ASR systems and of their functioning, while supporting the idea of efficiently integrating this technology to MD and TD workflows.

3 Related work

The interest in ASR technologies for dictation in fields such as translation is not new. Off-the-shelf ASR systems have been part of certain translators' toolbox for over a dozen years now (Bowker, 2002); in many cases, of those translators who once dictated with the aid of voice recorders and transcriptionists back in the 1960s and 1970s.

In the mid-1990s, research efforts to adapt ASR technology to human translation took place for the first time. Such developments focused on minimizing word error rates by combining ASR and machine translation (MT). Hybrid ASR/MT systems have access to the source text and use MT probabilistic models to improve recognition. A number of works have been conducted over the years, highlighting the various challenges of ASR/MT integration (Brousseau et al., 1995; Désilets et al., 2008; Dymetman et al., 1994; Reddy and Rose, 2010; Rodriguez et al., 2012; Vidal et al., 2006), and the potential benefits of using speech input for human translation and post-editing purposes (Garcia-Martinez et al., 2014; Mesa-Lao, 2014). Likewise, further efforts have been made by translation trainers and researchers to evaluate the performance of students and professionals when using off-the-shelf ASR systems for straight TD (Dragsted et al., 2009; Dragsted et al., 2011; Mees et al., 2013); and to assess and analyze professional translators' needs and opinions vis-à-vis ASR technology (Ciobanu, 2014; Zapata, 2012). But ASR systems are not all created equal, and it becomes necessary to investigate what type of system and what conditions of use are more appropriate for the needs of various users in a given domain.

There are three different types of ASR systems wrt. speakers: SI, speaker-dependent (SD) and SA. SI systems use data from many speakers across age, gender, sociolect and dialect to train acoustic models, as well as speaker normalization techniques such as Cepstral Mean and Variance Normalization, Vocal Tract Length Normalization and Maximum Likelihood Linear Transforms (see e.g. Uebel et al. (1999)). Normally, the speaker(s) who will use the system is not in the training data. SD systems are equivalent to SI systems, but use only training data from a single speaker who will also be the sole user of the system. This will produce better recognition performance than SI systems, but the drawback of SD systems is that the amount of training data necessary to train acoustic models is usually not available and time-consuming to collect.

SA systems constitute a middle road. The idea is to adapt an SI system to a specific user using only a little speaker-specific data. Speaker Adaptive Training (SAT) techniques such as Constrained Maximum Likelihood Linear Regression modify either the ASR model parameters or transform the training data directly. See Woodland (2001) for a review of adaptation techniques. Speaker-adaptation of an SI system practically happens in a supervised fashion where the user reads aloud a number of sentences. In this manner, the adaptation software has a gold standard to compare to ASR output and is able to learn a mapping function that optimizes ASR accuracy.

Training ASR systems is a computationally expensive process and training commercial systems can only take place on servers or clusters. Still, the training process can take days. Trained models can be embedded in a system on a computer or can be used from a server accessed through the cloud. The trade-off between embedded vs. cloud is one of computation vs.

latency/connectivity. The computation required in speech decoding (actual recognition) is also expensive. This is not a problem for computers connected directly to a power source, but for laptops and tablets, decoding drains the battery and consumes memory to such an extent that ASR is not a practical tool. Work on reducing memory usage and still achieve acceptable ASR accuracy has been conducted (e.g. in Lei et al. (2013)), but subjects such as reducing computation and implications for battery life have not been addressed.

If speech is streamed to a server, decoded and the output returned via the cloud or intranet, electrical and computational power is abundant. However, the client computer must have fast web access to stream sound to the server and receive text. Latency in ASR confuses users, who will stop dictating, repeat words, restart or speak slower than their natural rate of speech. The problem of battery lifetime can be alleviated by professional translators or physicians who use a desktop computer for dictation and manual revision. This chains the user to the workstation and is not appropriate for cases where mobility is desirable, e.g., physicians who will often have to dictate medical diagnoses while moving from one patient to the next; or translators who need to find ergonomic alternatives to prevent mental and physical fatigue, or even short- and long-term illnesses such as back pain or repetitive stress injury.

4 Research question

The two-part experiment was carried out particularly with translation and medical settings in mind, currently characterized by the extended use of keyboard-and-mouse graphical user interfaces. The underlying hypothesis is that speech input provides one of the most efficient means to perform TD and MD tasks, since ASR "has the potential to be a better interface than the keyboard for tasks for which full natural language communication is useful or for which keyboards are not appropriate" (Jurafsky and Martin, 2009).

But is ASR always beneficial for any task, for any user, in any environment and in any computational platform available today? This is the question that motivates this exploratory study, and is partially answered in the present paper.

5 Experimental setup

This experiment included a sample of English, French and Spanish speakers, as described below:

- English: four Indian-accented speakers (EN1, EN2, EN3, EN4) and one Spanish-accented speaker (EN5) (all non-native)
- French: one Spanish-accented speaker (FR1) and two Russian-accented speakers (FR2, FR3) (all non-native)
- Spanish: two Iberian-accented speakers (SP2, SP3) and two Latin-American-accented speakers (SP1, SP4) (all native)

All participants possess an excellent professional command of the experimental language, whether they speak it as a first, second, third or fourth language. The 12 participants (all graduate students or researchers), had in common at least a minimum level of familiarity with the notions of translation processes, computational linguistics and NLP. However, only a few reported they had hands-on experience with commercial or research-level ASR systems (and were therefore familiar with voice commands, etc.).

5.1 Methodology

Four tasks were involved in the main experiment: (1) typing; (2) reading aloud; (3) dictating with a commercial PC-based SA ASR system[1] on a laptop; and (4) dictating with a commercial cloud-based SI ASR system[2] on a tablet. Tasks 1 and 2 were control tasks, whereas tasks 3 and 4 were the experimental tasks[3].

A 200-word text was chosen for each language. The same text was used for all four tasks. The texts were selected (and amended) so that they would contain the same number of words, one title, two paragraphs and no foreign-language tokens that may not be recognized by an ASR system. For instance, in the English text, a foreign-language name was replaced by "John

[1] Dragon NaturallySpeaking Premium Edition, v.12.5., by Nuance Communications.

[2] Dragon Dictate, integrated in the Swype keyboard, by Nuance Communications.

[3] It was only possible to perform all 4 tasks with the English and French participants, since a PC-based ASR system in Spanish was not available for this experiment.

Smith" so that it would be easily recognized by the ASR systems. In addition, the three texts were relatively simple and contained no specialized terminology. They all contained a fair number of punctuation marks, which needed to be dictated (e.g. "full stop", "comma", "ellipsis", "open quote", "end of quote", "colon") during the experimental tasks (in addition to "new paragraph"). Furthermore, Translog II was used to display the 200-word text in the four tasks and to log the typing session (task 1). Although Translog II was primarily designed to investigate human translation processes, it can also be used to study reading and writing processes in general (Carl, 2012), as in the case of this experiment. This being said, the focus of this experiment was not on keystroke activity but rather on task times and ASR performance across various users, languages and devices.

The main experiment took place over two days. The experimental sessions were performed individually (i.e., one participant at a time). Control tasks were performed separately from experimental tasks (i.e., on different days). This would avoid mental and physical fatigue since each task involved the same text (i.e., typing it, reading it, dictating it on the laptop and dictating it on the tablet). Each task was timed using a stopwatch. No recording of the reading task (task 2) was made. As far as the experimental tasks are concerned (tasks 3 and 4), the transcriptions by the ASR systems both on the laptop and the tablet were saved as Word (.doc) documents.

To measure the word accuracy for the ASR systems, a simple online edit distance calculator[4] (aka. Levenshtein edit distance (Navarro, 2001) calculator) was used. Such a tool calculates the "cheapest" way to transform one string into another. The result obtained indicates the "total cost" or, in other words, the minimum total number of keystrokes what would be needed to edit a given text (in the case of our experiment, the output of the ASR system) to match another text (in our case, the original text).

Lastly, at a later date, a second experimental session took place with the participation of three informants (one per language) from the main experiment[5]. This time, participants were required to proofread and post-edit, using a laptop's keyboard, the texts they had produced earlier with the two ASR systems; in other words, to manually fix the ASR errors. This task was logged using InputLog, a research-level program designed to log, analyze and visualize writing processes (Leijten and Van Waes, 2013). InputLog analyses provide data such as total time spent in the document (i.e. reading through the text and manually fixing the ASR errors), total time of actual keystrokes (additions, deletions and substitutions), total characters typed, switches between mouse and keyboard, etc.

An overview of the results of the experiment and a discussion are provided in the following sections.

6 Results

6.1 Task times and accuracy

It is not surprising that speaking is faster than typing (Hauptmann and Rudnicky, 1990). Our data shows that participants, regardless of whether they were performing the experiment in their native language or in a foreign language, are consistently slower when typing than when reading out loud only. This being said, the reading times across participants and across languages are comparable with mean reading time of 84.74s and standard deviation (SD) of 0.78s. In other words, as it can be observed in Figures 3 and 4 below, it takes about the same amount of time to read a 200-word text in English, in French or in Spanish, whereas typing the same text can take 3-7 times longer.

Figures 3 and 4 also feature task times for ASR tasks. With the exception of EN3, task times for both ASR tasks are comparable (since essentially they involved doing exactly the same thing). ASR task times have longer duration than the reading task because the user needs to dictate punctuation marks and other editing commands. The difference between reading and dictation times (SRT) is statistically significant at p-value = 0.0022 measured across all participants. This is unsurprising when comparing SRT mean (128.3s) and SD (29.57s) to reading aloud. A Wilcoxon signed rank-test was used to calculate

[4] The tool, developed by Peter Kleiweg, is available for free at: http://odur.let.rug.nl/kleiweg/lev/.

[5] Unfortunately, the other nine participants were no longer available to perform this task.

the *p*-value because normal distribution of task times cannot be assumed and, with a small sample size, a robust method is needed to calculate statistical significance.

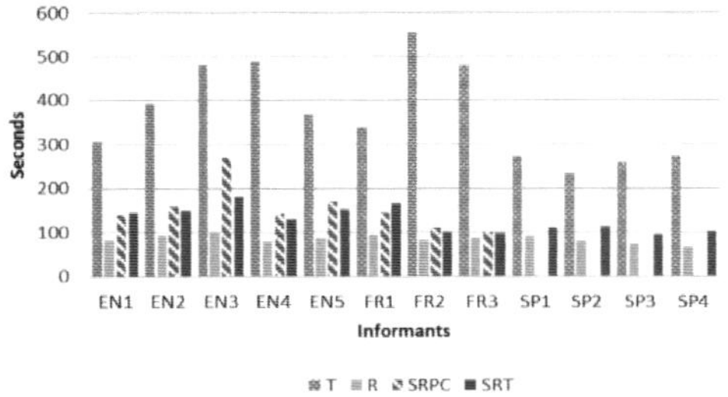

Figure 3. All task times (in seconds). T= typing; R= reading; SRPC: speech recognition on PC; SRT= speech recognition on tablet

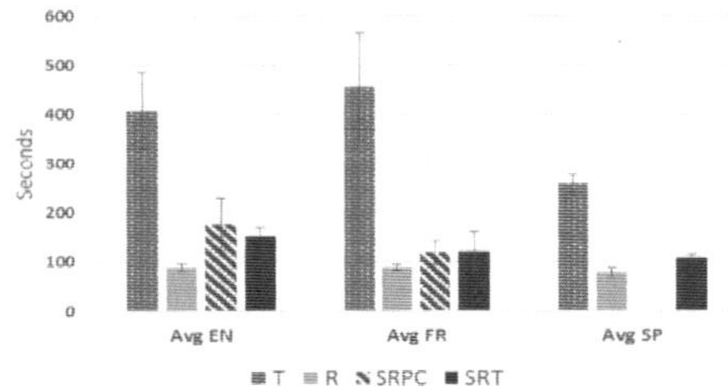

Figure 4. Average task times (in seconds) per language, displaying standard deviation bars.

Tables 1 and 2 show the WAcc for the PC-based system during task 3 in English and French respectively, for each non-native participant (see also Figures 5 and 6 below). It is important to note that the SA system was adapted with minimal training (for approx. 5 minutes) prior to performing the task.

	EN1	EN2	EN3	EN4	EN5
%WAcc-PC	89.2	86.56	80.7	78.97	86.31

Table 1. WAcc on laptop for English language

	FR1	FR2	FR3
%WAcc-PC	95.34	91.76	89.39

Table 2. WAcc on laptop for French language

For the Spanish language, ASR data was collected with the tablet only. Figure 5 displays very high WAcc rates with the cloud-based SI ASR system — with no previous training — used by native speakers of the language.

	SP1	SP2	SP3	SP4
%WAcc-T	99.09	97.04	98.85	94.18

Table 3. WAcc on tablet for Spanish language

Nonetheless, a poor performance of the cloud-based system is observed when used by non-native speakers, particularly Indian-accented English speakers. Figures 5 and 6 display the performance gap between the SA and SI ASR systems and is supported by the difference in means and SD in Table 4.

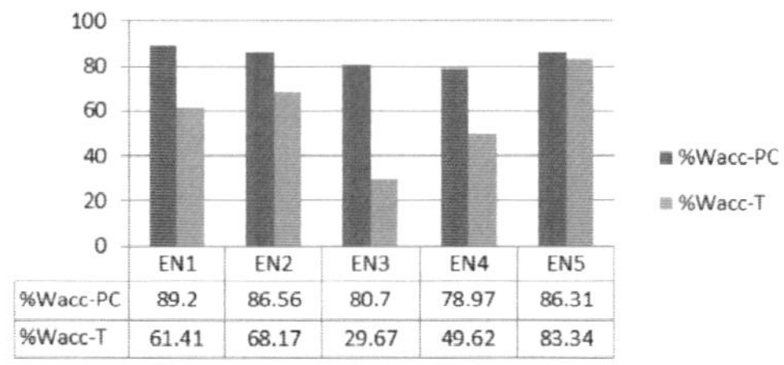

Figure 5. WAcc on laptop vs. tablet for English language

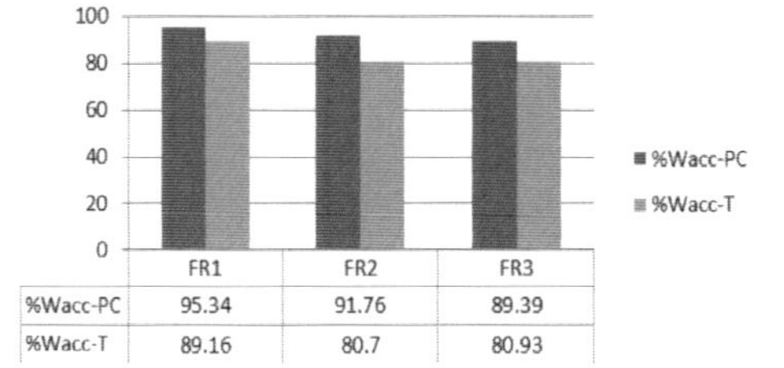

Figure 6. WAcc on laptop vs. tablet for French language

	EN	SP	FR
Mean (%)	58.44	97.26	83.60
SD (% points)	20.18	2.27	4.82

Table 4. WAcc statistics per language

6.2 Dictation workflow comparison

As mentioned in the methodology section, the focus of the main experiment was to collect data for task completion times and ASR WAcc rates. To compare MD and TD workflows using a transcriptionist to ASR-augmented MD and TD, a revision/post-editing phase must be included in our model of the workflow. ASR, whether SI or SA, is not perfect. We conducted an additional experiment in order to estimate the time and effort that would be required by the user to proof-read and edit the ASR output. This smaller experiment was carried out with informants EN5, FR1 and SP1, who manually post-edited, using a mechanical keyboard, the texts they had previously produced with the SA and SI ASR systems. Figure 7 below shows the time spent typing corrections with the keyboard versus the total time spent proofreading the document. The bars at 100% help illustrate the amount of time spent typing corrections (KT, dark blue) in comparison with the total time spent in the document (full bar).

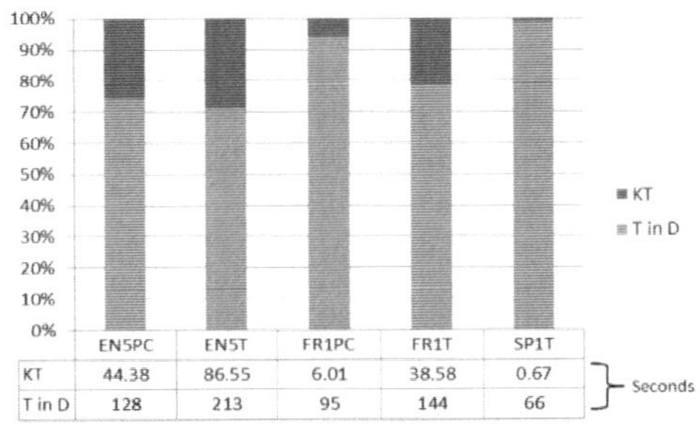

Figure 7. Total time spent typing vs. total revision time (all in seconds). KT= keyboard time; T in D= time in document

Lastly, we added the total revision time to the time dictating with ASR while dictating commands from Figure 3. In short, this indicates the total time a participant would need to carry out a dictation task from start to finish. Thus, as illustrated in Figure 8, this calculation allows us to figure out how much faster it may be to dictate with ASR and manually fix the ASR errors than it is to simply type the text on a mechanical keyboard, and to speculate about possible ways to reduce that time in order to near the reading-out-loud-only times.

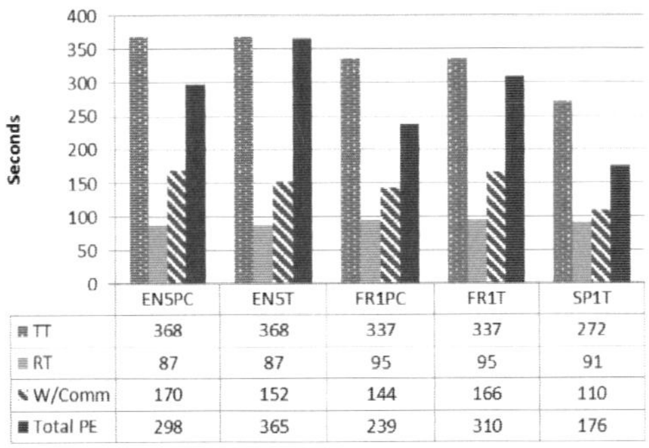

Figure 8. Total task time comparisons for participants EN5, FR1 and SP1 for both ASR systems. TT= typing time; RT= reading time; W/Comm= with commands; Total PE= total time after post-editing

Table 5 provides data on efficiency gains when reading out loud only as compared to typing, and when using ASR and manually post-editing as compared to typing. It also recalls the WAcc for each participant in the different ASR conditions. It can be observed, for instance, that participant EN5, who is a non-native speaker of English, can read out loud an English text 4.22 times faster than she can type the same text. However, with 83.34% WAcc (with the SI system) and 86.31% WAcc (with the SA system), the efficiency gains can be between 1.008 (almost null) and 1.234 respectively.

	T/R	T/Total PE	WAcc (%)
EN5PC	4.22	1.234	86.31
EN5T	4.22	1.008	83.34
FR1PC	3.52	1.41	95.34
FR1T	3.52	1.087	89.16
SP1T	2.99	1.545	99.09

Table 5. Efficiency gains comparison and WAcc for participants EN5, FR1 and SP1. T/R= efficiency gains when reading out loud vs. typing; T/Total PE= efficiency gains after post-editing ASR output vs. typing

In the following section, we provide a discussion on the results of this pilot experiment and formulate areas for future work.

7 Discussion and future work

We have confirmed in this experiment that speaking (or rather, reading aloud) is always faster (approx. 3-7 times) than typing; and we observed that, in terms of efficiency, non-native speakers of a language could benefit from ASR to perform dictation tasks only with an SA system; that native speakers get the best ASR performance (avg. 97% Wacc with the SI system); and that participants who are familiar with ASR technology may benefit considerably from it, regardless of the computational platform they are using (as was the case for EN5, FR1, SP1, SP2 and SP3). In addition, we observed that the extra time to dictate commands (e.g., punctuation marks) is significant and adds to the time needed to post-edit the ASR output. We have also observed that with relatively low WAcc rates (as it was observed for EN5 with the SI system, with 83.3% WAcc) the efficiency gains from ASR-augmentation disappear, but is not less efficient than typing. This being said, to perform certain tasks, punctuation and formatting commands might not always be necessary, or could be avoided using multimodal interaction.

Our experiment models ASR-augmented dictation workflows in two separate stages: a dictation stage and a post-editing stage. This follows the professional translation style taught at most universities: 1) skim the source text, 2) read and comprehend/prepare the source text, 3) create a draft target text, 4) post-edit target text. Our experiment models steps 3 and 4. However, there are many styles of text production and it is highly feasible that a translator or a physician would change errors on-the-fly rather than complete the dictation first and then proofread and edit the text. Because rereading ASR output to detect errors is unnecessary, post-editing task times (T in D, Figure 9) could be significantly reduced. To test this assumption, an experiment studying on-the-fly editing of dictated text will be conducted. It is a more accurate model of MD and TD workflows without third-party transcription stage and it would be possible to study the pros and cons of multimodal interaction using touch screens, gaze and mouse-and-keyboard. But also comparisons between mechanic keyboards, software keyboards and swipe keyboards will be possible.

The available software and hardware when conducting our experiments were a laptop and a tablet with an SA and an SI ASR system, respectively. The WAcc when using the tablet is consistently lower for non-native speakers of a language, as is expected for an SI system vs. an SA system. Some of the difference can also be due to the different microphones used: for the SI experiments with the tablet, the built-in microphone was used; for the SA experiments with the laptop, a Logitech h600 wireless headset was used. A control experiment with an SI system on the laptop and a SA system on the tablet will follow to shed light on this matter.

With a small number of participants, it is difficult to generalize and draw conclusions based on statistics. To add to our observations, additional experiments with a larger group of informants need to be conducted to make better use of statistical tools and analyses. In addition, larger-scale experiments would need to include longer texts, or several texts following each other, in order to investigate phenomena such as dictation fatigue. Lastly, it would be necessary to include other data collection methods and tools such as video and screen recording, eye-tracking and interviews, and to provide a wider picture of the usability of a particular system or interface by achieving a better understanding and assessment of the correlation between the different aspects of usability (effectiveness, efficiency and user satisfaction), and between objective and subjective usability measures (Hornbæk, 2006).

8 Conclusion

In this experiment, we examined the possibility for native and non-native speakers of a language to use speech as an input modality to dictate large volumes of texts, particularly in clinical documentation and translation workflows. In addition, we were interested in comparing two different ASR environments: a speaker-adapted ASR system installed on a laptop PC and a speaker-independent ASR system in a remote server accessible through a mobile device. We have observed that ASR-augmentation may not be counter-productive. For native speakers, speaker-adaptation does not seem to be necessary to realize efficiency gains, while it is appropriate for non-native speakers. According to our experiments, a WAcc above 83.3% is necessary for the ASR-augmented dictation workflow to be more efficient than typing. Furthermore, we have seen that small differences in WAcc can have a large impact on efficiency. Lastly, we acknowledge that the removal of out-of-vocabulary (OOV) words from the original English text (i.e. replacing a foreign name with "John Smith") may have biased the results in favour of the ASR solution because OOV words can have a large impact on WAcc. In real-life translation and medical dictation tasks with many proper names, pharmaceuticals and new terms, OOV words are more likely to occur frequently and that failed recognition of OOVs or recognition of different words can have a large impact on WAcc.

On one hand, as hospitals continue moving towards EMR systems and more efficient clinical documentation becomes necessary; and, on the other hand, as web-based translation tools and environments become more and more popular and efficient; it becomes essential to closely examine the different text-input modalities available in keyboard-less devices, as we move towards the era of mobile computing and ubiquitous information.

Acknowledgments

A special thanks to all anonymous participants for their time. We also acknowledge the assistance of Maheshwar Ghankot and guidance provided by Srinivas Bangalore and Michael Carl during the first set of experiments, and for their comments on an earlier version of this paper. This study was carried out within the framework of the translation data analytics project held in July-August 2014 at the Copenhagen Business School, in Denmark. The project was supported by the European Union's 7th Framework Program (FP7/2007-2013) under grant agreement 287576 (CASMACAT).

References

Bowker, Lynne. 2002. *Computer-Aided Translation Technology: A Practical Introduction*. Ottawa: University of Ottawa Press.

Brousseau, Julie, Caroline Drouin, George Foster, Pierre Isabelle, Roland Kuhn, Yves Normandin, and Pierre Plamondon. 1995. "French Speech Recognition in an Automatic Dictation System for Translators: The TransTalk Project." In *Proceedings of Eurospeech'95*. http://www.iro.umontreal.ca/~foster/papers/ttalk-eurospeech95.pdf.

Carl, Michael. 2012. "Translog - II: A Program for Recording User Activity Data for Empirical Reading and Writing Research." In *Proceedings of the Eight International Conference on Language Resources and Evaluation*, 4108–4112.

Ciobanu, Dragoş. 2014. "Of Dragons and Speech Recognition Wizards and Apprentices." *Revista Tradumàtica* (12): 524–538.

Désilets, Alain, Marta Stojanovic, Jean-François Lapointe, Rick Rose, and Aarthi Reddy. 2008. "Evaluating Productivity Gains of Hybrid ASR-MT Systems for Translation Dictation." In *Proceedings of the IWSLT2008*. http://www.mt-archive.info/IWSLT-2008-Desilets.pdf.

Dragsted, Barbara, Inge Gorm Hansen, and Henrik Selsøe Sørensen. 2009. "Experts Exposed." *Copenhagen Studies in Language* 38: 293–317.

Dragsted, Barbara, Inger M. Mees, and Inge Gorm Hansen. 2011. "Speaking Your Translation: Students' First Encounter with Speech Recognition Technology." *Translation & Interpreting* 3 (1): 10–43. http://www.trans-int.org/index.php/transint/article/viewFile/115/87.

Dymetman, Marc, Julie Brousseau, George Foster, Pierre Isabelle, Yves Normandin, and Pierre Plamondon. 1994. "Towards an Automatic Dictation System for Translators: The TransTalk Project." In *Fourth European Conference on Speech Communication and Technology*, 4. Citeseer. http://arxiv.org/abs/cmp-lg/9409012.

Garcia-Martinez, Mercedes, Karan Singla, Aniruddha Tammewar, Bartolomé Mesa-Lao, Ankita Thakur, M. A. Anusuya, Michael Carl, and Srinivas Bangalore. 2014. "SEECAT: ASR & Eye-Tracking Enabled Computer-Assisted Translation." In *Proceedings of the 17th Annual Conference of the European Association for Machine Translation*, 81–88.

Gingold, Kurt. 1978. "The Use of Dictation Equipment in Translation." In *La traduction, une profession. Actes du VIIIe Congrès mondial de la fédération internationale des traducteurs*, edited by Paul A. Horguelin, 444–448. Ottawa: Conseil des traducteurs et interprètes du Canada.

Gouadec, Daniel. 2007. *Translation as a Profession*. Amsterdam: John Benjamins.

Hauptmann, Alexander G., and Alexander I. Rudnicky. 1990. "A Comparison of Speech and Typed Input." In *Proceedings of the Speech and Natural Language Workshop*, 219–224.

Hétu, Marie-Pierre. 2012. "Le travail au dictaphone, une solution ergonomique?" *Circuit* 116 (summer 2012): 23.

Hornbæk, Kasper. 2006. "Current Practice in Measuring Usability: Challenges to Usability Studies and Research." *International Journal of Human-Computer Studies* 64 (2) (February): 79–102. doi:10.1016/j.ijhcs.2005.06.002. http://linkinghub.elsevier.com/retrieve/pii/S1071581905001138.

Jurafsky, Daniel, and James H. Martin. 2009. *Speech and Language Processing: An Introduction to Natural Language Processing, Computational Linguistics, and Speech Recognition.* 2nd ed. Upper Saddle River, New Jersey: Pearson Prentice Hall.

Lei, Xin, Andrew Senior, Alexander Gruenstein, and Jeffrey Sorensen. 2013. "Accurate and Compact Large Vocabulary Speech Recognition on Mobile Devices." *Interspeech* (August): 662–665. http://research.google.com/pubs/archive/41176.pdf.

Leijten, Mariëlle, and Luuk Van Waes. 2013. "Keystroke Logging in Writing Research: Using Inputlog to Analyze and Visualize Writing Processes." *Written Communication* 30 (3) (June 29): 358–392. doi:10.1177/0741088313491692. http://wcx.sagepub.com/cgi/doi/10.1177/0741088313491692.

Mees, Inger M., Barbara Dragsted, Inge Gorm Hansen, and Arnt Lykke Jakobsen. 2013. "Sound Effects in Translation." *Target* 25 (1) (January 1): 140–154. http://openurl.ingenta.com/content/xref?genre=article&issn=0924-1884&volume=25&issue=1&spage=140.

Mesa-Lao, Bartolomé. 2014. "Speech-Enabled Computer-Aided Translation: A Satisfaction Survey with Post-Editor Trainees." In *Workshop on Humans and Computer-Assisted Translation*, 99–103.

Navarro, Gonzalo. 2001. "A guided tour to approximate string matching". *ACM Computing Surveys*, 33(1): 31-88.

Oviatt, Sharon. 2012. "Multimodal Interfaces." In *The Human-Computer Interaction Handbook: Fundamentals, Evolving Technologies and Emerging Applications*, edited by Julie A. Jacko,

3rd ed., 415–429. New York: Lawrence Erlbaum Associates.

Pausch, Randy, and James H. Leatherby. 1991. "An Empirical Study: Adding Voice Input to a Graphical Editor." *Journal of the American Voice Input/Output Society* 9 (2): 55–66.

Reddy, Aarthi, and Richard C. Rose. 2010. "Integration of Statistical Models for Dictation of Document Translations in a Machine Aided Human Translation Task." *IEEE Transactions on Audio, Speech and Language Processing* 18 (8): 1–11. http://ieeexplore.ieee.org/stamp/stamp.jsp?arnumber=05393062.

Rodriguez, Luis, Aarthi Reddy, and Richard Rose. 2012. "Efficient Integration of Translation and Speech Models in Dictation Based Machine Aided Human Translation." In *Proceedings of the IEEE 2012 International Conference on Acoustics, Speech, and Signal Processing*, 2:4949–4952.

Romero-Fresco, Pablo. 2011. *Subtitling Through Speech Recognition: Respeaking*. Manchester: St. Jerome.

Uebel, Luis Felipe, and Philip C. Woodland. 1999. "An Investigation into Vocal Tract Length Normalisation." In *Sixth European Conference on Speech Communication and Technology*, 1–4. http://www.isca-speech.org/archive/eurospeech_1999/e99_2527.html.

Vidal, Enrique, Francisco Casacuberta, Luis Rodríguez, Jorge Civera, and Carlos D. Martínez Hinarejos. 2006. "Computer-Assisted Translation Using Speech Recognition." *IEEE Transactions on Audio, Speech and Language Processing* 14 (3). http://ieeexplore.ieee.org/stamp/stamp.jsp?arnumber=01621206.

Woodland, Philip C. 2001. "Speaker Adaptation for Continuous Density HMMs: A Review." In *ISCA Tutorial and Research Workshop (ITRW) on Adaptation Methods for Speech Recognition*.

Zapata, Julián. 2012. "Traduction dictée interactive : intégrer la reconnaissance vocale à l'enseignement et à la pratique de la traduction professionnelle." M.A. thesis, University of Ottawa. http://www.ruor.uottawa.ca/en/bitstream/handle/10393/23227/Zapata Rojas_Julian_2012_these.pdf?sequence=1.

Zapata, Julián, 2014. "Exploring Multimodality for Translator-Computer Interaction." In *Proceedings of the 16th International Conference on Multimodal Interaction*, 339–343. http://dl.acm.org/citation.cfm?id=2666280.

Inferring the location of authors from words in their texts

Max Berggren & Jussi Karlgren
Gavagai & KTH
Stockholm
{max, jussi}@gavagai.se

Robert Östling & Mikael Parkvall
Dept of Linguistics
Stockholm University
{robert, parkvall}@ling.su.se

Abstract

For the purposes of computational dialectology or other geographically bound text analysis tasks, texts must be annotated with their or their authors' location. Many texts are locatable but most have no explicit annotation of place. This paper describes a series of experiments to determine how positionally annotated microblog posts can be used to learn location indicating words which then can be used to locate blog texts and their authors. A Gaussian distribution is used to model the locational qualities of words. We introduce the notion of placeness to describe how locational words are.

We find that modelling word distributions to account for *several locations* and thus several Gaussian distributions per word, defining a filter which picks out words with high placeness based on their *local distributional context*, and aggregating locational information in a *centroid* for each text gives the most useful results. The results are applied to data in the Swedish language.

1 Text and Geographical Position

Authors write texts in a location, about something in a location (or about the location itself), reside and conduct their business in various locations, and have a background in some location. Some texts are personal, anchored in the here and now, where others are general and not necessarily bound to any context. Texts written by authors reflect the above facts explicitly or implicitly, through explicit author intention or incidentally. When a text is locational, it may be so because the author mentions some location or because the author is contextually bound to some location. In both cases, the text may or may not have explicit mentions of the context of the author or mention other locations in the text.

For some applications, inferring the location of a text or its author automatically is of interest. In this paper we show how establishing the location of a text can be done using the locational qualities of its terminology. Here, we investigate the utility of doing so for two distinct use cases.

Firstly, for detecting regional language usage for the purposes of real-time dialectology. The issue here is to find differences in term usage across locations and to investigate whether terminological variation differs across regions. In this case, the ultimate objective is to collect sizeable text collections from various regions of a linguistic area to establish if a certain term or turn of phrase is used more or less frequently in some specific region. The task is then to establish where the author of a text originally is from. This has hitherto been investigated by manual inspection of text collections. (Parkvall 2012, e.g.)

Secondly, for monitoring public opinion of e.g. brands, political issues, or other topic of interest. In this case the ultimate objective is to find whether there is a regional variation for the occurrence of opinionated mentions for the topic or topical target under consideration. The task is then to establish the location where a given text is written, or, alternatively, what location the text refers to.

In both cases, the system is presented with a body of text with the task of assigning a likely location to it. In the former task, typically the body of text is larger and noisier (since authors may refer to other locations than their immediate context); in the second task, the text may be short and have little evidence to work from. Both tasks, that of identifying the location of an author, or that of a text, have been addressed by recent experiments with various points of departure: knowledge-based, making use of recorded points of interest in a location, modelling the geographic distribution of topics, or using social network analysis to find additional information about the author.

This set of experiments focuses on the text itself and on using distributional semantics to refine the set of terms used for locating a text.

2 Location and words as evidence of locations

Most words contribute little or not at all to positioning text. Some words are dead giveaways: an author may mention a specific location in the text. Frequently, but not always, this is reasonable evidence of position. Some words are less patently locational, but contribute incidentally, such as the name of some establishment or some characteristic feature of a location.

Some locational terms are polysemous; some inspecific; some are vague. As indicated in Figure 1, the term *Falköping* unambiguously indicates a town in *Southern Sweden*, which in turn is a vague term without a clear and well defined border to other bits of Sweden. The term *Södermalm* is polysemous and refers to a section of town in several Swedish towns; the term *spårvagn* ("tram") is indicative of one of several Swedish towns with tram lines. We call both of these latter types of term *polylocational* and allow them to contribute to numerous places simultaneously.

Other words contribute variously to location of a text. Some words are less patently locational than named places, but contribute incidentally, such as the name of some establishment, some characteristic feature of a location, some event which takes place in some location, or some other topic the discussion of which is more typical in one location than in another. We will estimate the *placeness* of words in these experiments.

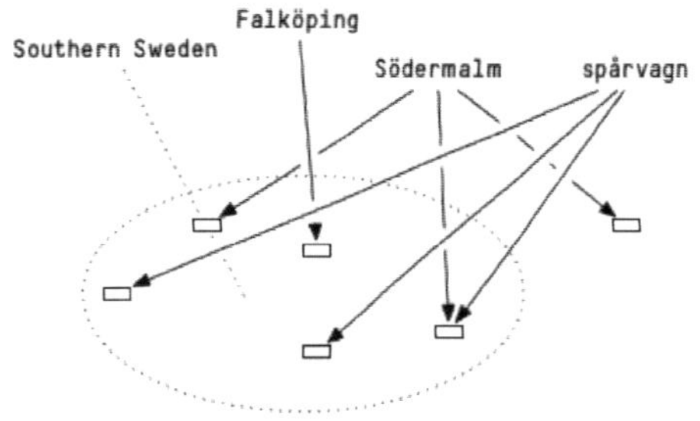

Figure 1: Some terms are polylocational

3 Mapping from a continuous to a discrete representation

We, as has been done in previous experiments, collect the geographic distribution of word usage through collecting microblog posts, some of which have longitude and latitude, from Twitter. Posts with location information are distributed over a map in what amounts to a continuous representation. The words from posts can be collected and associated with the positions they have been observed in.

First experiments which use similar training data to ours have typically assigned the posts and thus the words they occur in directly to some representation of locations - a word which occurs in tweets at $[N59.35, E18.11]$ and $[N59.31, E18.05]$ will have both observations recorded to be in the same city (Cheng et al. 2010; Mahmud et al. 2012). An alternative and later approach by e.g. Priedhorsky et al. (2014) is to aggregate all observations of a word over a map and assign a named location to the distribution, rather than to each observation, deferring the labeling to a point in the analysis where more understanding of the term distribution is known.

Another approach is to model *topics* as inferred from vocabulary usage in text across their geographical distribution, and then, for each text, to assess the topic and thus its attendant location visavi the topic model most likely to have generated the text in question (Eisenstein et al. 2010; Yin et al. 2011; Kinsella et al. 2011; Hong et al. 2012). We have found that topic models as implemented are computationally demanding, and the reported results show that they do not add accuracy to prediction. Since they build on a hidden level of "topic" variables they have little explanatory value to aid the understanding of localised language use.

In these experiments we will compare a list of known places with a model where the locational information of words is learnt from observing their usage. We compile this information either by letting the words vote for place or by averaging the information on a word-by-word basis. The latter model defers the mapping to known places until some analysis has been performed; the former assigns known places to words earlier in the process.

4 Test Data

These experiments have focused on Swedish-language material and on Swedish locations. Most Swedish-speakers live in Sweden; Swedish is mainly written and spoken in Sweden and in Finland. Sweden is a roughly rectangular country of about 450 000 km^2 as shown in Figure 2. Sweden has since 1634 been organised into 22 counties or *län* of between 3 000 km^2 and 100 000 km^2. The median size of a county is 10 545 km^2 which would, assuming quadratic counties, give a side of 100 *km* for a typical county.

We measure accuracy of textual location using the *Haversine distance*, the great-circle distance between two points on a sphere. We report averages, both mean and median, as well as percentage of texts we have located within 100 *km* from their known position.

Our test data set is composed of social media texts from two sources. One set is 18 GB of blog text from major Swedish blog and forum sites, with self-reported location by author - variously, home town, municipality, village, or county. The texts are mainly personal texts with authors of all ages but with a preponderance of pre-teens to young adults. The data are from 2001 and onward, with more data from the latest years. The data are concatenated into one document per blog, totalling to 154 062 documents from unique sources. Somewhat more than a third, 35%, have more than 10k characters.

The other set is 37 GB of blog text without any explicit indication of location. A target task for these experiments is to enrich these 37 GB of non-located data with predicted location, in order to address data sparsity for unusual dialectal linguistic items.

Figure 2: Map of Sweden

5 Baseline: the GAZETTEER model

For a list of known places we used a list[1] of 1 956 Swedish cities and 2 920 towns and villages as defined by Statistics Sweden[2] in 2010.

As the most obvious baseline, we identify all tokens found in this list, or gazetteer. Each such token is converted to a position through the Geoencoding API offered by Google[3]. The position with largest observed frequency of occurrence in the text is assumed to be the position of the text. Other approaches have taken this as a useful approach for identifying features such as Places of Interest mentioned in texts (Li et al. 2014). We call this approach the GAZETTEER approach.

6 Training Data

As a basis for learning how words were used we used geotagged microblog data from Twitter. About 2% of Swedish Twitter posts have latitude and longitude explicitly given,[4] typically those that have been posted from a mobile phone. We gathered data from Twitter's streaming API during the months of May to August of 2014, saving posts with latitude and longitude and with Sweden explicitly given as point of origin. This gave us 4 429 516 posts of about 630 MB.

7 Polylocational Gaussian Mixture Models

Given a set of geographically located texts, we record for each linguistic item – meaning word, in these experiments – the locations from the metadata of every text it occurs in. This gives each word a mapped geographic distribution of latitude-longitude pairs. We model these observed distributions using Gaussian 2-D functions, as defined by Priedhorsky et al. (2014). A 2-D Gaussian function will assume a peak at some position and allow for a graceful inclusion of hits at nearby positions into the model in a bell-like distribution.

[1] http://en.wikipedia.org/wiki/List_of_urban_areas_in_Sweden One named location ("När") was removed from the list since it is homographic to the adverbials corrresponding to the English *near* and *when*, causing a disproportionate amount of noise.

[2] *A locality consists of a group of buildings normally not more than 200 metres apart from each other, and must fulfil a minimum criterion of having at least 200 inhabitants. Delimitation of localities is made by Statistics Sweden every five years.* [http://www.scb.se]

[3] https://developers.google.com/.../geocoding/

[4] Determined by listening to Twitter's streaming API for about a day.

Many distributions could be envisioned here, but Gaussians have attractive implementational qualities and have a straightforward interpretation in terms of mapping to physical space.

In contrast to the original definition and and other similar following approaches, we want to be able to handle polylocational words. After testing various models on a subset of our data we find that fitting more than one Gaussian function—in effect, assuming that locationally interesting words refer to several locations–yields better results than fitting all locational data into one distribution. After some initial parameter exploration as shown in Figure 3, we settle on three Gaussian functions as a reasonable model: words with more than three distributional peaks are likely to be of less utility for locating texts. We consequently fit each word with three Gaussian functions to allow a word to contribute to many locations for the texts it is observed in.

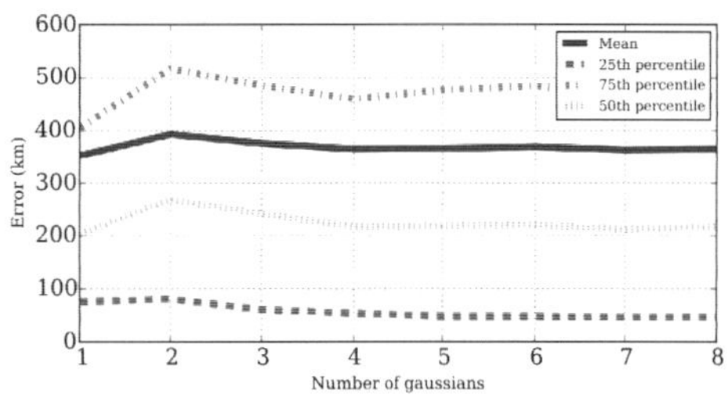

Figure 3: Effect of polylocational representations

8 The notion of placeness

In keeping with previous research on geolocational terms such as Han et al. (2014), we rank candidate words for their locational specificity. From the Gaussian Mixture Model representation, we take the log probability ρ in the mean of the Gaussian and transform it into a *placeness* score by $p = e^{\frac{100}{-\rho}}$. This is done for every word, for all three Gaussians. The score is then used to rank words for locational utility.

		Gaussian		
		1st	2nd	3d
Falköping		58	9	9
Stockholm		37	10	10
spårvagn	*"tram"*	36	18	15
och	*"and"*	16	15	9

Table 1: Example words and their log placeness

Table 1 shows the placeness of the three Gaussians for some sample words. The two sample named locations have high placeness for their first Gaussians, indicating that they have locational utility. "Stockholm", the capital city, which is frequently mentioned in conversations elsewhere has less placeness than has "Falköping", a smaller city. The word "tram" has lower placeness than the two cities, and the word "and" with a log placeness score of 16 can not be considered locational at all. Inspecting the resulting list as given in Table 2 which shows some examples from the top of the list, we find that words with high placeness frequently are non-gazetteer locations ("Slottsskogen"), user names, hash tags – frequently referring to events ("#lundakarneval"), and other local terms, most typically street names ("Holgersgatan"), spelling variants ("Ståckhålm"), or public establishments.

The performance of the predictive models introduced below can be improved by excluding words with low placeness from the centroid. This exclusion threshold is referred to as T below.

known places	hash tags	other
hogstorp	#lundakarneval	holgersgatan
nyhammar	#bishopsarms	margretegärdeparken
sjuntorp	#gothenburg	uddevallahus
tyringe	#westpride14	kampenhof
slottsskogen	#swedenlove1dday	ståckhålm
storvik	#sverigemotet	gullmarsplan
charlottenberg	#sthlmtech	tvärbanan

Table 2: Example words with high placeness

9 Experimental settings: the TOTAL and FILTERED models

We run one experimental setting with all words of a set, only filtered for placeness. We call this approach the TOTAL approach.

To refine the information from locational words further, we filter the words in the feature set to find the most locationally appropriate terms, in order to reduce noise and computational effort, but above all, in keeping with our hypothesis that the locational signal is present in only part of the texts. Backstrom et al. (2008) and following them, Cheng et al. (2010), using similar data as we do, also limit their analyses to "local" rather than "non-local" words in the text matter they process, modeling word locality through observed occurrences, modulated with some geographical smoothing. To find the most appropriate localised

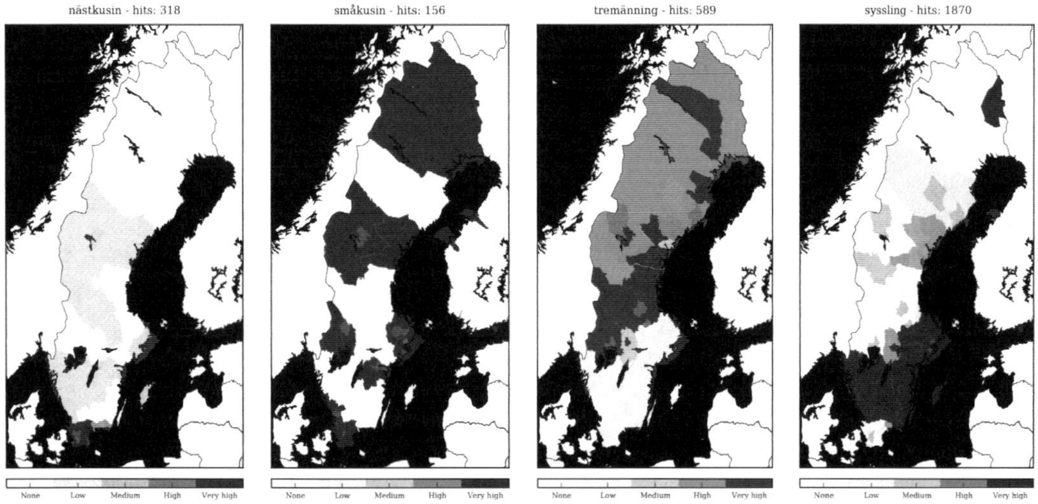

(a) Using labeled data set

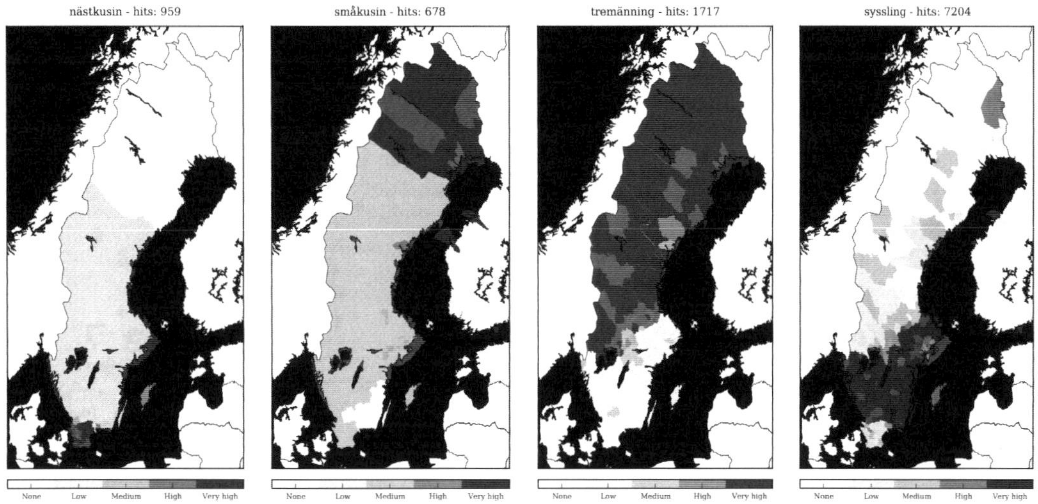

(b) Using enriched data set increases the data

Figure 5: Regional terminology for "second cousin"

linguistic items, we bootstrap from the gazetteer and collect the most distinctive distributional contexts of gazetteer terms. For this, we used context windows of six words before $(6+0)$, around $(3+3)$, and after $(0+6)$ each target word. These context windows were tabulated and the most frequently occurring constructions[5] are then ranked based on their ability to return words with high placeness. For each construction, the percentage of words returned with $\log T > 20$ is used as a ranking criterion. Using this ranking, the top 150 constructions are retained as a paradigmatic filter to generate usefully locational words. Constructions such as `lives in <location>` will be at the top of the list as shown in Figure 8.

Words found in the `<location>` slot of the constructions are frequency filtered with respect to N, the length of the text under analysis, with thresholds set by experimentation to $0.00008 \times N \leq f_{wd} \leq N/300$. This reduces the number of Gaussian models to evaluate drastically. Each text under consideration was then filtered to only include words found through the above procedure, reducing the size of the texts to about 6% of the original.

[5] In these experiments, the 900 most frequent constructions are used.

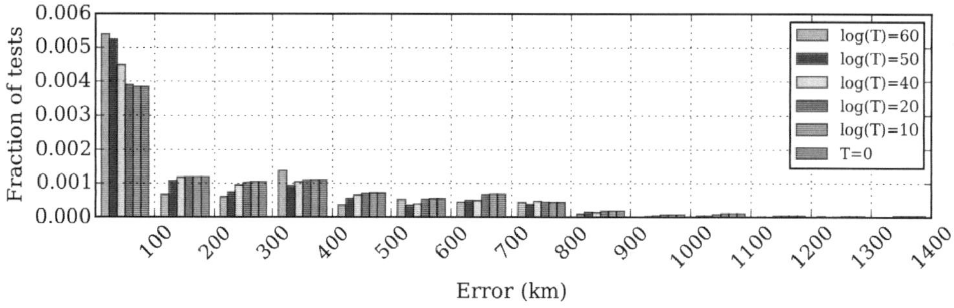

Figure 6: Comparing placeness thresholds for the FILTERED CENTROID model.

	Placeness	Error (km)		Percentile (km)			$e < 100\ km$	
	$\log T$	$\tilde{e}$	$\bar{e}$	25 %	50 %	75 %	Precision	Recall
FILTERED CENTROID	—	204	365	45	204	464	0.38	0.38
FILTERED CENTROID	10	204	365	45	204	464	0.38	0.38
FILTERED CENTROID	20	200	365	44	200	460	0.38	0.38
FILTERED CENTROID	40	145	333	32	145	396	0.44	0.32
FILTERED CENTROID	50	90	286	22	90	321	0.52	0.23
FILTERED CENTROID	60	70	271	13	70	330	0.53	0.04

Table 3: Comparing placeness thresholds for the FILTERED CENTROID model.

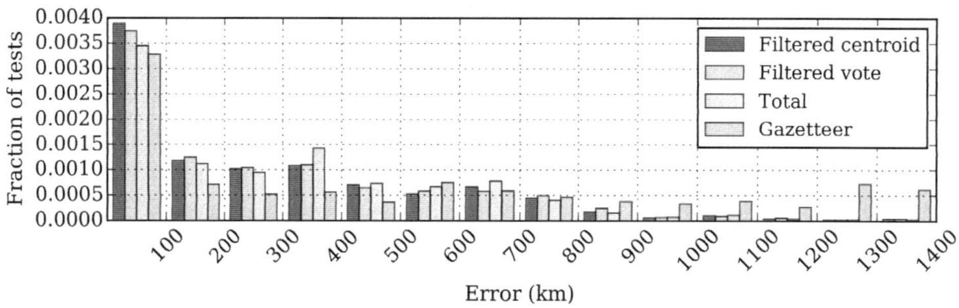

Figure 7: Comparing models with placeness threshold at $\log T = 20$.

	Placeness	Error (km)		Percentile (km)			$e < 100\ km$	
	$\log T$	$\tilde{e}$	$\bar{e}$	25 %	50 %	75 %	Precision	Recall
GAZETTEER	20	450	626	62	450	964	0.31	0.31
TOTAL	20	256	380	51	256	516	0.34	0.34
FILTERED CENTROID	20	200	365	44	200	460	0.38	0.38
FILTERED VOTE	20	208	377	58	208	467	0.37	0.36

Table 4: Comparing models: $\tilde{e}$ is the median error and $\bar{e}$ is the mean error in km.

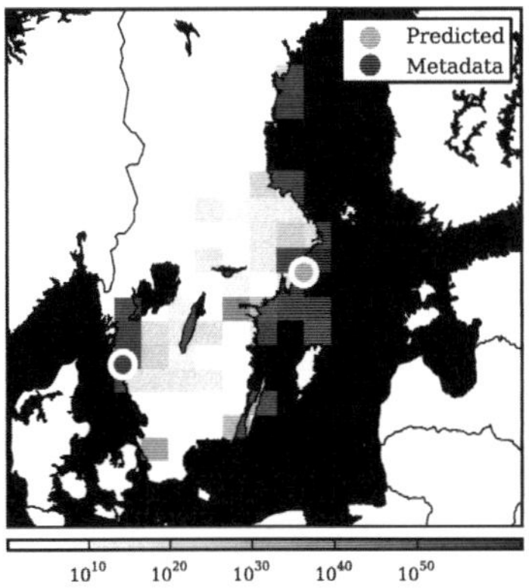

(a) All words of a text contribute to the predicted location •.

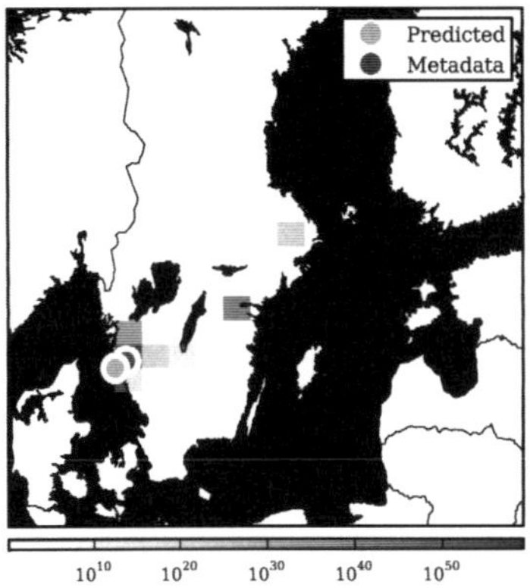

(b) Only words filtered through the distributional model contribute votes to yield a prediction • very close to the correct position •.

Figure 4: Comparison of grid and grammar.

10 Aggregating the locational information for filtered texts

The filtered texts are now processed in two different ways. Every unique word token in the Twitter dataset has a Gaussian mixture model i based on its observed occurrences, as shown in Section 8. This is represented by the three mean coordinates $\overline{\mu}^i$ and their corresponding *placenesses* $\overline{p}^i$.

$$\overline{\mu}^i = \begin{pmatrix} \mu_1 \\ \mu_2 \\ \mu_3 \end{pmatrix}^i \qquad \overline{p}^i = \begin{pmatrix} p_1 \\ p_2 \\ p_3 \end{pmatrix}^i$$

We compute a centroid for these coordinates, as an average best guess for geographic signal for a text. We do this with an arithmetic weighted mean. Given n words:

<location> mellan	<location> between
varit i <location>	been in <location>
bor i <location>	live(s) in <location>
var i <location>	was in <location>
vi till <location>	we to <location>
in till <location>	in to <location>
ska till <location>	going to <location>
<location> centrum	<location> centre
av till <location>	off to <location>
det av till <location>	go to <location>
hemma i <location>	home in <location>
till <location>	to <location>
upp till <location>	up to <location>

(a) In Swedish (b) Translated to English

Figure 8: Examples of locational constructions

$$M = \frac{\sum_{i=1}^{n} \overline{\mu}^n \cdot \overline{p}^n}{\sum_{i=1}^{n} \sum_{j=1}^{3} p_j^n}$$

Where $\overline{\mu}^n \cdot \overline{p}^n$ is the dot product[6]. We call this model FILTERED CENTROID

Alternatively, we do not average the coordinates, but select by weighted majority vote. We divide Sweden into a grid of roughly 50x50km cells. The placeness score of every locational word in a text is added to its cell. The centerpoint of the cell with highest score is assigned to the text as a location. We call this model FILTERED VOTE.

Figure 4 shows how filtering improves results, here illustrated by the FILTERED VOTE model. The top map shows how every word of a text contributes votes, weighted by their placeness, to give a prediction (●). The bottom map shows how when only words filtered through the distributional model are used, the voting yields a correct result in comparison with the gold standard (●) given by the metadata.

11 Results

As shown in Table 4 and Figure 7, the Gaussian models FILTERED CENTROID and FILTERED VOTE outperform the GAZETTEER model handily. Filtering words distributionally, in addition to reducing processing, improves results further. The FILTERED CENTROID model is slightly better than the FILTERED VOTE model , providing support for late discretization of locational information. A closer look at the effect, shown in Table 3 and in Figure 6, of feature selection with the placeness threshold shows the precision-recall tradeoff

[6] $\overline{\mu}^i \cdot \overline{p}^i = \mu_1^i p_1^i + \mu_2^i p_2^i + \mu_3^i p_3^i$ for this specific case.

contingent on reducing the number of accepted locational words.

These results are well comparable with the results reported by others: while direct comparison with other linguistic and geographic areas is difficult, Cheng et al. (2010) set a 100-mile ($\approx$ 160 km) success criterion for a similar task of geo-locating microblog authors (not single posts). They find that about 10% of microblog users can be localised within their 100-mile radius. Eisenstein et al. (2010) found they could on average achieve a 900 km accuracy for texts or a 24% accuracy on a US state level.

12 Regional variation

Returning to our use case we now use the FILTERED CENTROID model I............ to position and thus enrich a further 38% of our unlabeled blog collection with a location tag (setting the placeness threshold $\log T = 20$). This gives a noticeably better resolution for studying regional word usage as shown in Figure 5: the term for "second cousin" varies across dialects, and given the enriched data set we are able to gain better frequencies and a more distinct image of usage.

13 Conclusions

Our results show that inferring text or author location can be done with few knowledge sources. Given a list of known places and microblog posts with locational information we were able to pinpoint the location of more than a third of blog texts within 100 kms of their known point of origin. The notable results are three.

Firstly, that locational models trained on one genre can be used for inferring location of texts from another very different genre.

Secondly, that modelling words polylocationally (in the present case, using three locations) allowed us to use more diverse words than otherwise would have been possible.

Thirdly, that filtering the words by distributional qualities improved results. This point is useful to note even if other approaches than learning location from positioned texts is used: any gazetteer could be used to bootstrap locational constructions and to harvest other candidate terms from texts to enrich it.

Acknowlegdments

This work was in part supported by the grant SINUS (Spridning av innovationer i nutida svenska) from Vetenskapsrådet, the Swedish Research Council.

References

Lars Backstrom, Jon Kleinberg, Ravi Kumar, and Jasmine Novak. Spatial variation in search engine queries. In *17th international conference on World Wide Web*. ACM, 2008.

Zhiyyan Cheng, James Caverlee, and Kyumin Lee. You are where you tweet: a content-based approach to geolocating Twitter users. In *19th ACM international Conference on Information and Knowledge Management*. ACM, 2010.

Jacob Eisenstein, Brendan O'Connor, Noah A Smith, and Eric P Xing. A latent variable model for geographic lexical variation. In *Conference on Empirical Methods in Natural Language Processing*. ACL, 2010.

Bo Han, Paul Cook, and Timothy Baldwin. Text-based Twitter user geolocation prediction. *Journal of Artificial Intelligence Research (JAIR)*, 49:451–500, 2014.

Liangjie Hong, Amr Ahmed, Siva Gurumurthy, Alexander J Smola, and Kostas Tsioutsiouliklis. Discovering geographical topics in the Twitter stream. In *21st international conference on World Wide Web*. ACM, 2012.

Sheila Kinsella, Vanessa Murdock, and Neil O'Hare. I'm eating a sandwich in Glasgow: modeling locations with tweets. In *3rd international workshop on Search and mining user-generated contents*. ACM, 2011.

Guoliang Li, Jun Hu, Jianhua Feng, and Kian-lee Tan. Effective location identification from microblogs. In *30th IEEE International Conference on Data Engineering*. IEEE, 2014.

Jalal Mahmud, Jeffrey Nichols, and Clemens Drews. Where is this tweet from? Inferring home locations of Twitter users. In *6th International AAAI Conference on Web and Social Media*, 2012.

Mikael Parkvall. Här går gränsen. *Språktidningen*, October 2012. ISSN 1654-5028.

Reid Priedhorsky, Aron Culotta, and Sara Y Del Valle. Inferring the origin locations of tweets with quantitative confidence. In *17th ACM conference on Computer Supported Cooperative Work & Social Computing*. ACM, 2014.

Zhijun Yin, Liangliang Cao, Jiawei Han, Chengxiang Zhai, and Thomas Huang. Geographical topic discovery and comparison. In *20th international conference on World Wide Web*. ACM, 2011.

Automatic conversion of colloquial Finnish to standard Finnish

Inari Listenmaa
Chalmers Institute of Technology
Sweden
inari@chalmers.se

Francis M. Tyers
HSL-fakultehta,
UiT Norgga árktalaš universitehta,
N-9015 Norway
francis.tyers@uit.no

Abstract

This paper presents a rule-based method for converting between colloquial Finnish and standard Finnish. The method relies upon a small number of orthographical rules combined with a large language model of standard Finnish for ranking the possible conversions. Aside from this contribution, the paper also presents an evaluation corpus consisting of aligned sentences in colloquial Finnish, orthographically-standardised colloquial Finnish and standard Finnish. The method we present outperforms the baseline of simply treating colloquial Finnish as standard Finnish, but is outperformed by a phrase-based MT system trained by the evaluation corpus. The paper also presents preliminary results which show promise for using normalisation in the machine translation task.

1 Introduction

Most language technology tools are designed or trained based on standard language forms, where they exist. The application of these tools to non-standard language can cause a substantial decrease in quality for example in machine translation, parsing and part-of-speech tagging (Eisenstein, 2013). Non-standard language can have different orthographic conventions, along with different morphology, syntax and stylistics.

For language-technology researchers working on non-standard forms of language, there are two clear options: either create new tools to process non-standard text, or create tools to preprocess non-standard text, standardising it to be subsequently processed by existing tools.

This paper evaluates a number of methods for converting colloquial Finnish to standard Finnish and describes a parallel corpus for evaluation.

2 Related work

There are a number of areas of research related to the task of text normalisation. Text proofing tools, such as spelling and grammar checkers (Kukich, 1992) can be used to encourage adherence to particular orthographic or grammatical norms. Accent and diacritic restoration — for example in Scannell (2011) — is similar in that it aims to bring text closer to standard orthography in order to facilitate treatment by automatic tools. Another related area is machine translation between different written norms of the same language, for example between Norwegian Bokmål and Norwegian Nynorsk (Unhammer and Trosterud, 2009).

Scannell (2014) presents a method for normalising pre-standardised text in Irish to the modern standard. The method relies on a translation model consisting of word-to-word correspondences in addition to spelling rules. Each word-to-word mapping has the same conditional probability and a penalty is assigned to each spelling rule application. Decoding works by processing the source sentence word-for-word left-to-right, keeping track of the possible 'hypothesis' translations and their probabilities, and when the end of sentence is reached, the most probable is output.

2.1 Colloquial Finnish

Viinikka and Voutilainen (2013) describe the common meaning of the terms colloquial (*puhekieli*) and standard (*yleiskieli* or *kirjakieli*) Finnish: standard language is unified in morphology and vocabulary, following the regulations of a language board; colloquial language shows local and idiolectal variation, and has structures that are characteristic to spoken variety, such as discourse particles and incomplete clauses.

We illustrate the differences with the following example from our data set. Sentence 1 is the original colloquial version. The gloss shows the ac-

Colloquial	Normalised	Standardised
tai emmä tiiä olikse erikseen joku nuorisoalennus	tai en#minä tiedä oliko#se erikseen jokin nuorisoalennus	tai en minä tiedä oliko erikseen nuorisoalennus
toistaseks tullu kaks kysymystä	toistaiseksi tullut kaksi kysymystä	toistaiseksi on tullut kaksi kysymystä
ja sit 2009 just ennenku menin Japaniin	ja sitten 2009 juuri ennen#kuin menin Japaniin	ja sitten 2009 juuri ennen kuin menin Japaniin

Table 1: Example sentences from the parallel corpus. The # mark represents a missing word boundary.

tual word-by-word translation, and the translation shows similar style and register in English.

(1) *seiskakin* *oli* *vaan* *silleen* *et*
seven-ALSO was just like.that that
fonotaksista *päättelin*
phonotactics.ELA I.deduced

'also the seventh, it was like, I just deduced it from phonotactics'

For the normalised version,[1] we changed only morphology and vocabulary. On the lexical level, the word *seiska* 'number 7' is colloquial style, and in the standard translation it is replaced by the ordinal *seitsemäs* 'seventh'. Other changes in the normalised version target common morphological or phonological phenomena, such as restoring the reduced diphthong in *vaan* → *vain*. The original sentence and the normalised translation are shown below, aligned word by word.

(2) *seiskakin* *oli* *vaan* *silleen* *et*
seitsemäskin oli vain sillä#lailla että
fonotaksista *päättelin*
fonotaksista päättelin

The syntactic structure of the original sentence is markedly spoken; the word *seiska* is topicalised, and the main information "deduced from phonotactics" is in a subordinate clause. The translation into standard Finnish is shorter and more precise, leaving just the main information.

(3) *päättelin* *seitsemännenkin*
I.deduced seventh-ALSO
fonotaksista
phonotactics.ELA

'I deduced the seventh also from phonotactics'

[1]The normalised version is converted orthographically and lexically, but not syntactically or stylistically.

Section	Tokens		
	`dev`	`test`	`train`
Colloquial	1,003	1,012	5,103
Normalised	1,003	1,012	5,103
Standardised	1,000	991	4,982

Table 2: Statistics on sentences from the parallel corpus.

3 Corpus

Our evaluation corpus was created by manually translating texts in colloquial Finnish to standard Finnish. The corpus is freely available and published under the CreativeCommons CC-BY-SA 3.0 licence[2]. The texts were extracts from internet relay chat (IRC) conversations. We performed the conversion process in two steps, the first step involved simple orthographic normalisation, for example *oon* → *olen* 'I am'. Syntactic and stylistic conversions were not applied at this stage. The second conversion step normalised the text both orthographically and syntactically/stylistically. Table 1 presents an excerpt from each of the three parts of the corpus.

The corpus was split into three parts, development, testing and training. The development and testing portions contain approximately 1,000 words each, with the remaining approximately 5,000 words for training phrase-based and character-based models.[3] Table 2 gives statistics on the number of words in each section.

[2]https://svn.code.sf.net/p/apertium/svn/languages/apertium-fin/texts/normalisation/

[3]The corpus is split into 14 files of 500 words each. Files 01–02 were used for development; 03–04 for testing and 05–14 for training.

Input:	Mä oon Tomminkaa 'I am with Tommi'.		
Step 1	Mä oon Tomminkaa		apply rule 1:
	Minä oon Tomminkaa		mä → minä
Step 2	Mä oon Tomminkaa		apply rule 2:
	Minä oon Tomminkaa		oon → olen
	Mä olen Tomminkaa		
	Minä olen Tomminkaa		
Step 3	Mä oon Tomminkaa		apply rule 3:
	Minä oon Tomminkaa		(?+)nkaa → \1n kanssa
	Mä olen Tomminkaa		
	Minä olen Tomminkaa		
	Mä oon Tommin kanssa		
	Minä oon Tommin kanssa		
	Mä olen Tommin kanssa		
	Minä olen Tommin kanssa		
Step 4	Minä olen Tommin kanssa	-4.5811	rank candidates
	Minä oon Tommin kanssa	-7.8174	
	Mä olen Tommin kanssa	-8.0941	
	Mä oon Tommin kanssa	-8.8651	
	Minä olen Tomminkaa	-9.2045	
	Minä oon Tomminkaa	-12.4408	
	Mä olen Tomminkaa	-12.7176	
	Mä oon Tomminkaa	-13.4885	
Output:	Minä olen Tommin kanssa		

Table 3: Example trace of the normalisation method. Rules are applied in order to each of the possible candidate translations in turn. The candidates are then ranked using an n-gram language model of standard Finnish and either an n-best list or the best candidate is output.

4 Experiments

4.1 Rule-based normalisation

For the rule-based normalisation we applied a set of regular-expression based replace rules to the input text to produce all the possible candidate sentences in standard Finnish and then used a target-language model to rank the possible candidates. The candidate with the highest rank was selected as the normalised sentence. For the target-language model we used the Finnish side of the English–Finnish EuroParl parallel corpus (Koehn, 2005).

We developed two sets of rules:

- `rules-1`: 273 rules from Karlsson (2008)'s grammar of Finnish (§95–97). The rules took around one hour to implement.

- `rules-2`: 98 rules written by examining the development corpus, these rules also took approximately one hour to implement.

The rules included both simple one-to-one ('mä' → 'minä') and one-to-many ('emmä' → 'en minä') word correspondences, and also regular expression substitutions which could match a prefix or a suffix ('(?+)nkaa' → '\1n kanssa').

Table 3 gives an example trace of the system on a simple sentence using three replace rules.

4.2 Statistical machine translation

The statistical-machine translation approaches were implemented using the Moses toolkit (Koehn et al., 2007). The training set up was that used for the baseline system in the WMT shared tasks on machine translation.[4]

The target-language model corpus, trained using KenLM (Heafield, 2011), used was the same as in the rule-based experiments.

We trained models based on two approaches, the first being phrase-based machine translation (PBMT, Zens et al. (2002)) and the second on character-based machine translation

[4]`http://www.statmt.org/wmt11/baseline.html`

(CBMT, Nakov and Tiedemann (2012); Tiedemann (2009)).

For both approaches we trained two systems, the first used the *normalised* part of the corpus as the target language; the second used the *standardised* part of the corpus as the target language.

The idea behind this was that the *normalised* part of the corpus would be closer to the original colloquial text than the *standardised* part, making it easier to learn the alignment model.

Character-based

Nakov and Tiedemann (2012) present a method of statistical machine translation on the character level between related languages that takes advantage of phrase-based machine translation architecture. The method relies on preprocessing the input and output by inserting spaces in between the characters of words, for example the string 'mä meen Helsinkiin' would become 'm ä $ m e e n $ H e l s i n k i i n' with a unigram model, or 'mä ä$ $m me ee en n$ $H He el ls si in nk ki ii in' with a bigram model.

After preprocessing, the corpora are processed as with the phrase-based system, with the difference that the language model order is increased from 5 to 10-grams.

4.3 End-to-end translation

In order to evaluate how well the different normalisation strategies worked in combination with another language technology tool, we performed an end-to-end experiment involving machine translation. To evaluate this, we took the colloquial portion of the test corpus and manually translated it to English. For each of the best-performing systems we first passed the colloquial text through, and then translated the output to English using a widely-used online machine translation engine with Finnish to English. We compared the output to translating the text to English without the standardiser.

5 Results

Tables 4 and 5 present the results of the experiments.

The baseline was made by calculating the metric scores between the standardised 'reference' and the colloquial input. The results show that all conversion methods outperform the baseline.

Our rule-based method performs similarly to the character-based machine translation systems.

System	PER	WER	BLEU
Baseline	46.12	48.04	26.31
rules-1	38.27	41.19	32.65
rules-2	**38.17**	**35.25**	**36.41**
rules-c	36.56	39.68	34.68
CBMT-cn	43.09	48.34	33.55
CBMT-cs	46.22	52.27	29.21
PBMT-cn	**28.05**	**35.42**	**48.37**
PBMT-cs	27.95	36.13	46.76

Table 4: Results for the normalisation task. The system `rules-c` is the combination of the rules in `rules-1` and `rules-2`. The figures in bold are the best results for rule-based and SMT methods.

System	PER	WER	BLEU
Colloquial	41.02	69.57	12.11
Normalised	30.73	59.73	22.56
Standardised	33.88	61.61	19.49
rules-2	37.94	69.35	12.92
CBMT-cn	65.59	86.25	13.06
PBMT-cn	**35.69**	**65.14**	**17.75**

Table 5: Results for the Finnish to English translation task. The first three rows are the results from translating the sections of the corpus.

Both the character-based systems and the rule-based system achieve around half of the performance of the phrase-based system.

Out of the rule-based systems, the set of rules which was created by examining the development corpus outperforms both the set of rules from the grammar and the combined rules. The rules from the grammar capture more general tendencies, whereas the rules from the development corpus are more lexicalised. Since the testing corpus is small and only contains text from a single author, the higher performance of the second rule set could also be an due to overfitting.

It is interesting to note that MT systems trained on the normalised section of the corpus outperform those trained on the standardised corpus. One explanation for this could be that the corpus size is small, so that the word alignments are not as reliable on the standardised corpus which is by nature not a word-for-word conversion.

The systems for normalisation are able to improve out-of-vocabulary rates in many cases, most likely as the online statistical system that we used is trained on more formal texts. Frequent contractions such as *onks?* 'is there?', *oo* 'be.CONNEG'[5] and *vaa* 'only' are found untranslated in the output, but are easily converted by the systems.

6 Future work

Although a reasonable size for a test corpus, the corpus is still too small for wide-coverage experiments. We intend to expand the corpus size to at least 10,000 words. Another weakness of the corpus is that it contains text from a single author. We would ideally like to add texts from other authors and other colloquial genres—the challenge here is finding text that is both free of privacy issues and available to release under a free/open-source sence.

As for the methods, we would like to follow Scannell (2014) in incorporating 'translation' probabilities into our rule-based normalisation model. Our current model relies exclusively on the target-language model probability, however some rules may be more reliable or probable than others.

7 Conclusions

We have presented a parallel corpus of colloquial Finnish and standard Finnish – to our knowledge the first of its kind – and an evaluation of methods for converting colloquial Finnish to standard Finnish.

We have shown that converting from colloquial Finnish to standard Finnish substantially helps with the Finnish to English machine translation task.

Acknowledgments

We thank Joonas Kylmälä for translating the colloquial sentences into normalised and standardised versions.

References

Jacob Eisenstein. 2013. What to do about bad language on the internet. In *Proceedings of the 2013 Conference of the North American Chapter of the Association for Computational Linguistics*.

Kenneth Heafield. 2011. KenLM: faster and smaller language model queries. In *Proceedings of the EMNLP 2011 Sixth Workshop on Statistical Machine Translation*, pages 187–197, Edinburgh, Scotland, United Kingdom, July.

[5]The word *oo* is the negative form of the verb *olla* 'to be' in Finnish.

Fred Karlsson. 2008. *Finnish: An Essential Grammar*. Routledge, Abingdon, Oxon.

Philipp Koehn, Hieu Hoang, Chris Callison-Burch, Marcello Federico, Nicola Bertoldi, Brooke Cowan, Wade Shen, Christine Moran, Richard Zens, Chris Dyer, Ondrej Bojar, Alexandra Constantin, and Evan Herbst. 2007. Moses: Open Source Toolkit for Statistical Machine Translation. In *Demonstration session at the Annual Meeting of the Association for Computational Linguistics (ACL2007)*.

Philipp Koehn. 2005. Europarl: A parallel corpus for statistical machine translation. In *Proceedings of MT Summit*.

Karen Kukich. 1992. Techniques for automatically correcting words in text. *ACM Comput. Surv.*, 24(4):377–439, December.

Preslav Nakov and Jörg Tiedemann. 2012. Combining word-level and character-level models for machine translation between closely-related languages. In *Proceedings of the 50th Annual Meeting of the Association for Computational Linguistics*, pages 301–305.

Kevin Scannell. 2011. Statistical unicodification of african languages. *Language Resources and Evaluation*, 45(3):375–386.

Kevin Scannell. 2014. Statistical models for text normalization and machine translation. In *Proceedings of the Celtic Language Technology Workshop at COLING 2014*.

Jörg Tiedemann. 2009. Character-based PSMT for Closely Related Languages. In *Proceedings of 13th Annual Conference of the European Association for Machine Translation (EAMT09)*, pages 12–19.

Kevin Unhammer and Trond Trosterud. 2009. Reuse of free resources in machine translation between nynorsk and bokml. In *Proceedings of the First International Workshop on Free/Open-Source Rule-Based Machine Translation*, pages 35–42.

Jenni Viinikka and Eero Voutilainen. 2013. Ääniä ilmassa, merkkejä paperilla – puhutun ja kirjoitetun kielen suhteesta. *Kielikello*.

Richard Zens, Franz Josef Och, and Hermann Ney. 2002. Phrase-based statistical machine translation. In *KI - 2002: Advances in Artificial Intelligence. 25. Annual German Conference on AI, KI 2002*, volume 2479, pages 18–32. Springer Verlag.

Automatic Thematic Classification of the Titles of the Seimas Votes

Vytautas Mickevičius[1,2] Tomas Krilavičius[1,2]
Vaidas Morkevičius[3] Aušra Mackutė-Varoneckienė[1]
[1]Vytautas Magnus University, [2]Baltic Institute of Advanced Technology,
[3]Kaunas University of Technology, Institute of Public Policy and Administration
vytautas.mickevicius@bpti.lt, t.krilavicius@bpti.lt,
vaidas.morkevicius@ktu.lt, a.mackute-varoneckiene@if.vdu.lt

Abstract

Statistical analysis of parliamentary roll call votes is an important topic in political science as it reveals ideological positions of members of parliament and factions. However, these positions depend on the issues debated and voted upon as well as on attitude towards the governing coalition. Therefore, analysis of carefully selected sets of roll call votes provides deeper knowledge about members of parliament behavior. However, in order to classify roll call votes according to their topic automatic text classifiers have to be employed, as these votes are counted in thousands.

In this paper we present results of an ongoing research on thematic classification of roll call votes of the Lithuanian Parliament. Also, this paper is a part of a larger project aiming to develop the infrastructure designed for monitoring and analyzing roll call voting in the Lithuanian Parliament.

1 Introduction

Increasing availability of data on activities of governments and politicians as well as tools suitable for analysis of large data sets allows political science researchers to study previously under-researched subjects. As parliament is one the major foci of attention of the public, the media and political scientists, statistical analysis of parliamentary activity is becoming more and more prominent. In this field, parliamentary voting analysis might be discerned as getting increasing attention (Jackman, 2001; Poole, 2005; Hix et al., 2006; Bailey, 2007; Jakulin et al., 2009; Lynch and Madonna, 2012). Analysis of the activity of the Lithuanian parliament (the Seimas) is also becoming more popular. Voting of Lithuanian members of parliament (MPs) has been analyzed using various methods from both political science as well as statistical perspectives. Importantly, quite many different methods of statistical analysis have already been applied, such as multidimensional scaling (Krilavičius and Žilinskas, 2008), homogeneity analysis (Krilavičius and Morkevičius, 2011), cluster analysis (Mickevičius et al., 2014), and social networks analysis (Užupytė and Morkevičius, 2013).

This paper present results of an ongoing research dedicated to creating an infrastructure that would allow its user to monitor and analyze the data of roll call voting in the Seimas. The main idea of the infrastructure is to enable its users to compare behaviors of the MPs based on their voting results. However, overall statistical analysis of the MP voting on all the questions (bills etc.) during the whole term of the Seimas (4 years) might blur the ideological divisions that arise from differences in the positions taken by MPs depending on their attitudes towards the governmental policy or topics of the votes (Roberts et al., 2009; Krilavičius and Morkevičius, 2013). Therefore, one of the important tasks is creating the possibility to compare the voting behavior of MPs with regard to the topics of the votes and changes in the governmental coalitions. The latter objective is rather unproblematic as changes in the government are closely monitored by the media and information on the Seimas website (`www.lrs.lt`) allows extracting the information about MPs' belonging to factions, which can easily be matched with their position regarding the governmental coalition.

The other feature – possibility to monitor MPs' voting with regard to the topic of the vote – is more problematic to implement. (1) Votes on the floor of the Seimas are not thematically annotated by the Office of the Seimas, nor are there interest groups that are doing this (as in the US). Therefore, it is not possible to use any of such sources in classifying the votes. (2) Political science literature abounds with rather different approaches to the classification of political texts into thematic categories,[1] which requires making difficult subjective choices in selecting among them if one is about to include any of them into the infrastructure. (3) Even more problematic aspect is related to the vast quantities of votes in the parliament (counted in thousands) and the resulting requirement of automatic classification of them according to some selected topic scheme.

This paper presents research in progress which aims to find an optimal automatic text classifier for political texts (topics of parliamentary votes) in Lithuanian. The tasks tackled in the paper include: (1) To test the two most popular methods of natural language processing and feature selection – bag-of-words and n-gram; (2) To test the two most popular text classifiers – Support Vector Machines (SVM) and k nearest neighbors (k-NN); (3) To compare the efficiency of the selected text classifiers when using binary and non-binary feature matrices. Some attempts to classify Lithuanian documents were already made (Kapočiūtė-Dzikienė et al., 2012; Kapočiūtė-Dzikienė and Krupavičius, 2014), but they pursue a different problem, i.e. the first one works with full text documents, while the latter tries predicting faction from the record, not classify it.

The research is ongoing and the results are described in section 5 are partial. Future plans (see section 6) will cover more experiments with Lithuanian political texts.

2 Data

2.1 Data extraction

The data used for the study was extracted from the official Lithuanian parliament web site (`www.lrs.lt`). It consists of the titles of debates and votes that took place in the Seimas from 2008-11-17 to 2014-03-25 (`www3.lrs.lt/pls/inter/w5_sale.kad_ses`). The following rules were applied when collecting data: (1) debates from 2008-11-17 to 2014-03-25 were examined; (2) only debates with roll call votes were included; (3) in cases when single roll call votes were associated with several (usually very similar) titles of the debates (the so-called 'package voting'), these titles were merged and treated as one case.

Following these rules, the titles for 12211 roll call votes were identified in the time period analyzed and accordingly 12211 text documents (consisting of the titles of these votes) generated for further processing and analysis.

2.2 Preprocessing

In order to eliminate the influence of functional characters in the text analysis, the documents were normalized in the following way: (1) all punctuation marks were removed with no exceptions; (2) all multiple space characters (either intentional or not) were merged into one space character; (3) all numbers were removed; (4) all uppercase letters were converted to lowercase in order to eliminate the influence of word capitalization.

After the preprocessing a dictionary consisting of 2762 different words from the texts was generated. Here the word is defined as a set (or a substring) of symbols which is separated from the rest of text by one (in the beginning or the end of text) or two (in the middle) non-consecutive space characters.

Descriptive statistics of the text documents can be seen in table 1.

Length	In words	In characters
Minimum	2	19
Average	31	247
Maximum	775	6344

Table 1: Descriptive statistics of text documents.

Figures 1 and 2 show the frequencies of words and characters in the text documents.

2.3 Training and testing data

A set of 750 text documents (titles of votes) was selected out of the original data set to be used for training and testing of the classifiers. 500 documents were used for training of the classifiers and 250 documents were used to test the results.

These 750 titles of votes (text documents) were manually classified[2] into 7 aggregate

[1] Two major attempts are Manifesto Research Group (`manifestoproject.wzb.eu`) and Policy Agendas/Comparative Agendas (`www.comparativeagendas.info`) projects

[2] For the help in performing the classification authors thank Giedrius Žvaliauskas, researcher at the KTU Institute of Public Policy and Administration.

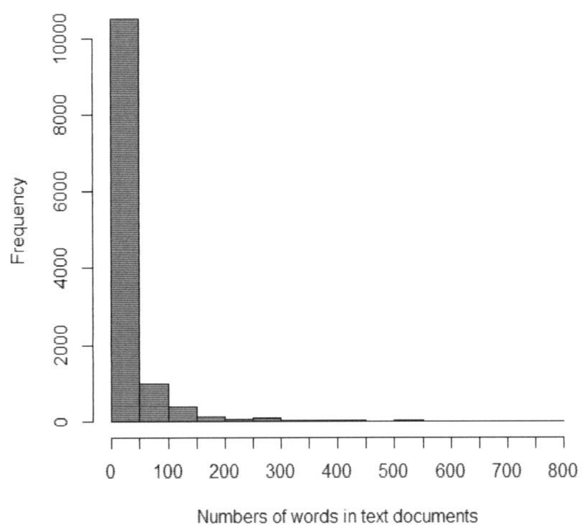

Figure 1: Distribution of words in the text documents.

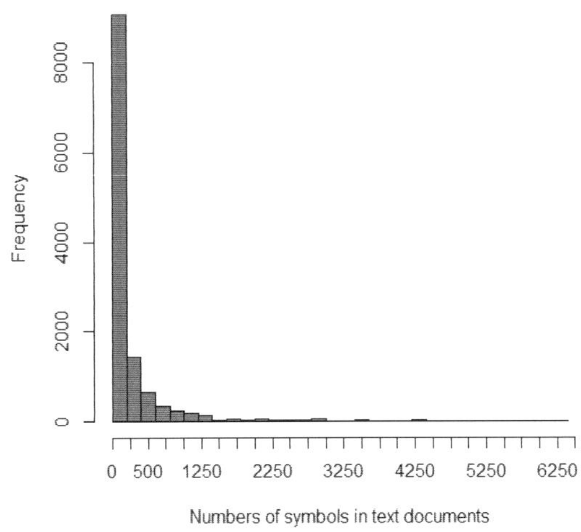

Figure 2: Distribution of characters on the text documents.

classes using the classification scheme of the Danish Policy Agendas project (`http://www.agendasetting.dk`). In order to avoid bias in automatic classification towards a more populous classes, the amounts of texts belonging to classes should not be significantly different, therefore titles of votes consisting the data set were not selected randomly: around 100 of votes for each class (aggregate topic) were selected from the debates of the last term of the Seimas (from 2012-11-16). See table 2 for the number of text documents in each class and the names of the classes.

Class	**No. of text documents**
Economics	126
Culture and civil rights	121
Legal affairs	106
Social policy	107
Defense and foreign affairs	82
Government operations	104
Environment and technology	103
Total	**750**

Table 2: Manual classification of documents.

3 Tools and methods

The research was performed using statistical package R (Team, 2013), a free software for statistical computing and graphics.

3.1 Features

Several popular feature representation techniques were used.

Bag-of-words is arguably the simplest and one of the most popular techniques for natural language processing. First of all, the dictionary of all unique words (for a definition of a word, see 2.2) in all of text documents is generated. Then a feature vector of length m is generated for each text document in the data, where m is a total number of unique words in the dictionary. Every element in the feature vector represents the count of appearance of a word in a text document for which the feature vector is generated. For example, if the 5th element of a feature vector is equal to 3, this indicates that the 5th word of the constructed dictionary occurs 3 times in a document under consideration.

***N*-gram.** Using this method documents are divided into character sets (substrings) of length n insomuch as the first substring contains all characters of the document from the 1st to n-th inclusive. Second substring contains all characters of the document from 2nd to $(n+1)$-th inclusive. This principle is used through the whole text document, the last substring containing characters from $(k-n+1)$ to k, where k is the number of characters in the text document. This process is applied to each given text document and a dictionary of unique substrings of length n (called n-grams) is generated. The set of feature vectors (feature matrix) is generated using the same principle as in the bag-of-words method, the only difference is that feature vectors contain counts of n-grams in a given text document instead of full words.

Sets containing series of characters is only one of several ways to use n-grams. Substrings can also be constructed of whole words, phonemes, syllables and other morphological units. The technique of using n-grams is advantageous in terms of flexibility as it does not require intensive data preprocessing, such as stemming, lemmatizing or removal of stop-words.

3.2 Text classifiers

Support Vector Machines (SVM) (Harish et al., 2010). This is a supervised classification algorithm (Vapnik and Cortes, 1995) that has been extensively and successfully used for the text classification tasks (Joachims, 1998). A document d is represented by a vector $x = (w_1, w_2, \ldots, w_k)$ of the counts of its words (or n-grams). A single SVM can only separate two classes – a positive class $L1$ (indicated by $y = +1$) and a negative class $L2$ (indicated by $y = -1$). In the space of input vectors x a hyperplane may be defined by setting $y = 0$ in the linear equation $y = f_\theta(x) = b_0 + \sum_{j=1}^{k} b_j w_j$. The parameter vector is given by $\theta = (b_0, b_1, ..., b_k)$. The SVM algorithm determines a hyperplane which is located between the positive and negative examples of the training set. The parameters b_j are adapted in such a way that the distance ξ – called margin – between the hyperplane and the closest positive and negative example documents is maximized. The documents having distance ξ from the hyperplane are called support vectors and determine the actual location of the hyperplane.

SVMs can be extended to a non-linear predictor by transforming the usual input features in a non-linear way using a feature map. Subsequently a hyperplane may be defined in the expanded input space. Such non-linear transformations define extensions of scalar products between input vectors, which are called kernels (Shawe-Taylor and Cristianini, 2004). In this paper linear kernel is examined, while analysis of non-linear kernels is included in the future plans (see section 6).

***K* Nearest Neigbors (*k*-NN) (Harish et al., 2010).** Let X be a document to classify. Using k-NN method distances between every document in a training dataset and document X are found. Out of all, k least distances are selected, considering the corresponding k documents nearest neighbors to document X. Document X is then assigned to a class that dominates in a set of k nearest neighbors.

This method has two modifiable parameters: dissimilarity measure (distance) and the number of nearest neighbors k. Euclidean distance is one of the most popular dissimilarity measure, calculated using formula 1.

$$d(X,Y) = \sqrt{\sum_{i=1}^{m}(x_i - y_i)^2}, \qquad (1)$$

here d is a distance between text documents X and Y, m is a number of features (length of feature vector), x_i and y_i – i-th feature (i-th element of feature vectors) of documents X and Y respectively.

The optimal number k of neighbors may be estimated from training data by cross validation (Hotho et al., 2005).

3.3 Testing results evaluation

As the actual classes of text documents in a training data set are known, it is possible to compare predicted classes with the actual ones. In order to evaluate testing results generated by a text classifier, formula 2 is applied.

$$ACC = \frac{\sum_{i=1}^{k} q_i}{k} \cdot 100\%, \quad x_i = \begin{cases} 1, & a_i = p_i \\ 0, & a_i \neq p_i \end{cases}, \qquad (2)$$

here ACC is the accuracy of the examined classifier, k is the number of documents in a testing data set, a_i is the i-th element of a vector that contains actual classes of the documents in a testing data set, p_i is the i-th element of a vector that contains predicted classes of the documents in a testing data set.

4 Experimental evaluation

4.1 Feature selection

For the analysis 5 dictionaries were generated out of 12211 text documents employing several variations of 2 natural language processing methods. While bag-of-words method is more or less straightforward and does not depend on changeable parameters, n-grams were analyzed in more depth – 3-grams and 4-grams were selected for the research discussed in this paper. Also, differences in classification effectiveness of n-grams as character sets and n-grams as word sets were analyzed. Descriptive statistics of the dictionaries generated can be seen in table 3.

Dictionary	No. of entries
Bag-of-words	2762
3-gram, chars	3730
4-gram, chars	10004
3-gram, words	12006
4-gram, words	16541

Table 3: Descriptive statistics of the dictionaries.

For every dictionary 2 feature matrices (10 feature matrices in total) were generated – one containing the counts of words in the feature vectors (as described in 3.1) and the other binary. Binary feature matrix is a variation of regular feature matrix where the feature is not the number of words in a document but the presence of a word in a document. Binary feature matrices were generated by converting all the elements greater than 0 (a word is not present in a document) to 1 (word is present in a document).

4.2 Automatic classification of documents

Out of every (10) feature matrices 750 documents were selected for training and testing of the classifiers (see 2.3 for the details). In order to achieve greater effectiveness training and testing was implemented in 6 iterations using cross-validation. First, all 750 selected documents were listed randomly. Then during each iteration document set was split 500 : 250 for training and testing classifiers, respectively. See table 4 for the details about data selection for each iteration.

No. of iteration	Training set	Testing set
1	1–500	501–750
2	51–550	1–50, 551–750
3	101–600	1–100, 601–750
4	151–650	1–150, 651–750
5	201–700	1–200, 701–750
6	251–750	1–250

Table 4: Data selection for cross-validation.

See results of experiments, in tables 5 and 6, for SVM and k-NN, correspondingly. The results show that n-grams representing sets of characters produce significantly better classification accuracy than n-grams representing sets of full words for both SVM and k-NN classifiers.

For SVM classifier, bag-of-words method of feature selection produced significantly better results than any of the analyzed n-gram variations, whereas k-NN classifier did not indicate any feature matrix as superior to the others. It is notable that increasing the number of nearest neighbors used in k-NN classifier produces worse results, therefore, 1-NN variation might be considered optimal.

The 5 best results achieved by the used classifiers are presented in table 7.

Features	Binary	Testing accuracy (%)
Bag-of-words	No	**70.7**
3-gram, chars	No	56.7
4-gram, chars	No	55.5
3-gram, words	No	48.5
4-gram, words	No	39.7
Bag-of-words	Yes	**70.5**
3-gram, chars	Yes	58.3
4-gram, chars	Yes	55.7
3-gram, words	Yes	48.3
4-gram, words	Yes	40.1

Table 5: Classification accuracy (%) with SVM.

Features	Binary	No. of nearest neighbors (accuracy, %)		
		1	3	5
Bag-of-words	No	**55.3**	46.3	45.5
3-gram, chars	No	54.1	47.1	43.8
4-gram, chars	No	52.7	47.4	43.5
3-gram, words	No	35.9	27.6	24.5
4-gram, words	No	30.9	22.9	21.6
Bag-of-words	Yes	57.6	46.7	43.7
3-gram, chars	Yes	**58.5**	51.8	48.8
4-gram, chars	Yes	54.8	47.8	45.4
3-gram, words	Yes	35.3	28.1	24.4
4-gram, words	Yes	30.3	22.3	21.8

Table 6: Classification accuracy (%) with k-NN.

5 Results and conclusions

1. **Support Vector Machines (SVM) classifier is more suitable for automatic classification of Lithuanian political texts (titles of the Seimas votes) than *k* nearest neighbors (*k*-NN) method.** During the experiments a maximum of 70.7% classification accuracy was achieved using SVM, with a maximum of k-NN method being 58.5%.

Classifier	Features	Binary	Testing accuracy (%)
SVM	Bag-of-words	No	**70.7**
SVM	Bag-of-words	Yes	**70.5**
1-NN	*3*-gram, chars	Yes	58.5
SVM	*3*-gram, chars	Yes	58.3
SVM	*3*-gram, chars	No	56.7

Table 7: Summary of the best classifiers.

2. **Bag-of-words method of feature representation is more suitable than n-grams while using SVM classifier.** The maximum accuracy combining SVM with bag-of-words technique was 70.7%, while the maximum accuracy combining SVM with any variation of n-gram was 58.3%.

3. **There is no significant difference between feature selection method when using k-NN classifier.** The maximum accuracies combining bag-of-words and n-gram with k-NN were 57.6% and 58.5% respectively.

4. **Using n-gram feature representation with political texts in Lithuanian language (titles of the Seimas votes), *3*-grams and *4*-grams should represent sets of consecutive characters, not sets of consecutive words.** *3*-grams consisting of characters produced maximum accuracy of 58.5%, while using *3*-grams consisting of words only 48.5% maximum accuracy was achieved. The corresponding maximums when using *4*-grams were 55.7% and 40.1%. Combined with k-NN classifier, n-grams consisting of words showed notably poorer results.

5. **Optimal number of nearest neighbors using k-NN method is 1.** Increasing number of nearest neighbors corresponds with deteriorating classification accuracy.

6. **No significant difference between the types of feature matrix (binary and non-binary) was detected.** Slightly better results were achieved using binary feature matrices with k-NN method, while the same matrices with SVM classifier produced nearly identical results.

6 Future plans

The results presented in this research paper are partial results of work-in-progress of creating a larger infrastructure of monitoring activities of the Lithuanian Seimas. The plans of further research in the field of automatic text classification are as follows:

1. Experiments with other classifiers, such as Multinomial Naive Bayes, Artificial Neural Networks, Logistic Regression, etc;

2. Experiments with other feature representation and selection techniques, such as tf-idf, w-shingling;

3. To use linguistically preprocessed data sets, such as stemmed or lemmatized dictionaries.

There are also plans to perform text classification on larger sets of data, including:

1. Analysis of titles of debates from all the sessions of the Lithuanian Parliament, regardless of the presence of roll call votes;

2. Employing additional documents (such as texts of the debated laws, bills, resolutions etc.) attached to the debates and votes.

It was also discovered that the problem of misclassification might be related with the fact that certain titles of the Seimas debates present classification challenge even for human coders. In other words, titles of the Seimas debates (and especially votes) can not be clearly assigned to one of the classes using only the title itself. More information about the debates and votes might be required. Also, classes (aggregate topics of Policy Agendas) themselves might require a critical review and stricter definitions.

The ultimate plan remains the same – to combine the results of automatic classification of debates (votes) with the analysis of roll call votes in the Seimas. This should result in a completion of the infrastructure designed for monitoring and analysis of the activity of the Lithuanian Parliament.

References

M.A. Bailey. 2007. Comparable Preference Estimates across Time and Institutions for the Court, Congress, and Presidency. *American Jrnl. of Political Science*, 51(3):433–448.

B.S. Harish, D.S. Guru, and S. Manjunath. 2010. Representation and Classification of Text Documents: a Brief Review. *IJCA,Special Issue on RTIPPR*, (2):110–119.

S. Hix, A. Noury, and G. Roland. 2006. Dimensions of Politics in the European Parliament. *American Jrnl. of Political Science*, 50(2):494–520.

A. Hotho, A. Nürnberger, and G. Paaß. 2005. A Brief Survey of Text Mining. *Jrnl for Comp. Linguistics and Language Technology*, 20:19–62.

S. Jackman. 2001. Multidimensional Analysis of Roll Call. *Political Analysis*, 9(3):227–241.

A. Jakulin, W. Buntine, T.M. La Pira, and H. Brasher. 2009. Analyzing the U.S. Senate in 2003: Similarities, Clusters and Blocs. *Political Analysis*, 17:291–310.

T. Joachims. 1998. Text Categorization with Support Vector Machines: Learning with Many Relevant Features. In *Proc. of ECML-98, 10th European Conf. on Machine Learning*, pages 137–142, DE.

J. Kapočiūtė-Dzikienė and A. Krupavičius. 2014. Predicting Party Group from the Lithuanian Parliamentary Speeches. *ITC*, 43(3):321–332.

J. Kapočiūtė-Dzikienė, F. Vaasen, A Krupavičius, and W. Daelemens. 2012. Improving Topic Classification for Highly Inflective Languages. In *Proc. of COLING 2012*, pages 1393–1410.

T. Krilavičius and V. Morkevičius. 2011. Mining Social Science Data: a Study of Voting of Members of the Seimas of Lithuania Using Multidimensional Scaling and Homogeneity Analysis. *Intelektinė ekonomika*, 5(2):224–243.

T. Krilavičius and V. Morkevičius. 2013. Voting in Lithuanian Parliament: is there Anything More than Position vs. Opposition? In *Proc. of 7th General Conf. of the ECPR Sciences Po Bordeaux*.

T. Krilavičius and A. Žilinskas. 2008. On Structural Analysis of Parlamentarian Voting Data. *Informatica*, 19(3):377–390.

M.S. Lynch and A.J. Madonna. 2012. Viva Voce: Implications from the Disappearing Voice Vote, 1865-1996. *Social Science Quarterly*, 94:530–550.

V. Mickevičius, T. Krilavičius, and V. Morkevičius. 2014. Analysing Voting Behavior of the Lithuanian Parliament Using Cluster Analysis and Multidimensional Scaling: Technical Aspects. In *Proc. of the 9th Int. Conf. on Electrical and Control Technologies (ECT)*, pages 84–89.

K.T. Poole. 2005. *Spatial Models of Parliamentary Voting*. Cambridge Univ. Press.

J.M. Roberts, S.S. Smith, and S.R. Haptonstahl. 2009. The Dimensionality of Congressional Voting Reconsidered.

J. Shawe-Taylor and N. Cristianini. 2004. *Kernel Methods for Pattern Analysis*. Cambridge University Press.

R Core Team, 2013. *R: A Language and Environment for Statistical Computing*. R Found. for Stat. Comp., Vienna, Austria.

R. Užupytė and V. Morkevičius. 2013. Lietuvos Respublikos Seimo Narių Balsavimų Tyrimas Pasitelkiant Socialinių Tinklų Analizę: Tinklo Konstravimo Metodologiniai Aspektai. In *Proc. of the 18th Int. Conf. Information Society and University Studies*, pages 170–175.

V. Vapnik and C. Cortes. 1995. Support-Vector Networks. *Machine Learning*, 2:273–297.

Sentiment analysis on conversational texts

Birgitta Ojamaa **Päivi Kristiina Jokinen** **Kadri Muischnek**

University of Tartu
{bl4606, kristiina.jokinen, kadri.muischnek}@ut.ee

Abstract

This paper describes ongoing work related to the analysis of spoken utterance transcripts and estimating the speaker's attitude towards the whole dialogue on the basis of their opinions expressed by utterances. Using the standard technology used in sentiment analysis, we report promising results which can be linked to the conversational participants' self-evaluation of their experience of the interaction.

1 Introduction

One of the popular research topics in current NLP is the sentiment analysis or opinion mining on texts corpora. Sentiment analysis has its roots in natural language processing and linguistics, and it appeared as the field of study in the early 2000s (Pang & Lee (2004, 2005) on document polarity analysis), and has become more popular due to widespread Internet usage and the texts freely available online on social media (Liu 2012: 1-2).

Sentiment analysis or opinion mining deals with using automatic analysis to find sentiments, emotions, opinions and attitudes from a written text towards a subject. This subject may be a product, an organisation, a person, a service or their attributes (Liu 2012: 1).

Based on the words associated with negative, neutral or positive sentiments, the documents are classified into positive, negative and neutral categories, and ratings for various aspects of a given topic (restaurant, movies) can be predicted.

Challenges with the short informal texts concern their unconventional characteristics as text: they contain shortenings, abbreviations, spelling mistakes, etc.

One of the interesting questions that we aim to study in this short paper is how well the standard techniques of sentiment analysis can be applied to conversational data. Since the utterances in conversations are short and produced alternatingly by the participants, transcribed dialogue texts resemble tweets or short SMS messages rather than long documents. However, face-to-face conversations are unique in that they are highly situational, and utterance meaning is constructed jointly by the participants in the dialogue context. The goal of this project was to use sentiment analysis on the conversational texts and compare the linguistic results with participant's own description of the interaction.

It must be noticed that the sentiment analysis we describe in this paper is not to be mixed with the participants' emotion analysis. Our goal is to study, if the sentiment analysis tools can be applied to conversational data and extract sentiments (positive and negative attitudes) that may be mapped onto the speakers' experience of the dialogue as a whole.

The short student paper is structured as follows. We introduce our data in Section 2, and discuss its cleaning and method in Section 3. We present results in Section 4, and discuss them with future prospects in Section 5.

2 Data

The texts used in this project are from the MINT (Multimodal INTeraction) project that deals with Artificial Intelligence and multi-modal agents (Jokinen and Tenjes 2012). One particular field where intelligent agents need a lot of development is the study of emotion and sentiment, not only in gestures, but language as well – for example in speech synthesis where it soon becomes important for an agent to learn different tones for communicating more effectively (Vainik 2014: 335).

The dialogues are first-encounter dialogues where the speakers are unfamiliar with each other and they are expected to make acquaintance with their partner. They are expected to describe their likings to the partner but not to start emotional arguments on due to social politeness rules.

Each utterance is a continuous vocalization by a speaker rather a grammatically "correct" sentence. We used the transcriptions of utterances in 23 dialogue files, altogether 2902 utterances. Although it might have been useful to divide the transcribed text according to the speakers, we did not do this due to the small amount of data.

Cleaning of the data included removing of the XML notation that was used in the transcriptions (made using Praat (Boersma 2001)), as well as the English translations of the text. In total, there were 2902 sentences or utterances. Since the Praat output texts are grouped by the speaker, the utterances had to be rearranged to display individual utterances by time.

The corpus is accompanied by self-evaluation of the participant's experience of the interactions. This is based on a questionnaire which the participants filled after each interaction, describing how well certain positive and negative adjectives (e.g. pleasant, stressful, interesting) describe their experience.

The method to clean the files was to:

1) clean some parts of code and all of the translated text manually;
2) remove code around the timestamps to sort the text using UNIX shell-script;
3) sort the text by timestamps using shell-script;
4) remove the remaining code using shell-script, leaving only text;
5) text segmentation using a Perl script[1]
6) morphological analysis/disambiguation using Filosoft's t3mesta in shell-script[2].

The final result of the cleaning was text separated into sentences by the markers <s> </s> and individual wordforms on each line. What was left is displayed in Figure 1. The utterances are annotated using tags <s> and </s>. A row begins with the word-form as it was used in text, followed by its lemma and inflectional endings, separated from the lemma by +. Then come the part of speech tags and morphological categories between double slashes //. English glosses for every word-form are added in the end of the row, translation of the whole utterance in the end of every utterance.

```
<s>
nüüd nüüd+0 //_Y_ ?, //  now
me mina+0 //_P_ pl n, // we
peame pida+me //_V_ me, //
must-1.pl
rääkima rääki+ma //_V_ma, //
speak-inf
</s>
'We must speak now'
```

1 Provided by Kaili Müürisep

2 www.filosoft.ee

```
<s>
*naer* naer+0 //_S_ sg n, //
laughter
</s>
'laughter'

<s>
jaa jaa+0 //_D_ // yes
</s>
'yes'
```

Figure 1. Text after cleaning and morphological analysis.

3 Finding lemmas

After cleaning the file, it was necessary to find the most frequently used lemmas to compile a suitable lexicon. Finding the most frequently used lemmas was done using another shell-script. Since the regular morphological ending of infinitive form of Estonian verb used in dictionariy entries (-ma) wasn't particularly useful for context, the verb stems were used. There didn't seem to be much variation amongst the texts, most of them shared the most frequent words, which are displayed in Figure 2.

```
1412 olema 'to be'
1033 mina 'I'
748 see 'this'
734 et 'that'
634 ja 'and'
524 siis 'then'
497 ei 'no'
470 nagu 'as, like'
362 jah 'yes'
360 naer 'laughter'
326 sina 'you'
```

Figure 2. The most frequent lemmas from all the texts together with their Estonian translations.

While comparing the vocabulary of the material with that of the general (written) Estonian, one could say that the differences can be described as general differences between written and spoken language – personal pronouns *mina* 'I' and *sina* 'you' are more frequent as well as various spoken language particles, e.g. *nagu* 'like', *noh*, *okei* 'okay'.

4 Compiling sentiment lexicons

The lexicon was separated into two categories: positive and negative words. Both of these categories were compiled by using the most prototypical lemmas (*good*, *bad*, *interesting*, *hard* etc.) and some frequent lemmas from the texts (such as conversational cues: *mhm*, *yes*, *okay*, etc). Altogether the dictionary was quite small: 46 words, most of those positive. Although some (such as Vainik (2014: 346)) have argued that splitting words by valence isn't enough for most applications, the decision was made to use just two lexicons, since there hasn't been much detailed research into emotional categories and corresponding words. Of course, statistical methods are very popular too. Figure 3 gives some positive and negative words from the lexicon.

```
Positive sentiment words

jajaa 'yes-yes'
julge 'brave'
legendaarne 'legendary'
lihtne 'simple'
meeldiv 'pleasant'


Negative sentiment words

häbi 'shame'
hull 'crazy'
igav 'boring'
imelik 'strange'
keeruline 'complicated'
```

Figure 3. Some words from the lexicons together with their English translations.

As mentioned, Estonian is a morphologically rich language, so there is a need to use the lemmas rather than operate on all the different word forms. To make the task easier, the word-forms used in text were all made (using shell-script) into lemma variants of the same word. Compared to Figure 1, Figure 4 might be hard to understand for an actual language speaker, but it keeps the lexicons concise and shouldn't change the meaning much, when already analysing only words, not phrases. At this stage, all the texts were joined together into one file.

```
oot kas siis keegi  teine
(oot kas siis kedagi teist)
wait if then anybody other
             -part   -part

siin ei ole    juures
(siin ei olegi  juures)
here no be-neg presence

näge või
(näha või)
see-inf  or

'wait, isn't anybody else
seen nearby'

vist    küll   jah
perhaps surely yes
'perhaps yes, sure'

väike naer
'some laughter'

ei aga mina ei tead    keegi
ei aga ma ei tea,      keegi
no but I  no know-neg
anybody

nagu ei
nagu ei
like  no
'no, but I don't know,
anybody like not...'
```

Figure 4. The text is lemmatized. Original text is in the parenthesis, followed by the English glosses. English translation is given in the end of every utterance.

5 Sentiment analysis

The sentiment analysis program was written in Python, using some of the code developed by the first autor for her bachelor thesis (Ojamaa 2014). The utterances were divided into four groups according by their sentiment: positive, negative, neutral and ambiguous.

Lexicons were read into lists and if matches were found, they were compared with the rest of the sentence to look for negation or other recognised sentiment words. Negation (formed by regular expression to account for three words that negate in Estonian: *ei, pole, mitte*) was allowed to influence words up to four words in the right- or left-hand context of the negation word. In the output of the program (the results file) the program displayed the sentiment evaluation for the sentences as well as the number of the sentence and the sentiment words found with their sentiment in context (since if negated, a positive word should have a negative polarity).

Out of 2902, the program annotated 576 sentences or 20% as positive, 38 or 1.3% as negative, and 3 as ambiguous. The rest or almost 79% of the utterances were either neutral or contained no sentiment.

6 Evaluation

200 analyzed sentences (utterances) were evaluated manually to see possible problems with the rules and lexicons. Of those, only 30 had got the wrong polarity tag, i.e. the overall correctness was 85%.

Of those 30, 20 erroneous decisions occurred because of the meta-comment "laughter" that was included in the positive lexicon, but in dialogues often signified awkwardness instead. The rest of the errors could feasibly be solved using regular expressions to find conversationally positive utterances (such as *mm* (a form of *mhm*) or *jaah* ('yees')). There was also a slight problem with negation, where the four word context might have been too large or punctuation should also have been taken into account. A few problems were caused by the small size of the lexicon assome sentiment words weren't recognized.

As mentioned, we can also compare the sentiment analysis results with the speaker's self-evaluation of the interaction. Comparing the results with data published by Jokinen and Tenjes (2012), where participants were mostly positive in their descriptions of their participating in the video collection, it seems that sentimental analysis is consistent with the results that point to the conclusion that the participants felt happy discussing in front of cameras and they could self-reflect on it later.

7 Discussion and Future work

This paper started to explore the use of standard sentiment analysis tools and methods in analyzing transcribed conversational data. The results show that the methods can be applied with fairly good classification results, and even though most sentences are neutral, the speakers are mostly positive when showing sentiment.

Still there are many issues to be taken into account and to be studied further. The text represents a spoken natural language, and there can be errors in speaking and in transcription. Estonian morphological analysis should also be more accurate, so as to improve the use of statistical methods and additional conversational cues when analyzing the texts.

Also, as mentioned, dialogues are joint efforts so we need to distinguish the two speakers, and take into account the fact that the speakers influence each other and their utterances are dependent on the previous utterances. The transcribed text should thus take into account the interaction context, and differentiate between the different speakers.

When dealing with spoken dialogues, speech signal is an clear source of predicting. We can also use speech signal analysis as the corpora contain videos from which the signal properties can be extracted.

References

Paul Boersma. 2001. Praat, a system for doing phonetics by computer. *Glot International* 5(9/10): 341-345.

Kristiina Jokinen and Silvi Tenjes. 2012. Investigating Engagement – Intercultural and Technological Aspects of the Collection, Analysis, and Use of Estonian Multiparty Conversational Video Data. Nicoletta Calzolari, Khalid Choukri, Thierry Declerck, Mehmet Uğur Doğan, Bente Maegaard, Joseph Mar (Ed.). *Proceedings of the Eight International Conference on Language Recourses and Evaluation* (LREC'12):2764 – 2769.

Diane Litman and Kate Forbes. 2003. Recognizing emotions from student speech in tutoring dialogues. *Workshop on Automatic Speech Recognition and Understanding*, ASRU '03. IEEE.

Bing Liu 2012. *Sentiment Analysis and Opinion Mining*. Morgan & Claypool. Synthesis Lectures on Human Language Technologies.

Birgitta Ojamaa. 2014. Tartu Ülikooli üliõpilaste tagasiside hoiakute analüüs. Bachelor's thesis.

Patrizia Paggio, Jens Allwood, Elisabeth Ahlsén, Kristiina Jokinen and Costanza Navarretta. 2010. The NOMCO Multimodal Nordic Resource – Goals and Characteristics. *Proceedings of the Seventh conference on International Language Resources and Evaluation* (LREC'10): 2968-2973

Bo Pang and Lillian Lee. 2004. A sentimental education: Sentiment analysis using subjectivity. *Procs of the Association for Computational Linguistics* (ACL): 271-278.

Bo Pang and Lillian Lee. 2005. Seeing stars: Exploiting class relationships for sentiment categorization with respect to rating scales. *Procs of the Association for Computational Linguistics* (ACL):115–124.

Ene Vainik. 2014. Kelle emotsioonile anda teksti ette lugedes hääl? Vaatlus mitmest perspektiivist. *Eesti Rakenduslingvistika Ühingu aastaraamat.* Vol 10 (2014): 335-351.

Adapting *word2vec* to Named Entity Recognition

Scharolta Katharina Siencnik
Department of Swedish /
Department of Philosophy,
Linguistics and Theory of Science
University of Gothenburg, Sweden
gussieka@student.gu.se

Abstract

In this paper we explore how word vectors built using *word2vec* can be used to improve the performance of a classifier during Named Entity Recognition. Thereby, we discuss the best integration of word embeddings into the classification problem and consider the effect of the size of the unlabelled dataset on performance, reaching the unexpected result that for this particular task increasing the amount of unlabelled data does not necessarily increase the performance of the classifier.

1 Introduction

Supervised NLP systems suffer from a fundamental data bottleneck problem: though unprecedented amounts of data and the computational power necessary for its processing have become available, supervised training requires data that has been annotated for a specific task. The process of annotation in turn requires human time and is thereby inherently connected to high costs, both in terms of time and money.

Enhancing supervised methods with unsupervised word representations can ameliorate this problem. Word representations can be trained on large unannotated corpora and can learn implicit semantic and/or syntactic information. This information can then be used to augment a small amount of annotated data, thereby reducing the amount of annotated data necessary or improving the accuracy of a classifier with a given amount of annotated data.

Different word representations have been shown to successfully improve various NLP tasks. For example, Miller et al. (2004) use word clusters during named entity recognition (henceforth NER) and Bansal et al. (2014) use continuous word representations as features for dependency parsing (for a larger overview cf. Bansal et al. (2014, p. 809)).

Naturally, the main goal of using word representations is adding further information to a classification task. How to make this information maximally relevant depends on the task given. Thus, whether we want two words to be considered similar depends on the task in which they are being classified (cf. Guo et al. (2014)). For example, Bansal et al. (2014) train their word representations on dependency context instead of raw linear context. In the following we will apply word vectors to the task of NER.

Vector based word representations have a successful history of use in information retrieval and computational semantics as an implementation of the long-standing linguistic hypothesis that words that occur in similar contexts tend to have similar meanings (Harris, 1954). More recently, word vectors have also been shown to be able to capture linguistic regularities of both semantic ('king' to 'man' is like 'queen' to 'woman') and syntactic nature ('ran' to 'run' is like 'laughed' to 'laugh') (Mikolov et al., 2013b).

We first discuss our method of extracting word vectors and adding them to the classification task before describing the task of NER and our more experiments more concretely. In the final discussion we primarily explore engineering options related to the incorporation of the word embeddings and the size of the unlabelled data set.

2 Extracting the word vectors

The method used to extract word vectors, *word2vec*, implements two models that take tokenised but otherwise non-processed text and derive a feature vector for every type in this data set. For this paper we used the continuous skip-gram model, a neural network model that avoids multiple hidden layers in order to allow extremely fast and efficient training, for example when compared to most clustering algorithms. During training, each word in the data set is used as an input to a log-linear classifier, which learns word representations by trying to predict words occurring within a certain range to either side of the word.[1] As those words occurring further away from the input word are less likely to be related to it, these words are given less weight (cf. Mikolov et al. (2013a, p. 4f.) for the original presentation).

Having chosen a word representation, an almost equally important choice regards the method by which the chosen feature is incorporated into a linear model. Using *word2vec* embeddings for syntactic parsing, Bansal et al. (2014) report that simply adding the relevant word vector to the feature vector during training does not yield improved results. One solution presented for this problem is clustering the word vectors (Guo et al., 2014). We adopt this solution using choose k-means clustering and introduce the clusters into the classification problem by adding a further feature representing the cluster of each word.

3 Named Entity Recognition

NER is a sequence prediction problem. Given a tokenised text, the task is that of predicting which words are locations, organisations or persons. To be able to distinguish multiple adjacent instances of the same type of named entity and a named entity spanning multiple words, a beginning-inside-outside (BIO) encoding is used (Sang and Veenstra, 1999).

Both training and testing data for the classifier were taken from the annotated CoNLL03 corpus (Sang and De Meulder, 2003). This data, which is a collection of news wire articles from the Reuters Corpus, is annotated with part-of-speech (POS), syntactic chunk and named entity tags. The features we extracted given one word in the data are: (1) tokens plus their POS tags in a window of ± 2 (2) token's syntactic chunk in a window of ± 1 (3) upper-cased tokens in a window of ± 2 (4) initial capitalization pattern of tokens in a window of ± 2 (4) the previous two predicted tags (5) the conjunction of the previous tag and the current token (6) prefixes and suffixes of the token (7) more elaborate word type information for the token (as employed by Zhang et al. (2003)).

A very simple implementation of evaluation was allowed by the CoNLL03 scoring method which evaluates whether the NER system correctly identified a full named entity. Furthermore, the evaluation script gives a clear presentation of performance in the different categories (person, location, organisation, miscellaneous), though we do not discuss the potential reasons for variations in performance in these categories here.

4 Experimental setup

All of our experiments were based on the RCV1 corpus which contains one year of Reuters English newswire from August 1996 to August 1997 (Lewis et al., 2004). Preprocessing of the RCV1 corpus involved the extraction of text from the news files as well as sentence and word tokenization, both of which we did using the NLTK toolkit.

In order to evaluate the effect of the size of the non-labelled corpus on performance we trained word embeddings on different subsets of RCV1. The smallest subset was the CoNLL03 corpus. Furthermore, we trained *word2vec* models on a quarter, half and three quarters of RCV1. In Table 1 below we give a rough estimate of the number of documents used for training each model (where a document contains between a few hundred and several thousand words) as well as the number of words represented with word vectors in the *word2vec* model. As could be expected given the Zipf distribution of words, the number of unique types does not grow linearly with the number of tokens in a model but begins to stagnate at a large number of documents.

This effect is fortified by necessary design choices: While training the CoNLL03 corpus we set the *word2vec* 'min_count' variable to one (which means that all tokens will be considered) whereas for the larger data sets it was set to the default value of five (only words occurring at least five times are represented) to reduce processing costs.

word2vec was reimplemented for use in Python by Rehurek and Sojka (2010). We use this implementation to build our models, using the default setting for vector dimensionality (100), as well as for the other parameters such as the number of training iterations and the size of the window.

[1]Bansal et al. (2014) report that the size of this range or window has a significant impact on the resulting word vectors. Large windows result in more semantically accurate groupings, whereas smaller windows result in the grouping of words with similar part-of-speech tags. Exploring various window magnitudes was unfortunately not within the scope of this paper.

data set	nr types	nr documents
CoNLL03	30 290	1 393
1/4 RCV1	145 824	~ 200 000
1/2 RCV1	221 066	~ 400 000
3/4 RCV1	289 345	~ 600 000
RCV1	356 843	~ 800 000

Table 1: Data set statistics.

The classification itself is a greedy implementation of the Linear Support Vector Classification algorithm as implemented in the scikit-learn software, using the default values (Pedregosa et al., 2011). Linear SVC was shown by Ratinov and Roth (2009) to perform comparably to more computationally complex and costly search algorithms such as beamsearch or Viterbi.

5 Discussion

During the following discussion of results when referring to performance we are referring to performance as indicated by the overall F-measure returned by the CoNLL03 evaluation script.

5.1 Cluster granularity

A practical challenge in generating clusters from word embeddings lies in choosing the relevant cluster granularity, i.e. the cluster granularity that maintains the information relevant to the classification task at hand.

Given the considerable time demands of generating clusters we performed all of our initial granularity experiments on the *word2vec* embeddings constructed from the smallest dataset, CoNLL03. Through our first experiment, we attained a rough idea of a task-adequate dimension of cluster granularity: We evaluated three dimensions of clusters (100, 1000 and 5000) extrinsically by considering their effect on the performance of the NER system. Granularity 1000 performed best, suggesting that this is the correct range of dimensionality.

In a next step, we manually inspected the clusters built at this granularity (again from the CoNLL03 *word2vec* model). Though they were rather noisy (e.g. numbers were included in almost every cluster[2]), they seemed to capture some regularities. In Example 1 we give two excerpts from clusters from this dataset, where the first is primarily a collection of person names (and some company names) and the second a collection of city names. Clusters at granularity 1000 from the larger datasets were similarly noisy.

(1) a. 0-6 1-15 1-7 1.4871 ... Alexia Angelica ... Jill Jimy Jolene Juliet KTM Kandarr ... Yamaha Yi Zina Zrubakova

b. AMSTERDAM ANKARA Auth ... VIENNA WARSAW WELLINGTON WINNIPEG

A solution to the cluster granularity problem proposed in many papers (e.g. Miller et al. (2004)) is the combination of multiple granularities, for example through hierarchical clustering. Surprisingly, for training on the CoNLL03 corpus the combination of different cluster granularities (we tried various combinations of 500, 1000 and 1500) did not improve accuracy. To ascertain the validity of this finding for all of our word embedding models, we repeated this experiment on the *word2vec* model built using half of the RCV1 corpus. Here, we found considerable improvement in performance, with a growth in performance for every added granularity (cf. Table 2), suggesting that further improvement could be achieved with an even greater number of clusters.[3]

granularity	performance
1500	82.83%
1000 + 1500	83.52%
500 + 1000 + 1500	83.81%

Table 2: Testing granularity with 1/2 RCV1.

5.2 Unlabelled corpus size

The second question we aimed to elucidate in this paper is what effect the size of the unlabelled corpus has on the performance of the NER system. Given our experimental set-up, this essentially boils down to the following question: Given an unlabelled corpus that is both periodically and stylistically similar to the testing data can we expect better performance the larger the corpus?

It is important to note that in particular in our experiments the size of the unlabelled corpus does

[2]To reduce this kind of noise, Turian et al. (2010) preprocess the data by removing all sentences that are less than 90% lowercase a-z (not counting whitespaces). In previous experiments we did not find this measure to improve performance.

[3]Limited processing power detained us from putting this hypothesis to the test.

not have a direct correlation to the percentage of word types occurring in the testing data that are also covered by the word embeddings model. This can be explained with reference to Table 1 and the setting of the *word2vec* 'min_word' variable discussed above. Whether choosing to train the model on all word types occurring in the training data as well as additional unlabelled data will improve performance by preventing the possibility of unknown words.

We did not find evidence that suggests a direct correlation between corpus size and performance. Rather, the improvement stagnated at around half of the RCV1 corpus. All results are given in Figure 1 and compared to the no cluster baseline; the F-measures given are achieved from adding clusters at granularity 1000, built from *word2vec* models trained on the various data sets, to the NER classifier.

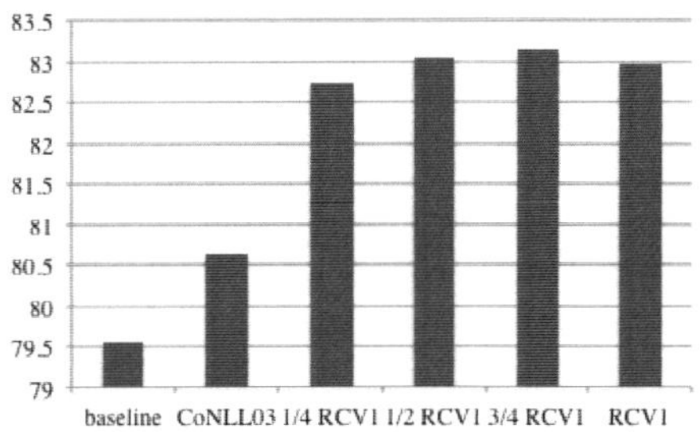

Figure 1: F-measures given in percent.

One possible explanation for the stagnating performance of the larger data set is that other training settings need to be employed for optimal training (e.g. higher vector dimensionality or more training iterations). Regardless of the validity of this explanation, the results suggest that optimal training of a word embeddings model for a certain task is a more complex problem than training it with the maximum amount of data.

6 Conclusion

In conclusion, we would like to present a summary of our results: In Figure 2 we show the Linear SVC baseline (a) in comparison to our lowest and our best performing experiment at cluster granularity 1000 (CoNLL03 and 3/4 RCV1, (b) and (c), respectively). Finally, we show the possible improvement through combination of multiple granularities by comparing the results of using 1/2 RCV1 with just 1000 clusters (d) and combining this granularity with 500 and 1500 (e).

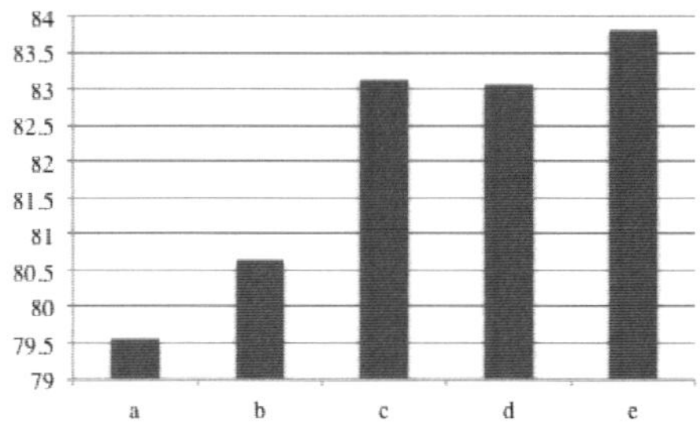

Figure 2: F-measures given in percent.

The graph reemphasises the two key observations discussed above:

1. Performance of the NER model improved with growth of the size of the unlabelled data set but only to a limit (here at around 300 000 types) at which it even started to drop.

2. Combining multiple cluster granularities led to our best improvement. It did not improve performance for smaller data sets.

We believe these findings adequately illuminate the complexity of optimally enhancing NLP tasks with unsupervised word representations of any kind.

There are naturally a number of ways this project could be replicated in a more sophisticated way to yield a yet more sophisticated understanding and therewith likely further gains in performance. For one, the performance by named entity class is potentially helpful data that was not considered here. For example, for result (e) in Figure 2 above, class-specific F-measures ranged from 74.77% (miscellaneous) to 91.47% (person). Interestingly, for the miscellaneous class few results fell over the baseline (74.02%) whilst this was the case for all results for the person class (baseline at 86.27%).

A further question worth exploring is how similar the unlabelled data needs to be to the testing data to achieve good results. Our data was from the same time period (important for named entities) and the same domain (newspaper articles). Exploring how much this can be altered to nevertheless maintain good results would be a valuable question to answer for insights on optimal training of word representation models.

Acknowledgments

This article is the result of course work produced during the Master's course in Language Technology at Gothenburg University for the Swedish Research Council's project 2012-5738 ("Towards a knowledge-based culturomics"). I would like to thank the Center of Language Technology for its generous funding towards my attendance at the 2015 NoDaLiDa conference.

References

Mohit Bansal, Kevin Gimpel, and Karen Livescu. 2014. Tailoring continuous word representations for dependency parsing. In *Proceedings of the 52nd Annual Meeting of the Association for Computational Linguistics (Volume 2: Short Papers)*, pages 809–815.

Jiang Guo, Wanxiang Che, Haifeng Wang, and Ting Liu. 2014. Revisiting embedding features for simple semi-supervised learning. In *Proceedings of the 2014 Conference on Empirical Methods in Natural Language Processing*, pages 110–120.

Zellig Harris. 1954. Distributional structure. *Word*, 10:146–162.

David D. Lewis, Yiming Yang, Tony G. Rose, and Fan Li. 2004. RCV1: A new benchmark collection for text categorization research. *Journal of Machine Learning Research*, 5.

Tomas Mikolov, Kai Chen, Greg Corrado, and Jeffrey Dean. 2013a. Efficient estimation of word representations in vector space. *CoRR*, abs/1301.3781.

Tomas Mikolov, Wen-tau Yih, and Geoffrey Zweig. 2013b. Linguistic regularities in continuous space word representations. In *Proceedings of the 2013 Conference of the North American Chapter of the Association for Computational Linguistics: Human Language Technologies*.

Scott Miller, Jethran Guinness, and Alex Zamanian. 2004. Name tagging with word clusters and discriminative training. In *Proceedings of Human Language Technologies*, pages 337–342.

Fabian Pedregosa, Gal Varoquaux, Alexandre Gramfort, Vincent Michel, Bertrand Thirion, Olivier Grisel, Mathieu Blondel, Peter Prettenhofer, Ron Weiss, Vincent Dubourg, Jake Vanderplas, Alexandra Passos, David Cournapeau, Matthieu Brucher, Matthieu Perrot, and Edouard Duchesnay. 2011. Scikit-learn: Machine learning in Python. *Journal of Machine Learning Research*, 12:2825–2830.

Lev Ratinov and Dan Roth. 2009. Design challenges and misconceptions in named entity recognition. In *Proceedings of the Thirteenth Conference on Computational Natural Language Learning*, Conference on Natural Language Learning 2009, pages 147–155.

Radim Rehurek and Petr Sojka. 2010. Software framework for topic modelling with large corpora. In *Proceedings of Language Resources and Evaluation Conference 2010 workshop New Challenges for NLP Frameworks*, pages 46–50.

Erik F. Tjong Kim Sang and Fien De Meulder. 2003. Introduction to the conference on natural language learning-2003 shared task: Language-independent named entity recognition. In *Proceedings of Conference on Natural Language Learning-2003*, pages 142–147.

Erik F. Tjong Kim Sang and Jorn Veenstra. 1999. Representing text chunks. In *Proceedings of the European Chapter of the Association for Computational Linguistics*, pages 173–179. Bergen, Norway.

Joseph Turian, Lev Ratinov, and Yoshua Bengio. 2010. Word representations: A simple and general method for semi-supervised learning. In *Proceedings of the 48th Annual Meeting of the Association for Computational Linguistics*, Association for Computational Linguistics 2010, pages 384–394.

Tong Zhang, Fred Damerau, and David Johnson. 2003. Updating an NLP system to fit new domains: an empirical study on the sentence segmentation problem. In Walter Daelemans and Miles Osborne, editors, *Proceedings of the Conference on Natural Language Learning-2003*, pages 56–62. Edmonton, Canada.

Active learning for sense annotation

Héctor Martínez Alonso Barbara Plank Anders Johannsen Anders Søgaard
Njalsgade 140, Copenhagen (Denmark), University of Copenhagen
alonso@hum.ku.dk, bplank@cst.dk, {ajohannsen, soegaard}@hum.ku.dk

Abstract

This article describes a real (non-synthetic) active-learning experiment to obtain supersense annotations for Danish. We compare two instance selection strategies, namely lowest-prediction confidence (MAX), and sampling from the confidence distribution (SAMPLE). We evaluate their performance during the annotation process, across domains for the final resulting system, as well as against in-domain adjudicated data. The SAMPLE strategy yields competitive models that are more robust than the overly length-biased selection criterion of MAX.

1 Introduction

Most successful natural language processing (NLP) systems rely on a set of labeled training examples to induce models in a supervised manner. However, labeling instances to create a training set is time-consuming and expensive. One way to alleviate this problem is to resort to *active learning* (AL), where a learner chooses which instances—from a large pool of unlabeled data—to give to the human expert for annotation. After each annotation by the expert, the system retrains the learner, and the learner chooses a new instance to annotate.

There are many active learning strategies. The simplest and most widely used is *uncertainty sampling* (Lewis and Catlett, 1994), where the learner queries the instance it is most uncertain about (Scheffer and Wrobel, 2001; Culotta and McCallum, 2005). Instead, in *query-by-committee* an entire committee of models is used to select the examples with highest disagreement. At the same time most studies on active learning are actually *synthetic*, i.e. the human supervision was just emulated by holding out already labeled data.

In this study, we perform a *real* active learning experiment. Since speed plays a major role, we do not resort to an ensemble-based query-by-committee approach but use a single model for selection. We evaluate two selection strategies for a sequence tagging task, supersense tagging.

2 Datapoint-selection strategies

Given a pool of unlabeled data U, a datapoint-selection strategy chooses a new unlabeled item u_i to annotate. We evaluate two of such strategies. They both involve evaluating the informativeness of unlabeled instances.

The first strategy (MAX) is similar to the standard approach in uncertainty sampling, i.e. the active learning system selects datapoint whose classification confidence is the lowest. The second strategy (SAMPLE) attempts to make the selection criterion more flexible by sampling from the confidence score distribution.

The two strategies work as follows:

1. MAX: Predict on U and choose u_i that has the lowest prediction confidence p_i, where p_i is the posterior probability of the classifier for the item u_i.
2. SAMPLE: Predict on U and choose u_i sampling from the distribution of the inverse confidence scores for all the instances—making low-confidence items more likely to be sampled. We calculate the inverse confidence score as $-log(p_i)$.

We apply both datapoint-selection strategies on two different subcorpora sampled from the same unlabeled corpus (cf. Section 3). Each $(strategy, subcorpus)$ tuple yields a system setup for an individual annotator. Table 1 describes the setup of our four annotators.

3 Data collection

An AL setup requires some annotated data to use as training seed for the first model, and as evalua-

Annotator	Strategy	Subcorpus
A_{S_1}	SAMPLE	C_1
A_{S_2}	SAMPLE	C_2
A_{M_1}	MAX	C_1
A_{M_2}	MAX	C_2

Table 1: Annotators and their setup, namely their instance selection strategy and the unlabeled subcorpus.

Domain	$\overline{SL}$	Seed	Test
Blog	16.44		100
Chat	14.61		200
Forum	20.51		200
Magazine	19.45		200
Newswire	17.43	400	200
Parliament	31.21		200

Table 2: Super-sense tagging data sets

tion test bench. We use previously available Danish sense-annotated data (Martínez Alonso et al., 2015). This dataset is a subset of the the ClarinDK corpus (Asmussen and Halskov, 2012) and has been annotated by two annotators and later adjudicated by a third. Table 2 shows the different domains that make up the initial annotated data and how much is used for training seed and for testing. We choose a conventional scenario where the initial system is trained only on an usual kind of text (newswire) in order to later assess the system's improvement on out-of-domain data.

In addition to the labeled data used for training seed and for testing, we use two unlabeled 10K-sentence subcorpora. These two subcorpora (C_1 and C_2) are randomly sampled from the ClarinDK corpus in order to obtain sentences of the same type that make up the labeled data, but ensuring that the sentences in C_1 and C_2 do not overlap with any of the labeled sentences described in Table 2. All the sentences in C_1 and C_2 are between 5 and 50 words long, in order to limit the strong bias for selecting longer sentences in AL for sequence prediction.[1]

4 Model

The features used in the model are the following. For each word w, we calculate:

a) 2-TOKEN WINDOW of forms, lemmas and POS tags before and after w, including w.
b) 2-TOKEN WINDOW of most-frequent sense tags for w.
c) BAG OF WORDS of forms and lemmas at the *left* and *right* of w, marked for directionality so words at the left are different from words at the right.
d) MORPHOLOGY of w, whether it is all alphanumeric, capitalized, contains hyphens, and its 3-letter prefix and suffix.
e) BROWN CLUSTER estimated from U. We generate the 2,4,6,8,10 and 12-bits long prefix of the cluster bitstring of w.[2]

The system is trained using search-based classification (SEARN) (Daumé et al., 2009)[3] using default parameters and one pass over the data. We use one pass over the data, thereby using strict online learning.

5 Evaluation

The goal of an AL setup is to augment the set of training instances. In this section we evaluate the performance of the AL-generated annotations during the annotation process in form of learning curves (Section 5.1). In order to gauge the robustness of a system trained on data obtained from AL, we break the evaluation down by domain (Section 5.2). Finally, we compare a system trained exclusively on annotated and ajudicated newswire data with systems trained on a combination of training seed and AL data. We evaluate all systems on micro-averaged F1.

5.1 Learning curves

This section describes the life-cycle for the AL setup for the four annotators. The system does one pass over the data and then retrains after each item. We evaluate against the entire test data that comprises different domains (Section 5.2).

We delimit the learnability space of the task between the most-frequent-sense (MFS) baseline at the bottom and an estimate of an upper bound (UB). We approximate the UB by training a system on the seed plus all the four AL-annotated datasets. Note that the data for UB is four times the data at the end point of any learning curve.

[1]The data will be made available at `clarin.dk` under *Danish Supersense Annotation.*

[2]We use Liang's implementation `https://github.com/percyliang/brown-cluster`

[3]SEARN in Vowpal Wabbit `https://github.com/JohnLangford/vowpal_wabbit/`

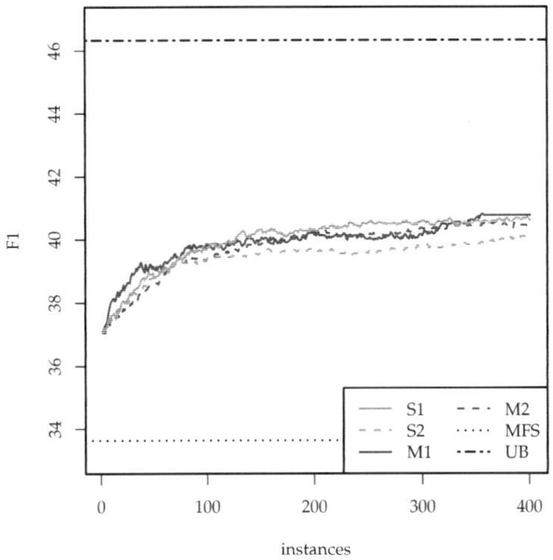

Figure 1: learning curves for the four annotators, delimited by the MFS baseline and the estimated upper bound (UB).

We observe that the MFS baseline (dotted line) is fairly low (33.63 F1). The system performance trained on seed starts at 37.06 F1. All learning curves show the same overall behavior with steeper learning for the first 150 instances. The differences are small, yet we can see that the SAMPLE approach surpasses the MAX strategy after 110 instances for one of the sub corpora. The most informative data during the initial iterations stems from annotator A_{M1} (MAX strategy), where we can observe the steepest increase. However, the MAX strategy results in *considerably* longer sentences (cf. $\overline{SL}$ in Table 4), thus is a major burden for the annotators compared to SAMPLE. In fact, A_{M1} could not finish the task in time, which is depicted by the straight line for the last 20 dots in the plot.

5.2 Performance across domains

The SAMPLE strategy turns out to be promising when evaluated on the entire test set, but only for one of the two subcorpora (Section 5.1). In this section, we look at the performance per domain.

Table 3 shows the domain-wise results for the last AL iteration of each annotator. We compare this to the most-frequent sense (MFS) baseline, as well to the original performance trained on only the seed data. The values for the annotators in Table 3 correspond with the last point of each learning curve in Figure 1, whereas the seed baseline is the common starting point (the intercept) for all learning curves.

We can see now that the seed baseline already beats MFS on all datasets except Chat, which is arguably very different from the newswire text that seed is sampled from. Overall, there is only a small difference in terms of performance between the two datapoint-selection strategies. The best strategy varies per domain.

			MAX		SAMPLE	
Dataset	MFS	Seed	$+A_{M_1}$	$+A_{M_2}$	$+A_{S_1}$	$+A_{S_2}$
Blog	25.6	37.2	40.5	**41.0**	*39.1*	39.4
Chat	36.1	*33.7*	39.8	*39.3*	40.1	**40.3**
Forum	31.1	33.4	**36.1**	35.9	*35.2*	35.5
Magazine	34.3	36.3	38.5	37.4	**38.6**	*36.8*
Newswire	31.5	37.2	**42.9**	40.5	41.2	*39.0*
Parliament	38.6	40.5	*45.0*	47.2	46.5	**47.5**
All	33.6	36.8	**40.8**	40.7	40.6	*40.1*

Table 3: Performance across domains for different training setups. The best system for each dataset is given in bold, and the worst system in italics.

Annotator	$\overline{SL}$	KL_{Seed-A}	KL_{A-Test}
A_{M_1}	43.36	0.026	0.027
A_{M_2}	42.65	0.019	0.027
A_{S_1}	26.16	0.035	0.054
A_{S_2}	26.24	0.017	0.022

Table 4: Descriptive statistics for the four generated datasets.

There are notable differences in terms of data characteristics between the resulting data samples. Table 4 shows descriptive statistics for the four resulting datasets, and how they relate to the seed training dataset and the overall test data. $\overline{SL}$ represents the average sentence length, KL_{Seed-A} is the Kullback-Leibler (KL) divergence from the seed dataset to each of the annotators', and KL_{A-Test} is the KL divergence from the annotators' datasets to the test data. We can see that there is a *big* difference in $\overline{SL}$ between the strategies. The system that use the SAMPLE strategy have a more variable sentence length but also much shorter sentences than MAX. It is still longer than the average sentence length in the unlabeled corpus, which is 21 tokens per sentence. This indicates that the selection strategy for SAMPLE is a compromise between the long-sentence bias of the MAX strategy and a purely random selection. Thus, we believe that the SAMPLE strategy is a viable alternative to the more common lowest-confidence strategy, because it can provide training data of competitive quality that is more varied and can provide more robust models.

5.3 Comparison with heldout data

In this last comparison, we gauge the effect of using adjudicated in-domain data instead of the same amount of AL-generated data. We remove the 200 newswire sentences from the test set and add them to the training seed. We train a system on the seed and these additional 200 adjudicated sentences (namely on all the 600 sentences of newswire data), and evaluate it across domains (all out-domain data). This system is compared to the result of the AL setup at the 200th iteration. The results in Table 5 show that even across domains it is more beneficial to have adjudicated in-domain data then the out-of-domain data annotated through active learning.

Dataset	Seed	+Newswire	MAX $+A_{M_1}$	MAX $+A_{M_2}$	SAMPLE $+A_{S_1}$	SAMPLE $+A_{S_2}$
Blog	33.7	**39.9**	39.1	39.0	39.0	38.5
Chat	33.4	**41.9**	38.6	37.5	38.2	36.8
Forum	36.3	**39.2**	35.8	35.3	35.2	35.4
Magazine	40.5	**42.8**	39.7	39.4	40.1	39.4
Parliament	36.8	**48.2**	43.5	47.3	46.5	46.3
All	33.9	**43.2**	39.7	40.3	40.4	39.8

Table 5: Cross-domain performance against heldout newswire data

The causes for the better performance of the +Newswire system are twofold. First, there is less noise in the data because of the two-round process of annotation and adjudication; and second, the bias of this system's annotation is the same as in the evaluation data. Note that the 200-instance data point is past the 150-instance convergence point for the learning curves in Figure 1.

6 Related Work

The AL models considered here are very standard. We take a small seed of data points, train a sequential labeling, and iterate over an unlabeled pool of data, selecting the data points our labeler is least confident about. In the AL literature, the selected data points are often those close to a decision boundary or those most likely to decrease overall uncertainty. This obviously leads to biased sampling, which can sometimes be avoided using different techniques, e.g., by exploiting cluster structure in the data.

Generally, active learning for sequential labeling has received less attention than for classification (Settles and Craven, 2008; Marcheggiani and Artieres, 2014). Our experiments were simple, and several things can be done to improve results, i.e., by reducing sampling bias. In particular, several techniques have been introduced for improving out-of-domain performance using active learning. Rai et al. (2010) perform target-domain AL with a seed of source-domain data. Among other things, they propose to use the source and target unlabeled data to train a classifier to learn what target domain data points are similar to the source domain, in a way similar to Plank et al. (2014). For more work along these lines, see Chan and Ng (2007) and Xiao and Guo (2013).

7 Conclusions

The systems that use the MAX selection strategy have a strong bias for the longest possible sentence, resulting from the low probability values obtained when calculating the prediction confidence of very long sequences. With few exceptions (e.g. an 11-word sentence on the 5th iteration for A_{M_1}), the systems exhaust the maximum-length sentences, and proceed to choose the longest available, and so forth.

We do not take our individual annotator's bias into consideration, but we believe that such bias plays a minor role in the differences of performance between MAX and SAMPLE. For instance, A_{S_2} is the only annotator that was directly involved in the creation of the annotated seed and test data, but has arguably the worst-faring system on overall F1, that is, regardless of how *good* (i.e. how similar in bias to the test data) an annotator is, the selection strategy is the main factor for the improvement rate of the system during active learning. Note however that the data annotated by A_{S_2} does indeed have the lowest KL divergences to the seed and test data in Table 4.

Using SAMPLE lowers the annotator time per sentence because sentences do get shorter, even though the performance is initially lower until the 150-instance convergence point. We propose that with the same amount of time an annotator can annotate more, shorter sentences for the same amount of words and obtain more varied annotations that yield more robust models. Very long sentences do not bring a major advantage, and this justifies sampling when it is necessary to strike a compromise between annotation time and model robustness.

References

Jørg Asmussen and Jakob Halskov. 2012. The clarin dk reference corpus. In *Sprogteknologisk Workshop*.

Yee Seng Chan and Hwee Tou Ng. 2007. Domain adaptation with active learning for word sense disambiguation. In *ACL*.

Aron Culotta and Andrew McCallum. 2005. Reducing labeling effort for structured prediction tasks. In *AAAI*.

Hal Daumé, John Langford, and Daniel Marcu. 2009. Search-based structured prediction. *Machine learning*, 75(3):297–325.

David D Lewis and Jason Catlett. 1994. Heterogenous uncertainty sampling for supervised learning. In *ICML*.

Diego Marcheggiani and Thierry Artieres. 2014. An experimental comparison of active learning strategies for partially labeled sequences. In *EMNLP*.

Héctor Martínez Alonso, Anders Johannsen, Anders Søgaard, Sussi Olsen, Anna Braasch, Sanni Nimb, Nicolai Hartvig Sørensen, and Bolette Sandford Pedersen. 2015. Supersense tagging for danish. In *Nodalida*.

Barbara Plank, Anders Johannsen, and Anders Søgaard. 2014. Importance weighting and unsupervised domain adaptation of POS taggers: a negative result. In *EMNLP*.

Piyush Rai, Avishek Saha, Hal Daume, and Suresh Venkatasubramanian. 2010. Domain adaptation meets active learning. In *Workshop on Active Learning for NLP, NAACL*.

Tobias Scheffer and Stefan Wrobel. 2001. Active learning of partially hidden markov models. In *In Proceedings of the ECML/PKDD Workshop on Instance Selection*.

Burr Settles and Mark Craven. 2008. An analysis of active learning strategies for sequence labeling tasks. In *EMNLP*.

Min Xiao and Yuhong Guo. 2013. Online active learning for cost sensitive domain adaptation. In *CoNLL*.

Uncovering Noun-Noun Compound Relations by Gamification

Johan Bos
Center for Language and Cognition
Oude Kijk in 't Jatstraat 26
University of Groningen
johan.bos@rug.nl

Malvina Nissim
Center for Language and Cognition
Oude Kijk in 't Jatstraat 26
University of Groningen
m.nissim@rug.nl

Abstract

Can relations described by English noun-noun compounds be adequately captured by prepositions? We attempt to answer this question in a data-driven way, using gamification to annotate a set of about a thousand noun-noun compound examples. Annotators could make a choice out of five prepositions generated with the help of paraphrases found in the Google n-gram corpus. We show that there is substantial agreement among the players of our linguistic annotation game, and that their answers differ in about 50% of raw frequency counts of the Google n-gram corpus. Prepositions can be used to describe the majority of the implicit relations present in noun-noun compounds, but not all relations are captured by natural prepositions and some compounds are not easy to paraphrase with the use of a preposition.

1 Introduction

English noun-noun compounds express a relation between the two nouns involved, but this relation isn't made linguistically explicit. So we can have *war crime* meaning a crime **in** a war, or *safety violations* meaning violations **of** safety, or *security guarantees*, meaning guarantees **for** security. In short: the relation between two nouns in a compound expression isn't specified and can take many different roles. This situation introduces an interesting problem for meaning interpretation: what semantic relation is expressed in a noun-noun compound?

There are mainly three different approaches that deal with this problem. The first family of approaches take a (usually small) fixed inventory of relations and use it to describe compounds based on well-established ontologies. The second line of research takes a set of English prepositions to describe compounds (in a way similar as we did above). This makes sense, as prepositions naturally describe a relation between two entities. The seminal work following this tradition is Lauer (Lauer, 1995), who, inspired by Levi's work on fixing a set of possible predicates for interpreting noun-noun compounds (Levi, 1978), developed an inventory comprising eight different prepositions: *of*, *for*, *with*, *in*, *on*, *at*, *about*, and *from*. The third set of attempts views compound interpretation as a paraphrasing task (Nakov, 2007). This would yield interpretations such as "a crime committed during a war" for our earlier example *war crime*.

None of the three approaches show clear advantages. On the one side of the spectrum, the fixed-vocabulary-approach faces the problem of being too strict. On the other end of it, paraphrasing is hard to control. Attempts at combining more than one approach for English (Girju, 2009) or German (Dima et al., 2014) still rely heavily on pre-constructed sets of relations/prepositions, the latter advocating a hybrid approach combining a semantic-relation and preposition-based method.

Given that the preposition-approach lies somewhere between these other two approaches, and can be taken in such a way that is entirely data driven, this is the approach that we will consider and use in this paper. While we are aware of its expressive limitations (prepositions might not be sufficient, and they might preserve some ambiguity of the compound), we still think it is interesting to test to what extent it can be carried out in (i) a completely data-driven fashion and (ii) using judgments by multiple speakers without linguistic training, thus making it extremely inexpensive and light, yet useful. To comply with (i), we make sure that prepositions are not derived from a fixed pre-compiled list, but rather acquired automatically, *case by case*, exploiting Google's n-grams to generate candidates. The compounds themselves are taken from an existing semantically annotated corpus, the Groningen Meaning Bank (Basile et al., 2012). Regarding (ii), we exploit crowd-sourcing and develop a game-with-a-purpose setting to collect data. The acquired data can then be analysed to investigate more closely the use of prepositions for interpreting noun noun compounds and the extent to which different people agree. Moreover, the data can be used to collect descriptive statistics on preposition use in this context that might give new insight into this approach.

2 Method

In this section we describe how we selected noun-noun compounds from a corpus (Step 1), generated potential prepositional relations for each compound (Step 2), and then manually annotated the preposition resembling the underlying meaning relation (Step 3). In what follows we will describe each step in further detail.

The first step is pretty straightforward and makes use of an existing parsed corpus of English texts, and simply looks for a sequence of exactly two nouns (i.e., the words before and after are not tagged as nouns). This excludes compounds comprising three of more nouns but this would only complicate the task (dealing with issues such as internal bracketing) and therefore this limitation allows us to put more focus on our key objectives. On a more detailed note, we take sequences that are tagged NN NN or NN NNS, as English grammar restricts the first noun to be of singular case.

The aim of the second step is to find a set of most likely prepositions that can be used to describe a noun-noun compound expression. This process is carried out with the aid of the Google n-gram corpus. Our starting point are 26 common English prepositions (this is considered to be a closed set, disregarding compound prepositions):

> *of, for, in, on, with, from, by, at, through, into, about, after, between, per, against, over, under, without, before, within, among, via, across, towards, toward,* and *around.*

Next, given a pair N_1–N_2 extracted from the corpus in Step 1, we compute the frequencies of the 4-gram N_2(s)–PREPOSITION–ARTICLE–N_1(s) in the four different singular/plural formations. We use MORPHA and MORPHG to generate all inflected forms of the nouns (Minnen et al., 2001). The articles that we insert in the 4-gram are *a, an* and *the*. For instance, the compound *expansion plan* would generate the following 4-gram patterns:

> plan of a expansion
> plan of an expansion
> plan of the expansion
> plans of a expansion
> ...
> plans for an expansions
> plans for the expansions

In case the number of resulting instances was lower than five, the empty places were filled up with the most frequently used prepositions overall computed for all compounds extracted from the Google n-gram corpus. These were: *of, from, on, for* and *by*. The total for a preposition given a compound is the sum of all frequencies obtained for each single query.

The third step is using the data generated in Step 2 in a GWAP, a *game with a purpose*, in order to collect human judgements. Wordrobe (Venhuizen et al., 2013), an existing internet-based GWAP architecture was used to launch a noun-noun compound annotation task in the shape of a game named *burgers* at `www.wordrobe.org`. Players of this game, not necessarily knowing anything about linguistic annotation, received a snippet of a text with the relevant noun-noun compound marked up in bold face, and were asked to select the most appropriate prepositions of the five candidates generated in Step 2. They were awarded points relative to the agreement of other players' choices for the same question (using add-1 smoothing initially). Players were instructed to hit the *skip* button in case none of the choices seemed to make sense.

A total of 1,296 game questions were generated on March 7, 2013 and released to the GWAP. We did not actively solliciated players, but instead relied solely on regular Wordrobe players or new players that found the game via social media or web links. This way, we gathered a total of 5,368 responses by 187 different GWAP players in the period between release and now (January 26, 2015).

3 Results

The number of annotations in our dataset is 5,195, for a total of 965 different compounds. This yields an average number of 5.4 annotations per compound (min=1, max=138). Most examples had between one and six GWAP players.

A small number of examples were *skipped* by the GWAP players (see previous section): 170 times, for a total of 75 different noun-noun compounds. In most cases these were ill-formed expressions caused by POS-tagging mistakes. Consider for instance the following compounds that were skipped by more than five different players: *capital city, attack north, camp north, c-130 aircraft,* and *accident north*. Except for *c-130 aircraft*, a name-noun compound, these are all mistakenly parsed as noun-noun compounds. This shows that the *skip* function in our annotation game does its job.

To get an idea of the effect of gamification, we took the 100 most frequently answered GWAP questions for further investigation. Within this set, we found that 51 times a preposition formed the majority class that was different from the most frequent preposition in the n-gram corpus found for the corresponding 4-gram patterns (see previous section). This indicates that the GWAP makes a real difference in choice of preposition for a compound.

Prep.	#selected	#majority	Example
about	46	8	security concerns(12)
across	7		border police(2)
after	3		capital city(2)
against	18	2	missile shield(11)
among	56		bird flu(53)
around	12	2	capital city(2)
at	122	19	border checkpoint(19)
before	8		bird flu(5)
between	6	1	government lines(2)
by	143	25	bomb attack(12)
for	1279	248	news agency(65)
from	296	31	bird flu(62)
in	592	65	car bomb(87)
into	17	2	cell research(5)
of	1879	344	death toll(62)
on	308	34	roadside bomb(37)
over	28	3	radio address(10)
per	12	2	capita income(9)
through	13	1	export trade(2)
toward	2		peace process(2)
towards	9		peace process(6)
under	21	1	car bomb(12)
via	7	2	audio messages(4)
with	300	44	bomb attack(26)
within	11		war crimes(2)
without	0		

Table 1: Choice of Prepositions by GWAP players.

In the whole dataset, 25 different prepositions were chosen by GWAP players, but obviously not all were used equally frequently. Its distribution is shown in Table 1. The second column in this table shows the total number of times a given preposition was chosen by a GWAP player. The third column shows the number of times the preposition had the majority of votes. The example in the fourth column is the one where the preposition was chosen in its highest score.

Perhaps unsurprisingly, *of* was picked most frequently. The least common prepositions selected by GWAP players were *across* (7), *between* (6), *after* (3), and *toward* (2). Perhaps this is because these prepositions express quite complex spatial or temporal relations. What Table 1 also shows is the number of times a preposition formed a majority class for a certain noun-noun compound. Relative majority has proven to be a simple but effective method for selected gold-standard values for word sense disambiguation in a GWAP setting (Venhuizen et al., 2013).

Recall that the GWAP players could select one preposition out of a set of five (extracted as described in Section 2). In the large majority of cases, either one (368 compounds) or two (374 compounds) prepositions were chosen. Three different ones were selected in 156 cases, four in 62, and five in 5 cases. Overall, we think this agreement is encouraging.

4 Discussion

It is hard to quantify the results that we obtained in terms of annotator accuracy. But taking a closer look at the results reveals some interesting and promising patterns. First of all, we show some examples of compounds that had unanimous decisions among various annotators (Table 2). Even relatively non-frequent prepositions like *against* were selected in complete agreement by the GWAP players.

Compound	Preposition	# Players
government forces	of	16
agriculture development	of	12
missile shield	against	11
agency chief	of	11
rescue teams	for	9

Table 2: Compounds with unanimous decisions.

Examples of compounds with only two different prepositions chosen by the players are shown in Table 3. In the top part of the table we report cases where one preposition is nevertheless dominant, while in the bottom part more difficult, ambiguous cases can be found.

Compound	prep1(#)	prep2(#)	prep3(#)	prep4(#)	prep5(#)	selected(%)	Total
bird flu	among(53)	before(5)	from(62)	in(16)	against(2)	from(0.45)	138
chemical company	for(5)	from(1)	in(3)	of(3)	within(1)	for(0.38)	13
death toll	in(2)	of(62)	on(6)	for(3)	with(1)	of(0.84)	74
defense official	from(3)	of(7)	at(2)	in(1)	with(1)	of(0.5)	14
background checks	for(1)	in(1)	into(1)	of(2)	on(1)	of(0.33)	6

Table 4: Cases where GWAP players picked at least one of each possible preposition candidate.

Compound	prep1	prep2	selected	# Players
roadside bomb	on(37)	in(2)	on(0.95)	39
assassination plan	for(16)	with(1)	for(0.94)	17
basketball game	in(1)	of(16)	of(0.94)	17
security concerns	about(12)	over(3)	about(0.8)	15
missile strike	of(7)	with(12)	with(0.63)	19
air strike	by(8)	from(9)	from(0.53)	17
army uniform	for(6)	of(7)	of(0.54)	13
army prison	for(5)	of(7)	of(0.58)	12
cell research	into(5)	on(6)	on(0.54)	11

Table 3: Compounds with two different choices.

The examples shown in this table show that in various cases more than one preposition seems accurate: *bomb* ***on*** *the roadside* or *bomb* ***in*** *the roadside* both express a spatial relation, and both prepositions would probably be accursate. Similarly, *concerns* ***about*** *security* or *concerns* ***over*** *security* seem both appropriate paraphrases of the compound. It also illustrates the fact that the more underspecified *of* is often chosen together with other, more specific prepositions. This shows both the advantage and disadvantage of using prepositions as relations: like other words, prepositions are ambiguous, and there is substantial overlap in meaning between the prepositions one finds in the English language. This makes them more flexible, but also less formal.

The data also supports the observation that prepositions that carry some logical meaning (such as negation) are unsuitable to describe relations between two entities found in noun-noun compounds. A clear case is *without*, that was never selected by a GWAP player (Table 1), whose lexical meaning could be paraphrased as *not with*. As negation is not related to any general kind of concept, a noun-noun compound would never be able to catch this aspect of meaning. Similarly, *after* and *before* carry some negation in their lexical meaning (as in *not at the same time*), and again the data supports this as they never formed the majority class.

Finally, in Table 4 we list those cases where all GWAP players selected at least one of each possible answers. Such a situation could be evidence that the relational meaning of a compound is hard to catch by a preposition. Certainly, the more players answered a specific question, the higher the chance that all possible candidates were selected at least once (for instance, taking into account the fact that players make mistakes). This seems to be the case for the first example in Table 4 where *before* and *against* are odd choices, but they are clearly outperformed by *among* and *from* that both seem adequate choices.

5 Conclusion

We showed that a data-driven approach to finding prepositions describing noun-noun compound relations is feasible. Simple raw frequencies of prepositional paraphrases aren't likely to get useful results. We demonstrated that a game with a purpose yields good results to find appropriate prepositions for this task. The results will be used to improve the Groningen Meaning Bank, a large corpus of semantically-annotated texts (Basile et al., 2012).

Compared to Lauer, we opted for a more data-driven choice of prepositions, rather than restricting ourselves to Lauer's set of eight prepositions. None of these prepositions would fit the compound *missile shield* but in our approach *against* would be selected as relation (see Table 2). We clearly benefit from such cases.

In future work it would be worthy to try to map prepositions to unambiguous relations, or attempt to group prepositions that bear similar meanings. One interesting way is to look at answer patterns in the data to disambiguate the very general preposition *of*, by taking into account other answers as well instead of just considering the majority class. Similarly, it would be interesting to see if one can predict idiosyncratic compounds such as *suicide bomber*, whose implicit relation is hard to catch by a preposition.

References

Valerio Basile, Johan Bos, Kilian Evang, and Noortje Venhuizen. 2012. A platform for collaborative semantic annotation. In *Proceedings of the Demonstrations at the 13th Conference of the European Chapter of the Association for Computational Linguistics (EACL)*, pages 92–96, Avignon, France.

Corina Dima, Verena Henrich, Erhard Hinrichs, and Christina Hoppermann. 2014. How to Tell a Schneemann from a Milchmann: An Annotation Scheme for Compound-Internal Relations. In Calzolari et al., editor, *Proceedings of the Ninth International Conference on Language Resources and Evaluation (LREC'14)*, Reykjavik, Iceland, may. European Language Resources Association (ELRA).

Roxana Girju. 2009. The syntax and semantics of prepositions in the task of automatic interpretation of nominal phrases and compounds: A cross-linguistic study. *Computational Linguistics*, 35(2):185–228.

Mark Lauer. 1995. Corpus statistics meet the noun compound: Some empirical results. In *Proceedings of the 33rd Annual Meeting of the Association for Computational Linguistics*, pages 47–54, Cambridge, Massachusetts, USA, June. Association for Computational Linguistics.

Judith Levi. 1978. *The Syntax and Semantics of Complex Nominals*. Academic Press.

Guido Minnen, John Carroll, and Darren Pearce. 2001. Applied morphological processing of English. *Journal of Natural Language Engineering*, 7(3):207–223.

Preslav Ivanov Nakov. 2007. *Using the Web as an Implicit Training Set: Application to Noun Compound Syntax and Semantics*. Ph.D. thesis, University of California, Berkeley.

Noortje Venhuizen, Valerio Basile, Kilian Evang, and Johan Bos. 2013. Gamification for Word Sense Labeling. In *Proceedings of the 10th International Conference on Computational Semantics (IWCS 2013) – Short Papers*, pages 397–403, Potsdam, Germany.

A multivariate model for classifying texts' readability

Katarina Heimann Mühlenbock, Sofie Johansson Kokkinakis
Department of Swedish, University of Gothenburg, Sweden
katarina.heimann.muhlenbock@gu.se, sofie.johansson.kokkinakis@gu.se

Caroline Liberg, Åsa af Geijerstam, Jenny Wiksten Folkeryd
Department of Education, Uppsala University, Sweden

Arne Jönsson, Erik Kanebrant, Johan Falkenjack
Department of Computer and Information Science, Linköping University, Sweden

Abstract

We report on results from using the multivariate readability model SVIT to classify texts into various levels. We investigate how the language features integrated in the SVIT model can be transformed to values on known criteria like vocabulary, grammatical fluency and propositional knowledge. Such text criteria, sensitive to content, readability and genre in combination with the profile of a student's reading ability form the base of individually adapted texts. The procedure of levelling texts into different stages of complexity is presented along with results from the first cycle of tests conducted on 8th grade students. The results show that SVIT can be used to classify texts into different complexity levels.

1 Introduction

Standardized international tests demonstrate a continuous deterioration for Swedish 15-year-olds when it comes to knowledge in mathematics, reading and science (OECD, 2014). The task of finding adequate texts to fit the individual student's reading level is by necessity one of the most challenging and important tasks for teachers today. To facilitate this, tools for teachers are needed that allow individual reading comprehension testing, presenting a reading profile for each student and suggestions of texts suitable with regard to genre, age and reading level. Essential to this endeavour is the ability to measure text complexity; which is what the SVIT model (Heimann Mühlenbock, 2013) is designed to do.

In this paper we will start in Section 2 by presenting how text complexity is measured, how the texts were selected and levelled, and how the tests were carried out. In Section 3 we present the first results from a subset of the tests carried out in the first year of the project. The correspondence between the text levelling and the students' results will be discussed in Section 4, and a final discussion on to which extent the results from the tests actually agree with the automatic selection and levelling of texts will follow in Section 5.

2 Method

The first task was to find adequate reading materials for each of the three school grades. Automated readability assessment has long rested upon very simplified heuristics for text complexity. Most measurements contain a factor that relates to a text's average sentence length and another factor related to the average word length (Flesch, 1948; Gunning, 1952; Senter and Smith, 1967; McLaughlin, 1969; Coleman and Liau, 1975; Kincaid et al., 1975). The underlying assumption is that the sentence length to some extent is correlated with the syntactic complexity and that the word length reflects the semantic load of a text. We used a more sophisticated method based on the SVIT model (Heimann Mühlenbock, 2013) for grading a bank of texts into appropriate levels. The first cycle of tests was devoted to investigating narrative texts, while texts concerning civics and science will follow in future studies.

After text selection, reading comprehension tests of narrative texts suiting students in the 4th, 6th and 8th grades in 74 Swedish schools were carried out on more than 4000 students. The schools were situated in three major Swedish municipalities, one for each grade. All the tests were given anonymously, and only the teacher was able to see the results from the individual students.

2.1 SVIT

Quantitative measures of readability are appealing since they are easy to perform computationally. The obvious drawback of measuring text phenomena at the surface level is that the results are purely descriptive and not interpretive. This is why readability researchers long struggled to find an easy and cost efficient way to devise a link between the quantitative textual properties and the qualitative characteristics. Eventually, the most widely known and used methods for readability measurement built upon formulas containing both a semantic and a syntactic variable. The semantic component is expected to be expressed in the vocabulary use, and more precisely in the texts average word length. The syntactic properties are accordingly anticipated to be found in the sentence structure through calculation of the average sentence length. The Swedish LIX Readability Index is based on these principles (Björnsson, 1968).

A multilevel theoretical readability framework considers additional levels of language and discourse. Chall (1958) proposed four different elements to be significant for a readability criterion; namely vocabulary load, sentence structure, idea density and human interest. Graesser et al (2011) distinguish five levels, including words, syntax, text base, situation mode,l and genre and rhetorical structure. The two theories are consistent in that they, in addition to vocabulary and syntactical properties, also consider the message intended to be conveyed in a text, through analysis of the idea density or text base. The genre structure refers to the category of text, while the situation model is assumed to capture the subject matter content of the text and inferences that are activated by the explicit text. Finally, the human interest level proposed by Chall is evidently strongly tied to the readers experiences and thus the least prone to external inspection.

The SVIT language model (Heimann Mühlenbock, 2013) includes a combination of properties at the surface, vocabulary, syntactical and idea density levels. The surface level measurement includes simple word and sentence length counts, but also measures of extra-long words (>13 characters), and token iteration. At the vocabulary level we find the vocabulary properties analysed in terms of word lemma variation and the proportion of words belonging to a Swedish base vocabulary (Heimann Mühlenbock and Johansson Kokkinakis, 2012). The syntactic level is inspected through measurements of mean distance between items in the syntactically parsed trees, mean parse tree heights, and the proportions of subordinate clauses and nominal modifiers. The idea density is supposed to be revealed through calculations of average number of propositions, nominal ratio and noun/pronoun ratio. Finally, it is assumed that the personal interest to some extent might be captured through the proportion of proper nouns in a text. We will focus on the results achieved for the most prominent features, i.e. those who were expected to be least mutually correlated. Some of the features listed in Table 1 are quite straightforward, while others need an explanation.

The *Lemma variation index* is calculated with the formula:

$$LVIX = \frac{\log(N)}{\log(2 - \frac{\log(U)}{\log(N)})}$$

where N = Number of lemmas and U = Number of unique lemmas

Words considered as *Difficult words* are those not present in category (C), (D), or (H) in the SweVoc base vocabulary. In category (C) we find 2,200 word lemmas belonging to the core vocabulary. Category (D) contains word lemmas referring to everyday objects and actions. Category (H), finally, holds word lemmas highly frequent in written text. In all, 4,700 word lemmas are included in these categories. The values in Table 2 refer to the mean percentage of the lemmas complementary to the mentioned categories.

The syntactic features *MDD*, *UA*, *AT*, *ET* and *PT* refer to properties in the dependency parsed sentences in the texts.

The *Nominal ratio* is achieved by calculating the proportion of nouns, prepositions and participles in relation to verbs, pronouns and adverbs.

2.2 Text selection method

In all, 22 texts from the LäSBarT corpus (Heimann Mühlenbock, 2013) and 31 texts from a bank of National reading tests were checked with the goal of finding suitable portions of narrative texts for the intended group of readers in the 4th, 6th and 8th Swedish school grades, which corresponds to students aged from 10 to 15 years.

2.3 Levelling texts

After the first manual check, the texts were graded into 7 levels of difficulty after multivariate analysis based on the SVIT model. The texts were classified manually after inspection of the SVIT values.

Level	Feature	Abbrev
Surface	Mean sentence length	MSL
	Mean word length in characters	MWL
Vocabulary	Lemma variation index	LVIX
	Difficult words	DW
Syntactic	Mean dependency distance	MDD
	Subordinate clauses	UA
	Prenominal modifier	AT
	Postnominal modifier	ET
	Parse tree height	PT
Idea density	Nominal ratio	NR

Table 1: SVIT features

Earlier experiments showed that for the task of differentiating between ordinary and easy-to-read childrens fiction, language features at the vocabulary and idea density levels were found to have the highest impact on the discriminative power. The features mirroring vocabulary diversity and difficulty, and idea density were given precedence when the metrics did not unambiguously point towards significant differences at the syntactic level.

For the students who attended 8th grade, six texts were selected based on the SVIT-values, ranging between 527 and 1166 words in length. The texts were then split into two groups (Group 1 and Group 2) with similar internal distribution between easier and more difficult texts. We will here present here the properties of the hardest and the easiest of the six texts, both present in Group 1. The two texts were not of equal length, but the students were allowed to read the texts and answer the questions at their own pace.

The easiest text (Text 1) was a short story retrieved from the collection of National reading tests, entitled *Att fiska med morfar* 'Fishing with Grandpa' by Ulf Stark. The most difficult text (Text 2) was also picked from the National reading tests. It is entitled *Populärmusik från Vittula* 'Popular music from Vittula', written by Mikael Niemi. Some of their respective values are shown in Table 2.

Based on the SVIT-values, we can derive the following information about the two texts:

Text 1 shows low average values regarding word and sentence lengths. At the vocabulary level, the word lemma variation is at medium level for the six texts. The syntactic complexity is very low, both regarding prenominal modifiers and parse tree height. The idea density level is below average.

Text 2 is slightly above average regarding word length. The word lemma variation index and percentage of difficult words are both considerably above average. The syntactic complexity is slightly above average for all features. Finally, the idea density is above average.

2.4 Testing method

Items testing two overall reading processes were constructed for each of the three texts (Langer, 2011; Luke and Freebody, 1999; Mullis et al., 2009; OECD, 2009):

1. Retrieve explicitly stated information and make straightforward inferences

2. Interpret and integrate ideas and information and reflect on, examine and evaluate content, language, and textual elements

In assessing the vocabulary knowledge of students, we focused on the receptive knowledge of subject and domain neutral content words in Swedish novels as test items. We used a reliable approach to create vocabulary tests similar to the Vocabulary Levels Test (VLT) (Nation, 2001). The test items were extracted from a frequency based vocabulary list of compiled corpora representing each level of text difficulty. The test items were presented in context in an authentic sentence taken from the text book. Three alternative meanings of the test item and one correct meaning were presented to the student. The alternative meanings (distractors) were similar to the test item regarding phonology or orthography.

332 students in the 8th grade in 5 schools in Gothenburg participated. The teachers were instructed to allow the students to read the texts and answer the questions at their own pace, which usually corresponded to a total time of one lesson per test. The tests were administered as paper questionnaires and the texts were read on paper.

3 Results from students' testings

The results presented here concern 94 students who performed all three tests on texts in Group 1, which included the two texts with SVIT-values exemplified in Table 2, deemed as the easiest and

Text	Surface features		Vocabulary features		Syntactical features					Idea density
	MSL	MWL	LVIX	DW	MDD	UA	AT	ET	PT	NR
Text 1	9.7	4.2	54.1	23.0	2.2	0.3	0.1	0.3	4.9	0.44
Text 2	11.3	4.8	69.8	33.0	2.1	0.3	0.3	0.4	5.5	0.70

Table 2: SVIT values

the most difficult. For each text, the students answered 12 questions regarding the content and 15 questions regarding the understanding of isolated words not present in the texts.

3.1 Text reading results

On average, students' performance on Text 1 was 74.2% correctness on content questions, and 68.3% on Text 2. These results indicate, that the texts were well adapted for the age group, but also that Text 2 was perceived as more difficult by the normally performing students.

For the low-performing students, the correlation between the results, i.e. correctness on content questions, and text complexity was even more obvious. 26 students scored <1 S.D. of the students' results. On average, they had 55.2% correctness on content questions for Text 1, and 37.0% correctness for Text 2. Furthermore, the 10 students who presented results <2 S.D. below normal scored on average 48.2% and 36.7%, respectively.

3.2 Vocabulary results

As could be expected, we found that there was a strong correlation between reading comprehension and vocabulary knowledge. The correlation was significant, 0.68 resp. 0.63 with Pearson's correlation at level 0.01.

4 Correspondence between readers and texts

When looking at the overall reading processes, it was found that among the 26 low-performing students, 12 showed reading profiles indicating that they were only able to correctly answer a few of the text-based and the interpretive and evaluative questions. They were assumed to work only on individual parts of the text and were most likely not able to grasp the big picture in the texts and how different aspects of the text were related. They all performed better on Text 1 than Text 2. Five students were found to perform pretty well on the text-based questions but not as good when it came to the interpretive and evaluative questions on Text 1. None of these students were able to correctly answer more than a few of the text-based and the interpretive and evaluative questions on Text 2. For the remaining low-performing students the results were more mixed. Four of them had a reading profile which implied rather good results on the text-based, interpretive and evaluative questions on Text 1, but did not grasp the content of Text 2. Finally, 5 students performed somewhat better on Text 2 than on Text 1, but were still not able to entirely comprehend the content of any of the two texts.

5 Discussion

We have presented an approach that investigates the extent to which automated text levelling with a multivariate analysis based on the SVIT language model really proved to correspond to students' actual reading performance. We found that the participating students performed better on the text judged as the easiest as opposed to the most difficult, with a mean difference in correctness of 5.9%. Furthermore, the low-performing students showed a significant difference in correctness of 18.2% between the two texts. These findings support the hypothesis that the SVIT readability model based on language features derived computationally, and present at deeper levels than the purely superficial, can devise a link between quantitative and qualitative text characteristics. Further studies investigating the efficiency on levelling texts from other genres than fiction will follow.

References

Carl Hugo Björnsson. 1968. *Läsbarhet*. Liber, Stockholm.

Jeanne S. Chall. 1958. *Readability: An appraisal of research and application*. Ohio State University Press, Columbus, OH.

Meri Coleman and Ta Lin Liau. 1975. A computer readability formula designed for machine scoring. *Journal of Applied Psychology*, 60:283–284.

Rudolf Flesch. 1948. A new readability yardstick. *Journal of Applied Psychology*, 32(3):221–233.

Arthur C. Graesser, Danielle S. McNamara, and Jonna M. Kulikowich. 2011. Coh-metrix. *Educational Researcher*, 40(5):223–234.

Robert Gunning. 1952. *The technique of clear writing*. McGraw-Hill International Book Co., New York, NY.

Katarina Heimann Mühlenbock and Sofie Johansson Kokkinakis. 2012. SweVoc – A Swedish vocabulary resource for CALL. In *Proceedings of the SLTC 2012 workshop on NLP for CALL*, pages 28–34, Lund, October. Linköping University Electronic Press.

Katarina Heimann Mühlenbock. 2013. *I see what you mean. Assessing readability for specific target groups*. Dissertation, Språkbanken, Dept of Swedish, University of Gothenburg.

J. Peter Kincaid, Robert P. Fishburne, Richard L. Rogers, and Brad S. Chissom. 1975. Derivation of new readability formulas (Automated Readability Index, Fog Count, and Flesch Reading Ease Formula) for Navy enlisted personnel. Technical report, U.S. Naval Air Station, Millington, TN.

Judith A. Langer. 2011. *Envisioning Knowledge. Building Literacy in the Academic Disciplines*. New York: Teachers' College Press.

Allan Luke and Peter Freebody. 1999. Further notes on the four resources model. Reading Online. http://www.readingonline.org/research/lukefreebody.html.

G. Harry McLaughlin. 1969. SMOG grading – a New Readability Formula. *Journal of Reading*, 12(8):639–646.

Ina V.S. Mullis, Michael O. Martin, Ann M. Kennedy, Kathleen L. Trong, and Marian Sainsbury. 2009. *PIRLS 2011 Assessment Framework*. PIRLS 2011 Assessment Framework.

Paul Nation. 2001. *Learning vocabulary in another language*. Cambridge University Press.

OECD. 2009. Pisa 2009 Assessment Framework. Key Competencies in reading, mathematics and science. Paris: OECD.

OECD. 2014. Pisa 2012. Results in Focus. What 15-year-olds know and what they can do with what they know. Paris: OECD.

R.J. Senter and E. A. Smith. 1967. Automated readability index. Technical report, Cincinnati Univ. Ohio, Cincinnati Univ. Ohio.

Enriching the Swedish Sign Language Corpus with Part of Speech Tags Using Joint Bayesian Word Alignment and Annotation Transfer

Robert Östling, Carl Börstell, Lars Wallin
Department of Linguistics
Stockholm University
SE-106 91 Stockholm
{robert,calle,wallin}@ling.su.se

Abstract

We have used a novel Bayesian model of joint word alignment and part of speech (PoS) annotation transfer to enrich the Swedish Sign Language Corpus with PoS tags. The annotations were then hand-corrected in order to both improve annotation quality for the corpus, and allow the empirical evaluation presented herein.

1 Introduction

While Swedish Sign Language (SSL) is a recognized language of Sweden, there are no NLP tools available for it. We used a novel method for part of speech (PoS) annotation transfer to create the first automatically PoS-tagged corpus of any sign language, by exploiting the existing translation of the corpus into written Swedish. We then manually corrected the resulting annotations, in order to provide high-quality data that could be used for e.g. future supervised PoS taggers.

2 Parts of Speech in Sign Languages

In early sign language (SL) linguistics, Supalla and Newport (1978) observed that consistent phonological patterns can distinguish PoS in phonologically and semantically related noun–verb pairs in American SL: nouns more often being restrained and repeated; verbs having a continuous articulation. A number of studies have similarly investigated nouns and verbs in a variety of SLs—e.g. Johnston (2001) for Australian SL; Hunger (2006) for Austrian SL; Kimmelman (2009) for Russian SL; and Tkachman and Sandler (2013) for Al-Sayyid Bedouin SL and Israeli SL—finding that e.g. manner, repetition, duration, size and mouthing[1] can differentiate nouns from verbs. However, extensive research of PoS in SLs is generally lacking (Schwager and Zeshan, 2008).

Turning to SSL, one study looked at morphosyntactic constraints differentiating e.g. verbs and adjectives (Bergman, 1983), and a recent overview of the linguistic structure of SSL lists 8 PoS (Ahlgren and Bergman, 2006)—based mainly on semantic and syntactic criteria identified in previous research—which is the set used in this work.

There are currently a number of ongoing SL corpus projects around the world, but few of them have extensive annotations for e.g. grammatical categories. One exception is the Auslan Corpus (Johnston, 2010), which features annotations of "grammatical classes" that to a large extent correspond to functional PoS (Johnston, 2014). However, the annotations in all of these SL corpora are done manually, which is rather time-consuming.

3 The Swedish Sign Language Corpus

The Swedish Sign Language Corpus (SSLC) (Mesch et al., 2012; Mesch et al., 2014) contains 25 hrs of partially transcribed, conversational data from 42 different signers of SSL. Its annotations mainly consist of a gloss for each sign (see 4.3), and a translation into written Swedish. The version used in our evaluations contains 24 976 SSL tokens, not sentence-segmented, and 41 910 Swedish tokens divided into 3 522 sentences.

Segmenting SSL data into sentences or utterances is no trivial task (Börstell et al., 2014), and there is currently no such segmentation in the SSLC. In order to use sentence-based word alignment models, we follow Sjons (2013) in using the Swedish sentences as a basis for segmentation.

[1] *Mouthing* refers to a mouth movement imitating that of a spoken word, i.e. as if silently articulating a word.

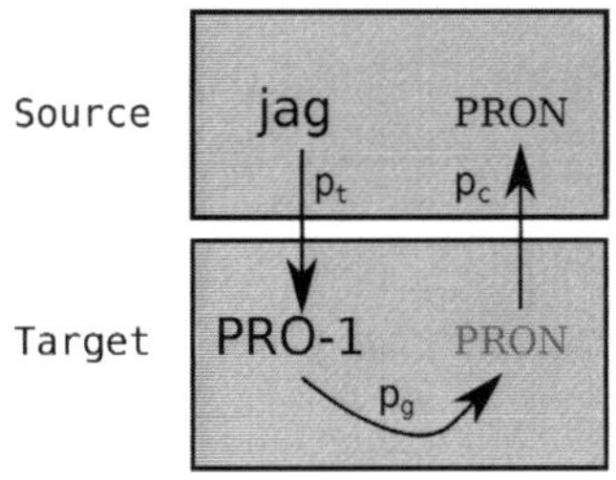

Figure 1: Circular generation model for joint word alignment and part of speech transfer, where Swedish *jag* 'I' is aligned to the SSLC gloss PRO-1. All variables are observed except the alignment and the target-side PoS tag (in grey).

4 Method

Since SSLC contains translations of each utterance into written Swedish, it is in effect a parallel corpus of Swedish and SSL. It has long been recognized that parallel corpora are useful for transfering annotation between languages (Yarowsky et al., 2001), and so our goal is to automatically transfer part of speech (PoS) tags from the Swedish translations to the SSL glosses. Given the relatively small size of the corpus, and the significant differences between the two languages, the error rate is expected to be high enough to warrant a final stage of manual correction.

4.1 Bayesian word alignment

Most previous research on word alignment has been building on the IBM models Brown et al. (1993) using Expectation-Maximization (EM) for inference. Recently, Bayesian models have been proposed as an alternative, offering a theoretically well-founded way of introducing soft constraints that encourage linguistically plausible solutions (DeNero et al., 2008; Mermer and Saraçlar, 2011; Riley and Gildea, 2012; Gal and Blunsom, 2013).

4.2 Alignment and part of speech transfer

Several authors, starting from Brown et al. (1993), have used word classes to aid word alignment in various manners. Toutanova et al. (2002) show that if both parts of a bitext are annotated with PoS tags, alignment accuracy can be improved simply by using a tag translation model $p(t_f|t_e)$ in addition to the word translation model $p(f|e)$.

Given that PoS tags improves the quality of word alignments, and that word alignments can be used to transfer PoS tags from one language to another, we use a model that jointly learns PoS tags and word alignment.

Figure 1 illustrates our *circular generation model*, so termed because a source language token is assumed to generate a target language token (through $p_t(f|e) = \theta_{te}$), which then generates its corresponding PoS tag (through $p_g(t_f|f) = \theta_{gf}$), which finally generates a PoS tag for the source language token (through $p_c(t_e|t_f) = \theta ct_f$).

We assume categorical distributions with Dirichlet priors:

$$\theta_t \sim \text{Dir}(\alpha_t); \theta_g \sim \text{Dir}(\alpha_g); \theta_c \sim \text{Dir}(\alpha_c)$$

These priors are symmetrical, except for α_c which is biased towards consistency between the tagsets. In our evaluations, we use $\alpha_c = 1000$ for consistent tag pairs, $\alpha_c = 1$ for others.

Inference in this model is performed using collapsed Gibbs sampling, where the alignment variable a_j (which links target token f_j to source token e_i) is sampled jointly with the target PoS tag t_{f_j}. The sampling equation is similar to those used by Mermer and Saraçlar (2011) and Gal and Blunsom (2013), with extra factors for the PoS tag dependencies. We also use the HMM-based word order model of Vogel et al. (1996), but as this does not directly interact with the PoS tags, we exclude it from Figure 1 for clarity.

From this model we obtain SSL part of speech tags in one of two different ways: directly from the model (the t_{f_j} variables), or by direct projection through the final alignment variables a_j. In both cases the sampling procedure is identical, the difference lies only in how the final PoS tags are read out.

4.3 Data processing

SSLC is annotated using the ELAN software (Wittenburg et al., 2006). Annotations are arranged into *tiers*, each containing a sequence of annotations with time slots. For the present study, two types of tiers are of interest: the signs of the dominant hand and the Swedish sentences. Signs are transcribed using glosses, whose names are most often derived from a corresponding word or expression in Swedish. Each gloss may also have a number of properties marked, such as which hand it was performed with, whether it was reduplicated, interrupted, and so on. The annotation conventions are described in further detail by Wallin et al. (2014).

The first step of processing is to group SSL glosses according to which Swedish sentence they overlap most with. Second, glosses with certain marks are removed:

- Interrupted signs (marked `@&`).
- Gestures (marked `@g`).
- Incomprehensible signs (transcribed as `XXX`).

Finally, some marks are simply stripped from glosses, since they are not considered important to the current task.

- Signs performed with the non-dominant hand (marked `@nh`).
- Signs held with the non-dominant hand during production of signs with the dominant hand. The gloss of the held sign (following a <> symbol) is removed.
- Signs where the annotator is uncertain about which sign was used (marked `@xxx`) or whether the correct gloss was chosen (marked `@zzz`).

In all, this is nearly identical to the procedure used by Sjons (2013, p. 14). Example 1 illustrates the output of the processing, with English glosses and translation added.

(1) STÄMMA OCKSÅ PRO-1 PERF BARN
be.correct also 1 PRF children
BRUKA SE SAGA^TRÄD PRO>*närv*
usually watch Sagoträdet 2
'I also have children—do you watch Sagoträdet?'

The Swedish translations were tokenized and PoS-tagged with Stagger (Östling, 2013), trained on the Stockholm-Umeå Corpus (SUC) (Ejerhed et al., 1992; Källgren, 2006) and the Stockholm Internet Corpus (SIC).[2]

4.4 Evaluation data

At the outset of the project, two annotators manually assigned PoS tags to the 371 most frequent sign glosses in the corpus. This was used for initial annotation transfer evaluations, and when the methods reached a certain level of maturity the remaining gloss types were automatically annotated, and the resulting list of 3 466 glosses manually corrected. Thus the initial goal of using annotation transfer to facilitate the PoS annotation was achieved, since all of the currently transcribed SSLC data now has manually verified annotations.

[2]`http://www.ling.su.se/sic`

PoS	SSLC	SUC
Pronoun	PN	DT, HD, HP, HS, PS, PN
Noun	NN	NN, PM, UO
Verb	VB	PC, VB
Adverb	AB	AB, HA, IE, IN, PL
Numeral	RG	RG, RO
Adjective	JJ	JJ
Preposition	PP	PP
Conjunction	KN	KN, SN

Table 1: PoS tags in the SSLC, and their counterparts in SUC.

In order to evaluate the performance of the annotation transfer algorithms, we use this final set of 3 466 annotated types as a gold standard.

4.5 Tag set conversion

As previously mentioned, we use the eight PoS categories suggested by Ahlgren and Bergman (2006) for SSL. The Swedish side is tagged using the SUC tagset, whose core consists of 22 tags (Källgren, 2006, p. 20). For direct tag projection and the tag translation priors in the circular generation model, the SUC tags are translated as in Table 1.

4.6 Task-specific constraints

SSLC contains various annotations that are useful for part of speech tagging. First of all, a few parts of speech are already apparent from the annotation: proper nouns (marked `@en`), pronouns (begin with PRO- or POSS-), and classifier constructions (marked `@p`, considered to be verbs). Second, the choice of gloss (in Swedish) correlates strongly with the SSL part of speech. In Example 1, for instance, the part of speech of most signs can be correctly guessed from the gloss alone, although sometimes this is not possible due ambiguity (e.g. *stämma* is ambiguous between noun and verb) or because the gloss name is not a Swedish word (e.g. PERF). We exploit this correspondence by requiring glosses to be tagged consistently with the SALDO morphological lexicon (Borin and Forsberg, 2009). That is, if the SALDO lexicon says that the name of a gloss is a Swedish word form with an unambiguous word class, this word class will always be assumed for the gloss. As can be seen from the baseline row in Table 2,

	Types		Tokens	
	Project	**Model**	**Project**	**Model**
baseline	$58.4 \pm 0.5\%$	$12.2 \pm 0.6\%$	$75.3 \pm 0.7\%$	$10.8 \pm 3.6\%$
constraints	$58.4 \pm 0.4\%$	$60.7 \pm 0.4\%$	$75.1 \pm 0.8\%$	$58.1 \pm 1.0\%$
circular	$64.7 \pm 0.5\%$	$68.3 \pm 0.4\%$	$77.4 \pm 0.8\%$	$77.6 \pm 0.7\%$
circular + bigrams	$64.8 \pm 0.3\%$	$68.4 \pm 0.3\%$	$77.3 \pm 0.7\%$	$77.6 \pm 0.7\%$
circular + constraints	$69.1 \pm 0.4\%$	$77.1 \pm 0.3\%$	$79.7 \pm 0.6\%$	$78.7 \pm 0.6\%$

Table 2: Token-level PoS tagging accuracy, using direct projection from the final alignment (projection) or for the joint models, the sampled PoS tag variables t_{f_j} (model). Note that in the former case, the PoS tag variables are ignored except during the alignment process. Figures given are averages $\pm$ standard deviation estimated over 64 randomly initialized evaluations for each configuration.

these constraints alone reach a fairly high level of accuracy.

5 Results

Table 2 shows the per-type and per-token accuracy for a number of different configurations, using both direct projection (*project*) and the sampled t_{f_j} PoS tag variables (*model*). While the model itself assigns tags on the token level, when obtaining the figures in Table 2 we ensure type-level tagging by assigning each token the majority tag of its type. This is also done for the *tokens* columns. Since the SSLC annotation does not contain glosses with ambiguous part of speech, using only token-level would introduce unnecessary noise.

The *baseline* model performs word alignment only, assigning random values to the PoS tag variables. Projection accuracy is fair (indicating that the word alignments are acceptable), but the much lower scores in the *model* columns represent an entirely random baseline. When the constraints described in Section 4.6 are enforced during sampling, the *model* scores increase as expected. Without coupling between the word alignment and PoS tags, the projected tags are not changed.

Using the circular generation model, the coupling between PoS tags and word alignment leads to better accuracy, as expected. This is also the case when using direct projection, indicating that the joint model increases word alignment quality (which we are unable to evaluate directly, lacking a gold standard word alignment).

Adding bigram dependencies between SSLC PoS tags allows the model to use (monolingual) contextual information, but this does not seem to affect the accuracy. The probable reason for this is that the coupling between Swedish and SSLC PoS tags is quite strong, and the contextual information can not significantly affect the final tagging.

The best results were obtained by using the circular model in conjunction with enforcing the task-specific constraints. The improvement when adding the constraints is particularly large on the type level, because this allows reasonable guesses for many of the rare types where there is not enough data for reliable word alignments. This is important for our goal, since we actually want type-based part of speech assignments.

The 77% accurate type-level tag list was manually corrected by two annotators (reaching consensus) in order to obtain the final tagging of the corpus, which is also used as the gold standard for the evaluation described in this section.

6 Conclusions

We have shown that annotation transfer, performed in a Bayesian model of joint word alignment and part of speech transfer, can be a useful tool when annotating a sign language corpus with parts of speech.

It should be stressed that our conclusions apply to this particular data set, which is rather untypical for annotation projection tasks, especially due to its limited size. Work carried out in parallel with the present study indicates that for longer parallel texts with better translations, other models may be more accurate. Since the primary aim of this study was to investigate methods for annotating the SSLC, rather than exploring annotation transfer in general, we are not currently concerned with other data.

References

Inger Ahlgren and Brita Bergman. 2006. Det svenska teckenspråket. In *Teckenspråk och teckenspråkiga: kunskaps- och forskningsöversikt*, volume 2006:29 of *Statens offentliga utredningar (SoU)*, pages 11–70. Ministry of Health and Social Affairs, March.

Brita Bergman. 1983. Verbs and adjectives: morphological processes in Swedish Sign Language. In Jim Kyle and Bencie Woll, editors, *Language in sign: An international perspective on sign language*, pages 3–9, London. Croom Helm.

Lars Borin and Markus Forsberg. 2009. All in the family: A comparison of SALDO and WordNet. In *NODALIDA 2009 Workshop on WordNets and other Lexical Semantic Resources – between Lexical Semantics, Lexicography, Terminology and Formal Ontologies*, pages 7–12, Odense, Denmark.

Carl Börstell, Johanna Mesch, and Lars Wallin. 2014. Segmenting the Swedish Sign Language corpus: On the possibilities of using visual cues as a basis for syntactic segmentation. In Onno Crasborn, Eleni Efthimiou, Evita Fotinea, Thomas Hanke, Julie Hochgesang, Jette Kristoffersen, and Johanna Mesch, editors, *Beyond the Manual Channel. Proceedings of the 6th Workshop on the Representation and Processing of Sign Languages*, pages 7–10, Reykjavík, Iceland. ELRA.

Peter F. Brown, Vincent J. Della Pietra, Stephen A. Della Pietra, and Robert L. Mercer. 1993. The mathematics of statistical machine translation: Parameter estimation. *Computational Linguistics*, 19(2):263–311, June.

John DeNero, Alexandre Bouchard-Côté, and Dan Klein. 2008. Sampling alignment structure under a Bayesian translation model. In *Proceedings of the 2008 Conference on Empirical Methods in Natural Language Processing*, pages 314–323, Honolulu, Hawaii, October. Association for Computational Linguistics.

E. Ejerhed, G. Källgren, O. Wennstedt, and M. Åström. 1992. The linguistic annotation system of the Stockholm-Umeå corpus project. Technical report, Department of Linguistics, University of Umeå.

Yarin Gal and Phil Blunsom. 2013. A systematic Bayesian treatment of the IBM alignment models. In *Proceedings of the 2013 Conference of the North American Chapter of the Association for Computational Linguistics: Human Language Technologies*, Stroudsburg, PA, USA. Association for Computational Linguistics.

Barbara Hunger. 2006. Noun/verb pairs in Austrian Sign Language (ÖGS). *Sign Language & Linguistics*, 9(1/2):71–94, January.

Trevor Johnston. 2001. Nouns and verbs in Australian sign language: An open and shut case? *Journal of Deaf Studies and Deaf Education*, 6(4):235–57, January.

Trevor Johnston. 2010. From archive to corpus: Transcription and annotation in the creation of signed language corpora. *International Journal of Corpus Linguistics*, 15(1):106–131.

Trevor Johnston. 2014. Auslan corpus annotation guidelines. Centre for Language Sciences, Department of Linguistics, Macquarie University.

Vadim Kimmelman. 2009. Parts of speech in Russian Sign Language: The role of iconicity and economy. *Sign Language & Linguistics*, 12(2):161–186.

Gunnel Källgren, 2006. *Manual of the Stockholm Umeå Corpus version 2.0.* Department of Linguistics, Stockholm University, December. Sofia Gustafson-Capková and Britt Hartmann (eds.).

Coşkun Mermer and Murat Saraçlar. 2011. Bayesian word alignment for statistical machine translation. In *Proceedings of the 49th Annual Meeting of the Association for Computational Linguistics: Human Language Technologies: short papers - Volume 2*, HLT '11, pages 182–187, Stroudsburg, PA, USA. Association for Computational Linguistics.

Johanna Mesch, Lars Wallin, and Thomas Björkstrand. 2012. Sign language resources in Sweden: Dictionary and corpus. In *Proceedings 5th Workshop on the Representation and Processing of Sign Languages: Interactions between Corpus and Lexicon*, Language Resources and Evaluation Conference (LREC), pages 127–130, Istanbul, Turkey.

Johanna Mesch, Maya Rohdell, and Lars Wallin. 2014. Annoterade filer för svensk teckenspråkskorpus. Version 2. `http://www.ling.su.se`.

Robert Östling. 2013. Stagger: An open-source part of speech tagger for Swedish. *North European Journal of Language Technology*, 3:1–18.

Darcey Riley and Daniel Gildea. 2012. Improving the IBM alignment models using variational Bayes. In *Proceedings of the 50th Annual Meeting of the Association for Computational Linguistics: Short Papers - Volume 2*, ACL '12, pages 306–310, Stroudsburg, PA, USA. Association for Computational Linguistics.

Waldemar Schwager and Ulrike Zeshan. 2008. Word classes in sign languages: Criteria and classifications. *Studies in Language*, 32(3):509–545, September.

Johan Sjons. 2013. Automatic induction of word classes in Swedish Sign Language. Master's thesis, Stockholm University.

Ted Supalla and Elissa L. Newport. 1978. How many seats in a chair?: The derivation of nouns and verbs in American Sign Language. In Patricia Siple, editor, *Understanding language through sign language research*, chapter 4, pages 91–132. Academic Press, New York, NY.

Oksana Tkachman and Wendy Sandler. 2013. The noun-verb distinction in two young sign languages. *Gesture*, 13(3):253–286.

Kristina Toutanova, H. Tolga Ilhan, and Christopher Manning. 2002. Extensions to HMM-based statistical word alignment models. In *2002 Conference on Empirical Methods in Natural Language Processing (EMNLP 2002)*, pages 87–94.

Stephan Vogel, Hermann Ney, and Christoph Tillmann. 1996. HMM-based word alignment in statistical translation. In *Proceedings of the 16th Conference on Computational Linguistics - Volume 2*, COLING '96, pages 836–841, Stroudsburg, PA, USA. Association for Computational Linguistics.

Lars Wallin, Johanna Mesch, and Anna-Lena Nilsson. 2014. Transkriptionskonventioner för teckenspråkstexter (version 5). Technical report, Sign Language, Department of Linguistics, Stockholm University.

Peter Wittenburg, Hennie Brugman, Albert Russel, Alex Klassmann, and Han Sloetjes. 2006. ELAN: a professional framework for multimodality research. In *Proceedings of the Fifth International Conference on Language Resources and Evaluation (LREC'06)*. `http://tla.mpi.nl/tools/tla-tools/elan/`.

David Yarowsky, Grace Ngai, and Richard Wicentowski. 2001. Inducing multilingual text analysis tools via robust projection across aligned corpora. In *Proceedings of the First International Conference on Human Language Technology Research*, HLT '01, pages 1–8, Stroudsburg, PA, USA. Association for Computational Linguistics.

Using Positional Suffix Trees to Perform Agile Tree Kernel Calculation

Gustavo Henrique Paetzold
University of Sheffield / Sheffield, United Kingdom
ghpaetzold1@sheffield.ac.uk

Abstract

Tree kernels have been used as an efficient solution for many tasks, but are difficult to calculate. To address this problem, in this paper we introduce the Positional Suffix Trees: a novel data structure devised to store tree structures, as well as the *MFTK* and *EFTK* algorithms, which use them to estimate Subtree and Subspace Tree Kernels. Results show that the Positional Suffix Tree can store large amounts of trees in a scalable fashion, and that our algorithms are up to 22 times faster than the state-of-the-art approach.

1 Introduction

A tree kernel is a type of convolution kernel that represents as features the substructures that compose a tree. They can be interpreted as a function $K(T_1, T_2)$, of which the value is a similarity measure between tree structures T_1 and T_2. Recently, tree kernels have become popular, and shown to be an efficient solution in tasks such as Question Classification (Moschitti, 2006), Relation Extraction (Zelenko et al., 2003), Named Entity Recognition (Culotta and Sorensen, 2004), Syntactic Parsing (Collins and Duffy, 2002), Semantic Role Labeling (Moschitti, 2006), Semantic Parsing (Moschitti, 2004), Glycan Classification (Yamanishi et al., 2007) and Plagiarism Detection (Son et al., 2006).

However efficient, tree kernels can be very difficult to calculate in a reasonable amount of time. Calculating $K(T_1, T_2)$ usually requires many verifications between node labels and can easily achieve quadratic complexity. Although algorithms of much lower complexity have been proposed (Moschitti, 2006), their performance can still be unsatisfactory in solving problems which involve large datasets.

In this paper, we present the findings of an ongoing work which focuses on proposing faster algorithms for the calculation of tree kernels. Our strategy uses a time-space tradeoff: we reduce processing time by querying syntactic patterns stored in a Positional Suffix Tree (PST), a novel data structure devised for the storage of trees and graphs. We introduce the the *MFTK* and *EFTK* algorithms, which use PST's to calculate Subtree (ST) and Subspace Tree Kernels (SST). Our experiments show that, while the *MFTK* algorithm is over 3.5 times faster than the state-of-the-art algorithm, the *EFTK* algorithm is over 22 times faster. We also demonstrate that PST's grow in log-linear fashion, scaling well to large tree datasets.

2 Positional Suffix Trees

In order for us to create faster algorithms for the calculation of tree kernels, we have conceived the Positional Suffix Tree: an adaptation of the well known Suffix Tree (Weiner, 1973). Its goal is to store tree structures, such as syntactic parses, and allow efficient search for patterns in them. In other words, it is a tree that stores other trees. To avoid confusion, throughout the rest of the paper we will refer to PST nodes as "trie nodes".

Each trie node of the PST represents a tree node of a certain label in a given position. In constituency parses, for an example, a trie node could represent an "*NP*" (Noun Phrase) node as the leftmost child of an "*S*" (Sentence) node. A PST trie node is composed of the following components:

- **Label:** The identifier of the tree node being represented, such as "*DT*".
- **Tree ID Set:** A set containing the identifiers of each and every tree added to the PST which contains the tree node in question.
- **Children:** A vector of size n, where n is the *the largest number of children parented by*

the tree node in question. In each position i of the children vector is stored a hash structure H that maps the set of tree node labels L to the trie nodes that represent them. The L set contains all the labels of child nodes observed in position i parented by the tree node in question.

As an example, consider the trie node that represents the "**NP**" node highlighted in the three parse trees of Figure 1.

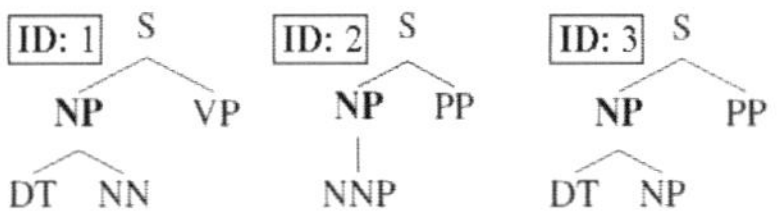

Figure 1: Parse trees with "NP" node

Figure 2 illustrates such trie node.

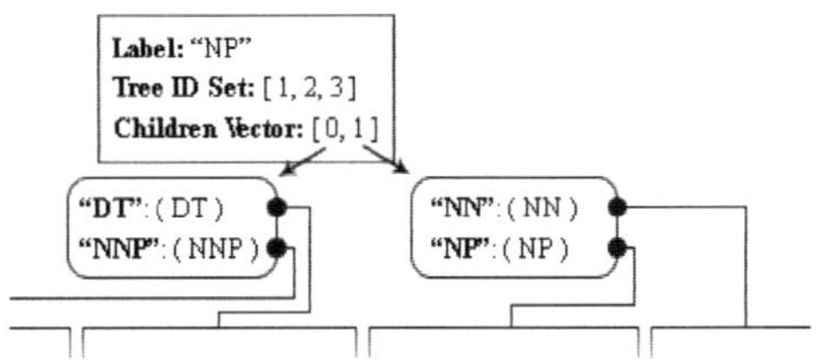

Figure 2: Valid PST trie node

Differently from standard Suffix Trees, the PST node labels can be of any hashable type, any node can have one or more children, and the ordering of a trie node's children is not determined by the alphabetical order of their labels, but rather the position in which the children nodes appear in each tree individually.

3 Tree Kernel Modeling

Our algorithms calculate two types of kernels: the Subtree and the Subspace Tree Kernels. Given two tree structures, the Subtree Kernel (Vishwanathan and Smola, 2004) represents the overlap of "subtrees" between them, which consist of every non-leaf node along with all its descendants. The Subspace Kernel (Collins and Duffy, 2002), on the other hand, represents the overlap of "subspace trees", which are all subtrees and their generalized versions, where some or all of their leaves can be non-terminals. While the *EFTK* algorithm explores those definitions directly, the *MFTK* algorithm explores the ST/SST model of Moschitti (2006), in which the kernel value between two trees is represented as:

$$K(T_1,T_2) = \sum_{n_1 \in N_{T_1}} \sum_{n_2 \in N_{T_2}} \triangle(n_1,n_2) \quad (1)$$

Where N_{T_i} is the set of nodes of tree T_i, and $\triangle(n_1,n_2)$ is a function that represents the similarity between nodes n_1 and n_2, subject to the following rules:

- $\triangle(n_1,n_2) = 0$ if $n_1 \neq n_2$
- $\triangle(n_1,n_2) = \alpha$ if $n_1 = n_2$ and both n_1 and n_2 are leaf nodes.
- Otherwise:

$$\triangle(n_1,n_2) = \alpha \prod_{j=1}^{nc(n_1)} \left(\sigma + \triangle\left(c_{n_1}^j, c_{n_2}^j\right)\right) \quad (2)$$

Where α is a decay factor and $\sigma \in \{0,1\}$. When $\sigma = 0$, $K(T_1,T_2)$ calculates the ST Kernel, and when $\sigma = 1$, the SST Kernel.

4 Algorithms

4.1 PST Storing Algorithm

The recursive algorithm below adds a node N_t of a given tree identified by ID in position i of the children vector of trie node N_{pst}.

Algorithm *AddNode*(N_t, ID, i, N_{pst}):

```
C = N_pst.Children
L = N_t.Label
if L in C[i]:
   then N = C[i][L]
   else N = new PSTNode()
          N.Label = L
          C[i][L] = N
Add ID in N.TreeIDSet
for j in [0, ||N_t.Children||]:
          C_t = N_t.Children[j]
          AddNode(C_t, ID, j, N)
```

4.2 The *MFTK* Algorithm

The *MFTK* (Much Faster Tree Kernel) algorithm calculates both ST and SST Kernels depending on the σ parameter. Unlike state-of-the-art algorithms, it does not calculate $K(T_i,T_j)$ individually, but rather $K(T_i,\{T_1,\ldots,T_n\})$ directly. It receives as input a target tree T_i and a PST containing all subtrees, each with an individual ID, of every source tree T_j. It also requires a hash M, which maps the subtrees' IDs to its respective tree T_j. The algorithm below creates a valid PST and M map.

Algorithm *CreatePST*($T_i, T_1, \ldots, T_n$):

```
PST = new PST()
M = new Hash()
for i in [1,n]:
        for c in T_i.Nodes:
                ID = new ID()
                AddNode(c, ID, 0, PST.Root)
                M[ID] = i
return PST, M
```

Given a PST, a map M, α and a $\sigma \in \{0,1\}$, the following algorithm calculates $K(T_i, \{T_1, T_2, \ldots, T_{n-1}, T_n\})$.

Algorithm *Score*($PST, M, T_i, \{T_1, \ldots, T_n\}, \alpha, \sigma$):

```
K = new Hash()
for j in [1,n]:
        K[j] = 0
for c in T_i.Nodes:
        S_s = MFTK(c, PST.Root, 0, α, σ, nil)
        for M_atch in S_s.Keys:
                S = S_s[M_atch]
                K[M[M_atch]] += S
return K
```

The function *MFTK*, described in the algorithm below, uses the PST to estimate kernel values. It receives a tree node N_t, a trie node N_{pst}, a position i, parameters α and σ and an auxiliary static hash *Ss*. It returns a hash $S_s[N_t]$ which maps a subtree ID M_{atch} to its ST/SST score.

Algorithm *MFTK*($N_t, N_{pst}, i, \alpha, \sigma, S_s$):

```
if S_s is nil:
    then Ss = new Hash()
S_s[N_t] = new Hash()
C_pst = N_pst.Children[i][N_t.Label]
for ID in C_pst.TreeIDSet:
        S_s[N_t] = α
for j in [0, ||N_t.Children||]:
        N_tc = N_t.Children[j]
        MFTK(N_tc, C_pst, j, α, σ, S_s)
        M_iss = {S_s[N_t].Keys}-{S_s[N_tc].Keys}
        for ID in Ss[N_tc].Keys:
                S_s[N_t][ID] *= σ + S_s[N_tc][ID]
        for ID in M_iss:
                S_s[N_t][ID] *= σ
return R_esult = S_s[N_t]
```

4.3 The *EFTK* Algorithm

The *EFTK* (Even Faster Tree Kernel) algorithm uses a very unique strategy: instead of using the model of Moschitti (2006), it calculates the number of common subtrees between two tree structures directly. The *EFTK* can only calculate the ST Kernel. It employs the same *CreatePST* and *Score* routines described in Section 4.2, but instead of the *MFTK* function, it applies the one below.

Algorithm *EFTK*(N_t, N_{pst}, i, S_s):

```
C_pst = N_pst.Children[i][N_t.Label]
if S_s is nil:
   then S_s = C_pst.TreeIDSet
   else S_s = S_s ∩ C_pst.TreeIDSet
for j in [0, ||N_t.Children||]:
        C_t = N_t.Children[j]
        if C_t.Label in C_pst.Children[j].Keys:
           then EFTK(C_t, C_pst, j, S_s)
           else S_s = {}
R_esult = new Hash()
for ID in Ss:
        R_esult[ID] = 1
return R_esult
```

5 Experiments

5.1 Performance Comparison

In this experiment, we conduct a performance comparison between the *MFTK* and *EFTK* algorithms, the baseline QTK (Quadratic Tree Kernel) and the state-of-the-art FTK (Fast Tree Kernel), both of which were proposed by Moschitti (2006).

We have chosen to estimate the processing time taken by the algorithms to calculate the kernel values between the constituency parses produced by the Stanford Parser (Klein and Manning, 2003) of 500 test and 5452 training questions. The datasets were devised for the task of Question Classification (Li and Roth, 2002). The algorithms were implemented in Python, and ran in a computer with a quad-core Intel® Core i7-4500U 1.8GHz and 8Gb of RAM running at 1600MHz. Since the time taken by both FTK and *MFTK* to calculate ST and SST kernels do not vary, we choose to present the performance results for ST kernel calculation only. Figure 3 illustrate the results obtained for increasing portions of the training set, and Figure 4 the average time taken to calculate $K(T_i, T_i)$ for T_i of different node sizes.

The *MFTK* algorithm is on average 3.54 times faster than FTK for different corpus sizes, while

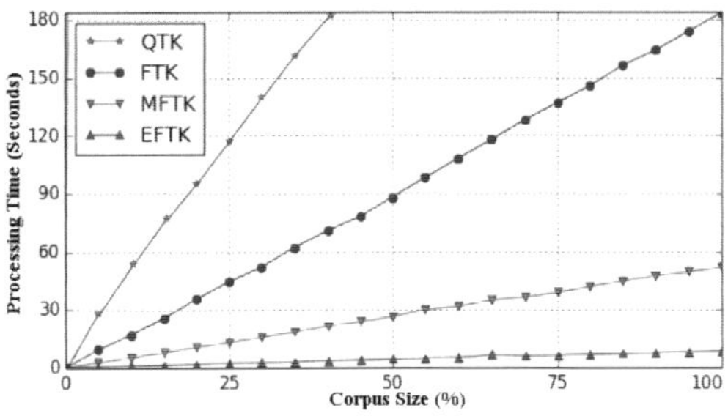

Figure 3: Processing time over different portions of the dataset

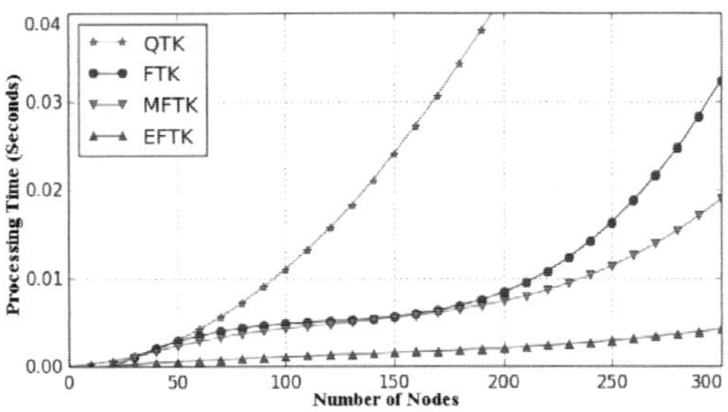

Figure 4: Processing time over trees of different node sizes

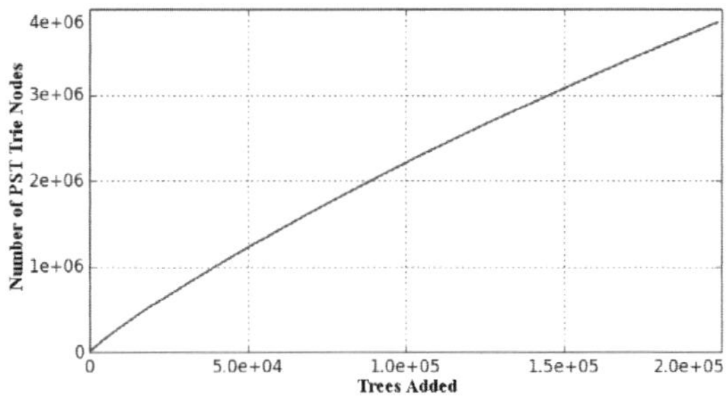

Figure 5: Number of trie nodes over the numbers of trees stored

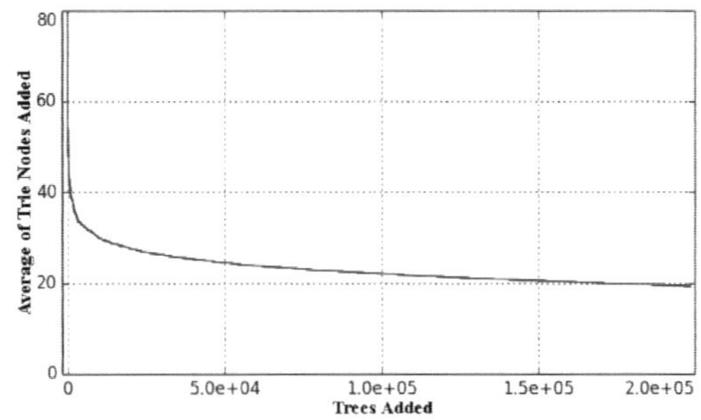

Figure 6: Average number of new trie nodes over the number of trees stored

the *EFTK* algorithm is on average 22.15 times faster. It can also be noticed that, while the processing time of *EFTK* grows almost linearly as the number of nodes rise, the FTK shows a square-like behavior, which is also outperformed by the *MFTK* algorithm.

5.2 Storage Scalability

In this experiment, we evaluate how well Positional Suffix Trees scale with respect to large datasets. To that purpose, we chose to store a dataset of 200k constituency parses of sentences taken from Wikipedia and Simple Wikipedia (Paetzold and Specia, 2013) in a PST, and collect statistics about its size. The PST was implemented in Python and the script ran in the same computer used in the experiment of Section 5.1. Figure 5 shows the number of trie nodes in the PST as the number of stored trees rise, and Figure 6 illustrates the average number of new PST trie nodes added after each tree is stored.

It is noticeable that the curve in Figure 5 shows a convergence pattern, which is in conformity with what is observed in Figure 6, where it is shown that the number of average new nodes tends to converge to an ever lower amount. Such phenomena provide evidence that the PST can indeed store large amounts of tree structures in a scalable fashion, since the more trees are added, the less it needs to grow to represent them.

6 Conclusions and Future Work

In this paper we have introduced the Positional Suffix Tree, a data structure designed to store trees and graphs, and also two algorithms which use them to estimate Subtree and Subspace Tree Kernel values: the *MFTK* and the *EFTK*.

Our experiments revealed that, while the *MFTK* algorithm calculates both ST and SST Kernels in nearly half an order of magnitude faster than state-of-the-art algorithms, the *EFTK* algorithm calculates ST Kernels over an order of magnitude faster. We have also found that the PST provides a scalable storage solution for syntactic parse trees.

In the future we intend to devise algorithms for other kernels, such as the Partial Tree Kernel (Moschitti, 2006), and also explore ways to calculate approximate, faster to estimate, versions of such kernels.

Acknowledgments

I would like to thank the University of Sheffield for supporting this project.

References

Michael Collins and Nigel Duffy. 2002. New ranking algorithms for parsing and tagging: Kernels over discrete structures, and the voted perceptron. In *Proceedings of the 40th Annual Meeting on Association for Computational Linguistics*, ACL '02, pages 263–270, Stroudsburg, PA, USA. Association for Computational Linguistics.

Aron Culotta and Jeffrey Sorensen. 2004. Dependency tree kernels for relation extraction. In *Proceedings of the 42nd Meeting of the Association for Computational Linguistics (ACL'04), Main Volume*, pages 423–429, Barcelona, Spain, July.

Dan Klein and Christopher D. Manning. 2003. Accurate unlexicalized parsing. In *In Proceedings of the 41st Annual Meeting of the Association for Computational Linguistics*, pages 423–430.

Xin Li and Dan Roth. 2002. Learning question classifiers. In *Proceedings of the 19th International Conference on Computational Linguistics - Volume 1*, COLING '02, pages 1–7, Stroudsburg, PA, USA. Association for Computational Linguistics.

Alessandro Moschitti. 2004. A study on convolution kernels for shallow semantic parsing. In *Proceedings of the 42Nd Annual Meeting on Association for Computational Linguistics*, ACL '04, Stroudsburg, PA, USA. Association for Computational Linguistics.

Alessandro Moschitti. 2006. Efficient convolution kernels for dependency and constituent syntactic trees. In *ECML*, pages 318–329, Berlin, Germany, September. Machine Learning: ECML 2006, 17th European Conference on Machine Learning, Proceedings.

Gustavo H. Paetzold and Lucia Specia, 2013. *Proceedings of the 9th Brazilian Symposium in Information and Human Language Technology*, chapter Text Simplification as Tree Transduction.

Jeong-Woo Son, Seong-Bae Park, and Se-Young Park. 2006. Program plagiarism detection using parse tree kernels. In *Proceedings of the 9th Pacific Rim International Conference on Artificial Intelligence*, PRICAI'06, pages 1000–1004, Berlin, Heidelberg. Springer-Verlag.

S V N Vishwanathan and Alex Smola. 2004. Fast kernels for string and tree matching.

Peter Weiner. 1973. Linear pattern matching algorithms. In *Proceedings of the 14th Annual Symposium on Switching and Automata Theory (Swat 1973)*, SWAT '73, pages 1–11, Washington, DC, USA. IEEE Computer Society.

Yoshihiro Yamanishi, Francis Bach, and Jean-Philippe Vert. 2007. Glycan classification with tree kernels. *Bioinformatics*, 23(10):1211–1216.

Dmitry Zelenko, Chinatsu Aone, and Anthony Richardella. 2003. Kernel methods for relation extraction. *Journal of Machine Learning Research*, 3:2003.

Helping Swedish words come to their senses: word-sense disambiguation based on sense associations from the SALDO lexicon

Ildikó Pilán
Språkbanken, Dept. of Swedish, University of Gothenburg
Gothenburg, Sweden
ildiko.pilan@svenska.gu.se

Abstract

This paper describes a knowledge-based approach to word-sense disambiguation using a lexical-semantic resource, SALDO. This hierarchically organized lexicon defining senses in terms of other related senses has not been previously explored for this purpose. The proposed method is based on maximizing the overlap between associated word senses of nouns and verbs co-occuring within a sentence. The results of a small-scale experiment using this method are also reported. Overall, the approach proved more efficient for nouns, since not only was the accuracy score higher for this category (56%) than for verbs (46%), but for nouns in 22% more of the cases was a sense overlap found. As a result of an in-depth analysis of the predictions, we identified a number of ways the system could be modified or extended for an improved performance.

1 Introduction

Word-sense disambiguation (WSD) aims at computationally determining the correct sense of a word in a given context (Agirre and Edmonds, 2007). Research in the area began already around the 1950s, being that the successful completion of this task is a prerequisite for a large number of complex Natural Language Processing (NLP) applications (Navigli, 2009). Navigli (2009) as well as Agirre and Edmonds (2007) offer a detailed overview of WSD methods. Such techniques can be classified, among others, based on the amount of knowledge-sources required, i.e. knowledge-based vs. statistical approaches. A wide-spread knowledge-rich method for WSD is the *Lesk algorithm* (Lesk, 1986), based on the overlap between information available about a sense in a lexical resource and the context which the target word appears in. The Lesk algorithm has received a lot of interest and different modified versions of it have also been tested, e.g. Banerjee and Pedersen (2002), Miller et al. (2012), Ekedahl and Golub (2004).

Numerous previous studies deal with WSD for English (Navigli, 2009), but there are significantly fewer examples of WSD for other languages in the literature. The SENSEVAL-2 Workshop (Edmonds and Cotton, 2001) aimed at the extension of WSD to a number of different languages, including a Lexical Sample task for Swedish. Kokkinakis et al. (2001) describe the Swedish data and report the results of the participating systems using this material. The Swedish dataset included altogether 10241 instances selected from the Stockholm-Umeå Corpus (SUC) (Ejerhed and Källgren, 1992) with an average polysemy of 3,5 senses per lexeme. The best performing system for Swedish (Yarowsky et al., 2001) achieved an overall precision of 74,7% for mixed-grained distinctions, where verbs were significantly harder to disambiguate than nouns (a precision of 63,4% compared to 76,9% respectively). A subsequent attempt at Swedish WSD, based on Random Indexing and word co-occurrence, is described in Hassel (2005). This system obtained an accuracy of about 80% on a small dataset comprised of 133 instances, aiming at distinguishing three senses of the word *resa*, namely the senses "journey", "to travel" and "to raise".

In the following, we describe the first results obtained with a knowledge-based WSD system under development using *SALDO* (Borin et al., 2013), a Swedish lexical-semantic resource. Exploring this lexicon for WSD is particularly interesting, since its structure differs considerably from WordNet (Fellbaum, 1998), a common alternative employed for this task. Unlike WordNet, SALDO covers all parts of speech (POS) and it is based on association relations among hierarchically organized word senses. Our WSD method builds on the idea that by taking into consideration the overlap between a list of associated senses of nouns and verbs occurring within a sentence, we can disambiguate their senses.

In this paper, we first present SALDO and our test data in section 2. Section 3 provides details about our knowledge-based WSD method, whilst results are presented in section 4. Section 5 includes a thorough analysis of errors and finally, section 6 concludes the paper and outlines directions for further research.

2 Resources used

Our main resource, SALDO was used both as basis for the sense inventory and as source of information about associations between senses. This lexicon contains hierarchically organized word senses where the top node, *PRIM*, is an artificial node whose children consist of 43 core senses. Instead of textual definitions, each sense is defined in terms of another manually selected sense, a mandatory primary descriptor (PD), and one (or more) optional secondary sense descriptors. Each descriptor is a more central semantic neighbor of a given entry. Centrality is determined in terms of frequency, stylistic unmarkedness, morphological complexity and directional semantic relations (e.g. hyperonyms as descriptors of their hyponyms). Due to the structure of SALDO, each sense can be characterized by a a list of *ancestors* (or *semantic path*) consisting of all the primary descriptors encountered while moving upwards in the hierarchy until reaching the top node (*PRIM*). We indicate different SALDO senses with a superscript digit following the word throughout this paper.

In absence of a dataset annotated with SALDO senses for a variety of parts of speech, we evaluated our method on a set of sentences collected via a corpus query tool, *Korp* (Borin et al., 2012b), checking manually whether the predicted senses were correct. Our system made sense predictions for each noun and verb in the sentence, but we only inspected the sense of one target item per sentence. As targets for WSD we used 5 polysemous nouns and equally many verbs suggested by native speakers based on their intuitions. We considered 10 sentences for each item which resulted in 100 test sentences in total. The amount of our test data was limited due to time constraints and the cost of manual sense annotation and error analysis. Our target items and the English equivalent of their first sense (*Eng*) are listed in Tables 1 and 2. The tables include also the number of senses (*# senses*) in SALDO and the average number of senses per POS category (*Avg*).

POS	Lemma	Eng	# senses	Avg
noun	mål	"goal"	7	**4**
	val	"choice"	4	
	glas	"glass"	3	
	ask	"ash tree"	2	
	lov	"permit"	4	

Table 1: Target nouns to disambiguate.

POS	Lemma	Eng	# senses	Avg
verb	läsa	"read"	2	**3.2**
	flyga	"fly"	2	
	ersätta	"substitute"	2	
	spela	"play"	8	
	väcka	"arouse"	2	

Table 2: Target verbs to disambiguate.

The sentences constituting our test set were randomly selected via Korp from the *LäsBarT* corpus (Heimann Mühlenbock, 2013), a collection of easy-to-read newspaper and fiction texts. Since the semantic paths of all nouns and verbs in a sentence were considered by our WSD method when looking for overlaps (without the introduction of a more limited window size) we opted for using a corpus that typically contains shorter sentences than other corpora do, to increase the feasibility of a manual error analysis. Since sentences were randomly selected, the distribution of senses was uneven in the 10 example sentences per lemma.

3 Method

The knowledge-based WSD method proposed relies on maximizing the overlap between the ancestor senses of nouns and verbs appearing within a sentence-long context. By looking at shared senses higher in the SALDO hierarchy, we aim at capturing the idea of semantic relatedness, potentially a shared domain.

In the first step of our WSD, the list of ancestors for each noun and verb in the sentence is collected via *Karp* (Borin et al., 2012a), an online infrastructure for Swedish lexical resources. We access Karp through its web-services using a base form search with a lemma and a POS, provided for each token via the Korp annotation pipeline. Then, the ancestor-overlap for combinations of sense pairs for each pair of lemmas is computed. The comparison does not take place only within the same POS category, i.e. noun and verb senses are compared also to each other. Since for longer paths the absolute number of overlaps would be higher, we introduced a normalization step: the number of overlapping ancestors in the paths of the two senses compared is divided by the summed length of these paths. In a subsequent step, the scores from the pair-wise comparison are summed for each sense and the sense maximizing the overlap with other senses is suggested as disambiguated sense. If no overlap is found, the fallback strategy is choosing the first sense from SALDO. In the case of multi-word expressions (MWE), the corresponding lemma and sense is comprised of more than one word, e.g. *spela_roll* "matter". For such lemmas, the following word is checked in the sentence, in attempt to identify the MWE. If a match is found, the multi-word sense is chosen as prediction.[1]

4 Results

The results of our experiment are presented in Table 3 in terms of the number of correct predictions and fallback predictions for the 10 test sentences per each target item. The amount of correct fallback predictions is indicated in parenthesis, a missing value meaning zero. We also included a baseline accuracy, the average accuracy for nouns and verbs in general (*Avg acc*) and the overall accuracy of the system. We used as baseline our fallback, that is always opting for sense number 1.

The average accuracy of the system over all 100 sentences tested was 51% for disambiguating lemmas with an average polysemy of 3.6, which was only a 1% improvement over the baseline. Although the verbs tested had, on average, almost one sense less to choose from (Table 2) and a higher baseline, the accuracy of our system was 10% lower for verbs than for nouns. In the case of nouns, the system achieved an accuracy of 56% which was 10% above the baseline, whilst for verbs the performance remained 8% below the baseline. Moreover, overlaps were much more common for nouns, where in only 8% of the cases was the fallback of choosing sense number 1 used (in absence of an overlap), out of which none were correct guesses. Verbs tended to create fewer overlaps, 15 out of 50 predictions were fallbacks. For verbs, 20% of correct predictions were obtained with the fallback strategy, which suggests that the overlap-based method proposed is more suitable for nouns. This, however, would need to be confirmed by further experiments on a larger dataset.

Our system's performance compared to the best system in the SENSEVAL-2 task (Yarowsky et al., 2001) remains rather low (17,4% lower for verbs and 20,9% lower for nouns, see section 1). However, the knowledge resource, the sense inventory, as well as the target lemmas and the corpus used were different, which makes a direct comparison hard.

5 Error analysis

To acquire a better understanding about why the system failed to disambiguate senses in certain cases and how the results could be improved, we performed a detailed error analysis of our test sentences. This showed that there are a number of different reasons behind the inaccurate predictions, some of the most common causes being: the insufficient amount of context, the limited number of ancestors, disregarded paradigmatic information, a lack of evidence of common domain or topic, undetected multi-word expressions and the absence of frequency information for a sense.

In the following, we provide an example for some of these categories. Besides the target lemma to disambiguate, we consider also the senses of other nouns and verbs in the sentence that were involved in producing the overlap, highlighting some factors that aided or inhibited successful disambiguation.

One of the potential pitfalls of our approach was the lack of a sufficient amount of context for producing a useful overlap. In the sentence *Sen kommer han på att han behöver en* ***ask***. "Then he remembers that he needs a **box**.", the noun *ask* could be either "box" or "ash tree". Since both verbs are rather generic, none of them produces an overlap with any of the senses of *ask*. In such cases frequency and word co-occurrence informa-

[1] MWE senses were excluded from the counts in Tables 1 and 2 since currently the system cannot detect discontinuous MWE, which results in a rather low MWE recall.

POS	Nouns					Verbs				
Lemma	mål	val	glas	ask	lov	läsa	flyga	ersätta	spela	väcka
# correct predictions	6	5	5	5	7	5	4	4	3	7
# fallbacks (# correct)	1	1	2	0	0	1	2	4 (4)	0	8 (6)
Avg acc (baseline)	56% (46%)					46% (54%)				
Overall acc (baseline)	51% (50%)									

Table 3: WSD results on 100 test sentences.

tion might improve WSD.

Information about the paradigm, i.e. which inflectional pattern a word follows, could also reduce ambiguity in certain cases. In *Nästan hälften av socialdemokraterna i* ***valet*** *tjänar mer än 400 tusen kronor om året.* "Almost half of the socialdemocrats in the **election** earns more than 400 thousand Swedish crowns per year.", the guessed sense for the word *val* was *val*^{2} "whale" (PD: *djur*^{1} "animal"). The base form of this sense (*val*) is the same as that of the correct sense *val*^{4} "choice" (PD: *välja*^{1} "choose"), however, *val*^{2} is a common gender noun, whilst *val*^{4} is of neuter gender. Consequently, the inflected word form in the sentence above, containing the neuter definite ending *-et*, would have been able to rule out *val*^{2}.

There are cases in which the prediction is wrong since information from SALDO is not sufficient for disambiguation, even though the context would be enough for a human to identify a common domain or topic and thus, the correct sense. Consider the example of *Smutsiga grytor, tallrikar och* ***glas*** *trängdes på diskbänken.* "Dirty pots, plates and **glasses** crowded the sink.". Our system used the fallback strategy and guessed *glas*^{1} "glass" (PD: *material*^{1} "material"), instead of the correct solution *glas*^{2} "glass" (PD: *dricka*^{1} "drink") since no overlap was found among the correct senses *gryta*^{1} "pot" (PD: *kärl*^{1} "vessel"), *glas*^{2} "glass" (PD: *dricka*^{1} "to drink") and *tallrik*^{1} "plate" (PD: *mat*^{1} "food"). All these nouns belong to the same topic that could be labeled as *kitchen*, but this is not always reflected in their ancestors. This example would suggest that our system could benefit from the integration of additional information about the domain to which each word sense belongs.

Furthermore, we can find examples where an incorrect prediction could be avoided if a more sophisticated method for detecting multi-word units was used in a step preceding WSD. In *Tiden* ***spelar*** *egentligen inte så stor roll.* "The time does not really **matter** so much.", the verb *spela* and the noun *roll* together form a MWE meaning "matter". SALDO contains a corresponding sense (*spela_roll*^{1}), however, since there are intervening words between the two parts of the expression, our system fails to detect this multi-word unit and, thus, the correct sense. Instead, *spela*^{3} "act" (PD: *teater*^{1}) and *roll*^{1} "part" (PD: *spela*^{3}) is chosen based on the overlap of ancestors.

6 Conclusion and future work

We presented a WSD method for Swedish based on overlap counts between word senses from SALDO, a lexicon previously unexplored for this purpose. We achieved 51% accuracy on a dataset with 3.6 average senses per lemma. We found that this approach was more successful for disambiguating nouns than verbs both in terms of accuracy (56% vs 46%) and the amount of overlap found (92% vs 70% of the test items respectively). A detailed error analysis showed that incorporating, among others, strategies handling the absence of overlap and information about topics or domains in this approach could contribute to achieving a more accurate performance. Addressing these areas of improvement could make this WSD system more useful for several NLP tasks including, but not limited to machine translation, sentiment analysis and summarization.

In the future, a number of directions for extending our method could be investigated such as considering secondary descriptors in the overlap counts and taking into consideration dependency relations during disambiguation. The performance of our system would need to be measured on a larger dataset labeled by multiple annotators and disambiguating the sense of adjectives and adverbs with this method could also be explored. Integration with other knowledge resources and vector space models may also be interesting directions to pursue.

References

Eneko Agirre and Philip Glenny Edmonds. 2007. *Word sense disambiguation: Algorithms and applications*, volume 33. Springer.

Satanjeev Banerjee and Ted Pedersen. 2002. An adapted Lesk algorithm for word sense disambiguation using WordNet. In *Computational linguistics and intelligent text processing*, pages 136–145. Springer.

Lars Borin, Markus Forsberg, Leif-Jöran Olsson, and Jonatan Uppström. 2012a. The open lexical infrastructure of Språkbanken. In *LREC*, pages 3598–3602.

Lars Borin, Markus Forsberg, and Johan Roxendal. 2012b. Korp-the corpus infrastructure of Språkbanken. In *LREC*, pages 474–478.

Lars Borin, Markus Forsberg, and Lennart Lönngren. 2013. SALDO: a touch of yin to WordNet's yang. *Language Resources and Evaluation*, 47(4):1191–1211.

Philip Edmonds and Scott Cotton. 2001. SENSEVAL-2: overview. In *The Proceedings of the Second International Workshop on Evaluating Word Sense Disambiguation Systems*, pages 1–5. Association for Computational Linguistics.

Eva Ejerhed and Gunnel Källgren. 1992. The linguistic annotation of the Stockholm-Umeå Corpus project. Technical report, University of Umeå.

Jonas Ekedahl and Koraljka Golub. 2004. Word sense disambiguation using Wordnet and the Lesk algorithm. *Projektarbeten 2004*, page 17.

Christiane Fellbaum. 1998. *WordNet*. Wiley Online Library.

Martin Hassel. 2005. Word sense disambiguation using co-occurrence statistics on random labels. In *Proceedings of Recent Advances in Natural Language Processing 2005*, Borovets, Bulgaria.

Katarina Heimann Mühlenbock. 2013. *I see what you mean*. Ph.D. thesis, University of Gothenburg.

Dimitrios Kokkinakis, Jerker Järborg, and Yvonne Cederholm. 2001. Senseval-2: the Swedish framework. In *The Proceedings of the Second International Workshop on Evaluating Word Sense Disambiguation Systems*, pages 45–48. Association for Computational Linguistics.

Michael Lesk. 1986. Automatic sense disambiguation using machine readable dictionaries: how to tell a pine cone from an ice cream cone. In *Proceedings of the 5th annual international conference on Systems documentation*, pages 24–26. ACM.

Tristan Miller, Chris Biemann, Torsten Zesch, and Iryna Gurevych. 2012. Using distributional similarity for lexical expansion in knowledge-based word sense disambiguation. In *COLING*, pages 1781–1796.

Roberto Navigli. 2009. Word sense disambiguation: A survey. *ACM Computing Surveys (CSUR)*, 41(2):10.

David Yarowsky, Silviu Cucerzan, Radu Florian, Charles Schafer, and Richard Wicentowski. 2001. The John Hopkins SENSEVAL-2 system descriptions. In *Proceedings of SENSEVAL-2 Second International Workshop on Evaluating Word Sense Disambiguation Systems*, pages 163–166, Toulouse, France, July. Association for Computational Linguistics.

Using sub-word n-gram models for dealing with OOV in large vocabulary speech recognition for Latvian

Askars Salimbajevs
Tilde, Vienibas gatve 75a, Riga, Latvia
askars.salimbajevs@tilde.lv

Jevgenijs Strigins
Tilde, Vienibas gatve 75a, Riga, Latvia
jevgenijs.strigins@tilde.lv

Abstract

In the Latvian language, one word can have tens or even hundreds of surface forms. This is a serious problem for large vocabulary speech recognition. Inclusion of every form in vocabulary will make it intractable, but, on the other hand, even with a vocabulary of 400K, the out-of-vocabulary (OOV) rate will be very high. In this paper, the authors investigate the possibility of using sub-word vocabularies where words are split into frequent and common parts. The results of our experiment show that this allows to significantly reduce the OOV rate.

1 Introduction

The Latvian language is a moderately inflected language, with complex nominal and verbal morphology. Latvian also has a selection of prefixes that can modify nouns, adjectives, adverbs, and verbs either in a qualitative or a spatial sense. There is no definite or indefinite article in Latvian, but definiteness can be indicated by the endings of adjectives.

Because of these properties, one word in Latvian can have tens or even hundreds (in the case of verbs) of surface forms. A successful large vocabulary speech recognition system must be able to recognize most (if not all) of these forms. This means that the vocabulary of the system must be really huge and contain about a million or more source forms. Speech recognition with such a vocabulary can be computationally intractable on most consumer hardware. On the other hand, reducing vocabulary size increases the OOV rate and significantly degrades the quality of recognition. For example, an out-of-vocabulary word is known to generate between 1.5 and 2 errors (Schwartz et al., 1994).

In this paper, the authors explore the sub-word approach, i.e., prefixes and endings, which are mostly common for all words, are split and treated as separate words. This splitting greatly reduces vocabulary size, but can introduce other problems.

There have been many efforts in using word decomposition and sub-word based language models (LM) for dealing with OOV in inflective languages such as Arabic (El-Desoky et al., 2013; Choueiter et al., 2006), Czech (Ircing et al., 2001), Estonian (Alumae, 2004), Finnish (Siivola et al., 2003), Russian (Oparin, 2008; Shin et al., 2013), Turkish (Yuret and Biçici, 2009), and Slovenian (Maučec et al., 2009). However, the authors could not find any reports on similar efforts for Latvian.

Significant improvement in the OOV rate was reported in all cases, but the changes in WER were not as dramatic. The exception was the Finnish language (Siivola et al., 2003), where an astonishing improvement from 56% to 31% was achieved.

Significant improvement was also observed for the Estonian language (Alumae, 2004); WER dropped by about 6.5% absolute with the morpheme language model (LM) and by more than 10% absolute when using the interpolated morpheme and class LM.

Different approaches for selecting sub-word units have been explored. These can be divided into two groups: (1) data-driven methods (Maučec et al., 2009; Siivola et al., 2003; Singh et al., 2002) and (2) supervised methods with some embedded language knowledge (e.g., morphological analyzers, stemmers) (Alumae, 2004; Choueiter et al., 2006; El-Desoky et at., 2013; Ircing et al., 2001; Shin et al., 2013). In this work the authors investigate methods from both groups.

2 Word n-gram language models

Word n-gram language models (LM) are probabilistic models that attempt to predict the next word based on the previous *n-1* words. To approximate the underlying language in this way, the assumption that each word depends only on the previous *n-1* words must be made. This assumption is very important, because it massively simplifies the estimation of such a model from the given data.

To estimate an n-gram language model, a large text corpus is used. For an estimated model, probabilities are calculated in the following way:

$$P(w_i | w_{i-1}, \dots, w_{(i-n)+1}) = \frac{cnt(w_{(i-n)+1}, \dots, w_{i-1}, w_i)}{cnt(w_{(i-n)+1}, \dots, w_{i-1})}$$

where *cnt* is the count of given word sequences in a text corpus.

N-gram models do not recognize different inflected forms of the same word and treat them as separate words. For a closed vocabulary system, this means:

- If an inflected form is not presented in the training corpus, then it will not be recognized correctly.
- The full vocabulary of such a LM will contain about a million or more surface forms. The number of n-grams will be more than 200 million for 3-gram model. Because of high memory and computational resource requirements, speech recognition with such a LM will be too slow or even impossible on most consumer hardware. Therefore, vocabulary must be cut, and the model must be pruned, which will result in high OOV rates and increased perplexity (increased LM confusion on test data).
- Estimation of model of this size requires a huge amount of training data in order to get reliable probability estimates for all possible surface forms.

3 Sub-word n-gram language models

Sub-word based search vocabularies and language models can reduce the OOV rate of a speech recognition system by decomposing whole words into smaller units. These smaller units are selected to be common for a large number of words.

Using sub-word vocabulary requires the following steps to be taken:

- Decomposition: The original words need to be decomposed into smaller sub-word units. The units need to be common for many words, so that the new sub-word vocabulary size is clearly smaller than that of the whole word vocabulary.
- Pronunciation Generation: In this step sub-word unit pronunciations are being added to the speech recognition engine. In general, deducing the pronunciation of a sub-word unit from the pronunciation of a whole word is often challenging and even impossible in some cases. However, Latvian has a strong correspondence between written form and phoneme sequence, and this makes it possible to use a grapheme-based approach in this step.
- Language Model Training: A new language model needs to be trained for recognition of sub-word units. A model is usually trained on the same text corpus that was used for deriving the vocabulary.
- Word Reconstruction: After decoding, the recognized sub-words need to be recombined in order to obtain a valid word sequence.

3.1 Unsupervised word decomposition

One approach to decomposing words into sub-word units is to use probabilistic machine learning methods. In this paper, the authors use *Morfessor* 2.0 (Creutz and Lagus, 2005; Virpioja et al., 2013) – a family of methods for unsupervised learning of morphological segmentation. The *Morfessor* model is trained on a text corpus, and then this corpus is segmented using this model. The result is a corpus made from sub-word units, which can be used to train an n-gram language model and derive a vocabulary of noticeably smaller size (see Table 1).

Using this vocabulary, the output of the speech recognizer will be a sequence of sub-word units. In order to reconstruct the surface forms, a separate hidden-event language model (Stolcke et al., 1998) is used. This model is trained on a corpus in which the places where the word was divided are treated as hidden events and are marked using special connector tags. Applying it to a sequence of sub-word units produces a sequence of the most likely sub-word units and connector tags from which full words can be reconstructed.

3.2 Word decomposition using a stemmer

Another approach is to perform decomposition by separating stems and endings only. Forms with different prefixes will still be treated as separate words.

Decomposition is done using the Latvian stemmer developed by Pinnis and Skadiņš (2012) for their machine translation experiments. The stemmer outputs the stem for any given word. Endings can then be obtained by comparing the stem and the original word.

The Latvian stemmer can be run in two modes: (1) short mode, where only short basic endings are cut, and (2) full mode, where full endings are recognized.

In order to simplify word reconstruction, every ending is marked. After decoding, words can be reconstructed by simply concatenating stems and their marked endings.

4 Set-up and results

4.1 Data and experiments

In this work, the authors used a 22 million sentence text corpus, which was collected by crawling Latvian web news portals. The corpus is used for training the *Morfessor* model and extracting vocabularies.

Sub-word vocabularies are extracted by performing a word decomposition on the text corpus and taking the 100 thousand most frequent units. For comparison, the full vocabulary of this corpus contains approximately 1.5 million surface forms.

Also, vocabularies of the 100, 200, and 400 thousand most frequent surface forms were extracted as a baseline.

For evaluation, a small 23-minute long annotated speech corpus from 10 speakers was used.

4.2 OOV experiments

First, OOV rates for different methods were calculated on the evaluation corpus transcripts. As shown in Table 1, even with a 400K vocabulary, OOV is still very high – 7.15%. Both of the proposed methods, which use sub-word units instead of words, show a significant reduction of the OOV rate in the test corpus, while using a much smaller vocabulary.

Vocabulary containing sub-word units from *Morfessor* output almost completely solves the OOV problem, despite being the smallest among other vocabularies.

Method	**Size**	**OOV, %**
Baseline	100K	11.2 %
Baseline	200K	8.7 %
Baseline	400K	7.15 %
Stemmer (short)	100K	2.6 %
Stemmer (full)	100K	1.5%
Morfessor	76K	**<0.01 %**

Table 1: OOV rate comparison

4.3 Experiments with speech recognition

In order to evaluate the influence of sub-word vocabularies on the speech recognition task, the authors set up the following speech recognition system:

- The system uses the HMM-GMM (4000 senones and 90000 Gaussians) approach and is based on the *Kaldi* toolkit (Povey et al., 2011)
- The acoustic model is trained on a 100-hour long Latvian Speech Recognition Corpus (Pinnis et al., 2014)
- Grapheme-based pronunciations
- fMLLR speaker adaptation

For systems with sub-word vocabularies, training set transcripts were also split using the previously described models and tools and were used during the retraining of the acoustic models, so that the model is more adapted for recognizing sub-word units.

For language modeling, we used the same 22 million sentence text corpus. 3-gram models were used in all experiments, except for the *Morfessor*-

based system, where 6-gram models were also trained. All models are pruned with equal parameters. The results of the speech recognition are shown in Table 2.

Despite the reduction in the OOV rate, no significant improvement in WER has been achieved. On the contrary, the baseline system with a 200K vocabulary showed the best results, while the *Morfessor* based system showed only a very small improvement (1%) in comparison to the baseline 100K system. For systems using decomposition with a stemmer, an increase in the WER was observed.

Method	WER, %	
	Sub-word units	Words
Baseline, 100K	-	40.49 %
Baseline, 200K	-	**38.26 %**
Morfessor	38.79 %	39.43 %
Morfessor, 6-gram LM	39.33 %	39.60 %
Stemmer (short)	35.30 %	42.02 %
Stemmer (full)	**35.26 %**	43.11 %

Table 2: Word error rate comparison

5 Discussion

Intuitively, any OOV improvement should also result in improvement of recognition quality. For example, the same 200K baseline system shows about 27% WER on a subset of evaluation data with no OOV words. However, experiments performed in this work showed mostly negative results, despite big improvement in the OOV rate.

One possible reason for this is the fact that sub-word units are difficult to discriminate acoustically. For example, when using the stemmer (short mode) for decomposition, the WER for stems is 33% and around 37% for endings. For comparison, the stemmer in full mode produces shorter, more morphologically correct stems and longer endings, and, as a result, WER for stems increased to 35%. The same reason can also be applied to *Morfessor*-derived "morphemes". This means that a more careful selection of sub-words is needed and that more morphologically correct decomposition will not guarantee a better result.

Another reason for such results can be the fact that the context of the units gets expanded after splitting words, i.e., 3-grams for sub-word units covers only some part of 3-grams for whole words and is more comparable to 2-gram word models. It can be concluded that more powerful language models are needed for sub-word vocabularies.

In order to test this hypothesis, the authors trained a 6-gram model for *Morfessor* sub-word units. However, only a tiny increase in WER has been achieved. This result is counterintuitive, and more careful analysis is needed in future work.

The authors also experimented with different pruning parameters, but classic word models still showed better results.

6 Conclusion

In this paper, the authors presented a report of the current research on the use of sub-word vocabularies for large vocabulary speech recognition for Latvian. This approach significantly reduces the OOV rate.

The authors explored two different methods: (1) fully unsupervised and data driven word decomposition using the *Morfessor* tool and (2) word decomposition using a stemmer.

Despite the fact that both methods have demonstrated significant reduction in OOV rates (almost 0% in the case of *Morfessor*), speech recognition results can be described as negative, because the best results were obtained using the baseline word based system.

In future work, the authors plan to investigate better ways for selecting acoustically distinguishable sub-word units and to explore methods that would compensate for a weaker LM when using sub-word units.

Acknowledgments

The research leading to these results has received funding from the research project "Information and Communication Technology Competence Centre" of EU Structural funds, contract nr. L-KC-11-0003 signed between the ICT Competence Centre (www.itkc.lv) and the Investment and Development Agency of Latvia, research No. 2.4 "Speech recognition technologies".

References

Alumäe, T. (2004). Large Vocabulary Continuous Speech Recognition for Estonian Using Morphemes and Classes. In K. Sojka, Petr and Kopeček, Ivan and Pala (Ed.), *Text, Speech and Dialogue. Lecture Notes in Computer Science* (pp. 245–252). Springer Berlin Heidelberg. doi:10.1007/978-3-540-30120-2_31

Choueiter, G., Povey, D., Chen, S. F., & Zweig, G. (2006). Morpheme-Based Language Modeling for Arabic Lvcsr. *2006 IEEE International Conference on Acoustics Speech and Signal Processing Proceedings*. doi:10.1109/ICASSP.2006.1660205

Creutz, M., & Lagus, K. (2005). *Unsupervised Morpheme Segmentation and Morphology Induction from Text Corpora Using Morfessor 1.0. Publications in Computer and Information Science, Report A81, Helsinki University of Technology* (pp. 1–27).

El-Desoky Mousa, A., Kuo, H. K. J., Mangu, L., & Soltau, H. (2013). Morpheme-based feature-rich language models using Deep Neural Networks for LVCSR of Egyptian Arabic. In *ICASSP, IEEE International Conference on Acoustics, Speech and Signal Processing - Proceedings* (pp. 8435–8439). doi:10.1109/ICASSP.2013.6639311

Ircing, P., Krbec, P., Hajic, J., Psutka, J., Khudanpur, S., Jelinek, F., & Byrne, W. (2001). On large vocabulary continuous speech recognition of highly inflectional language czech. In *European Conference on Speech Communication and Technology (EUROSPEECH)*.

Maučec, M. S., Rotovnik, T., Kačič, Z., & Brest, J. (2009). Using data-driven subword units in language model of highly inflective Slovenian language. International Journal of Pattern Recognition and Artificial Intelligence. doi:10.1142/S0218001409007119

Oparin, I. (2008). *Language models for automatic speech recognition of inflectional languages*. University of West Bohemia.

Pinnis, M., Auziņa, I., & Goba, K. (2014). Designing the Latvian Speech Recognition Corpus. In *Proceedings of the 9th edition of the Language Resources and Evaluation Conference (LREC'14)* (pp. 1547–1553).

Pinnis, M., & Skadiņš, R. (2012). MT Adaptation for Under-Resourced Domains – What Works and What Not. In Human Language Technologies – The Baltic Perspective - Proceedings of the Fifth International Conference Baltic HLT 2012 (Vol. 247, pp. 176–184). Tartu, Estonia, Estonia: IOS Press.

Povey, D., Ghoshal, A., Boulianne, G., Burget, L., Glembek, O., Goel, N., … Vesely, K. (2011). The Kaldi Speech Recognition Toolkit. In *IEEE 2011 Workshop on Automatic Speech Recognition and Understanding*. IEEE Signal Processing Society.

Schwartz, R., Nguyen, L., Kubala, F., Chou, G., Zavaliagkos, G., & Makhoul, J. (1994). On Using Written Language Training Data for Spoken Language Modeling. In *Proceedings of the Workshop on Human Language Technology* (pp. 94–98). Stroudsburg, PA, USA: Association for Computational Linguistics. doi:10.3115/1075812.1075830

Shin, E., Stüker, S., Kilgour, K., Fügen, C., & Waibel, A. (2013). Maximum Entropy Language Modeling for Russian ASR. In *Proceedings of the International Workshop for Spoken Language Translation (IWSLT 2013)*. Heidelberg.

Siivola, V., Hirsimäki, T., Creutz, M., & Kurimo, M. (2003). Unlimited Vocabulary Speech Recognition Based on Morphs Discovered in an Unsupervised Manner. In *European Conference on Speech Communication and Technology (EUROSPEECH)* (pp. 2293–2296).

Singh, R., Raj, B., & Stern, R. M. (2002). Automatic generation of subword units for speech recognition systems. *IEEE Transactions on Speech and Audio Processing*, *10*, 89–99. doi:10.1109/89.985546

Stolcke, A., Shriberg, E., Bates, R., Ostendorf, M., Hakkani, D., Plache, M., … Lu, Y. (1998). Automatic detection of sentence boundaries and disfluencies based on recognized words. *ICSLP*. doi:10.1.1.53.7127

Virpioja, S., Smit, P., Grönroos, S.-A., & Kurimo, M. (2013). Morfessor 2.0: Python Implementation and Extensions for Morfessor Baseline. *Aalto University Publication Series SCIENCE + TECHNOLOGY, 25/2013*.

Yuret, D., & Biçici, E. (2009). Modeling Morphologically Rich Languages Using Split Words and Unstructured Dependencies. In *ACL-IJCNLP 2009*.

Analysing Inconsistencies and Errors in PoS Tagging in two Icelandic Gold Standards

Steinþór Steingrímsson
The Árni Magnússon Institute for Icelandic Studies
Reykjavík, Iceland
steinst@hi.is

Sigrún Helgadóttir
The Árni Magnússon Institute for Icelandic Studies
Reykjavík, Iceland
sigruhel@hi.is

Eiríkur Rögnvaldsson
University of Iceland
Reykjavík, Iceland
eirikur@hi.is

Abstract

This paper describes work in progress. We experiment with training a state-of-the-art tagger, *Stagger*, on a new gold standard, *MIM-GOLD*, for the PoS tagging of Icelandic. We compare the results to results obtained using a previous gold standard, *IFD*. Using *MIM-GOLD*, tagging accuracy is considerably lower, 92.76% compared to 93.67% accuracy for *IFD*. We analyze and classify the errors made by the tagger in order to explain this difference. We find that inconsistencies and incorrect tags in *MIM-GOLD* may account for this difference.

1 Introduction

For some years a new gold standard, *MIM-GOLD*, for training PoS taggers has been under development (Loftsson et al., 2010; Helgadóttir et al., 2012). This corpus contains approximately one million tokens of text from various sources from the period 2000–2009.

State-of-the-art PoS tagging accuracy for Icelandic, 92.82%, was achieved by Loftsson and Östling (2013), using the Averaged Perceptron Tagger *Stagger* without an external lexicon. All PoS taggers tested so far for Icelandic have been developed or trained and tested on the Icelandic Frequency Dictionary (*IFD*) (Pind et al., 1991).

In this paper we describe the training and testing of *Stagger* on *MIM-GOLD*. Results are compared to the results for training and tagging *IFD* reported by Loftsson and Östling (2013). Tagging errors made by *Stagger*, when tagging the two gold standards, are examined and classified to explain the difference in tagging accuracy.

In Section 2 we describe the two corpora used for training and tagging. In Section 3 we describe training and tagging of *MIM-GOLD* with *Stagger*. In Section 4 we discuss the results. In Section 5 we report on the analysis of errors made by *Stagger* when tagging the two corpora, and in Section 6 we conclude.

2 Resources

2.1 The IFD corpus

The *IFD* contains 100 fragments of text published for the first time in 1980–1989. Each fragment contains about 5,000 tokens. There are five categories of text in the corpus, approximately equally sized, four of which (80%) are literary texts from published books. The fifth category contains non-fictional texts from various sources. The tagset used in *IFD* is based on the traditional Icelandic analysis of word classes and grammatical categories, with some exceptions where that classification has been rationalized. The tagset contains about 700 possible tags of which 639 occur in *IFD*. The size of the tagset mirrors the morphological complexity of Icelandic. The corpus was tagged with a combination of automatic methods and manual checking. In the work on training and testing *Stagger* on *IFD* (Loftsson and Östling, 2012), the authors used a reduced tagset of 565 tags and a corrected version of *IFD* (Loftsson, 2009). 15.9% of the word forms in the *IFD* are ambiguous as to the tagset within the *IFD*. This figure is quite high, which illustrates the complex inflectional morphology of Icelandic. We will show in Section 5 that many of the errors made by the taggers when tagging Icelandic are due to this high ambiguity rate.

2.2 The MIM-GOLD corpus

The foundation for the building of *MIM-GOLD* is the Tagged Icelandic Corpus (*MIM*), which was released in the spring of 2013, both for search[1]

[1] http://mim.arnastofnun.is/

and download[2]. This corpus contains 25 million running words from various genres dating from the first decade of the 21st century (Helgadóttir et al., 2012). The compilation of *MIM-GOLD* has been described in two papers (Loftsson et al., 2010; Helgadóttir et al., 2014). *MIM-GOLD* contains about one million tokens which were sampled from 13 text types in *MIM*. The largest contributions are newspaper texts, text from published books and blog text. Other text classes include text from various websites, law text, text from school essays, text written-to-be-spoken, text from adjudications, text from radio news scripts and e-mails. *MIM-GOLD* is thus twice the size of *IFD* and the texts are more varied. About 80% of the texts in *IFD* are literary texts compared to less than 25% in *MIM-GOLD*.

The texts were tagged with the program *CorpusTagger*, which was developed for sentence segmentation, tokenization and tagging of *MIM-GOLD* (Loftsson et al., 2010). Five different individual taggers were used, after which *CombiTagger* (Henrich et al., 2009) was applied to select a single tag. All the taggers used were trained or developed using *IFD*. The *IFD* tagset was therefore used with some adjustments. Three different correction phases have been applied to the tagging of *MIM-GOLD*. In the first phase, systematic ways of error detection were applied in the form of noun phrase (NP), prepositional phrase (PP), and verb phrase (VP) error detection programs described by Loftsson (2009). In the second correction phase, all the tags in *MIM-GOLD* were checked manually. The third phase was carried out in a semi-automatic manner using *IceTagger* (Loftsson, 2008). The tags output by *IceTagger* were compared with the (presumed) correct tags in the corpus. If a difference was found, the line containing the discrepancy was marked as an error candidate and inspected manually. The total number of tags corrected in all three phases was just under 130.000.

Some adjustments were made to the tagset of *IFD* for *MIM-GOLD*, in line with the reduction of the *IFD*-tagset reported for the experiment with *Stagger*. Named entity classification for proper nouns was removed and all number constants were labelled with a single tag. Two other modifications were made. Tagging and tokenization of abbreviations was modified, and foreign names in *IFD* were tagged as proper nouns and provided with a gender in a similar fashion to Icelandic names. There is, however, considerable inconsistency in the tagging of foreign names in *MIM-GOLD*. During the second correction phase foreign names were tagged as proper nouns and marked for gender, if they were common and exhibited Icelandic inflection. When gender was difficult to decide they were tagged with unspecified gender. During the third correction phase this decision was modified such that foreign names were simply classified as foreign words. As a result foreign names in *MIM-GOLD* are classified in three different ways: As foreign words; as proper nouns with gender specified or as proper nouns with gender unspecified. As a part of further correcting the tagging of *MIM-GOLD* it is necessary to tackle this inconsistency. Since the texts in *IFD* date from the period 1980–1989 and are mainly literary texts no e-mail addresses or web addresses occur in the text. For *MIM-GOLD* a new tag was used for these entities.

2.3 The Database of Icelandic Inflection

In experiments with tagging Icelandic, extended lexicons have been derived from the Database of Icelandic Inflection (*BÍN*)[3] (Bjarnadóttir, 2012). This was done in the experiment with training and testing *Stagger* on *IFD* and is also used in the experiment reported here.

3 Experiment

The experiment with training and testing *Stagger* on *IFD* reported by Loftsson and Östling (2013) was repeated for *MIM-GOLD*. We evaluated the version of *Stagger* using linguistic features (LF) and the unknown word guesser *IceMorphy* (Loftsson, 2008) and added an extended lexicon based on *BÍN*. We did not add word embeddings (WE) as was done in the original experiment. Results are shown in Table 1. Average unknown word ratio for the *IFD* corpus when using *BÍN* is 0.97% and for the *MIM-GOLD* corpus 3.43%.[4]

4 Results

As shown in Table 1, overall accuracy for *IFD* is 93.67%. Comparable result for *MIM-GOLD* is

[2]`http://malfong.is/`

[3]*BÍN* contains about 270,000 paradigms with about 5.8 million inflectional forms. It is available at `http://bin.arnastofnun.is/`

[4]Loftsson and Östling used folds 1–9 of the *IFD* corpus for training and testing and fold 10 for development. In the present experiment we used all folds for training and testing.

Corpus	Unknown words	Known words	All words
IFD	58.31	94.02	93.67
MIM-GOLD	68.97	93.61	92.76

Table 1: Tagging accuracy when tagging *IFD* and *MIM-GOLD* using 10-fold cross-validation.

92.76%. Accuracy for known words is higher for *IFD* (94.02%) than for *MIM-GOLD* (93.61%), but accuracy for unknown words is higher for *MIM-GOLD* (68.97%) than for *IFD* (58.31%). The higher accuracy for known words in *IFD* can be explained by a greater number of tagging errors and more inconsistencies in *MIM-GOLD*. Higher accuracy for unknown words in *MIM-GOLD* are explained, at least in part, by a higher number of unknown tokens in *MIM-GOLD* that are relatively easy for the tagger to tag correctly, such as web addresses, e-mails and foreign words. In the next Section we will perform error analysis to try to explain this difference in accuracy.

5 Error analysis

Manning (2011) trained and tested the Stanford PoS tagger (Toutanova et al., 2003) on standard splits of the Wall Street Journal (WSJ) portion of the Penn Treebank for PoS tagging. In order to understand how tagging accuracy could be improved, Manning analyzed the errors made by the tagger, and suggested that the largest opportunity for further progress comes from improving the linguistic resources from which taggers are trained. To get a rough breakdown of how the linguistic resources can be improved, Manning did a small error analysis, taking a sample of 100 errors which the Stanford tagger made when tagging the WSJ. We did a similar analysis to try to explain the difference in tagging accuracy when *Stagger* was trained and tested on the two Gold standards, as described in Section 3. We took a random sample of 300 errors from each corpus. The errors were divided into six classes, as shown in Table 2.

Class of error	IFD (%)	MIM-GOLD (%)
Unknown	8.00	16.33
Improvable tagging	38.00	31.33
Insufficient context	36.00	29.67
Ambiguous tags	11.33	7.00
Inconsistency	1.00	4.67
Gold standard error	5.67	11.00
Total	**100.00**	**100.00**

Table 2: Percentage of different PoS tagging error types.

1. **Unknown words/word forms:** The word either did not appear in the training data, so the tagger had to rely on context features, or the word form did not appear with the tag it has in this context. The most common errors in this category are proper nouns tagged as common nouns. Other errors include adverbs tagged as nouns, and incorrect gender or case for words with case inflection.
2. **Improvable tagging:** This category has errors for which we could imagine a tagger finding the right tag, either by looking at the context of a few more words or looking at particular features of surrounding words. The most common errors in this category are incorrect case or gender tags for nouns and adjectives. Often there were wrong tags, even though the tagger tagged adjacent words correctly, and there should be agreement for case or gender with the word in question. In many of these errors the case is determined by a preceding verb.
Example of failure in agreement in two adjacent words: "í guðrækilegum *[correct: singular; tagged as: plural]* umvöndunartóni *[correct: singular; tagged as: singular]*" (e. *in a tone of religious disapproval*).
3. **Insufficient contextual knowledge:** The determination of the correct tag requires broad contextual knowledge, such as (i) incorrect case with prepositions where semantics are required for the correct case; (ii) long distance assignment of case, gender or person; (iii) incorrect tagging of lower case word forms in multiword named entities.
Example of long distance assignment of person: "Ég nefndi *[correct: 1st person; tagged as: 1st person]* síðast tvö af þessum orðum og boðaði *[correct: 1st person; tagged as: 3rd person]* ..." (e. *The last time, I talked about two of these words and announced ...*)
4. **Ambiguous tags:** Unclear or ambiguous tags, in the context, such as (i) verb tense, where a verb has the same form for past and present tense and it is unclear which is being

used; (ii) words that are commonly used in either of two genders, and (iii) examples where it is not clear whether plural or singular forms are being used, e.g. in headlines.
Example of the homonymic past and present form: "Meðan ég elti *[In corpus: past tense; Tagged as: present tense]* hann." (e. *While I chase/chased him.*)

5. **Gold standard inconsistency:** Due to discrepancy in annotation of particular word classes.
6. **Gold standard errors:** In *MIM-GOLD* there are two common error types responsible for the majority of errors in this category. 11 of the 33 errors were unanalyzed tags where a correct tag could easily be determined and is determined correctly by the tagger. 6 errors were due to split sentences, because of incorrectly determined sentence breaks. Other error types were found in both *MIM-GOLD* and *IFD*.

The above classification is subjective and other researchers might have classified a few of the errors differently, in particular when choosing between the categories *improvable tagging* and *insufficient contextual knowledge*.

For our purposes, the most important categories are the last two, where the gold standard is wrong or inconsistent.

	IFD (%)	**MIM-GOLD** (%)
Correct tag	93.67	92,76
Unknown	0.51	1.18
Improvable tagging	2.40	2.27
Insufficient context	2.28	2.14
Ambiguous tags	0.72	0.51
Inconsistency	0.06	0.34
Gold standard error	0.36	0.80
Total	**100.0**	**100.0**

Table 3: Tagging categorization in the corpora.

6 Discussion and further work

Generalizing from our sample and looking at the percentage of tags in the tagger output that falls into each category, we see a clear difference between the corpora (Table 3). We confirmed that there is statistically significant difference ($p<0.001$) in error types between the two corpora by performing a chi-square test. The proportion of words falling into the category *insufficient contextual knowledge* is roughly the same. The same applies to *improvable tagging*. Unknown words are more common in *MIM-GOLD*. This can be explained by the fact that the texts in this corpus come from more varied sources than the texts in *IFD*. *Ambiguous tags* are somewhat more common in *IFD*, this can possibly be explained by *IFD* containing mostly literary texts. The lower score for 10-fold validation is likely explained by the high rate of wrong tags and inconsistencies in *MIM-GOLD*, 1.14% of the total compared to 0.42% in *IFD*, a difference of 0.72% compared to 0.91% difference in tagging accuracy.

Results from the tagging experiment show lower tagging accuracy for *MIM-GOLD* than *IFD*. We have shown that this may, at least in part, be explained by a higher number of inconsistencies and incorrect tags in *MIM-GOLD* than *IFD*. To determine the most cost-efficient way of reducing these errors, a further error analysis should be carried out and decisions made, based on that data, as to where we should focus our efforts. When the tagging accuracy in *MIM-GOLD* has been improved, experiments will be made to merge the two corpora in training data-driven taggers.

Acknowledgments

The correction of MIM-GOLD was funded in part by the Institute of Linguistics at the University of Iceland and the Ministry of Education, Science and Culture. The authors would also like to thank Hrafn Loftsson for assistance in training Stagger.

References

Kristín Bjarnadóttir. 2012. The Database of Modern Icelandic Inflection. In *Proceedings of "Language Technology for Normalization of Less-Resourced Languages", workshop at the* 8th *International Conference on Language Resources and Evaluation, LREC 2012*, Istanbul, Turkey.

Sigrún Helgadóttir, Ásta Svavarsdóttir, Eiríkur Rögnvaldsson, Kristín Bjarnadóttir, and Hrafn Loftsson. 2012. The Tagged Icelandic Corpus (MIM). In *Proceedings of the workshop Language Technology for Normalization of Less-Resourced Languages, SaLTMiL 8 – AfLaT, LREC 2012*, pages 67–72, Istanbul, Turkey.

Sigrún Helgadóttir, Hrafn Loftsson, and Eiríkur Rögnvaldsson. 2014. Correcting errors in a new gold standard for tagging icelandic text. In *Proceedings of the 9th International Conference on Language Resources and Evaluation (LREC 2014)*, Reykjavik, Iceland.

Verena Henrich, Timo Reuter, and Hrafn Loftsson. 2009. Combitagger: A system for developing combined taggers. In *Proceedings of the 22nd International FLAIRS Conference, Special Track: "Applied Natural Language Processing"*, Florida, USA.

Hrafn Loftsson and Robert Östling. 2013. Tagging a morphologically complex language using an averaged perceptron tagger: The case of icelandic. In *Proceedings of the 19th Nordic Conference of Computational Linguistics (NODALIDA-2013), NEALT Proceedings Series 16*, Oslo, Norway.

Hrafn Loftsson, Jökull H. Yngvason, Sigrún Helgadóttir, and Eiríkur Rögnvaldsson. 2010. Developing a PoS-tagged corpus using existing tools. In *Proceedings of "Creation and use of basic lexical resources for less-resourced languages", workshop at the 7th International Conference on Language Resources and Evaluation, LREC 2010*, Valetta, Malta.

Hrafn Loftsson. 2008. Tagging Icelandic text: A linguistic rule-based approach. *Nordic Journal of Linguistics*, 31(1):47–72.

Hrafn Loftsson. 2009. Correcting a PoS-tagged corpus using three complementary methods. In *Proceedings of the 12th Conference of the European Chapter of the ACL (EACL 2009)*, Athens, Greece.

Christopher D. Manning. 2011. Part-of-speech tagging from 97% to 100%: is it time for some linguistics? In *Computational Linguistics and Intelligent Text Processing*, pages 171–189. Springer.

Jörgen Pind, Friðrik Magnússon, and Stefán Briem. 1991. *Íslensk orðtíðnibók [The Icelandic Frequency Dictionary]*. The Institute of Lexicography, University of Iceland, Reykjavik, Iceland.

Kristina Toutanova, Dan Klein, Christopher D. Manning, and Yoram Singer. 2003. Feature-rich part-of-speech tagging with a cyclic dependency network. In *Proceedings of the 2003 Conference of the North American Chapter of the Association for Computational Linguistics on Human Language Technology*, NAACL, Edmonton, Canada.

From digital library to n-grams: NB N-gram

Magnus Breder Birkenes **Lars G. Johnsen**
Arne Martinus Lindstad **Johanne Ostad**
The National Library of Norway
P.O.Box 2674 Solli
NO – 0203 Oslo, Norway
{magnus.birkenes, lars.johnsen, arne.lindstad, johanne.ostad}@nb.no

Abstract

At the National Library of Norway, we are currently developing a service comparable to the Google Ngram Viewer (Michel et al., 2010; Lin et al., 2012; Aiden and Michel, 2013) called NB N-gram. It is based on all books and newspapers digitized up to and including 2013, as part of the large scale digitization project at the National Library of Norway. Uni-, bi- and trigams have been generated on the basis of this text corpus containing some 34 billion words. In this paper, we sketch the background of NB N-gram and illustrate some applications of it.

1 Background

In 2006, the National Library of Norway initiated an ambitious digitization program, with the goal of digitizing its entire collection. The collection contains all material collected under the legal deposit act, and includes among other things books, newspapers, periodicals, magazines, journals, music, films, posters and maps; basically anything published in the public domain in more than 50 copies. The collection contains material in many different languages.

The aim of the digitization program is to make the entire collection available for viewing purposes in a way that does not challenge intellectual property rights. To this end, agreements have been made, that make it possible to give access to the digitized content. *Bokhylleavtalen* ("The Bookshelf agreement") from 2012 gives the National Library right to make all books published up to and including the year 2000, available to users with a Norwegian IP-address.

The National Library has also made agreements with newspapers that make it possible to give access to a number of newspaper titles in digital format in Norwegian libraries. Some titles are also available outside public libraries to all users. Another example is an agreement made with the major public broadcaster in Norway (NRK), where open and free access for everyone is given to more than 36,000 radio programs. This includes radio broadcast news from the 1930s onward.

2 NB N-gram

In order to present an alternative and linguistically and historically more interesting take on the material, the thought developed that a statistical approach to the contents in the Digital National Library would be interesting.

NB N-gram gives both researchers and the general public the possibility to look at linguistic and cultural trends in this material, by connecting text and metadata (year, language information).

2.1 Generating n-grams

For copyright reasons, it is impossible to give access to full text versions of the material in the collection, but from the material underlying the n-gram viewer, the digitized text has been extracted, and uni-, bi- and trigrams have been generated from a base consisting of 34 billion words (11 billion words from 230,000 books, and 23 billion words from some 540,000 newspapers, spanning the period 1810-2013).

The texts in the Digital National Library are stored in XML format (ALTO XML) and were converted to plain text and then tokenized. Frequencies were counted for each single unique n-gram, but only texts in Norwegian Bokmål and Norwegian Nynorsk were considered in the first revision. The language classification relies upon information from the national bibliographical system BIBSYS, which is mostly, but not always, correct (an automatic detection using character n-grams would probably provide more exact results). The resulting data set consists of a collection of n-tuples on the form (n-gram, year, language, frequency).

2.2 Technical Implementation of NB N-gram

Building upon this material, NB N-gram consists of three components: a frontend, a backend and an n-gram database. Essentially, it is a web application written in Python/Flask.[1] The user enters search terms that the backend converts into valid SQL statements. The backend then returns the results from the database as a JSON object. The chart is drawn entirely on the client-side, using nvd3.[2]

The database is the single-most important component: We chose sqlite3 for retrieval speed and portability.[3] The database contains tables for each unique n-gram (unigram, bigram and trigram), which are connected to tables containing frequency information on these n-grams for both languages covered (Norwegian Bokmål and Norwegian Nynorsk), as shown in Figure 1 below.

freq	year	lang	first
60	2008	nno	lingvistikk
60	2008	nob	lingvistikk
120	2008	all	lingvistikk

Figure 1: Sample from the database

One frequency table holds all absolute frequencies for a particular n-gram for each year (from 1810 to 2013). Another table, used for wildcard-search (more on that in section 3.2), contains the summed frequencies for all years. We have chosen to store as much information as possible: Since we are dealing with tables containing several hundred millions of entries, doing some operations on the fly (like aggregating numbers for the two languages and then sorting on them) has proven to be way too time-consuming. As a result, we store most of the numbers (only the relative frequency is computed). With the help of indices, a query is very fast, even on slower HDDs (ca. 0.1 seconds).

3 User Interface

3.1 Basics

NB N-gram has a simple user interface that was created also with visually impaired users in mind. Thus all elements scale well on all devices and graphs can be shown either in colors or in grayscale.

The most central element to the user interface is the chart. By default, the chart shows the frequency representation of the four classic authors in the Norwegian literary canon. Frequencies are given as relative frequencies, but an option for showing absolute frequencies is also included.

3.2 Search

Above the chart the user will find a search box, where search terms may be entered, separated by commas (like in the Google Ngram Viewer), each search term resulting in a separate graph. Figure 2 shows a sample search in the newspaper material using the three search terms "EEC", "EF" and "EU" (different abbreviations for the political institution now known as the European Union) with spikes in 1972 and 1994, when the two referendums on Norwegian EU membership were held.

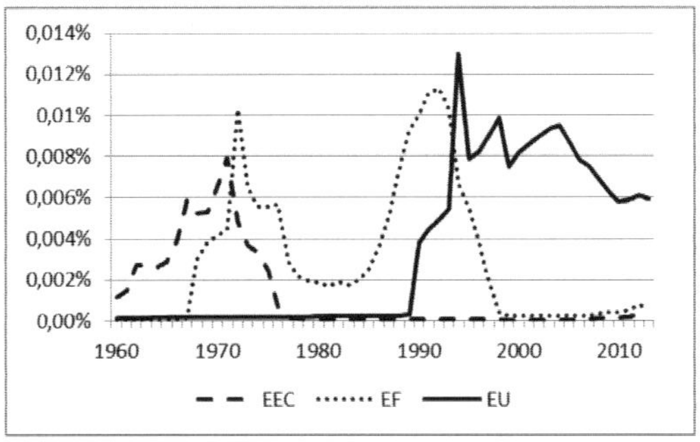

Figure 2: Trend lines for "EEC", "EF", "EU".

A search term may contain one single *n*-gram (from unigram up to the size of a trigram) or the combination of many n-grams, using the + operator. In this way, a search for *hest+hesten+hester+hestene* 'horse, the horse, horses, the horses' results in a graph with all inflectional forms of the word *hest* 'horse'.

A wildcard search is also possible: Similar to the Google Ngram Viewer, using a wildcard in a

[1] http://flask.pocoo.org/
[2] http://nvd3.org/
[3] https://sqlite.org/

search term will plot the ten most frequent n-grams matching that criterion. Technically speaking, "most frequent" is here defined as the n-gram having the highest total frequency across the whole period. Unlike the Google Ngram Viewer, NB N-gram also allows wildcards inside words: for example, the search term **else* will result in ten graphs showing the most frequent words ending in the derivational suffix *–else* within the period 1810-2013.

3.3 Smoothing

In order to compensate for variation from year to year, NB N-gram uses a smoothing algorithm similar to that of the Google Ngram Viewer. Thus, a smoothing of 4 (which is the default) means that the frequency of a particular year is computed as the average of the relative frequency in the four years before and the four years after, divided by nine.[4]

3.4 Customized views

The user interface itself allows for certain customizations: The default range (1810 to 2013) may be decreased in order to focus on a special period (for example a decade). Also, clicking on the bullet points in the legend allows for blending out (and in) individual graphs.

3.5 Download of Raw Data

The statistical data underlying the graphs – both relative and absolute frequencies – can be downloaded as .csv-files (comma-separated text). Also the graphics can be downloaded, as scalable high-quality .svg-files.

3.6 Inspecting the underlying material in NB Bokhylla

Clicking on a graph gives the user the possibility to show examples of the search terms in context through NB Bokhylla. If you are in Norway, you get access to all material published before 2001. If you are outside of Norway, only sources not protected by copyright are shown.

4 Further perspectives

In this paper, we outlined the background of NB N-gram and showed some of its applications.[5] In the future, we hope to provide additional functionality such as linguistic annotation and genre-based search (based on Dewey classification). We also want to look at the possibility of including other languages from our material, such as Sami and Kven.

Acknowledgments

We would like to thank our colleagues at the National Library of Norway for input and technical assistance.

References

Erez Aiden and Jean-Baptiste Michel. 2013. *Uncharted: Big Data as a Lens on Human Culture*. Penguin, New York.

Yuri Lin, Jean-Baptiste Michel, Erez Lieberman Aiden, Jon Orwant, William Brockman and Slav Petrov. Syntactic Annotations for the Google Books Ngram Corpus. Proceedings of the 50th Annual Meeting of the Association for Computational Linguistics Volume 2: Demo Papers (ACL '12) (2012)

Jean-Baptiste Michel, Yuan Kui Shen, Aviva Presser Aiden, Adrian Veres, Matthew K. Gray, William Brockman, The Google Books Team, Joseph P. Pickett, Dale Hoiberg, Dan Clancy, Peter Norvig, Jon Orwant, Steven Pinker, Martin A. Nowak, and Erez Lieberman Aiden. Quantitative Analysis of Culture Using Millions of Digitized Books. Science (Published online ahead of print: 12/16/2010).

Google Ngram Viewer Documentation: `https://books.google.com/ngrams/info`

[4] Google Ngram Viewer Documentation: `https://books.google.com/ngrams/info`

[5] A beta version of NB N-gram is available via the following link: `http://www.nb.no/sp_tjenester/beta/ngram_1`

The Corpus of American Norwegian Speech (CANS)

Janne Bondi Johannessen
The Text Laboratory & MultiLing, University of Oslo / P.O. Box 1102
Blindern, 0317 Oslo, Norway
jannebj@iln.uio.no

Abstract

This paper contains a description of the Corpus of American Norwegian Speech, a new tool for heritage language research. We present the background for its existence, the linguistic contents and its main technical features. The demonstration will show the corpus in use, focussing on problems that are specific to heritage language research, and how the corpus can be searched to provide relevant data.

1 Introduction

The American Norwegian language is a dying language. It is therefore important to record it and make it available for research. The best way to do this, is to transcribe the recordings, morphologically tag the transcriptions and make them available in a searchable corpus, The Corpus of American Norwegian Speech (CANS). The Text Laboratory at the University of Oslo (UiO) has developed many speech features for its corpus system Glossa (Johannessen et al. 2008), which is already used for many other speech corpora, so it has been a relatively easy task to put one more corpus into the same architecture. The Glossa architecture has proved to be a valuable corpus search system, and is used for many corpus projects outside the UiO, most recently the Finland Swedish speech corpus Talko. Glossa is currently undergoing further development under the CLARIN umbrella and the Norwegian project Clarino.

The paper is structured as follows: Section 2 gives some background on the American Norwegian heritage language, while Section 3 describes the main features of the corpus, first with a presentation of the informants in the corpus in numbers, then with a list of the special metadata of these heritage informants, and finally with the way the corpus has been transcribed and annotated. Section 4 presents some examples of search possibilities, and Section 5 sums up the paper.

2 The Norwegian Heritage language in America

Norwegian emigration to America started in 1825, and by 1930, 850 000 people had left for the new world, i.e. the USA and Canada, approximately the same as the whole population of Norway in 1800. Most settled in the Midwest. In these rural areas, whole communities had a Norwegian population, and for a long time they had their own schools, churches and newspapers, thereby keeping the language alive. Researchers have been interested in the American Norwegian language at several points in time. Didrik Arup Seip and Ernst W. Selmer did recordings in the 1930s, Einar Haugen in 1940s, Arnstein Hjelde in the 1990s, and the present author with colleagues in the 2010s.

Research into heritage language has recently become a major field of linguistics, Rothman (2009:159) defines this way: "A language qualifies as a heritage language if it is a language spoken at home or otherwise readily available to young children, and crucially this language is not a dominant language of the larger (national) society." The last years an annual workshop series has been established (the last was held in 2014 at UCLA), and in 2012 a special issue of *Norsk Lingvistisk Tidsskrift* was devoted to Norwegian heritage language (for both, see References).

Heritage languages usually differ from their mother languages (if these are a majority language elsewhere), in that they have a rather large number of loanwords, and that their phonology, morphology and syntax may have features from the neighbouring language or at least are different from those of their mother language.

For these reasons, studying heritage language may bring new knowledge on the human language capacity. It is interesting to see which linguistic features that change, and how, and even to compare the changes with the language of first and second acquisition of the mother language. It is obvious that a good corpus of heritage language is a valuable resource for such research.

3 The CANS corpus

3.1 The contents of the corpus: informants and numbers

The corpus will be growing as there are many recordings that are in the process of being transcribed and annotated for corpus adaption, but at the moment the corpus consists of 131 000 words based on the speech of 36 informants from 13 different speakers from Illinois, Iowa, Minnesota, South Dakota and Wisconsin. The speakers range in age from 67 to 96, but the majority are in their 80s. Since none of them have transferred the language to the next generation, this language is dying. The recordings are from the fieldwork conducted by the present author, from the 2010s.

3.2 Metadata on informants

For each informant, a variety of metadata is available, and searchable. This includes place and state of informant, age, year of birth, language of instruction at school, how much contact they have with Norway, how many times they have visited Norway, whether they read Norwegian, whether they have Norwegian as their mother tongue (L1), which generation immigrant they are, area in Norway where ancestors came from, number of words in the interview, and year of recording. The heritage corpus-specific metadata has been selected by consulting researchers who were using the corpus from the start (see Acknowledgments).

3.3 Transcriptions

All the recordings have been transcribed in two ways: a phonetic-like one and a standard orthographic one. The phonetic transcription was done first via the free software Transcriber and later by Elan. The result of this manual transcription has then been translated to orthographic transcription using a semi-automatic Dialect Transliterator, developed at the Text Laboratory. This transliterator uses a "bi-lingual" word list consisting of dialectal, phonetically written word forms and their standard orthographic equivalents, and which is a result of previous transliterations. It translates each phonetically written form to an orthographic word. The result is then inspected manually, checking the two transcription equivalents and comparing the transcriptions to the original audio versions.

After manual inspection and correction, the new transliterated set of phonetic and orthographic text is fed back into the transliterator, improving the word list for further use for that particular dialect or language variety. Whenever a word in its phonetic transcription is not found in the word list, the same word is used for transliteration, to be given an orthographic form later in the manual inspection. At this stage, certain other annotations are also added, see for example Section 3.5.

The two transcriptions are strictly aligned word by word, and linked together in Glossa, and the user can choose to search in only one of them, or in both simultaneously. (See list of web sites at the end of this paper.)

3.4 Tagging

The CANS corpus has been tagged with a TreeTagger (Schmid 1994, 1995) trained on a speech version of the Oslo-Bergen tagger, developed for a speech corpus of the Oslo dialect, and then measured by 10-fold cross validation at an accuracy of 96, 9 % (Søfteland and Nøklestad 2008). The accuracy has not been measured for the CANS corpus, but with its high number of English loan words and dialectal word order, the result is likely not as good.

3.5 Other annotation

Since CANS contains heritage language it has many loanwords. These have been annotated manually in the transliteration process with the tag x. Even if the corpus contains only about 130 000 words, the number of words tagged with x is nearly 4000.

4 Searching the CANS corpus

The corpus can be searched using words, parts of words or word combinations and by annotations. The metadata can also be used as search filters, see Johannessen et al. (2012) and (2014) for a general introduction to the corpus search features.

In this paper the focus is on what is special for the CANS corpus.

Figure 1 illustrates a search for the x-tagging described in Section 4.5; the x is chosen from the Criteria menu that filters any search given in the word-box above it. (The box can be empty, too, as it is here.)

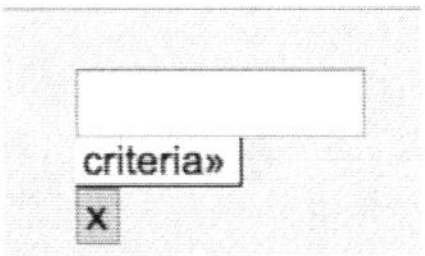

Figure 1: Searching for x-tagged words

This search gives 3857 hits. One is illustrated below, in Figure 2. (The orthographic transcription is on the first line, followed by the phonetic one on the second.)

å jeg driver og **raiser** noe hester

å e driv å **reiser** no hæsster

'Oh, I raise some horses.' (blair_WI_01gm)

Figure 2: One of the results from the search for x-tagged words (*raise* is an English loanword; the Norwegian equivalent is *avle.*)

Other typical words tagged with x are interjections like *oh, huh, right*, and words that have replaced Norwegian ones, like *cousin* (instead of fetter), *back* (tilbake), *figure* (think), *telle* (fortelle).

An example of filtering a search by informant metadata is given in Figure 3, where informants are specified to be fourth generation immigrant. This box comes in addition to the general word-box, this time searching for the word *ikke* 'not'.

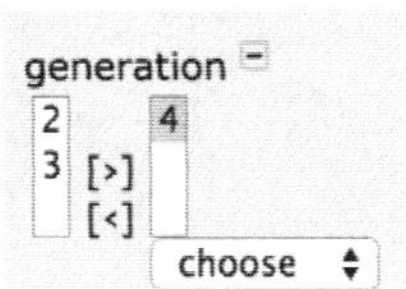

Figure 3: Filtering a search by speaker's generation

The search yielded 467 results divided amongst 7 informants. It can be filtered further, e.g. by the home county of the ancestors, age or any other metadata.

5 Conclusion

This paper has presented the Corpus of American Norwegian Speech, a heritage language corpus. The paper has focussed on heritage languages in general and American Norwegian in particular, and the most central details of the corpus. Some statistics on the informants were offered, the special metadata of these heritage informants were presented, and transcription and annotation were briefly presented. Finally, some illustrations of search possibilities were given. For more general speech corpus features of CANS, the readers are referred to Johannessen et al. (2012, 2014). Expansions of the corpus are expected, as there is presently some funding for more transcriptions. The corpus may also be expanded with other heritage Scandinavian languages.

Acknowledgments

The Corpus of American Norwegian Speech could not have been developed without several people. The most important ones are the American Norwegians who have willingly sat down in front of a camera to talk with their fellow heritage speakers and the researchers. Signe Laake and Arnstein Hjelde have been excellent collaborators and company at fieldwork on several occasions from 2010 to 2014.

The people at the Text Laboratory, UiO, have a major role in the corpus development. Kristin Hagen has taken the responsibility for technical decisions and coordinating work. Joel Priestley has designed the corpus interface and is chief programmer for all the specific speech features. Eirik Olsen, André Kaasen and Eirik Tengesdal have been vital in observations and suggestions related to transcription.

The collection of material, i.e. fieldwork and recordings, has been funded by The Research Council of Norway (RCN) under the project Norwegian Dialect Syntax; the Department of Linguistics and Scandinavian Studies, UiO. Transcriptions have been funded partly by the Text Lab, UiO, by the University of Tromsø (thanks are due to Marit Westergaard and Merete Anderssen, who have also given input on search options and metadata in the corpus), and by the RCN project LIA, no. 225941. The fieldwork was partly supported by the RCN through its Centres of Excellence funding scheme, project no. 223265.

References

Johannessen, Janne Bondi, Lars Nygaard, Joel Priestley, and Anders Nøklestad. 2008. Glossa: a Multilingual, Multimodal, Configurable User Interface. In: *Proceedings of the Sixth International Language Resources and Evaluation (LREC'08)*. Paris: European Language Resources Association (ELRA). http://www.hf.uio.no/iln/tjenester/kunnskap/sprak/glossa/LREC-glossa_2008.pdf

Johannessen, Janne Bondi, Joel Priestley, Kristin Hagen, Anders Nøklestad, and Andre Lynum. 2012. The Nordic Dialect Corpus. In *Proceedings of the Eighth International Conference on Language Resources and Evaluation*. European Language Resources Association, p. 3388-3391. http://dblp.uni-trier.de/db/conf/lrec/lrec2012.html

Johannessen, Janne Bondi, Øystein Alexander Vangsnes, Joel Priestley, Kristin Hage,. 2014. A multilingual speech corpus of North-Germanic languages. In Raso, Tommaso; Mello, Heliana (eds.): *Spoken Corpora and Linguistic Studies*. John Benjamins Publishing Company, p. 69-83. https://www.benjamins.com/#catalog/books/scl.61.02joh/fulltext

Norsk Lingvistisk Tidsskrift [Norwegian Linguistics Journal]. 2012. Special issue on the Norwegian Language in America (edited by Janne Bondi Johannessen and Joe Salmons).

Rothman, Jason. 2009. Understanding the Nature and Outcomes of Early Bilingualism: Romance Languages as Heritage Languages. *The International Journal of Bilingualism* 13: 155-163.

Schmid, Helmut. 1995. Improvements in Part-of-Speech Tagging with an Application to German. *Proceedings of the ACL SIGDAT-Workshop*. Dublin, Ireland.

Schmid, Helmut. 1994. Probabilistic Part-of-Speech Tagging Using Decision Trees. *Proceedings of International Conference on New Methods in Language Processing*, Manchester, UK.

Søfteland, Åshild and Anders Nøklestad. 2008. Manuell morfologisk tagging av NoTa-materialet med støtte fra en statistisk tagger. In Johannessen, Janne Bondi og Kristin Hagen (eds.) *Språk i Oslo. Ny forskning omkring talespråk*. Novus, Oslo.

Web sites

5th Annual Workshop on Immigrant Languages in the Americas, UCLA, October 17-19, 2014. http://tekstlab.uio.no/WILA5/index.html

CLARIN: http://www.clarin.eu/

Clarino: http://clarin.b.uib.no/

Corpus of American Norwegian Speech (CANS): http://tekstlab.uio.no/glossa/html/?corpus=amerikanorsk

DialectTransliterator: http://omilia.uio.no/scandiasyn/translit/

Elan: https://tla.mpi.nl/tools/tla-tools/elan/

Glossa corpus search and processing tool: http://www.hf.uio.no/iln/english/about/organization/text-laboratory/services/glossa.html

Oslo-Bergen Tagger: http://tekstlab.uio.no/obt-ny/english/index.html

Talko: http://www.sls.fi/doc.php?category=2&docid=943

Text Laboratory: http://www.hf.uio.no/iln/english/about/organization/text-laboratory/

TreeTagger: http://www.ims.uni-stuttgart.de/projekte/corplex/TreeTagger/

Transcriber: http://trans.sourceforge.net/en/presentation.php

Open-Domain Semantic Parsing with Boxer

Johan Bos
Center for Language and Cognition
University of Groningen
johan.bos@rug.nl

Abstract

Boxer is a semantic parser for English texts with many input and output possibilities, and various ways to perform meaning analysis based on Discourse Representation Theory. This involves the various ways that meaning representations can be computed, as well as their possible semantic ingredients.

1 Introduction

In this paper I present the capabilities of the open-domain semantic parser Boxer. Boxer is distributed with the C&C text processing tools (Curran et al., 2007), and its main characteristics were first described in my earlier work (Bos, 2008). The roots of the current version of Boxer go back even further, long before Boxer was officially released to the community (Bos et al., 2004; Bos, 2001).

Boxer distinguishes itself from other semantic parsers in that it produces formal meaning representations (compatible with first-order logic) while reaching wide coverage, and is therefore used in a range of applications (Basile et al., 2012; Bjerva et al., 2014). To get an idea of what Boxer does, consider the input and output in Figure 1.

```
John did not go to school .

 __________________
|x1                |
|..................|
|named(x1,john,per)|
|    ____________  |
|   |e2 x3       | |
| ¬ |............| |
|   |go(e2)      | |
|   |agent(e2,x1)| |
|   |school(x3)  | |
|   |to(e2,x3)   | |
|   |____________| |
|__________________|
```

Figure 1: Example of Boxer's input and output.

Here, the input is a simple sentence, and Boxer's output a formal interpretation of this sentence: there is a person x_1 named "john", and it is not the case that there is a school-going-event e_2 that involves the entities x_1 (John) and a school (denoted by entity x_3). But Boxer has a lot more to offer, and what this paper contributes (and adds with respect to previous publications) is a fine-grained description of the many possibilities that Boxer provides for the formal semantic analysis of text processing.

2 Interface Formats

The input of the Boxer system is a syntactic analysis in the form of a derivation of combinatorial categorial grammar, CCG (Steedman, 2001). This input can be augmented in order to incorporate information of external language technology components. The output is a meaning representation, produced in a variety of standard formats.

2.1 Input

Boxer requires a syntactic analysis of the text in the form of CCG-derivations, every sentence corresponding to one CCG derivation. The derivation itself is represented as a `ccg/2` Prolog term, comprising a sentence identifier and a recursively built structure of combinatorial rules (such as `fa/3`, `ba/3`, and so on), and terminals (the lexical items). All combinatorial rules of CCG are supported, including the generalized composition rules and the type-changing rules introduced in CCGbank (Hockenmaier and Steedman, 2007).

The terminals are captured by a Prolog term consisting of the CCG category (Boxer implements about 600 different lexical category types), the token, its lemma, and part-of-speech. Information of external tools can also be included here, such as word sense disambiguation, thematic role labelling, noun-noun compound interpretation, or reference resolution.

```
sem(1,[1001:[tok:'John',pos:'NNP',lemma:'John',namex:'I-PER'],
       1002:[tok:did,pos:'VBD',lemma:do,namex:'O'],
       1003:[tok:not,pos:'RB',lemma:not,namex:'O'],
       1004:[tok:go,pos:'VB',lemma:go,namex:'O'],
       1005:[tok:to,pos:'TO',lemma:to,namex:'O'],
       1006:[tok:school,pos:'NN',lemma:school,namex:'O'],
       1007:[tok:'.',pos:'.',lemma:'.',namex:'O']],
    b2:drs([b1:[]:x1],
           [b1:[1001]:named(x1,john,per,nam),
            b2:[1003]:not(b3:drs([b3:[]:e1,b3:[]:x2],
                                  [b3:[1004]:pred(e1,go,v,0),
                                   b3:[]:role(e1,x1,agent,1),
                                   b3:[1006]:pred(x2,school,n,0),
                                   b3:[1005]:rel(e1,x2,to,0)]))])).
```

Figure 2: Boxer's output in Prolog format, for "John does not go to school."

Any parser can be used to support Boxer, as long as it produces CCG derivation in the required Prolog format. The standard parser used in tandem with Boxer is that of the C&C tools (Clark and Curran, 2004). Alternatively, other parsers can be used, such as EasyCCG (Lewis and Steedman, 2014). The lemmas can be provided by off-the-shells tools like morpha (Minnen et al., 2001).

2.2 Output

The standard output is a meaning representation in the form of a Discourse Representation Structure (Kamp and Reyle, 1993). This output is standard shown in Prolog format, but can also be produced in XML (with the `--format xml` option). Output can also be suppressed, with `--format no`, in case only human-readable output is wanted.

For the user's convenience, the meaning can also be displayed in boxed format (with the `--box true` option), as shown above. In combination with `--instantiate true`, this yields convenient names for discourse referents that appear in the boxes. Additionally, with the `--ccg true` option, a pretty-printed version of the input CCG-derivation is presented to the user.

3 Semantic Frameworks

3.1 Semantic Theory

The backbone of Boxer's meaning representations is provided by Discourse Representation Theory, DRT (Kamp and Reyle, 1993). Boxer follows the theory closely (`--theory drt`), except with respect to (i) event semantics, where it adopts a neo-Davidsonian approach, and (ii) the analysis of sentential complements, where Boxer follows an analysis based on modal logic (Bos, 2004).

By default, Boxer produces a meaning representation for every sentence in the input. However, with `--integrate true` it computes a single meaning representation spanning all sentences, with separate boxes corresponding to all sentences. Instead, using `--theory sdrt`, a Segmented Discourse Representation Structure is produced, following SDRT (Asher, 1993).

3.2 Meaning Translations

The meaning representations of Discourse Representation Theory can be shaped in different ways, and Boxer supports several of these possibilities. The standard representations are DRSs (Discourse Representation Structures, the boxes, selected with `--semantics drs`). Alternatively DRSs can be shown as Projective DRSs (Venhuizen et al., 2013) using `--semantics pdrs`, where each DRS is labelled with a pointer, and each DRS-condition receives a pointer to the DRS in which it appears.

For some applications and users with different mind-sets, Boxer comes with an option to translate DRSs into other types of meaning representation. First of all, with `--semantics fol`, Boxer supports the well-known translation from boxes to first-order logic (Kamp and Reyle, 1993; Bos, 2004), or to DRSs in the form of graphs (Basile and Bos, 2013), when invoked with `--semantics drg`. Secondly, the meaning representations can be translated into flat logical forms, as proposed in Jerry Hobbs's framework (Hobbs, 1991), with `--semantics tacitus`. Note that not all of these translations are necessary meaning-preserving, becauce of the differences in expressive power between the formalisms.

4 Meaning Details

The devil is in the detail. Indeed, to get the most out of Boxer, it is important to know what features it offers to compute meaning representations.

4.1 Linguistic Features

Copula Notorious among computational semanticists is the analysis of the copula. Boxer gives two options: to interpret the copula as were it an ordinary transitive verb (`--copula false`), or by introducing an equality symbol between two entities (`--copula true`). The latter option has as advantage that certain inferences can directly be drawn, but as disadvantage that some nuances of meaning are lost (i.e., the distinction between *John is a teacher* and *John was a teacher*).

Multiword Expressions Boxer provides two ways to represent compound proper names. With `--mwe no` a compound name such as *Barack Obama* is represented by two naming conditions (with the non-logical symbols `barack` and `obama`), and with `--mwe yes` as a single naming condition (with symbol `barack~obama`).

Noun–Noun Compounds Noun–noun compounds are interpreted as two entities that form a certain relation. By default, Boxer picks the generic prepositional *of*–relation. With `--nn true`, Boxer attempts to disambiguate noun-noun compound relations by selecting from a set of prepositional relations (Bos and Nissim, 2015). For instance, *beach house* would be interpreted as: house(x) $\wedge$ beach(y) $\wedge$ at(x,y).

Reference Resolution By default Boxer doesn't resolve pronouns or other referential expressions, but with `--resolve true`, Boxer attempts to resolve pronouns, proper names and definite descriptions (currently using a rule-based approach). The foundational algorithm to accomplish this is based on Van der Sandt's theory of presupposition projection (Van der Sandt, 1992). The discourse referents of the selected antecedents are unified with those of the referential expression.

Thematic Role Labelling As mentioned above, Boxer follows a neo-Davidsonian approach to event semantics. This means that events (usually triggered by verbs) introduce discourse referents, and these are related to discourse referents of participants by two-place relations, the thematic roles. Standard (`--roles proto`) these roles are picked from a set of five proto-roles: agent, theme, topic, recipient, and experiencer. A more fine-grained inventory of roles is employed with `--roles verbnet`, producing thematic roles as provided by VerbNet (Kipper et al., 2008). This is done by mapping the obtained proto-roles to VerbNet roles, using a simple deterministic approach in the semantic lexicon of Boxer.

4.2 Logical Features

Eliminating Equality In some cases equality symbols can be elimated from the meaning representation, resulting in a logically equivalent logical form. This is possible, for instance, when the two variables within an equality relation are bound by discourse referents introduced in the same DRS as the equality condition. Equality conditions are introduced by a range of lexical entries, but in the final meaning representation they don't play a fundamental role. With `--elimeq true` such equality conditions are removed and their corresponding discourse referents unified.

Modal Modal expressions (as introduced by modal adverbs or modal verbs) can be made explicit in the meaning representation by invoking `--modal true`. This triggers two additional complex DRS-conditions formed by the unary box and diamond operators from modal logic, expressing necessity (univerally quantifying over possible worlds) and possibility (existentially quantifying over possible worlds). This option also has an effect on the translation to first-order logic, and when used in combination with `--semantics fol` the translation to modal first-order logic is used (with reification over possible worlds).

Tense The standard reference textbook for Discourse Representation Theory has an extensive analysis of various tenses found in the English language (Kamp and Reyle, 1993). Boxer aims to reproduce this analysis with `--tense true`. This involves additional relations and discourse referents related to the events introduced by the text.

5 Conclusion

I have outlined a large set of possibilities that the semantic parser Boxer offers. These concern input and output modalities, as well as the level of detail of meaning interpretation. I will demonstrate a selection of these features at the conference.

References

Nicholas Asher. 1993. *Reference to Abstract Objects in Discourse*. Kluwer Academic Publishers.

Valerio Basile and Johan Bos. 2013. Aligning formal meaning representations with surface strings for wide-coverage text generation. In *Proceedings of the 14th European Workshop on Natural Language Generation*, pages 1–9, Sofia, Bulgaria.

Valerio Basile, Johan Bos, Kilian Evang, and Noortje Venhuizen. 2012. Negation detection with discourse representation structures. In *The First Joint Conference on Lexical and Computational Semantics (*SEM 2012 Shared Task)*, pages 301–309, Montreal, Canada.

Johannes Bjerva, Johan Bos, Rob Van der Goot, and Malvina Nissim. 2014. The meaning factory: Formal semantics for recognizing textual entailment and determining semantic similarity. In *Proceedings of the 8th International Workshop on Semantic Evaluation (SemEval 2014)*, pages 642–646, Dublin, Ireland.

Johan Bos and Malvina Nissim. 2015. Uncovering noun-noun compound relations by gamification. In Beáta Megyesi, editor, *Proceedings of the 20th Nordic Conference of Computational Linguistics*.

Johan Bos, Stephen Clark, Mark Steedman, James R. Curran, and Julia Hockenmaier. 2004. Wide-Coverage Semantic Representations from a CCG Parser. In *Proceedings of the 20th International Conference on Computational Linguistics (COLING '04)*, pages 1240–1246, Geneva.

Johan Bos. 2001. DORIS 2001: Underspecification, Resolution and Inference for Discourse Representation Structures. In Patrick Blackburn and Michael Kohlhase, editors, *ICoS-3, Inference in Computational Semantics*, pages 117–124.

Johan Bos. 2004. Computational Semantics in Discourse: Underspecification, Resolution, and Inference. *Journal of Logic, Language and Information*, 13(2):139–157.

Johan Bos. 2008. Wide-Coverage Semantic Analysis with Boxer. In J. Bos and R. Delmonte, editors, *Semantics in Text Processing. STEP 2008 Conference Proceedings*, volume 1 of *Research in Computational Semantics*, pages 277–286. College Publications.

Stephen Clark and James R. Curran. 2004. Parsing the WSJ using CCG and Log-Linear Models. In *Proceedings of the 42nd Annual Meeting of the Association for Computational Linguistics (ACL '04)*, pages 104–111, Barcelona, Spain.

James Curran, Stephen Clark, and Johan Bos. 2007. Linguistically Motivated Large-Scale NLP with C&C and Boxer. In *Proceedings of the 45th Annual Meeting of the Association for Computational Linguistics Companion Volume Proceedings of the Demo and Poster Sessions*, pages 33–36, Prague, Czech Republic.

Jerry R. Hobbs. 1991. SRI international's TACITUS system: MUC-3 test results and analysis. In *Proceedings of the 3rd Conference on Message Understanding, MUC 1991, San Diego, California, USA, May 21-23, 1991*, pages 105–107.

Julia Hockenmaier and Mark Steedman. 2007. CCG-bank: a corpus of CCG derivations and dependency structures extracted from the Penn Treebank. *Computational Linguistics*, 33(3):355–396.

Hans Kamp and Uwe Reyle. 1993. *From Discourse to Logic; An Introduction to Modeltheoretic Semantics of Natural Language, Formal Logic and DRT*. Kluwer, Dordrecht.

Karin Kipper, Anna Korhonen, Neville Ryant, and Martha Palmer. 2008. A large-scale classification of English verbs. *Language Resources and Evaluation*, 42(1):21–40.

Mike Lewis and Mark Steedman. 2014. A* ccg parsing with a supertag-factored model. In *Proceedings of the 2014 Conference on Empirical Methods in Natural Language Processing (EMNLP)*, pages 990–1000, Doha, Qatar, October. Association for Computational Linguistics.

Guido Minnen, John Carroll, and Darren Pearce. 2001. Applied morphological processing of english. *Journal of Natural Language Engineering*, 7(3):207–223.

Mark Steedman. 2001. *The Syntactic Process*. The MIT Press.

Rob A. Van der Sandt. 1992. Presupposition Projection as Anaphora Resolution. *Journal of Semantics*, 9:333–377.

Noortje Venhuizen, Johan Bos, and Harm Brouwer. 2013. Parsimonious semantic representations with projection pointers. In *Proceedings of the 10th International Conference on Computational Semantics (IWCS 2013) – Long Papers*, pages 252–263, Potsdam, Germany.

Extracting Semantic Frames using hfst-pmatch

Sam Hardwick
University of Helsinki

Miikka Silfverberg
University of Helsinki

Krister Lindén
University of Helsinki

{sam.hardwick, miikka.silfverberg}@iki.fi, krister.linden@helsinki.fi

Abstract

We use `hfst-pmatch` (Lindén et al., 2013), a pattern-matching tool mimicking and extending Xerox `fst` (Karttunen, 2011), for demonstrating how to develop a semantic frame extractor. We select a FrameNet (Baker et al., 1998) frame and write shallowly syntactic pattern-matching rules based on part-of-speech information and morphology from either a morphological automaton or tagged text.

1 Introduction

`pmatch` is a pattern-matching operation for text based on regular expressions. It uses a context-free grammar on regular expression terminals, which allows for recursive, self-referencing rules which would not be possible in a fully regular formalism. The matched patterns may be efficiently tagged, extracted and modified by the rules.

Large-scale named-entity recognisers (NERs) have been developed in `pmatch` for Swedish and Finnish. Here we demonstrate a bottom-up approach to using it to identify the frame "Size" in FrameNet.

2 A Semantic Frame

A semantic frame (Fillmore, 1976) is a description of a *type* of event, relation or entity and related participants. For example, in FrameNet, a database of semantic frames, the description of an `Entity` in terms of physical space occupied by it is an instance of the semantic frame `Size`. The frame is evoked by a lexical unit (LU), also known as a frame evoking element (FEE), which is a word (in this case an adjective) such as "big" or "tiny", descriptive of the size of the `Entity`. Apart from `Entity`, which is a core or compulsory element, the frame may identify a `Degree` to which the `Entity` deviates from the norm ("a **really** big dog") and a `Standard` to which it is compared ("tall **for a jockey**").

Lexical Unit (LU)	Adjective describing magnitude (large, tiny, ...)
Entity (E)	That which is being described (house, debt, ...)
Degree (D), optional	Intensity or extent of description (really, quite, ...)
Standard (S), optional	A point of comparison (for a jockey, ...)

Table 1: The semantic frame *Size*.

For example:

$$\left[_{\text{Size}} \left[_{\text{E}} \text{He}\right] \text{is} \left[_{\text{D}} \text{quite}\right] \left[_{\text{LU}} \text{tall}\right] \left[_{\text{S}} \text{for a jockey}\right]\right]$$

Figure 1: A tagged example of *Size*

3 A Rule

A `pmatch` ruleset consists of a number of named regular expressions and functions, exactly one of which is the top-level rule which is named `TOP` or is introduced with the directive `regex`. For example:

```
define my_colours {green} | {red};
define TOP my_colours EndTag(colour);
```

Listing 1: Introducing `pmatch` syntax

The effect of the directive `EndTag()` is to tag whatever is matched by its rule (here shown with an unintentional effect):

```
The light went <colour>green</colour>
and the mechanism was
trigge<colour>red</colour>.
```

To avoid tagging the "red" at the end of "triggered", we need to add a word boundary to the rule. This could be accomplished by defining eg. `W` to be whitespace (`Whitespace`), punctuation (`Punct`) or the limit of input (`#`). `W` may then be interpolated in rules when we want to capture whitespace inside the pattern, or checked for with run-time context checking just to make sure there is a word boundary at the edge of our rule (`LC()` and `RC()` check left and right contexts respectively).

A simple and common syntactic realisation of the `Size` frame is a single noun phrase containing one of the LUs, such as "the big brown dog that ran away". Here we'd like to identify "big" as `LU`, "brown dog" as `Entity` and the combination as `Size`. Our first rule for identifying this type of construction might be

```
define LU {small} | {large} |
  {big} EndTag(LU);
define Size1 LU (Adjective)
  [Noun].t(Entity);
define TOP Size1 EndTag(Size);
```

Listing 2: A simplified first rule

This ruleset has been simplified for brevity – it has only a few of the permitted LUs, and word boundary issues have not been addressed.

The `[].t()` syntax in the definition of `Size1` is a tag delimiter that controls the area tagged as `Entity`. The extra `Adjective` is optional, which is conveyed by the surrounding parentheses.

We can verify that our rules extract instances of our desired pattern by compiling them with `hfst-pmatch2fst` and running the compiled result with `hfst-pmatch --extract-tags`. In the following we have inputted the text of the King James Bible from Project Gutenberg (`gutenberg.org`) and added some extra characters on both sides for a concordance-like effect:

```
...
there lay a <Size><LU>small</LU>
round <Entity>thing</Entity></Size>
...
there was a <Size><LU>great</LU>
<Entity>cry</Entity></Size> in Egypt
...
saw that <Size><LU>great</LU>
<Entity>work</Entity></Size> which
...
```

`pmatch` may be operated in various modes. In `locate` mode the position and length of each match is given, and only the outermost tag is supplied. `match` mode (which is the default) tags and outputs running text, and `extract` mode does the same but omits parts of the input that aren't matched by a rule. Matches may also be extracted via an API call, for example in order to achieve the above-seen concordance effect.

A natural next step is to add optional non-core elements, such as an adverb preceding the LU being tagged as `Degree` and a noun phrase beginning with "for a" following it as `Standard`.

```
define Size1 [Adverb].t(Degree)
  LU (Adjective) [Noun].t(Entity)
  [{for a} NP].t(Standard);
```

Listing 3: Extending the rule with optional elements

Here are some examples this rule finds in the British National Corpus (Consortium, 2007).

```
...
presence of an <Size>
  <Degree>arbitrarily</Degree>
  <LU>small</LU> <Entity>
  amount</Entity></Size> of dust
...
one <Size><LU>small</LU>
  <Entity>step</Entity>
  <Standard>for a man</Standard>
  </Size>
...
```

We can see that in "small amount of dust" we might want to tag not just the immediate noun as `Entity` but the entire noun phrase (which could be implemented up to a context-free definition of a noun phrase), and in "one small step for a man" a common indirect use of the `Standard` construction.

The FrameNet corpus itself is a good source for finding more cases.

As well as correct matches, such as "small

round thing" in the biblical example, we have metaphorical meanings of `Size`, such as "great cry". This may or may not be desired – perhaps we wish to do further processing to identify the target domains of such metaphors, or perhaps we wish to be able to annotate physical size and physical size only.

3.1 Incorporating Semantic Information

Size is a very metaphorical concept, and syntactic rules as above will produce a large amount of matches that relate to such uses, eg. "a great cry" or "a big deal". If we wish to refine our rules to detect such uses, there are a few avenues for refinement.

First of all, some LUs are much more metaphorical than others. During the rule-writing process, a training set taken from a corpus (ideally a tagged corpus, but in this case taken from from a collection of appearances of the LU) is subjectively perused for more or less metaphorical cases.

A "great man" is almost certainly a metaphorical use, whereas a "large man" is almost certainly concrete. Accuracy may be improved by requiring "great" to be used together with a common concrete complement, like "great crowd". Improvements are rejected or accepted on the basis of performance on the training set.

There are also semantic classifications of words, such as WordNet (Miller, 1995). We may compile the set of hyponyms of *physical entity* and require them to appear as the nouns in our rules.

```
define phys_entity
  @txt"phys_entity.txt";
! a list of singular baseforms
! can be expanded to include
! eg. plurals by suitably composing
! it with a dictionary automaton
define phys_entities
  phys_entity .o. noun_baseform_expander;
```

Listing 4: Reading an external linguistic resource

3.2 Incorporating Part-of-speech Information

We have hitherto used named rules for matching word classes, like `Noun`, without specifying how they are written. Even our collection of LUs might need some closer attention – for example "little" could be an adverb.

Considering that in writing our rules we are effectively doing shallow syntactic parsing, even a very simple way to identify parts of speech may suffice: a morphological dictionary. For example, a finite-state transducer representing English morphology may be used to define the class of common nouns as in listing 5.

```
! The file we want to read
define English @bin"english.hfst";
! We compose it with a noun filter
! and extract the input side
define Noun English .o.
 [?+ "<NN1>" | "<NN2>"].u;
! (NN1 is singular, NN2 plural)
```

Listing 5: Using a dictionary to write POS rules

If we have the use of a part-of-speech tagger, we may write our rules to act on its output, as in table 6.

```
define Noun LC(W) Wordchar+
 ["<NN1>"|"<NN2>"] RC(W);
```

Listing 6: Using tags in pre-tagged text

4 Increasing Coverage

Having considered for each rule where `Degree` and `Standard` may occur, coverage may be evaluated by also finding those cases where a LU is used as an adjective but hasn't been tagged, eg.

```
define TOP Size1 | Size2 | ...
 [LU].t(NonmatchingLU);
```

The valid match is always the longest possible one, so `NonmatchingLU` will be the tag only if no subsuming `SizeN` rule applies.

For example in

```
the moving human body is
<NonmatchingLU>large</NonmatchingLU>
obtrusive and highly visible
```

We see another realisation of the frame: the `Entity` being followed by a copula, and the `LU` appearing to the right. We could write the rule `Size2` to capture this, adding positions for non-core elements either by linguistic reasoning or by searching the corpus.

References

Collin F. Baker, Charles J. Fillmore, and John B. Lowe. 1998. The Berkeley FrameNet project. In *Proceedings of the 36th Annual Meeting of the Association for Computational Linguistics and 17th International Conference on Computational Linguistics -*

Volume 1, ACL '98, pages 86–90, Stroudsburg, PA, USA. Association for Computational Linguistics.

The BNC Consortium. 2007. *The British National Corpus*. Oxford University Computing Services, version 3 (BNC XML) edition.

Charles J. Fillmore. 1976. Frame semantics and the nature of language. *Annals of the New York Academy of Sciences: Conference on the Origin and Development of Language and Speech*, 280(1):20–32.

Lauri Karttunen. 2011. Beyond morphology: Pattern matching with FST. In Cerstin Mahlow and Michael Piotrowski, editors, *Systems and Frameworks for Computational Morphology*, volume 100 of *Communications in Computer and Information Science*, pages 1–13, Berlin Heidelberg. Springer.

Krister Lindén, Erik Axelson, Senka Drobac, Sam Hardwick, Juha Kuokkala, Jyrki Niemi, Tommi Pirinen, and Miikka Silfverberg. 2013. HFST – a system for creating NLP tools. In Cerstin Mahlow and Michael Piotrowski, editors, *Systems and Frameworks for Computational Morphology*, volume 380 of *Communications in Computer and Information Science*, pages 53–71, Berlin Heidelberg. Springer.

George A. Miller. 1995. Wordnet: A lexical database for English. *Communications of the ACM*, 38(11):39–41.

discoursegraphs: A graph-based merging tool and converter for multilayer annotated corpora

Arne Neumann
Applied Computational Linguistics
SFB 632 / EB Cognitive Science
Universität Potsdam, Germany
`arne.neumann@uni-potsdam.de`

Abstract

`discoursegraphs` is a Python-based converter for linguistic annotation formats which facilitates the combination of several, heterogeneous layers of annotation of a document into a unified graph representation. The library supports a range of syntax and discourse-related formats and was successfully used to revise and merge a multilayered corpus (Stede and Neumann, 2014).

1 Introduction

In an ideal world, we would like to have an easy-to-use annotation tool that supports a wide range of annotation tasks, uses a standard-compliant interchange format and which can be easily extended – in a novice friendly programming language. While there has arguably been progress in the field of general-purpose annotation software in recent years (e.g. `brat` (Stenetorp et al., 2012) and `WebAnno` (Yimam et al., 2013)), hierarchical and higher order annotation remains the domain of specialised programs (e.g. `RSTTool` (O'Donnell, 2000) and `MMAX2` (Müller and Strube, 2006)) using idiosyncratic file formats, written and last maintained by brave colleagues in the dark ages of computer history.

To honor the contributions of these fellow minds, I have implemented a simple and easily extendable toolkit called `discoursegraphs`, which can convert a number of syntax and discourse-related annotation formats and is able to merge these annotations into a single graph for further exploration or transformation into other, more sustainable formats. The library is free and open-source software and is available from its repository[1]. It can also be installed directly via Python's `pip` package manager[2].

2 Related Work

There are numerous converters for linguistic annotations, but they usually only convert between a limited set of file formats and are geared towards specific projects or focus on one type of annotation (e.g. *treetools*[3] for Treebank formats). To the best of my knowledge, there's only one other off-the-shelf converter that supports merging heterogeneous annotations into a unified data structure: `SaltNPepper` (Zipser et al., 2010; Zipser et al., 2014). Despite its wide range of import and export formats (and its recent addition of merging capabilities), I chose to write my own toolkit for the sake of simplicity and maintainability.[4]

3 System Architecture

`discoursegraphs` is implemented in Python 2.7 and uses the `NetworkX` library (Hagberg et al., 2008) to represent annotated documents as graphs.

`DisourseDocumentGraph` is the fundamental data structure of the library. It is a directed graph with (possibly) multiple edges between nodes. Each token in a document is represented by a node with token-level features (e.g. part-of-speech tag and lemma) encoded as attribute-value pairs.

All nodes and edges belong to at least one annotation layer (with possible sub-layers, e.g. `'syntax'` vs. `'syntax:category'`, `'syntax:token'` or

[1] `https://github.com/arne-cl/discoursegraphs`

[2] `https://pip.pypa.io`

[3] `https://github.com/wmaier/treetools`

[4] *SaltNPepper* is a versatile, mature library – there's even an annotation tool based on it (Druskat et al., 2014) – but it is also rather heavy-weight. The core of *SaltNPepper* (not including importers and exporters) already consists of roughly 60,000 lines of Java, while *discoursegraphs*' core consists of only 750 lines of Python.

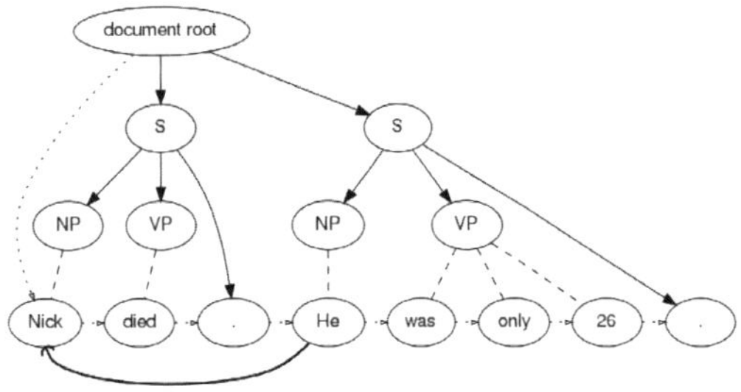

Figure 1: Example document containing two sentences with syntax and coreference annotation.

'rst' vs. 'rst:nucleus'), which they can be easily queried for.

Annotations are expressed as additional nodes (e.g. for elements in a constituency parse tree) and directed edges between them. Both annotation nodes and edges can have additional attributes stored in attribute-value pairs. Namespaces are used in order to allow conflicting annotations to be merged. For example, a token node may have two part-of-speech annotations associated with it (e.g. 'penn:vbz' and 'brown:doz').

The toolkit relies on four basic types of edges (Figure 1) to model linguistic annotations ranging from syntax to semantics, discourse phenomena and information structure:

- **spanning relation**: one span root node with outgoing edges to all (token) nodes the span covers – signifies a contiguous span of tokens, e.g. a phrase or a named entity [dashed line without arrow]
- **dominance relation**: a hierarchical annotation, e.g. from a noun phrase to a noun in a constituent structure [solid line with black arrow]
- **pointing relation**: a non-hierarchical relation, e.g. for linking coreferent entities [bold solid line with curved arrow]
- **precedence relation**: a path, starting from the document root node through all tokens in the order they occur in the document and ending at the last token [dotted line with unfilled arrow]

While typed edges are not strictly necessary to represent linguistically annotated data in graphs[5], they avoid ambiguity – especially when working with unknown corpora or when multiple tools have to work on the same dataset, cf. Neumann et al. (2013).

3.1 Importers

discoursegraphs includes importers for the following tools and formats: (i) constituent and dependency structures: Tiger-XML (Mengel and Lezius, 2000), Penn Treebank (Prasad et al., 2008) and CoNLL 2009/2010 (Hajič et al., 2009; Farkas et al., 2010), (ii) rhetorical structure: RSTTool's (O'Donnell, 2000) rs3 and rst/dis formats, (iii) pointing relations (e.g. coreference, connectives): MMAX2 (Müller and Strube, 2006) and ConAno (Stede and Heintze, 2004), and (iv) annotations of spans of text: EXMARaLDA (Schmidt, 2004).

Additional importers can easily be implemented by parsing an input format (e.g. with lxml[6]) and adding its tokens as nodes to a DisourseDocumentGraph. Afterwards, annotation nodes and edges can be added. To simplify the development of complex converters, you can add annotations iteratively and use the library's visualisation and document statistics functions (cf. Section 4) to check if the resulting graph matches your expectations.

3.2 Exporters

The library also provides a number of exporters for (i) general purpose graph formats like dot (Ellson et al., 2002), GEFX[7], GML[8] and GraphML (Brandes et al., 2013), (ii) the linguistic interchange formats CoNLL 2009 and PAULA XML 1.1 (Zeldes et al., 2013), (iii) the neo4j graph database[9] – both regular export via the geoff format, as well as live upload of annotated graphs to a running neo4j instance, and (iv) EXMARaLDA's exb format.

4 Usage

The API of the library has been kept deliberately simple. These five lines are all it takes to parse a document with two different annotation layers (syntax and rhetorical structure) into document graphs, merge them and convert them into a format that can be read by neo4j:

[5] For example, the ISO-standardised *Linguistic Annotation Framework* (ISO 24612, 2012) does allow type annotations on edges, but does not require them.

[6] http://lxml.de/

[7] http://gexf.net/format/

[8] http://www.fim.uni-passau.de/en/fim/faculty/chairs/theoretische-informatik/projects.html

[9] http://neo4j.com/

```
import discoursegraphs as dg
docgraph = dg.read_tiger('in.xml')
rstgraph = dg.read_rs3('in.rs3')
docgraph.merge_graphs(rstgraph)
dg.write_geoff(docgraph, 'out.geoff')
```

Document conversion and annotation merging is also available via a command-line interface. Beyond merging, the API provides functions for basic document statistics and graph visualisations (using the browser-based IPython (Pérez and Granger, 2007) notebook[10] and its dot plugin[11]).

`discoursegraphs` provides functions to select nodes and edges based on their properties (e.g. membership in a layer, edge type, annotations etc.). Combined with the graph manipulation capabilities of *NetworkX*, this e.g. allows the user to extract meaningful substructures from multi-level annotated documents or to create trees that combine syntactic and discourse information for kernel-based machine learning, as in Joty and Moschitti (2014).

5 Future Work

I plan to extend `discoursegraphs` with im- and exporters for further interchange formats, i.e. GrAF (Ide and Suderman, 2007), FoLiA (van Gompel and Reynaert, 2013) and especially Salt (Zipser et al., 2010), in order to leverage `SaltNPepper`'s broader variety of supported formats, which would in turn also allow users to use merged corpora in the `ANNIS` linguistic query and visualisation tool (Krause and Zeldes, 2014).

Acknowledgments

This work was supported by Deutsche Forschungsgemeinschaft as part of the funding for project D1 in the Collaborative Research Center 632 'Information Structure' (Univ. Potsdam, HU Berlin and FU Berlin). I would also like to thank Matthias Bisping, Yulia Grishina and Tatjana Scheffler for testing the software and reporting bugs.

References

Ulrik Brandes, Markus Eiglsperger, Jürgen Lerner, and Christian Pich. 2013. Graph markup language (GraphML). In Roberto Tamassia, editor, *Handbook of Graph Drawing and Visualization*. CRC Press.

Stephan Druskat, Lennart Bierkandt, Volker Gast, Christoph Rzymski, and Florian Zipser. 2014. Atomic: an open-source software platform for multi-level corpus annotation. In *Proceedings of the 12th edition of the KONVENS conference Vol. 1*. Universität Hildesheim.

John Ellson, Emden Gansner, Lefteris Koutsofios, Stephen C North, and Gordon Woodhull. 2002. Graphviz–open source graph drawing tools. In *Graph Drawing*, pages 483–484. Springer.

Richárd Farkas, Veronika Vincze, György Móra, János Csirik, and György Szarvas. 2010. The CoNLL-2010 shared task: learning to detect hedges and their scope in natural language text. In *Proceedings of the Fourteenth Conference on Computational Natural Language Learning—Shared Task*, pages 1–12. Association for Computational Linguistics.

Aric A. Hagberg, Daniel A. Schult, and Pieter J. Swart. 2008. Exploring network structure, dynamics, and function using NetworkX. In Gäel Varoquaux, Travis Vaught, and Jarrod Millman, editors, *Proceedings of the 7th Python in Science Conference (SciPy2008)*, pages 11–15, Pasadena, CA USA.

Jan Hajič, Massimiliano Ciaramita, Richard Johansson, Daisuke Kawahara, Maria Antònia Martí, Lluís Màrquez, Adam Meyers, Joakim Nivre, Sebastian Padó, Jan Štěpánek, et al. 2009. The CoNLL-2009 shared task: Syntactic and semantic dependencies in multiple languages. In *Proceedings of the Thirteenth Conference on Computational Natural Language Learning: Shared Task*, pages 1–18. Association for Computational Linguistics.

Nancy Ide and Keith Suderman. 2007. GrAF: A graph-based format for linguistic annotations. In *Proceedings of the Linguistic Annotation Workshop*, pages 1–8. Association for Computational Linguistics.

ISO 24612. 2012. *Language Resource Management – Linguistic Annotation Framework*. International Standards Organization, Geneva, Switzerland.

Shafiq Joty and Alessandro Moschitti. 2014. Discriminative Reranking of Discourse Parses Using Tree Kernels. In *Proceedings of the 2014 Conference on Empirical Methods in Natural Language Processing (EMNLP)*, pages 2049–2060. Association for Computational Linguistics.

Thomas Krause and Amir Zeldes. 2014. ANNIS3: A new architecture for generic corpus query and visualization. *Literary and Linguistic Computing*.

Andreas Mengel and Wolfgang Lezius. 2000. An XML-based Representation Format for Syntactically Annotated Corpora. In *Proceedings of the 2nd International Conference on Language Resources and Evaluation (LREC 2000)*.

Christoph Müller and Michael Strube. 2006. Multi-level annotation of linguistic data with MMAX2. In

[10] `http://ipython.org/notebook.html`

[11] `https://github.com/cjdrake/ipython-magic`

Sabine Braun, Kurt Kohn, and Joybrato Mukherjee, editors, *Corpus technology and language pedagogy: New resources, new tools, new methods*, pages 197–214. Peter Lang.

Arne Neumann, Nancy Ide, and Manfred Stede. 2013. Importing MASC into the ANNIS linguistic database: A case study of mapping GrAF. In *Proceedings of the Seventh Linguistic Annotation Workshop (LAW)*, pages 98–102. Association for Computational Linguistics.

Michael O'Donnell. 2000. RSTTool 2.4: a markup tool for Rhetorical Structure Theory. In *Proceedings of the 1st International Conference on Natural Language Generation (INLG 2000)*, pages 253–256. Association for Computational Linguistics.

Fernando Pérez and Brian E. Granger. 2007. IPython: a system for interactive scientific computing. *Computing in Science and Engineering*, 9(3):21–29.

Rashmi Prasad, Nikhil Dinesh, Alan Lee, Eleni Miltsakaki, Livio Robaldo, Aravind K Joshi, and Bonnie L Webber. 2008. The Penn Discourse TreeBank 2.0. In *Proceedings of LREC 2008*.

Thomas Schmidt. 2004. Transcribing and annotating spoken language with EXMARaLDA. In *Proceedings of the LREC-Workshop on XML based richly annotated corpora, Lisbon*, pages 69–74.

Manfred Stede and Silvan Heintze. 2004. Machine-assisted rhetorical structure annotation. In *Proceedings of the 20th international conference on Computational Linguistics*, page 425. Association for Computational Linguistics.

Manfred Stede and Arne Neumann. 2014. Potsdam Commentary Corpus 2.0: Annotation for Discourse Research. In *Proceedings of the Ninth International Conference on Language Resources and Evaluation (LREC'14)*, Reykjavik, Iceland. European Language Resources Association (ELRA).

Pontus Stenetorp, Sampo Pyysalo, Goran Topić, Tomoko Ohta, Sophia Ananiadou, and Jun'ichi Tsujii. 2012. brat: a Web-based Tool for NLP-Assisted Text Annotation. In *Proceedings of the Demonstrations Session at EACL 2012*, Avignon, France. Association for Computational Linguistics.

Maarten van Gompel and Martin Reynaert. 2013. FoLiA: A practical XML Format for Linguistic Annotation-a descriptive and comparative study. *Computational Linguistics in the Netherlands Journal*, 3:63–81.

Seid Muhie Yimam, Iryna Gurevych, Richard Eckart de Castilho, and Chris Biemann. 2013. WebAnno: A Flexible, Web-based and Visually Supported System for Distributed Annotations. In *ACL (Conference System Demonstrations)*, pages 1–6.

Amir Zeldes, Florian Zipser, and Arne Neumann. 2013. PAULA XML Documentation: Format Version 1.1. Research Report, hal-00783716, https://hal.inria.fr/hal-00783716.

Florian Zipser, Laurent Romary, et al. 2010. A model oriented approach to the mapping of annotation formats using standards. In *Workshop on Language Resource and Language Technology Standards, LREC 2010*.

Florian Zipser, Mario Frank, and Jakob Schmolling. 2014. Merging data, the essence of creation of multi-layer corpora. In *Postersession der Sektion Computerlingustik auf der 36. Jahrestagung der Deutschen Gesellschaft für Sprachwissenschaft (DGfS)*.

Omorfi—Free and open source morphological lexical database for Finnish

Tommi A Pirinen
Ollscoil Chathair Bhaile Átha Cliath
ADAPT Centre — School of Computing
Dublin City University, Dublin 9
tommi.pirinen@computing.dcu.ie

Abstract

This demonstration presents a freely available open source lexical database omorfi. Omorfi is a mature lexicographical database project, started out as a single-person single-purpose free open source morphological analyser project, omorfi has since grown to be used in variety of applications including spell-checking, statistical and rule-based machine translation, treebanking, joint syntactic and morphological parsing, poetry generation, information extraction. In this demonstration we hope to show both the variety of end-user facing applications as well as the tools and interfaces for computational linguists to make the best use of a developing product. We show a shallow database arrangement that has allowed a great variety of contributors from different projects to extend the lexical database while not breaking the continued use of existing end-applications. We hope to show both the best current practices for lexical data management and software engineering with regards to continuous external project integration of a constantly developing product. As case examples we show some of the integrations with following applications: Voikko spell-checking for Windows, Mac OS X, Linux and Android, statistical machine translation pipelines with moses, rule-based machine translation with apertium and traditional xerox style morphological analysis and generation. morphological segmentation, as well as application programming interfaces for python and Java.

1 Introduction

Omorfi[1] (open morfology for Finnish), as a project is centred around morphological analysis of Finnish. Morphology is a core for many if not most natural language processing systems, especially in the case of such morphology-heavy language as Finnish. However, the detail and even the formatting of the result of morphological processing varies from application to application. In order to produce all the different formats of output and details of data, one needs to maintain a large database of all the bits and pieces of lexical information that is necessary to produce the wanted readings, and that is exactly what omorfi has become over the years. What we have in the current version of omorfi, is a lexical database of roots, morphs and combinatorics, that can be *weaved* for use of different applications, documentations, and automatic test suites by use of simple scripting. The database is easy to maintain and update for linguists and contributors. It is robust enough to support a wide range of applications without the progress of each application and changes to their specific data bearing a negative effect to other applications.

2 Database

The word *database*, in context of omorfi is currently used in a very liberal sense, while we have structured our data in a manner that resembles relational database to the extent that it could be converted into a one by quite simple and fast process, we have opted to stick with basic *tab-separated-values* format for basically two reasons: firstly, computational linguists and computer scientists are already well-versed to handle this type of files with ease and efficiently on the command-line, they integrate with the basics of unix taught to any computational linguist in the past 20 years or

[1] https://github.com/flammie/omorfi/

so (Church, 1994), and the expected improvement in the use of real relational databases comes from the complexity of dozens of tables and billions of rows of data, whereas lexicon will likely not reach even million of root-words any time soon. For easy editing the TSV files are importable and exportable to all the commonly available free office products: e.g., LibreOffice[2] and OpenOffice.

3 Application Data Format Generation

The application of morphs and morphotactics is based on *finite state morphology* as documented by Beesley and Karttunen (2003). In order to be able to compile our lexical database into a finite-state automaton format for efficient processing, we generate a *lexc* file representation of the data, and compile it using *HFST* (Lindén et al., 2011) software that is available as a free and open source system. The translation from tab-separated-values into lexc is done by python scripts, an example of formats is in listings 1 and 2. Transformation is pretty straight-forward and easy to maintain.

```
lemma   homonym new_para    origin
Aabel   1       N_STADION   unihu
...
talo    1       N_TALO      kotus
...
Öösti   1       N_TYYLI     unihu
```

Figure 1: Lexical data in lexeme database, consisting of a *unique key* of lemma and homonym number, a paradigm for inflection and source of origin, which is all the obligatory information for each word to be added in the database. The origin's main importance is copyright's rather than linguistic information or database structure; in origins *unihu* refers to a yet unnamed project in University of Helsinki and *kotus* stands for Nykysuomen sanalista by kotus (RILF; research institute of languages in Finland)

The additional data can be added to each lexeme using the lemma and homonym number as an identifier, these data are stored in a separate TSV file that is joined to the database in figure 1 to produce a master database. E.g., a named-entity recognition project would add lines from `Aabel 1 first` to `Öösti 1 geo` into a file of named entity classes to add "first name" information to *Aabel* and "geographical place" information to *Öösti*. Then it can be accessed e.g., to generate readings of `PROPER=FIRST` and `PROPER=GEO` into the lexc code to be added to a specific named-entity categorising automaton, or the master database can be queried for this information when the given lemma is seen in the analysed text.

4 Applications

The applications we are demonstrating in this paper are: statistical machine translation, rule-based machine translation, spell-checking and correction, morphological segmentation, analysis and generation.

For statistical machine translation, we are using moses[3] (Koehn et al., 2007). There are at least two ways morphological processing can be used in moses pipeline:*segmentation* (Dyer et al., 2008) and *factorisation* (Koehn and Hoang, 2007). In segmentation approach, the word-forms are reduced to smaller units, such as morphs, or just words (i.e. root morphs with sufixes intact but compounds broken), applying traditional statistical machine translation methods to morphs is supposed to improve the translation quality by decreasing the amount of unseen tokens and matching the morphs to many non-Finnish word-forms more regularly (e.g., aligning suffixes to preposition). In factored translation, results of morphological analysis are stored in a vector, each component of which can be used at any point of statistical machine translation: typical components of the vector are e.g., lemma, part-of-speech and full morphosyntactic description.

For rule-based machine translation setting we combine omorfi with apertium[4] (Forcada et al., 2010). In apertium's shallow rule-based machine translation, omorfi is used for morphological analysis, disambiguation and morphological generation.

For spell-checking we use voikko.[5] In spell-checking and correction omorfi is used to locate misspelled words and to find most likely corrections given mispelling (Pirinen and Lindén, 2014).

The morphological analysis and segmentation are tasks that the above-mentioned end-user programs depend on, but we also provide an API ac-

[2] http://libreoffice.org

[3] http://www.statmt.org/moses/

[4] http://apertium.sf.net

[5] http://voikko.sf.net

```
LEXICON Nouns
[WORD_ID=Aabel][POS=NOUN][PROPER=FIRST]:0Aabel N_STADION        ;
...
[WORD_ID=talo][POS=NOUN]:0talo  N_TALO  ;
...
[WORD_ID=Öösti][POS=NOUN][PROPER=GEO]:0Ööst  N_TYYLI ;
```

Figure 2: Lexical data in lexc-compatible format for compilation.

cess for python and Java as well as convenience bash scripts on top of direct access to the automata.

Given this wide array of applications it is obvious how importance of lexical data management has gotten to more central position as the project has progressed: maximal coverage of word-forms for machine translation is not invariably a good thing for spell-checker.

Acknowledgments

The research leading to these results has received funding from the European Union Seventh Framework Programme FP7/2007-2013 under grant agreement PIAP-GA-2012-324414 (Abu-MaTran).

Omorfi consists of a large body of work from numerous academic and open source contributors, including: Inari Listenmaa, Francis M Tyers, Ryan Johnson, and Juha Kuokkala.

References

Kenneth R Beesley and Lauri Karttunen. 2003. Finite-state morphology: Xerox tools and techniques. *CSLI, Stanford*.

Kenneth Ward Church. 1994. Unix™ for poets. *Notes of a course from the European Summer School on Language and Speech Communication, Corpus Based Methods*.

Christopher Dyer, Smaranda Muresan, and Philip Resnik. 2008. Generalizing word lattice translation. Technical report, DTIC Document.

Mikel L. Forcada, Mireia Ginestí Rosell, Jacob Nordfalk, Jim O'Regan, Sergio Ortiz-Rojas, Juan Antonio Pérez-Ortiz, Gema Ramírez-Sánchez, Felipe Sánchez-Martínez, and Francis M. Tyers. 2010. Apertium: a free/open-source platform for rule-based machine translation platform. *Machine Translation*.

Philipp Koehn and Hieu Hoang. 2007. Factored translation models. In *EMNLP-CoNLL*, pages 868–876.

Philipp Koehn, Hieu Hoang, Alexandra Birch, Chris Callison-Burch, Marcello Federico, Nicola Bertoldi, Brooke Cowan, Wade Shen, Christine Moran, Richard Zens, et al. 2007. Moses: Open source toolkit for statistical machine translation. In *Proceedings of the 45th Annual Meeting of the ACL on Interactive Poster and Demonstration Sessions*, pages 177–180. Association for Computational Linguistics.

Krister Lindén, Erik Axelson, Sam Hardwick, Tommi A Pirinen, and Miikka Silfverberg. 2011. Hfst—framework for compiling and applying morphologies. *Systems and Frameworks for Computational Morphology*, pages 67–85.

Tommi A Pirinen and Krister Lindén. 2014. State-of-the-art in weighted finite-state spell-checking. In *Computational Linguistics and Intelligent Text Processing*, pages 519–532. Springer.

A Tool for Automatic Simplification of Swedish Texts

Evelina Rennes
SICS East Swedish ICT AB, Sweden
evelina.rennes@liu.se

Arne Jönsson
SICS East Swedish ICT AB, Sweden
arne.jonsson@liu.se

Abstract

We present a rule based automatic text simplification tool for Swedish. The tool is designed to facilitate experimentation with various simplification techniques. The architecture of the tool is inspired by and partly built on a previous text simplification tool for Swedish, CogFLUX. New functionality, new operation types, and new simplification operations were added.

1 Introduction

The task of automatic text simplification aims to reduce the overall complexity of a text, in order to enhance comprehension for a human reader, or to improve further processing performed by a computer program. The simplification of texts have previously been performed manually, but since this is a very time consuming and expensive task, the possibility to automatically create simplifications of texts would result in more accessible information, to a relatively low cost. Recent years' increase in computer power, and the availability of high quality linguistic resources and language processing tools enable faster, better, and more powerful tools for natural language processing needed for more advanced text simplification.

The group of people that might benefit from a text simplification tool is not homogeneous and therefore, it is important to account for the differences between these groups, and perhaps also look for the individual needs among the group members. The simplification tool can be used to study such individual simplication needs.

Although automatic summarization has been pointed out as a possible method of simplifying a text (Margarido et al., 2008; Smith and Jönsson, 2011), simplifications are not always shorter than the originals. For example, a simplification operation applied to a syntactically complex sentence might result in a longer sentence with a less complex grammatical structure, and some readers might benefit from more extensive explanations of terms or certain phenomena in order to gain full understanding of a text.

1.1 Text Simplification in Swedish

A study on simplification operations for Swedish was made by comparing the phrase structures of a text written in Standard Swedish to a manually simplified version of the text, and subsequently extracting simplification operations (Decker, 2003). This work resulted in 25 extracted simplification rules. The rules were grouped into two subsets: rules that delete or replace sub-phrases and rules that add new syntactical information to the text. The CogFLUX system (Rybing et al., 2010), implemented the first subset of this rule set. Abrahamsson (2011) developed the tool further by adding another subset of the rules, and an additional synonym replacement module.

Simplification through synonym replacement has been investigated by evaluating and comparing different methods for choosing alternative synonyms (Keskisärkkä and Jönsson, 2012). In that work, the success of the simplification used measures such as readability metrics, average word length, proportion of long words, and replacement error ratio. Synonym replacement was also the main interest in a study of simplification of Swedish medical texts (Abrahamsson et al., 2014), that replaced difficult medical terms with synonyms that were considered easier, by applying the two Swedish readability metrics LIX and OVIX to the texts. The difficulty of a given word was estimated by taking into account both the frequency of the word in a general corpus, but also the frequency of substrings of words. The result showed that the resulting text was slightly more difficult according to LIX, while being more readable according to OVIX.

2 The tool

The architecture of the text simplification tool presented in this paper is inspired by and partly built on CogFLUX (Rybing et al., 2010).

2.1 Layout

The applet, in its current state, consists of two main fields. An upper white field where the original text is inserted, and a lower white field contains the output of the simplification.

By the use of check boxes, the user decides what simplification operation to apply to the text.

The tool surrently supports the following simplifications: passive-to-active, quotation inversion, rearranging to straight word order, sentence split, synonym replacement, and the simplification rules extracted by Decker (2003). For our current experimental purposes, the first five are divided into three groups, corresponding to the estimated level of simplification.

- Low
  - Sentence Split
  - Quotation Inversion
- Medium
  - Low level operations +
  - Passive-to-active
  - Straight word order
- High
  - Medium level operations +
  - Synonym replacement

The user, or experimenter, can easily try either the pre-defined groups, or any combination of simplifications.

2.2 Linguistic Resources

The linguistic resources used in this project were the SUC3 corpus and the Synlex synonym lexicon.

The Swedish Language Bank (*Språkbanken*), has since the seventies developed and stored a large collection of Swedish text corpora. One of these is the Stockholm-Umeå Corpus (Ejerhed et al., 2006), which is a balanced corpus consisting of one million words, annotated with part-of-speech tags, morphological features and citation form

The synonym replacement module was built on the work of Abrahamsson (2011) using the Synlex lexicon (Kann, 2004), with an included frequency list. Synlex is a free linguistic resource containing about 80000 synonym pairs. The collection of synonym pairs was constructed in cooperation with voluntary Internet users, by giving suggestions of possible synonyms and giving the users the possibility to rate the correctness of the suggestion of a given synonym pair.

2.3 Preprocessing

For tagging we use Stagger (Östling, 2013), a fairly new part-of-speech tagger based on the averaged perceptron (Collins, 2002). It is currently the most accurate tagger for Swedish. Per-token accuracy is estimated to about 96.6 % (10-fold cross validation on SUC 3.0).

For syntactic analysis we use MaltParser 1.2 (Nivre et al., 2006) as the latest version, MaltParser 1.7.2, does not produce phrase structure trees, which in the current phase of the project is needed for interpretation of the rules. However, future functionality might benefit from dependency parsing, which can be turned on with a simple switch.

2.4 Simplification

The simplification rules were formalized to fit *X-rules*, the syntax notation script used in CogFLUX (Rybing et al., 2010). Originally, there were two different types of possible operations, replace (REPL) and delete (DEL). For this project, two additional operation types were created for the purpose of this study, SHIFT and SPLIT. After each operation type there is a target phrase, i.e. the type of phrase that is to be manipulated, followed by an arrow pointing towards the substitute phrase. In the REPL operation the substitute phrase consists of the replacement phrase structure, while the DEL operation completely removes the target phrase. The notation of the SHIFT operation is slightly different. Given a target phrase (to the left of the arrow), the second part of the rule indicates what part of the structure that will change position. This specific operation handles changes of word order, and in order to avoid erroneous rearrangement of words, this operation is only triggered by certain syntactic tags, for example the passive tense. The SPLIT operation simply splits a sentence into two when the condition to the left is fulfilled.

A functionality that was added to the *X-rules* script is the possibility to add dependency tags to the part-of-speech tags. This was made in order to make full use of the information provided by the parser. Another additional development was the introduction of the "?" tag, which is able to represent one, many or no tags of any sort.

All the syntactic rules that were previously applied in the CogFLUX project were included in this project.

This work did not take into account all the simplification operations suggested by the previously conducted literature overview, but limited the applied operations to 4 rules. Other operations were not included in this first iteration due to the nature of the actions: they are either too complex for the tool in its current state, or they cannot be easily included without a foregoing text analysis. The aim is, however, to continue the development of the simplification tool, and eventually apply all the proposed operations.

The syntactic simplification applied in this project consisted of 4 separate rules:

- Changing from passive to active voice

  To transform a sentence from passive to active voice in Swedish, the subject of the passive sentence must become the object of the active sentence. The s-ending must be deleted and the preposition *av* (*by*, for example *the cookie was eaten* ***by*** *the boy*) must be removed. In order to perform this, a sequence of operations were applied when a sentence of passive voice was detected:

  SHIFT//S-NP(SS) VB/VP ? PP(AG) $\rightarrow$ S-PP NP &P(#)

  input: *The huge cookie was eaten by both Kalle and Stina in the dining room.*
  output: *Both Kalle and Stina ate the huge cookie in the dining room.*

- Quotation Inversion

  The quotation inversion changes the place of the speaker in a quotation, from *[quotation], said X* to *X said: [quotation]*) (Bott et al., 2012).

  The quotation inversion operation is triggered by quotation marks followed by specific words from a lexicon that might indicate a quotation (such as *said, exclaimed, whispered*, etc. and the quotation (specified by the quotation marks) switches place with the verb phrase and the noun phrase, such as:

  input: *"Go to bed!" said Kalle.*
  output: *Kalle said: "Go to bed!"*

- Rearranging to straight word order

  This rule shifts the word order of clauses initiated with adverbs or adjectives.

  SHIFT//S-AVP/AP VB/VP NP(SS) ? $\rightarrow$ S-NP(SS) AVP &P(#) (1)
  SHIFT//S-AVP/AP VB/VP NP(SS) ? $\rightarrow$ S-AVP ? &P(#) (2)

  The application of this simplification operation might result in the following example:

  input: *Yesterday bought Kalle a new car.**
  output: *Kalle bought a new car yesterday.*

- Sentence split

  The SPLIT operation splits a sentence in two. In the example rule below, a clause that is consisting of two clauses joined with a conjunction, is split at the word marked as a conjunction and two separate sentences are created, inserting a full stop as an end of sentence marker.

  SPLIT//S-S KN S $\rightarrow$ KN &P(#)

  The rule type is dynamic and the breaking point can easily be changed by changing the second part of the rule.

3 Conclusion

This report described a framework for syntactical and lexical text simplification for Swedish. The architecture of the tool is inspired by and partly built on a previous text simplification tool for Swedish, CogFLUX, but has been modified with new functionality. Two new operation types were added, SHIFT and SPLIT, and four new simplification operations were applied: changing from passive to active word order, quotation inversion, rearranging to straight word order, and sentence split.

The tool is mainly intended to be used for experiments on rule based text simplification techniques.

Acknowledgments

This research was supported by SICS East Swedish ICT AB.

References

Emil Abrahamsson, Timothy Forni, Maria Skeppstedt, and Maria Kvist. 2014. Medical text simplification using synonym replacement: Adapting assessment of word difficulty to a compounding language. In *Proceedings of the 3rd Workshop on Predicting and Improving Text Readability for Target Reader Populations (PITR)@ EACL*.

Peder Abrahamsson. 2011. Mer lättläst - påbyggnad av ett automatiskt omskrivningsverktyg till lätt svenska. Bachelor's thesis, Linköping University.

Stefan Bott, Horacio Saggion, and Simon Mille. 2012. Text simplification tools for spanish. In *Proceedings of the Eight International Conference on Language Resources and Evaluation (LREC'12)*.

Michael Collins. 2002. Discriminative training methods for hidden markov models: Theory and experiments with perceptron algorithms. In *Proceedings of the ACL-02 Conference on Empirical Methods in Natural Language Processing*, Stroudsburg, PA, USA. Association for Computational Linguistics.

Anna Decker. 2003. Towards automatic grammatical simplification of swedish text. Master's thesis, Stockholm University.

Eva Ejerhed, Gunnel Källgren, and Benny Brodda. 2006. Stockholm Umeå Corpus version 2.0.

Viggo Kann. 2004. Folkets användning av lexin – en resurs. Technical report, KTH Nada.

Robin Keskisärkkä and Arne Jönsson. 2012. Automatic text simplification via synonym replacement. In *Proceedings of The Fourth Swedish Language Technology Conference*.

Paulo R. A. Margarido, Thiago A. S. Pardo, Gabriel M. Antonio, Vinícius B. Fuentes, Rachel Aires, Sandra M. Aluísio, and Renata P. M. Fortes. 2008. Automatic summarization for text simplification: Evaluating text understanding by poor readers. In *Companion Proceedings of the XIV Brazilian Symposium on Multimedia and the Web*.

Joakim Nivre, Johan Hall, and Jens Nilsson. 2006. Maltparser: A data-driven parser-generator for dependency parsing. In *Proceedings of the Fifth International Conference on Language Resources and Evalutation*, pages 2216–2219.

Robert Östling. 2013. Stagger: an open-source part of speech tagger for swedish. *Northen Europea Journal of Language Technology*, 3.

Jonas Rybing, Christian Smith, and Annika Silvervarg. 2010. Towards a rule based system for automatic simplification of texts. *Proceedings of SLTC*.

Christian Smith and Arne Jönsson. 2011. Automatic Summarization As Means of Simplifying Texts, an Evaluation for Swedish. In *Proceedings of the 18th Nordic Conference of Computational Linguistics (NoDaLiDa-2010)*.